NATIONAL CONSTRUCTION LAW MANUAL

First Edition

by
James Acret

With love,
this book is inscribed to
Laiah Lee.

ACKNOWLEDGMENTS

The author acknowledges the assistance of Laiah Lee, who converted airy words into those mysterious ranks and files of ones and zeroes. Bill Mahoney, converted the ones and zeroes to a text and put it into the reader's hands. Rod Moss, Art O'Leary, and Mark Benjamin read the manuscript and made many helpful suggestions. Jim Rigelhaupt understood.

TABLE OF CONTENTS

BNi Building News

EDITOR-IN-CHIEF
William D. Mahoney, P.E.

TECHNICAL SERVICES
Susanne Westphal
Edward E. Kleimola
Wade T. Ryer

COVER DESIGN
Robert O. Wright

BNI Publications, Inc.

LOS ANGELES
10801 NATIONAL BLVD.
LOS ANGELES, CA 90064

ANAHEIM
1610 S. CLEMENTINE STREET
ANAHEIM, CA 92802

BOSTON
77 WEXFORD STREET
NEEDHAM HEIGHTS, MA 02194

WASHINGTON, D.C.
502 MAPLE AVENUE WEST
VIENNA, VA 22180

ISBN 1557011710

NATIONAL CONSTRUCTION LAW MANUAL
1997 EDITION

Table of Contents

CHAPTER 1

CONTRACTS

CHAPTER 1

§ 1.01 What is a Contract

In its classic legal definition, a contract is simply a *promise* that the law will enforce. In the business of construction, a contract is usually easily recognized, consisting as it does of a preprinted text labeled "*contract*", "*subcontract*", "*agreement*", or "*purchase order*". Yet an enforceable contract may also be formed in other ways, without writing, without a handshake, over the telephone, or even without words.

Construction contract promises deal with the performance of work and the payment of money. If we take as an example a contract to build a hospital, the contractor *promises* to build the hospital according to drawings and specifications and the owner *promises* to make the jobsite available and to make progress payments to the contractor as the work advances. The *contract documents*, including drawings and specifications, may run to 1,000 pages or more, each page containing an assortment of promises that work will be performed as specified. The specifications almost always refer to codes, standards, ASTM's and technical reports that contain thousands of pages more, all of which are incorporated into the contract documents as promises of the contractor.

As we shall see, and as experienced contractors know very well, despite these thousands of pages of technical writing and hundreds of thousands of words supported by drawings, sketches, and illustrations, it still seems impossible to give a completely accurate and unambiguous description of the physical characteristics of a complicated building. Therefore, even the most elaborately articulated contract is subject to interpretation. Moreover, judges are not satisfied merely to enforce the promises explicitly included in the contract documents, but the law implies additional conditions that seem necessary to carry the intentions of the parties into effect.

> One would expect that a prime contractor and a subcontractor dealing with an $11,200,000 sheet metal job would be pretty sure whether they had entered into a contract or not. In the case of *Allied Sheet Metal v Kerby Saunders*, 619 NYS2d 260 (AD 1994), they were not. The subcontractor had prepared a document entitled

"scope sheet" dated November 26, 1986 that dealt with the fabrication and installation of a heating ventilation and air conditioning system in a hospital. The scope sheet was signed by the contractor's vice-president and identified the project, the work to be performed, the job number, and the contract price. The court held that the scope sheet was not a contract, since there was no indication that the document was intended to be anything more than a memorandum of the work that was covered by the subcontractor's bid. The court pointed out that parties would not ordinarily commit themselves to an $11,200,000 project without a formal writing.

§ 1.02 Competent Parties

An enforceable contract requires at least two parties, and they must both be competent to contract. Children, insane and intoxicated persons are not competent to enter into an enforceable contract. A corporation whose charter has been revoked for failure to pay taxes is not competent to contract. A person who has no authority to act on behalf of another party cannot bind that other party to a contract.

The superintendent of a park district and the president of an engineering company agreed that the engineering company would perform inspection work for the park district and prepare drawings for the repair of a building. The superintendent, however, had no authority to bind the park district because the Park District Code prohibited contracts without approval of the park district board. The court therefore held that the supposed contract was void from the beginning, and the engineering company had no right to be paid for its work even though the park district may have benefited from the work. *DC Consulting Engrs, Inc. v Batavia Park Dist*, 143 Ill App 3d 60, 492 NE2d 1000 (1986). The court said:

> [W]hen an employee of a municipal corporation purports to bind the corporation by contract without prior approval, in violation of applicable statute, such a contract is utterly void . . . such a contract cannot be validated by principles of ratification or estoppel.

§ 1.03 Legal Object

For a contract to be enforceable, it must have a legal object. A contract to ship cocaine, or to divide the loot from a bank robbery, could be unenforceable. A contract to build a structure in violation of the zoning laws would be unenforceable. A contract by an unlicensed contractor or uncertified or unregistered architect or engineer may be unenforceable by the unlicensed person. A contract to fix prices, or refrain from competition, is illegal and unenforceable.

> In *Richmond Co. v Rock-A-Way, Inc.*, 404 So 2d 121 (Fla. Dist Ct App 1981), two contractors were contemplating bidding for a recreation project. Let us call them Alpha and Beta. Alpha proposed that Beta refrain from bidding the job as a prime contractor, but submit a subcontract bid to Alpha. Alpha then agreed that if it was the low bidder, and was awarded the contract, it would sub the work to Beta rather than to any of Beta's competitors. Beta welshed on the deal, and bid the job as a prime contractor. The court dismissed Alpha's claim against Beta for breach of contract. Anti competitive agreements between contractors are void. Such agreements are against public policy because they tend to extinguish competition.

§ 1.04 Letters of Intent

A letter of intent may or may not be a contract. It depends upon whether the parties to the letter of intent manifested an intention to be bound.

> In *Quake Construction, Inc. v American Airlines*, 181 Ill App 3d 908, 537 NE2d 863 (1989), Jones Brothers Construction Co. was employed by American Airlines to manage an airport project. Quake submitted a bid and received a "letter of intent" from American Airlines. The letter stated that American intended to award the contract to Quake. Quake obtained sub bids and attended a preconstruction meeting, but then was terminated by Jones. The court found that the letter of intent was ambiguous and that it would be necessary to consider conversations and conduct of the parties to determine whether the letter of intent was an enforceable contract or not. The Court of Appeal ordered the lower court to examine the

conduct and the conversations of the parties to determine whether they intended to be bound by the letter of intent.

Letters of intent are enforceable under the Uniform Commercial Code. Versions of the Uniform Commercial Code have been adopted in all states. The UCC applies to sales of merchandise. The UCC applies to a construction contract, when the dominant feature of the contract is a sale of goods even though the performance of some construction services is contemplated.

In *J Lee Gregory v Scandinavian House*, 433 SE2d 687 (Ga. Ct App 1993), the owner of an apartment building delivered a letter of intent to a window company accepting the window company's proposal and authorizing measurements for windows. The window company delivered working drawings after which the parties fell into a dispute over the terms of payment. The owner then awarded the work to another contractor and the window company sued. HELD: The predominant character of the transaction was a sale of windows even though the window company was also to install the windows. The UCC governed the transaction. Under the UCC, the letter of intent was an enforceable contract.

§ 1.05 Certainty

An uncertain contract cannot be enforced. Although courts will attempt to interpret a contract so as to give it sufficient certainty to be enforced, they are not always able to do so. More than one construction contract has been held unenforceable for uncertainty. A contract to build a building for a specified sum of money was deemed too uncertain to be enforced when there were no drawings or specifications, and no designation of the basic characteristics of the building such as square footage, number of stories, and building materials to be used. Likewise, a contract to install tenant improvements for a specified price where the nature of the improvements had not been described was deemed to be unenforceable.

A homebuilding contract was too uncertain to be enforced. The contract stated:

> The buyer herein agrees to construct at such time as he chooses residences of not less than 1200 square feet on the parcels facing Gault Street.

The court held the contract was too uncertain to be enforced.

> A promise to erect buildings where the dimensions and plans are not specified, or which refers to plans and specifications as part of a contract although no plans and specifications are attached . . . are all too vague, and are not of sufficient definiteness . . . to be enforceable.

Colorado Corp. v Smith, 121 Cal App 2d 374, 263 P2d 79 (1953).

§ 1.06 Consideration

A contract to be enforceable must be supported by consideration. A promise to make a gift is not enforceable. If I were improvident enough to promise to give my nephew a pony for Christmas, the nephew could not enforce that promise.

The consideration for a construction contract is easily found: it consists on one side of the promise to build and on the other side of the promise to pay. In most commercial contracts the consideration is an exchange of money for some product or service, such as the provision of lumber or landscaping or janitorial services at a specified price. The consideration to support the enforceability of a contract may be any legal detriment. A non-competition agreement consists of a promise on one side, essentially, to do nothing: (to refrain from engaging in a particular business). Since the promisor thereby agrees to refrain from doing an act that it is legally otherwise entitled to do, the promise is legal consideration. On the other hand, a promise to refrain from robbing a liquor store would not qualify as legal detriment and therefore would not be valid consideration for the payment of protection money, because to rob the store is something that the promisor is not legally entitled to do.

Just as a contract, to be enforceable, must be supported by consideration, so also must a change order to a contract be supported by consideration. If there is no consideration, the change order is unenforceable.

> Thermoglaze contracted to furnish and install 444 windows for $88,960. The owner specified that the windows were to be white. After 195 had been installed, the owner's wife complained about the white color and wanted to change to bronze. The contractor

promised to replace the white windows with bronze, and solicited additional lucrative work on other properties. The owner refused to commit to the additional work and the contractor refused to honor its promise to change the white windows to bronze. The owner refused to pay for the windows and the contractor sued. HELD: The promise to change to bronze windows was not supported by consideration and therefore the contractor was entitled to be paid for the white windows. *Thermoglaze, Inc. v Morningside Gardens Co.*, 23 Conn. App 741, 583 A2d 1331, *cert denied* (Feb. 21, 1991).

A promise to perform something that the promisor is already obliged by contract to perform is not supported by consideration. This is a situation that can come up in connection with change orders.

In *J&R Elec Div v Skoog Constr Co.*, 38 Ill App 3d 747, 348 NE2d 474 (1976), an electrical subcontractor was obliged by the terms of a subcontract to install switchgear to be purchased by the project owner. When the time came to install the switchgear, subcontractor contended that it had not seen the addendum that included the switchgear in the contract. The contractor then wrote a letter promising to reimburse the subcontractor for the switchgear. The contractor refused to pay for the switchgear, and the subcontractor sued. HELD: The purported modification of the contract embodied in the letter was not supported by consideration, since the subcontractor was already obliged to install the switchgear. By, in effect, agreeing to perform some work that it was already obliged to perform, the subcontractor did not incur legal detriment and therefore there was no consideration for the prime contractor's promise to pay additional compensation.

§ 1.07 Illusory Contract

Suppose a subcontractor, on a handshake, agrees to install a roofing assembly for $10,000, but reserves the right to cancel the contract at any time for any reason or no reason. This is an example of an *illusory* contract. It appears that the contract is supported by consideration on both sides: the promise to pay $10,000 is the legal detriment that supports the promise to install the roof, which furnishes the legal detriment on the other side. But, in law, such a contract is not enforceable because it is not supported by consideration, since the subcontractor reserved the right to cancel the deal at any time for any reason or no reason, its promise is *illusory*. (It should be noted, though, that a contract in writing is *presumably* supported by consideration.)

Now let's take a hypo. (*Hypo* is law school lingo for a hypothetical situation.) Suppose a subcontractor agrees to build a roof for $10,000 but reserves the right to cancel the contract at any time for any reason or no reason. At 55% completion, having been paid $5,000, the roofer stops work and refuses to continue, exercising its right to cancel the contract. The owner employs another roofer to finish the job, but it costs $6,000. Is the owner entitled to recover $1,000 damages from the roofer? No. The roofer reserved the right to cancel the contract at any time, and part performance did not destroy that right.

Now suppose the roofer has performed 50% of the work and, unpaid, cancels the contract, and sues the owner for $5,000. *Judgment for the roofer.* Although the roofer reserved the right to cancel the contract, by rendering part performance, it cured the *illusory* nature of the contract, and was entitled to proportionate compensation.

Now suppose the roofer has completed 50% of the work and been paid $5,000, and the *owner* cancels the contract. Is the roofer entitled to sue the owner for the profit it anticipated upon completion of the entire work? No. Since the roofer had the right to cancel the contract at any time, the contract was *illusory*, and therefore the owner also had the right to cancel the contract at any time.

Illusory contracts are sometimes encountered in construction law practice because owners are tempted to write into their contracts an option to terminate a contractor's performance with or without cause at any time. The temptation is understandable. It is a risky thing for an owner to terminate a contractor's performance for cause. An owner who throws a contractor off a job is likely to be sued. If it is determined that the action was not justified, the owner may become liable for substantial damages. One way to avoid this difficulty is to reserve the right to terminate the contract without cause. This, however, makes the contract illusory because the owner, in effect, may perform the contract or not at its sole option. The undesired side effect is that the contract becomes unenforceable, and therefore the contractor, as well as the owner, can terminate performance at any time with or without cause. This could be an attractive option for a contractor in the process of losing money on a job.

An illusory contract is unenforceable because it lacks *mutuality*. A contract, to be valid, must be *mutually* enforceable, which is to say, either party may enforce it. If an owner, for example, reserves an unqualified right to terminate a contract, the contract is illusory and lacks mutuality and therefore is not binding on either party.

> In *City of Pocatello v Fidelity & Deposit Co.*, 267 F 181 (CCA Idaho 1920), a contract for construction of a city water supply was at issue. The city reserved the right to terminate the contract if, for any reason, it failed to sell the bonds to finance the project. The parties fell into dispute over the city's refusal to grant an extension to the contractor, and the contractor refused to proceed with the work. The city performed the work by other means and filed suit against the contractor. HELD: The contract was unenforceable because it lacked mutuality. The city had the option to terminate the contract at any time and had in effect the right to escape liability to the contractor regardless of work performed by the contractor.

§ 1.08 Mutual Assent

The formation of a contract requires a manifestation of mutual assent. Manifestation of mutual assent is not to be confused with a meeting of the minds. A *meeting of the minds* implies a perfect understanding by each party of the intentions of the other party. Such perfect understanding is possible, perhaps, but seldom achieved in a construction contract. It is a commonplace observation that the expectations of an owner may differ considerably from the product that a contractor intends to deliver, even though the parties may have signed a well articulated contract with detailed drawings and specifications. Therefore it is not the secret, unexpressed intentions and beliefs of the parties that govern the formation of a contract, but the outward manifestation of that intent. It is only by considering the words actually used by the parties, and not what the parties had in mind when they used those words, that a court can interpret and enforce contractual obligations.

§ 1.09 Offer and Acceptance

Contracts are usually formed by offer and acceptance. For example, S: "I will sell you my horse for $500." B: "Done!" This is a contract. It is a manifestation of mutual assent supported by consideration between competent parties and for a legal object. The contract is sufficiently certain to be enforceable and, indeed, is hardly subject to misinterpretation. If it is objected that the contract does not sufficiently describe the time for performance, the law will supply a reasonable time.

An offer often elicits a *counter-offer* rather than an unqualified acceptance. For example, S: "I'll sell you my horse for $500." B: "I'll give you $400." S: "Done." In this example, the counter-offer was accepted and a contract formed. Now suppose, S: "I'll sell you my horse for $500." B: "I'll give you $400." S: "No deal." B: "OK I'll give you $500." Here, no contract has been formed because the counter-offer "I'll give you $400" terminated the offer, which could not thereafter be accepted. Now suppose, S: "I'll sell you my horse for $500." B: "I'm sorry I was late. The traffic was terrible today." S: "I withdraw my offer." B: "I accept your offer." Here, no contract was formed because the offer was withdrawn before it was accepted.

§ 1.10 Delivery

Mutual assent to the terms of a contract is usually indicated by the signatures of both parties to the contract document. Is a contract formed when the document has been signed by both parties, or only when a signed copy has been delivered to both parties? As a general rule, it is the signature *and delivery* of a document that forms a binding contract. There are, however, exceptions. It is possible for a party to manifest assent to a contract document short of delivering a signed copy to the other party.

> In *MJ Oldenstedt Plumbing v K-Mart*, 257 Ill App 3d 759, 195 Ill Dec. 906, 629 NE2d 214 (1994), contractor accepted subcontractor's bid in a telephone conversation and stated that a written agreement would follow by mail. When the subcontractor received the written form, the subcontractor signed the form but never delivered it to the contractor. Nevertheless, the subcontractor commenced performance of the work, and informed the contractor that it would deliver a copy of the signed document. HELD: A contract was formed. It was reasonable for the contractor to believe that the subcontractor had agreed to the terms of the document and therefore the subcontractor was estopped to deny the agreement.

§ 1.11 Contracts Without Words

It is quite possible to make a contract without any words at all. An ordinary gas station offers a commonplace example of such a contract. The gas pump has a price on it. A customer comes in and pumps ten gallons of gas. An enforceable contract has arisen here because a customer, by actions, has promised to pay for the gas. One way to explain this contract is to say that the availability of the gas pump with the price stated on the register constitutes an offer to sell gas for that price, and pumping constitutes the acceptance of the offer and a promise to pay.

> In *Wattie Wolfe Co. v Superior Contractors, Inc.*, 417 P2d 302 (Okla. 1966), Superior Contractors, Inc., without benefit of a written contract, performed backfilling, compacting, and paving over a sewer line on an air force base job. The utilities subcontractor denied that the sub-subcontract for backfilling, compacting, and paving covered the entire line. Superior Contractors, Inc. had backfilled, compacted, and paved the entire line without objection from the utilities subcontractor. HELD: The subcontractor accepted the benefits of the transaction and its conduct manifested the existence of a contract covering the entire project. Therefore, a contract is implied from the conduct of the parties.

§ 1.12 Options

An offer may ordinarily may be withdrawn at any time before it has been accepted, leaving the parties in the same position as if the offer had never been made. However, an offeror may contract to keep the offer open. Suppose S: "I'll sell you my horse for $500, and I agree to keep this offer open for ten days." After five days, S revokes the offer. On the ninth day, B accepts the offer. *No contract!* S had the right to withdraw the offer in spite of the promise to keep it open for ten days. A promise is not enforceable unless it is supported by consideration. Here, B gave no consideration for the promise to keep the offer open for ten days.

B, however, could *take an option* on the horse by rendering consideration for the promise to keep the offer open for ten days. If the parties agree that the offer will be kept open for ten days, and if B pays S a dollar (or some other consideration) for the option, then S is rendered legally powerless to revoke the offer.

§ 1.13 Mistake

Under narrowly circumscribed rules, conduct that would otherwise result in the formation of a contract does not do so if the assent of one of the parties was procured through a mistake of fact. The policy of the law here is to prevent a party from unfairly taking advantage of a mistake by another party. Suppose, for example, that B offers to buy a horse named Man of War from S for $100,000. Because of the price, S knows that B is laboring under the mistaken impression that Man of War is the winner of the triple crown. The horse that is the object of this transaction, though, is just an ordinary horse. S would not be able to enforce the contract of sale because S knew, or should have known that B's promise was induced by a material mistake of fact.

Now suppose S submits a bid of $100,000 to K to perform the plumbing work on a school job. In figuring its bid, S made a clerical error in addition by transposing numbers so that the cost of 3/4 inch pipe was figured at 57 cents a foot rather than 75 cents a foot as result of which the amount of the bid was $12,500 lower than intended. K receives four other bids for the same scope of work one of which is $104,000, another is $111,000, and the other two are somewhat higher. K accepts S's low bid of $100,000. S now refuses to perform the work on the ground that it really intended to bid $112,500 and, through a clerical mistake, the bid was only $100,000. Here, S would be required to perform the work because K had no reason to know that S's bid was induced by a clerical mistake. K can show that it is not unusual for plumbing bids for school work to vary by as much as 20%.

Now suppose the same situation, but S by clerical error omitted the cost of 3/4 inch pipe entirely from its bid, which was $80,000. Other bids were $104,000, $111,000, $116,000, and $135,000. Here, S introduces evidence that a wide variation in bids is highly unusual and that K should therefore have known that there was something wrong with S's bid and that, in fact, it was probably induced by some kind of mistake. Under such circumstances, K could not take advantage of S's mistake by accepting the bid. Even though it might appear that a contract had been formed, in this case, there would be no contract because S's apparent assent to the contract was vitiated by clerical error, or *mistake*.

Now let us assume the erroneous $80,000 bid alerts K to the likelihood of error, so, before bid opening time, K calls S on the phone and says the bid looks low and S should recheck. A few minutes later S calls K back and says the figures have been rechecked and S is satisfied with them and therefore the bid stands. K is now faced with a dilemma. K still suspects that there may be something wrong with S's figures, but on the other hand K knows that a dozen of other prime contractors are bidding the job and that S has submitted a bid to all prime bidders and, therefore, if K doesn't use S's bid and the other prime bidders do use S's bid, K won't get the job. With some trepidation, K uses the bid and the job is awarded to K. S now refuses to perform, claiming mistake. Here, the law would enforce the contract simply because it was reasonable under the circumstances for K to take S's word that the bid was a legitimate bid, and not induced by mistake. S's representation here is an example of *estoppel*. Having deliberately induced K to believe that its bid was legitimate, S would not be allowed to falsify that statement by claiming the bid was induced by mistake.

> In *Kutsche v Ford*, 222 Mich 442, 192 NW 714 (1923), contractor mistakenly omitted from its estimate a $7,000 figure for plastering. The school board nevertheless attempted to accept the bid. HELD: The contractor is relieved of its bid. District should not be allowed to profit from the contractor's mistake.

Error of Judgment

The fact that a party makes an error of judgment in agreeing to be bound by contract will not allow that party to escape from the obligation of a contract. Suppose, for example, that B agrees to buy a spec home from S in the mistaken belief that the market for housing is about to rise. In fact, before the close of escrow, the market falls. B cannot escape from the contract because it now appears that it will be unprofitable because of an error in judging the market. This is an error in judgment, rather than an error of fact, and it is only an error of fact that vitiates a contract. By the same token, a framing subcontractor would not be relieved of the consequences of a bid because of a sudden increase in lumber prices.

Mistake in Law

Suppose B agrees to buy Blackacre for $500,000 mistakenly believing that Blackacre is zoned R-4. Blackacre is actually zoned R-1. Such a mistake would not vitiate the contract because it is a mistake of law rather than a mistake of fact. Suppose that O employs K to build a one-story house on Blackacre under the mistaken belief that the zoning law prohibits construction of a two-story house in the neighborhood. Such a mistake of law would not vitiate the contract.

Now suppose B agrees to buy Blackacre under the mistaken belief it is zoned R-4, and S shares that mistaken belief. This is known as a mutual mistake of law. If parties enter into a contract under a mutual mistake of law, both wrongly believing the law to be the same thing, and under circumstances where neither party would have made the contract had it known the true state of the law, then the supposed contract does not come into existence since the agreement would never have been made if both parties had known the true state of the law.

§ 1.14 Duress

An agreement procured by *duress* is not enforceable. The law would not enforce a contract signed at gun point. To create an enforceable legal obligation, consent must be freely given.

In rare circumstances, the law recognizes that a contract may be vitiated by *economic duress*. In the construction industry, this may occur when a contractor is desperate for money and therefore signs a full release in exchange for partial payment. If the contractor can show that there was no good faith dispute as to the amount earned under the contract, that the contract had been fully performed, and that the contractor simply had to have some money to meet payroll, otherwise go out of business, the release could be invalidated by economic duress. It is only rarely, though, that the economic pressures of doing business in the construction industry rise to the level of economic duress.

The courts recognize that it is not unusual for contractors to operate under economic pressure, and that it would be difficult for parties to conduct business if releases could be easily nullified simply because they were signed under economic pressure.

> In *Vulcan Painters, Inc. v MCI Constructors, Inc.*, 41 F3d 1457 (11th Cir 1995), subcontractor had submitted seven claim letters seeking damages for delay at a time when it was low on cash to cover its payroll. Subcontractor negotiated for a $50,000 payment. Immediately after the negotiations were completed, subcontractor's president left town and was not in the office when a final release was faxed by the contractor. The president directed the controller to execute the release, using the signature stamp of the president, but did not read the document until weeks later. HELD: The release was valid and enforceable. The president executed the document

without having read it, and cannot set up duress or ignorance of the contents of the document to avoid the obligation.

A contract signed under compelling fear of economic loss is not enforceable.

In *Thomas Constr Co. v Kelso Marine, Inc.*, 639 F2d 216 (5th Cir 1981), subcontractor submitted an oral bid to supply redi-mix for a hospital project. The oral bid was confirmed by the subcontractor in writing. After the hospital job was awarded to the prime contractor, the subcontractor demanded a higher price. The prime contractor was over a barrel because there was no economically feasible alternate source, and signed a purchase order increasing the price. HELD: Economic duress precluded the formation of an enforceable contract. The prime contractor was compelled by fear of economic loss to sign the purchase order.

In *Willms Trucking v JW Constr*, 442 SE2d 197 (SC Ct App 1994), a contractor who had signed a release filed an action against a project owner for breach of a written change order. When contractor began to excavate the site of a mini warehouse facility it was discovered that unsuitable soil was present and that "muck and fill work" would be required. The parties signed a change order for the muck and fill work, but the owner refused to pay for it and eventually terminated the contract. HELD: The release was enforceable. The contractor executed the release under duress because it was under great pressure to pay its subcontractors and suppliers.

A contract extracted under a threat of stopping work may be unenforceable if the agreement is produced by economic duress.

In *Hotel Constructors, Inc. v Seagrave Corp.*, 574 F Supp 384 (SDNY 1983), a hotel owner signed two construction contract modifications: the first increased the contract price by $750,000 and the second added another $100,000. Work on the curtain wall subcontract had progressed to a point where it would not be feasible for another subcontractor to take over performance of the work. The curtain wall subcontractor threatened to stop work unless the owner agreed to the price increases. HELD: The modifications, signed under duress, were unenforceable.

§ 1.15 Contract Induced by Fraud

A contract induced by fraud is not enforceable.

Suppose K says to S, a plumbing subcontractor, "If you'll take this job for $100,000 you'll make a lot of money". S, believing this to be true, signs the contract. S, on further reflection, determines that the job is a loser and attempts to cancel the contract on that ground. Here, the contract would be enforceable because it was based on K's statement of opinion, and not on a representation of fact.

Now suppose K tells S that the soil to be excavated by S contains no rock and therefore S will make a lot of money by contracting to perform excavation and grading work for $100,000. In fact, K has seen a soils report that shows that the soil contains rock. Here, since S's assent to the contract was procured by a misrepresentation of fact, believed by S to be true, the contract is not enforceable.

> In *Taylor and Jennings, Inc. v Bellino Bros Constr Co.*, 106 AD2d 779, 483 NYS2d 813 (1984), subcontractor agreed to lay 3,200 lineal feet of concrete sewer pipe and to install 21 manholes for the prime contract unit price less 10 percent. The unit price recorded in the subcontract was based on fraudulent misrepresentations by the prime contractor as to the unit prices contained in the prime contract document. Subcontractor accidentally saw the prime contract unit prices and thus discovered that the amounts had been misrepresented by the prime contractor. HELD: The subcontract was void for fraud and therefore the subcontractor was entitled to recover the reasonable value of its performance.

§ 1.16 Bidding

Construction contracts are often put out for bid. The owner may, and often does, reserve the right to reject the low bid, or reject all bids. Such an invitation to bid is, in legal contemplation, an invitation to make an offer. The owner, of course, is not legally bound to accept any offer.

An unaccepted bid is merely an offer, and not a contract.

In *Heritage Pools, Inc. v Foothills Metro Recreation & Park Dist*, 701 P2d 1260 (Colo. Ct App 1985), bidders on a recreational pool construction project were required to list their subcontractors. The park district required the low bidder to substitute a more experienced subcontractor for Heritage Pools, Inc., the listed subcontractor. After the substitution of the subcontractor had been agreed to, the district awarded the work. The replaced subcontractor filed an action against the park district, alleging that it was a third party beneficiary of the contract between the park district and the contractor. HELD: Bids, as mere offers, do not impose contractual obligations until accepted. The prime contractor's bid was not accepted until after the subcontractor had been "substituted out" and therefore Heritage Pools was merely an incidental party, and not a third party beneficiary. The listing of Heritage Pools in the prime contractor's bid did not constitute an independent bid by Heritage Pools to the park district.

An invitation to bid may expressly provide that the owner will contract for a project with the lowest responsible bidder. In such a case, the invitation to bid may be treated as an offer that can be accepted and therefore ripen into a contract.

Public agencies have occasionally attempted to award a contract to a second low bidder deemed "more responsible" or "more qualified". They cannot do so without violating competitive bidding laws adopted in most states.

In *Swinerton & Walberg Co. v City of Inglewood-Los Angeles Civic Center Auth*, 40 Cal App 3d 98, 114 Cal Rptr 834 (1974), a city awarded a construction contract to the second low bidder on the ground that the second low bidder was more qualified to perform the work than the low bidder. HELD: The city had promised to award the contract to the lowest responsible bidder, and the low bidder reasonably had detrimentally relied on that promise when it went to the expense of preparing its bid. Therefore the low bidder was entitled to recover damages from the city in an action based on promissory estoppel.

§ 1.17 Ethics of Bidding

"It costs money to bid a job." For this reason it is considered unethical to award a contract to a favored bidder who did not submit the lowest bid. It is also unethical to give a favored bidder a "last look" at competitive bids so as to enable that favored bidder to submit the low bid. To do so is to take unfair advantage of a bidder's work and expertise because, after all, if the bidder knew that its bid was to be used only to check the validity of a competitor's number, the bidder would never incur the trouble, expense, and potential liability of figuring the job and submitting a bid. Do these "ethical" considerations find support in the law? They do to a large degree. For an owner to invite bids with no intention of awarding a contract to the low bidder, but merely to check the figures of a favored, pre-selected contractor would be actionable fraud, for the owner, either expressly or implied, promises to award the contract to the low bidder, or at least to give fair consideration to all bidders. To issue an invitation to bid when the contractor has been already pre-selected would be a sham.

Public agencies must give fair consideration to bids.

> In *King v Alaska State Hous Auth*, 633 P2d 256 (Alaska 1981), the authority undertook an urban renewal project and announced that property owners in the project area would be given preferential consideration as redevelopers. Owner submitted a proposal but the authority awarded the redevelopment contract to a competing redeveloper. HELD: When it solicited bids, in exchange for a bidder's investment of time and resources in preparing a bid, the authority impliedly promised to consider the bid honestly and fairly. A breach of that implied promise would entitle a bidder to recover the costs incurred in preparing the bid. Here, there was no reasonable basis for the authority's decision to award the contract to the competing redeveloper.

§ 1.18 Promissory Estoppel

An unaccepted bid is an unaccepted offer. Normally, an unaccepted offer can be withdrawn at any time by the offeror. Application of the doctrine of *promissory estoppel*, however, may prevent this.

Customary and accepted construction industry bidding practices provide an interesting example of the workings of the free enterprise system. Trade contractors hesitate to expose their bids until the last possible moment for fear that the prime contractor may reveal the bid to another more favored subcontractor. (A practice known as *bid shopping*.) Therefore trade contractors telephone their bids to contractors mostly during the last hour before bid opening time. For a moderate size job, this means that something over 100 trade contractors may telephone their bids to some dozen or so prime contractors in a period of 60 minutes. Since bids are not always "comparable" (for example, some bids may contain exclusions, some subcontractors may submit a single bid for two trades) the reader will not be surprised to learn that mistakes occur.

Let us say that a dozen prime bidders have submitted their bids to an owner by 2:00 on a Friday afternoon (the bid opening time). The owner now has twelve *offers* to consider. Can the owner pick and choose which offer to accept, or must it accept the lowest responsible bid? Most public agencies are bound by statute to award the contract to the lowest responsible bidder. But even a private owner, taking bids for a hotel or a warehouse, may be obliged to award the contract to the lowest responsible bidder. But, you will say, there is no contractual obligation for the owner to make such an award. The invitation to bid was not an offer -- the prime contractors' bids are not acceptances -- therefore, no contract has been formed.

Here, the owner's obligation to award the contract to the lowest responsible bidder is based on a legal doctrine called *promissory estoppel*. The doctrine states that when a party should know that its conduct will cause another to rely upon it in a definite and substantial way, then the party may not be allowed to falsify the promise that is implied by that conduct. Here, the owner knew that prime contractors would be induced to expend significant resources in bidding the job in reliance on the statement that the contract would be awarded to the lowest responsible bidder. Therefore, under the doctrine of promissory estoppel, the owner is required to do just that: award the contract to the lowest responsible bidder. The effect of the application of the doctrine of promissory estoppel is to convert the owner's invitation to bid into an *option*: an offer that cannot be withdrawn without the consent of the optionee (the lowest responsible prime bidder).

> In *Marbucco Corp. v City of Manchester*, 137 NH 629, 632 A2d 522 (1993), the city took bids for replacement of the windows at a public library. The invitation to bid required a base bid with eight

alternates. Plaintiff was the low bidder, but the city awarded the contract to another bidder who had submitted an unsolicited alternate #9. The low bidder sued the city to recover the cost of preparing its bid and the profit it would have made if the contract had been awarded to the low bidder. HELD: Plaintiff reasonably relied on the city's promise to award the contract to the lowest responsible bidder and therefore plaintiff was entitled to recover damages under the theory of promissory estoppel. Alternate #9, which was proposed by the bidder itself and not available to any other bidders, went beyond the bounds of a mere informality or irregularity.

The doctrine of promissory estoppel also applies to sub-bids. A prime contractor who uses a low sub-bid in compiling its own bid to the owner is obliged by the doctrine of promissory estoppel to award the subcontract to the low sub-bidder. Otherwise the prime bidder would be taking advantage of the low sub-bid to obtain the award of the prime contract, and the low sub-bidder would have incurred the trouble and expense of bidding the job for nothing.

In *Drennan v Star Paving Co.*, 51 Cal 2d 409, 333 P2d 757 (1958), Star Paving telephoned to Drennan a paving sub-bid of $7,131.60. This was the lowest bid, and Drennan computed its bid for a school job accordingly. Drennan was the low prime bidder and the school district awarded the project to Drennan. The following morning, Star informed Drennan that it had made a mistake on its bid, and eventually Star refused to perform the work for less than $15,000. Drennan, after shopping for several months, contracted the work for $10,948.60. Drennan sued for the difference. HELD: Drennan was entitled to recover the difference between Star's bid and the paving cost. Here, the subcontractor made a promise that Drennan relied on in a definite and substantial manner. Star should have anticipated such reliance. Such a promise, even if unaccepted, will be enforced if injustice cannot be avoided in any other way.

Now let us suppose that a prime contractor submits its "standard form" subcontract document to a low responsible sub-bidder. The sub-bidder refuses to sign the form because it objects to certain obnoxious (to the subcontractor) provisions in the subcontract form. No contract is formed until both parties have signed the same form. But under the doctrine of promissory estoppel, the parties have an obligation to negotiate in good faith a subcontract document that is fair to both sides. In determining the good faith of the negotiations, the courts rely upon expert testimony as to trade practice dealing with currently accepted forms of subcontract documents.

> In *Hawkins Constr Co. v Reiman Corp.*, 245 Neb 131, 511 NW2d 113 (1994), Hawkins relied upon Reiman's low paving bid and, after being awarded the prime contract, sent Reiman a 17-page Subcontract Agreement that contained non-standard terms that were found objectionable by Reiman. After unsuccessful negotiations, Hawkins hired another subcontractor at a higher price. HELD: It was unreasonable for Hawkins to expect Reiman to agree to non-standard provisions contained in the subcontract form. Therefore Reiman was relieved of the duty to perform in accordance with the bid.

An essential element of the doctrine of promissory estoppel is reasonable reliance by the prime contractor on the subcontractor's bid. Suppose that a prime contractor receives a rebar bid of $139,511. At the same time, the prime contractor has received a number of other bids all of which are more than 20 percent higher. Would the prime contractor be justified in relying on such a bid, and using it in compiling its own bid? Should the prime contractor deduce that the bid is too low and therefore probably the result of a mistake?

> In such a case, *C&K Engineering Contractors v Amber Steel Co.*, 23 Cal 3d 1, 587 P2d 1136, 151 Cal Rptr 333 (1978), the prime contractor called the low bidder to say that its bid was "a hell of a lot lower" than 20 percent below the other bids for the same work, and asked the sub-bidder to recheck. Sub-bidder rechecked, and confirmed the bid. HELD: Here, the prime contractor complied with the trade custom of warning subcontractors of unusually low bids, and the sub-bidder, having confirmed its bid, was bound to pay the difference between the cost ($242,171) and its bid. The prime contractor was awarded judgment for $102,660.

The development of the doctrine of promissory estoppel is a good example of the way common law courts evolve legal doctrine in the interest of fairness. Under ordinary contract doctrine, a contract is only formed by an unconditional and explicit manifestation of mutual assent, usually by the mechanism of an offer followed by an acceptance. The doctrine of promissory estoppel was evolved by the courts to avoid injustice by supporting the ethical concepts of the construction industry.

§ 1.19 Auctions

At most auctions, the auctioneer reserves the right to withdraw an item from sale if it fails to fetch a predetermined price. However, if an auction is expressly declared to be *without reserve*, an item must be sold to the highest bidder regardless of the amount of the bid.

In the first case, the auctioneer is considered to be inviting bids, or offers, and when an item is knocked down it constitutes acceptance of the bidder's offer. In the second case, when the item goes on the block it is considered to be an irrevocable offer to sell to the highest bidder, and the high bid is deemed to be the acceptance of that offer to sell.

§ 1.20 The Battle of Forms

Most prime contractors evolve a form of subcontract that they consider to be effective in protecting their interests. These are sometimes drafted by lawyers and often evolve, painfully, clause by clause, from experience. Subcontractors, as well, usually have their own preprinted forms that give adequate protection to their interests. This sets the scene for the *battle of forms*, which may begin with a subcontractor submitting a written proposal that converts into a written contract if the contractor signs it. The prime contractor is seldom so complacent as to sign the subcontractor's form, but tenders its own form which is to be accepted when signed by the subcontractor. More often, the prime contractor sends an unsigned form to the subcontractor, thus reserving for itself the privilege of being the last to sign the document that creates the contractual relationship.

Let us suppose now that a contractor, having received two signed subcontract forms from a subcontractor, places its signature on both forms but fails to return a fully executed copy to the subcontractor. A week later, the subcontractor discovers an error in its estimate and promptly cancels the subcontract. *No contract!* When the subcontractor signed and returned the two forms it thereby extended an offer which could be accepted by the prime contractor not only by signing, *but also returning* a copy of the subcontract form to the subcontractor. If the prime contractor could accept the offer merely by signing a copy of the form without returning it to the subcontractor, there would be a lack of mutuality since the prime contractor could then abide by the contract or not, as might be dictated by its own developing interests.

Now let us assume the same situation in which the prime contractor signs both copies of the proffered subcontract form but fails to return one copy to the subcontractor. Nevertheless, the project manager schedules the subcontractor to start work on June 1, which subcontractor does. Now assume that one of the parties (it makes no difference whether it is the prime contractor or the subcontractor) seeks to cancel the contract. It may not legally do so. *A contract has been formed.* By its conduct in scheduling the commencement of the subcontractor's work, the contractor accepted the subcontractor's offer. By starting work, the subcontractor acknowledged that acceptance.

> In *MJ Oldenstedt Plumbing v K-Mart*, 257 Ill App 3d 759, 195 Ill Dec. 906, 629 NE2d 214 (1994), it was held that delivery was not an essential element to the formation of a subcontract, when the subcontractor signed its copy but never delivered it to the prime contractor. By signing its copy of the contract and commencing work, the subcontractor accepted the terms of the written contract.
>
> In *Central Indus Eng. Co. v Strauss Constr Co.*, 98 Cal App 3d 460, 159 Cal Rptr 564 (1979), prime sent to sub a form of contract calling for a 15 percent retention and including a "pay if paid" clause. Sub returned the documents with a letter changing the 15 percent retention to a 10 percent retention and deleting the pay if paid clause. Prime filed the letter along with its copy of the subcontract document. Prime then made progress payments to sub, withholding 10 percent rather than 15 percent. HELD: Prime had accepted the proposed modification by its conduct in not objecting to it and in withholding 10 rather than 15 percent as retention.

Now let us suppose that a contractor signs and sends to a plumbing subcontractor two subcontract forms. The forms provide that the subcontractor will supply a plumbing system and supply seismic strapping for all pipe, and that the subcontractor will not be entitled to receive payment until it has paid for all materials supplied to the job. The subcontractor crosses out and initials those provisions, signs the form and sends it back to the contractor. The contractor retains the form in its file but does not initial the strikeouts. Subcontractor performs the work but does not install the seismic strapping. The contractor makes progress payments but refuses to make the final payment until the subcontractor has paid for all pipe.

Here, a contract was formed when the parties manifested their mutual assent by performance. The prime contractor's offer to enter into a contract was rejected when the subcontractor modified the form. The question is whether the prime contractor accepted the modification of the form. By its actions, the contractor did so by accepting performance without seismic strapping. From this it may be inferred that the contractor was aware of the modifications and therefore, by its conduct, accepted the subcontractor's offer to enter into the modified contract and therefore acquiesced in the deletion of the payment provision.

§ 1.21 Modification

Every contract is subject to modification (particularly, it seems, every construction contract). Project owners and architects are notorious for changing details of construction as the physical development of structures previously known only by drawings, sketches, and descriptions becomes available for inspection. This desire to improve upon the structures and facilities envisioned by the drawings requires a *modification* to the contract (the legal term is "*modification*"; the construction lingo is "*change order*" or "*extra*").

Occasionally an owner (or a misguided owner's lawyer), determined to avoid *extras*, writes a contract clause that prohibits *modifications*. For example,

> This will be a no extras contract. The contractor acknowledges that the contract documents define a complete and buildable project and that the contractor will construct the entire work and obtain a certificate of occupancy without requesting any extra compensation whatsoever. The contractor will not be entitled to extra compensation in the absence of a written extra work order signed by both parties.

Such language may indeed protect the owner from unwanted extras, but it may also prevent the owner from ordering extra work that is wanted, or needed, for a final product that will fulfill the owner's needs. Consider the following scenario:

> Contract provides that under no circumstances will the contractor receive extra compensation. Owner decides to increase the manufacturing capacity of the assembly line and issues a change order for additional wiring and switch gear to accommodate additional machinery. Contractor refuses to figure the cost of the change order or to perform the additional work. Owner's lawyer advises that the only way to obtain performance of the extra work would be to employ another contractor. This, owner finds, would be impractical and prohibitively expensive. The *no extras* clause gave the contractor tremendous leverage to negotiate a fat price for the extra.

In law, once a contract has been formed, each party has the right to stand on the contract. So long as one party performs its side of a contract, the other party is legally obliged likewise to perform. A party cannot unilaterally change the terms of a contract because to do so would be a breach. In our example the contractor had the right to carry out the promise it had made to install the electrical system per the contract documents, and the owner had no right to change that promise.

We can see, then, that from an owner's point of view one of the most important provisions that should be included in a construction contract is a provision that the owner reserves the right to increase, reduce, or change the scope of the work.

In the absence of such a clause, a contract can only be modified by a manifestation of mutual assent supported by consideration. The requirements for *modification* of a contract are the same as the requirements for the *formation* of a contract.

> As part of a highway construction project, contractor was required to clear timber and was entitled to retain the timber that it cleared. A subcontract provided that subcontractor would supply clearing and grubbing for $1,200 per acre. Contractor orally permitted the subcontractor to do as it pleased with the timber. The timber was then appropriated by a third party, and subcontractor offered to complete the job for $1,700 an acre. Contractor did not respond to subcontractor's offer, and subcontractor completed performance. HELD: There was no enforceable oral or written

> modification to the subcontract since the contractor never accepted the subcontractor's proposal to increase the cost of the work and therefore the alleged modification was not fully executed by both parties.

Westfork Constr Co. v Nelson, Inc., 877 P2d 481 (Mont. 1994).

In construction industry usage, modification is usually accomplished by a written change order in which the parties agree that the contractor will perform a change in the work in exchange for negotiated compensation. (In the case of a *deletion*, the parties agree to a reduction in the contract price in exchange for removing items from the scope of the work.) The modification is supported by consideration because the contractor performs more (or less) work for an increase (or decrease) in the contract price.

One may occasionally encounter a change order that is not supported by consideration. Suppose, for example, that an architect issues a field order calling for upgraded paint. The field order specifies that there will be no change in the contract price or the contract time. Contractor accepts the field order by signing it. Later, the contractor informs the owner that it will not change the paint unless it receives additional compensation. Here, the contractor's position is sustained by law because the modification, since it was not supported by consideration, is unenforceable. (Such an outcome would be avoided by a contract clause providing that the contractor would comply with all field orders issued by the architect and that the question of compensation, if any, would be resolved in a manner specified by the contract documents.)

> An electrical subcontract for a school project provided that the owner would purchase switchgear, but the installation and final connection of the switchgear would be performed by the subcontractor. The subcontractor, claiming it had not seen the addendum that introduced the switchgear requirement, persuaded the prime contractor to sign a letter that called for reimbursement for the installation of the switchgear. HELD: The alleged modification was not supported by consideration and therefore was unenforceable.

J&R Elec Division v Skoog Constr Co., 38 Ill App 3d 747, 348 NE2d 474 (1976).

It is said that a claim for extra work requires proof of five elements.

> A judgment of $4,902.72 for extra work performed by a contractor on a contract to build a home addition was affirmed. The court explained that the contractor, in order to recover for extra work, had the burden of proving 1) the work was outside the scope of the work defined by the contract, 2) the owner ordered the extras, 3) the owner expressly or impliedly agreed to pay for the extras, 4) the extras were not furnished by the contractor as a voluntary act, and 5) the extras were not rendered necessary by the negligence of the contractor.

Kern v Rafferty, 131 Ill App 3d 728, 476 NE2d 52 (1985).

A contractor is not entitled to extra compensation merely because the work covered by the contract is made more expensive due to unforeseen conditions.

> Soil at a dam site contained more moisture than anticipated. The owner had provided bidders with geotechnical data, but bidders were instructed to make their own investigation and no price adjustment would be made for unforeseen conditions. HELD: A party who agrees to complete construction for a fixed cost must absorb any losses resulting from unforeseen conditions. The contract squarely placed the risk of uncertainty as to soil conditions on the contractor. There can be no recovery for extra work if the work is covered by the terms of the contract. The contractor is not entitled to additional compensation merely because its work was made more expensive by moist soil conditions.

Green Constr Co. v Kansas Power & Light Co., 1 F3d 1005 (10th Cir 1993).

§ 1.22 Oral Modification

Suppose Calvin signs a contract to build a hotel for Oscar for $10,000,000 and to complete the work by June 1. On February 1, it looks to Oscar as if Calvin is falling behind schedule. He therefore agrees to give Calvin a bonus of $100,000 if the job is finished by June 1. This modification would not be legally enforceable, because the promise to pay $100,000 on one side is not supported by any consideration on the other side. All Calvin has to do to earn the $100,000 is something he was already legally obliged to do anyway: finish the job on time.

A written contract is subject to oral modification, but only if the modification has been fully performed on one side. Suppose a written contract to sell a horse for $500 on June 1. Buyer offers to pay seller an additional $50 if seller will keep the horse and feed it until July 1. Seller agrees. This oral modification of a written contract would not be enforceable until fully performed on one side. By feeding the horse for an extra month, seller would be entitled to enforce the oral modification.

The reason for these rules is to prevent the fraud or misunderstanding that could be encouraged by allowing oral modification of written contracts. The integrity of written contracts could become no stronger than one person's word against another! Full performance on one side, however, gives evidence of the authenticity of an oral modification.

Controversies often arise about whether a contractor is entitled to be paid for an *unwritten extra*. For example, owner asks contractor to increase the size of patio slab and contractor agrees to do so for $5.00 a square foot. Contractor performs but owner reneges. Here, the oral modification would be enforceable since it is supported by performance by the contractor.

> Subcontractor agreed to furnish concrete construction for payment to be computed by measuring the concrete inside the forms. Before performance began, the parties agreed orally to compute the price on the basis of cubic yardage of concrete delivered to the job. HELD: Plaintiff alleged adequate consideration for the oral modification and full performance on plaintiff's part enabled plaintiff to state a cause of action for additional compensation.

DL Godbey & Sons Constr Co. v Deane, 39 Cal 2d 429, 246 P2d 946 (1952).

§ 1.23 Written Change Order Requirement

Many construction contracts contain a provision that the contract can be modified only by a written change order. Under some circumstances, the written change order requirement is enforced by the courts. Under other circumstances, it may be held that the written change order requirement has been waived or rescinded.

Subcontracts for construction of an apartment building provided that extra compensation would not be paid without an express written change order. HELD: Blacktop subcontractor and drywall subcontractor were not entitled to extra compensation since their extra work was not supported by written change orders.

Hayle Floor Covering v First Minn. Constr, 253 NW2d 809 (Minn. 1977).

In *Acoustics, Inc. v Trepte Constr Co.*, 14 Cal App 3d 887, 92 Cal Rptr 723 (1971), the court said:

> Compliance with contractual provisions for written orders is indispensable in order to recover for alleged extra work . . . subordinate field personnel cannot waive the mandatory contract requirement that ordered changes or additions or extras be approved in writing by the state architect . . . The contract provisions show explicitly that Mr. Omelia had no authority to order the performance of disputed work . . . or order changes in the construction. . . .

92 Cal Rptr at 740.

It is often held that the written change order requirement is waived.

The contract for construction of a 40-unit apartment complex required that all change orders be in writing. The contractor discovered that certain additional work was needed in order to properly complete the project. The owner's representative said, "Get the project done. Get it done. We'll take care of it later." Contractor then performed extra work to conform the project to actual topography and actual boundaries that were not properly depicted on the drawings, and to install drainage culverts required by municipal regulations. HELD: The oral modification was enforceable. The contractor acted in good faith; owner had knowledge of the performance of the additional work and promised to pay for it.

Eastline Corp. v Marion Apartments, Ltd., 524 So 2d 582 (Miss 1988).

> A contract to build a home provided that extra work orders must be in writing and executed before the extra work was performed. The owner requested, and the contractor performed, extra work as required by changes in the plans and specifications. HELD: The parties waived the written change order requirement. The owner was estopped to enforce the written change order requirement since the contractor had installed the extra work at the owner's request.

Harrington v McCarthy, 91 Idaho 307, 420 P2d 790 (1966).

It is sometimes held that an owner is *estopped* to enforce a written change order requirement.

> On a coke battery project, contractor submitted over 1,300 revisions to an electrical subcontractor, 20 percent of which arrived after the projected completion date of the work. The revisions led to massive changes in the scope of the work. The subcontract contained a written change order requirement which the subcontractor requested be waived. The contractor never responded to the request for waiver. HELD: The contractor was estopped to enforce the written change order requirement. The revisions were performed at the request of the contractor and the revisions to the plans were marked "approved for construction". If the contractor had intended to enforce the written change order requirement, it was under a duty to notify the subcontractor of that intention.

EC Ernst, Inc. v Koppers Co., 626 F2d 324 (3d Cir 1980).

§ 1.24 Abandonment

It sometimes occurs that the parties to a construction contract make changes to the scope of the work that are so extensive that the courts hold that the contract has been *abandoned.* It may also be held that the parties have abandoned a written change order requirement.

> A homeowner and a home building contractor made 33 changes to the scope of the work, but at no time followed the requirement that change orders be reduced to writing. HELD: The contractor was entitled to recover the reasonable value of its work. The

conduct of the parties indicated that they intended to abandon the provisions of the written contract.

Campbell v Blount, 24 NC App 368, 210 SE2d 513 (1975).

The price of a subcontract was increased from $2,933,610 to a total of $4,551,239.21 by changes required because of poor engineering. HELD: Where the scope of work greatly exceeds that called for by a contract, abandonment of the written contract may be implied from the acts of the parties. Under such circumstances the subcontractor would be entitled to the reasonable value of its work.

Daugherty Co. v Kimberly-Clark Corp., 14 Cal App 3d 151, 92 Cal Rptr 120 (1971).

A contract for remodeling a paper mill contained a guaranteed maximum price of $4,789,000. Hundreds of changes were made because of complicated defective mechanical drawings. Judgment for the contractor $2,836,270.81 was AFFIRMED. The change in the scope of the work was of such magnitude that the parties implicitly mutually abandoned the contract. The parties ignored the written change order requirement. While the original contract price was $4,789,000, the contractor eventually performed work worth $8,194,713.02. When a construction contract is abandoned, the contractor should receive its *quantum meruit*, the reasonable value of its work based on its total costs.

C Norman Peterson Co. v Container Corp. of Am, 172 Cal App 3d 628, 218 Cal Rptr 592 (1985).

§ 1.25 Contracts That Must be in Writing

In the sixteenth century the English Parliament adopted a *statute of frauds* requiring that certain contracts be in writing. The purpose of the statute was to prevent fraud by placing some limitations on the types of contracts that may be oral. The statute of frauds still survives, in expanded versions in most states. The statute does not actually require that the *contract* be in writing to be enforceable, but that some *evidence* of the contract exist that is signed by the party to be bound therewith.

Thus the purpose of the statute, prevention of fraud, could be served by a letter, signed by the party to be bound, *describing* an oral agreement between two parties.

The following types of contract are required, in most states, to be in writing to be enforceable:

Real estate contracts. Contracts to sell real estate, leases, agreements to pay commissions to real estate brokers.

Contracts to make a will. An agreement that a certain person will inherit property.

Contract that can't be performed in less than one year. An agreement must be in writing if by its terms it cannot be performed within one year. An example would be an agreement, made in 1995, to transfer title to a vehicle in 1997.

Promise to answer for the debt or default of another. A guarantee that a debtor will pay a debt must be in writing to be enforceable. Likewise, surety bonds, such as payment and performance bonds, must be in writing to be enforceable.

Contract for sale of goods in excess of 50 pounds in value. The amount, expressed in dollars, varies from state to state: $5,000 is the order of magnitude.

Consumer contracts. Many states require that certain consumer contracts be in writing: examples are automobile sale contracts, gymnasium contracts, dancing school contracts and home improvement contracts.

> A plumbing subcontractor refused to perform work in an office building because of doubts about the financial responsibility of the prime contractor. In order to induce the subcontractor to perform, the owner of the building signed the subcontract document. HELD: The subcontract was not covered by the statute of frauds. The owner's signature was an original undertaking rather than a guarantee that the contractor would perform its obligations under the contract.

Otto Contracting Co. v Schinella & Son, 179 Conn. 704, 427 A2d 856 (1980).

§ 1.26 Parol Evidence Rule

"Parol evidence" is a confusing term. The word "parol" suggests "oral". The term "parol evidence", however, has nothing to do with "oral", but deals with statements (or conduct) during the negotiation of a written contract. The parol evidence rule, like the rule against oral modification of a written contract, protects the sanctity of the written word.

The parol evidence rule is based on the common sense assumption that when persons have taken the trouble to reduce an agreement to writing, the meaning of the agreement should be determined from the material contained within the four corners of the instrument, and not from consideration of the negotiations that preceded the execution of the instrument.

Suppose a contractor agrees to diligently and expeditiously remodel owner's home. Owner testifies that during the negotiation of the contract, before the contract was signed, contractor promised to finish the job by June 1. Contractor objects to the introduction of this testimony, contending that the evidence should be excluded because it violates the parol evidence rule. What was said during negotiations, contractor asserts, is irrelevant. It's the written contract that counts!

It is often said that the parol evidence rule is a rule for interpretation of contracts disguised as a rule of evidence. In our example, the issue that is really at stake is: what is the true meaning of "diligently and expeditiously". Does diligently and expeditiously mean by June 1? Or by June 1, provided the job is not delayed by rain? Or by June 1, come hell or high water?

> A contract for construction of a school required that the work be completed by a specified date. The contractor filed an action against the school district seeking compensation for acceleration of the schedule. The contractor offered evidence that in a pre-bid conference, school officials had stated that it would be permissible to finish the project any time up until eleven months after the specified completion date. HELD: The evidence was not admissible. The contract was integrated, and the evidence would have contradicted explicit provisions of the contract documents.

Lower Kuskokwim Sch Dist v Alaska Diversified Contr,Std of Pract, Interpretation by Arch or Eng, Inc., 734 P2d 62 (Alaska 1987),*cert denied*, 110 S Ct 725 (1990).

A stadium contractor accepted a supplier's oral bid for seating materials. Forty days later, the supplier reneged. The contractor purchased materials elsewhere and sued for the difference. HELD: The supplier waived the statute of frauds defense. The supplier knew the contractor would rely on its bid but took 40 days to renege. Moreover, in the usual course of business, contractors rely on oral bids received over the telephone.

HB Alexander & Son, Inc. v Miracle Recreation Equip Co., 314 Pa Super 1, 460 A2d 343 (1983).

The parol evidence rule applies to written agreements that appear to be "integrated". By this word is meant that the parol evidence rule only applies if the written instrument appears to be the final and complete expression of the agreement of the parties. A written contract that appears to be fragmented or partial, or to omit certain terms, is not subject to the parol evidence rule. An example of such a "non-integrated" contract would be one which specifies contractor will perform as agreed, when the words "as agreed" refer to agreements reached in conversation during the negotiation of the contract. (The integration can sometimes be achieved by an "integration clause" which specifically provides the written contract is the final and complete agreement of the parties and that the interpretation of the contract is not to be influenced by evidence of communication between the parties prior to the date of execution.)

How is one to know whether a contract is "integrated" or not? A document can appear to be complete and integrated even though it is not. For example, suppose a contract calls for conveyance of "the Tulare property". Although the document does not disclose it, seller owns two properties Tulare: one is a farm and the other is a gold mine. Buyer contends that the subject of the contract is the gold mine, but seller contends it is the farm. Seller wants to introduce evidence of conversations that dealt with irrigation, pest control, and other agricultural subjects rather than drifts, shafts, and assays.

In order to determine whether a contract that appears to be integrated is really integrated, a court must provisionally accept evidence of the conversations of the parties in order to determine whether the proffered statements are such as would naturally have been made by the parties under the circumstances: in other words, to determine whether the evidence is persuasive. If the court finds the evidence persuasive it will determine the contract was not "integrated", admit the evidence, and interpret the contract accordingly. The necessity of admitting evidence in order to determine whether a contract is integrated prevents the parol evidence rule from having much bite with modern courts. That the written words of a contract are sacred is a tarnished concept in modern law.

> The contract to outfit the interior of a theater included a payment schedule. Construction of the theater was delayed by the owner so the payment schedule took effect before it was time for the interior contractor to perform. After disputes, the interior contractor left the job. HELD: The owner was entitled to introduce parol evidence to explain that the parties intended for payments to be dependent upon work performed.

Fredericks v Filbert Co., 189 Cal App 3d 272, 234 Cal Rptr 395 (1987).

> Homeowner signed a cost plus contract with no guaranteed maximum. The court allowed the homeowner to testify that the contractor had agreed to a guaranteed maximum price. AFFIRMED. Parol evidence was admissible because the contract was silent on the subject of a guaranteed maximum, and the parol evidence did not alter or contradict the terms of the contract. Here, the proffered evidence merely supplied a missing element.

Petrus v Bunnell, 129 So 2d 702 (Fla. Dist Ct App), *cert denied*, 135 So 2d 742 (Fla. 1961).

> In *Quake Constr, Inc. v American Airlines*, 181 Ill App 3d 908, 537 NE2d 863 (1989), a contractor issued a letter of intent for an airport job. The court held that the language of the letter of intent was ambiguous and therefore parol evidence was admissible to ascertain whether the parties intended to be bound by the letter of intent or not.

> In *Pacific Gas & Elec Co. v GW Thomas Drayage & Rigging Co.*, 69 Cal 2d 33, 442 P2d 641, 9 Cal Rptr 561 (1968), the court held that parol evidence was admissible to show that the terms of a contract were ambiguous. The court said:

> The test of admissibility of extrinsic evidence to explain the meaning of a written instrument is not whether it appears to the court to be plain and unambiguous on its face, but whether the offered evidence is relevant to prove a meaning to which the language of the instrument is reasonably susceptible. . . . Although extrinsic evidence is not admissible to add to, detract from, or vary the terms of a written contract, these terms must first be determined before it can be decided extrinsic evidence is being offered for a prohibited purpose.

442 P2d at 644, 69 Cal Rptr 644.

§ 1.27 Interpretation of Contracts

Modern history shows that prerequisite to a market economy is a system of laws not the least vital of which is the law of contracts. An economic freedom prized in the democratic system of government is freedom to contract. Indeed, the construction industry offers a compelling example of the economic vitality fostered by the law of contracts.

By freedom of contract we mean simply the freedom to choose the promises we will extract in exchange for the promises we will make. A myriad of reported cases deal with the interpretation of contracts.

Montaigne said:

> There is more ado to interpret interpretations than to interpret things, and more books upon books than upon any other subject; we do nothing but comment upon one another.

"Of Experience", *Essays (1580-88)*.

Intention of the Parties

The freedom of contract is given practical effect by the dominant rule of interpretation: that a contract will be interpreted so as to carry into effect the intention of the parties. The importance of this rule of interpretation will be seen if we compare it to other possible rules: for example, that a contract should be interpreted so as to maximize the taxes enjoyed by the state or so as to support the principles of an organized religion.

Words of the Contract

In seeking to arrive at the true meaning of a contract, courts resort first of all, to the words of the contract.

> Disputed language in a contract to construct a mobile home park was the phrase "turn-key construction job". The court held that the term "turn-key construction job" made the contractor responsible to provide the design and construction of the project. The phrase was unambiguous and therefore extrinsic evidence as to the meaning of the term was inadmissible.

Mobile Home Envts v Barton & Barton, 432 F Supp 1343 (D Colo. 1977).

> Subcontract to clear acreage for a highway project provided that the subcontractor was bound to the prime contractor to the same extent that the prime contractor was bound to the state, and that if the subcontractor made a claim for extra compensation, the amount to be paid to the subcontractor would be no more than the amount recovered by the prime contractor from the state. Subcontractor was entitled to retain the timber it cleared, but the timber was appropriated by a third party. The prime contractor made a claim against the state and recovered $22,359.63 in settlement, which it paid to the subcontractor minus markup of $2,500. HELD: The subcontractor was bound by the unambiguous terms of the contract and could not recover any more than the amount recovered by the prime contractor from the state.

Westfork Constr Co. v Nelcon, Inc., 877 P2d 481 (Mont. 1994).

If the words utilized in a contract are clear and free of ambiguity, then they clearly express the intention of the parties and no interpretation is necessary. If, however, the words are ambiguous, fairly susceptible to more than one interpretation, then the courts resort to a hierarchy of rules of interpretation.

Interpretation by the Parties

The practical interpretation by the parties to a contract is given great weight. Parties, by their conduct in the performance of a contract, often clear up ambiguous language. Suppose, for example, that a contract provides for construction of a project in 250 days. This is ambiguous, because it could be interpreted as 250 working days or 250 calendar days. Contractor submits a schedule to the owner that shows the contract complete in 250 working days. Owner acknowledges receipt of the schedule and does not object to it. Here, the parties by their conduct have clarified the ambiguity and we know that "250 days" means "250 *working* days".

> A subcontract provided that subcontractor would supply quality control testing services for an estimated $44,000 to be ". . . Invoiced on a Unit Price Basis, either at a cost per hour or cost per test. . . ." After 15 months, prime contractor refused to make further payments. By that time, the unit price billings and payments had exceeded the estimate by $8,617.64. HELD: The intention of the parties was indicated by the fact that the contractor paid invoices for 15 months based on unit cost charges. This made it clear that the $44,000 was only an estimate, and not a guaranteed maximum price.

Professional Serv Indus v JP Constr, Inc., 241 Neb 862, 491 NW2d 351 (1992).

Technical Words and Trade Usage

Technical words when used in a contract are given a technical interpretation. If a word is defined by trade usage, and the contracting parties are members of the trade, then the trade interpretation prevails. For example, the term "smooth and level" may carry an established trade usage such as, plus or minus 1/10 of a foot in ten feet. "Slope to drain" may have an established trade usage that defines the degree of slope.

> A contract provided for "turn-key" construction of a residence with a guaranteed maximum price of $85,000. HELD: The word "turn-key" has an accepted meaning in the construction industry. The contractor was required to complete the work so that the house was ready for occupancy by the owner.

Blue v RL Glosson Contracting, Inc., 173 Ga. App 622, 327 SE2d 582 (1985).

The plans for the construction of a medical clinic contained details illustrating two alternate reinforcement schemes. Trade practice in the area dictated that rebar should be installed per scheme 1 rather than per scheme 2. HELD: The contractor was charged with knowledge of trade standards and practices in the community.

Fortec Constructors v United States, 760 F2d 1288 (Fed Cir 1985).

Specifications required contractor to paint "all previously painted or varnished surfaces". The contractor figured the job assuming that a baked enamel surface was not included in the surfaces to be painted. Trade usage supported the contractor's interpretation. HELD: When a trade usage is well established, well defined, and well recognized, the government will be presumed to be aware of it. The contractor was therefore entitled to receive an equitable adjustment of the contract price.

Gholson, Byars & Holmes Constr Co. v United States, 173 Ct Cl 374, 351 F2d 987 (Ct Cl 1965).

Interpretation by Architect or Engineer

A contract provision may give an architect or an engineer the power to interpret contract provisions or to resolve ambiguities in the contract documents. Such provisions are enforceable when they deal with technical construction issues.

Paragraph 35 of a construction contract provided that final approval of the project would be determined by the project engineer. The engineer issued a certificate of completion and contractor applied for final payment. The county refused to pay, and instead conducted a second final inspection and produced a list of discrepancies. After the contractor had corrected those discrepancies, the county made a third final inspection and still refused to make the final payment. HELD: The engineer was qualified as arbitrator under the contract and the county was bound to make final payment.

United Pac Ins Co. v County of Flatheat, 499 F2d 1235 (9th Cir 1974).

When an engineer exercises judgment in favor of its own employer and against a contractor, the courts are reluctant to uphold a contract provision making the decision of the engineer final and binding.

> Contractor claimed compensation for additional expenses caused by unanticipated subsurface conditions. Under a clause in the contract documents, the chief engineer of the Transit Authority was authorized to determine every question and determination was to be final and conclusive. The contract also gave the engineer the final decision with respect to compensation for unanticipated subsurface conditions. HELD: "To give to the Engineer who is obligated to the City, the power to conclusively bind the contractor on legal determinations and, in effect, expose the contractor to the risks of performing, without compensation, work outside the intent of the contract . . . would . . . be tantamount to 'confer[ing] upon the municipality the unilateral power to modify the agreement and to impose on the contractor risks which he did not assume as part of his bargain.'"

Thomas Crimmins Contracting Co. v City of New York, 138 AD2d 138, 530 NYS2d 779 (1988), *affd*, 74 NY2d 166, 542 NE2d 1097, 544 NYS2d 580 (1989).

At minimum, when an engineer's decision is final, the engineer must afford due process to the contractor.

> Contract for construction of a dam provided the state engineer would decide disputes between contractor and the state. The contract provided that engineer's decision was "final and conclusive unless it is fraudulent or capricious or arbitrary or so grossly erroneous as necessarily to imply that faith." The engineer denied contractor's claims. HELD: The decision of the engineer was not enforceable because the engineer did not give the contractor due process. The engineer relied on factual material in making its decision, but failed to advise the contractor in advance. Thus, the contractor did not have a reasonable opportunity to refute the evidence that the engineer relied upon.

Zurn Eng v State, 69CalApp 3d798,138Cal Rptr478, *cert denied*,434 US985 (1977).

Satisfaction Clause

Suppose a contract provision requires work to be performed to the satisfaction of the architect, and the architect is honestly dissatisfied with the contractor's performance, but the dissatisfaction is unreasonable. Will the satisfaction clause be enforced? Courts hold that a contractor has properly performed its work if a reasonable person would be satisfied, even though the architect, engineer, or owner may be dissatisfied.

> Subcontractor supplied aluminum walls for a Chevrolet plant. The contract provided that the work, including artistic effect, was subject to approval by the architect and that final acceptability would rest strictly with the owner. In bright sunlight, the walls did not appear to have a uniform finish and the owner rejected the work. The jury was instructed that satisfaction clauses are to be determined by objective criteria. HELD: The "reasonable person standard" applies when the work involves commercial quality, operative fitness, or mechanical utility. The "good faith standard" applies when the work must satisfy personal aesthetics or fancy. Here, the contract called for a mill finish wall and it was difficult if not impossible to achieve a uniform finish with such aluminum. Therefore the "reasonable person" test was correctly applied.

Morin Bldg Prods Co. v Baystone Constr, Inc., 717 F2d 413 (7th Cir 1983).

Performance Specification

If a specification requires that a contractor use a particular product, and also requires that the contractor achieve a specified performance, the particular specification controls.

> A contract for air conditioning work required that the contractor utilize a particular size and quality of air conditioning equipment. The contract also required that the system establish at least a 30-degree variation from outside temperature for cooling and a 50-degree variation for heating. The subcontractor built the job as specified, but it did not achieve the cooling requirement. HELD: The subcontractor did not assume responsibility for the adequacy of the plans and specifications to meet the purpose of achieving a 30-

degree variation for cooling. The owner impliedly represented that if the contractor followed the specifications the desired performance would be achieved.

Kurland v United Pac Ins Co., 251 Cal App 2d 112, 59 Cal Rptr 258 (1967).

Legal versus Illegal

A contract will be interpreted so as to make its performance legal rather than illegal. For example, a contract provision requiring at least three bids for every trade would be interpreted so as to require three bids from licensed trade contractors.

Interpretation Against Party Who Caused Ambiguity

An ambiguous term in a contract is construed against the party who caused the ambiguity to exist: the party who drafted the contract. This rule is enforced with particular rigor in cases where a contract is offered by a party of greater bargaining strength to a party of less bargaining strength on a "take it or leave it" basis (for example, an insurance policy). Likewise, a printed subcontract form tendered by a prime contractor to a subcontractor will be interpreted, if ambiguous, against the prime contractor who could have prevented the ambiguity by more careful drafting.

The Alaska State Housing Authority prepared specifications for gravel surfacing material that were ambiguous. Contractor installed material that complied with contractor's interpretation and the housing authority required replacement. This delayed the job and the housing authority assessed liquidated damages. HELD: Since the specifications were ambiguous, the housing authority, as drafter, was responsible for the delay in completion. Therefore the housing authority is not entitled to assess liquidated damages against the contractor, but must pay the contractor for the additional costs resulting from its demand that the contractor replace the original gravel surfacing materials.

Alaska State Hous Auth v Walsh & Co., 625 P2d 831 (Alaska 1985).

A contractor sold lots to a home buyer and agreed to build a house on the lots for "cost plus 10 percent". The contractor billed the owner for 10 percent of the cost of the lots, as well as 10 percent

> of the cost of the construction work. Contractor had failed to make clear to the owner that he expected to charge 10 percent of the cost of the lots, and failed to establish that there was a trade custom for the owner to pay such an amount. HELD: The contract was ambiguous, and ambiguities in a contract are construed most strictly against the author, in this case, the contractor.

Don Nelson Constr Co. v Landen, 198 Neb 533, 253 NW2d 849 (1977).

Pay When Paid Clause

Subcontract documents often include a provision that the prime contractor will pay the subcontractor only from funds received by the prime contractor from the owner for work performed by the subcontractor. Since the enforcement of such a clause can lead to injustice, courts are inclined to interpret such a clause so that it applies only to the *timing* of the payment to the subcontractor, and not to the subcontractor's *entitlement* to payment.

In interpreting "pay when paid" clauses, courts may resort to several rules of interpretation. One is the rule that ambiguities are construed against the drafter. Since pay when paid clauses are almost invariably drafted by the prime contractor, this rule works against interpretation as a "pay if paid" clause.

Another rule is that courts construe a condition in a contract as a condition concurrent rather than a condition precedent. A condition precedent is a condition (an event) that must occur before a right arises. A condition concurrent is an event that is scheduled to occur simultaneously with, concurrently with, or at the same time as, another event. For example, a contract provides that a contractor will provide an owner with shop drawings. The law implies a condition concurrent that when the owner receives shop drawings, the owner will process them with reasonably promptness. If the owner rejects the shop drawings or requests further information, the law implies that the contractor will supply the necessary information within a reasonable time. These events (the provision of shop drawings, processing the shop drawings, providing further information) are construed as conditions concurrent. Thus, for example, even if the owner fails to process shop drawings promptly, when the owner does process them, the contractor is obliged to supply whatever further information is needed. If the owner's obligation were construed as a condition precedent, then the failure of the owner to process shop drawings promptly would relieve the contractor of any obligation to supply the additional required information. To give such a condition to a contract would create great confusion and inconvenience. Courts do not construe a condition as a condition precedent unless the language employed leaves virtually no other possibility.

Suppose that contractor is to receive a progress payment when framing is completed and another progress payment when the roof is on. Contractor finishes the framing but fails to install the roof. Is the failure to install the roof a condition subsequent that destroys the contractor's entitlement to the progress payment for framing? Is payment of the framing progress payment a condition precedent to contractor's obligation to install the roof? Or are performance of the work and progress payments conditions concurrent?

The courts usually avoid construing a promise as a condition subsequent since that would destroy rights that have already arisen. In doubtful cases a promise is construed as a condition precedent rather than as a condition subsequent. Thus the failure to make a progress payment might be viewed as a condition precedent to the contractor's obligation to proceed with additional work, but not as a condition subsequent that would destroy the owner's right, already arisen, to have the contractor correct defective framing work.

Courts prefer to construe contractual obligations as conditions concurrent that the parties are simultaneously obliged to perform.

> *Condition precedent found.* A painting purchase order provided "payment of purchaser by Owner shall be a condition precedent to Vendor's right to receive payment thereunder". HELD: The language is unambiguous and must be enforced. Where commercial parties expressly agree that a specified occurrence shall be condition precedent to the enforceability of an obligation, and there is no ambiguity arising out of other language in the contract, the only question for the court is whether the condition precedent has been complied with. Since the condition precedent did not occur, the painting subcontractor had no right to receive payment.

David Fanaros, Inc. v Dember Constr, 195 AD2d 346, 600 NYS2d 226 (1993).

In a California case, seemingly relatively unambiguous language was construed as a pay *when* paid provision.

The subcontract provided: "To pay to the Subcontractor upon receipt of each payment received from the owner, the proportions of said payment allowed to Contractor on account of subcontractor's work, to the extent of subcontractor's interest therein." Because of disputes between owner and prime contractor, the owner withheld payment. HELD: "Courts should avoid an interpretation which will make a contract 'unusual, extraordinary, harsh, unjust or inequitable. . . .'" 105 Cal Rptr at 582. "[A]ny ambiguity of a contract should be strictly construed against the party who prepared it." 105 Cal Rptr at 584.

Yamanishi v Bleily & Collishaw, Inc., 29 Cal App 3d 457, 105 Cal Rptr 580 (1972).

A paving subcontract provided that the prime contractor would make final payment to the subcontractor when the architect accepted the subcontractor's work and upon the contractor's receipt of full payment from the owner. The architect accepted the work, but the owner failed to pay the contractor in full. HELD: The payment clause established the timing, rather than the entitlement, to payment. A provision denying payment to a subcontractor until the contractor has received payment from an owner merely fixes a reasonable time for payment and, absent unambiguous language, does not set a condition precedent.

Aetna Cas & Sur Co. v Warren Bros Co., 355 So 2d 785 (Fla. 1978).

Clause enforced. Framing and drywall subcontract provided: "Final Payment shall not become due unless and until the following conditions precedent to Final Payment have been satisfied: . . . (c) receipt of Final Payment for Subcontractor's work by Contractor from Owner. . . ." HELD: The contract clearly stated that payment from owner was a condition precedent to the contractor's obligation to pay the subcontractor and thus shifted the risk of nonpayment from prime contractor to subcontractor.

Pace Constr Corp. v OBS Co., 531 So 2d 737 (Fla. Dist Ct App 1988).

Typewriting Controls Printing

In these days of standardized form contracts, all too frequently the parties do not carefully read the entire text of contract documents. They are often tempted to skip over the fine print and read more carefully the material that is inserted into the form by typewriting or handwriting. In the event of inconsistency, the courts will enforce the typewritten or handwritten provisions. A handwritten provision, in turn, controls typewritten provisions.

> A contract to build 109.5 miles of pipeline from Bethany, Missouri to Mason City, Iowa was typewritten except for handwritten paragraph 2.03 which read "Contractor shall not be liable under any circumstances or responsible to [owner] for consequential loss or damages of any kind whatsoever including but not limited to loss of use, loss of product, or loss of revenue or profit". Another typewritten paragraph provided that the contractor would pay the owner for damages sustained by owner's property arising out of the operations of the contractor. HELD: The handwritten provision, which was clear and unambiguous, controlled and modified the typewritten provision.

Wood River Pipeline Co. v Willbros Energy Servs Co., 241 Kan 580, 738 P2d 866 (1987).

> In *Batson-Cook Co. v Poteat*, 147 Ga. App 506, 249 SE2d 319 (1978), a standard printed contract form prepared by a prime contractor included a broad indemnity clause under which a subcontractor agreed to indemnify the prime contractor against all claims arising from subcontractor's negligence regardless of whether the injury was caused in part by the prime contractor. Typed on the printed form was a provision that the subcontractor assumed no responsibility for the negligence of the prime contractor. HELD: Since the provisions were in conflict, the typewritten provision prevailed over the printed material.

Drawings and Specifications

Many construction contracts contain a "precedence clause" defining the order of precedence of various contract documents in the event of conflict. For example, it may be provided that in the event of conflict between the drawings and specifications, the drawings control. The precedence clauses come into play only when there is actual conflict between the various parts of the contract documents, and not where an omission in one document is supplied by another.

> A contract for construction of a boiler plant provided that drawings would control any contrary provisions in the specifications. The drawings indicated that the entire boiler room was to be painted. HELD: The drawings controlled.

ACME Builders, Inc. v Facilities Dev Corp., 51 NY2d 833, 413 NE2d 1165, 433 NYS2d 749 (1980).

> A contract to remodel a housing project provided that in case of conflict between specifications and drawings, the specifications would control. The contractor sought additional compensation for installation of concealed raceways as required by the drawings. The technical specifications did not include raceways. HELD: There was no conflict. The drawings controlled.

Housing Auth of Sanford v Boyce Constr Co., 358 So 2d 35 (Fla. Dist Ct App 1978).

Duty to Inquire

If there is an obvious ambiguity in plans and specifications, a contractor bidding those plans and specifications has a duty to inquire as to the proper interpretation.

> A contract for site work, drainage and utility work contained a glaring error. It provided that "90 yards" of backfill would be required for hundreds of structures. The contractor nevertheless bid the job, figuring 90 yards of backfill. In the event, 11,000 yards of backfill were required and the contractor sought to recover $100 per yard for the extra work. HELD: The contractor had a duty to clear up the obvious ambiguity before submitting its bid.

> > A contractor who fails to inquire into a patent ambiguity may not successfully make a claim for contract payments based on the contractor's

> interpretation of the ambiguous language in the contract, no matter how reasonable its interpretation may be. *Fortec Constructors v United States*, 760 F2d 1288, 1291 (Fed Cir 1985).

D'Annunzio Bros v New Jersey Transit Corp., 245 NJ Super 527, 586 A2d 301 (1991).

Surrounding Circumstances

Courts take the circumstances surrounding the formation of a contract into account. In order to interpret an ambiguous phrase a court may attempt to put itself into the position of the party. For example, a provision that contractor will perform work diligently and expeditiously can take on a special meaning if the contract is for construction of a football stadium and the season is approaching.

§ 1.28 Performance

The obligation of a contract is extinguished by performance. Performance that is defective or delayed, however, may be a breach of contract and, if unexcused, gives the innocent party a cause of action for breach of contract.

> A plumbing contractor installed a sewer pipe as instructed by homeowner. The pipe was installed at a level that was too low to permit gravity flow into the city sewer system. HELD: Since the plumber performed as instructed, performance was proper.

Kubista v Jordan, 228 Neb 244, 422 NW2d 78 (1988).

> *Workmanlike performance.* Owner sued contractor for defective construction of a project to convert a garage into a room with an addition. HELD: Performance of the contractor was workmanlike and therefore the owner was not entitled to recover damages.

Mahler v Bellis, 231 Neb 161, 435 NW2d 661 (1989).

§ 1.29 Performance by Subcontractor

A prime contractor is responsible for defective performance by a subcontractor.

Wisler sold a spec house to Sabella in October 1955. Between November 1, 1958 and February 1, 1959 a sewer lateral began to leak, causing the house to settle. The market value of the house declined from $18,200 to $10,000. HELD:

> As the general contractor, Wisler is held responsible for the defective plumbing even though the work might have been completed by a subcontractor.

Sabella v Wisler, 59 Cal 2d 21, 377 P2d 889, 27 Cal Rptr 689 (1963).

§ 1.30 Excuse for Nonperformance

A material breach of contract on one side excuses further performance on the other side. If L employs K to install a slate roof, and K instead willfully installs a composition roof, K's material breach of contract would excuse O's duty to perform. O's duty to pay for the roof would be excused by the material breach of contract.

Subcontractor agreed to install a steel guardrail on a highway project for $103,086.85. The contract provided that all work was to be completed on October 1, 1973. When the site was not ready for installation of the guardrail until July 1974 the subcontractor refused to perform. HELD: Failure to have the site ready for the guardrail work was a material breach of the subcontract, and this discharged the subcontractor's duty to perform.

RG Pope Constr Co v Guard Rail, Inc. 219 Va 111, 244 SE2d 774 (1978).

Concrete subcontractor for a project at Kelly Air Force Base fell behind schedule and severely delayed work of other subcontractors. The prime contractor terminated the subcontractor's performance.

> In Texas, the general rule is that reciprocal promises in a contract, absent intentions to the contrary, are presumed to be mutually dependent and the breach of one will excuse the performance of the other. . . . Furthermore, a party who is in default or breach cannot maintain a suit for breach of a contract.

HELD: The subcontractor's breach of contract justified the prime contractor in terminating performance.

DEW, Inc. v Depco Forms, Inc., 827 SW2d 379 (Tex. Ct App 1992).

§ 1.31 Substantial Performance

If the performance of a contractor is defective and yet the other party to the contract receives substantially all the benefits that it expected, the breach of contract may be excused under the doctrine of substantial performance.

The doctrine of substantial performance applies when

- The breach of contract is unintentional,
- The actual performance is equivalent to, or better than, the promised performance or,
- The deviation from the promised performance is slight and can be compensated in damages.

An example of substantial performance is delayed performance. A contractor's delay in completion of a project can normally be compensated in damages.

For another example, suppose that a contract calls for installation by an electrical subcontractor of #14 wire, but the contractor installs #12 wire. Here the deviation is not only slight, it is beneficial to the owner and therefore the doctrine of substantial performance would excuse the breach.

In another example, suppose a plumbing contractor installs a grade of pipe that deviates slightly from the grade required by the specifications. To remove and replace the pipe with the correct grade would be virtually impossible, because it would be necessary to dismantle parts of the building in order to do so. It is possible to estimate the damages sustained by the owner by computing the diminution in the market value of the building caused by the installation of the non-compliant pipe. The doctrine of substantial compliance would apply in such a case.

A masonry subcontract required the subcontractor to parge the inner face of a brick wall and to use specified galvanized ties. Subcontractor did not use the specified ties and did not parge the walls. Prime contractor never objected. Prime contractor withheld payment. HELD: A contractor may not recover payment for construction work without showing complete and strict performance of all terms. Failing in such complete performance, the contractor may nevertheless recover in *quantum meruit* if it shows substantial performance of the contract and a good faith endeavor to fully perform. Here, the trial court properly determined that the subcontractor attempted to perform in good faith in view of evidence that no objection was made by the general contractor.

Hayeck Bldg & Realty Co v Turcotte, 361 Mass 785, 282 NE2d 907 (1972).

Contractor agreed to install a 50 x 72 foot steel building for $11,000. Owner refused to pay, complaining of a cracked concrete ramp, leaks at the base of wall panels, and sliding door problems. Contractor admitted the defects and calculated the cost of repair would be $1,225. HELD: Contractor substantially performed and was entitled to recover the balance of the contract less $1,225 offset for cost of repairs.

Koland, Inc. v Hanggi, 320 NW2d 502 (ND 1982).

Contractor agreed to design and construct a plant for processing mustard seeds. Owner withheld $25,000 from the contract price because water penetrated the storage bins making mustard seeds unusable. HELD: Generally speaking, when a contractor has substantially performed a construction contract, the contractor may recover the contract price less the expense of repairing any defects. If the contractor has failed substantially to perform, it may not recover under the contract at all. Here, the contractor did not substantially perform since the defects were the result of the contractor's negligent design and construction.

Merrill Iron & Steel v Minn-Dak Seeds Ltd, 334 NW2d 652 (ND 1983).

Contractor constructed a concrete water slide at Thunder Mountain Rapids and recovered judgment against the owner for $202,000. Although there were cracks in the slide, they did not interfere with the use of the slide and the contractor did not perform in an unworkmanlike manner. AFFIRMED. The contractor substantially performed.

WE Erickson Constr, Inc. v Congress-Kenilworth Corp., 115 Ill 2d 119, 503 NE2d 233 (1986).

A home building contract required galvanized rod iron pipe, lap welded "of Reading manufacture". Nine months after completion, owner discovered some pipe was procured from a different manufacturer. Architect ordered the contractor to re-pipe, which would have required demolition of areas of work that had already been completed. HELD: The omission of the specified brand was not willful or fraudulent and the brand used was of the same quality, appearance, and market value as the specified brand. Contractor substantially performed.

Jacobs & Young v Kent, 230 NY 239, 129 NE 889 (1921).

In *In re Triple M Contractors, Inc.*, 94-3 BCA P 27003 (1994), a contractor was required to remove and replace 8,700 feet of concrete gutter. HELD: Although the gutter originally installed would have performed the purpose of carrying water away from a security fence, the useful life would have been reduced by five years or 20%. The installation of such gutters did not achieve substantial performance.

§ 1.32 Part Performance

Suppose an owner withholds a progress payment from a contractor, claiming that structural steel welds are defective. Contractor walks off the job and files suit to recover the progress payment plus the 10% retention and the profit that it would have made if it had been able to complete the work. The court decides that the welds are indeed defective and the owner was justified in withholding the progress payment. The breach was material. Does this mean that the contractor is entitled to no payment for its part performance and therefore must disgorge any progress payments already received from the owner? No. The contractor may retain appropriate compensation for part performance. A party is not allowed to gain more from the breach of a contract than it would have gained from the full performance of the contract. To require the contractor to disgorge would give the owner a windfall, since it would receive the benefit of the part performance without being required to render any compensation. The court would compute the damages sustained by the breach of contract, including damages for the delay and expense of obtaining another contractor to complete the work, and would deduct from the owner's damages the value of the part performance offset by the progress payments already made.

A contractor wrongfully ejected from a job is entitled to be paid the reasonable value of its work.

> In *Pan Am Realty Trust v Twenty-One Kings, Inc.*, 297 F Supp 143 (DVI 1968), *affd*, 408 F2d 937 (3d Cir 1969), owner failed to obtain financing and instructed contractor to stop work. The contractor sought to recover for work performed and architectural fees. HELD: A contractor who is wrongfully forbidden to complete work may treat the contract as rescinded and maintain an action for *quantum meruit.* The Restatement (Second) of Contracts, section 468(1), provides that a party who has rendered part performance for which there is no defined return performance fixed by the contract can get judgment for the value of the part performance rendered.

The issue becomes more complicated when the question is whether a contractor who has breached the contract, and has not substantially performed, is entitled to be paid for part performance. Should the property owner receive a windfall because the contractor committed a breach of contract? If the contractor is to be compensated, how should the compensation be determined?

> The contract price of a home building contract was $50,000 to be paid $5,000 upon signature of the contract, $15,000 when the subfloor was installed, $15,000 when the house was "locked in", and $15,000 upon completion. The owners withheld the third payment, claiming that the house was not "locked in". Contractor stopped work. The trial court determined that the building was not locked in, but the owners insisted they would withhold the third payment until the contractor performed some work that was not necessary for the building to be locked in. The trial court award 80% of $50,000 and subtracted from the amount of the judgment $20,000 that the owners had already paid plus $4,100 paid to another contractor for correcting defective work. The 80% award was based on a determination that the work was 80% complete. REVERSED.

> Where a breaching contractor has not achieved substantial performance, the basis of recovery is to prevent the unjust enrichment of the owner or the "feeling that the landowner is not entitled to a windfall merely because he has contracted with a man who has breached his contract". 653 SW2d at 148. Damages should be awarded under a quasi contract theory based on the benefit conferred upon the owner. Here, the trial court failed to determine the value of the house as constructed or to take into account the $22,900 that the owners paid a replacement contractor to finish the work.

Pickens v Stroud, 9 Ark App 96, 653 SW2d 146 (1983).

The opposing policies of the law: that a breaching party should not be able to recover on the contract and that a property owner should not be unjustly enriched at the expense of a contractor -- were discussed by the 9th Circuit Court of Appeals in a case decided in 1991.

> CSE subcontracted work at Vandenburg Air Force Base to Palmer for $220,162. The contract price was increased by a change order to $235,137. After part performance, Palmer breached the contract and left the job. CSE by then had paid $114,758.98 and thereafter spent $126,673.56 to finish the job. This was $6,295.54 more than the adjusted contract price. The district court should have awarded the $6,295.54 to the owner, but instead determined the value of Palmer's part performance was $204,845.26 for which Palmer had only been paid $114,758.98, and awarded to Palmer the difference minus the $6,295.54 overrun sustained by CSE. Thus Palmer recovered some $80,000 for its part performance, and also received an award of attorneys fees and costs. REVERSED. A breaching party cannot obtain damages for breach of contract from an innocent party. In such a case, if the innocent party suffered damages because of the breach, the innocent party should recover from the breaching party. But on the other hand, if a breaching party has conferred a benefit upon an innocent party, the law should avoid the unjust enrichment that would occur if the breaching party were paid nothing for its services. The trial court should have followed the Restatement (Second) of Contracts, section 374 comments A and B (1981). A breaching party may recover for part performance, but the

amount of recovery is limited to the amount by which the innocent party's gain exceeded its loss and is also limited to no more than a ratable portion of the total contract price. Thus the innocent party can never wind up paying a total that exceeds the contract price. Here, the trial court in error made such an award to the breaching party. A contractor should not be allowed to stop performing at any time and sell its part performance to an owner who agreed only to pay for full performance.

United States ex rel Palmer Constr, Inc. v Cal State Elec, Inc., 940 F2d 1260 (9th Cir 1991).

§ 1.33 Remedies for Breach of Contract

Most contracts have for their objective the economic betterment of the contracting parties. Therefore, a breach of contract usually causes economic damage to the innocent party. The purpose of the law is to require the breaching party to pay compensation to the innocent party. The basic purpose is to put the innocent party in as good a position as it would have occupied if the contract had been performed.

Three types of remedy are available to compensate for a breach of contract.

Damages

The remedy most commonly selected by the courts is to award money (called "damages") to the innocent party. Most economic wrongs can be rectified by a monetary award in an amount that is sufficient to put the innocent in the position that it would have occupied if the contract had been performed. For example, if B pays S $15,000 for a new Chevrolet, and S fails to deliver, a court would award B a sufficient amount of money to buy a new Chevrolet. The amount could be more or less than $15,000 but it would be enough to put B in the same position it would have enjoyed if S had delivered.

Cement supplier failed to deliver contracted cement due to a severe shortage, and as a result the contractor was unable to fulfill its own construction contracts. Verdict to contractor $1,175,974. REVERSED. Blue book equipment rental rates may be used as a guide to show damages resulting from idle equipment, provided the

> result is not unreasonable. Here, contractor received an award greater than it could have obtained by performing its projects. If Blue book figures are admitted into evidence the jury should be instructed to counter balance the blue book amounts by subtracting decreased costs resulting from non-use of the equipment.

Arcon Constr Co v South Dakota Cement Plant, 412 NW2d 876 (SD 1987).

Specific Performance

There are circumstances under which an award of money damages will not truly compensate for a breach of contract. For example, suppose B pays S $50,000 for a 1928 Chevrolet in mint condition. This is an item that is not readily available in the market. B paid for a unique item. In such circumstances, a court might order S to deliver the unique automobile. Such an order would be called an order for *specific performance* of a contract. The court would have the power to order the sheriff to take S into custody and hold S until the order was obeyed.

Restitution

A third remedy available for breach of contract is *restitution*. While the objective of damages is to put the innocent party in the position it would have occupied if the contract had been performed, the purpose of restitution is to put the parties back in the position that they occupied before the contract was formed. If restitution were awarded in the hypo proposed above, the $50,000 would be returned to B, and S would keep the car.

> In *Building Rentals Corp. v Western Cas & Sur Co*, 498 F2d 335 (9th Cir 1974), the court pointed out that the remedy of restitution is utilized to put an injured party in as good a position as it held before the contract was made. A sub-subcontractor stopped performance when progress payments were not made by the subcontractor. The trial court erroneously determined the amount of restitution by applying the percentage of job completion to the total contract price rather than by figuring the value of the materials furnished by the sub-subcontractor. The contract price may be evidence of reasonable value but does not finally determine the value of the performance or limit the sub-subcontractor's recovery. The proper measure of reasonable value is the amount for which such services

and materials could have been purchased at the time and place the services and materials were supplied.

A striking result of the restitution remedy is that it may enable a contractor, by rescinding its contract, to convert a losing project into one that produces a profit.

Prime contractor failed to perform its promise to pay subcontractor for crane usage. The subcontractor walked off the job. HELD: The subcontractor who stopped performance was entitled to recover *quantum meruit* value of work and equipment furnished under the contract, regardless of whether the subcontractor would have been able to recover damages for breach of contract. The impact of *quantum meruit* is to allow a party to recover the value of its services and materials supplied regardless of whether it would have lost money on the contract and therefore would have been unable to recover in a suit on the contract. The measure of recovery for *quantum meruit* is the reasonable value of performance. While a contract price may be evidence of reasonable value it does not measure the value of performance or limit recovery.

United States v Algernon Blair, Inc., 479 F2d 638 (4th Cir 1973).

Punitive Damages

For the most part damages for breach of contract are limited to compensatory damages. Punitive damages, however, may be awarded in cases of malice or oppression. The purpose of punitive damages is to punish and to deter.

An owner was unable to use an addition to its retail showroom because of a recurring moisture problem. The jury awarded compensatory damages of $8,711.69 and punitive damages of $6,500. REVERSED. The award of punitive damages for breach of contract was error. Although some construction defects could be considered to be a form of fraud or misrepresentation because they were undisclosed and latent, no public interest would be served by imposing punitive damages. None of the defects endangered public safety, and the parties were of equal bargaining power.

Sandock v Borkholder Co, 396 NE2d 955 (Ind. Ct App 1979).

> Contractor filed suit against an owner for wrongfully removing the contractor from a pipeline project. HELD: The contractor was proceeding with due diligence when the owner terminated performance. Nevertheless, punitive damages may not be awarded for breach of contract, even a malicious breach. A tort must be present. Contractor was not therefore entitled to punitive damages.

Delhi Pipeline Corp. v Lewis, Inc., 408 SW2d 295 (Tex. Ct App 1966).

Despite the rule that punitive damages may not be awarded for a mere breach of contract, homeowners are often successful in recovering damages from contractors who abuse their trust.

> Contractor delivered a defective house to homeowner three months late. Judgment that included punitive damages was AFFIRMED. To sustain punitive damages there must be evidence that contractor acted with reckless indifference to the rights of homeowner or acted in intentional and wanton violation of those rights. Here, the builders made no substantial repairs and took advantage of homeowners. The acts of the contractor rose above simple negligence and supported a finding of reckless or intentional conduct.

Tessman v Tiger Lee Constr Co, 228 Conn. 42, 634 A2d 870 (1993).

> A jury awarded homeowners $5,400 compensatory damages and $28,000 in punitive damages. REVERSED. 1) The compensatory damages should have been measured either as the difference between the fair market value of the home as built and its value if it had been constructed according to the contract, or as the cost to repair defective construction, whichever is less. There was no adequate evidence of compensatory damages. 2) Punitive damages are not available for breach of contract, absent independently tortious conduct.

Pogge v Fullerton Lumber Co, 277 NW2d 916 (Iowa 1979).

In some states, punitive damages may be awarded for a malicious breach of contract.

> A judgment of $14,144 in compensatory damages and $105,000 punitive damages was AFFIRMED. Subcontract for a school roof specified use of materials available only from supplier. Subcontractor ordered materials and supplier accepted the order and processed it in the context of a longstanding business relationship. Then an employee of the supplier, knowing that it would cause the subcontractor to lose its contract, wantonly and maliciously canceled the order. HELD: The award of punitive damages was justified.

Custom Roofing Co v Alling, 146 Ariz. 388, 706 P2d 400 (1985).

> Subcontractor encountered differing site conditions and requested a change order. Contractor stated it would investigate the problem and adjust the contract price after the project was completed. Contractor, however, made no investigation and did not adjust the contract price. In an action for breach of contract, the trial court awarded $66,500 in compensatory damages and $133,000 in punitive damages. AFFIRMED. Punitive damages may be awarded in a breach of contract case where the actions of the defendant are malicious, fraudulent, oppressive, or reckless.

Albuquerque Concrete v Pan Am Services, 118 NM 140, 879 P2d 772 (1994).

§ 1.34 Owner's Damages for Defective Construction

There are two possible ways to measure the economic damage done to an owner by defective construction: one is the cost to correct the defect and the other is to measure the diminution in the market value of the owner's property caused by the defective construction. In some situations these amounts will be virtually identical, but sometimes the disparity is striking.

Let us assume that the defect is a leaking roof. Assume the cost of correction is $15,000. Such being the case, a willing buyer would subtract $15,000 from the purchase price in order to have the funds available to fix the roof. Now assume the construction defect is installation of undersized duct work in the air conditioning system. As a practical matter, with proper sized ducting the system could reduce the ambient temperature by 22°F: as built, only a 20°F reduction will be achieved. The cost of correction would be $100,000 because it would be necessary to remove ceilings and break through walls. The influence on the market value of the building, however, might be negligible.

To actually correct the duct work would be economic waste. Therefore courts normally award the cost of correction or the diminution in value *whichever is less*.

> Owner claimed defective performance of a contract for construction of an ice skating rink. Judgment for owner $29,500 AFFIRMED. The purpose of damages for breach of contract is to restore the innocent party to its former position and to give it the benefit of its bargain. This objective can be obtained either by awarding to the owner the cost remedying defective work or the difference in value between the project as constructed and the value if constructed as promised. Here, the Master found it would not involve unreasonable economic waste to remedy the defective work, as the cost of correction was less than 5% of the total contract price.

MW Goodell Constr Co v Monadnock Skating Club, Inc., 121 NH 320, 429 A2d 329 (1981).

Some courts hold that a contractor is not entitled to compute damages as the diminution in value when the contractor has committed a willful breach of contract.

> Contractor deviated from plastering and heating plans in constructing houses in a subdivision. The trial court awarded costs of correction. AFFIRMED. A contractor is not entitled to application of the "value theory" unless the contractor has substantially performed in good faith. Here, the contractor intentionally deviated from drawings and breached the contract. Therefore the trial court properly awarded the cost of correction.

Shell v Schmidt, 164 Cal App 2d 350, 330 P2d 817 (1958), *cert denied*, 359 US 959 (1959).

Many courts hold that the cost of correction is the proper measure of damages in the absence of economic waste.

Contractor failed to slope garage floor three inches from rear to front so as to facilitate water drainage. The trial court awarded damages of $1,296 (the cost to the contractor of constructing the floor) plus $20 to level the floor. REVERSED. Damages should have been such as to put the owner in the position it would have occupied had the contract been properly performed. The preferred measure of damages is the cost of reconstruction in accordance with the contract, if the reconstruction is possible without economic waste. If reconstruction would cause unreasonable waste, the difference in value should be awarded.

Johnson v Garages Etc., Inc., 367 NW2d 85 (Minn. 1985).

Home building contractor did not install styrofoam insulation or footing drains because the homebuilder felt they were unnecessary. Cost of correction damages of $5,700 AFFIRMED. Diminution in value applies as a measure of damages only when a breach of contract is immaterial or when the contractor unintentionally deviates from a nonessential contract requirement. Here, the builder intentionally breached the contract and therefore the damages were properly measured by the cost of installing the items that were left out.

Roudis v Hubbard, 176 AD2d 388, 574 NYS2d 95 (1991).

If a breach of contract is willful, some courts will award the cost of correction even if it exceeds the diminution in market value. Other courts, however, subscribe to the theory that the law should encourage breaches of contract that are economically beneficial. Assume, for example, that a contract requires fill from pit A. Pit A is distant from the jobsite and fill from that source would cost $10 per cubic yard. By chance the contractor discovers that fill of equal quality is available at $1.00 per cubic yard from pit B, a nearby jobsite that is looking for a dump for its exported fill. Contractor willfully breaches the contract by supplying fill from pit B. The cost of correction would be $25 per cubic yard. Such a correction, however, would be wildly uneconomic. It would be a total waste of money. Therefore most courts would not award damages even for the willful breach. Thus the law encourages *economic* breaches of contract.

§ 1.35 Contractor's Damages for Breach by Owner

The damages recoverable by a contractor for breach of contract by an owner are calculated to compensate the contractor for economic loss caused by the breach. Therefore the measure of damages depends upon the nature of the breach. If an owner delays or disrupts a contractor's performance, the contractor may recover as damages the increased cost of performance. If an owner prevents a contractor from performing or completing the work of the contract, then the contractor is entitled to be paid the value of work actually performed plus the profit that it would have enjoyed if it had been allowed to fully perform the contract.

> Guerini was the subcontractor for installation of imitation sandstone and performance of concrete work on a government post office job in Puerto Rico. The contractor notified Guerini that it was time to start work on the subcontract, but when Guerini arrived in Puerto Rico the project had not progressed to the point where there was any substantial amount of work available to be performed. Frustrated by inadequate derrick power, delays, and improper foundations, Guerini terminated performance. The trial court excluded prospective profits from the consideration of the jury on the ground that prospective profits were contingent and speculative. REVERSED. A witness testified the contract price was $64,750 and it would have cost $55,012 to perform the work. Therefore Guerini, if allowed to proceed with the work, would have made a profit of $9,700. This is the amount Guerini should recover.

Guerini Stone Co v PJ Carlin Constr Co, 240 US 264 (1916).

> A jury awarded a carpet contractor $206,376.25 for not performing a carpet installation contract of $382,060, which the owner canceled without good cause. The contractor introduced evidence that it anticipated a 40% profit on such contracts. HELD: The appropriate award would have been $136,824.

Lanes Floor Coverings, Inc. v IBM Corp., 131 AD2d 729, 516 NYS2d 956, *appeal denied*, 70 NY2d 610, 516 NE2d 1223, 522 NYS2d 110 (1987).

§ 1.36 Owner's Damages for Delay

Delay in the completion of a construction project is damaging both to the owner and the contractor. The owner is damaged by the inability to make economic use of its improved property. The contractor is damaged by the expense of running the job during the period of delay. Among expenses and losses that may be incurred by an owner because of delay in the completion of a construction project are extended supervision and inspection expense, interest on money borrowed to finance the construction work, rent that the owner could have obtained by renting out the completed project, and profit that the owner could have made by utilizing the completed project in its business.

Rental value, construction interest, and profit that could have been made by utilizing the finished project are three different economic measures of the same loss. To award an owner construction loan interest, and rental value, and lost profit, would be to award a triple recovery for the same loss, since interest, rent, and profit are nothing more than three different measures of return on capital. The preferred, and usually most accurate, measure of damages for delay in the completion of a construction project is the rental value: the reasonable rent that could have been obtained during the period of the delay.

For certain types of projects, however, rental value is difficult to determine. It would be difficult to produce evidence of the market rental value of a sewer, a bridge, or a school building. For this reason, it is customary for the parties to public construction contracts to agree that the contractor will pay the owner a liquidated amount of damages for each day of delay in the completion of the project. Such provisions are known as liquidated damages provisions.

> A renter advanced a $6.5 million loan for the construction of Essex House, an apartment building in New York City. The borrower defaulted and the lender took over the project and finished the work. The trial court awarded $798,416.81 including interest, taxes, and insurance during the period of delay. The Supreme Court said that loss of rent is an alternate and superior measure of damages, but interest, insurance, and taxes (not to exceed rental value) are also a proper measure of damages for delay in the completion of a building.

Prudence Co v Fidelity & Deposit Co, 297 US 198 (1936).

A townhouse purchaser who loses a favorable rate of interest because of construction delays may be entitled to recover damages for that loss.

> An agreement provided that seller would construct and deliver a townhouse on a specified closing date. After substantial delays in completion caused by heavy rainfall, the purchase closed at a mortgage rate of 12%. HELD: The buyer was properly awarded the difference in interest rates.

Appollo v Reynolds, 364 NW2d 422 (Minn. 1985).

> A contract to build a mill provided that damages for delay in completing the mill would be $50 per day to be deducted from the contract price. Architects, fixing the amount of the final certificate for payment, deducted $50 per day for 27 days: $1,350. HELD: The parties, by fixing liquidated damages, showed their intention to fix damages for delay at a particular sum. The liquidated damages clause did not impose a penalty, but was a reasonable enforceable estimate of the actual damages.

Hennessy v Metzger, 152 Ill 505, 38 NE 1058 (1894).

In cases in which some delay is caused by contractor and some is caused by owner, liquidated damages may be apportioned.

> A utility contract with a liquidated damages clause was delayed 83 days, with 18 days chargeable to the developer and 65 to the contractor. HELD: The contractor was required to pay liquidated damages for 65 days of delay, and was not relieved of that duty by the fact that developer caused part of the delay.

Keith v Burzynski, 621 P2d 247 (Wyo. 1980).

§ 1.37 Waiver

Waiver is defined as the intentional relinquishment of a known right. Let us suppose that a construction contract provides that in the event the progress of the work is delayed by inclement weather or some other cause beyond the control of the contractor, the contractor will give written notice to the owner within ten days after the commencement of the delay, and that in the absence of such a written notice the contractor waives any right to an extension of time. On June 1 a rainstorm creates muddy conditions that delay excavation and grading operations for 14 days. Contractor shuts down the job, but fails to request an extension of time. Another storm on July 1, and yet another on August 1, cause similar problems. In response to a phone call from contractor's project manager, owner then issues a change order that extends the contract time by 35 working days because of inclement weather. Another storm on December 1 causes further delay, but this time the owner refuses to grant an extension of time on the ground that the contractor failed to make a timely written request. Here, the contractor would be legally entitled to the extension of time since the owner, by its conduct, has *waived* the written notice provision. By conduct the owner led the contractor reasonably to believe that it would not insist on strict compliance with the written notice requirement. (In anticipation of such events contracts sometimes contain *anti-waiver* clauses that provide that failure of the owner to insist on strict compliance with contract requirements in one case will not waive the owner's right to insist on strict compliance in another case.)

The doctrine of waiver may also work against a party claiming an extension of time. By failing to request an extension of time in writing, a contractor may waive its right to have the time extended.

> Construction of a building was delayed by change orders among other causes. The contract provided that the contractor would request extensions of time in writing. HELD: Failure to request extensions of time for delays caused by the owner waived the contractor's right to claim an extension of time for extra work performed at the request of the owner.

Roberts v Security Trust & Sav Bank, 196 Cal 557, 238 P 673 (1925).

> A provision in a subcontract for erection of a metal building required the subcontractor to make a claim for interference in writing within five days, and also provided that a claim for interference was waived unless so submitted. Subcontractor filed suit to recover damages caused by congestion of the jobsite and interference that allegedly caused the subcontractor to perform its work at 35% efficiency. HELD: Since the interference claim was not made within five days, it was deemed to be waived.

Allen-Howe Specialties Corp. v United States Constr, Inc., 611 P2d 705 (Utah 1980).

Let us suppose a contract contains a provision that the contractor will not be entitled to additional compensation for extra work without a written change order. Owner requests contractor's project manager to increase the size of the paved section of the parking lot. Project manager agrees to do so for a price. Project manager asks the owner to issue a written change order. Owner tells project manager not to worry about that, no written change order is necessary and the extra work will be paid for. Contractor performs the extra work. Owner then refuses to pay since no written change order was issued. Here, the owner expressly *waived* the contract requirement. The written change order requirement was inserted into the contract for the benefit of the owner, and the owner therefore had the power, intentionally, to waive the requirement.

> Home building contract provided that claims for extra costs must be supported by a written change order executed before the work was performed. The parties changed the plans and the owner requested the contractor to perform extra work. The contractor performed the extra work without written change orders. HELD: The parties waived the provision requiring that all changes be reduced to writing before the work was performed. Moreover, the owner was *estopped* to rely on the written change order provision to avoid liability.

Harrington v McCarthy, 91 Idaho 307, 420 P2d 790 (1966).

> The owner of a Chinese restaurant requested that the contractor, reconstructing the exterior of the existing structure, revise the plans and perform extra work. The written agreement required prior written authorization for changes in the scope of the work. HELD: The owner waived the written change order requirement by orally approving the performance of extra work.

Huang Intl., Inc. v Foose Constr Co, 734 P2d 975 (Wyo. 1987).

> A painting contract in connection with a shopping center project provided that no extra work would be performed without written

agreement. Subcontractor testified that the contractor's agent stated that change orders did not have to be in writing. HELD: The contractor's agent could legally covenant to waive the written change order stipulation in the contract.

> There is nothing sacrosanct about a written agreement. Granted that writing makes for specificity and clarity, reduces changes for errors, and allows for constant reference as to what was agreed upon, it nevertheless holds no superior position over an oral compact in the realm of authoritative utterances, except for when the Statute of Frauds intervenes or is invoked. 136 A2d at 83. Minds may meet in the field of oral concord as well as between the borders of parchment or paper. *Id* 84.

Wagner v Graziano Constr Co, 390 Pa 445, 136 A2d 82 (1957).

A breach of contract may be waived by a party who does not promptly insist on performance.

The employee of a contractor who was injured on the job filed an action against the building owner. The owner filed a cross-complaint against the contractor, alleging it had breached its contract by failing to provide insurance that was required by the contract. The contract provided that certificates of insurance would be filed with the owner before the commencement of the work. The contractor did not file the certificates of insurance. HELD: Owner waived the contractual obligation to provide certificates of insurance when it failed to require those certificates before the commencement of work or before contractor was paid in full for a completed job.

Geier v Hamer Enters, 226 Ill App 3d 372, 589 NE2d 711 (1992).

A slight breach of contract at the beginning of performance might justify an owner in removing a contractor from a job, whereas a similar breach later in the performance might be deemed insubstantial. Breach by the contractor does not terminate the contract as a matter of course, but is grounds for termination at the

> option of the owner. A notice of termination should clearly indicate to the contractor that the owner considers the contract terminated. If the owner, with knowledge of a breach of contract, continues to accept performance from the contractor, this conduct may constitute a waiver of the breach.

Whitney Inv Co v Westview Dev Co, 273 Cal App 2d 594, 78 Cal Rptr 302 (1969).

§ 1.38 Estoppel

The legal concept of *estoppel* has three elements: 1) a party by words or conduct induces another party to believe; 2) the other party does believe; and 3) the other party relies on that belief to its detriment.

It is sometimes said that a party, having induced another to believe that certain stated facts are true, is not permitted then to falsify those facts.

Suppose an owner requests that a contractor accelerate installation of a parking lot so that a stadium can be ready for business on opening day. Owner asks how much the contractor will charge for the acceleration. Contractor states that the acceleration will actually save money and therefore there will be no additional charge. Contractor then accelerates the work, the parking lot is ready for opening day, and contractor sends owner a bill for acceleration expense. Here, the contractor would be *estopped* to claim the additional compensation. Contractor led owner to believe that the acceleration would be at no expense to the owner. The owner did believe that representation and relied upon it to its detriment. (*Detriment* lies in the fact that the owner could have avoided the extra expense by electing not to accelerate.) Contractor is therefore *estopped* to falsify the representation that the acceleration would be at no additional expense.

The concepts of *waiver* and *estoppel* are closely related. The reader will recall the example in which an owner waived the right to insist on ten days written notice of delay in the progress of the job by granting extensions of time in three instances where no written request was made. This conduct waived the right to insist on written notice in the fourth instance. This is also an example of *estoppel* since the owner by its conduct led the contractor to assume they would not insist on the written notice requirement, and the contractor relied on the representation implied by that conduct to its detriment by failing to give ten days written notice of the fourth delay; therefore the owner was *estopped* to falsify the implied representation that it would not insist on the written notice requirement.

> Generally speaking, four elements are required for application of the doctrine of estoppel: 1) the party to be estopped must be apprised of the facts; 2) the party to be estopped must intend that its conduct shall be acted upon, or must so conduct itself that the party asserting the estoppel has a right to believe that the conduct was so intended; 3) the party asserting the estoppel must be ignorant of the true state of facts; 4) the party asserting the estoppel must rely on the other party's conduct to its injury.

Millan v Restaurant Enters Group, 14 Cal App 4th 477, 18 Cal Rptr 2d 198 (1993).

§ 1.39 Anticipatory Repudiation of Contract

Anticipatory repudiation of contract is a legal term that describes the express repudiation by one party of its obligations under a contract. Suppose, for example, B agrees to buy a horse from S for $500. B has to take delivery of the horse on June 1 and pay for it on June 10. On May 30, B tells S that it still wants the horse, but is not going to pay for it. B has thus unequivocally and unconditionally stated to S that B intends to break the contract. Under these circumstances S, of course, could not be expected to deliver the horse. Delivery of the horse, in fact, would be excused under the rubric *anticipatory repudiation of contract*. An anticipatory repudiation of contract excuses counter performance.

Of course, to excuse further performance the anticipatory repudiation must be a *material* breach. Suppose, for example, contractor informs owner that because of union rules it will not be able to install a revolving door in a hotel, but the owner will be required to procure the installation of the door directly from the vendor and subtract the cost from the contract price. Failure to install the revolving door is a technical breach of contract, yet it would not be such a material breach so as to allow the owner to repudiate the entire contract for the construction of the hotel.

> Contractor was employed to install a gravel driveway. Muddy conditions interfered with the work and, after two false starts, the contractor waited for the ground to dry. The owner twice inquired and was promised that contractor would "get right on it". Forty-five days after the contract was signed, contractor promised to be on site

> to install the gravel driveway on the following day. Contractor failed to appear. HELD: The contractor's conduct constituted an anticipatory repudiation of the contract. It was reasonable for the owner to conclude that the contractor would never complete performance. Here, conduct constituted anticipatory repudiation.

Wholesale Sand & Gravel, Inc. v Decker, 630 A2d 710 (Me 1993).

§ 1.40 Prospective Failure of Consideration

A *prospective failure of consideration* excuses counter performance even by a party that is itself in breach of contract. *Failure of consideration* denotes an extremely material breach of contract. It means that the very consideration bargained for by the promisee will not be delivered.

Suppose a contract calls for construction of a hotel and an access road. Without the access road, the hotel will be economically useless. Owner breaches the contract for construction of the hotel by shorting the contractor $50,000 on a $200,000 progress payment. The following month, creditors levy on contractor's assets and contractor goes out of business. The owner is faced with a prospective failure of consideration in that contractor will not now be able to install the access road. This excuses any further performance of the contract by owner, even though owner was in breach at the time when the prospective failure of consideration occurred.

> Contractor agreed to build a housing complex on a turn-key basis in 540 days. When 50% of the contract time had expired only 6% of the work had been completed. Owner terminated contractor's performance. HELD: A prospective failure of consideration discharges the non-defaulting party's duties under a contract. The owner was under no obligation to make further payments to the contractor, even though the contract time had not expired. One is not required to perform a useless act when it is clear that the promised equivalent will not be returned.

First Natl. Bank v Indian Indus, 600 F2d 702 (8th Cir 1979).

> A contract to paint a 23-building 115-unit apartment complex was plagued by delays and difficulties. Contractor stated that subcontractor would not be paid for past or future work. Contractor

> politely ordered subcontractor to leave the job. HELD: The statement that subcontractor would not be paid could have been treated as an anticipatory breach of contract. Subcontractor was justified in leaving the job permanently.

Martell Bros v Donbury, Inc., 577 A2d 334 (Me 1990).

§ 1.41 Implied Conditions Concurrent

Contracting parties often take certain things for granted, but they are not included within the four corners of the contract document. For example, a contractor will assume that the owner will make the jobsite available to the contractor even though that is not specifically provided in the contract. A contractor may also assume that an owner will make decisions promptly when such decisions are needed for the orderly progress of the work.

Since such obligations often are not expressly included in a contract, the courts imply them. Such conditions as are necessary to make a contract conformable to usage and to make the benefits of the contract available to both parties are implied, and known by the courts as *implied conditions concurrent*. It is an implied condition, for example, that a contractor will maintain an orderly workforce, will construct the project according to building codes and conform to safety regulations.

> Contractor was employed to repair a building that was partly destroyed by the 1906 San Francisco earthquake. Without the contractor's consent, the owner took over the jobsite, tore down some brick work, and occupied the building. The courts said:
>
> > In every building contract there are implied covenants to the effect that the contractor shall be permitted to proceed with the construction of the building in accordance with the other terms of the contract without interference by the owner, and shall be given such possession of the premises as agreed upon. Such terms are necessarily implied from the very nature of the contract, and a failure to observe them, not consented to by the contractor, constitutes a breach of contract on the part of the owner entitling the contractor to rescind, although it may not amount

> to a technical prevention of performance. [The owners] cannot ignore their own obligations under the contract and, at the same time, seek to hold [contractor] to its terms.

Gray v Bekins, 186 Cal 389, 199 P 767 (1921).

> In general, where plans, specifications and conditions of a contract do not otherwise provide, there is an implied covenant that the owner of the project is required to furnish whatever easements, permits or other documentation are reasonably required for the construction to proceed in an orderly manner.

Coac, Inc. v Kennedy Engineers, 67 Cal App 3d 916, 136 Cal Rptr 890 at 892 (1977).

In a contract with no contrary provisions, compliance with the applicable building code is implied requirement.

> As a part of a home building contract, contractor constructed a well. The water produced by the well was turbid, discolored, and contained salts, irons, dissolved solids and bacteria. The water was unfit for domestic consumption. HELD: Existing law, including municipal ordinances, form a part of the contract. The contract did not specify the quantity or quality of water to be produced by the well; nevertheless, the contract impliedly required that the well meet the water requirements established by state law.

Koval v Peoples, 431 A2d 1284 (Del. Super Ct 1981).

> Homebuyers agreed to purchase a lot on which vendor agreed to build a house. After homebuyers took occupancy, the interior walls and ceilings cracked because of sinking foundations. Vendor had failed to install a sufficient number of piers, and the footings were inadequate to support the house, which became unlivable. HELD: It was an implied term of the contract that the home would be constructed upon sufficient foundations. There was an implied

> covenant that the house would be built on a foundation sufficient to sustain it.

Phillips v Wick, 288 SW2d 899 (Tex. Ct App 1956).

§ 1.42 Impossibility

Performance of a contract is excused if impossible. For example, suppose an owner signs a contract with a roofing contractor to re-roof the owner's warehouse. After the contract has been signed, but before work has begun, the warehouse is destroyed by an earthquake. Performance therefore becomes impossible and both sides are excused from performance.

> A contract to repair Cooper Lake Dam required hauling rock across a frozen lake. Thin ice conditions made the hauling impossible. The owner nevertheless insisted that the contractor continue to perform. Owner made suggestions as to methods to be used by the contractor to perform the contract. Contractor filed to suit to recover the costs of attempting to perform, as required by the owner, contractual obligations that were impossible. HELD: Contractor was entitled to recover costs reasonably incurred after notifying owner that ice conditions made performance impossible.

Chugach Elec Assn v Northern Corp., 562 P2d 1053 (Alaska 1977).

When an owner ejects a prime contractor from a construction project, further performance by the subcontractors may become impossible. Are subcontractors then entitled to recover from prime contractor the profit that they anticipated from performance of subcontract work? The answer, in the first instance, depends upon whether subcontract document includes a clause dealing with cancellation of the prime contract. Many subcontract documents contain a provision that if the owner terminates the prime contractor's performance, the prime contractor is excused from further performance of the subcontract. In the absence of such an explicit provision, the subcontractor's right to recover compensation may depend upon whether termination of the prime contract was the fault of the prime contractor.

> Through no fault of prime contractor, owner terminated prime contractor's performance of a construction project. Subcontractor then sued prime contractor for profits that the subcontractor

anticipated. HELD: The termination of the general contract was not the prime contractor's fault, so the subcontractor was not entitled to recover its lost profits. Supervening impossibility of performance puts an end to recovery, regardless of defendant's prior breach of contract.

Manganaro Bros v Gevyn Constr Corp., 610 F2d 23 (1st Cir 1979).

Subcontractors employed to perform excavation and foundation work for a school administrative center filed an action against the prime contractor after a newly elected school board voted to cancel the prime contract. Judgment for subcontractors AFFIRMED. Subcontractors had commenced performance under oral agreements. The agreements did not provide that the prime contractor would be relieved from its obligation to pay for subcontract work if the district canceled the prime contract. Courts should not create contracts for the parties. If the obligation to perform is absolute, impossibility of performance is no excuse for non-performance if the impossibility could reasonably have been anticipated. Here, the jury found that the board's action was justified and that cancellation of the prime contract did not release the prime contractor from its obligation to subcontractors.

Calvin v Koltermann, Inc., 563 SW2d 950 (Tex. Ct App 1977).

Instances of true legal impossibility are few and far between. Suppose, for example, that a warehouse project burns down when 60% complete. It will be difficult and expensive, but not impossible, for the prime contractor to perform the contract. The contract requires the prime contractor to deliver to the owner a completed project, and that obligation is not excused by the destruction of the partially completed project. Here, the law assumes that if the contractor had wanted to be excused from performance by such an event, that term would have been inserted into the contract.

Work performed by a contractor constructing an irrigation pump system that was damaged by "forces of nature" without the fault of either the owner or the contractor. The loss was the contractor's misfortune and the contractor's responsibility, even though this part of the work had been accepted as complete. One who contracts to erect a structure must bear loss resulting from accidents to or destruction of the project before completion of the work.

Sornsin Constr Co v State, 180 Mont. 248, 590 P2d 125 (1978).

Temporary impracticability does not discharge the obligations of the parties to a construction contract.

Contractor was unable to commence construction when, unknown to either party, a construction moratorium had been enacted before the contract was signed. The maximum period that the ordinance would have delayed construction was eleven months. An eleven month delay would not have been unreasonable under the circumstances. HELD: The owner breached the contract by repudiating its obligation to perform. Temporary impracticability merely suspended the duty to perform. Temporary impracticability did not discharge the owner's duty to perform its side of the contract.

GW Anderson Constr Co v Mars Sales, 164 Cal App 3d 326, 210 Cal Rptr 409 (1985).

In some states, *extreme impracticability* excuses performance.

Sewer contractor encountered unstable soil and was directed by the engineer to utilize crushed stone to stabilize the area. The contractor completed 93% of the project but was unable to finish because crushed stone would not stabilize the soil. City, upon engineer's advice, then terminated the contractor's performance on the ground that contractor failed to continue with the work. The contractor was awarded its retention, lost profits, and delay damages $129,446. AFFIRMED. Under Oklahoma law, contractor's performance was excused. Although performance was not strictly impossible, it was excused by impracticability arising from extreme and unreasonable difficulty, loss, and expense.

Miller v City of Broken Arrow, Okla., 660 F2d 450 (10th Cir 1981), *cert denied*, 455 US 1020 (1982).

Many construction contracts deal with potential destruction of the project by requiring either that the prime contractor, or the owner, supply builders risk insurance. In the AIA contract documents, for example, it is provided that owner will purchase builders risk insurance naming the prime contractor as an additional insured, and in the event of damage to or destruction of the project while under construction, the owner, acting as trustee, will collect the insurance proceeds which will then be used to pay for costs of reconstruction.

> A highway bridge was destroyed by fire when it was nearly completed. Contractor had failed to provide fire fighting equipment. HELD: Contractor agreed without qualification to build the bridge for a stipulated price. The contract was indivisible and therefore, under common law, the contractor was required to rebuild the bridge at its own expense. The fire was foreseeable because the bridge utilized dry creosote poles, the weather was dry, and construction personnel were permitted to smoke.

Reece Constr Co v State Highway Comm., 6 Kan App 2d 188, 627 P2d 361 (1981).

§ 1.43 Commercial Frustration

Performance of a contract may be excused if its basic purpose is frustrated. An early example occurred when the coronation of an English king was postponed. Those who had agreed to pay big money for the privilege of having a window seat for the procession were excused from the obligation to pay for those seats. The transaction was rendered meaningless by the postponement.

In one case, a contractor agreed to obtain all gravel needed to build a road from a designated pit. When the project was about 60% complete, the contractor encountered ground water. The additional expense did not excuse the contractor's obligation to perform.

Assuming that equally appropriate gravel could be obtained less expensively from another source, the contractor here might have elected to breach the contract by utilizing another source. In such case the owner's damages for the breach of contract would be negligible, nominal, or nonexistent. The rule would come into play that a party should not be able to gain more from the breach of a contract than from its performance. The effect of these rules dealing with damages for breach of contract is that the law may sometimes tolerate so-called "economic" breaches of contract.

> A highway department decided not to install concrete median barriers on a highway under construction. The subcontractor who had been employed to install the median barriers filed suit against the prime contractor to recover profit that was lost when 25,800 linear feet of median barrier was deleted. At the time when barriers were deleted the subcontractor had produced and delivered about half. By then, contractor had paid the subcontractor at the contract price for all barriers produced and delivered. HELD: When, after a contract is made, a party's principal purpose is substantially frustrated without its fault by the occurrence of an event the non-occurrence of which was a basic assumption on which the contract was made, the party's remaining duties to render performance are discharged. Restatement (Second) of Contracts, section 265 (1981).
> Here, the contractor was not responsible for the highway department's decision and the contingency could not have reasonably been foreseen. Subcontractor was also aware of the prime contract provision that gave the highway department the power to delete work. Therefore contractor was not liable to subcontractor for deletion of the barriers from the work.

Chase Precast Corp. v John J Paonessa Co, 409 Mass 371, 566 NE2d 603 (1991).

§ 1.44 Third Party Beneficiary Contract

It is possible, and occasionally quite practical, for a contract to be signed by three parties all of whom have an interest in a transaction or project. This is uncommon, though, and most contracts have but two parties. There are circumstances, however, when a contract signed only by two parties can be enforced by a third person who is not a party to the contract. These are called *third party beneficiary contracts*.

A promissory note can be endorsed by the payee to a third party who can then enforce the note according to its terms. This is not an example of a third party beneficiary contract but of an *assignment*. A third party beneficiary contract is from its very inception intended expressly for the benefit of a third party. For example, when a person enrolls a son or daughter in college and pays the tuition, a contract is formed that is expressly for the benefit of the student and the contract is thereafter enforceable by the student, as well as by the parent.

That a person will incidentally benefit from the performance of a contract does not make the person a third party beneficiary. For example, if O specifies Frigidaire appliances for a home, Frigidaire benefits from the contract, but this does not mean Frigidaire may enforce the contract. Here, Frigidaire would be described as an *incidental beneficiary* since the main purpose of the contract was to fulfill O's desire for a new home and not to provide sales to Frigidaire.

A typical construction subcontract may be expressly intended for the benefit of a third party. S, for example, enters into a contract with K to install a plumbing system in a home that K will build for O. Here, O is no mere incidental beneficiary but is the party expressly intended to receive the ultimate benefit of S's performance. Therefore the subcontract is considered by some courts to be a third party beneficiary contract, enforceable by O.

The courts are far from unanimous in their views as to whether a particular type of contract is a third party beneficiary contract or not. Quite a number of cases have held that a project owner is a third party beneficiary of a subcontract that provides for construction of a part of the project, while other courts have held that the relationship between owner and subcontractor does not rise to the level of a third party beneficiary contract.

> Steelform subcontracted to install a roof on a building owned by Gilbert. Gilbert filed an action against Steelform claiming the right to enforce a contractual warranty given by Steelform to the prime contractor. HELD: Under Cal Civ Code § 1559 Gilbert was a third party beneficiary of the contract and therefore was entitled to sue for breach of the implied warranty of fitness. Steelform subcontracted to perform a part of the work that the general contractor had the duty to perform under the prime contract.

Gilbert Fin Corp. v Steelform Contr Co, 82 Cal App 3d 65,145 Cal Rptr 448 (1978).

> Owner employed a contractor to design and build a house with an auxiliary solar heating system, and deposited $1,000 with the contractor to be used for lot survey, plans and specifications. Contractor employed an architect to design the house and the solar

heating system. HELD: The owner, even though not specifically identified in the contract between the contractor and the architect, must have been known to the architect and the contract was a third party beneficiary contract. Therefore the owner stated a good cause of action for improper design of the auxiliary solar heating system.

Keel v Titan Constr Corp., 639 P2d 1228 (Okla. 1981).

Road building contractors agreed, in their contract with the county, to insure the least practicable interference with traffic and to refrain from isolating places of business from access to the roadway. HELD: The contract provisions clearly established an intention to create a right primarily and directly benefiting the third party landowners, who therefore could claim the right to enforce the access provisions of the contract.

Legare v Music & Worth Constr, Inc., 486 So 2d 1359 (Fla. Dist Ct App 1986).

Hospital owners attempted to enforce a $35.9 million fixed price subcontract for mechanical work. The prime contract provided (Article 1.1.2) "nothing contained in the Contract Documents shall create any contractual relationship between the Owner . . . and any Subcontractor or Sub-subcontractor". HELD: The contract language prevented the owner from maintaining an action against the subcontractor on a third party beneficiary theory.

Pierce Assocs. v Nemours Found, 865 F2d 530 (3d Cir 1988), *cert denied*, 109 S Ct 3218 (1989).

Unit owners of a commercial condominium where they conducted an antique business sold all unoccupied units in the building to a developer, who contracted with a contractor to renovate the building. Owners filed an action against the contractor alleging the contractor's work was faulty, unworkmanlike, and uncompleted. HELD: The unit owners failed to show that the developer and the contractor intended that the unit owners would receive an enforceable benefit under the contract, and therefore the owners were not entitled to pursue a third party beneficiary claim against the contractor.

FO Bailey Co v Ledgewood, Inc., 603 A2d 466 (Me 1992).

Contractors, subcontractors, and material suppliers occasionally claim to be third party beneficiaries of construction contracts, architectural contracts, surety bonds, and construction loan agreements, usually with indifferent success.

> A sub-subcontractor who manufactured customized windows for a school project filed a third party beneficiary claim against the prime contractor after the subcontractor filed for bankruptcy. HELD: The language of the subcontract did not reveal any intention between the contractor and the subcontractor to benefit the sub-subcontractor and therefore there is no third party beneficiary contract.

Coast to Coast Mfg. v Carnes Constr, Inc., 145 Ariz. 112, 700 P2d 499 (1985).

> A general contractor on a utilities construction project provided performance bonds guaranteeing that the contractor would perform the work required by the contracts. The contractor became insolvent and left material suppliers unpaid. The material suppliers failed to enforce their mechanics lien rights, but brought this action against the surety on the performance bonds to recover payment for materials supplied to the projects. HELD: The performance bonds do not show any intent to benefit the material suppliers. The project owners (the utilities) that required the contractor to post the performance bond had no legal responsibility to pay the material suppliers and therefore the material suppliers fail to state a third party beneficiary cause of action.

Cretex Cos. v Constr Leaders, Inc., 342 NW2d 135 (Minn. 1984).

> Contractor for construction of a sewer line under the Great South Bay filed a third party beneficiary action against the engineer who designed and supervised the project. HELD: The contract between the engineer and the county provided that the services of the engineer be provided directly to the county, and therefore the contractor was not an intended third party beneficiary.

Edward B Fitzpatrick Jr. Constr Corp. v County of Suffolk, 138 AD2d 446, 525 NYS2d 863, *appeal denied*, 73 NY2d 703, 534 NE2d 315, 537 NY2d 477 (1988).

Sewer contractor filed a third party beneficiary action against attorneys who had prepared contract documents for a township. The contract provided that the owner would obtain all necessary rights of way before issuing a notice to proceed. HELD: The contractor had a right to rely on the notice to proceed as indicating that the necessary rights of way had been obtained. The provisions of the contract were such as to make the contractor an intended third party beneficiary of the contract between the township and its attorneys.

RJ Longo Constr v Schragger, 218 NJ Super 206, 527 A2d 480 (1987).

Home building contractor contracted to build a $15,900 house financed by a construction loan conditioned on an FHA commitment. The FHA certified final inspection but the construction lender refused to make the final construction disbursement to the contractor because the owners were eight months behind in making their payments on the mortgage. Contractor filed a third party beneficiary action against lender under the construction loan agreement between the lender and the owners. HELD: The evidence failed to show that the contractor was a third party beneficiary. The text of the agreement showed no intention to secure any benefit to the contractor. While the contractor may have benefited incidentally from the construction loan agreement, the construction loan agreement was not expressly for the benefit of the contractor.

Winnebago Homes v Sheldon, 29 Wis. 2d 692, 139 NW2d 606 (1966).

Subcontractor for excavating an airport runway claimed to be third party beneficiary of the contract between the prime contractor and the airport authority. HELD: Subcontractor was not a third party beneficiary.

APAC-Carolina v Greensboro-High Point, 110 NC App 664, 431 SE2d 508 (1993).

§ 1.45 Assignment

The rule is that rights under a contract are assignable. Non-assignability is the exception. Rights under a contract are assignable absent a contract provision prohibiting assignment and unless a party to the contract had an objective reason to repose a particular trust and confidence in the performance of a particular promisor.

> After signing a remodeling contract with homeowner, contractor sold its contracting business to one of its employees. The employee, as assignee, performed the remodeling work with the assistance of the original contractor, who had agreed to work for the former employee for one year and to help finish the remodeling project. HELD: The employee was entitled to enforce the contract. The owner had the benefit of the original contractor's personal services in performing the work, and made no complaint.

Strand v Courier, 434 NW2d 60 (SD 1988).

It is fairly common for a contractor to assign its payments under a construction contract to a vendor or to a financial institution. An assignment of all payments to be received under a construction contract is valid without the consent of the other party to the contract. An assignment, however, of part of the proceeds places a burden on the payor because it requires the payor to distinguish between payments due to the assignor and those due to the assignee, and therefore a partial assignment requires consent of the promisor.

An assignment to a financial institution may be as security for payment of a debt, or it may be an outright assignment accompanied by notice to the promisor that all payments are to be made to the financial institution. Such an assignment is called *factoring*. The assignee in such a case is a *factor*.

An assignment carries with it the benefits of a contract, but does it also impose upon the assignee the burden of performing the contract? One who assigns rights under a contract may also *delegate* duties, but the *delegatee* is not bound to perform the duties of the contract unless it manifests its agreement to do so.

Prime construction contracts often provide that in the event the contractor materially breaches the contract and the owner therefore terminates the contractor's performance and ejects the contractor from the job, the contractor will assign to the owner all of its rights under the project subcontracts. In this case, the owner steps into the shoes of the contractor and may require the subcontractors to finish the job. The subcontractors, assuming proper documentation, are required as a part of their subcontract documents to consent in advance to such an assignment.

> A paving subcontractor obtained a judgment of $115,651.13 against a developer after the developer terminated the prime contractor's performance. The unpaid subcontractor had pulled off the job, refusing to continue without assurances of payment. After a conversation with developer, subcontractor completed the project and developer terminated the general contractor's performance and took over the work. The prime contract provided that termination of the prime contract resulted in the assumption of "obligations, commitments and unsettled claims that contractor had previously undertaken or incurred in good faith in connection with the project". HELD: Developer assumed the duty to pay the general contractor's debt. Subcontractor was a creditor-beneficiary of that obligation and was entitled to assert a direct cause of action against the developer.

Pike Indus v Middlebury Assocs., 136 Vt. 588, 436 A2d 725 (1981).

When a financial institution makes a construction loan, it takes a mortgage or a deed of trust as security for the repayment of the loan. In the event that the developer who signed a deed of trust goes into default, then the construction lender can foreclose the mortgage or the deed of trust and take possession of the development.

Part of the loan documentation usually includes an assignment of the construction contract as additional security for the payment of the loan. The contractor is required to consent in advance to this assignment. (The lender usually also takes an assignment, as security, of the contract between the owner and the project architect.)

The loan documentation provides that if the lender declares a default, it then has the right to require the contractor to perform the balance of construction. The loan documentation, of course, does not delegate the developer's duties under the contract to the lender, nor does the lender consent in advance to any such delegation. Nevertheless, under the rubric, *he who accepts the benefit must take the burden*, the construction lender cannot enforce the contractor's obligation to perform the construction contract without performing, on behalf of the developer, the developer's obligation to pay for the work. In fact, the failure to make progress payments would excuse counter-performance by the contractor.

A distinction must be made between assigning a construction contract that has not yet been fully performed and assigning a *cause of action* that has arisen after performance of the contract has been completed. The cause of action may be assignable even if the performance of the contract is not assignable.

> Architect performed architectural services for renovation of 72 apartment units under a standard AIA contract form that provided "neither the Owner, nor the Architect shall assign, sublet or transfer any interest in this agreement without the written consent of the other". After renovations were completed and after the architect was paid in full, the owner sold the apartment complex to purchaser, and executed a blanket assignment of all leases and contract rights associated with the project. Purchaser filed an action against the architect claiming defective design was a breach of contract. The trial court found that the assignment was invalid based on the provision in the AIA contract document. REVERSED. The non-assignability clause prohibited the transfer of any "interest in this agreement". This prohibited the assignment of the performance of the executory contract. It did not prohibit the assignment of the right to sue for damages for breach of the fully executed contract.

Ford v Robertson, 739 SW2d 3 (Tenn. Ct App 1987).

§ 1.46 Illegality

Courts will not enforce illegal contracts. For example, suppose that S, a shipper, and C, a carrier, enter into a contract to transport marijuana. S pays for the carriage in advance but C refuses to perform. Can S sue C for a return of its money? *No.* Courts will not become participants in illegal conduct by enforcing such contracts. The law leaves such parties where it finds them.

Suppose a dozen contractors agree to rig bids so as to divide all highway jobs between them according to a predetermined ratio. Such a price fixing agreement would be illegal under the Sherman Act and would violate competitive bidding statutes and therefore would, of course, not be enforced by the courts.

Richmond Co. and Rock-A-Way, Inc. agreed that Richmond would refrain from bidding a recreation area job and in return, Rock-A-Way, if it were awarded the prime contract, would employ Richmond as a subcontractor. Rock-A-Way got the job but welshed on the deal. The trial court dismissed Richmond's claim. AFFIRMED. The agreement was void. Such agreements extinguish competition for the prime contract and eliminate any competition for the subcontract, and therefore are against public policy and unenforceable.

Richmond Co v Rock-A-Way, Inc., 404 So 2d 121 (Fla. Dist Ct App 1981).

Contractors and subcontractors established a bid depository program under which member subcontractors agreed they would not submit bids to prime contractors who were not participants in the bid depository program. Prime contractors agreed that they would not use bids from outside subcontractors unless they were received more than four hours before bid opening time. HELD: The agreement was a violation of the state's Cartwright Act since it established a boycott of non-member prime contractors.

People v Inland Bid Depository, 233 Cal App 2d 851, 44 Cal Rptr 206 (1965).

A form of illegality that is dangerous to contractors is encountered when a public agency violates competitive bidding laws. A contract issued by a public agency without complying with applicable competitive bidding statutes may be void and unenforceable. This may mean that the contractor, having performed its work in good faith, will not be paid for its work because payment would be illegal.

A county road commissioner agreed to buy crushed rock from plaintiff. Agreement was made by an exchange of letters. Under applicable statutes, the road commissioner did not have the power to contract. Such contracts were to be awarded by the Board of Supervisors after competitive bidding. HELD: Contract is void and unenforceable. A public agency is not bound by such dealings even though it has received substantial benefits under the contract.

Bear River Sand & Gravel Corp. v Placer County, 118 Cal App 2d 684,

258 P2d 543 (1953).

A developer needed permits to construct a marina on Arcadia Lake. A consultant offered to "take care of the mayor". The developer paid $7,000 to the consultant who was supposed to pass the money on to the mayor. Just before the final vote, the consultant demanded an additional $10,000. The developer refused to pay the $10,000 and the project was rejected. The developer then sued the consultant and the mayor for extortion and fraud. HELD: The contract between the developer and the consultant was illegal and unenforceable.

An-Cor, Inc. v Reherman, 835 P2d 93 (Okla. 1992).

In violation of competitive bidding statutes a county paid $42,151.90 for tunneling, repairing bunkers, repairing hoists and related work. A taxpayer sued the contractor, seeking an order that the contractor disgorge the money. HELD: The contract, which did not comply with competitive bidding requirements, is void and cannot be ratified. The contractor is presumed to know the law and therefore is required to reimburse the money to the county. To hold otherwise would nullify competitive bidding requirements.

Miller v McKinnon, 20 Cal 2d 83, 124 P2d 34 (1942).

Long, a licensed general contractor, obtained a construction loan commitment, $2,650,000, from South Bay Savings and Loan Association. The loan was approved after Long arranged for a $26,500 kickback to be paid to McAllister, South Bay's vice-president in charge of construction loans. After McAllister left his employment with South Bay, South Bay refused to fund the loan since Long had contributed only $20,000 to a $2.65 million deal. Long obtained judgment on a jury verdict for $2,341,609 plus costs and attorneys fees for breach of the construction loan agreement. REVERSED. The loan was linked to an illegal kickback. Under California Penal Code § 639 it is a felony to offer anything of value to an officer of a financial institution for procuring an extension of credit. A party to an illegal contract cannot ratify it, cannot be

> estopped from relying on the illegality, and cannot waive its right to urge the defense.

Long v South Bay Sav & Loan Assn, 10 Cal App 4th 947, 12 Cal Rptr 2d 896 (1992).

A special form of illegality is contracting by an unlicensed contractor. Many state license laws treat unlicensed, or improperly licensed, contractors as if they were drug dealers. An unlicensed contractor is deprived of the right to sue in court to recover payment for its work. The contractor may be unable to recover compensation, even for proper performance, even when the non-licensure is temporary or inadvertent. The interpretation is so severe that a contractor that inadvertently allows its license to expire for a short period of time during the progress of a job may be prohibited from recovering compensation for any part of the work, even work performed during the period of proper licensure.

> A construction contractor's license lapsed for a period of five weeks during which it was acting as a painting subcontractor on a housing authority job. Unpaid, the subcontractor filed an action against the contractor for breach of contract. HELD: The contract was illegal under the California Contractors License Law and the contractor was not entitled to recover judgment.

Bierman v Hagstrom Constr Co, 176 Cal App 2d 771, 1 Cal Rptr 826 (1959).

> A licensed Oregon contractor undertook to build a home in the State of Washington. Homeowner, who had formerly been a licensed contractor in California, allegedly represented that it would act as general contractor and would take care of all licensing requirements. Contractor, unpaid, filed suit to recover $32,500. HELD: Contractor is barred by the Washington contractors license statute from maintaining an action against the homeowner for breach of contract.

Frank v Fischer, 108 Wash 2d 468, 739 P2d 1145 (1987).

> An unlicensed interior decorator undertook to perform painting work and to furnish and decorate the owner's office. An arbitrator awarded $1,648.59 for the painting work. AWARD VACATED.

> The decorator required a contractor's license to perform the painting work. A party to an illegal contract cannot obtain judicial assistance in enforcing the contract, and the submission of the illegal contract to arbitration does not purge it of illegality.

Franklin v National C Goldstone Agency, 33 Cal 2d 628, 204 P2d 37 (1949).

Contractors who bid federal work are not required to comply with state licensing requirements. Federal law is supreme, and cannot be nullified by state statute. It is federal policy to award work to the lowest responsible bidder, and the determination of responsibility is left to the federal government.

> The State of Arkansas fined an air force base contractor for working as a contractor in the state without a license. REVERSED. The Armed Services Procurement Act sets the guidelines for federal determination of "responsibility" and it does not require state licensing. To apply Arkansas contractor license requirements to a federal contractor would give the state a power of review over the federal determination of responsibility and would frustrate the policy of selecting the lowest responsible bidder.

Leslie Miller, Inc. v Arkansas, 352 US 187 (1956).

Some courts hold that an unlicensed contractor who has been paid must disgorge the payments, while other courts leave the parties where they find them.

> Owner, aware that contractor was unlicensed, employed contractor under an oral contract to construct a trailer park. Dissatisfied with the work, owner sued the contractor for breach of contract. HELD: An unlicensed contractor may not retain payments made under a contract which requires him to perform in violation of the license law. Contractor was required to refund all payments.

Mascarenas v Jaramillo, 806 P2d 59 (NM 1991).

> Owner sought to recoup money paid to architect on the ground that architect was unlicensed. HELD: Although the architect would not be able to obtain a *quantum meruit* judgment against the owner, the owner could not use the license statute as a sword to recoup

> monies already paid in exchange for the allegedly unlicensed services.

Sutton v Ohrbach, 198 AD2d 144, 603 NYS2d 857 (1993).

A few courts will allow *quantum meruit* recovery to an unlicensed contractor in order to prevent the unjust enrichment of the owner.

> Unlicensed contractor filed suit against owner to recover for services performed pursuant to a contract for a building to house a beauty shop. Ark Code An § 17-22-103 (supp 1987) prohibits unlicensed contractors from bringing an action to enforce a contract for more than $20,000. HELD: Even if the contract claim was void, contractor was entitled to recover under a plea of *quantum meruit*. A *quantum meruit* plea is a claim for unjust enrichment and does not involve the enforcement of a contract.

Sisson v Ragland, 294 Ark 629, 745 SW2d 620 (1988).

Occasionally a performance bond surety, faced with default by its principal, will take over performance of a construction contract. Such a takeover may violate the contractor's license law and prevent the surety from recovering compensation for its work.

> After a contractor defaulted on an apartment construction project, the surety took over completion. The unlicensed surety filed an action against the electrical subcontractor seeking damages in excess of $100,000. HELD: Since the surety was unlicensed, it was precluded from filing an action against the allegedly defaulting electrical subcontractor. The contractor's license requirement applies to performance bond sureties as well as to other parties who undertake to perform construction work.

GenIns Co of Am v St.Paul & Marine Ins Co,
38CalApp3d760,113CalRptr613(1974).

Wrong License

In order to recover compensation for its work, a contractor must be properly licensed in the proper trade. Thus, a licensed HVAC contractor is not properly licensed for the performance of plumbing work. If an HVAC contractor bids a complete mechanical package, including plumbing, it cannot comply with the licensure requirements by merely employing a properly licensed subcontractor to perform that portion of the work. The appropriate licenses must be in the name of the contracting party.

Enforcement by Innocent Party

Suppose a homeowner innocently signs a contract with an unlicensed contractor. The homeowner can still enforce the contract for two reasons: 1) the license law was enacted for the protection of the homeowner (and persons similarly situated), and 2) the homeowner is innocent of wrongdoing.

Unlicensed Subcontractor

Suppose K, properly licensed, employs S, unlicensed, to perform plumbing work on a hotel project. A dispute arises between the owner and K, who files suit against the owner to recover the balance of the contract price. By this time the job is finished and K has paid S in full for all of the plumbing work. Owner defends K's suit by alleging and proving that S was unlicensed. In such a case, some courts would not permit K to recover from owner the portion of the contract price allocable to work performed by S. Nor would K be able to recover back from S the payments already made for the illegal plumbing work, since in cases of illegality the court leaves the parties where it finds them. Prudent prime contractors therefore assure themselves of the proper licensure of subcontractors whom they employ.

Substantial Compliance

In an attempt to prevent the unjust enrichment of project owners at the expense of unlicensed contractors, courts in some states have developed a doctrine of substantial compliance in order to relieve contractors of the consequences of technical violations of the Contractors License Law.

> A contractor whose roofing license had been issued on July 28, 1987 became unlicensed on September 16, 1990 when its license was canceled for failure to renew its financial responsibility bond. Contractor learned of the cancellation in January of 1991 and immediately supplied the missing bond. The license was reinstated January 26, 1991. On December 20, 1990, while unlicensed, the contractor had agreed to perform work for owner. Owner paid only

> 50% of the contract price. HELD: The contractor did not willfully violate the licensing statute and was fiscally responsible and competent at all times during the performance of the contract. The contractor substantially complied with the licensing requirements and is entitled to recover payment for the balance of its work. The New Mexico licensing statute was not intended as an unwarranted shield for the avoidance of a just obligation.

Koehler v Donnelly, 114 NM 363, 838 P2d 980 (1992).

A number of states have enacted consumer protection laws that impose special requirements for home building and home remodeling contracts between contractors and owners. Whether a home improvement contract that violates such a statute is enforceable depends on the terms of the statute.

> Contractor and homeowner signed a remodeling contract for $84,687.41. Three months later the contractor increased the price to $117,470.57, claiming that homeowner orally agreed to pay that amount. HELD: Enforcement of the oral extra work order is prohibited by Conn. Gen Stat § 20-429 (Statute of Frauds) which requires that home improvement contracts be in writing.

Caulkins v Petrillo, 200 Conn. 713, 513 A2d 43 (1986).

> Licensed contractor Asdourian entered into a home remodel contract with homeowner Araj. The oral contract violated Cal Bus & Prof. Code § 7159 which requires that home improvement contracts be committed to writing. Violation of § 7159 is a misdemeanor. HELD: Generally speaking, such a contract is void, but the rule will not be applied in its fullest rigor under all circumstances. Here, homeowner Araj was a real estate investor and not an unsophisticated homeowner and the contract is enforceable.

Asdourian v Araj, 38 Cal 3d 276, 696 P2d 95, 211 Cal Rptr 703 (1985).

Building Codes

A contract to perform construction in violation of building codes is illegal and unenforceable. If not so expressed, it is an implied condition of every construction contract that the construction will comply with applicable codes. It is sometimes said *the law is a part of the contract.* Contractor will therefore perform as required by building codes, zoning laws, safety regulations, noise abatement ordinances, anti-pollution laws, wage-hour laws and all other statutes and ordinances that apply to the work. Likewise it is the owner's obligation to provide drawings and specifications that comply with zoning laws, energy conservation regulations and handicapped/access requirements.

§ 1.47 Express Warranty

Many construction contracts include a warranty against defective work and materials. It is usually provided that contractor, at no expense to the owner, will promptly remedy any defects as to which the contractor is given notice within one year. This traditional one year warranty is often confused by contractors with the statute of limitations. Contractors sometimes believe that they are not responsible for construction defects that are brought to their attention more than one year after the completion of the project. This is not true. An owner has the right to file a suit against a contractor for construction defects that appear more than one year after the completion of the project. The right to sue is not cut off until the statute of limitations expires. The statute of limitations does not begin to run until the cause of action arises in favor of the owner, and the cause of action does not usually arise until the owner discovers (or reasonably should have discovered) the defect. Thus if the defective compaction of a fill results in cracking of a concrete slab that occurs, and is discovered by the owner, three years after completion of the work, the statute of limitations begins to run upon the discovery of the defect and the owner has one or more years after the discovery of that defect to file suit (the period dictated by the statute of limitations adopted by the state where the project is located).

The statute of limitations for breach of written contract varies from state to state (four years is typical). A promise contained in a written construction contract is governed by the statute of limitations for breach of written contract and therefore, in our example, an owner would have four years from discovery of the cracked slab to file an action to recover damages for the breach.

> In 1960 contractor signed a design-build contract. The roof began to leak approximately one year after completion. The roof blistered. Repairs failed. Eventually it was necessary to remove and replace the entire roof. Owner obtained judgment on a verdict for $13,687.92. AFFIRMED. The contract included a provision that

the contractor would remedy any defects due to faulty workmanship or materials which appear within one year from the date of occupancy of the project. Contractor contended that since the defects first appeared more than one year after occupancy the suit was barred. HELD: It is more reasonable to interpret such a warranty provision as extending, rather than limiting, the contractor's liability for faulty construction. The warranty provision in no way impaired the contractor's obligation to perform in a workmanlike manner. Whether the defect appeared within one year of occupancy was immaterial to the owner's right of recovery.

Burton-Dixie Corp. v Timothy McCarthy Constr Co, 436 F2d 405 (5th Cir 1971).

Bank filed a claim for breach of express warranties of workmanship and materials against a contractor. Judgment for treble damages $960,000 was AFFIRMED. The Texas Deceptive Trade Practices -- Consumer Protection Act applied since this was a sale of consumer goods and services for commercial or business use, and the bank was entitled to mandatory treble damages.

McAllen State Bank v Linbeck Constr Co, 695 SW2d 10 (Tex. Ct App 1985).

A roof on a state building was installed over Zonolite (a lightweight insulated concrete) in accordance with specifications provided by the manufacturer. Architects relied on the published specifications and the roof was built by an installer approved by the manufacturer. Manufacturer approved the roof and issued a ten-year warranty. Almost immediately, the roof leaked. The manufacturer disclaimed liability claiming the leaks were caused by excessive moisture in the underlying Zonolite material. Judgment of $100,000 actual damages and $1,000,000 punitive damages was AFFIRMED. Manufacturer had experienced similar problems with Zonolite but continued to specify the installation. HELD: Where a manufacturer has actual knowledge of recurring problems the law imposes upon it a duty to change the specifications, withdraw them, or warn of the dangers inherent in following the specifications. Punitive damages were proper since the manufacturer intentionally and willfully induced consumers to utilize expensive roofing systems that were not watertight.

Stephen v GAF Corp., 242 Kan 152, 747 P2d 1326 (1987).

> A builder boasted to an owner that a pole barn "would stand until [owner's] three-year-old son was old enough to take over the farm". The roof collapsed. HELD: Builder was liable under its oral warranty of fitness.

Krohnke v Lemer, 300 NW2d 246 (ND 1980).

Manufacturers often promote their building materials with brochures, standard specifications, and warranties distributed, for the most part, to architects, engineers, and developers. Such manufacturer literature may constitute a warranty enforceable by the consumer of the materials.

> A building owner's breach of warranty claim can proceed on the allegation that the manufacturer of roofing materials made specific recommendations in marketing literature upon which the owner relied.

Chenango County Indus Dev Agency v Lockwood Greene Engrs, Inc., 114 AD2d 728, 494 NYS2d 832 (1985).

> Even though homeowners and manufacturer did not deal directly with each other, if the homeowners relied upon a brochure prepared by the manufacturer that promised that the manufacturer would replace or repair defects resulting from poor workmanship, then the warranty was enforceable.

Herman v Bonanza Bldg., Inc., 223 Neb 474, 390 NW2d 536 (1986).

§ 1.48 Implied Warranty

The law of implied warranty developed as a part of the law dealing with *sales*. For example, when a merchant sells a loaf of bread, the sale carries with it an implied warranty that the product is of merchantable quality and fit for its intended purpose. Such a warranty also applies to the sale by a developer of new homes or condominiums, which are covered by an implied *warranty of habitability*. An implied warranty is not a warranty expressed in words, either oral or written words, but is a warranty implied from the fact of the sale itself. Since the very purpose of a home is habitation, the law implies that a merchant who sells a new one warrants *habitability*. A home is not *habitable* if the roof leaks, if the wind blows through it, if the heating system is defective, or if it importantly fails to comply with building code requirements.

> Despite soils reports showing a high water table in certain areas of a subdivision, a builder constructed homes with basements that were not waterproof, and leaked. Home buyers filed an action for damages against builder alleging breach of warranty. HELD: To construct basements below the water table, which resulted in seepage and water damage causing the houses to be uninhabitable, constituted a breach of the implied warranty of habitability.

Anderson v Bauer, 681 P2d 1316 (Wyo. 1984).

> Four years after purchasing a home for $55,000 from builder/vendor, purchasers noticed a dip in the kitchen floor. Testing showed the foundations were sinking because the house was built on soil composed of deteriorating tree trunks, wood, and other biodegradable materials. Judgment for purchasers $57,466 AFFIRMED. An implied housing merchant warranty imposes a contractual liability on a housing builder/vendor that a house will be constructed in a workmanlike manner free from material defects. Responsibility should be placed upon the party best able to prevent and bear the loss.

Caceci v DiCanio Constr Corp., 72 NY2d 52, 526 NE2d 266, 530 NYS2d 771 (1988).

In some states the courts have held that the implied warranty of habitability may be enforced by a so-called *remote purchaser*, which is to say, a purchaser other than the original home buyer. Courts in other states do not agree.

> Lack of privity of contract between a builder/vendor and a buyer was not a good defense because the implied warranty of habitability exists independent of contract. Builder/vendor had a duty to provide a habitable home, and breach of that duty was a tort which did not

require privity of contract. (Slide-related structural damage to a home that was built on unstable ground.)

Degnan v Executive Homes, Inc., 215 Mont. 162, 696 P2d 431 (1985).

Plaintiffs purchased a four-year-old home that proved to have defective central air conditioning, and recovered judgment of $3,555 against the contractor who originally built and sold the home. AFFIRMED. The implied warranty of habitability is usually applied to latent defects in a new home sold by a builder. However, it may be applied to remote purchasers on a case by case basis depending on the age of the building, uses to which the building has been put, the maintenance of the building, the nature of the defects, and the expectations of the parties. Here, although the home was four years old, it had been occupied only for two short periods prior to occupancy by plaintiffs.

Gaito v Auman, 313 NC 243, 327 SE2d 870 (1985).

After a house settled, cracks appeared in sheetrock, the floor began to sink away from the interior walls, brick veneer began to crack and doors would not close properly. The foundations were sinking. Inspection showed that the footings had been built on fill. The central issue in the case was whether a subsequent purchaser could pursue a cause of action under the doctrine of implied warranty. HELD: The extension of the doctrine of implied warranty to subsequent purchasers is based on sound legal and policy considerations. A builder holds itself out as competent to build habitable dwellings, and common experience teaches that latent defects may not manifest themselves for a considerable period after the original purchaser has sold the property. The ordinary buyer is not a position to discover hidden defects in a structure.

Terlinde v Neely, 275 SC 395, 271 SE2d 768 (1980).

Some courts do not accept what appears to be the majority rule, and deny an action in implied warranty to remote purchasers.

> In an action by remote townhome purchasers against a builder/developer seeking damages for defective siding, judgment for the builder/developer was AFFIRMED. The implied warranty of habitability arises out of a contract between the builder and the initial buyer. There is no hint in the case law that it arises out of the general duty to build a reasonably fit house. A builder therefore is not liable to a remote purchaser who has no privity with the builder. The remote purchasers could not be third party beneficiaries to the implied warranty, since the remote purchasers were unknown persons at the time when a warranty was given.

Foxcroft Townhome Owners Assn v Hoffman Rosner Corp., 105 Ill App 3d 951, 435 NE2d 210 (1982), *affd*, 96 Ill 2d 150, 449 NE2d 125 (1983).

The New Hampshire Supreme Court, joining the majority, stated that the doctrine of implied warranty is available to remote purchasers in Idaho, Arizona, Illinois, New Jersey, Oklahoma, Mississippi, Texas, Arkansas, South Carolina, Indiana, Wyoming, and New Hampshire. Jurisdictions still requiring privity are New York, Georgia, Minnesota, Missouri, South Dakota, Florida, Connecticut, and Colorado.

> A garage was built in 1977 and six months later the original property owner sold to subsequent purchasers, who filed action against the builder to recover damages resulting from structural problems including separation and bowing of trusses. The trial court dismissed the claim, holding that subsequent purchasers could not recover under a theory of implied warranty. REVERSED. Implied warranties are imposed by law on the basis of a public policy to protect purchasers from latent defects. This principle applies equally to subsequent purchasers as to original purchasers. Contractor should not be relieved of liability simply because property changes hands. A contractor should expect that a house it builds might be sold within a short period of time. The doctrine of implied warranty should be extended to protect subsequent purchasers for a reasonable time from damages arising from latent defects.

Lempke v Dagenais, 130 NH 782, 547 A2d 290 (1988).

West Virginia extends the doctrine of implied warranty of habitability to cover remote purchasers. *Sewell v Gregory*, 371 SE2d 82 (W Va 1988). California does not. *Huang v Garner*, 157 Cal App 3d 404, 203 Cal Rptr 800 (1984). California, however, extends the doctrine of implied warranty to cover work performed by a subcontractor, as well as work performed by a prime contractor. *ACED v Hobbs-Sesack Plumbing Co*, 55 Cal 2d 573, 360 P2d 897, 12 Cal Rptr 257 (1961).

Some builders attempt to avoid liability under the doctrine of implied warranty by disclaimers. Such disclaimers, however, are regarded with disfavor and are effective only if expressed in unmistakable language.

> Storm drain built by developer continued to fail causing extensive damage to common areas, which became veritable swamps of standing water. Judgment for townhouse owners $25,443.03 AFFIRMED. The purchase agreement provided a one-year express warranty and stated that the warranty was in lieu of any other express or implied warranty, including the warranty of merchantability and the warranty of fitness for a particular purpose. This disclaimer did not effectively remove the implied warranty of *habitability*.

Briarcliffe W Townhouse Owners Assn v Wiseman Constr Co, 134 Ill App 3d 402, 480 NE2d 833 (1985).

§ 1.49 Implied Warranty That Plans Are Suitable For Construction

The vigor and resiliency of the doctrine of implied warranty is reflected in the so-called *Spearin doctrine* which holds that an owner who supplies plans to a contractor impliedly warrants to the contractor that the plans are suitable for construction.

> A contractor agreed to build a dry dock at the Brooklyn Navy Yard in accordance with plans and specifications prepared by the navy. Contractor relocated a six-foot brick sewer as required by the plans. A year after relocation the six-foot sewer broke during heavy rainfall because of a dam in a seven-foot sewer, downstream, that was owned by the city. The dam was not shown by the plans. The dry dock was flooded. Contractor refused to continue with the work unless the government took responsibility for the necessary clean-up.

The government eventually annulled the contract. HELD: If a construction contractor is bound by contract to build according to plans and specifications provided by the owner, the contractor is not responsible for the consequences of defects in the plans and specifications. There is an implied warranty that if the plans and specifications are followed, the resulting construction will be satisfactory. The contractor's duty to check plans did not impose on the contractor the obligation to determine their adequacy to accomplish the purpose in view.

United States v Spearin, 248 US 132 (1918).

Plans and specifications supplied by the state for construction of a storm sewer failed to reveal adverse soil conditions known to the state. HELD: A contractor who is misled by incorrect plans issued by a public agency is entitled to recover extra compensation for work necessitated by conditions being other than as represented. "The furnishing of misleading plans and specifications by the public body constitutes a breach of an implied warranty of their correctness." 370 P2d at 340.

Souza & McCue Constr Co v Superior Court, 57 Cal 2d 508, 370 P2d 338, 20 Cal Rptr 634 (1962).

§ 1.50 Strict Liability

Strict liability is a tort concept that developed from the law of warranty. The legal concept, sometimes known as *products liability*, is a social policy invented by United States courts in order to do justice between producers and consumers.

The law of negligence, to be considered in a later chapter, is based on the idea that wrongdoing should be punished, and that a wrongdoer who by a wrongful act harms an innocent party should, as a form of punishment, be required to pay compensation to the innocent party. To require a negligent driver who hits a pedestrian to pay for the pedestrian's medical expenses and pain and suffering is a form of retribution that may discourage further wrongdoing.

Strict liability, unlike *negligence*, does not depend upon wrongdoing and has no element of punishment. Economic doctrine recognizes that those who produce and market products do so at a profit, and social justice requires that if the product causes damage to a consumer, the producer should pay the consumer's damages, so that the cost of such damages will become a part of the price of the product and thus the cost of injuries to consumers will be spread among all consumers. The doctrine serves to spread risk by including the cost of injuries to consumers in the price of the products they consume. Whether this idea is good social policy or not is much debated, but nevertheless the doctrine of strict liability holds a producer liable for damages caused to consumers by defective products whether the producer was negligent or not. It is only necessary to prove that the consumer was injured by a defect in the product, and not that the product was negligently designed or manufactured.

> Fireproofing material that contained asbestos was sold to a contractor and installed in a shopping center. The shopping center owner filed an action against the manufacturer of the fireproofing material alleging that the value of the building was diminished by the presence of the defective fireproofing material and seeking to recover expenses incurred for inspection, testing, and removal of the material. The trial court ruled that the damages were solely economic losses and that the fireproofing material had not caused any physical harm to the building. REVERSED. The material caused physical harm to the building and not only to the product itself. This type of injury is actionable under the doctrine of strict liability.

Northridge Co v WR Grace & Co, 162 Wis. 2d 918, 471 NW2d 179 (1991).

> Stored merchandise was damaged by the collapse of suspended refrigeration lines. The Celsius that attached the hanger rods to the ceiling became brittle and corroded at sub-zero temperatures. HELD: The subcontractor who undertook the obligation to design, supply, and install the Celsius was subject to the doctrine of strict liability, as was the sub-subcontractor who undertook to supply and install the Celsius. Both the subcontractor and the sub-subcontractor were in the same position as if they were sellers. The test for determining the applicability of the strict liability doctrine is not the sale of a product, but the placing of a product in commerce.

Commercial Distribution Center, Inc. v St. Regis Paper Co, 689 SW2d 664 (Mo. Ct App 1985).

Some courts have held that subcontractors are not subject to the doctrine of strict liability.

> An action by a homeowners association alleged strict liability against numerous subcontractors. HELD: No California case has applied the doctrine of strict liability to a subcontractor. The consumer is protected by the liability of the developer. The subcontractor does not control the final product, which is affected by work done by the developer and other subcontractors. A developer is usually better capitalized and more likely to be insured than a subcontractor.

La Jolla Homeowners Assn v Superior Court (Quality Roofing, Inc.), 212 Cal App 3d 1131, 261 Cal Rptr 146 (1989).

> A home buyer was severely lacerated when she leaned on a soapdish which had been purchased by and installed by a subcontractor to the subdivider who built the home. HELD: Subcontractor is not liable under the doctrine of strict liability because the subcontractor was not a "seller" of the soapdish. The Restatement (Second) Torts, § 402A(1)(a) provides that a seller of a defective product is liable to a consumer for physical harm if "the seller is engaged in the business of selling such a product". Here, the subcontractor was not a "seller" within the meaning of the Restatement.

Monte Vista Dev Corp. v Superior Court (Wiley Tile Co), 226 Cal App 3d 1681, 277 Cal Rptr 608 (1991).

Having intervened in the market place with the doctrine of strict liability, the courts found themselves entangled of necessity in the evaluation of the design elements of all kinds of products. Manufacturers may defend an allegedly defective design by pointing out the life safety benefits of the design. As a crude example, airbags sometimes cause injuries and their inclusion in an automobile could be considered to be a design defect except for the fact that they save lives.

Suppose that a manufacturer of an elastomeric roofing material introduces a new product after careful research and design. Despite the care taken by the manufacturer, the product fails and consumers are injured by water intrusion that damages ceilings, drywall, carpet, and furniture. The manufacturer, though not negligent, would be liable under the theory of strict liability.

Now suppose that the elastomeric roofing material was used in building 100 tract homes that were developed and built by a subdivider. In such a case, the subdivider as well as the manufacturer of the elastomeric material would be liable for damages, since the subdivider, as a mass homebuilder, is in a position analogous to that of a manufacturer.

> A subdivider employed a subcontractor to install radiant heating systems in homes in a subdivision. Unable to purchase copper pipe because of shortages that occurred during the Korean War, the subcontractor utilized coated steel tubing that had been approved by the FHA. Eight years after installation, the heating system failed because the steel pipe corroded. A remote purchaser obtained judgment against the subdivider for $5,073. AFFIRMED. Regardless of negligence, the subdivider was liable to the remote purchaser on the theory of strict liability.

Kriegler v Eichler Homes, Inc., 269 Cal App 2d 224, 74 Cal Rptr 749 (1969).

Some courts hold that the doctrine of strict liability does not apply to an occasional homebuilder.

> Builder constructed only two single-family homes between 1978 and 1980. HELD: The doctrine of strict liability applies only to mass homebuilders. An occasional homebuilder should not be subject to the doctrine of strict liability because it cannot protect itself by spreading the risk of defective construction among a large number of residences.

Oliver v Superior Court (Regis Builders, Inc.), 211 Cal App 3d 86, 259 Cal Rptr 160 (1989).

The doctrine of strict liability does not apply against architects and engineers.

> A soils engineer prepared a report to certify rough grade for five residential lots but went on to say that the report did not include any finished lot grading and that residential foundation construction

should be in accordance with acceptable methods approved in writing by the engineer. Subdivider proceeded with fine grading and installed foundations without further consultation from the soils engineer. HELD: There was no evidence that the soils engineer was negligent, and engineers are not subject to the doctrine of strict liability.

> Those who sell their services for the guidance of others in their economic, financial, and personal affairs are not liable in the absence of negligence or intentional misconduct . . . the services of experts are sought because of their special skill . . those who hire such persons are not justified in expecting infallibility, but can expect only reasonable care and competence. They purchase service, not insurance. 115 Cal Rptr at 101.

Swett v Gribaldo, Jones & Assocs., 40 Cal App 3d 573, 115 Cal Rptr 99 (1974).

CHAPTER 2

CONSTRUCTION CONTRACTS

Chapter 2

§ 2.01 Modern Construction Contracts

The construction contract as it has developed in the second half of the twentieth century is an instructive artifact of the enterprise system. The well-drafted document, governing, as it does, the economic relationships of the parties, is exquisitely sensitive to, and crafted to respond to, the statutes and regulations of the state and the common law as developed by the courts. Thus the contract responds to: the fact that the physical characteristics of construction are governed, in exquisite detail, by building codes; the fact that the professional activities of architects, engineers, and contractors are regulated by licensing agencies; the fact that under ancient English legal doctrine, a party who has been injured by a breach of contract is entitled to recover only such damages as were reasonably foreseeable under the circumstances at the time when the contract was formed. A hypothetical archeologist of the future, presented with a form construction contract, could deduce, in broad outline, the customs, laws, and regulations of modern economic life.

One of the first inferences to be drawn from the examination of a construction contract is that the parties to it are free to select the terms that are to govern their relationship or, failing to reach such an agreement, are free to decline to deal with one another at all. From this it follows that the terms of the contract are subject to negotiation, and may be modified subject only to the exhaustion of the ingenuity of the parties and their representatives.

The precise expression of the contract is only rarely prescribed by law. In some states a statute prescribes the language of a provision to be included in every construction contract informing consumers that contractors are required to be licensed by the state. Other than in such rare instances, however, the parties are free to invent any language. As is only natural, though, certain forms of expression have become customary.

The expression of a construction contract is influenced more by the bargaining strength and the knowledge of the parties than by any other two factors. Knowledge, here, consists of construction knowledge and legal knowledge. A party with superior construction knowledge has an important advantage in negotiating the provisions of the plans and specifications. The party with superior legal knowledge has the advantage of understanding the rules by which courts interpret contracts, and the ways in which certain contract terms have been interpreted in past cases.

§ 2.02 Basic Obligations

The basic obligation of a prime contractor is to build the project as per the plans and specifications, on schedule, and on budget. The basic obligation of the owner is to pay the contract price. The performance obligations of the contractor are usually spelled out in exquisite detail, while the obligation of the owner to pay the contract price is expressed with admirable brevity. Other obligations of the owner that are implied by the very existence of the contractual relationship, the obligations to provide proper plans and specifications, to provide proper access to the jobsite, to process shop drawings and provide the contractor with needed information are referred to only in passing or omitted from the express terms of the contract altogether. The striking disparity between the expression of the obligations of the contractor and the obligations of the owner is explained by the fact that the language of the construction contract is usually provided by the owner rather than by the contractor. This privilege is engrossed by the owner simply because of the competition between contractors for the relatively small number of projects that are available to be performed.

The rubric under which the law defines these unexpressed obligations of the owner is "implied conditions of cooperation". It is an implied condition of every contract that the parties will cooperate with each other so that the basic objectives of the contract may be achieved, and that neither party will do anything to deprive the other of the fundamental benefits of the contract. The basic obligation of the contractor to provide construction that complies with the building codes is usually expressed in considerable detail, while the obligation of the owner to provide access to the jobsite and "buildable plans" is treated with silence.

§ 2.03 The Scope of the Work

The vast bulk of many construction contracts concerns itself with an exquisitely detailed depiction in words, figures, and drawings (and sometimes, nowadays, in electronic data) of the work to be performed by the contractor. Crucial as they are, these descriptions of the work are only vaguely understood by most project owners, who must rely upon their professional advisors, the architects and engineers, to prepare the construction documents. Architects and engineers in their turn rely upon their consultants for structural, soils, electrical, and mechanical systems, and the specialists who design those systems are often compelled to rely for the most crucial information upon the representations and advice of trade contractors and materials manufacturers.

With respect to description of the scope of the work, the construction contract is analogous to a pyramid. At the very apex of the pyramid is a provision in the agreement signed by owner and contractor to the effect that the contractor will perform the work called for by the drawings and specifications in a good and workmanlike manner.

The next level of the pyramid is the specifications, which may be contained on a single sheet of paper or many thousands of sheets according to the nature of the project and the inclinations of the owner. The specifications in turn are supported by the drawings which, again, may consist of a simple sketch or thousands of pages. These documents are themselves supported by the applicable building codes (usually about a thousand pages) which in their turn are again supported by tens of thousands of pages of industry standards promulgated and frequently revised by industry groups such as the American Concrete Institute (colloquially, the ACI's), the American Society of Testing Materials (ASTM's), the Uniform Building Code (UBC), the National Electrical Code (NEC), and on, and on, and on.

Despite these many references (and it is no exaggeration to say that they would fill an entire library), disputes still arise from the apparently irremediable uncertainty that inheres in any attempt to describe with absolute certainty the physical nature of a construction project. When such issues must be resolved in court the outcome depends upon the credibility of expert testimony and the ingenuity of counsel.

Implied warranty of workmanlike construction. Even though a contract may not so specify, there is a warranty, implied by law, in every construction contract, that the contractor will perform the work in a workmanlike manner. "Workmanlike construction" is a matter of trade practice that varies from time to time and from location to location and is, again, a matter to be proved by the testimony of architects, engineers, contractors, superintendents, field supervisors, and craftspeople. The legal benchmark here is the average performance of a qualified contractor or tradesperson. This standard may be, and often is, modified by a provision that all work will be performed in accordance with the highest and best standards of performance.

Implied warranty of contract documents. Offsetting in some cases the implied warranty of workmanlike performance is the implied warranty that the owner will supply contract documents (plans and specifications) that are buildable, and not misleading. (This rule of law is known as the *Spearin doctrine*. It is named after the United States Supreme Court case in which the implied warranty was applied to contract documents supplied by the navy to a government contractor.) A moment's consideration will show that the Spearin doctrine may come into conflict with the implied warranty of workmanlike performance. Here, the Spearin doctrine should normally prevail because of the convention that architects and engineers by their superior training and education are given final authority to control construction, and this authority cannot be undermined by every jobsite superintendent who thinks he knows how to run a job simply because he has had 50 years of experience in the trades. It goes without saying that the superintendent operating within his area of expertise is as likely, perhaps more likely, to be right than the architect. But the conventions must be observed nevertheless and for good reason. The function of the architect is to protect the owner's investment while the superintendent is sometimes motivated by less altruistic concerns.

Performance specifications. The specifications may be written on a descriptive basis or on a performance basis. A descriptive specification prescribes the exact item to be supplied by the contractor while a performance specification leaves the selection of the exact item up to the contractor but prescribes the exact performance to be achieved by the item. For example, a specification may prescribe the physical characteristics of a beam by calling out its size and material, or may require that the beam support a specified load and leave the size, dimensions and materials to the discretion of the contractor. An example of the fallacy "more is better" may occur when a spec writer calls out both the physical characteristics of an item and its performance. Does the construction meet both criteria? This may be impossible because the item described may not perform as required so the item supplied by the contractor will violate the performance side of the specification or the descriptive side. In a well-known case of this type the contract documents described an air conditioning system in detail as to chillers, air handling equipment, and duct work and went on to provide that the system would reduce the ambient temperature by 30 degrees. The contractor installed the system as described but it did not achieve the required reduction in ambient temperature. The court held the contractor had not committed a breach of contract because an implied warranty ran from the owner to the contractor that if the contractor installed the system described by the specification it would perform as required. The principle at stake here is that the work must be controlled by the designer rather than by the contractor. If it were to be held that the performance specification controls over the descriptive specification, then the contractor would be at liberty to cheapen the job to its liking as long as the required performance was attained.

The tension between descriptive and performance specifications is also found in the building codes, which typically describe a system but go on to say that the description is not meant to frustrate the ingenuity of architects and engineers, who may submit for approval by the public agency systems that do not comply with the descriptions supplied by the code, as long as specified performance requirements are attained.

The duty to warn. Instances arise in which a contractor, or more often a subcontractor, observes an error in contract documents. A contractor or a subcontractor bidding a job may be inclined to figure it precisely as detailed because to figure the job as it should be built would increase the bid and the contractor or subcontractor would thereby forfeit any chance of being the low bidder. One option available to the contractor or subcontractor then is to figure the job precisely as specified,with the expectation that a change order can be negotiated at the appropriate time. Courts have held that a contractor confronted with obviously erroneous contract documents has a duty to call the error to the owner's attention before signing the contract. A contractor or subcontractor may, however, be tempted to seek a competitive advantage by remaining silent.

The dragnet clause. The dragnet clause is much favored by owners and architects for inclusion in prime contracts (and by prime contractors for inclusion in subcontracts): it provides that the contractor (or subcontractor) will provide a complete and workable project (or system), that requirements may be scattered throughout the contract documents and may be included on the drawings and omitted from the specifications or included in the specifications but omitted from the drawings but nevertheless must be provided no matter where found in the contract documents. The dragnet clause is a particular danger to subcontractors who may bid a job based upon a takeoff of only those parts of the drawings and specification that normally apply to their trade. By following this practice a plumbing subcontractor, for instance, may miss piping that is displayed only on the HVAC drawings. Dragnet clauses that would lead to harsh or inequitable results may be difficult to enforce.

Satisfaction clauses. It may be provided that all construction will be performed to the satisfaction of the owner, the architect, or the engineer. Let us suppose now that a contractor supplies work as described by the contract documents that meets the standards of trade practice but the owner is not satisfied. The inquiry here is not whether the owner, in fact, is satisfied, but whether the owner, as a reasonable person, should be satisfied. Satisfaction clauses are normally interpreted as "reasonable" satisfaction clauses and the contractor is not held to the standard of providing absolute subjective satisfaction.

It is sometimes argued that a distinction should be made for aesthetic matters and questions of artistic effect. In such cases, the quality of performance is very much a question of judgment and it may be reasonable for the owner to impose a personal satisfaction requirement on a work of art.

Design-build. Many problems associated with the scope of the work, and some other problems too, are eliminated by the design-build system. Here, the contractor, rather than the owner, employs the architect and takes responsibility for designing the project.

§ 2.04 Contract Price

Of all the clauses in a construction contract the one of greatest interest to, and virtually the only clause of benefit to the contractor is the one that establishes the owner's obligation to pay for the work. Virtually all the other provisions of a construction contract are there for the protection and benefit of the owner.

Lump sum contract. The lump sum contract is one under which the contractor undertakes to produce a finished project for a specified sum of money. This type of contract is well adapted to competitive bidding, a system under which a contract is awarded to the lowest responsible bidder. In the simplest form of competitive bidding, all bids are exactly the same except for the amount, and the work is awarded to the contractor who bids the lowest amount.

Cost plus contracts. In a cost plus contract, the owner agrees to pay to the contractor the cost of the work plus a fee. The fee may be expressed as a percentage of cost (for example, cost plus 10%) or may be fixed irrespective of cost. In fixed fee contract, the owner agrees to pay to the contractor the cost of the work plus a specified sum (for example, cost plus fixed fee of $150,000).

Alternates. A contract may contain alternates from which the owner may choose at specified prices. For example, alternate "one" might consist of an elevator to be added to the scope of the work for a specified amount of money to be added to the contract price. Specification of alternates can complicate the competitive bidding process, since the identity of the low bidder may depend on the array of alternates accepted or rejected by the owner.

Allowances. An allowance, properly speaking, is the estimated cost of some designated portion of the work that is included in the contract price, with a provision that if the actual cost of that portion of the work is greater or less than the estimate, the difference will be added to or subtracted from the contract price. Items such as fixtures or carpets that have not been selected may conveniently be included in the scope of the work and the contract price by this means.

Guaranteed max. Construction industry jargon is somewhat inconsistent in the application of the term "guaranteed max". The expression is a contraction of the term "guaranteed maximum" and usually refers to a provision that the total price of a *cost plus* contract will not exceed a *guaranteed maximum price.* The term "guaranteed max" is, however, often used as a synonym for a "fixed price" or "hard dollar" contract.

Share savings. As an incentive to economy, an owner sometimes offers a bonus to a contractor in the form of a share of the amount saved by the owner if the total cost of a contract is less than the guaranteed maximum price.

§ 2.05 Change Orders

All contractors contend, and most architects and engineers acknowledge, that there has never been a perfect set of contract documents and that something is invariably either omitted or wrongly or ambiguously displayed on the drawings and specifications. It also seems inevitable that architect and owner, closely observing the process by which the ideas they previously expressed only in writing are converted by the contractor into palpable, material form, want changes. That changes will be wanted is foreseen, and a method for achieving changes is provided in the contract documents. A properly drafted change order clause gives the owner the *power* to *order* the contractor to change the work.

In the process of implementing a change order, the question of price will arise. A *deductive* change order reduces the contract price, while a change order that adds to the scope of the work increases the price. It is unwise from the owner's point of view to require advance agreement as to the amount by which the contract price will be increased or reduced, since that would give the contractor unjustified leverage. The contractor could simply gouge, or refuse to agree to the change.

Pricing change orders. Pricing change orders may be a time consuming and annoying exercise to contractors and subcontractors. The activity consumes the time of project managers and estimators that could be better devoted to performing the work. Moreover, it is an unprofitable activity if the owner decides the price is too high and decides not to issue the change order. Portions of the work must sometimes be delayed while it is determined whether a change order will be issued or not. It is understandable, then, that the owner, in the interest of expediting a project, may reserve the power to issue change orders before a price has been agreed to. The contract usually provides that in such cases the contract price will be equitably adjusted. Even in the absence of such a provision, the law implies such a promise when the contractor, at the request of the owner, increases the scope of the work with no demonstrated intention of making a gift. Under one popular provision, the contractor is required to document its costs on a daily or weekly basis, and the owner reimburses the costs monthly plus a specified percentage of costs to cover overhead until the final price of the change can be agreed to. Processing changes in this manner can become an administrative nightmare as the contractor is required to assemble supporting cost data from subcontractors who may be none too cooperative if they believe they are losing money processing change orders.

Difficulty is always encountered in defining the line that divides "cost" from "overhead". Contract language defining "cost" may run to several densely worded paragraphs.

A clause that is sometimes favored by owners provides that if the parties cannot agree to the price of a change order, the contractor will perform the work as ordered. The price will be agreed to later, and meanwhile the contractor will maintain job progress without stopping or slowing the work. It may be difficult, though, even impossible, to enforce such a provision, because such a clause puts the contractor at the mercy of the owner.

Written change order requirement. Many contracts provide that the contractor will not be paid for changes in the absence of a written change order. The law will not enforce such a provision if the owner requests extra work and promises to pay for it and the contractor performs it. This is because, in most states, a written contract can be modified by an *executed oral agreement*. "Executed oral agreement" is defined as an oral contract that has been executed (or performed) on one side. Thus the parties, in such a case, are held to have modified the contract by annulling the written change order requirement.

Theories of *waiver* and *estoppel* are also used by the courts to avoid enforcement of written change order requirements. It is possible for an owner to *waive* a provision that is inserted in the contract for the owner's benefit. Thus a court may hold that an owner has waived, or intentionally relinquished, the right to enforce the requirement that change orders be reduced to writing.

The concept of *estoppel* may also be invoked. Let us suppose that owner requests, and pays for, a series of small changes. Then owner requests a big change, but refuses to pay for it, relying on the provision that change orders to be enforceable must be reduced to writing. Here, the *estoppel* may be applied since the owner, by its conduct, has led the contractor to believe that it will pay for unwritten change orders, and may not be permitted, in law, to falsify that belief.

§ 2.06 Progress Payments

The construction industry operates on progress payments. Contractors and subcontractors are not expected to have the resources to finance their own work for more than a few weeks at a time, nor are owners expected to pay in advance for work that has not yet been performed.

Milestone payments. The contract price may be divided into a series of payments to be made when certain milestones are achieved. For example, a series of payments totaling 100% may be paid in increments when the foundation is complete, when framing is complete, when the roof is on, when drywall is hung, and when the project passes final inspection and receives a certificate of occupancy. A plumbing subcontract might be scheduled for payments when the ground work is in, when piping is completed, and when the fixtures are hung.

Percentage of completion. Under one popular system, progress payments are made according to percentage of completion. Here, owner and contractor agree at the outset that specified values are assigned to different portions of the work and that the contractor will bill the owner monthly for the percentage of value that is proportional to the percentage of completion of that portion of the work. For example, if it is agreed that the framing is worth $100,000 and that the contractor has performed 60% of the framing, then the contractor may bill $60,000 for framing. Thus, progress billings are calculated against the schedule of values that has been agreed to by the parties in advance.

A contractor may attempt to exploit this system by *front loading* or *front end loading* the schedule of values. If a contractor is allowed to overstate the value of items of work that will be performed early on, then the profit may be extracted from the job at the beginning. This, of course, means that later stages of the job must be performed at a loss and raises the possibility that the contractor may become insolvent in the later stages.

Retention. As a form of security that the contractor will complete the job, the owner usually withholds a 10% retention from the contractor's progress payments. Prime contractors in turn withhold the 10% retention from subcontractors. Early trades, however, are sometimes unwilling to allow 10% to be retained from their contract earnings until the end of the job, so the customary 10% retention is subject to negotiation by the early trades.

The 10% retention is scheduled to be paid when the period for recording claims of mechanics lien has expired. This gives the owner an opportunity to foreclose the possibility of mechanics liens being recorded by subcontractors or material suppliers before the last payment is disbursed to the prime contractor.

Extra work. "Extra work" is work performed by a contractor that was not included within the scope of the work that was agreed to be performed in return for payment of the contract price. When a contractor performs extra work at the request of the owner, the contractor usually expects to be paid for it. A contractor that performs extra work at the request of an owner is usually entitled to receive payment under one legal theory or another. In most states, courts hold that a written contract may be modified by an oral contract. If the contract contains a covenant against oral modifications, then the courts may hold that the owner has waived the requirement that extra work be authorized in writing, or is estopped to enforce it.

When extra work is ordered by an unauthorized employee of the owner, however, the owner may escape liability to pay for it. Many construction contracts restrict authority to order extra work to certain named individuals, and such clauses are enforceable.

Scope of the work. Owners and contractors often fall into dispute about precisely what is included within the scope of the work defined by the contract documents. Drawings, for example, often do not attempt to depict every element of every system to be installed by a contractor, and leave some items to be inferred. For example, it may be inferred that a wire must be run from a switch to the piece of equipment that is controlled by the switch, and yet that wire may not be expressly displayed on the drawings. Therefore the contractor may consider installation of the wire to be extra work, while the owner may in good faith believe that the wire is included. The issue may be addressed by a clause of the contract to the effect that the contractor will produce a complete and operable system including all items and elements that may be inferred from the items and elements that are displayed on the drawings. A subcontractor, however, will argue that those items should only be included within the scope of the work that would be taken off by the subcontractor's estimator in figuring the job. Items that would not normally be taken off by the subcontractor's estimator will not be included in the subcontract price and therefore should not be considered to be within the scope of the work.

§ 2.07 One-Year Warranty

Although there are many variations, the warranty clause of a construction contract usually provides that the contractor will repair or replace, without charge, defective materials, equipment, or workmanship for a period of one year. The one-year warranty clause is often accompanied by an exculpatory clause, that provides the specified warranty is in lieu of all other express or implied warranties. Thus, a clause that appears to be giving something to the owner may sometimes be made to subtract from rights that the owner would otherwise have under doctrine of implied warranty. Courts are reluctant to give this type of exculpatory clause full effect.

It is sometimes believed, erroneously, that a warranty clause reduces, rather than increases, the responsibilities of the contractor. A failure to fulfill the requirements of the contract documents is a breach of contract. If a contractor breaches the contract, for example, by supplying an inferior quality of piping material, the contractor would be responsible to correct that breach even if it were not discovered by the owner until after the expiration of the one-year warranty. When properly understood, therefore, the conventional one-year warranty adds little, if anything, to a contractor's responsibilities.

Many contracts provide that the contractor will collect and deliver to the owner the warranty documents that apply to materials and equipment incorporated into the job. This enables the owner to call directly upon the manufacturer of air conditioning equipment, for example, for warranty service.

§ 2.08 Indemnity

Indemnity clauses are usually imposed on the contracting party of the lesser bargaining strength. Thus the contractor may be required to indemnify the owner, and sometimes even the architect, against claims and liability. Subcontractors are customarily required to indemnify the prime contractor and the owner against claims and liability.

It is important to understand that indemnity is a three-party concept. The three parties are the indemnitor, indemnitee, and the claimant. For example, an indemnity clause will customarily require the prime contractor to indemnify the owner against claims made by an injured worker. Here, the worker is the claimant, the contractor is the indemnitor, and the owner is the indemnitee.

The word "indemnity" is sometimes misused in construction contracts by those who would attempt to build additional protection into an indemnity clause by including a promise to "indemnify" against defective workmanship and materials. The proper concept, here, is "warranty", and not "indemnity". A warranty is an undertaking that work and materials will be of workmanlike and merchantable quality, whereas an indemnity is an undertaking to protect the indemnitee against third party claims. It is possible that a third party claim could arise out of defective material. For example, a worker might sustain injury because of a cross grained rafter. An indemnity clause would protect the owner against the worker's claim, while a warranty clause would cover the cost of repairing the rafter.

Some courts have held that an indemnity clause should not interpreted to indemnify a person against its own wrongful conduct on the ground that such an indemnity would tend to encourage carelessness. The prevailing view, though, is that indemnity is analogous to insurance. There is no social policy against insurance even though it is arguable that an uninsured person might conduct business more carefully than one covered by insurance. Therefore there is no social policy against an indemnity clause that protects the indemnitee against claims arising out of its own negligent conduct. Courts are still reluctant, however, to interpret an indemnity clause so as to protect an indemnitee against claims arising out of its own misconduct in the absence of clear language. Many indemnity clauses, therefore, do make it very clear that such protection is extended. Many forms of indemnity clause go so far as to require a contractor to indemnify an owner against claims and liability arising out of or related to performance of the work even in the absence of negligent conduct by the contractor. Thus, the analogy to insurance is complete, since an insurance company agrees to defend and indemnify the insured against claims absent any possible negligence or misconduct by the insurance company.

Another issue that may be confronted in the interpretation of an indemnity clause is the question of whether the indemnitor must pick up the costs of defense. Some clauses explicitly require the indemnitor to defend the indemnitee. An indemnity against "claims" as well as against "liability" is usually interpreted to include defense costs.

An indemnitee may be perplexed about whether to actually entrust its defense to an indemnitor, particularly if the financial resources of the indemnitor are questionable and most particularly if the indemnitor and the indemnitee are alleged by the claimant to be joint tortfeasors. A defendant in a lawsuit might well question the quality of a defense to be provided by a co-defendant, who might be expected to defend itself by attempting to pin blame on other defendants. This problem is resolved by observing the rules against conflict of interest that apply to lawyers. Since lawyers may not represent conflicting interests, the indemnitor must employ independent counsel to vigorously defend the position of the indemnitee.

These indemnity problems, to the extent that they deal with indemnity against claims for bodily injury or physical damage to property, are best handled by insurance. If the indemnitor obtains coverage denoted "blanket contractual" or "liability assumed by contract", then the indemnitor's insurance company is required to provide the defense and indemnity specified in the indemnity clause. To put it another way, the indemnity clause is then backed by insurance. Many indemnity clauses in construction contracts are therefore supported by insurance clauses that require the indemnitor to carry appropriate coverage and to provide the indemnitee with evidence of such coverage. The overall effect is to transfer the risk from the indemnitee's insurance carrier to the indemnitor's insurance carrier.

Most insurance policies cover bodily injury and physical injury to tangible property. Potential claims are left uncovered that do not fall under those rubrics. Let us say, for example, that a subcontractor makes a claim against an owner, alleging that the owner negligently supplied unbuildable drawings. Here we have a claim arising out of the work against an owner who is an indemnitee under the prime contract, but a claim that would not be covered by insurance against bodily injury or physical injury to tangible property. Is prime contractor/ indemnitor required by the indemnity clause to defend the owner against such an uninsured claim? A broadly worded indemnity clause could be interpreted to cover such claims.

Most states prohibit construction contract indemnity provisions that require a contractor or subcontractor to provide indemnity against claims and damages arising from the sole negligence of the indemnitee. Such statutes, however, do not make it unlawful for a contractor or subcontractor to provide *insurance* against such claims and damages.

§ 2.09 Property Insurance

In the event of damage to or destruction of the project by fire, earthquake, flood, or other peril, the questions to be resolved are 1) is the contractor excused from further performance; 2) is the project to be rebuilt; 3) is it the owner of the project or the contractor who is at risk. Absent a clause excusing further performance, the contractor is required to rebuild because destruction of the project does not make performance of the contract *impossible* albeit more expensive.

If the risk of damage or destruction is on the contractor, then the contractor should insure the risk. Builders risk insurance is available to protect the contractor's interest in the continued existence of the project. If the project is destroyed by fire, then, the contractor could use the proceeds of the insurance to rebuild.

If the risk of damage or destruction is on the owner, then the contract may provide that the owner will use the proceeds of insurance to pay to the contractor the cost of rebuilding.

Now let us suppose that a project is destroyed by a fire ignited by a welder employed by a steel fabricating subcontractor. Suppose that the owner's builders risk insurance company pays the cost of reconstruction. Under these circumstances the insurance carrier is *subrogated* to the owner's rights to recover the cost of rebuilding from the subcontractor. Again, the subcontractor's liability insurance carrier will indemnify the subcontractor against this loss. Many construction contracts provide that the owner's insurance carrier will "waive subrogation". Under the approach taken by the AIA general conditions, the owner provides builders risk insurance and the owner's insurance carrier waives subrogation rights against the contractor and all subcontractors.

§ 2.10 Liability Insurance

A liability insurance carrier undertakes that if a claim is made against the insured for bodily injury or property damage, the insurance carrier will defend the insured against the claim and pay the claim if the insured is found liable.

It is in the interest of the project owner to shift liability, if possible, to the contractor and its insurance carrier. It is in the interest of the prime contractor to shift liability, in turn, to its subcontractors and their insurance carriers. This may be accomplished by indemnity agreements backed by insurance. The prime contract document imposes a specific liability insurance requirement on the prime contractor and on subcontractors, and the prime contractor and subcontractors are required to name the owner as an additional insured on their policies. Prime and subcontractors are generally required to supply certificates of insurance, and appropriate endorsements, showing that the owner is named additional insured and the insurance of the prime contractor and subcontractors is primary. This means that the insurance of the prime and subcontractors is to be exhausted before resort may be had to the insurance of the owner.

Parallel provisions run between the prime contractor and subcontractors, who are required to name the prime contractor and the owner as additional insureds on their policies, and to provide certificates of insurance and endorsements to demonstrate that such coverage exists. The certificate of insurance and the endorsement should provide that the insurance carrier will not cancel or reduce coverage without giving 30 days advance written notice to the owner.

§ 2.11 Default

"Default" is a material failure to perform in accordance with the requirements of a contract. Default, therefore, is a breach of contract: but not a trivial breach. Moreover, default is a breach of contract that is unexcused. Performance of a contract is excused by a material breach. This is simply a reflection of a common sense axiom that one party to a contract cannot insist on full performance by the other party, while at the same time ignoring its own obligation of performance.

Default by contractor. The law gives a project owner three basic options in response to default by a contractor. The first option is to allow the contractor to continue to perform but withhold from progress payments an amount calculated to compensate the owner for economic loss caused by the default. The second option is to terminate the contractor's performance, employ a replacement contractor to finish the job, and sue for the amount by which the cost of finishing the work exceeds the contract price. The third option is to *rescind* the contract. Rescission is an option seldom exercised by an owner because the legal effect of rescission is literally to cancel the contract itself, and not just to terminate continued performance of the contract. After rescission, the law attempts to put the parties back in the position they occupied before the contract was formed. This resolves itself into payment, by the owner to the contractor, of the reasonable value of the contractor's performance. It is usually more advantageous to the owner to keep the terms of the contract alive and to sue for damages for breach of contract.

A typical default clause provides that if the contractor fails to perform as specified by the contract documents, the owner will give written notice of default, and if the contractor fails to cure the default within a specified period of days or hours, the owner may remove the contractor from the job. A well articulated default clause will also permit the owner to assign subcontracts to a substitute, takeover, replacement contractor. The well articulated clause will require subcontractors to consent in advance to this assignment. When exercising its rights under a default clause, the owner may pick and choose its subcontracts with due regard to the obligations of the contractor that the owner must assume when taking control of the subcontract. One who takes the benefits of a contract is usually required, by law, to also accept the burdens. Thus an owner exercising a contractual right to take an assignment of rights under a subcontract will also find itself bound to perform the obligations of the prime contractor to that subcontractor. It may be more sound economically for an owner to reject a particular subcontract and employ a different subcontractor to finish the work. The contractor is required to turn over its materials, tools, equipment, and subcontracts to the owner who may utilize them in finishing the work. A typical clause goes on to provide that if the total cost of the work exceeds the contract price the contractor will, upon demand, pay the difference to the owner; contra wise, if the total cost is less than the contract price, the owner will pay the surplus to the contractor on demand. Because of this provision, a few owners have found themselves in the ironic position of making a payoff to a defaulting contractor because their takeover was so efficient it left the owner with a surplus of funds.

It is important for a project owner terminating a contractor's performance to rigorously follow the provisions of the termination clause with respect to notice. Since the consequences of termination are severe, termination provisions are strictly enforced. A contractor whose performance is terminated is, of course, unable to perform the contract, and is not even in a position to correct defective construction. Therefore, improper termination gives a contractor a defense to accusations of construction defects, since the termination prevented the contractor from correcting the defects. (*Prevention of performance* is a recognized defense to a claim of breach of contract.)

Default by owner. Default by owner usually takes the form of failure to make a progress payment. If the failure to make a progress payment is unexcused, and prolonged, it is by definition a material breach of contract since, from a contractor's point of view, the only reason for performing a construction contract is to get paid. The contractor's options are 1) stop work, but remain ready, willing, and able to continue performance; 2) terminate performance and sue for the contract value of work already performed plus the profit reasonably anticipated for completion of the job; 3) terminate performance and rescind the contract. Rescission is a very attractive option for a contractor since it removes all contract provisions including obnoxious ones, such as a requirement that the work be performed on schedule or a requirement that no extra work will be paid for unless ordered in writing. After rescission, the law attempts to put the parties in the position they would have occupied if the contract had never been formed, and this usually means that the contractor is entitled to be paid the reasonable value of its work regardless of the provisions of the contract.

(Rescission of a contract does not, however, terminate an arbitration clause.)

Default clauses usually provide that contractor will give written notice to the owner before stopping work, in order to give the owner an opportunity to cure the default by making payment.

No stop clause. A no stop clause provides that in the event of a dispute the contractor will not slow or stop the work, but will continue working on the project until completion, and resolve the dispute then. From the contractor's point of view, such clauses are very dangerous because the enforcement of such a clause can require the contractor to empty its treasury by continuing performance without receiving progress payments. Some courts have held, with questionable justification, that by agreeing to a no stop clause a contractor gives up the right to rescind a contract even though the owner may have committed a material, unexcused breach.

§ 2.12 Liquidated Damages

Many construction contracts contain clauses that specify (or *liquidate*) the damages that will be sustained by the owner if completion of the project is delayed. Courts are generally reluctant to enforce liquidated damages clauses because the amount may be such as to penalize a contractor for breach of contract rather than merely to compensate the owner for its actual loss sustained because of delay. This goes against the general objective of the law of contracts, which is to compensate actual loss, rather than to punish wrongdoing.

Some state legislatures have adopted statutes directing the courts to liberally enforce liquidated damages provisions. In states where such legislation has not been adopted, though, the clause should be drafted so as to make it clear that the amount to be paid by the contractor for each day of delay is not a penalty. First of all, then, the clause should not refer to the payment as a "penalty", but should make it clear that the amount to be paid was negotiated by the parties as a reasonable forecast of the actual damages that would be suffered by the owner from a delay in performance.

§ 2.13 Extensions of Time

Most construction contracts specify a date for completion of the project and also provide that if construction is delayed by inclement weather, flood, fire, riot, civil commotion, or other such *force majeure* then the time for performance of the contract will be extended.

Many contracts also provide that if the time required to perform the contract is extended by change orders issued by the owner, the number of days is to be specified as part of the change order.

Critical path. It may also be provided that the time for performance will not be extended unless the delay is to work that is on the critical path, which is to say that total contract time will not be extended because the contractor is delayed in performing some item of work that, by being delayed, does not hold up the performance of other items of work. This type of clause can lead to disputes about "float" time.

Float refers to a period of time during which the contractor has the option of either performing, or not performing, an item of work and still not delaying the ultimate completion of the job. For example, a contractor may elect to pour a patio slab at the beginning, in the middle, or at the very end of a job if the pour does not delay the start of any other portion of the work. So, does the float belong to the owner or to the contractor? Suppose the contractor cannot start construction of the patio cover until the slab has been poured. It will take four working days to form and pour the slab and another five working days to construct the cover. The entire work must be completed by June 1. The contractor decides to wait until May 20 to pour the slab but rains that day delay the completion of the project until June 10. The owner may argue that the contractor should have expedited the pour so as to avoid the risk that rain would delay the ultimate completion of the job. The contractor will argue that it merely used the float, as it was entitled to do in planning the job.

Requests for extensions of time. A contract may provide that a contractor is only entitled to an extension of time if it makes a written request promptly after the commencement of a delay. Courts may be reluctant to enforce such clauses when their application would appear to be unjust, and, as in the case of the written change order requirement, these provisions may be *waived* by the owner, who may also be *estopped* to enforce them.

§ 2.14 No Damages for Delay

A clause favored by many owners is one that provides that in the event that performance of a contract is delayed by an act of the owner, the contractor, upon prompt application, will be entitled to an extension of time but *no damages for delay*. This type of provision can put the contractor at the mercy of the owner and therefore courts enforce it with reluctance. It is often held that such a clause is enforceable only if the delay is of the type that was in the contemplation of the parties at the time when the contract was negotiated. Application of this test often excludes a particular cause of delay from the universe of those that may have been within the contemplation of the parties at the time when the contract was negotiated. It has often been held that a no damages for delay clause does not apply to delays caused by acts of the owner.

§ 2.15 Anti Waiver Clauses

We have noticed that courts may attempt to avoid the harsh application of a written change order requirement by invoking the doctrine of *waiver* (defined, legally, as the intentional relinquishment of a known right). As is logical, then, an owner may include in the contract documents an anti waiver clause the effect that the owner will not be held to have waived any provision of the contract documents except if the waiver be in writing signed by the owner. May the owner waive the application of the anti waiver clause? One can only say that courts do not like to enforce contract provisions that permit one party to sacrifice the interest of another party for its own gain, and are quite ingenious at avoiding what they perceive to be unjust results.

§ 2.16 Final Payment as a Release

Some courts have held that when an owner makes final payment to a contractor the owner impliedly releases the contractor from all claims known, or that should be known to the owner at the time when the payment is made. This issue may be controlled by a clause specifying that final payment either does, or does not, constitute release of all claims.

§ 2.17 Compliance with Laws

A contract clause may require that the contractor comply with all laws, statutes, rules and regulations of public authority including building codes and safety regulations. Such a clause may be considered superfluous, since even without such a clause it is implied that the law is a part of the contract. The clause may appear to apply in an instance where the drawings and specifications require the contractor to install an item of work in a manner that violates building codes. Which part of the contract is to be enforced? Many courts hold that a construction contract includes an implied warranty by the owner that the contractor can build according to the plans and specifications without violating building codes.

§ 2.18 Contractor to Report Errors

A contract may provide that the contractor will promptly report to the owner or the architect any error on the drawings or in the specifications, including any failure to comply with codes. Under some contract clauses the contractor accepts a positive duty to scrutinize the drawings and specifications and determine that they are buildable. This clause violates the conventions and traditions of the industry which are to the effect that the contractor is not as knowledgeable as the architect and the engineer and should accept direction from them. It also transfers from the architect to the contractor the duty of coordinating the drawings (that is to say, making sure that beams do not interfere with duct work and so forth). The contractor may unwittingly lend dignity to such a clause by selling an owner on the contractor's "value engineering" program. The object of "value engineering" is to cheapen the cost of a job without reducing its quality by recommending more efficient or less expensive systems to the owner.

§ 2.19 Value Engineering

It is undoubtedly true that architects and engineers sometimes specify systems that could be replaced by other, less expensive systems, and it is often arguable that the quality of a less expensive system is just as good. A contractor's knowledge of such systems may be superior to the knowledge of a particular architect, so sometimes owners encourage contractors to "value engineer" by offering them a portion of the savings. Value engineering clauses can inspire sophisticated debates about the relative qualities of building systems.

§ 2.20 Competent Workers

This clause provides that the contractor and its subcontractors will supply an adequate number of skilled and competent workers to the project. An additional clause often provides that the job superintendent is subject to the approval of the owner, and will not be changed without the owner's approval.

§ 2.21 Union Labor

It is sometimes provided that the project workers will be union members and that the contractor and its subcontractors will abide by specified master labor agreements. It may also be provided that in the event presence of the contractor or a subcontractor on the project causes picketing or other labor trouble, the contractor or subcontractor will do whatever is necessary to remove the picket line and expedite the work.

§ 2.22 Or Equal

Public works contracts often provide that if an item of material or equipment is designated by a brand name it will be deemed to be followed by the phrase "or equal". The purpose of such a clause is to secure to the public agency the advantages of competitive bidding, and to prevent the favoritism and corruption that could occur if a public officer were allowed to direct business to a specified "sole source". The contractor may be required to submit its "or equals" to the public agency for consideration within a specified period of time after the award of the contract, and the clause may establish the criteria by which the proposed equal is to be judged.

§ 2.23 Insolvency

It is sometimes provided that the owner may cancel the contract if the contractor becomes insolvent or files for bankruptcy. The owner's supposed reserved right to cancel a contract in the event of bankruptcy may be frustrated by a trustee in bankruptcy, who has the right to affirm, and enforce, the contracts of the bankrupt contractor.

§ 2.24 Right to Demand Bond

The owner may reserve the right to demand that the contractor furnish a performance bond at any time during the progress of the work, provided that the owner pays the premium. The reservation of a right to demand bond may have a tincture of cynicism to it because the owner may reserve such a right against the possibility of a dispute, knowing that it will likely be impossible for the contractor to obtain a bond to guarantee the continued performance of a partially completed project which has already fallen into dispute. Therefore the true purpose of reserving such a right may be to enable the owner to establish a clear, material default such as would justify the owner in removing the contractor from the job.

§ 2.25 Bond Provisions

The provisions of a construction contract often are, and from the owner's point of view always should be, incorporated into the bond. The function of a performance bond is to require the surety company to guarantee that the contractor will properly perform the contract. Enforcement of a performance bond may be frustrated, however, if the contract is materially changed by extra work orders, since such a material change may *exonerate* the bond. A bond may also be exonerated if the owner prepays the contractor, since prepayment reduces the contractor's motivation to continue performance. A contract clause may avoid these defenses by providing that changes to the scope of the work or prepayment will not exonerate the bond, and such clauses may be made effective by a provision in the bond that incorporates the contract provisions into the text of the bond.

§ 2.26 Scheduling

It may be provided that the contractor will provide the owner with a schedule, and that the contractor will maintain the schedule. The schedule may be required to show when the various portions of the work will begin and end and what items of work are on the so-called *critical path*. The clause may require the contractor periodically to revise the schedule to reflect the actual progress of the work, and may provide that if the contractor falls behind schedule the contractor will supply additional forces to accelerate the work, or that the owner may provide such additional forces on its own and deduct the cost thereof from the contractor's progress payment. It is also sometimes provided that the schedule to be supplied by the contractor will not propose that the work be finished before the date specified for completion in the contract documents, since the owner may fear that the contractor could then make a claim against the owner for delay if the work is not finished by the accelerated date.

§ 2.27 Pay When Paid -- Pay If Paid

Many subcontracts provide that the prime contractor will make progress payments to the subcontractor only when the prime contractor has received payments from the owner. The purpose of such a clause is to prevent the prime contractor from having to go into its own funds to finance the construction. The courts often perceive such clauses as inequitable so they are construed, if possible, to relate to the *timing* of payment rather than to the *entitlement* to payment. The well drafted clause, from the prime contractor's point of view, will provide that the prime contractor will make payment to the subcontractor only from funds received by the owner in payment for the subcontractor's work, and that the receipt of funds from the owner is a *condition precedent* to the prime contractor's obligation to make any payment to the subcontractor. Most courts, sometimes reluctantly, will enforce such provisions if they are clear and explicit.

§ 2.28 Backcharges

A prime contract may provide that the owner may withhold from progress payments an amount sufficient to pay the cost of correcting any defective work. Construction industry lingo for such withholds is "backcharges". The subcontract clause may, in turn, provide that the prime contractor may pass such backcharges on to the responsible subcontractor.

§ 2.29 Backcharges for Delay

If an owner backcharges a prime contractor for delay, the prime contractor may resort to a subcontract clause that authorizes the prime contractor to distribute backcharges among responsible subcontractors and provides that the prime contractor's allocation will be final so long as it is made in good faith.

§ 2.30 Scope of Subcontract Work

It may be provided that work to be performed by a subcontractor may be scattered throughout the drawings and specifications and that in the event of any disagreement between subcontractors as to the responsibility for a particular item of work, the prime contractor will decide the dispute and its decision will be final.

§ 2.31 Dispute Resolution

Reflecting the perception that litigation is ruinous, many contracts include provisions for methods of alternate dispute resolution. The most popular methods are mediation and arbitration.

The function of a mediator is to assist parties in negotiating an acceptable resolution to their disputes. The function of an arbitrator is to listen to the parties present their cases and then issue an enforceable award resolving the dispute.

Since many disputes involve not only the owner and the contractor, but also the architect, engineer, and subcontractors, it is important that arbitration and mediation clauses be coordinated so as to sweep into the dispute resolution process all potential parties. One effective procedure is to appoint an arbitrator (or a dispute review board) in advance so that disputes may be resolved promptly, as they arise, during the progress of the job rather than, as is the usual case, after the completion of the work.

§ 2.32 Consumer Contracts

Many states impose special requirements for construction contracts with consumers (read "homeowners"). Among such requirements may be found the following:

- Restrictions on the amounts of down payments.
- Explanations of mechanics lien laws and their potential dangers to homeowners.
- "Buyer's remorse" provisions permitting the homeowner to cancel a contract within some specified period of time.
- A warning that an arbitration provision supplants the right to a jury trial and a requirement that an arbitration clause be in bold face type and countersigned by the consumer.
- A notice that contractors are required by the state to be licensed and that consumers may receive assistance from the state licensing agency.

CHAPTER 3

CONTRACTORS LICENSE LAW AND ILLEGALITY

Chapter 3

§ 3.01 License Requirement

The legislatures of 33 states have seen fit to enact statutes under which persons who engage in the business of contracting are required to be licensed by an agency of the state. Qualifications for licensure include experience in the construction trades, passing an examination, and minimum financial strength.

Since a corporation or a partnership can have construction experience and pass an examination only through its personnel, licensure of the firm usually depends upon the qualifications of a responsible officer or employee. The responsible officer or employee is required not just to take the test or sign the license application, but also to participate in the operations of the company to such a degree that he or she can exercise appropriate control. The purpose of this exercise of control is to make certain that the licensed contractor complies with the requirements of the license law.

A contractor whose responsible managing employee performs no functions is not properly licensed.

> In *Rushing v Powell*, 61 Cal App 3d 597, 130 Cal Rptr 110 (1976), plaintiff and defendant obtained a joint license by using a scheme under which plaintiff gave defendant $6,000 worth of equipment for the use of its name in the contracting business. Defendant performed absolutely no functions with respect to the conduct of the business. HELD: The purported license was a nullity and plaintiff had no right to seek the assistance of the court to recover money allegedly due from defendant on a swimming pool contract.

To engage in the contracting business without a duly issued license is to commit a misdemeanor that is punishable by fine, imprisonment, or both. Prosecution for contracting without a license is handled by public prosecutors and the cases are decided by judges and juries.

Federal contracting is exempt. Federal agencies adopt their own rules and regulations for determining the qualifications of contractors working on the federal work. If state licensing laws were applied to contractors performing federal work, the state would thereby interfere with the national government's right to pick and choose contractors. Therefore, under the supremacy clause of the U.S. Constitution, contractors and subcontractors working on federal jobs are not required to be licensed.

> A subcontractor on a project to repair streets at Little Rock Air Force Base filed an action against the prime contractor. Subcontractor was unlicensed. The trial court found that Arkansas' contractors license requirement did not apply to work performed on a federal project, and awarded the subcontractor $19,479. AFFIRMED. The federal government establishes qualifications for contractors, and to allow state regulators to affect the qualifications would undermine the supremacy clause of the U.S. Constitution.

Airport Constr & Materials, Inc v Bivens, 279 Ark 161, 649 SW2d 830 (1983).

§ 3.02 Conduct of the Contracting Business

Contractors are required by law to complete construction contracts diligently and in a workmanlike manner for the stated price, to carry workers compensation insurance, to pay the prevailing wage where that is such a legal requirement, and to perform construction work in accordance with building codes and only after issuance of required permits. For violations of such laws contractors are not only subject to prosecution, imprisonment, and fine, but also to suspension or revocation of their contractors licenses. Disciplinary action against a contractors license, and the license of the responsible managing officer or employee, is administered after a hearing before officials of the contractors licensing agency of the state.

Persons who do not normally consider themselves to be contractors, such as decorators, landscapers, and tree trimmers, may find themselves within the scope of licensing requirements.

> In *Franklin v National C Goldstone Agency*, 33 Cal 2d 628, 204 P2d 37 (1949), an unlicensed interior decorator entered into an oral agreement to furnish and decorate an office. The work undertaken by the decorator included painting. Unpaid, the decorator pursued

> arbitration proceedings against the owner and recovered an arbitration award that included $1,648.59 for painting. The trial court confirmed the award. REVERSED. The decorator required a contractors license to perform the painting work. Submission of an illegal contract to arbitration does not purge it of illegality.

Contractors license legislation is consumer protection legislation. In most states the contractors licensing officials concentrate on protecting homeowners against predatory practices and incompetence.

The contractors licensing agency of the state issues, renews, suspends and revokes licenses, administers examinations, investigates complaints, prosecutes offenders, administers disciplinary action and responds to inquiries from the public. These functions are financed by fees paid by contractors when they apply for issuance, change, or renewal of a license.

§ 3.03 The Doctrine of Illegality

Contracts infected by illegality are unenforceable. A clear example would be a contract between illicit drug dealers for the transportation of cocaine. Suppose the shipper welshes on an agreement to pay a carrier for the transportation. Can the carrier go to court, and sue the shipper for the shipping charges? The failure to pay the shipping charges is a clear breach of contract, but it is the breach of a contract that the law will not enforce. To enforce such a contract would involve the courts in drug dealing. Therefore the law leaves the parties to an illegal contract where it finds them.

In many states the courts apply the doctrine of illegality to the attempted enforcement of a construction contract by an unlicensed contractor. (The doctrine may also be applied against the enforcement of a contract by an unlicensed architect or engineer.) In these states, an unlicensed contractor finds the doors of the courts are closed, and this makes it impossible for an unlicensed contractor to recover compensation for construction work. The doctrine of illegality is so strong that is has even been upheld in cases where there was evidence that a project owner intentionally lured an unlicensed contractor into the performance of work so as to get it for free.

> Contractor Wessman sought out Hydrotech, a New York corporation that manufactures and installs patented equipment

> designed to simulate ocean waves. Wessman employed Hydrotech to install equipment in a California amusement park. The project owners promised that Wessman would arrange for a contractors license, and the owners induced Hydrotech to enter into the contract by promising payment which the owners never intended to make. HELD: Cal Bus & Prof Code § 7031 bars all actions, however characterized, which seek compensation for unlicensed work. The prohibition operates even when the person for whom the work was performed knew that the contractor was unlicensed.

Hydrotech Sys v Oasis Water Park, 52 Cal 3d 988, 803 P2d 30, 277 Cal Rptr 517 (1991).

The strict enforcement of the doctrine of illegality may cause what appears to be flagrant injustice, especially where the lack of licensure is a technical one, caused perhaps by negligence or inattention in promptly paying a license renewal fee. Strict enforcement may be justified (or in some case required by the legislature) on the ground that it is necessary in order to effectively enforce the licensure requirement. Some larger states register hundreds of thousands of contractors, and yet it is estimated that hundreds of thousands more operate without licenses. Effective monitoring of their activities by state deputies is virtually impossible. It must be admitted that strict enforcement of the doctrine of illegality, indeed, does act as a strong deterrent to unlicensed activity.

The harsh application of the doctrine of illegality makes it imperative that contractors rigorously insure full compliance with state licensing requirements.

§ 3.04 Effect on Parties Dealing with Unlicensed Contractor

Contractors license laws are enacted for the protection of project owners, and therefore an owner does not incur any penalty for contracting with an unlicensed contractor.

> In *Domach v Spencer*, 101 Cal App 3d 308, 161 Cal Rptr 459 (1980), an unlicensed contractor defended itself against a homeowner's claim by alleging that it was an unlicensed contractor. The homeowner recovered a judgment of $10,276 against the contractor for unworkmanlike performance. AFFIRMED. The contractor asserted that homeowners could not recover judgment

> since they were parties to an illegal contract. Plaintiffs, however, were within the class for whose benefit the statute was enacted and could not be regarded as being *in pari delicto*.

On the other hand, a supplier or subcontractor who supplies materials to, or provides services for, an unlicensed contractor, may be affected by the doctrine of illegality. Such a supplier or subcontractor may lose its right to recover compensation for its work or materials.

> An unlicensed contractor failed to pay for materials supplied by plaintiff, which notified the owner of the amount due and recorded a mechanics lien on the owner's property. The owner showed that the contractor was unlicensed and the trial court entered judgment for the owner. AFFIRMED. Since the contractor was unlicensed, the contract between the owner and the contractor was null, void, and unenforceable. Since owner did not owe contractor an unpaid balance, the supplier's lien could not be enforced.

Brown v Mountain Lakes Resort, Inc, 521 So 2d 24 (Ala 1988).

A person dealing with an unlicensed contractor, in some circumstances, upon learning of the nonlicensure, may rescind the contract.

> A property owner (vendor) entered into an agreement to sell nine lots to an unlicensed contractor and subordinate one-half of the purchase price until the contractor had built a home on the lot and had closed a sale of the home. After part performance, the vendor repudiated the contract. Judgment for vendor AFFIRMED. Vendor was in the class of intended beneficiaries of the legislation, since the vendor, having subordinated one-half of the purchase price, had an interest in the contractor's construction skills.

Gross v Bayshore Land Co, 710 P2d 1007 (Ala 1985).

Some states hold that the doctrine of illegality does not apply to an action between contractors, since contractors are not among the class of persons to be protected by the legislation.

> In *Parker v Vista Constr Concepts, Inc*, 134 Misc 2d 1, 511 NYS2d 458 (Sup Ct 1986), an unlicensed subcontractor was permitted to recover compensation from a prime contractor on the ground that the New York City code prohibits enforcement of contracts against owners, but does not prohibit enforcement of contracts between a subcontractor and a prime contractor.

Some states do not enforce the doctrine of illegality, but allow an unlicensed contractor to recover compensation on the basis of *quantum meruit*.

> In *Sisson v Ragland*, 294 Ark 629, 745 SW2d 620 (1988), an unlicensed contractor sought to recover *quantum meruit* damages for services performed in construction of a building to house a beauty shop. The trial court dismissed the action on the ground that the contractor was unlicensed. REVERSED. *Quantum meruit* is a claim for unjust enrichment and does not involve the enforcement of contracts.

Other states prohibit a *quantum meruit* award to an unlicensed contractor.

> In *Triple B Corp v Brown & Root, Inc*, 106 NM 99, 739 P2d 968 (1987), the court entered judgment for a contractor in an action in which an unlicensed subcontractor sought to recover compensation for work performed for the contractor. HELD: The Arizona statute, § 60-13-30, legislatively authorizes unjust enrichment claims against persons who receive work performed by unlicensed contractors.

In some states, the doctrine of illegality applies to unlicensed engineers and architects as well as to unlicensed contractors. In such states, an unlicensed engineer may be unable to recover compensation for engineering services performed.

> In *Wheeler v Bucksteel Co*, 73 Or App 495, 698 P2d 995 (1985), an unregistered engineer sought to recover compensation for industrial engineering services. Judgment on jury verdict for engineer REVERSED. The Professional Engineer Registration Act is designed to protect the public against incompetent engineers. The statute prohibits precisely the acts that were performed by plaintiff and for which it sought payment. Even though the statute did not

> expressly limit the engineer's right to sue, the court will not enforce a contract entered into in violation of the statute.

A construction contract may be illegal if it includes design functions to be performed by an unlicensed architect or engineer.

> A nonprofit corporation, as owner, contracted with a manufacturer of prefabricated modular housing for the design and construction of a drug and alcohol treatment facility. Owner paid a 2% deposit and the manufacturer commenced architectural drawing and site engineering. Owner then learned manufacturer was not properly licensed to perform architectural or engineering services and cancelled the contract. HELD: The manufacturer must refund the deposit. The manufacturer argued that the entire contract was not void because architectural and engineering services were only incidental. However, the court pointed out that without the architectural and engineering services the units could not have been built. Public policy prohibits rewarding the manufacturer for illegal, unlicensed contractor.

Kansas City Community Center v Heritage Indus, 972 F2d 185 (8th Cir 1992).

§ 3.05 Substantial Compliance

Courts in many states, in order to avoid injustice, apply the doctrine of substantial compliance when nonlicensure is technical and the public has received the essential protection afforded by the law. An example of technical noncompliance would be the failure by two licensed contractors, acting as a joint venture, to secure an additional license for the joint venture. In such a case the public would be protected by the individual licensure, and little protection would be added by an additional license in the name of the joint venture.

> Contractor filed an action against owner for breach of an excavating and grading contract. The contractor had possessed a contractors license when the contract was signed. Fifteen months thereafter, the license expired. Contractor continued to perform, unlicensed, from June 30, 1963 to April 28, 1964. The contractor renewed its license on June 26, 1964 after the job was finished. HELD: The court should not transform the statute into an

> unwarranted shield for an avoidance of just obligations. The responsibility and competence of the managing officer were officially confirmed throughout the period of performance, because the managing officer had a contractors license throughout that time. Contractor substantially complied with the requirements of the license law.

Latipac, Inc v Superior Court, 64 Cal 2d 278, 411 P2d 564, 49 Cal Rptr 676 (1966).

> In *Roth v Thompson*, 113 NM 331, 825 P2d 1241 (1992), the New Mexico Supreme Court held that the elements of the substantial compliance doctrine are 1) contractor held a valid license at the time of contracting, 2) contractor readily secured a renewal of the license, and 3) the responsibility and competence of the contractor's managing officer were officially confirmed throughout the period of performance. Here, subcontractor's efforts to obtain a license when work under its subcontract was nearing completion did not satisfy the elements of the doctrine.

§ 3.06 Strict Enforcement of the Doctrine of Illegality

In states where the doctrine of illegality is strictly enforced, its application can be harsh indeed. In one case, for example, a painting contractor allowed its license to expire for a period of two weeks because of inattentiveness in mailing in a required renewal application and fee. During the period of nonlicensure, the contractor was performing a job that lasted approximately ten months. Because of the two week nonlicensure, though, the court refused to permit the contractor to recover any compensation whatever for the work performed during the ten month job.

In another case, a licensed prime contractor who unknowingly employed an unlicensed subcontractor was denied access to the court to recover, from the owner, for work performed by the properly licensed prime contractor. Since the balance due included compensation for work performed by an unlicensed subcontractor, recovery was denied.

On the other hand, a New York court has held that nonlicensure is no defense to enforcement of an *arbitration award* unless the nonlicensure appears on the face of the award.

Confirmation of an arbitration award in favor of a contractor and against a homeowner was AFFIRMED. The homeowner contended the award violated public policy because it included compensation for work performed while the contractor was unlicensed. HELD: Nothing on the face of the award indicated whether the contractor was a home improvement contractor or when the contractor obtained a contractors license. Therefore the award was properly confirmed.

Hirsch Constr Corp v Anderson, 180 AD2d 604, 580 NYS2d 314 (1992).

Bonding companies sometimes are tempted to "take over" the performance of a construction contract on behalf of a defaulting contractor. Such activity, however, is illegal if the surety does not hold a contractors license.

Surety took over completion of an apartment construction project on behalf of a prime contractor who had become insolvent. Surety filed suit for damages against its electrical subcontractor. HELD: The unlicensed surety was precluded from filing an action against the allegedly defaulting electrical subcontractor. A performance bond surety, as any other party, is required to have a license before undertaking to perform construction work.

General Ins Co of America v St Paul & Marine Ins Co, 38 Cal App 3d 760, 113 Cal Rptr 613 (1974).

§ 3.07 Owner Builder Exemption

Most states exempt from the contractors license requirement an owner who is working to improve his or her own property. If the property is intended for sale, however, the owner builder exemption may not apply. Thus, land developers and subdividers may be required to have contractors licenses.

§ 3.08 Recoupment

The doctrine of illegality prevents the courts from awarding compensation to unlicensed contractors. However, the courts are split on the question of whether enforcement of the doctrine requires an unlicensed contractor to disgorge money voluntarily paid for unlicensed work. In some states, an unlicensed contractor must refund payments received for unlicensed work.

> In *Mascarenas v Jaramillo*, 806 P2d 59 (NM 1991), an owner paid an unlicensed contractor for construction of a trailer park, then discovered that work did not conform to code requirements and filed suit to recover the cost of correction. HELD: Owner is entitled to recover not only the cost of correction, but to obtain a refund of all monies paid to the unlicensed contractor. As a matter of public policy, an unlicensed contractor may not retain payments made under a contract for performance of work in violation of the Construction Industries Licensing Act.

> In *Sutton v Ohrbach*, 198 AD2d 144, 603 NYS2d 857 (1993), owner sought to recoup money paid to unlicensed architects. HELD: Even though the architects would not have been able to enforce their contract to extract payment from the owner, the owner could not use the licensing statute to recoup monies already paid in exchange for architectural services.

> In *Marshall-Schule Assocs v Goldman*, 137 Misc 2d 1024, 523 NYS2d 16 (Civ Ct 1987), an owner paid a $10,000 retainer to an unlicensed interior design firm. The court held that the work described by the agreement went far beyond mere interior design, and required licensure as an architect. HELD: The owner was entitled to recoup the $10,000 retainer fee.

§ 3.09 Trade Contractors

Most states distinguish between general contractors and trade contractors, and require licensure in a proper specialty. In a typical statutory pattern, general contractors are permitted to perform work only if more than two trades are required for the work. Work that requires only one trade, for example masonry work or roofing work, is to be performed by a contractor with the appropriate specialty license. A specialty contractor, for example, an electrical contractor, is not allowed to take a contract requiring performance of work in other trades, such as plumbing or concrete work.

§ 3.10 Consumer Protection Laws

Many states have enacted special provisions for the protection of homeowners. For example, a contractor who solicits home improvement work, such as masonry or patio work, from door to door, is in some states required to give the customer notice of a "cooling off period" during which the customer can cancel the contract without penalty. Some states also impose special requirements on home improvement contracts, such as regulations that limit the amount of the down payment that a contractor may legally receive for home improvement work.

Whether a contract that does not comply with consumer protection laws is enforceable is a matter of state law. In some states such contracts are unenforceable, and in other states they may be enforceable depending on circumstances.

> In *Asdourian v Araj*, 38 Cal 3d 276, 696 P2d 95, 211 Cal Rptr 703 (1985), contractor violated the home improvement contract provisions of the State of California (Cal Bus & Prof Code § 7159) which require that home improvement contracts be reduced to writing. While it is true that generally a contract that violates a regulatory statute is void, the rule is not inflexible. HELD: Here, where the owner was a sophisticated real estate investor, the contractor is entitled to be paid for its work, even though the provisions of the statute were violated.

> In *Caulkins v Petrillo*, 200 Conn 713, 513 A2d 43 (1986), the court reached an opposite conclusion. Contractor signed a contract for remodeling a home for $84,687.41. Contractor contended that homeowners orally consented to a revised contract amount of $117,470.57. HELD: Conn Gen Stats § 20-249 prevents enforcement of an oral contract for home improvements.

§ 3.11 Other Forms of Illegality

It is generally held that a contract with a public agency that fails to comply with competitive bidding requirements is void and unenforceable. It is also been held that contractors must disgorge the proceeds of such contracts.

> In *Bear River Sand & Gravel Corp v Placer County*, 118 Cal App 2d 684, 258 P2d 543 (1953), county road commissioners agreed

to buy crushed rock from plaintiff. Contract was formed by an exchange of letters. The road commissioner, however, had no legal power to contract. Such contracts were required to be let by the board of supervisors after competitive bidding. HELD: A public agency is not bound by such dealings even though it may have received substantial benefits from the *ultra vires* act.

In *Miller v McKinnon*, 20 Cal 2d 83, 124 P2d 34 (1942), the county paid $42,151.90 to repair bunkers, remove and repair hoists, and drive a tunnel. The contract was awarded without competitive bidding. A taxpayer sued for a return of the money. Judgment of dismissal REVERSED. Such a contract is void and cannot be ratified. There may be no quasi contractual recovery and therefore the contractor must disgorge the payments. To hold otherwise would nullify the competitive bidding requirement.

Corruption takes many forms. In one case, a developer unsuccessfully attempted to recover a bribe when it did not produce its desired results. In another, a construction loan agreement tainted by an attempted kickback was held to be unenforceable.

In *An-Cor, Inc v Reherman*, 835 P2d 93 (Okla 1992), a developer agreed to "take care of the mayor" by paying a $7,000 bribe. Just before the final vote on the development project, a consultant demanded an additional $10,000 out of which the consultant would "take care of the mayor". The developer balked, the project was rejected. HELD: The contract was illegal and the developer could not recoup the bribe.

In *Long v South Bay Sav & Loan Assn*, 10 Cal App 4th 947, 12 Cal Rptr 2d 896 (1992), developer Long agreed to trade his condominium in Newport Beach for a construction loan officer's condominium in Las Vegas. The trade fell through, and developer then paid a $26,500 brokers commission to a third party with the understanding that the commission would be kicked over to McAllister. McAllister recommended approval of a $2,650,000 construction loan, and the savings and loan association approved it. McAllister then left the lender, which then refused to fund the construction. Developer obtained judgment on a jury verdict for

$2,341,609. REVERSED. The loan was inextricably linked to the illegal kickback. (Cal Pen Code § 639 makes it a felony to pay a commission to an officer of a financial institution for procuring an extension of credit.) A party to an illegal contract cannot ratify it, cannot be estopped from relying on the illegality, and cannot waive its right to the defense of illegality.

CHAPTER 4

TORTS

Chapter 4

§ 4.01 Torts

In the chapter on contracts we dealt mainly with legal obligations undertaken voluntarily. Toward the end of the chapter we discussed the topics of implied warranty and strict liability. These two doctrines, unlike the law of contract, impose obligations that are not voluntarily undertaken. Thus, the doctrines of implied warranty and strict liability shade imperceptibly into the topic of the present chapter, *Torts*. The law of torts deals with obligations imposed by law regardless of whether the parties agree to them or not.

The concept of *negligence* (which is one of many torts) is based on the idea that it is a social wrong for one person through carelessness to injure another person, and that the wrongdoer should make amends by paying compensation to the innocent party. For a commonplace example, a driver who runs a stop light and runs down a pedestrian must pay compensation to the pedestrian even though the driver may have intended no harm.

§ 4.02 Negligence

Negligence is want of due care. "Due care" flows from the concept that every person should conduct affairs in such a way as to avoid injury to others. Due care is the degree of care that the ordinary person would exercise in conducting affairs. A failure to exercise due care is defined as negligence.

Let us suppose that an excavation contractor raises dust that spoils some work that has been carefully performed by a painting contractor nearby. The first step in determining whether the excavator might be responsible for the damage would be to determine whether the excavator violated the standard of due care. This would depend upon such factors as weather, wind, and whether the excavator had reason to know of the presence of wet paint in the vicinity of the project. Expert witnesses would give evidence as to the standard of conduct usually adhered to by excavation and grading contractors in the area.

An important element of due care is *foreseeability.* Conduct is deemed negligent that an ordinarily prudent person would foresee creates, or increases, a risk of harm. But a defendant is not held to the duty of eliminating all risk. For example, it can be argued that K, by building a two-story, instead of a one-story, structure increases the risk that a person could be injured in a fall from the second story. It is foreseeable that persons will fall from windows and that their injuries will be greater if they fall from second story rather than first story windows. This does not mean, though, that construction of a two-story house is negligent. All life involves some risk. The social utility of allowing the construction of multi-story buildings, as permitted by the building codes, outweighs the risk thus created. Again, in the natural order of things, persons conducting themselves in a careful manner don't fall from windows absent intervening negligent conduct.

> A university employed a design consultant to provide technical advice for construction of student residences. After the buildings were finally occupied, a large chunk of the facade fell into the courtyard. Fortunately, no one was injured. The university filed suit against the consultant alleging negligence. The trial court dismissed the action on the ground that the design consultant had no duty independent of the contract. REVERSED. The project affected a significant public interest since it called for housing facilities on a crowded college campus. The effect of the public interest here gives rise to a duty of reasonable care independent of the provisions of the contract.

Trustees of Columbia Univ v Mitchell/Giurgola Assocs, 109 AD2d 449, 492 NYS2d 371 (1985).

> A contractor stated a valid cause of action against an engineer, alleging that negligent design caused the contractor to incur higher costs than bid for the construction of a sewer treatment facility. HELD: Contractor stated a good cause of action, as it was part of a definable class that would foreseeably rely on the engineer's plans.

Reliance Ins Co v Morris Assoc, PC, 607 NYS2d 106 (App Div 1994).

> A contractor filed suit against an air conditioning equipment manufacturer, alleging that delay in delivery of equipment caused the contractor to sustain $30,000 in liquidated damages payable to the owner because of delay in completion of the project. The trial court dismissed the action. REVERSED. 1) The policy of the law is

to hold persons liable for injury caused through want of ordinary care. 2) The supplier's conduct directly affected the contractor's ability to timely perform. 3) The supplier could reasonably have foreseen delay. 4) The delay caused the contractor to be assessed for the liquidated damages. 5) There was a close connection between the delay of the manufacturer and the liability for liquidated damages.

Chameleon Engg Corp v Air Dynamics, Inc, 101 Cal App 3d 418, 161 Cal Rptr 463 (1980).

A tenant suffered second and third degree burns after placing feet in a bathtub without first testing the water temperature. HELD: The contractor who built the apartment complex had a duty to provide a proper hot water temperature control, and the failure to fulfill that duty was negligence.

Tirella v American Properties Team, Inc, 145 AD2d 724, 535 NYS2d 252 (1988).

Some courts hold prime contractors responsible for the negligence for their subcontractors.

A father and two children died of asphyxiation caused by a malfunctioning gas heater. Contractor employed a licensed plumbing contractor to install the heater. Subcontractor modified the heater, installing a 35,000 BTU burner in a 25,000 BTU heater. An accumulation of soot eventually caused carbon monoxide to enter the home, causing the deaths. Verdict for plaintiff AFFIRMED. A contractor supervises the entire project and is responsible for dangerous conditions created by the negligence of a subcontractor. The contractor had a duty to inspect the gas appliance and failed to do so.

Dow v Holly Mfg Co, 49 Cal 2d 720, 321 P2d 736 (1958).

A homeowner was injured by falling waist-deep into a hole when the ground in the homeowner's yard caved in. Settling was caused by a broken and uncapped sewer stub. Neither the contractor nor the sewer and water subcontractor was aware of the existence of the stub, which was not shown on the city's plans and was not disclosed by wetness above the six-foot level to which subcontractor excavated. HELD: Actionable negligence requires a legal duty to protect homeowner from injury, failure to discharge that duty, and the injury proximately caused by the undischarged duty. Here, neither contractor nor subcontractor knew, or had reasonable opportunity to acquire knowledge about, the broken stub.

Wilson v F&H Constr Co, 229 Neb 815, 428 NW2d 914 (1988).

A worker was electrocuted when scaffold came into contract with a power line. Widow sued architect who had been hired by contractor to prepare construction drawings and design foundation. HELD: "An architect, in the absence of a duty specially imposed by contract or course of conduct, has no duty to take affirmative action to protect workers from hazards on the jobsite which are either known or readily visible." 648 A2d at 329.

Frampton v Dauphin Distribution Serv Co, 648 A2d 326 (Pa Super 1994).

§ 4.03 Negligence Per Se

The Congress of the United States and the legislatures of the states adopt laws that are known as *statutes*. County Boards of Supervisors and City Councils, as they are generally called, adopt *ordinances*. Federal agencies, such as the Federal Communications Commission, and state and local regulatory authorities, such as Industrial Safety Commissions, in their turn are authorized to adopt *regulations*. All these enactments have the force of law.

When a statute, ordinance, or regulation has a purpose of protecting persons or property against injury, and when a person violates that statute, ordinance, or regulation and as result injures somebody, then the prohibited conduct is called *negligence per se*. The act is negligent by definition. The wrongdoer will not be heard to say the conduct was reasonable that violated a statute, ordinance, or regulation duly adopted by a legislative body.

(Although the word *statute* technically refers to laws adopted by Congress and the state legislatures, it may also be used as a generic term to include ordinances and regulations, and we shall use the term in that sense.)

For violation of a statute to be *negligence per se*, the statute must have been adopted for the protection of persons or property. Violation of a parking ordinance, for example, would not be negligence per se because parking ordinances are adopted for public convenience and revenue rather than for the protection of persons and property. For example, suppose D fails to feed a parking meter and as a result a police officer slips on a banana peel and suffers injury. Here, although it might be said that the violation of the parking ordinance caused the injury, the violation would not be negligence *per se* because the ordinance was adopted for revenue and not for the protection of persons against injury.

Now assume that D parks in a red zone near a corner, which obstructs the view of a motorist who therefore suffers injury in a collision. Parking in the red zone would be considered negligence *per se* because the purpose of the red zone was to promote public safety.

Suppose S sold a used bulldozer to B without collecting the sales tax on it, and B later used the bulldozer to excavate a slope, causing a landslide that injured P. It could be argued that the illegal sale caused the injury, yet the sales tax statute was adopted for revenue purposes and not for public safety purposes and therefore S would not be liable to P.

If, though, D should fail to install a handrail as required by the building code and P, for lack of a handrail, falls and sustains injury, the conduct of D would be negligent *per se* since the violation of the ordinance caused the very injury that the ordinance was designed to prevent.

> Remote purchasers filed action against building designer and project engineer alleging defects including insufficient shear walls, insufficient fire retardation, and deviation from approved plans. Many defects violated the 1961 Uniform Building Code. HELD: The UBC was intended to protect subsequent purchasers and code violations by the designers would be negligence per se.

Huang v Garner, 157 Cal App 3d 404, 203 Cal Rptr 800 (1984).

> Subsequent purchasers filed action against home builder alleging negligent construction. HELD: Allegations of building code violations constituted negligence per se.

Oates v JAG, Inc, 314 NC 276, 333 SE2d 222 (1985).

A home sustained damage from fire allegedly caused by defective construction of a flue running from a basement furnace to the fireplace. HELD: Omission of clay liner in the flue was violation of the building code and negligence per se.

Foster v Bue, 749 SW2d 736 (Tenn 1988).

In an action against land surveyors, plaintiffs alleged that defendant surveyors violated licensing statutes by preparing plans for a construction project without having an engineering license. HELD: Unlicensed preparation of plans does not constitute negligence per se.

Tydings v Loewenstein, 505 A2d 443 (Del Super Ct 1986).

Contractor and subcontractor built an elaborate wooden spiral staircase as requested by plaintiff homeowner. After living with the staircase for one and a half years, plaintiff replaced it with a staircase of a different design. Building code violations were then discovered. HELD: Failure to exercise due care is presumed if a defendant violated a statute, the violation caused damages, the damages resulted from an occurrence the statute was design to prevent, and the person who suffered damage was of the class of persons for whose protection the statute was adopted. Here, requirements prescribing the height and width of the stairs and the height of the handrail were to insure the safety of persons using the staircase and not to prevent property owners from incurring costs associated with the remediation of building code violations.

Morris v Fortran, 22 Cal App 4th 968, 27 Cal Rptr 2d 585 (1994).

§ 4.04 Proximate Cause

A person is legally responsible for negligent conduct only if the conduct is the *proximate cause* of an injury. The term "proximate cause" simply defines the type of causation recognized by law to impose liability.

Suppose K installs a light fixture in the living room of a house under construction. Six months later O, homeowner, suffers injury from a fall sustained while changing the bulb in the fixture. Here we have a case of direct factual causation since it is true that but for the fact that K installed the light fixture O would not have sustained injury. Despite factual causation, though, K's conduct was not the *proximate cause* of O's injury because it was not foreseeable that the conduct of K would increase the legal risk of harm to O.

Now suppose that K negligently installed the light fixture by anchoring it to the ceiling with only two bolts, rather than the three required by the building code. The conduct of K was, indeed, negligent but the injury sustained by O was not the type of injury that the ordinance was adopted to prevent. Therefore the negligent conduct by K was not the proximate cause of O's injury. O, indeed, would have sustained the injury even if K had used three bolts to anchor the fixture.

On the other hand, let us suppose that the fixture, inadequately anchored, falls on O's head. Although a normal person would have suffered only a minor injury, O sustains a severe injury because a pre-existing disease had required surgical removal of part of O's skull. Here, K would be liable for the full damages sustained by O even though it might not have been foreseeable that the injury caused by the negligent conduct would be so severe

> Owner alleged flooding in building was caused by survey engineer's negligent setting of stakes that were used to determine elevations for a drainage system. HELD: The stakes were not in place when the floor was poured and the flooding was due to design defects attributable to the architect. Therefore, the flooding was not caused by acts of the engineer.

Dollar Rent-A-Car Sys v Nodel Constr Co, 172 Mich App 738, 432 NW2d 423 (1988).

> A worker who fell off a loading dock filed suit against an architect to recover damages. The worker unequivocally testified in his deposition that when he walked toward the end of the loading dock he tripped over rubber bumper strips that had been installed to prevent handtrucks from rolling off the dock. HELD: Since the architect did not design the rubber bumper strips or their location,

the actions of the architect were not the proximate cause of the injuries.

Hansen v Ruby Constr Co, 155 Ill App 3d 475, 508 NE2d 301 (1987).

Homes were damaged by landslides and water runoff. Homeowners accused an engineer of negligent preparation of the site plan. The evidence showed that the engineer had designed a drainage system for the subdivision but the developer did not construct the drainage system. HELD: Negligence of the engineer could not have been a proximate cause of the damage.

Brickman v Walter Schoel Engg, 630 So 2d 424 (Ala 1993).

Now let us suppose that O is transported to the hospital in an ambulance and suffers additional injury because of a traffic accident. K would not be liable for the additional injury because, in legal contemplation, the addition injury was the result of an independent intervening cause.

Plaintiff sued a contractor for injuries she sustained when she slipped on ice that had accumulated on a sidewalk constructed by the contractor. HELD: The property owner's negligence in failing to remove the ice after receiving several complaints was an intervening cause which relieved the contractor of liability.

Lynch v Norton Constr, Inc, 861 P2d 1095 (Wyo 1993).

Plaintiff was stopped in a traffic lane when a drunk driver crossed the median strip and struck plaintiff's automobile. HELD: Even if the contractor modifying the intersection where the accident occurred had breached a duty of care to the plaintiff, the drunk driver's actions were an intervening cause.

Billman v Frenzel Constr Co, 635 NE2d 435 (Ill App Ct 1993).

A contractor was employed to convert an alley into a pedestrian sidewalk. The gas company located and exposed its lines. The contractor then covered the gas lines with earth, concealing them from view. Subcontractor, working thereafter, snagged a rusty pipe with a backhoe. Uninformed by the contractor of the fact that the gas lines had been covered, and informed by the gas company that the pipe was 30 inches below the surface, subcontractor concluded the rusty pipe was not a gas line. An explosion ensued. At trial, the jury apportioned 25% liability to contractor and 75% to subcontractor. Contractor appealed, claiming that subcontractor's negligence was a superseding cause. HELD: To be a superseding cause, the intervening negligence must in no way be caused by another party's negligence. Here, the jury could have concluded that the contractor's negligent grading of the alley and failure to inform the subcontractor of the location of the gas lines contributed to the accident and therefore the subcontractor's negligence could not have been a superseding cause.

Farmington Plumbing & Heating Co v Fischer Sand & Aggregate, Inc, 281 NW2d 838 (Minn 1979).

§ 4.05 Contributory Negligence

The doctrine of contributory negligence holds that one whose negligence contributes to his or her own injury is not legally entitled to recover damages from another who also negligently contributes to injury. Under the doctrine, for example, a person who negligently failed to wear a seatbelt would not be able to recover compensation from a driver who negligently caused a collision if the failure to wear a seatbelt contributed to the injury.

The doctrine of contributory negligence, with its "all or nothing" results, has been replaced in most states by the doctrine of comparative negligence under which liability is proportional to fault.

An architect sued a surveyor alleging the surveyor prepared a plat that did not properly locate property lines and corners. The trial court held that contributory negligence of the architect barred recovery. REVERSED. The surveyor was negligent in failing to ascertain how the architect intended to use the survey, and the architect was contributorily negligent in failing to inform the surveyor of the intended use. However, surveyor negligently certified that it had carefully surveyed the property when it had not actually done so. The surveyor's negligent certificate was the

> proximate cause of increased construction costs for which the architect sought to recover and the architect was not contributorily negligent when it relied on the plat for construction purposes, since the architect could reasonably assume that the surveyor would fulfill its obligations.

Bell v Jones, 523 A2d 982 (DC 1986).

§ 4.06 Comparative Negligence

In most states courts have abandoned the doctrine of contributory negligence in favor of *comparative negligence* which allocates liability among negligent parties proportionate to the degree of negligence. Suppose defendant negligently runs a red light and collides with plaintiff, who is negligently driving at night without illuminated headlights. Plaintiff's damages are $90,000. If the jury weighs plaintiff's negligence at 40% and defendant's negligence at 60%, then plaintiff could recover from defendant $54,000. If in the same accident defendant suffered $200,000 damages, it could recover from plaintiff $80,000.

A worker is injured by falling on rebar left uncapped, contrary to safety regulations, by a rebar contractor. The prime contractor, responsible under a contract with the owner for jobsite safety, failed to discover and correct the uncapped rebar and a cross-grained rafter (installed by a framing contractor) that caused the fall. In such a case, amounts of comparative negligence would be assigned by a jury. Under what has been called by some as the "deep pockets" rule, the injured worker would be entitled to recover 100% of its damages from any one of the three defendants. That defendant would thereafter seek contribution from the other defendants so that the amount paid by each defendant would match the jury's assignment of comparative fault. (The calculations do not end here. Also to be taken into account are the workers compensation laws, discussed later in this chapter, the indemnity clauses in the contracts between owner, contractor, and subcontractors, and the effect of insurance coverage.)

> A chicken barn collapsed. Responsibility was apportioned 55% to the designer, 15% to the manufacturer of building materials, and 30% to the chicken farmer. HELD: Under the Minnesota statute it was proper to assess 70% of the damages against the designer even though the designer was only 55% negligent, since the faulty design was found to be the direct cause of the loss.

Jack Frost, Inc v Engineered Bldg Components Co, 304 NW2d 346 (Minn 1981).

> A "dream house" was completed at a total cost of $550,000. The house leaked. Some rooms could not be heated above 60 degrees. The homeowners deemed the house uninhabitable, moved out, and sold it for $315,000. Referee found that architect, engineer, and contractor were solely responsible for some defects and jointly responsible for others. HELD: Since none of the defendants offered evidence as to how to apportion damages, the *single injury rule* applies. When separate and independent acts of negligence of two or more persons are the direct cause of a single injury and it is impossible to determine apportionment of liability, the actors are jointly and severally liable.

Paine v Spottiswoode, 612 A2d 235 (Me 1992).

§ 4.07 Attractive Nuisance

If a burglar falls through the roof of a store during an attempted burglary, the owner of the store is not liable for the burglar's injuries even if the roof was in a dangerous condition. This is because a property owner is not normally responsible for the safety of trespassers.

This rule is modified by the doctrine of *attractive nuisance*. This makes a property owner responsible for injuries to children who may be injured because of the existence of attractive, but dangerous, places to play. It is well known that children like to make playgrounds of partly completed buildings. Property owners are responsible to prevent youngsters from using jobsites as dangerous playgrounds.

> A 12-year-old stepped on the end of a piece of board while playing on scaffolding at a residence. The board tilted, and injury resulted from a fall. HELD: The scaffolding was an attractive nuisance.

Crain v Sestak, 262 Cal App 2d 478, 68 Cal Rptr 849 (1968).

Many states have adopted *recreational use statutes* to encourage landowners to open their property for recreational use by exempting them from liability for injuries sustained by recreational users of their land.

> Plaintiff, friends and 14-year-old sister, Bambi, celebrating the Fourth of July at Malibu Beach, gained access to the roof of a building under construction. Two loose boards connected the roof with that of an adjoining building also under construction. Bambi crossed to the other building and screamed for help. Plaintiff fell two stories after guiding her back to safety. The trial court granted non-suit based on a recreational use statute. REVERSED. The exemption from liability for property owners permitting recreational use of their land did not apply. The legislature did not intend to encourage builders to allow public access to places unsuitable for recreation, such as rafters and roofs of new homes.

Potts v Halsted Fin Corp, 142 Cal App 3d 727, 191 Cal Rptr 160 (1983).

§ 4.08 Workers Compensation

Workers compensation laws have been adopted in all states for the protection of workers who may be injured in the course and scope of their employment. Here, social policy is that the product of the manufacturer should not be tainted with the blood of the worker. The economic theory is that the price of manufactured products should include the cost of medical care and rehabilitation of workers who may be injured while producing the product.

The workers compensation system is "risk spreading" policy similar to the peculiar risk doctrine. The peculiar risk doctrine, however, was evolved by the courts while the workers compensation system has been decreed by Congress and the state legislatures. The cost of workers compensation is imposed on the employer and included in the price of the product, and therefore the ultimate beneficiary of the product, the consumer, pays for medical care and rehabilitation as a part of the price of the product. Risk is further spread among employers by the existence of a mandatory insurance system in which each employer is required to participate. In return for the payment of the premium, the employer receives a workers compensation insurance policy that protects the employer against workers compensation claims. The law mandates that the employer either purchase the insurance or furnish evidence of self insurability. The establishment of a self insurance program (and the evidence of financial responsibility required for self insurability) are so onerous that all but the largest and richest employers are forced by the law to purchase workers compensation insurance either from private insurance companies or from insurance companies that are, in effect, state agencies.

It was decided by the authors of the workers compensation laws that workers would be entitled to receive compensation without having to show that the employer was negligent. Workers compensation is designed to be swift, certain, and effective. In exchange for the social benefit of swift, certain, and effective compensation, however, the employer was protected against lawsuits from workers seeking compensation for injuries sustained during employment. The employer is therefore protected from worker litigation, although the employer's insurance carrier may become involved in workers compensation hearings to determine the degree of injury, degree of disability, and amount of compensation to be paid. These amounts to be paid to the injured worker are determined by schedule. The hearings deal with evaluation of medical reports, evidence of degree of disability and rehabilitation costs.

Cases arise in which an employer is, in fact, negligent and this negligence is the proximate cause of an injury to a worker. In such cases, the employer is protected from litigation by the workers compensation system and the worker is denied the opportunity to recover damages for pain and suffering, or any greater damages that are prescribed by the workers compensation schedule.

Under the peculiar risk doctrine, however, an injured worker may be able to sue the project owner for such damages, even though the project owner is not blamed for negligent conduct, but is only liable because of the peculiar risk doctrine. Some courts have held that this defies logic, and have therefore held that the peculiar risk doctrine does not apply in favor of a worker who receives workers compensation. In states that follow this rule, however, the peculiar risk doctrine would still apply in favor of persons, other than workers, who sustain injuries in jobsite accidents.

§ 4.09 Exclusive Remedy Doctrine

The doctrine that workers injured in the course and scope of their employment may not file civil lawsuits against their employers, but must resort to the workers compensation system to satisfy their claims, is known as the *exclusive remedy doctrine*. For such injuries, workers compensation is said to be the exclusive remedy. The exclusive remedy doctrine, however, applies only to the employer of the injured worker. Therefore, if a worker is injured on a jobsite because of the negligence of a party other than the employer, the worker may recover compensation from that negligent party.

Let us return to our hypo about the worker who sustains a fall because of a cross grained rafter installed by a framing subcontractor and is injured by rebar negligently left uncapped by a reinforcing steel subcontractor. The injured worker may recover workers compensation from its employer, the roofing subcontractor, but may also file an action against the framer, the rodbuster, and the general contractor. The worker might also file an action against the supervising architect, and take advantage of the peculiar risk doctrine to also sue the project owner. None of these potential defendants would be protected by the exclusive remedy doctrine.

Let us now suppose that one reason the roofer sustained the fall was because the employer failed to enforce a safety regulation requiring safety belts. The employer, though negligent, is protected against civil litigation by the exclusive remedy doctrine. However, in some states, the exclusive remedy doctrine would not prevent the other defendants from filing cross-complaints against the roofing contractor for comparative equitable contribution.

> Employees of subcontractor fell from scaffolding, accepted workers compensation benefits, and pursued claims against the general contractor for the warehouse conversion project. The general contractor sought indemnity from the subcontractor/employer. Summary judgment for subcontractor AFFIRMED. There was no express indemnity agreement between the parties, and the Workers Compensation Act, Mass Gen Laws Ann Ch 152, § 23 (1986 id) provides that an employee who receives workers compensation releases all claims or demands at common law against the employer. To hold an employer liable to indemnify a third party would be a radical departure from the reasonable expectations of the parties, and to imply an indemnity agreement here would defeat the exclusivity provisions of the Workers Compensation Act.

Larkin v Ralph O Porter, Inc, 405 Mass 179, 539 NE2d 529 (1989).

> A subcontractor dug a trench according to instructions of the contractor's superintendent. The trench collapsed and injured an

employee of the contractor. Employee sued the subcontractor, who filed a third party complaint for indemnity or contribution against the contractor. Subcontractor testified that trenching was dangerous but contractor's superintendent said, "don't worry about it -- we'll take care of it if anything happens". The injured employee received workers compensation benefits from the contractor. HELD: An employer, here, the contractor, who complies with workers compensation laws is protected from all claims of contribution.

Williams v White Mountain Constr Co, 749 P2d 423 (Colo 1988).

§ 4.10 Peculiar Risk Doctrine

The rule that a person is not responsible for injuries negligently inflicted by its independent contractors is modified by the *peculiar risk doctrine*. During its early development this doctrine was known as the *ultra hazardous activity* doctrine, which held that a person cannot escape liability for injuries inflicted from the conduct of an ultra hazardous activity by employing independent contractors to conduct the activity. Operations such as tunneling and blasting were deemed ultra hazardous because they carry a special risk of serious harm.

The courts never succeeded in drawing a line around the activities deemed "ultra hazardous", and as more and more persons were held liable for injuries negligently inflicted by their independent contractors, the doctrine changed its name to *peculiar risk.*

Owners of construction projects are often subjected to liability under the peculiar risk doctrine. This doctrine holds that an owner who employs a contractor to perform an activity that the owner should recognize carries with a *peculiar* risk of harm has a duty to take measures to insure that the contractor performs those operations carefully.

Courts have found that excavation is risky, trenching is risky, roofing is risky, framing is risky, and electrical and painting work also have their special risks. The peculiar risk doctrine has expanded so far that it is said that the doctrine applies unless there is some good reason not to apply it, so that norm is for a project owner to be legally responsible for injuries inflicted by its independent contractors on workers, visitors, and passers-by.

Here, the basis of liability is not *negligence* (the absence of due care), but the existence of a *peculiar risk.* The *negligence*, if any, is that of an independent contractor. The defendant is liable not for its wrongful conduct, but because of its status as a person engaged in an enterprise that the law defines as involving peculiar risk.

> Plaintiff, an employee of a wrecking company, wrecking a brewery, was injured when struck in the shoulder by a 500-pound steel panel that was pushed over by a bulldozer. The jury found that the plaintiff worker was contributorily negligent 5%, the brewery's negligence was 20%, and the negligence of the wrecking company was 75%. HELD: The brewery is liable for the negligence of the wrecking company under the peculiar risk doctrine, which is a well recognized exception to the rule that one who employs an independent contractor is not liable for injuries caused by the negligence of the contractor. The brewery should have recognized that demolition requires special precautions. Having failed to insure that such precautions be taken, the brewery is liable for the wrecking contractor's failure to take such precautions.

Aceves v Regal Pale Brewing, 24CalApp 3d502, 595 P2d 619, 156 CalRptr 41 (1979).

> An unshored trench nine feet deep caved in, killing a worker employed by a subcontractor. HELD: The peculiar risk doctrine applied as a matter of law. Trenching creates a peculiar risk of harm unless special precautions are taken.

Jimenez v Pacific W Constr Co, 185 Cal App 3d 102, 229 Cal Rptr 575, *review denied*, (Nov 25, 1986).

> Plaintiff worker, employed to paint radar domes, failed to tie into a safety line and was injured in a fall from a 55-foot dome. The court apportioned negligence 30% to plaintiff, 25% to the government, and 45% to the contractor. Plaintiff recovered $795,446.33 of which the United States was held liable for $425,733.87 and obtained judgment over against the contractor for $272,400.35. AFFIRMED. The government knowingly permitted the contractor to use inexperienced and careless crew members without requiring adequate safety precautions, and is liable under the

peculiar risk doctrine. The government is therefore responsible for all damages other than the 30% attributable to the worker's comparative negligence and is entitled to indemnity from the contractor for its proportion of negligence.

Rooney v United States, 634 F2d 1238 (9th Cir 1980).

The application of the peculiar risk doctrine to a non-negligent property owner who employs an independent contractor has been criticized because it may result in a duplicate recovery to the worker or a windfall to a workers compensation insurance carrier. It may also have the anomalous result of imposing liability on a non-negligent owner while exempting from liability a negligent employer/contractor or employer/subcontractor.

The peculiar risk doctrine and the workers compensation system both serve the same social policy: to put the risk of worker injuries on the employers and owners who benefit from the work performed, even in the absence of negligence.

An employer is liable for payment of workers compensation whether it is negligent or not. Therefore the workers compensation system protects a negligent employer from liability to a worker while the peculiar risk doctrine would impose that liability on the non-negligent project owner.

An insulation worker went to the edge of a roof panel to trim excess insulation, the panel buckled, and the worker was thrown to the ground. HELD: The peculiar risk doctrine does not apply. Employees of independent contractors are not in the protected class, since they are protected by the workers compensation system.

Stockwell v Parker Drilling Co, 733 P2d 1029 (Wyo 1987).

A licensed roofing contractor was employed to reroof a rental duplex owned by a schoolteacher who ascertained that the contractor was licensed and carried workers compensation insurance. Plaintiff was directed by his foreman to carry buckets of tar up a ladder. Plaintiff fell and was burned. Plaintiff obtained workers compensation benefits and also sued the schoolteacher/owner under the peculiar risk doctrine. The trial court denied the owner's motion for summary judgment. REVERSED. A minority of American

> courts apply the peculiar risk doctrine in favor of an employee of an independent contractor. But the workers compensation system serves the same social purposes as the peculiar risk doctrine. The workers compensation law protects a negligent employer against indemnity claims from the property owner with the anomalous result that a non-negligent owner's liability may be greater than that of a negligent employer. The working of the peculiar risk doctrine in such a case penalizes an owner who hires experts to perform dangerous work rather than assign the activity to its own inexperienced employees.

Privette v Superior Court, 5 Cal 4th 689, 854 P2d 721, 21 Cal Rptr 2d 72 (1993).

§ 4.11 Comparative Equitable Contribution

If more than one party engages in negligent conduct that proximately causes injury, the parties are known as "joint tortfeasors". The injured party may pick and choose among joint tortfeasors and may sue one or all of them. If the injured party recovers judgment against more than one joint tortfeasor, the party may collect the entire amount of the judgment from whichever defendant the injured party may select. (This is known, by some, as the "deep pockets" theory.)

A joint tortfeasor that has satisfied more than its proportionate share of the judgment may, however, secure reimbursement from another joint tortfeasor according to the proportion of liability assigned by the jury. Thus, in our hypo, the jury may have assigned 10% to the worker, 40% to the roofing subcontractor, 20% to the framer, 20% to the rodbuster, and 10% to the owner. Supposing that the worker recovers the entire judgment (less 10% deducted for comparative negligence) from the owner, the owner would be entitled to recover proportionate amounts from its joint tortfeasors under the doctrine of comparative equitable contribution.

When the owner, in our example, seeks to recover from the roofing subcontractor its 40% share, the roofing subcontractor interposes the exclusive remedy defense. In some states, the exclusive remedy defense does not prevent a joint tortfeasor from recovering its proportionate share of liability from another joint tortfeasor.

§ 4.12 History of Comparative Equitable Indemnity

At common law (which, in this case, means up through the first half of the twentieth century) judges kept the law of torts quite simple. A negligent person was considered to be a wrongdoer, and got little sympathy. Under the doctrine of contributory negligence, a person whose negligence contributed to an accident was not entitled to receive any compensation. The rule of no compensation was applied harshly, rather than on a comparative basis, so that a slightly negligent victim was prevented from recovering compensation even from a grossly negligent perpetrator.

Contributory negligence was never a defense to an intentional tort, such as assault, battery, or fraud. The courts later began to hold that the defense of contributory negligence should not be available to a defendant who had been guilty of wanton and willful misconduct.

In the second half of the twentieth century judges and state legislatures began to work toward a more perfect, sensitive, and sophisticated system. Influential were the workers compensation laws that had been adopted in all states. Under these statutes, employers (even though non negligent) were required to pay workers (even though negligent) who were injured on the job. Compensation was awarded as a matter of social policy rather than to punish wrongdoing, and employers were required to purchase insurance to cover the losses. The insurance premiums, it was perceived, would then be built into the cost of the goods, and the risk of injury would be spread among the purchasers of those goods in a socially beneficial way. This analogy had its influence in the development of the concept of comparative responsibility.

The rule at common law was that there was no right of contribution between joint tortfeasors. Thus, if a plaintiff recovered judgment against two defendants for the same injury (for example, a bystander injured in an accident caused a motorist driving the wrong way on a one-way street hitting a car that ran a red light) the bystander could satisfy the judgment in full by levying on the assets of one defendant who was not then entitled to partial reimbursement from the other defendant. The attitude of the courts was that both defendants were wrongdoers and so the law would leave them where it found them.

Questions of joint responsibility and contribution are particularly characteristic of construction industry torts, since defective construction often results from the combined negligence of architects, engineers, prime contractors, and subcontractors.

In recent decades, the courts of most states have ceased to regard joint tortfeasors as outlaws and have embraced the notion of comparative negligence supported by the concept of *comparative equitable indemnity*, while the rule of joint and several liability is retained for the benefit of injured plaintiffs.

Under the rule of joint and several liability, a plaintiff may still pick and choose in enforcing a judgment against defendants jointly responsible for injury. This means the plaintiff is entitled to recover full compensation from a defendant with deep pockets without being put to the trouble of attempting to collect a proportionate share from each defendant.

Under the doctrine of comparative negligence, however, juries determine the proportionate fault of the plaintiff and each defendant. A "deep pocket" defendant that has paid more than its proportionate share may then recoup from other joint tortfeasors their proportionate shares under the doctrine of comparative equitable indemnity. So in the end more perfect justice is achieved.

Meanwhile, deep pocketed entities such as automobile manufacturers and government agencies, have agitated for tort reform and in some states have succeeded in getting the "deep pockets" rule of joint and several liability modified or annulled by legislative action.

It is always difficult to predict the results of reform. Legal reform invariably entails unintended, and often the opposite of intended, results. It was soon found that the rule against contribution between joint tortfeasors had promoted settlements, because under that rule a defendant could settle with a plaintiff and not be exposed to liability to another tortfeasor seeking to recoup a proportionate share of damages from its former co-defendant. Under the rule of comparative equitable indemnity, it became impossible for a defendant to settle with a plaintiff and buy peace from its co-defendants. The legislative solution in some states has been the creation of "good faith settlement hearings" that allow a defendant to submit its proposed settlement with a plaintiff to a court for determination that the settlement is "in the ballpark" and therefore protects the settling defendant from comparative equitable indemnity claims. As we shall see, the good faith settlement hearings themselves have become exquisitely complex and the subjects of many appeals.

A good faith settlement is one that is not calculated to harm anyone and that results in a defendant making a fair contribution to compensating the plaintiff for its damages. The determination of a good faith settlement in a construction dispute requires first, an estimate of the plaintiff's damages, second, an allocation of those damages among the defendants, third, an evaluation of the probability that the settling defendant will be held liable, and fourth, an evaluation of any indemnity rights that may be transferred to the plaintiff as part of the consideration for settlement.

In construction cases, damages must be allocated among the various trades so that the excavation contractor is not asked to contribute to roof repairs.

Indemnity rights. A determination of good faith settlement protects a defendant from comparative equitable indemnity claims, but not from indemnity claims under an express indemnity agreement. Since most construction subcontract documents include express indemnity clauses under which the subcontractor undertakes to indemnify the prime contractor and the property owner against claims, subcontractors may be unwilling to settle unless a part of the settlement package includes a waiver by the prime contractor of its indemnity claims against the subcontractor.

On the other hand, a prime contractor seeking to achieve a good faith settlement may assign to the owner its express indemnity claims against subcontractors, and the value of such indemnity claims must be taken into account in determining whether the settlement is in good faith.

With such complex issues at stake, it has been difficult to prevent good faith settlement hearings from developing into mini trials, in which the non-settling defendants argue tenaciously in order to prevent a defendant from "getting out cheap". The motivation of the non-settling defendants is not unaffected by the prospect that the plaintiff may utilize settlement funds to finance the cost of increasing the aggressiveness of its pursuit of the non-settling defendants.

Insurance coverage disputes may also be dragged into the good faith settlement hearings because a settling defendant may assign to the plaintiff its rights against an insurance company which may have declined coverage of the plaintiff's claim against the settling defendant. The value of this assignment must then also be taken into account.

§ 4.13 Assumption of the Risk

Assumption of the risk is a defense to a claim for compensation for an injury caused by the negligence of the defendant. A baseball fan, for example, who sits near homeplate, assumes the risk of being hit by a baseball. A downhill skier assumes the risks that normally attend that sport. One who helps a lumberjack fell a tree by pulling on a rope to induce the tree to fall in the direction of the pull may be said to assume the obvious risk of injury when the tree falls in the intended place.

> A firefighter slipped and fell on a wet stairway during a fire safety inspection. Plaintiff noticed that a flight of concrete stairs was wet but nevertheless climbed the stairway to proceed with the inspection. He exercised special caution traversing the stairway but nevertheless slipped and fell. The trial court granted summary judgment for defendant. AFFIRMED. One who has knowledge and appreciation of a particular danger created by the defendant's negligence and voluntarily chooses to encounter it assumes the risk of the hazard. Plaintiff saw the risk, exercised special caution, but was nevertheless injured. HELD: The doctrine of assumption of the risk is a complete defense, even after the adoption of comparative negligence.

Donohue v San Francisco Hous Auth, 230 Cal App 3d 635, 281 Cal Rptr 446 (1991).

> Homeowner O'Brien employed Mitch Elam to cut down four redwood trees, having heard that Mitch was skilled in removing trees. Mitch decided to "freefall" one of the trees. To prevent the tree from falling on a garage, Mitch employed plaintiff to pull on a rope. (Plaintiff was expected to plan and follow an "escape route".) The tree fell, plaintiff failed to escape and was seriously injured. He expected the tree to come down slowly but, because its branches had been removed, the expected "parachute effect" was not present and the tree fell faster than expected. HELD: That risk, the plaintiff did not assume. (Owner O'Brien was held liable to plaintiff under the peculiar risk doctrine. As a matter of law, felling a tree creates a peculiar risk that a person standing under the tree will be hurt.)

Maehl v O'Brien, 231 Cal App 3d 674, 283 Cal Rptr 23 (1991).

Assumption of the risk is a defense to a claim of strict liability as well as a claim of negligence.

> Plaintiff let go the handle of a half-inch drill motor to grab a mullion. The drill hung up and plaintiff was thrown to the ground. Plaintiff was aware of safety instructions that require the operator always to grip the side handle of the tool. HELD: The doctrine of assumption of the risk applies to actions founded on strict products liability.

Milwaukee Elec Tool Corp v Superior Court (Vondrasek), 10 Cal App 4th 403, 6 Cal Rptr 2d 423, *review tranferred to Court of Appeals by*, 840 P2d 954, 13 Cal Rptr 2d 849 (1992).

§ 4.14 Releases and Disclaimers

Those who rent horses, skis, and the use of bungee jumping equipment are often asked to sign releases of liability. If the release language is clear, conspicuous, intelligible, unambiguous, and if the customer is given an opportunity to read it before signing, such releases of liability are given effect by the courts.

> Lawyer Guido was injured in a fall from a horse. She testified in a deposition that she did not feel comfortable signing something that said "release" on the top. She signed it, however, after being told by her instructor that it did not mean anything and was just for insurance purposes. HELD: The release is enforceable. Plaintiff was asking the court to rule that a practicing attorney can rely on the advice of an equestrian instructor as to the validity of release that she executed without reading.

Guido v Koopman, 1 Cal App 4th 837, 2 Cal Rptr 2d 437 (1991), *review denied* (Feb 26, 1992).

On the other hand, a disclaimer of liability buried in fine print among the provisions of a contract may be unenforceable, particularly if the party disclaiming liability is a professional (such as an architect) and the other party to the contract is a consumer (such as a homeowner). A disclaimer in a *contract of adhesion* will not be enforced. A contract of adhesion is a standard form offered on a take it or leave it basis to a person of inferior bargaining power. For example, a customer may be asked to sign a contract when employing a stockbroker. An inconspicuous provision in such a contract relieving the broker of liability for improper trading would not be enforceable against the consumer.

In *Henrioulle v Marin Ventures, Inc*, 28 Cal 3d 512, 573 P2d 465, 143 Cal Rptr 247 (1978), the court held invalid an exculpatory clause dealing with the liability of an apartment building owner to a tenant for personal injury. The court applied six criteria in holding the clause invalid: 1) the clause exculpates a business that is suitable for public regulation, 2) the service provided is of great importance and practical necessity to the public, 3) a party holds itself out as willing to perform the service for any member of the public, 4) the party possesses a decisive advantage in bargaining, 5) the contract is standardized, and there is no provision that the customer may pay an additional fee and obtain additional protection, and 6) the person or property of the customer is under the control of the business and subject to risk of carelessness.

In *Solidification, Inc v Minter*, 305 NW2d 871 (Minn 1981), a contractor agreed to raise a concrete slab floor in a warehouse by pumping grout into the floor. The contract included an exculpatory clause to the effect that the contractor would attempt to avoid clogging the sewer but it would not accept responsibility "should this occur". Judgment for owner AFFIRMED. Exculpatory clauses in contracts between private parties are valid but will be strictly construed. The clause is ambiguous as to the contractor's responsibility "should this occur" and therefore the clause did not relieve the contractor of its own negligence.

In *Trenton Constr Co v Straub*, 310 SE2d 496 (W Va 1983), homeowners sought damages for moisture problems, claiming that contractor was required to install a visqueen vapor barrier under the house. The contractor defended on the ground that the owner's architect had, by letter, accepted the completed construction and approved all work as being done in a workmanlike manner. HELD: The homeowners were not bound by the release. The defect was concealed and could not have been discovered by due diligence. Here, the absence of the visqueen barrier was discovered only when homeowners removed a portion of the bathroom floor in order to relocate the fixtures in the room.

§ 4.15 Economic Loss

Economic loss is a legal term that describes damages that are not caused by physical injury. Examples of physical injury are bodily injury and property damage caused by an automobile accident. An example of economic loss is loss of income sustained by the owner of a delivery truck while the truck is in the shop after a recall to correct a defect in the brake system. Economic loss is the type of loss sustained because of the failure of a product to perform as represented or as anticipated. This type of loss can be, and usually is, compensated in an action for breach of contract or breach of warranty.

Some states do not allow a plaintiff to recover damages for economic loss under a negligence theory. "Economic loss" here is defined as frustration of the plaintiff's economic expectations from the use of a product. For example, an owner who employs a contractor to construct a warehouse does so with certain economic expectations to be enjoyed from the use of the warehouse. If the building does not perform as expected, the owner will suffer economic loss (sometimes measured as the reduction in the reasonable rental value of the building). The owner may recover such damages from the contractor as damages for breach of contract.

Restaurants, bars, and motels filed suit against a bridge contractor to recover for losses they sustained when a bridge was closed because of cracking and deterioration. Summary judgment dismissing claims AFFIRMED. The law does not recognize the cause of action in negligence in favor of a person who has suffered only economic loss. Implied warranty does not extend to third parties who suffer only economic loss.

Nebraska Innkeepers, Inc v Pittsburg-Des Moines Corp, 345 NW2d 124 (Iowa 1984).

Homeowners employed contractor for a "package deal" including land, design, and construction of a house and pool. The pool settled, water pipes broke, soil under the pool eroded, and the pool and house foundations cracked. Homeowners filed an action against the architect and pool installer who had been employed by the contractor. HELD: The loss was purely economic and therefore not compensable in a negligence cause of action. When a project "injures itself" because one of its component parts is defective, a purely economic loss results for which no action in tort will lie.

Sensenbrenner v Rust, Orling & Neale Architects, Inc, 236 Va 419, 374 SE2d 55 (1988).

The supplier of roofing materials persuaded a project engineer to specify its material. The roofing material deteriorated, but there was no evidence of damage to any property other than the defective roof itself. The project general contractor brought an action against the supplier seeking to recover the cost of replacing the defective roof. HELD: The cost to repair or replace defective property is economic loss, and since there was no privity between contractor and supplier, the contractor's negligence claim was properly dismissed.

State v Mitchell Constr Co, 108 Idaho 335, 699 P2d 1349 (1984).

Homeowners association sued a manufacturer of asphalt shingles for the cost of repairing and replacing shingles that blistered. The owners recovered judgment $40,679 actual damages plus $250,000 punitive damages. REVERSED. South Carolina follows the majority rule under which tort liability can be imposed only in cases of personal injury or property damage. Under contract law, parties negotiate the allocation of risk. Recovery of damages for economic loss should be left to contract and warranty law. If intangible economic loss were actionable under a tort theory, the provisions of the Uniform Commercial Code dealing with assignment of risk, warranties, and disclaimers would be rendered meaningless.

2000 Watermark Assoc v Celotex Corp, 784 F2d 1183 (4th Cir 1986).

Subsequent owners of buildings sued the builder and architect alleging physical deterioration of the buildings. HELD: Absent a contractual relationship, there can be no recovery for economic loss.

Lake Placid Club Attached Lodges v Elizabethtown Builders, Inc, 131 AD2d 159, 521 NYS2d 165 (1987).

Suppose that the HVAC system of a hotel is inadequate. O, who contracted with K for the building, has now sold the building to B. If B makes a claim against K for reduction in the reasonable rental value of the hotel because of the HVAC, in some states K could interpose the *economic loss* defense. The defense is based on the theory that economic expectations should be protected only by contract law, and not by negligence law.

Now let us suppose that B files an action against K for water damage sustained because of a defective roof. Here, the economic loss defense would not apply because the nature of the loss is not purely economic, but rather is physical injury to tangible property.

The economic loss defense is of special importance to architects and engineers. Suppose, for example, that an office building develops a reputation for inadequate elevatoring and as a result the landlord must make rental concessions to the tenants. B, the third owner of the building, brings an action against E, the architect's elevator consultant. Since B is seeking compensation for disappointed economic expectations from the use of the building, the economic loss defense could apply.

Suppose K submits a bid to O to construct a hotel in accordance with drawings prepared by A. During the course of construction it is discovered that the drawings have not been adequately coordinated, and therefore numerous changes are required to allow the mechanical systems to be installed without interfering with the structural elements of the building. In order to overcome these problems K is forced to employ an assistant superintendent and a field engineer, but completion of the job is still delayed for six months as a result of which the contractor sustains additional expenses for field overhead and home office overhead. K makes a claim against A for these losses, alleging that A's negligence (or professional malpractice) caused foreseeable damage to K's economic interests. Since K has no contract with A, the economic loss defense could apply.

Many states that recognize the economic loss defense make an exception for cases in which a defendant furnishes information that it should know will be relied upon by third parties in the conduct of their affairs. Since architects should anticipate that contractors will rely on information supplied by architects in estimating costs of construction, they may not use the economic loss defense in such states.

The economic loss rule is not recognized in most states. In most states, owners and contractors have been permitted to recover economic damages from manufacturers, contractors, architects, and engineers on negligence theories.

> Contractor was delayed in the construction of a water line project because of the negligence of an engineer who failed to call out fittings necessary for laying pipe through an "S" curve. The jury returned a verdict of $381,000. AFFIRMED. The requirement of privity of contract to maintain an action for economic loss has been abolished in Montana. A contractor may recover purely economic loss against an engineer when the engineer knew or should have foreseen that the particular plaintiff or an identifiable class of plaintiff was at risk in relying upon information supplied.

Jim's Excavating Service v HKM Assoc, 878 P2d 248 (Mont 1994).

> A sub-subcontractor filed an action against a contractor for negligence in ordering changes that required tens of thousands of hours of extra work and caused the sub-subcontractor to incur $5,545,900 in expense. Contractor sought to dismiss the complaint on the ground that the sub-subcontractor could not recover purely economic damages in tort. HELD: When plaintiff's damages are reasonably foreseeable and the injury is proximately caused by defendant's negligence, courts have endeavored to create exceptions to the economic loss doctrine to allow recovery. A defendant owes a duty of care to take reasonable measures to avoid the risk of causing economic damages to a particular plaintiff whom the defendant knows is likely to suffer damages from its conduct.

Dynalectric Co v Westinghouse Elec Corp, 803 F Supp 985 (DNJ 1992).

> A general contractor filed an action against an air conditioning equipment manufacturer alleging that the manufacturer delayed the delivery of equipment to an air conditioning subcontractor and, by failing to promptly fill the subcontractor's purchase order, delayed the prime contractor's performance of a job with the Corps of Engineers resulting in the assessment of liquidated damages of $30,000. The trial court dismissed the complaint. REVERSED. The policy of this state is to hold persons liable for economic loss

caused to another through want of ordinary care. The factors taken into account in determining liability were 1) the supplier's conduct directly affected the contractor's ability to timely perform, 2) the supplier could have foreseen the consequences of the delay, 3) because of the delay the contractor suffered damages, and 4) there was close connection between the acts of the supplier and the damages suffered by the contractor.

Chameleon Engg Corp v Air Dynamics, Inc, 101 Cal App 3d 418, 161 Cal Rptr 463 (1980).

A subcontractor who installed a fire detection system filed an action against the engineer who had prepared the specifications for the installation. The engineer approved catalogue cuts for UV detectors as submitted by the subcontractor, even though they did not meet the requirements of the contract documents. After the system was installed, the owner rejected it. HELD: South Dakota recognizes a cause of action for economic damage for professional negligence absent privity of contract. The damage to the subcontractor was foreseeable by the engineer.

Mid-Western Elec v DeWild Grant Reckert, 500 NW2d 250 (SD 1993).

§ 4.16 Intentional Torts

Deliberate injury of one person by another, if not justified, is an intentional tort. *Battery*, for example, is an intentional physically touching another person. In the field of construction law, the most important intentional torts are *fraud* and *libel*.

Fraud is sometimes also known as *misrepresentation* or *deceit*. *Libel* is also called defamation. Defamation is *libel*, if written, and *slander* if oral.

§ 4.17 Fraud

The elements of *fraud* are 1) a misrepresentation of fact, 2) intended to deceive, 3) that actually does deceive the plaintiff, 4) who relies the misrepresentation, 5) in a detrimental way. Thus, suppose that D tells B that a building is founded on rock when D knows very well that the building is founded on uncompacted fill. B buys the building, which later requires extensive repair because of settlement of the fill.

B could recover damages from D for fraud since D made an intentional misrepresentation of a material fact that was believed by B, and upon which B relied in deciding to buy the building.

It is sometimes difficult to distinguish between fraud and a sales pitch. For example, "this house is well built" is a statement of opinion, rather than a statement of fact, and therefore such a statement might be considered "puffing" but not a misrepresentation of fact.

> Bond holders filed an action against engineers who had advised a power company that was planning to construct two nuclear power plants financed by the sale of revenue bonds. In connection with the bond offerings, the power company prepared statements that contained the opinions of engineers and accountants as to the structural and financial feasibility of the project. The project was terminated because of decreased power demands and the inability to obtain sufficient financing to continue the project. Bond holders sued engineers alleging they supplied inaccurate information and fraudulent recommendations. HELD: Since the engineers gave information to the power company knowing that the power company would pass the information on to the bond holders, they had a duty to refrain from fraudulent misrepresentations even absent privity or a fiduciary relationship.

Haberman v Washington Pub Power Supply Sys, 109 Wash 2d 107, 744 P2d 1032 (1987).

> Subsequent purchasers of a house filed an action against a builder seeking to recover the cost of repairing defects in a septic system. The original contractor for the septic system refused to finish the job and the builder took over. The engineer who designed the system inspected it and certified the "as built" system to the health department, but thereafter the builder altered or destroyed portions of the system. HELD: The builder knowingly made affirmative fraudulent representations and plaintiffs were entitled to recover the cost of remedying the defects.

Herz v Thornwood Acres "D", Inc, 86 Misc 2d 53, 381 NYS2d 761 (Justice Ct 1976), *affd*, 91 Misc 2d 130, 397 NYS2d 358 (Sup Ct 1977).

A promise of future conduct does not rise to the level of misrepresentation.

In *RC Constr v National Office Sys*, 622 So 2d 1253 (Miss 1993), contractor filed an action against a subcontractor for breach of contract and misrepresentation. Subcontractor had telephoned a bid that the contractor had used in preparing its own bid. After being awarded the project, the contractor solicited the subcontractor for a better price but never informed the subcontractor that its bid had been accepted. HELD: 1) The contractor failed to accept the bid and therefore no contract was formed. 2) The subcontractor's promise to provide furniture for the project at a specified cost did not amount to a misrepresentation.

Contractor was employed to install concrete sewer pipe and manholes at unit prices. Subcontractor agreed to perform the work on behalf of the contractor at 10% below the unit prices contained in the prime contract. Subcontractor entered into the contract based on contractor's misrepresentations as to the true unit prices, which subcontractor only discovered after observing the contents of the prime contract by accident. The evidence showed that the contractor did not obtain the owner's consent to subbing the work out, and hid from the owner the subcontractor's presence on the job site by covering up the decals on the subcontractor's trucks. Judgment for subcontractor $68,163.23 plus interest AFFIRMED. The contract was void for fraud and the subcontractor was entitled to recover the *quantum meruit* value of its work.

Taylor & Jennings, Inc v Bellino Bros Constr Co, 106 AD2d 779, 483 NYS2d 813 (1984).

After a hospital was substantially completed, the city refused to allow the hospital to open because the wall paneling installed in the rooms and corridors had a flame spread rating of more than 15. The paneling actually had a rating of 255. The architect had selected the panel after being advised by the manufacturer that the paneling was not fire rated. Although the statement was technically true, it was nevertheless fraudulent because it was misleading in that it failed to disclose the high fire spread characteristics of the paneling. Where

> one has made a true statement and subsequently acquires new information rendering it untrue or misleading, the information must be disclosed in order to avoid liability for fraud.

St. John Hosp v Corbetta Constr Co, 21 Ill App 3d 925, 316 NE2d 51 (1974).

§ 4.18 Fraudulent Concealment

An element of fraud is usually an intentional misrepresentation of fact. Fraud, however, may also consist of an intentional concealment of a fact or facts that a person is under a duty to disclose. Suppose, for example, that a project owner knows that a high water table exists on property that is designated for construction, and will interfere with the contractor's work. Under such circumstances, the owner has an obligation to disclose the presence of the high water table to the contractor.

> A City's chief engineer had knowledge from past projects of highly unstable soil conditions along the route of a projected sewer line, and directed an independent soils testing firm to take its borings at preselected locations which avoided the area of greatest unsettled conditions. Contractor sought damages for fraudulent breach of contract. HELD: It is the general rule that by failing to impart knowledge of difficulties to be encountered in a project, the owner will be liable for misrepresentation if the contractor is unable to perform according to the contract provisions. Exculpatory contract provisions will not protect an owner against liability for active concealment.

Salinas, City of v Souza & McCue Constr Co, 66 Cal 2d 217, 424 P2d 921, 57 Cal Rptr 337 (1967).

> After removing, straightening, beveling and stockpiling 120,540 feet of pipe at 25 cents per foot, a contractor stopped work and alleged that the owner had misrepresented job conditions. The owner had misrepresented the depth of the pipe, and did not disclose that the pipeline contained oil and other materials. HELD: The contractor was entitled to rely on the owner's representations and did

not have an independent duty to examine the pipeline before entering into the contract. Moreover, the contractor did not waive its cause of action for fraud by continuing performance after discovering that the job conditions had been misrepresented.

Fiedler v McKea Corp, 605 F2d 542 (10th Cir 1979).

§ 4.19 Fraudulent Inducement of Contract

Although a mere statement of opinion is not fraud, a misrepresentation of a state of mind is a misrepresentation of fact, and not a statement of opinion. Assume, for example, that D promises to mow P's lawn every week while P is on vacation. At the time when D makes the promise, it has no intention whatever of fulfilling that promise but actually intends to steal P's lawnmower. This would be *fraudulent inducement of contract* sometimes known as *promissory fraud.* The promise was an implied misrepresentation of fact: the fact that D actually intended to perform as promised.

Suppose that D, hoping to get construction work performed for free, intentionally seeks out an unlicensed contractor, P, and signs a contract promising to pay P for construction work. At the time when the contract is signed, D has no intention of making any payments under the contract. This would be an instance of fraud in the inducement of a contract since D impliedly represented its intention to fulfill the terms of the contract. (In some states an unlicensed contractor can recover damages for fraud, although it is disabled by the doctrine of illegality from enforcing a contract which it is unlicensed to perform.)

In one case a jury found a contractor, who was two months late in completing the construction of a house, guilty of fraudulent inducement of contract. The jury concluded that, at the time the contractor entered into the construction contract which included a completion date of November 1, the contractor had no intention of finishing the job on time. The jury in that case awarded substantial punitive damages in addition to compensatory damages.

In *Kuchta v Allied Builders Corp*, 21 Cal App 3d 541, 98 Cal Rptr 588 (1971), a court awarded punitive damages to homeowners on the ground that contractor had fraudulently induced homeowners to enter into a contract for construction of an outdoor patio and living area. The contractor knew, but failed to disclose to homeowners, that the plans did not meet the local building code. As a result of the code violations, owners were required by the city to restore the property to its original condition. HELD: Fraudulent inducement to enter a contract is a tort, and the trial court correctly instructed the jury that it was entitled to award punitive damages for fraud.

§ 4.20 Negligent Misrepresentation

Negligent misrepresentation is an actionable tort, but it is not fraud. The distinction is the difference between a mistake and a lie. If a misrepresentation is merely negligent, and not intentional, it is treated as any other form of negligence. A person has a duty to avoid exposing others to unreasonable risk of harm by making statements of fact that may be untrue. Before making a statement of fact, a person has a duty to make a reasonable investigation to determine whether that fact is true or not.

For example, suppose that O tells K, an excavation and grading contractor, that Blackacre contains no rock. O's statement is based on the opinion of a soils engineer who has drilled ten test holes on Blackacre and who is familiar with the geology of the area. Suppose, though, that despite the drilling and the geological knowledge, K encounters rock. Is O in this case guilty of negligent misrepresentation? *No.* O carefully investigated the subsurface conditions before making the statement of fact.

Now suppose, O, the owner of Blackacre, tells K that there is no subsurface rock on the property, but O has no particular reason to believe this to be the fact. One who makes a representation of fact with no reason to believe that the representation is either true or untrue makes a negligent misrepresentation.

In *Myers & Chapman, Inc v Thomas G Evans, Inc*, 323 NC 559, 374 SE2d 385 (1988), *rehg denied*, 324 NC 117, 377 SE2d 235 (1989), a subcontractor was held liable for negligently misrepresenting, on an application for payment, that $11,247 worth of specialty items (sophisticated electronic devices) had been purchased and stored for the work. HELD: The subcontractor's failure to inquire as to the specifics of the application for payment and the subcontractor's admission of lack of knowledge as to whether or not the items were actually on hand supports a finding of gross negligence.

In *Arnold N May Builders, Inc v Bruketta*, 100 Ill App 3d 722, 426 NE2d 1246 (1981), a contractor assured a farmer that a cattle confinement building would be ready by winter and that the owner did not need to winterize its feedlot. The building was not completed until spring of the following year. Many cattle died from exposure and others lost weight. Judgment for the owner $38,641.68 was AFFIRMED. Contractor negligently misrepresented the completion date.

In *Aliberti LaRochelle & Hodson Engg Corp v Federal Deposit Ins Corp*, 844 F Supp 832 (D Me 1994), an engineering company was held liable for negligently misrepresenting to a construction lender the cost of constructing a motel/condominium project. The engineer should have known the project could not be built for $918,000.

§ 4.21 Damages for Fraud and Misrepresentation

A plaintiff who is damaged by intentional or negligent misrepresentations may recover compensatory damages. Compensatory damages are intended to compensate the injured party for loss sustained because of the misrepresentation. For example, damages for misrepresenting the absence of rock from an excavation site would be the cost of removing and disposing of the rock. If the contractor were able to sell the rock, or crush it and utilize it as building material, the excess cost of removing the rock would be offset by the sales revenue. The object of compensatory damages in such a case is to put the injured party in the position it would have occupied, economically, if the misrepresentation had not been made.

For intentional misrepresentation, or fraud, the courts may also award *punitive*, or *exemplary* damages. The purpose of punitive damages is not to compensate the injured party for its injury, but to punish a wrongdoer and set an example to others.

In order to deter wrongful conduct, a jury must take into account the economic condition of the defendant. An award of $20,000 might serve to deter a small trader from repetition of misconduct whereas it could require an award of $1,000,000 or more to really get the attention of the board of directors of a large corporation.

Therefore the amount of punitive damages is left pretty much to the discretion of the jury. Excessive awards of punitive damages, however, are often overturned by the courts on appeal.

There are those who consider it anomalous that punitive damages are awarded as a windfall to the plaintiff rather than, as a traffic fine would be, to the state. Punitive damages are a favorite target of those who would reform the tort system.

§ 4.22 Libel and Slander

Libel and slander are disparagement. Libel is written disparagement and slander is oral disparagement. Libel and slander are false disparagement, so truth is a complete defense.

One who falsely accuses another of criminal conduct is guilty of the tort. It is also libelous or slanderous to falsely accuse a person of incompetence in the conduct of a business or profession.

> In *Quality Granite Constr v Hurst-Rosche*, 632 NE2d 1139 (Ill App Ct 1994), an engineer certified a project was 100% satisfactorily completed, but later wrote the owner a letter stating the contractor may be considered in default because of failure to complete the project in a timely manner, substandard workmanship, and inability to interpret the contract documents. Contractor obtained a verdict against the engineer for libel. AFFIRMED. The contractor submitted evidence that it had complied with the plans and specifications. The letter was defamatory on its face because it accused the contractor of an inability to perform properly its trade or profession. Engineers have no blanket immunity from liability for libel.

A statement that would otherwise be libelous may sometimes be *justified*. For example, it is part of an architect's duty to its client to advise the client against contracting with an incompetent contractor. If an architect gives an honest opinion based on a reasonable investigation and reputation in the construction community, it may be justified in advising that a contractor is not qualified to perform a certain job even though the advice is based partly on hearsay.

> In *Riblet Tramway Co v Ericksen Assocs*, 665 F Supp 81 (DNH 1987), an engineer employed by the state to review bids for a ski lift renovation project opined that it would be risky to employ the low bidder because the low bidder was inexperienced in working with triple chairlift systems. HELD: The consultant's statements of opinion were not defamatory. The consultant did not misrepresent the bidder's level of experience.

Statements that would otherwise be slanderous may also be *privileged.* For example, any testimony given in court or any statement made by a lawyer as a part of litigation or arbitration proceedings is privileged. The rationale for this so-called *litigation privilege* is that litigants should have the utmost freedom in presenting their cases without fear of being sued for libel or slander. If litigants could be sued for statements made in the course of litigation every lawsuit would then be pregnant with another lawsuit, in which case litigation would be virtually endless.

§ 4.23 Damages

Damages for libel and slander are computed so as to compensate the injured party for loss caused by the false statement. For example, if a contractor lands a job by falsely accusing a competitor of incompetence or dishonesty, a part of compensatory damages would be the profit that the contractor could have obtained if it had been awarded the contract. Courts also award punitive, or exemplary damages for libel and slander, as an example to others and to deter future misconduct.

§ 4.24 Malicious Prosecution and Abuse of Process

One of life's unpleasant experiences is to become a defendant in a lawsuit. If the potential liability is uninsured, the cost of defense can be crushing. Defending a suit distracts from the better things in life and forces one into the company of lawyers whose acquaintance one might otherwise avoid. It is natural for a defendant who has won an unjust lawsuit to contemplate revenge by inflicting litigation on the unsuccessful former plaintiff. The desire for retribution is not always nullified by the consideration that by becoming a plaintiff, the former defendant inflicts continued litigation upon himself.

Courts do not encourage malicious prosecution cases because they imply litigation can be truly endless. The plaintiff in a malicious prosecution action is required to show that the defendant's suit was without probable cause and "favorable termination" of the former suit on the merits. In most states, malice is inferred from the lack of probable cause, and it is not necessary to prove that the former plaintiff actually sought to inflict harm on the former defendant.

Since favorable termination is a requirement of the cause of action for malicious prosecution, a defendant in a lawsuit is not permitted to file a cross-complaint for malicious prosecution.

Abuse of process is the illegitimate use by a plaintiff of the process of the court. "Process" in this sense includes writs of attachment, subpoenas, instructions to the sheriff, and claims of mechanics lien. An example of an abuse of process would be for a person who had performed no work on and supplied no materials to a construction project to record a claim of mechanics lien on that project in order to put economic pressure on the project owner to achieve some ulterior purpose, for example, to induce the owner to sell the property at a bargain price. Favorable termination is not a requirement of the cause of action for abuse of process and therefore such a claim may be filed as a cross-complaint in the very litigation that provides the occasion for the abuse of process.

CHAPTER 5

CLAIMS

Chapter 5

§ 5.01 Owner's Damages for Delay

If a contractor delays the completion of a construction project, the owner will suffer monetary damages from being deprived of the economic value of the completed project.

The object of investment is revenue. An owner who invests capital, for example, in the construction of a hotel does so in order to enjoy the revenue that the investment can produce. To make the investment ties up capital the cost of which is usually measured as interest. If the owner borrows the money to build the project, then the owner must pay interest on that borrowed money. If the owner already has the money for the project set aside, then borrowing is not necessary but the owner will lose what it could have made by depositing the money with the bank at interest. One measure of an owner's damages for delay is, therefore, the interest that the owner could have made by depositing its money with the bank.

During a period of delay, an owner also suffers damages in the form of real estate taxes paid for the ownership of unproductive property. Putting the two elements together, then, one way of measuring an owner's damages for delay is interest and real estate taxes paid during the period of the delay.

Property owners often refinance their property after the completion of construction. In a market in which interest rates are rising, the increased cost of interest caused by a delay in the completion of the construction may be an element of damages.

> Because of delayed completion of an addition to a hospital, the owner refinanced at a much higher rate than would have been available if the project had been completed on time. The owner also incurred additional interest expense for its construction loan, which remained in effect during the period of delay. HELD: It was proper to award the owner damages for interest incurred during the extended period of construction, since such additional interest costs were predictable at the time when the contract was signed. However, the increase of the refinancing interest rate was caused by

> factors of supply and demand rather than by the delay, and would thus be compensable only if the parties had contemplated the increased interest rates during the period when the contract was formed.

Roanoke Hosp Assn v Doyle & Russell, Inc, 215 Va 796, 214 SE2d 155 (1975).

> It has been held that a townhouse purchaser may recover increased interest rates incurred because of a delay in completion of the townhouse by the townhouse developer.

Appollo v Reynolds, 364 NW2d 422 (Minn 1985).

§ 5.02 Reasonable Rental Value

A preferred method of measuring an owner's damages for delay is to compute the reasonable net rental value. For example, it should be easy to compute the reasonable rental value of an apartment building by summing the rental values of each apartment. Net rental value is obtained by subtracting the costs of management and maintenance, such as cost of management fees, utilities, and insurance premiums.

An owner may attempt to recover reasonable rental value plus construction loan interest plus real estate taxes as damages for delay, but such an award would be excessive because reasonable rental value by definition includes sufficient revenue to pay interest and taxes.

> A foreclosing construction lender on Essex House, an apartment hotel in New York City, filed an action against sureties on a bond that had guaranteed the developer would complete construction according to the requirements of the contract documents, and on schedule. HELD: Interest on investment along with taxes and insurance premiums are losses flowing from the failure to receive a finished building on time. Loss of rent is an alternate, and superior measure of damages; interest, insurance premiums, and taxes combined, not to exceed rental value, are also a proper measure of damages for delay in the completion of a construction project.

Prudence Co v Fidelity & Deposit Co, 297 US 198 (1936).

> Contractor failed to complete installation of a water and sewer system for a mobile home park on time. HELD: An award of $40,500 for lost rental income caused by the delay was proper.

Landmark, Inc v Stockmen's Bank & Trust Co, 680 P2d 471 (Wyo 1984).

§ 5.03 Liquidated Damages

Parties may agree that if the contractor fails to finish the job on time the contractor will pay liquidated damages, usually expressed in terms of dollars per day of delay. In this case the term "liquidated" describes the fact that the amount of damages per day has been agreed to in advance. Such a provision in a contract is sometimes loosely referred to as a *penalty clause*. This reflects the idea that the contractor is penalized for delay. Some courts are reluctant to enforce a penalty clause even though they would enforce a liquidated damages clause. The law abhors penalties because they can be unjust. The law, however, encourages liquidated damages agreements if they represent a good faith attempt by the parties to predict actual damages and, by liquidating them, save the trouble, expense, and uncertainty of proving the amount after a dispute has arisen.

Liquidated damages are especially appropriate in some cases where it is difficult to calculate reasonable rental value. How much, for example, is the reasonable rental value of a freeway bridge? How does a charity estimate the rental value of a soup kitchen? The contracts for such projects should include liquidated damages provisions.

> A contract to build a mill contained a provision that $50 per day would be deducted from the contract price as a liquidated damages for delay in completion of the project. The contract provided that the damages would be considered to be liquidated damages and not a penalty. The architect, in fixing the amount of the final certificate for payment, deducted $1,350 for 27 days of delay. HELD: A careful study of the contract reveals that the parties intended to fix liquidated damages, rather than a penalty, and therefore the owner was justified in withholding the $50 per day for each day of delay.

Hennessy v Metzger, 152 Ill 505, 38 NE 1058 (1894).

A question sometimes arises as to whether liquidated damages may be apportioned in cases where part of the delay is caused by the contractor and part by the owner. Better reasoned cases hold that liquidated damages may be apportioned.

> A contract between a developer and a utility contractor contained a liquidated damages provision. Construction was delayed for 83 days, of which 18 days were chargeable to the developer. The trial court apportioned the fault and assessed liquidated damages for 65 days of delay against the contractor. AFFIRMED. The fact that developer caused some of the delay did not preclude recovery of liquidated damages.

Keith v Burzynski, 621 P2d 247 (Wyo 1980).

Where a property owner ejects a contractor from a job, its entitlement to liquidated damages may be jeopardized. This is because by removing a contractor from the job the owner prevents the contractor from completing the work within the stipulated time.

> In *Twin River Constr Co v Public Water Dist No 6*, 653 SW2d 682 (Mo Ct App 1983), it was held that the trial court wrongly awarded liquidated damages to an owner against a contractor for a period after the owner had terminated the contractor's performance and taken over performance of the work with its own employees.

In early law, courts were reluctant to award liquidated damages and held that if an owner prevented a contractor from completing a construction project on time by causing some delay, it waived the right to recover liquidated damages.

> In *United States v United Engg & Constructing Co*, 234 US 236 (1914), our Supreme Court dealt with a federal government contract for construction of a pumping plant for a navy dry dock. The government changed the plans and thereby caused delays of two years. The work was also delayed by subcontractors. The government assessed 240 days of liquidated damages at $25 per day as provided in the contract. HELD: In accordance with the English rule, when the contractor agrees to do a piece of work within a given time and when performance is prevented by act of the owner, the entitlement to liquidated damages is waived.

In a surprising number of cases, the amount of liquidated damages stipulated in a construction contract is less than the actual damages that the owner would suffer because of delay. In such cases, owners have been known to argue that where the owner caused part of the delay, liquidated damages may not be awarded, but actual damages (greater than the amount of liquidated damages) are recoverable in their place. Such an argument receives little sympathy from the courts, since the effect would be to reward an owner for its own wrongdoing.

> A contract for construction of a law school dormitory provided for $2,000 per day liquidated damages. The liquidated damages clause limited the total amount of liquidated damages to $50,000. The owner sought to recover actual delay damages of $390,000, arguing that the owner had contributed to the delay. HELD: If the owner could have asserted its own culpability in delaying completion of the project to defeat the liquidated damages clause, and to recover its actual damages for delay, it would have profited from its own wrong. Such a result would be as inequitable as illogical.

XLO Concrete Corp v John T Brady & Co, 104 AD2d 181, 482 NYS2d 476 (1984), *affd*, 66 NYS2d 970, 489 NE2d 768, 498 NYS2d 799 (1985).

§ 5.04 Contractor's Damages for Delay

The law recognizes that a contractor may suffer damages if an owner interferes with or delays the progress of the contractor's work. A contractor, figuring a job, includes *labor units* and *overhead.* Labor units represent the contractor's estimated costs of performing certain kinds of work. For example, an electrical subcontractor might figure $1.00 per foot for the labor of installing conduit and wire under specified conditions. Most contractors are well aware of their overhead costs, which can be expressed as a percentage of sales. Overhead consists of certain fixed expenses that are incurred whether the contractor takes in any money or not: rent, utilities, and the salaries of executives, secretaries and estimators. If such items add up to $100,000 in a year when the contractor's revenue was $1,000,000, then overhead is 10% of revenue. A contractor who figures a job, and wants that job to earn enough to carry its share of overhead will then add 10% to the estimated cost of the job. (This, in fact, will produce a little less than 10% of revenue, since cost is presumably less than revenue.)

If an owner, by breach of contract, delays the completion of a project the law recognizes that the damages for that breach of contract should include an amount to compensate the contractor for the cost of operating its business during the period of delay. Overhead as an element of damages for delay is computed by the *Eichleay* formula. The Eichleay formula expresses the relationship between overhead for the project under construction and the contractor's total overhead during the contract period. For example, if work on the contract begins January 1 and ends October 30, the contractor figures its total earnings from the project during that period of time and also figures its total earnings from all projects during the same period of time. The overhead charged to the project is then computed according to that same ratio. If project earnings were found to be 20% of all earnings, then the amount of overhead charged to the project would also be 20%.

Lawyers, judges and CPA's have amused themselves with much esoteric debate about the Eichleay formula which is, after all, only a rough, common sense way of estimating a loss. One line of argument against the Eichleay formula runs that it is only "unabsorbed" home office overhead that should be charged to the owner. It is, of course, possible that a contractor's home office can be fully "absorbed" on profitable work even during a period when a particular project is suffering from delay. Use of the Eichleay formula is, however, justified by the fact that it probably represents a reasonable approximation of the expectations of the parties (if they had thought about it) at the time when the contract was signed.

> A federal post office and courthouse job in Albany called for the contractor to complete a $2,968,000 contract in 365 days. The government caused 969 days of delay. The contracting officer awarded the contractor $333,084 on its claim for unabsorbed home office overhead. The amount was computed using the Eichleay formula, which the court defined as follows:
>
> > The Eichleay formula requires three steps: 1) to find allocable contract overhead, multiply the total overhead cost incurred during the contract period times the ratio of billings from the delayed contract to total bills of the firm during the contract period; 2) to get the daily contract overhead rate, divide allocable contract overhead by days of contract performance; and 3) to get the amount recoverable, multiply the

daily contract overhead rate times days of government-caused delay.

Application of the Eichleay formula requires 1) compensable delay, 2) contractor was required to stand by the work and could not take other jobs or reduce its staff during the period of the delay. HELD: When a contractor satisfies the prerequisites for application of the Eichleay formula, that formula is the exclusive means available for calculating unabsorbed home office overhead. The contractor may not recover interest for equity capital applied to the performance of the project, and may not attempt to show that a larger percentage of home office effort was applied than the fraction yielded by application of the Eichleay formula.

Wickham Contracting Co v Fischer, 12 F3d 1574 (Fed Cir 1994).

In *Conti Corp v Ohio Dept of Admin Svcs*, 90 Ohio App 3d 462, 629 NE2d 1073 (1993), the court of claims entered judgment of $347,734.09 for a contractor for delay in renovation and reconstruction of a building on the Youngstown State University campus. Asbestos removal had halted the project for 140 days. HELD: It was proper for the trial court to utilize the Eichleay formula. The formula is proper based on the simplicity of the formula, the widespread use of the formula, and the credible testimony of witnesses.

The number produced by the Eichleay formula is only one component of a contractor's damages for delay in the construction of a project. It costs the contractor a calculable amount of money to keep a job open regardless of the amount of work performed during any particular day. Among such expenses are the daily cost of a field superintendent, a job shack, job telephone, jobsite clerk or secretary, field engineer, and daily equipment rental for such items as cranes, trucks, and loaders. Insurance premiums, when measured as a fraction of work under construction, may also represent a compensable daily cost.

§ 5.05 Contractor's Damages for Disruption

A contractor may seek to recover damages for disruption from an owner under legal theories of *interference*, *warranty*, and *implied covenant*. *Interference* is a breach of contract by which an owner interferes with a contractor's prosecution of the work. Suppose an owner orders a contractor to stop a part of the work, for example electrical work, pending redesign. Such an order would disrupt the job. It would cause the electrical subcontractor to demobilize and this might in turn interfere with the progress of drywall work, plumbing, and other trades. Such interference would be a breach of an implied condition, for every contract carries with it implied (if not expressed) conditions that neither party will interfere the other party's performance. The interference of the owner would in turn cause the prime contractor to breach its contract with the electrical subcontractor, for the subcontract would also include an implied condition that the prime contractor will make the jobsite available so that the subcontractor can perform its work in a normal and productive manner.

Another cause of action that can arise in favor of a prime contractor against an owner is founded on warranty law. An owner *impliedly warrants* to a contractor that the drawings (usually prepared by an architect employed by the owner) describe a buildable project and have been properly coordinated. (By "coordinated" is meant that the mechanical and architectural systems have been carefully reviewed so as to make certain that the various elements do not interfere with each other: thus, HVAC duct work does not occupy space required for structural steel.)

A construction contract also carries with it the *implied covenant* that the owner (usually through the architect) will promptly supply information needed by the contractor to resolve conflicts or ambiguities in the drawings so the contractor will not have to stop work while waiting for information.

> A jury awarded a contractor \$16.24 million for delay in the construction of a \$52.3 million advanced waste water treatment plant. AFFIRMED. The project was delayed for 15 months beyond its original 1,200-day completion deadline. A major cause of delay followed from a change in the firm that provided engineering services. This made it difficult for the contractor to obtain job information. HELD: The county impliedly warranted that the contractor, if it complied with the contract documents, would be able to complete the job in the contemplated period of time.

Frank Briscoe Co v Clark County, 857 F2d 606 (9th Cir 1988), *cert denied*, 490 US 1048 (1989).

§ 5.06 Measure of Damages for Disruption

Actionable interference (or breach of warranty) causes a reduction in the efficiency and productivity of the operations of prime contractor and subcontractors. This usually hits the bottom line in the form of increases in labor expense. Assume an electrical subcontractor figured $1.00 a foot for the cost of labor to install conduit and wire. A worker discovers that a certain conduit run cannot be installed because existing duct work interferes with it. The journeyman and an apprentice therefore stop work, seek out the working foreman who confers with the superintendent to assign different work. The workers are instructed to return their tools to the toolbox and the materials to the yard, and equip themselves to install switchgear in another area of the jobsite. After the workers reach the new work area it takes them awhile to become oriented to the physical conditions and to understand the relationship of shop drawings to the work they are to perform. After the conflict with the duct work is resolved the workers can return to their original task after assembling the appropriate tools and materials, at which time the orientation process is repeated as the workers study the architect's instructions for resolution of the conflict.

In figuring labor units it is probable that the subcontractor anticipated what it considered to be a normal amount of conflict in the drawings. The subcontractor testifies, though, that it encountered many more such conflicts than had been anticipated at the time when the subcontractor prepared its bid, and that the overall effect was to cause the cost of installing conduit and wire to increase from $1.00 a foot to $1.80 a foot. This represented only 55% of expected productivity and caused an 80% increase in labor costs. From this could be computed the monetary damages sustained by the subcontractor because of the owner's failure to furnish coordinated drawings.

If this lack of coordination, together with other disruption caused delay in the completion of the work then the subcontractor's damages would include an element of home office overhead computed according to the Eichleay formula and extended jobsite expense for such items as field supervision and jobsite telephone expense. The total damages for interference and delay would be the sum of the interference element added to the overhead elements. The subcontractor will wish to add profit to the total damage figure, but this is not permitted by the law. The law only awards compensation for loss, and does not recognize profit as an element of damages for breach of contract. Many arbitrators, though, if they are not bound to follow the law, do award profit as an element of damages, reasoning that a contractor's entire motivation for being in business is to make a profit, and that a breach of contract should not require the contractor to devote its resources to unprofitable work.

§ 5.07 Pass Through Claims

The reader may have wondered how a subcontractor might be able to pursue a claim against a project owner with whom the subcontractor has no contractual relationship. Such a claim may be "passed through" the prime contractor, who does have a contractual relationship with the owner. The theory is that the owner, by breach of its contract with the prime contractor, causes the prime contractor to breach its contract with the subcontractor. When the subcontractor makes its claim against the prime contractor, the prime contractor passes it through by making a claim against the owner. The prime contractor often includes the subcontractor's claim with a claim of its own against the owner.

In some states a subcontractor may make a direct claim against the owner under theories of negligence and breach of warranty.

> A contractor filed action against a harbor owner to recover costs incurred by a dredging subcontractor, alleging that the owner had inaccurately represented soil conditions. HELD: Contractor had the right to assert the subcontractor's claims against the harbor under the changed conditions clause in the general contract, as the subcontract incorporated that provision. Contractor was potentially liable to subcontractor and therefore could have raised parallel claims against the harbor. The fact that the subcontractor had exonerated the contractor from liability for cost overruns in exchange for contractor bringing the claim did not deprive the contractor of its standing to pursue the claim on the subcontractor's behalf.

Umpqua River Navigation Co v Crescent City Harbor Dist,
618 F2d 588 (9th Cir 1980).

> Work on a sewer contract was delayed by failure of the district to provide right of way. The prime contractor recovered $40,323.49 from the sanitation district, and two subcontractors recovered a total of more than $7,000 against the prime contractor. (The subcontractors' judgments were conditional upon the contractor collecting its judgment from the sanitation district.) HELD: The

contractor had a right to recover damages from the district on behalf of its subcontractors on the theory that the district's breach caused the contractor to incur liability to the subcontractors.

DA Parrish & Sons v County Sanitation Dist No 4, 174 Cal App 2d 406, 344 P2d 883 (1959).

§ 5.08 Acceleration and Constructive Acceleration

Suppose that a project owner orders a contractor to accelerate its work and finish a project on June 1 rather than, as scheduled, on September 1. Under the contract documents, the contractor had the right to schedule the work for a September 1 completion, so the order to accelerate is a breach of contract. Acceleration, however, may be costly to the contractor. The contractor may have to employ additional journeymen and apprentices, and may perhaps have to resort to employing those less skilled or less well-motivated than the contractor's regular workers.

Acceleration can also cause inefficiency because of a phenomenon known as "trade stacking". Suppose that normal sequence for construction of hotel rooms is framing followed by plumbing followed by electrical work followed by drywall followed by finish plumbing followed by finish electrical followed by finish carpentry. Because of acceleration, though, the drywall starts to get out ahead of the plumbing and electrical work. This will cause the plumber and the electrician to send crews into the same rooms where the drywaller is working. The crews try to work around each other. This causes a loss of productivity that translates into damages for the prime contractor and the trade contractors.

Constructive acceleration occurs when the date for completion of a project remains as scheduled but the amount of work is increased. This may occur because the owner orders the contractor to perform extra work without granting an extension of time to perform the work, or when the owner refuses to grant extensions of time for excusable delays. Constructive acceleration has the same effect on efficiency and productivity as acceleration, and damages for constructive acceleration are computed in the same way as damages for disruption.

§ 5.09 Total Cost

Many cases have held that a plaintiff is entitled to recover damages from a defendant if it is reasonably certain that the damages have been sustained, even though it may not be possible to prove the amount of damages with complete precision.

This principle finds expression in the willingness of courts to accept the *total cost* method of computing damages. Let us suppose that a contractor's efficiency and productivity have been affected by the breaches of contract by an owner. Suppose the owner supplies the contractor with uncoordinated contract documents and therefore it is frequently necessary for the contractor to stop work in specified areas of the project in order for the architect or the engineer to clarify or redesign the drawings. The efficiency of the contractor's operation is degraded when it is necessary to remove crews from one part of the jobsite and mobilize them in another area. Although the contractor has records of hundreds of instances when crews were forced to stop work and remobilize elsewhere, the timesheets and payroll records of the workers do not disclose the exact loss of productivity or the precise damages flowing from each incident. The contractor is, however, able to show that labor costs increased from an estimated $100,000 to an actual $150,000. The contractor introduces into evidence the estimate that it prepared and shows that the contract price is based on the estimate. Expert testimony establishes that the estimate was reasonable and that if the owner had supplied proper plans the labor costs would have been no more than the estimated amount. The contractor then subtracts the estimated labor cost from the total labor cost actually incurred, and the remainder is the damages sustained by the contractor because of the owner's breaches of contract that reduced the contractor's productivity.

> Contractor’s subcontractor filed an action against a prime contractor alleging that the prime contractor breached the contract by failing to make proper excavations for foundation work and by failing to provide the proper quantity and quality of lumber. Subcontractor introduced a statement prepared by a CPA that showed all costs on the project. From this was subtracted the amount that had been paid to the subcontractor, and judgment was entered for the difference.

Continental Cas v Shaffer, 173 F2d 5 (9th Cir 1949), *cert denied*, 338 US 820 (1949).

> Construction of a coal fired electricity generating plant was projected to require 37 months and 4.5 million hours of labor. The project actually required 48 months and nearly 9 million hours of labor. The jury came in with a verdict of $26.2 million in favor of the contractor and against the power district. AFFIRMED. The reasons for the delays and cost overruns were numerous, complex, and interrelated. Once the fact of damages is established, considerable leeway is permitted in determining the amount of damage. The jury properly utilized the total cost method for computing the amount of damages.

Nebraska Pub Power Dist v Austin Power, Inc, 773 F2d 960 (8th Cir 1985).

§ 5.10 Modified Total Cost

It is not always true that a contractor's estimate is perfect, nor is it always true that all loss of productivity was caused by breaches of contract by the owner. A contractor may therefore introduce its estimate but point out some errors in the estimate that caused the contractor to lower the contract price. The contractor may also point out that certain losses in productivity were not caused by the owner, but rather by poor supervision and coordination of the work by the contractor. When the errors in the estimate and the losses of productivity that are the fault of the contractor are taken into account, the contractor's damages caused by the owner become less than the difference between the total cost of the project and its estimated cost. This method of computing damages, where the contractor reduces its claim by taking responsibility for its own blunders and inefficiency, is *modified total cost*. Modified total cost is preferred by courts over the total cost theory of computing damages.

> Jury awarded $141,175 to a contractor based on the *modified total cost method*: total cost minus costs that the subcontractor or its subcontractors caused to be incurred. Once the fact of damage has been established, the plaintiff is obliged to produce only the best evidence available that will afford the jury a reasonable basis for estimating the dollar amount of the loss.

Seattle W Inds v David A Mowat Co, 110 Wash 2d 1, 750 P2d 245 (1988).

In *Municipality of Anchorage v Frank Coluccio Constr Co*, 826 P2d 316 (Alaska 1992), the court stated that, in a modified total cost analysis, the procedure is to look at all the money that was spent, subtract all the money that was paid, and then take a deeper look. Damages are calculated by starting with the contractor's costs in excess of what it was paid, then attempting to back out any costs that are not attributable to the property owner.

§ 5.11 Restitution

In reaction to a material breach of contract, a contractor may select from four courses of action:

Temporary termination. Temporarily stop performance, remaining ready, willing, and able to resume performance when the breach has been cured.

Terminate performance. Terminate performance and sue for damages for breach of contract.

Rescission. Rescind the contract and seek restitution of the consideration it has rendered.

Continued performance. Ignore the breach and continue to perform under protest until the job is finished and then sue for damages for breach of contract.

A material breach of contract excuses further performance on the common sense rationale that a party cannot insist that the other party punctiliously perform its obligations under a contract while at the same time failing to render counter-performance.

If an owner fails to live up to its side of a contract by failing to make progress payments, and the failure to make progress payments is unexcused, then the contractor has the option of continuing the job or stopping work.

If the contractor decides to stop work, then it has the option of standing on the contract or rescinding the contract.

If the contractor stands on the contract, its damages will be the contract price based on a percentage of completion plus the profit it would have enjoyed had it not been for the owner's breach.

If the contractor rescinds the contract, its damages will be the reasonable value of the work performed. Thus it is possible, by rescission, for a contractor to turn a losing contract into a profitable one.

> In *BL Metcalf Gen Contractor, Inc v Earl Erne, Inc*, 212 Cal App 2d 689, 28 Cal Rptr 382 (1963), the court pointed out that there is distinction between rescission and termination. It is contemplated that upon rescission the parties return those things of value which they have received from each other, and resume the *status quo*. Termination, however, contemplates the right of contracting party to terminate further performance because of a breach by the other party. When a party to a contract has committed a material breach, the other has the right and option to determine what remedy it will pursue: it may rescind the contract or terminate performance.
>
> In *McConnell v Corona City Water Co*, 149 Cal 60, 85 P 929 (1906), the court said that a contractor, faced with a breach of contract by the owner, may pursue any of three remedies: 1) rescind the contract and seek to recover the reasonable value of the work performed, 2) keep the contract alive and remain ready and able to perform it, or 3) terminate performance and sue for the profit it would have realized if it had not been prevented from performing.
>
> In *Myers v Western Realty & Constr, Inc*, 130 Ariz 274, 635 P2d 867 (1981), an electrical subcontractor stopped work when the prime contractor failed to make a progress payment. Judgment for the subcontractor was AFFIRMED. An action in quantum meruit is proper where, after non-payment, the subcontractor rescinds the contract.
>
> A subcontractor was entitled to rescind and recover in quantum meruit the value of labor and equipment furnished when prime contractor refused to fulfill its obligation to pay for the subcontractor's use of the crane. The impact of quantum meruit is to

> allow the subcontractor to recover the value of services rendered irrespective of whether it would have made money or lost money on the contract.

United States v Algernon Blair, Inc, 479 F2d 638 (4th Cir 1973).

§ 5.12 Abandonment

Most construction contracts contain a clause that allows the owner to issue change orders requiring the contractor to change the scope of the work. A change order that reduces the scope of the work is called a deductive change order, usually resulting in a decrease in the contract price. Other change orders increase the scope of the work and call for an increase in the contract price. Occasionally an owner may make such dramatic increases in the scope of the work that the stage is set for application of the legal concept of *abandonment*. In one case, for example, the owner of a processing plant continually issued orders to change the work without following the procedures established by the contract documents for such change orders, to such an extent that the scope of the work was increased by more than 50%. Here, the court held that the parties had *abandoned* the contract. The court then ordered the owner to pay the contractor the reasonable value of the work because, since the contract had been abandoned, the contract price no longer applied.

> Extras of $1.6 million were ordered on a $2.9 million contract. HELD: Abandonment of the contract may be implied from the acts of the parties where the scope of work undertaken greatly exceeds that called for under the contract.

Daugherty Co v Kimberly-Clark Corp, 14 Cal App 3d 151, 92 Cal Rptr 120 (1971).

CHAPTER 6

MECHANICS LIENS

Chapter 6

§ 6.01 Development of the Law

The nation's first mechanics lien law was enacted by the Maryland General Assembly in 1791 to facilitate the construction of the new capital city of Washington. It is said that the law was enacted at the urging of Thomas Jefferson and James Madison. All 50 states now have mechanics lien statutes. The mechanics lien statutes may have grown out of maritime law, which granted a lien against a ship to those who furnished material or labor to the vessel. The early common law also granted a lien to mechanics who increased the value of personal property committed to their possession, while the European civil law has long recognized a lien right in a builder. It may be that the system of mechanics liens was motivated by the desire to build up a new and rapidly growing country. Without a strong private banking system, the new nation relied upon laborers and material suppliers for credit. The mechanics lien statutes serve to encourage workers and material suppliers to devote their assets to the construction of buildings and other structures. (Under New Jersey's new law, the "old" term "mechanics lien" has been replaced by the term "construction lien".)

§ 6.02 Security for a Debt

The mechanics lien is a form of security for the payment of a debt, and is similar in its function to a mortgage or a deed of trust. The legislative purpose of the mechanics lien is to prevent injustice. The statutes are aimed to prevent the unjust enrichment of a property owner at the expense of a contractor or material supplier who has contributed to the value of the owner's property by furnishing work or materials to a construction project.

Consider the case of a contractor who installs a new parking lot for the owner of a convenience store. The new parking lot increases the value of the owner's property. If the owner avoids paying for the work, it is a clear case of unjust enrichment. Of course, the contractor could sue the owner for the debt, but the contractor might be unable to collect a judgment because of the owner's insolvency. The purpose of the mechanics lien statutes is to prevent this injustice by giving to the contractor a mechanics lien as a form of security for the payment of the debt.

The function of a mechanics lien is similar to the function of a mortgage. Each serves as a form of security for the payment of a debt. In the case of a mortgage, the debt is consensual. The debt usually arises when the borrower signs a promissory note undertaking to repay money advanced by a financial institution. At the same time the borrower signs a mortgage that provides that in case the borrower doesn't repay the debt the financial institution can foreclose on the property.

A mechanics lien, on the other hand, is not consensual. It is not supported by a promissory note or by a mortgage signed by the borrower. The mechanics lien arises of its own accord, by force of law, immediately when the lien claimant first furnishes work, equipment, or materials that improves the property of the owner.

§ 6.03 The Other Side of Unjust Enrichment

As between a prime contractor and an owner, the enforcement of a claim of mechanics lien can prevent unjust enrichment. It is plainly evident that the law should not encourage an owner who would unfairly fail to compensate a contractor for its work, since then the owner would enjoy the benefits of the contractor's performance. This is because it is impossible for a contractor to repossess a building or other structure erected upon property belonging to the owner. The cost of dismantling the building would exceed the value of the salvable materials. Economic waste would result. In justice, then, the contractor is allowed to follow its resources on to the owner's property through the foreclosure of the lien which, in effect, forces the owner to fulfill its contractual obligation to pay for the work. But it doesn't end there.

Since the mechanics lien right is given, in most states, to all who contribute to the project, including subcontractors, materialmen, sub-subcontractors and their materialmen, there is a potential that injustice may be done to the owner. Suppose, for example, that an owner employs a contractor to build a swimming pool for $20,000. The pool being satisfactorily completed, the owner pays the $20,000 to the prime contractor after which the company that installed the decking work records a claim of lien for $5,000. Here it may be argued that it is the decking contractor that has been unjustly enriched, since the owner pays the price of the subcontractor's poor judgment in advancing credit to the defaulting prime contractor.

Some states, for example, New Jersey and Georgia, prohibit lien claimants from collecting from the owner a greater amount than the owner contracted to pay for a completed work of improvement. In such states, the owner can never be required to "pay twice" as a result of a filing of a claim of lien.

Owners, construction lenders and title companies have made their case to the legislatures of most states, which have enacted statutes that require those who would establish mechanics lien rights to give written preliminary notices to the owners of the projects they improve, and sometimes to the project construction lenders and prime contractors also. The function of the preliminary notices is to enable the owners, construction lenders and prime contractors to administer progress payments in such a way as to avoid the possibility of liens.

The interest of the construction lender in avoiding mechanics lien claims will become clear from our discussion of priorities. If a mechanics lien claim takes priority over the lien of a mortgage securing a construction loan, the value of the lender's security is reduced by the amount of the claim of lien. The prime contractor's interest in avoiding mechanics lien claims rests upon the simple fact that the prime contractor has a statutory, and also usually a contractual, duty to protect the owner's project from mechanics lien claims. Therefore, when a claim of lien is recorded, the owner subtracts the amount of the claim from the prime contractor's next progress payment. Therefore it is to the prime contractor that usually falls the primary operational responsibility for processing progress payments in such as a way as to avoid mechanics lien claims.

§ 6.04 Mechanics Lien: A Cloud on Title

When a mortgage is recorded in the county recorder's office, it notifies anyone who is interested in purchasing or otherwise dealing with the property that a financial institution has a lien on the property that must be taken into account. When a claimant records a claim of mechanics lien in the county recorder's office (or, in some states, *files* a claim of lien in the county clerk's office), this action has the same effect as the recording of a mortgage or a deed of trust. A person interested in buying the property would then know that it would take title subject to the claim of mechanics lien.

In Maryland, a claim of mechanics lien can be established only by court order after the owner has had an opportunity to be heard. A claimant must file a petition to establish a mechanics lien in court. This petition constitutes notice to potential purchasers of the land that the petitioner claims a mechanics lien against the property.

We have said that a mechanics lien attaches to property immediately when a claimant has supplied work, equipment, or materials to a project. The lien, then, arises before the document claiming the lien has been recorded. Therefore, the mere fact that a construction project is in progress means that title to property is clouded -- not because anybody has recorded a claim of lien, but because somebody *might* record a claim of lien. For this reason, owners find it difficult or impossible to sell or borrow against property when construction work is in progress.

§ 6.05 The Question of Priority

In many states, mechanics lien claims take priority not from the time when they are recorded, but rather from the commencement of construction work on the project. In New York, for example, claims of lien have priority over a mortgage, building loan mortgage, or conveyance that was recorded after the work of improvement began but within four months of its completion. The building loan mortgage may take priority over mechanics liens, however, if it contains a trust covenant. In Texas and California, claims of mechanics lien relate back to the visible commencement of construction on the land. In Florida, claims of lien generally take their priority from the date of recording of the claim of lien. Thus, in most states, if construction work visibly commences on a construction project on January 2, and a painting contractor starts work the following October and records a claim of lien in December, the claim of lien takes its priority from January 2. In other states, a claim of mechanics lien takes priority when the claimant first delivered work or materials to a project. In our example, then, the claim of the painting contractor would take its priority from the commencement of painting work in October rather than from the commencement of construction work in January.

The issue of priority is of vital importance to lien claimants. Assume that property is encumbered by a first mortgage and a second mortgage. The owner defaults. The holders of both mortgages foreclose. Property is sold at public auction. The money from the sale is insufficient. Under these circumstances, the holder of the first mortgage is paid 100% of the money from the sale and the holder of the second mortgage gets nothing.

In the same way, if a mechanics lien has priority over a mortgage, the mechanics lien claimant may receive 100% of its claim while the holder of the mortgage may get nothing. And, vice versa, if the mortgage had been recorded before the commencement of construction work, the mortgage would have priority over the deed of trust and the holder of the mortgage could be paid 100% of its claim while the mechanics lien claimant could get nothing.

§ 6.06 The Sheriff's Sale

The enforcement of a mechanics lien is in five steps. In the first step, the claimant provides work, equipment, or materials that improve the owner's property, and an unrecorded lien attaches to the property. In the second step, the lien claimant provides preliminary notices to the property owner and to the construction lender, as required in most states. In the third step, the unpaid claimant records a claim of lien in the county recorder's office. In the fourth step, the claimant brings its foreclosure case to trial and the court enters a judgment of foreclosure in which the sheriff is ordered to sell the property to the highest bidder at public auction, and use the proceeds of the sale to pay the claim. In the judgment of foreclosure the court determines the priority of the mechanics lien claim and the priority of other, competing, liens or mortgages. In the fifth step, after advertisement, the sheriff sells the property to the highest bidder at public auction, and distributes the proceeds of the sale according to the priorities as determined by the court.

All mechanics lien claims share the same priority. Thus if there are two mechanics lien claims, one of which is for $25,000 and the other of which is for $75,000, and the sheriff has $50,000 to distribute, 25% of that amount goes to the one claimant and 75% to the other.

Now let us assume that Blackacre, our hypothetical parcel of real property, is encumbered by a mortgage of $100,000 and two claims of mechanics lien, one for $25,000 and the other for $75,000. In order to make foreclosure effective, the lien claimants must join the holder of the mortgage in their foreclosure action. If the court determines that the mechanics lien claims have priority over the mortgage, and the sheriff's sale produces $100,000 or less, the holder of the mortgage gets nothing: its claim is wiped out by the foreclosure of the mechanics lien claims. If on the other hand the mortgage or deed of trust has priority over the mechanics lien claims, then lien claimants are wiped out. Thus it is said that, in foreclosure, a claim of mechanics lien is only as good as the owner's equity in the property. The *equity*, of course, is determined by subtracting existing encumbrances (usually mortgages) from the value of the property.

§ 6.07 Construction Loans

Most construction projects are built with borrowed money. The financial institutions that lend money for construction usually do so on the security of a mortgage. The major legal documents supporting a construction loan are a promissory note, a mortgage, and a construction loan agreement. The promissory note records the amount of loan and the borrower's promise to repay it. The mortgage, a document that is recorded in the county recorder's office, gives the lender the right to foreclose if the borrower fails to repay the loan. The construction loan agreement, which is a lengthy document, provides that the borrower will use the proceeds of the loan to construct the project according to plans and specifications that are incorporated into the construction loan agreement. Since the lender relies upon the improved value of the property as security for the repayment of the loan, the lender has a vital interest in insuring the construction of a quality project in accordance with the schedule that is incorporated into the contract.

Taken together, the mortgage and construction loan agreement impose upon the borrower an array of duties deemed essential by the lender for the protection of its security. Typical such duties include the obligation to build according to the plans and specifications and to the satisfaction of the architect, the duty to advance the project on schedule, the duty to pay for all work and materials incorporated into the project, the duty to avoid the recording of mechanics liens, the duty promptly to pay real estate and other taxes, the duty to avoid violation of any building or zoning laws, the requirement to insure the project against fire, flood, or other damage with insurance policies issued by insurance carriers that are approved by the lender, and the duty to deposit additional funds in the construction loan account if the lender should feel insecure.

The failure of the borrower to fulfill any of these obligations is a default under the mortgage document that gives the lender the right to foreclose.

§ 6.08 Progress Payments

It is customary for all construction work to be paid for progressively, during the progress of the work. It would be a rare owner who would be willing to pay 100% of the contract price in advance and then trust the contractor to build the project lien-free, on schedule, and on budget. The owner customarily makes monthly progress payments to the contractor based on the value of the work accomplished during the previous month. From the amount of each progress payment the owner usually withholds a 10% retention partly as leverage to insure that the contractor will finish the project and partly as security against mechanics lien claims. In most cases, the payment schedule is dictated by the construction lender. The construction loan agreement allows the borrower to draw construction loan funds monthly, for 90% of the value of the work accomplished during the previous month.

Adherence to this system produces an arithmetic balance between the amount of money advanced by the lender at any point in time and the value of the project which stands as security for the loan, since the value of the security increases as the project is built. The value of the security is increased by the value of the bricks and mortar that are introduced upon the property.

§ 6.09 Optional Advances

As we have seen, in some states mechanics lien claims take their priority from the commencement of visible construction work on the jobsite. In some states a claim of lien takes priority from the date when the *claimant* started to supply work or materials to the project. In one state, Maryland, mechanics lien claims take their priority from the day when judgment of foreclosure is entered. In all states, a mechanics lien claimant will hope to establish priority over the mortgage securing the construction loan. If the construction loan mortgage takes priority over the mechanics lien claim, the owner might have no equity in the property and therefore there would be bidders at the sheriff's sale.

In the first instance, the priority of the mortgage securing the construction loan is determined by the date of its recording in the county recorder's office. But even if a mortgage securing a construction loan was recorded before any construction work began, claims of mechanics lien will have priority over "optional advances", if any, disbursed by the lender to the borrower.

As we have noted, construction loan funds are customarily disbursed monthly during the progress of the work. So long as these disbursements are obligatory, they take priority over mechanics lien claims. However, disbursements that are optional lose their priority.

Assume that a construction loan agreement provides that the owner will remove the effect of any recorded claim of mechanics lien within ten days. Assume the owner fails to do so and the lender complains about it. Assume that the lender nevertheless grudgingly continues to make disbursements from the construction loan account in order to keep the job going. Assume that the construction loan agreement provides that the lender has the right to withhold disbursements in the event of a default under the construction loan agreement. Here, the disbursements made after the lender learned of the default would be optional advances, since they were disbursements from the loan account that the borrower could not legally require the lender to pay.

The priority of the mortgage securing the construction loan is then divided into two parts: the amount securing obligatory advances has priority over mechanics lien claims and the amount securing optional advances is inferior to, and subject to, the mechanics lien claims.

The student who compares the provisions of a typical construction loan agreement with the vicissitudes of a construction project (particularly a troubled construction project) is likely to conclude that the borrower can scarcely avoid defaults and therefore the typical construction loan disbursement will likely be characterized as an optional advance. The law treats each optional advance as if it were a new loan made by the lender with knowledge of the establishment of mechanics lien rights, which therefore take priority over the new loan represented by the optional advance. From an operational point of view, the truth of the matter is that the advance of construction loan draws by the lender is not truly optional. The lender knows very well that without a monthly infusion of construction loan funds, all work on the job will come to a halt. An uncompleted construction project produces no revenue, and therefore the borrower who depends upon the revenue from a construction project to make the payments on a mortgage securing a construction loan will go into default if the project is not completed. A construction lender that forecloses on a partially completed construction project will almost inevitably suffer severe loss because the value of the partially completed project is almost never sufficient to cover the amount of the loan.

§ 6.10 Mechanics Lien Releases

The most direct and obvious way to avoid mechanics lien claims is to make certain that every potential lien claimant receives its share of every progress payment. Payment, obviously, is a good defense to a claim of mechanics lien.

One way that the owner can insure payment of a subcontractor is to make a direct payment to that subcontractor and then subtract the amount of the payment from the earnings of the prime contractor.

A common variation of this technique is to make payment both to the prime and the subcontractor by means of a joint check, which is to say, a check payable jointly to prime and sub. This gives the subcontractor an opportunity to protect its own interests by refusing to endorse the joint check until paid by the prime contractor. A flaw in the system occurs, however, if the prime contractor makes payment to the subcontractor with a check that is later returned by the bank for insufficient funds. Now the subcontractor, although it endorsed the joint check, has not been paid. Thus the subcontractor may still resort to the foreclosure of a mechanics lien claim.

Owners, in order to guard against this scenario, may include a notation on the back of the check to the effect that endorsement of the check acknowledges payment of the full face amount of the check, and each endorser releases all mechanics lien rights against the project through the date of the check.

The owner's most severe risk is the claim of mechanics lien that "comes out of nowhere". Such a claim could be recorded by a material supplier to a sub-subcontractor, for example, who was never present on the job because the sub-subcontractor picked up the materials from the supplier's yard. How was the owner to know that this material supplier might lien the job?

It might occur to the owner that it would be good policy to require the contractor and all subcontractors, as a part of their contract documents, to waive mechanics lien rights. In most states, however, such an advance, or "executory" waiver, is void and invalid.

In states that have adopted a preliminary notice system, this problem is solved because the only claimants who may assert mechanics lien claims are those who have given the proper preliminary notices. The owner in such cases identifies those claimants who have established the right to record a claim of lien by making a roster of those who have given preliminary notices. The owner is then in a position to insure that all the potential mechanics lien claimants receive their share of every progress payment.

In processing progress payments, the owner may rely on releases instead of, or in addition to, direct payment or joint checks. The form of release depends upon state law. In California, for example, the form of release is dictated by the legislature, and non-conforming forms are invalid.

A mechanics lien release may be conditional or unconditional. An unconditional release acknowledges payment for all work and materials delivered to the job and fully and unconditionally releases all mechanics lien rights. A conditional release, however, is not effective until the check representing a progress payment has cleared the bank.

Releases given in exchange for progress payments usually apply to all work and material delivered to the job before the date of the payment period to which the progress payment applies. It is therefore necessary for personnel who are processing progress payments to verify that the amount of the check tendered in payment matches the amount stated on the release, and that the date of the release matches the period for which the progress payment is tendered.

In some states, Illinois, for example, it is a crime to fraudulently obtain a waiver of lien from a subcontractor and fail to pay for it within 30 days after receiving the final payment.

§ 6.11 Effective Releases

Let us suppose that an owner requires a prime contractor to execute a mechanics lien release and deliver it to the owner before the owner will make final payment for construction work performed by the prime contractor. The prime contractor signs and delivers the release, but the payment is never made. The prime contractor then records a mechanics lien claim, and files an action to foreclose it. At the trial, the owner introduces the release in evidence and argues that the action should be dismissed because the contractor released its claim of lien.

In such a case, the release would be ineffective. A release is a form of contract by which one party promises not to make a claim or enforce a right. But to be enforceable a contract must be supported by consideration. Here, the consideration for the contract failed, and therefore the release is ineffective, because the owner failed to make the promised payment in exchange for the release.

Now let us suppose that a prime contractor induces a subcontractor to sign and deliver a release by explaining that the owner won't make the next progress payment to the prime contractor until the prime contractor has delivered releases from all subcontractors. The subcontractor gives the release to the prime contractor, who delivers it to the owner. After reviewing this and other releases, the owner issues the next progress payment to the prime contractor, but the prime contractor fails to make payment to the subcontractor. Subcontractor records a claim of lien and files an action of foreclosure. At the trial, the owner introduces the release in evidence and moves for a dismissal. Here, the court would grant the motion. Although the subcontractor did not get paid, nevertheless the owner relied upon the release to its detriment, by making a payment to the prime contractor. This detrimental reliance would make it inequitable to enforce the claim of lien. The subcontractor delivered the release to the prime contractor for the very purpose of inducing the owner to make a progress payment. Once the owner has detrimentally relied on the release by making the progress payment, the subcontractor would be estopped from denying the effectiveness or validity of the release.

Here, the subcontractor might have insured its payment, or avoided releasing its right to claim a lien, by signing a conditional release. A conditional release is one that specifies its effectiveness is conditioned upon payment of a certain amount. The owner could then insure payment either by making direct payment to the subcontractor or by issuing a check payable jointly to the prime contractor and the subcontractor.

§ 6.12 Release Bond

In many states it is possible to remove the effect of a recorded claim of lien by recording in the county recorder's office a release bond. The release bond is executed by a principal and surety who agree that they will pay any amount that the court finds due on the claim of lien. The release bond therefore becomes a substitute for the security afforded by the claim of lien, and from the date of recording, the effect of the claim of lien is removed from the owner's title.

For an owner or construction lender with excellent bonding capacity, to record a release bond is an attractive way to free the title to property from a recorded claim of lien and thereby make it possible to sell or refinance the property. Many owners, however, lack the bonding capacity to be able to obtain a release bond without posting collateral with the surety. This would mean, for example, that in order to obtain a $100,000 release bond an owner would be required not only to pay an annual premium of perhaps $800 to $1,000 but also would be required to post $100,000 collateral with the surety in order to protect the surety against any possible loss from issuing the bond.

§ 6.13 Title Company Indemnity

The effect of a claim of lien may sometimes be avoided by an owner who has a good relationship with a title company through the use of a title company indemnity agreement. This procedure is available to good customers of title companies who are financially responsible. If a developer wishes to sell or refinance property that is encumbered by a claim of lien, the developer may induce a title company to write a policy of title insurance that ignores the claim. The title company may be willing to do so if the developer signs an agreement to indemnify the title company against any loss that it might sustain as a result of issuing the policy without disclosing the claim of lien.

§ 6.14 Motion to Release Lien

The courts recognize that the recording of a claim of mechanics lien can cause hardship to a property owner. In most states a claim of lien may be recorded without any judicial scrutiny and without posting a bond to guard the owner against loss in the event that the claim of lien is unjustified. A prompt remedy is therefore needed to enable an owner to invoke the jurisdiction of a court to remove an unjustified lien. A motion to release a claim of lien is therefore available in most states by means of which an owner may seek prompt judicial action and, in a proper case, the court will issue an order releasing the lien.

§ 6.15 Constitutionality of the Mechanics Lien Statutes

Whether a claim of mechanics lien is subject to constitutional attack is a question of some debate. A recent case decided by the United States Supreme Court dealing with attachment, and not with mechanics liens, established some principles of due process that have lead some authorities to question the continued viability of the mechanics lien remedy. In most states the county recorder will record a claim of lien tendered by anyone who has the recording fee, and thus the owner's property is encumbered without the protection that would be afforded by any pre-lien judicial scrutiny. The recording of a lien may have a severe impact on the economic well-being of an owner, because the recording may be a breach of an owner's obligations under a mortgage, and moreover the recording may make it impossible for the owner to sell or refinance the property. It may therefore be questioned whether the recording of a claim of lien without judicial scrutiny violates due process of law. The argument is particularly cogent in states where, as we have seen, the lien claimant may be a stranger to the owner.

§ 6.16 Enforcement Procedures

There is considerable variation from state to state in the time limits, documents, and procedures for claiming and enforcing claims of mechanics lien. The following exposition is therefore generalized, and the student should refer for particulars to the laws of the state where the project is located.

Most states, in order to guard against "secret" liens, require that a lien claimant give a preliminary notice to the property owner, and sometimes also to the prime contractor and construction lender. The purpose of the notice is to inform the owner that the potential claimant is furnishing work or materials to the project and, if unpaid, reserves the right to record a claim of lien. The notice discloses the name and address of the potential claimant and the type of work or materials being supplied, and sometimes includes an estimate of the value of the work or materials to be supplied. The notices may be given personally or by mail. Some states require that the notices be given by certified mail.

A claimant who fails to give the required preliminary notice within the time specified by statute loses the right to claim a mechanics lien. The claimant loses lien rights even if it is shown that the owner had actual knowledge of the fact that the claimant was supplying work or materials to the project. This is because the purpose of the notice is not only to convey knowledge, but also to notify the owner that the claimant reserves the right to record a claim of lien.

Claim of lien. The claim of mechanics lien that is recorded in the county recorder's office is usually a simple document that includes the name of the claimant, the amount of the claim, and a description of the property where the project is located. The claim of lien also includes the name of the owner of the property and a description of the type of work or materials supplied by the claimant.

The claim of lien is required to be recorded within a period of time, usually 30 to 90 days, after the completion of the entire work of improvement.

Notice of completion. A notice of completion is a document that may be recorded by a property owner in order to reduce the amount of time within which a claim of lien may be recorded. This document gives notice that the construction project has been completed and therefore notifies potential lien claimants that they must look to their rights. The notice of completion must be recorded within a few days, usually ten, after the completion of the project and thereby reduces the time limit for recording a claim of lien, for example, from 90 days to 30 days.

Owners sometimes misunderstand the function of a notice of completion. The function is not to signify acceptance of, or satisfaction with, the contractor's work but the fact that the job is finished and work has stopped.

Notice of cessation. It sometimes occurs that a contractor walks off a job or is thrown off a job and the work stops. The owner now needs to employ another contractor to finish the work. But the owner also needs to know if there are any mechanics lien claims. By recording a notice of cessation, the owner can start the time running for recording lien claims even though the job is not complete.

Foreclosure suit. Since a recorded claim of mechanics lien clouds the owner's title, the claimant should diligently prosecute the claim to foreclosure. Therefore a short statute of limitations is provided, usually 90 days, for filing foreclosure suit.

Notice of lis pendens. A mechanics lien foreclosure suit is filed in the courthouse while a claim of mechanics lien is recorded in the county recorder's office. A person searching title and finding a recorded mechanics lien is entitled to assume that the lien has expired unless there is evidence in the county recorder's office that suit has been filed within the statutory time. The recorded notice of lis pendens fulfills this function, as it gives notice that suit has been filed and therefore that a person dealing with the property will take title subject to the outcome of the foreclosure suit. It is important to the claimant that the notice of lis pendens contain names of all owners of the property, since the failure to name an owner would leave that owner free to deal with the property free of the mechanics lien claim.

§ 6.17 Stop Notices

For obvious reasons mechanics liens are not permitted on public property. It would be anomalous indeed for a police station or a city hall to be sold at public auction to the highest bidder. Legislatures in many states have, however, provided those who have mechanics lien rights on private projects with stop notice rights on public projects. A stop notice is a lien that attaches not to real property but to money. The law envisions that a public agency, when it undertakes a construction project, sets aside a certain amount of money to pay for the work. By giving a stop notice to the public agency, the person who contributes work or materials to the project may obtain what might be loosely described as a lien on the fund of construction money. The ultimate end result of the enforcement of a stop notice is for the court to order the public agency to pay the money to the claimant. The agency, of course, withholds this money from the prime contractor's progress payments, and thus the filing of a stop notice on a public project is about as welcome to the agency and the prime contractor as would be the recording of a mechanics lien to the owner and prime contractor on a private project.

In many states the law does not require a public agency to pay a stop notice claimant unless the agency thereafter has remaining in the construction account a sufficient amount to finish the project.

§ 6.18 Stop Notice Procedures

The stop notice procedures and time limits are analogous to those established for mechanics liens. Similar preliminary notice requirements are imposed. There is a short statute of limitations for filing an enforcement action. If more than one stop notice is filed and the agency has insufficient funds to pay all, the funds are divided pro rata among the claimants. The prime contractor may release the funds by filing a release bond with the public agency.

§ 6.19 Stop Notices on Private Projects

Legislatures in some states have given stop notice rights on private, as well as public projects. The stop notice remedy extends to private projects in California, Indiana, Mississippi, New Jersey, and New Mexico. Here, the stop notice applies to construction funds in the hands of the owner and also to construction funds in the hands of the construction lender. A stop notice to a construction lender must be supported by a bond, given by the claimant, that insures against damages to the lender and the project owner in the event the stop notice is determined to be invalid. The function of the stop notice is to intercept funds before they are paid to the prime contractor.

The filing of a stop notice is extremely unwelcome to a construction lender, since it portends the possibility of a judgment being entered against the lender. The filing of a stop notice is a breach of the construction loan agreement and therefore the lender has the right to insist that the borrower immediately remove it, or deposit sufficient funds in the construction loan account to satisfy the stop notice and at the same time insure that there is sufficient money remaining in the construction loan account to finish the project. This theoretical right, however, is often unenforceable because the owner may not have funds at hand. The rights of stop notice claimants take priority over the right of the construction lender to utilize the funds in the construction loan account for the completion of the project. The construction lender has this dilemma: whether to withhold construction funds from the borrower/builder and be left the defaulted and uncompleted construction project as security for its loan, or to ignore the stop notice, keep the job going and defend against the claim in court. The most rational decision often is to ignore the stop notice and keep the job going.

§ 6.20 Equitable Lien

Let us suppose that a contractor who is negotiating with an owner for the construction of an apartment building project wants assurances that the owner has adequate financing to pay the contract price. The owner has arranged construction financing with a savings and loan association. The contractor calls the loan officer and verifies the fact that the savings and loan association has set aside $700,000 in a construction loan account to pay for the cost of constructing the project. Since the contract price is $650,000, the contractor relies on the construction loan funds for payment, signs the contract with the owner, and starts work. During the course of the project, the owner runs into financial difficulties and fails to pay real estate taxes and insurance premiums for the project. In order to protect its interests, the savings and loan association (as it is permitted to do by the construction loan agreement) withdraws money from the construction loan account to pay the taxes and insurance premiums. As a result, the construction loan account is reduced by $100,000 and the owner is unable to make the last payment of $50,000 to the contractor.

Upon the completion of the project, the owner is required by the construction loan agreement to pay off the construction loan with the proceeds of a takeout loan. The takeout loan does not fund, however, because of a mechanics lien claim recorded by the project architect. The construction loan therefore goes into default and the savings and loan association forecloses the mortgage securing the construction loan. The savings and loan association then sells the project to a third party and uses the proceeds of the sale to satisfy the balance due on the loan. Under these circumstances, does the savings and loan association have any financial responsibility to the contractor?

The savings and loan association has made no contractual promises to the contractor, but its role in the project was confined to providing construction financing.

The contractor argues that it should have an equitable lien on the construction loan funds because the construction work performed by the contractor increased the value of the project that was the security for the loan, and the savings and loan association got the benefit of the contractor's work when the project was sold after foreclosure of the mortgage. Moreover, the contractor performed its work in reliance on the construction funds, and that reliance was partly induced by the loan officer who confirmed the existence and amount of the construction loan account. Under such facts, the contractor has an *equitable lien* on the construction loan account which is recognized and enforced by the courts. An equitable lien may also arise in favor of subcontractors and material suppliers. A subcontractor or supplier, before performing work on a project, may check with the financial institution to see whether funds are available to pay for the work or materials. If such a claimant justifiably relies on assurances from a financial institution that construction loan funds are available, an equitable lien may arise under state law in favor of the subcontractor or supplier.

The end result of the successful enforcement of a claim of equitable lien is that the construction lender is required to pay the amount of the lien to the claimant. In New York, the mechanics lien law contains trust fund provisions under which all funds paid to an owner, contractor, or subcontractor for the improvement of real estate constitute trust funds held by the party receiving them as trustee for parties who provide labor or materials to the trustee. Thus an owner receiving construction loan funds from a construction lender, or a contractor receiving construction funds from an owner, does not have an interest in those funds until the claims of all trust beneficiaries have been settled. A contractor therefore cannot take money it received to build a house and use it to pay office rent or the salary of a secretary. The money must first be used to pay subcontractors, laborers, and material suppliers.

The trust fund law creates a fiduciary relationship and prohibits diversion of the funds to purposes not directly related to the improvement of the property.

The trustee is required by New York law to keep books of account showing the allocation of income and expense to each trust it administers. Failure to keep the required records is presumptive evidence that the trustee diverted the funds.

§ 6.21 Payment Bonds

An owner or a construction lender, wary of mechanics liens and stop notices, may require a prime contractor to furnish a payment bond. Although this raises the price of the construction project by the amount of the premium on the payment bond, therefore adding something on the order of one-half of one percent to the price of construction, the bond guarantees that the prime contractor will see to the payment of all claims that might ripen into mechanics lien or stop notice claims. Thus the payment bond guarantees not only that the prime contractor will pay its own direct subcontractors and suppliers, but also sub-subcontractors, and their suppliers. (The payment bond is usually combined with a performance bond that guarantees the prime contractor will perform all work required under the contract, and the combined premium for the two bonds runs between $7.00 and $10.00 per thousand.)

§ 6.22 The Miller Act

The Miller Act (40 U.S.C. § 270(a)ff.) requires prime contractors on federal work to furnish payment bonds for the protection of those who supply work or materials to federal projects. The bond protects the claims of subcontractors and their subcontractors, and it does not protect the claims of subcontractors or material suppliers beyond the second tier. Material suppliers who supply materials to other material suppliers are not covered.

Recovery under the Miller Act payment bond does not require that materials actually be incorporated into the work. Recovery is allowed if materials are supplied for the work, the material supplier had a good faith belief that the materials were intended for the specified work, and the claimant has not been paid.

The courts are divided on the question of whether delay damages are recoverable under the Miller Act. As a general rule, attorneys fees are not recoverable.

In order to protect its claim, any claimant other than a supplier or a subcontractor with a direct contractual relationship with the prime contractor must give a 90-day notice to the prime contractor. This notice must be given by registered mail within 90 days after the claimant has completed its work on the project, or supplied its last materials to the project.

The notice must include the amount of the claim and the name of the party who ordered the work or material. An action to enforce rights under a Miller Act bond must be brought within one year after the claimant last furnished work or materials.

Most states have enacted their "Little Miller Acts" for the protection of the claims of those who supply services or materials to state and local public works projects.

§ 6.23 Cumulative Remedies

Mechanics lien claims, stop notices, equitable liens and payment bond claims are cumulative remedies. A claimant may rely upon all remedies, and enforce them concurrently.

CHAPTER 7

ARBITRATION

Chapter 7

§ 7.01 Enforceability of Arbitration Agreements

Construction contracts more often than not include arbitration clauses requiring that disputes arising out of or related to the performance of the contract or the interpretation thereof be decided by arbitration. Up until the 20's and 30's, common law courts were generally hostile to arbitration agreements and held that, although arbitration awards were enforceable, arbitration agreements were not. Therefore a party to an arbitration agreement could ignore the arbitration clause and resolve its disputes in court. All this changed when Congress adopted the Federal Arbitration Act in 1925. Since then most states have adopted versions of the Uniform Arbitration Act. Arbitration agreements are now enforceable in all states except Nebraska.

This means that if a party to an agreement containing an arbitration clause files suit against the other party, the defendant may file with the court a petition to compel arbitration, and the court will order the parties to arbitrate their dispute as required by the arbitration clause in the contract.

> Plumbing subcontractor filed a lawsuit against a general contractor, who filed a motion to compel arbitration in accordance with an arbitration clause in the subcontract document. Motion was denied by the trial court. REVERSED. The court must grant an application for an order to proceed with arbitration whenever the parties have agreed to arbitrate and the court is satisfied there is no substantial issue as to whether such an agreement was made.

Beemik Builders & Constructors v Huber Plumbing, 476 So 2d 780 (Fla Dist Ct App 1985).

§ 7.02 Waiver of Right to Compel Arbitration

The parties may, of course, expressly waive their right to compel arbitration of a dispute. Waiver of the right to compel arbitration may also be inferred from conduct. If parties litigate their dispute to final judgment there can be no doubt that both parties have waived the right to compel arbitration.

Upon being served with a lawsuit, the party who wishes to preserve its right to resolve the dispute by arbitration should promptly file a petition to compel arbitration, because if the party files an answer to the plaintiff's complaint and goes on to defend the lawsuit the courts will, at some point, find that the defendant has waived the right to compel arbitration.

> Subcontractor filed suit against a prime contractor for $29,230.08 allegedly due as a balance for subcontract work. The prime contractor answered the complaint, subcontractor requested a trial date, a trial date was set, and the subcontractor made a motion for summary judgment. After all these court proceedings had occurred, the prime contractor made a motion to compel arbitration. The motion was denied. AFFIRMED. The contractor waived its right to arbitration by failing to request arbitration until a late stage of the lawsuit.

Bramcon Gen Contractors, Inc v Wigley Constr Co, 774 SW2d 826 (Tex Ct App 1989).

> Owner filed suit against a contractor alleging negligent construction of a roof on a warehouse and office facility. The contractor filed an answer and a third party complaint seeking indemnity from a subcontractor, and served numerous interrogatories on the owner. The contractor then moved to stay the litigation pending arbitration. The trial court denied the motion. REVERSED. Participation in litigation does not waive the right to demand arbitration absent a showing of prejudice to the adverse party. Examples of prejudice would be the expense of a long trial, loss of helpful evidence, steps taken in litigation to the detriment of a party, or use of discovery procedures not available in arbitration to the prejudice of the party opposing arbitration. Here, in the absence of a finding of prejudice, the denial of the motion to compel arbitration was improper.

Servomation Corp v Hickory Construction Co, 316 NC 543, 342 SE2d 853 (1986).

> After ten months defending a lawsuit by a hospital, and after filing a motion for summary judgment, obtaining discovery, and

> taking depositions, and after losing its motion for summary judgment, a contractor demanded arbitration. HELD: The contractor waived its right to arbitration by participating in litigation. It never brought up the request for arbitration until after it lost its motion for summary judgment. The contractor's actions were inconsistent with any intent to assert its right to arbitrate.

St. Mary's Medical Center v Disco Aluminum Prods Co, 969 F2d 585 (7th Cir 1992).

§ 7.03 Scope of Arbitration Clause

Most arbitration clauses are written with a broad scope so as to include arbitration of all disputes that might arise. It is usually considered disadvantageous to employ an arbitration agreement of narrow scope because then the parties might find themselves involved in arbitration and litigation at the same time. Since an advantage of arbitration is to provide for the swift, simple and efficient resolution of disputes it would be anomalous for the parties to have to arbitrate and litigate different aspects of the same dispute. Nevertheless, arbitration clauses of narrow scope are sometimes encountered such as, for example, might require arbitration only of disputes dealing with interpretation of drawings and specifications.

> Subcontractor filed suit against general contractor to recover payments allegedly due under a contract to perform concrete work. Contractor demanded arbitration. The demand for arbitration was denied. HELD: The only dispute subject to arbitration were those specified for arbitration under the contract. The parties agreed to arbitrate particular issues, such as variations in pay required by alteration work, but they nowhere agreed to arbitrate a dispute dealing with the subcontractor's entitlement to progress payments.

Havens v Safeway Stores, 235 Kan 226, 678 P2d 625 (1984).

A contract for construction of a church included a clause providing for arbitration of all claims and disputes arising out of, or relating to, the contract or the breach thereof. Contractor demanded arbitration, claiming $362,462.28 under a change order. The arbitrator determined that the change order was not signed by trustees who were authorized by the church and therefore the change order was invalid, however the arbitrator allowed the contractor to recover based on quantum meruit. The arbitrator awarded $263,310.97 based on quantum meruit. The trial court confirmed the award. REVERSED. The arbitrator did not have jurisdiction to adjudicate disputes that were not based on the parties' contract.

Trustees/Asbury United Meth Church v Taylor&Parrish, Inc,452SE2d847(Va 1995).

§ 7.04 Enforceability of Arbitration Award

A dispute submitted to arbitration is decided by an *award*. The award is similar to a court judgment but is not directly enforceable. Enforcement is achieved by filing a court petition to confirm the arbitration award. Arbitration awards are usually confirmed in summary proceedings, after which the court judgment, containing the same terms as the award, is enforceable like any other court judgment.

§ 7.05 Deference to the Arbitration Agreement

The statutes governing arbitration, and the courts, generally defer to the agreement of the parties as to matters of arbitration procedure. Therefore most of the arbitration procedures established by statute may be overridden by the agreement of the parties, who are thus encouraged to devise systems of dispute resolution that are to their own liking. Thus, disputes are resolved by a single arbitrator unless the parties elect to have two or more arbitrators. Disputes (in most states) are decided without depositions and discovery unless the parties call for discovery in their arbitration agreement.

§ 7.06 Self-Designed System

The law encourages parties to devise their own variations and modifications to the arbitration system. For example, *subject to the agreement of the parties*, which is to say, in the absence of any contrary agreement, the arbitrator of a dispute is appointed by a court upon the petition of one of the parties. It is customary, however, for the parties to designate the arbitrator, or a method for the selection of the arbitrator, in advance. For example, an arbitrator may be appointed in accordance with the rules of the American Arbitration Association. In another common form of agreement, each party selects an arbitrator and the two arbitrators thus selected mutually appoint the third arbitrator.

In many states, absent any contrary agreement by the parties, arbitration is conducted without depositions and discovery, and an arbitrator's decision is enforceable even if it is contrary to law. The parties may, however, in the arbitration agreement, provide for depositions and discovery and may provide that the decision of the arbitrator must be in accordance with law. The student should therefore remember that any description of the arbitration system is a description of the usual, or customary, operation of the system which, in most respects, is subject to being changed by the agreement of the parties.

§ 7.07 Incorporation of Arbitration Agreement in Construction Documents

Although an arbitration agreement to be enforceable must be in writing, it is not necessary that the writing be signed by the parties, but only that the parties have manifested a mutual intention to be bound by the writing. Thus, in construction documents, an arbitration clause is often included in general conditions that, in turn, are incorporated not only in the prime contract but also in the subcontract documents: thus is achieved the desired result that a dispute between prime contractor and owner, that may also involve work performed by one or more subcontractors, may be resolved by an arbitration proceeding that includes all of the necessary parties.

> A subcontract provided that the prime contractor had the same rights and remedies against the subcontractor as the owner and against the prime contractor under the provisions of the prime contract with respect to the work to be performed by subcontractor. HELD: This language was sufficient to incorporate the arbitration clause of the prime contract documents, and the subcontractor was entitled to arbitrate its delay claim against the prime contractor.

Turner Constr Co v Midwest Curtainwalls, Inc, 187 Ill App 3d 417, 543 NE2d 249 (1989).

Many construction disputes include a contention by a prime contractor or a subcontractor that design, or inspection, or observation of construction, or provision of information, review of shop drawings, or some other architectural or engineering function was performed in a negligent manner. It is good policy, therefore, for the arbitration clause in the general conditions to include a provision that the architect or engineer will become a party to the arbitration and be bound by the award upon the demand of the owner, the prime contractor or a subcontractor. The American Institute of Architects and its insurance advisors prefer to exempt architect and engineer from arbitration proceedings that include the prime contractor and subcontractors, so the arbitration clause found in the AIA general conditions prohibits joinder of architect or engineer in arbitration proceedings between owner, contractor and subcontractors. The standard form of agreement between owner and architect for architectural services, however, does provide for arbitration of disputes between owner and architect.

Envision a dispute between an owner and a prime contractor, subject to arbitration, in which the prime contractor claims to be entitled to extensions of time and extra compensation because of defective uncoordinated drawings. If the arbitration agreement permits the owner to do so, it would like to join the architect in the arbitration proceedings so that the architect could defend its own performance. Absent joinder of the architect, the arbitration award will only determine legal responsibility as between prime contractor and owner. If the arbitrator decides that the prime contractor is entitled to extensions of time and extra compensation because of defective and uncoordinated plans, the award will be in favor of the prime contractor and against the owner. The owner would thereafter commence a separate arbitration proceeding against the architect to recoup for the expense and delay caused by the defective uncoordinated drawings.

Envisioning the possibility of being involved in two separate arbitration proceedings to resolve that which in essence is a single dispute, many owners insist on an arbitration clause that is as comprehensive as the disputes that are likely to arise, and therefore provide that architect, engineer, subcontractors and material suppliers are all required, upon the demand of any party, to participate in arbitration proceedings and be bound by the award provided that they have signed any document that incorporates the arbitration provisions of the general conditions.

> A performance bond incorporated by reference the terms of a construction contract between an owner and a prime contractor for the construction of a warehouse addition. Owner, claiming faulty construction, filed a demand for arbitration against both the contractor and the surety company. The surety sought declaratory judgment that the surety was not compelled to participate in the arbitration proceedings. HELD: Sureties are required to arbitrate issues relating to a performance bond where the performance bond incorporates by reference a contract containing an arbitration clause.

Hoffman v Fidelity & Deposit Co, 734 F Supp 192 (DNJ 1990).

§ 7.08 Selection of the Arbitrator

The selection of the arbitrator is the most important step in any arbitration proceeding. Among the qualities desired in a good construction arbitrator are integrity, experience, impartiality, knowledge of construction, knowledge of construction law, patience, judicial temperament, diligence, and good humor. It is a rare arbitrator who combines all of these qualities, and therefore major construction disputes are often assigned to a tribunal of three arbitrators one of whom is a lawyer, one a contractor or subcontractor, and one a design professional.

The American Arbitration Association, which is the primary provider of arbitration services to the construction industry, subject to the agreement of the parties, usually appoints three arbitrators to hear major cases. For smaller cases, the American Arbitration Association usually provides a single arbitrator who may be a lawyer, contractor, architect or engineer as may be designated by the parties.

Under the AAA rules, arbitration proceedings are initiated by one party filing a demand for arbitration naming the other party or parties as respondent or respondents. The American Arbitration Association administrator reviews the demand for arbitration and any answering statement filed by other parties, to determine the nature of the dispute in order to select appropriate nominee-arbitrators. The nominees are then placed on a list which is sent to the parties, who are invited to strike the names of any nominee-arbitrators deemed undesired. From the remaining nominees, then, the American Arbitration Association appoints the arbitrator or arbitrators.

If all nominee-arbitrators are stricken or unavailable, the AAA presents another list. It sometimes occurs that a party, desiring to obstruct proceedings, strikes all nominees. In cases when an arbitrator or tribunal of arbitrators cannot be appointed after the submission of two lists, the AAA makes an administrative appointment of the arbitrator or arbitrators.

The selection of the arbitrator, however, can be controlled by the parties who may, and often do, devise other methods. In some cases, the parties agree upon the identity of the arbitrator at the time when the contract is signed. Another common method is for each party to appoint an arbitrator, and the two "partisan" arbitrators thus selected appoint the third, or *neutral* arbitrator. The dispute is then decided by an award signed by any two arbitrators. Unlike the neutral arbitrator, though, party-appointed arbitrators are expected to represent the point of view of the party who appointed them. In such cases, all issues of procedure are decided by the neutral arbitrator and the partisan arbitrators serve as advocates rather than as neutral, impartial adjudicators.

An arbitrator or potential arbitrator who discovers any possible conflict of interest must promptly disclose it. The parties may, and sometimes do, waive such conflicts, but in the absence of such a waiver an arbitration award may be vacated by a court of law based on conflict of interest, bias, prejudice, or an impression of possible bias.

The arbitration statutes provide that if for any reason the method selected by the parties for appointment of the arbitrator should fail, the arbitrator will be appointed by a judge.

> In *Delma Engg Corp v K&L Constr Co*, 6 AD2d 710, 174 NYS2d 620, *affd*, 5 NY2d 852, 181 NYS2d 794 (1958), the arbitration clause required arbitration under the rules of the New York Building Congress. At the time of the dispute the congress no longer administered arbitrations, so the court was authorized to appoint three arbitrators from the panel formerly used by the congress.
>
> In *In re Dutchess Community College*, 57 AD2d 555, 393 NYS2d 77 (1977), an arbitration clause provided that disputes relating to the contractor's performance would be determined by the architect in accordance with the construction industry arbitration rules of the American Arbitration Association. The contractor's motion to disqualify the architect as an arbitrator was denied. HELD: The architect was not disqualified from acting as a sole arbitrator even though it had been retained by the owner.
>
> In *Naclerio Contracting Co v City of NY*, 116 AD2d 463, 496 NYS2d 444 (1986), *affd*, 69 NY2d 794, 505 NE2d 625, 513 NYS2d 115 (1987), a sewer construction contract provided that the city's sewer commissioner had the power to review and determine any and all questions in relation to the contract and its performance. HELD:

A party will not be compelled to arbitrate a dispute before an arbitrator who is a party to the dispute. A party cannot serve as an arbitrator in its own case.

§ 7.09 Arbitration Proceedings

Arbitration proceedings closely resemble court proceedings, but they are less formal. An arbitrator sits at the head of the table (or at a head table) and the parties face each other across the table. The parties are almost always represented by lawyers who introduce evidence much as they would in court through the testimony of witnesses and the introduction of exhibits. Witnesses testify under oath, and they are subject to cross examination. Arbitrators are not required to follow the rules of evidence (absent a contrary provision in the arbitration clause) but receive such evidence as they deem appropriate and reliable. Arbitrators may exclude evidence that is cumulative or of slight value when compared to the time and trouble of producing it.

In construction arbitration, much testimony is given by expert witnesses. The parties themselves are often experts, and the arbitrator or one or more of the arbitrators may also have extensive expertise. For example, an arbitration dealing with structural engineering problems may feature a structural engineer as one of the arbitrators.

After opening statements, the claimant presents its evidence and rests. The respondent then presents its evidence and rests. Thereafter claimant and respondent present rebuttal evidence until the parties and the arbitrator are satisfied with the state of the record and, after final arguments, the arbitrator takes the matter under submission. An award in writing must be rendered within the time permitted by law or by the agreement of the parties (usually 30 days).

Arbitration proceedings may be recorded by a court reporter at the option and expense of the parties. Each party contributes an equal share to the fees of the neutral arbitrator usually paid daily or weekly in advance. The award may require the losing party to reimburse the fees of the neutral arbitrator to the prevailing party. If the arbitration agreement so provides, the arbitrator may award attorneys fees to the prevailing party.

A visit to the jobsite is often an important part of arbitration proceedings.

It sometimes occurs that a party, dissatisfied with some aspect of an arbitration proceeding, seeks interlocutory court review. Most courts, however, resist being brought into an interlocutory review of arbitration proceedings because of the expense and delay that this entails. Arbitrators are expected to make their own decisions on matters of evidence and procedure subject to possible review at the time when the award is brought before the court to be vacated or confirmed.

In order to afford due process, the arbitrators should not take evidence except when both parties are present. Parties may often stipulate that arbitrators may make a jobsite visit without the parties being present, but absent such a stipulation, such a jobsite visit should not be undertaken unless the parties are present.

It is obviously improper for an arbitrator to receive evidence from one party unless the other party is present, and able to observe the production of evidence and produce its own evidence to meet the evidence produced by the other party.

> In an arbitration between a subcontractor and a contractor arising out of construction of a school building, a dispute was submitted to arbitration under a written agreement. The agreement explicitly provided that the arbitrators were authorized to visit the jobsite provided all three of them were to be present at the time of the visit. One of the arbitrators examined the jobsite alone, without the presence of the other arbitrators, and one of the arbitrators had an ex parte conversation with one of the parties to the dispute concerning the case. AWARD VACATED. Arbitrators had no right to consider facts not submitted into evidence at the hearings. It was misconduct for an arbitrator to seek evidence through an independent investigation, and the visit by one of the arbitrators to the jobsite was a specific violation of the arbitration agreement.

Fred J Brotherton, Inc v Kreielsheimer, 8 NJ 66, 83 A2d 707 (1951).

Although one case has held that an arbitrator may consult an outside attorney in reaching a decision, such a practice should probably be avoided.

> In *Griffith Co v San Diego College for Women*, 45 Cal 2d 501, 289 P2d 476 (1955), a dispute between a contractor and a college owner was submitted to arbitration before a panel of three arbitrators. One of the arbitrators conferred with an outside attorney

before the award was made. The outside attorney drafted the opinion for the arbitrators to sign. HELD: This was not misconduct. The arbitrator had informed both of the other arbitrators that it intended to seek legal confirmation of whatever opinion was arrived at, and neither arbitrator made any objection. The court held that it is entirely proper for arbitrators to obtain from disinterested persons of acknowledged skill such information or advice in reference to technical questions submitted to them as may be necessary to enable them to come to correct conclusions, provided that the award is the result of their own judgment after obtaining such information.

Due process requires that arbitrators give the parties a fair opportunity to present their cases. There are occasions when due process requires arbitrators to grant a continuance.

In *Omego Cont, Inc v Maropakis Cont, Inc*, 160 AD2d 942, 554 NYS2d 664 (1990), a dispute between a contractor and a subcontractor was submitted to arbitration. On the second day of hearings, the subcontractor presented its case. After the contractor's attorney advised the arbitrator that the contractor would be late because of car trouble, the arbitrator denied a request for continuance and later denied a request to reopen the hearings. AWARD VACATED. The decision to grant or refuse a continuance is within the discretion of an arbitrator, but in this case the refusal to continue the matter foreclosed the presentation of material and pertinent evidence and therefore the arbitrator abused its discretion by refusing to grant the continuance.

In *Bay State York Co v Canter Constr Co*, 5 Mass App Ct 192, 360 NE2d 900 (1977), in an arbitration between a contractor and an owner, hearings were postponed several times at the request of contractor's attorney. The arbitrators finally denied the request for a further adjournment. AWARD CONFIRMED. Refusal to grant another continuance, requested by the contractor so that the contractor could employ new counsel to replace the attorney it had discharged, was not an abuse of discretion. The contractor had delayed the proceedings several times and the arbitrators might have believed that the discharge of counsel was mere pretext to further delay the proceedings.

Arbitrators have wide discretion as to the introduction of evidence, and may either receive evidence that would not be admissible in court (for example, hearsay evidence) or may refuse to hear cumulative evidence.

> In *JJK Constr, Inc v Rosenberg,* 141 AD2d 507, 529 NYS2d 339 (1988), a contractor's action to foreclose a mechanics lien against an owner was submitted to arbitration and the arbitrator awarded $120,600 plus 9% interest to the contractor. AWARD CONFIRMED. The owner demanded that the contractor produce its original payroll records, and the arbitrator declined to order that the records be produced. HELD: An arbitrator is not bound by substantive laws and procedures governing litigation.

§ 7.10 The Expense of Arbitration

A supposed advantage of arbitration is that arbitration proceedings are less expensive than court proceedings: and so, indeed, they usually are. Bear in mind, however, that the arbitrators and any arbitration administrator (such as the American Arbitration Association or JAMS/ Endispute) must be paid by the parties, whereas the salaries of judges and the cost of administering the judicial system are largely paid out of the public treasury. Therefore, the resolution of a lengthy construction dispute by arbitration may cost more than court proceedings would cost, even though arbitration proceedings of reasonable length are indeed less expensive than comparable court proceedings.

Much of the expense of court proceedings is imposed by two things that are usually not present in arbitration proceedings: discovery and motion practice. Modern discovery is often abused to burden the opposing party rather than used in a true search for information. In most states, discovery is not permitted in arbitration except as otherwise agreed by the parties. It is not customary for arbitrators to entertain motions.

> In *Lutz Engg Co v Sterling Engg & Constr Co,* 112 RI 605, 314 A2d 8 (1974), a contractor in the midst of arbitrating a dispute with a subcontractor sought a court order for depositions and discovery. HELD: A party to an arbitration proceeding has no right to discovery. Discovery purportedly in aid of arbitration proceedings will not in reality aid, but would introduce hardship. Arbitration

once undertaken should continue freely without being subjected to a judicial restraint that would tend to render the proceedings neither one thing nor the another, but transform them into a hybrid, part judicial, and part arbitrational.

§ 7.11 Speed

One reason for the rapidly growing popularity of arbitration and other methods of alternate dispute resolution is that litigation is slow and, in many states, it is getting slower. As Congress and the state legislatures modify, strengthen, and improve the criminal justice system, the civil calendar loses judicial time to the criminal calendar, which causes delay in the processing of civil disputes. Civil judges in many states are being overwhelmed with impossible workloads with many judges disposing of 20 or 30 motions every day, which does not allow much time for careful judicial study and reflection.

Under ordinary circumstances it may take 20 or 30 days to appoint an arbitrator and another 60 to 90 days for final resolution of a construction dispute provided the parties do not agree to continuances. Arbitrators are usually reluctant to grant continuances even if they are agreed to by both parties. Speedy arbitration is often frustrated, however, by the inability of the parties and their attorneys to give accurate estimates of the number of hearings required for the resolution of a dispute. If the parties estimate that five hearings will be required the matter is set down for five hearings. If more hearings are required they will have to await available time on the calendars of the parties and the arbitrators. Under-estimation of the number of hearings required is by far the most significant factor that delays arbitration proceedings.

Nevertheless, it is only a rare case that is not resolved in less than a year when the civil calendars in the courts of some states are reaching four, five or more years.

§ 7.12 Remedies and the Award

An arbitration award must be in writing signed by the neutral arbitrator, or a majority of arbitrators. The award should finally resolve all disputes between the parties, and is usually expressed in monetary terms. Unless the agreement of the parties provides otherwise, an arbitrator is not required to write an opinion or give reasons for an award. Many arbitrators are reluctant to write opinions because of an exaggerated fear that the content of the opinion might give the losing party grounds to attack the award. This is a source of frustration to some parties, especially losing ones who have a hard time understanding how they might have lost a case of such obvious merit.

Although they usually express their awards in monetary terms, arbitrators are not so limited. They may make interlocutory orders for the preservation of the subject of a dispute or for the preservation of evidence. Arbitrators may grant injunctive relief. For example, an arbitration award may require a contractor to remove mechanics lien claims recorded by subcontractors against the owner's property, and thereupon order the owner to make a certain payment or payments to the contractor. An arbitrator could also issue an award requiring the contractor to repair defective work. An arbitrator could issue an award requiring a contractor to sign paperwork needed for a certificate of occupancy. An arbitrator could issue an award prohibiting a contractor from stopping work, or prohibiting an owner from ejecting a contractor from a job.

> In *David Co v Jim W Miller Constr, Inc*, 428 NW2d 590 (Minn Ct App 1988), *affd*, 444 NW2d 836 (Minn 1989), an arbitrator in a construction defect dispute between a property owner and a contractor awarded the owner $884,476 in return for which the owner was ordered to convey the title to the property to the contractor, or, in default thereof, the owner was to pay the contractor $497,925. AWARD CONFIRMED. The power to create a remedy is an indispensable part of an arbitrator's jurisdiction. Arbitrators may give innovative, even unique remedies.

There are certain provisional remedies, however, that are not available in arbitration and to obtain which a party must seek the intervention of a court. For example, an arbitrator could not issue a writ of attachment or a writ of execution or authorize the recording of a notice of lis pendens. In most states, however, a party may apply to a court for provisional remedies while at the same time proceeding to resolve a dispute by arbitration.

> In *Marsch v Williams*, 23 Cal App 4th 238, 28 Cal Rptr 2d 402 (1994), an arbitration panel appointed one of its members as a receiver to supervise the dissolution of a partnership. REVERSED. The arbitrators had no power to appoint a receiver. Receivership is a proceeding jealously guarded by the courts. A party to an arbitration

agreement seeking the appointment of a receiver should apply to the court, and not to the arbitrator, for such relief.

An arbitration award may not normally be vacated because of an error in law. Arbitrators are often laypersons, not learned in the law and may base their awards on broad concepts of justice and equity.

In *Hembree v Broadway Realty & Trust Co*, 151 Ariz 418, 728 P2d 288 (1986), a developer sought to vacate an arbitration award that gave compensation to a homeowner for a defective roof. The developer argued that the arbitrator's interpretation of the law of implied warranty was erroneous. HELD: Whether the theory of implied warranty was applicable to the case was a question for the arbitrator. A court not may inquire as to whether errors of law were made by an arbitrator in reaching its decision.

In *Trident Tech College v Lucas & Stubbs, Ltd*, 285 SC 98, 333 SE2d 781 (1985), *cert denied*, 474 US 1060 (1986), the college obtained a large arbitration award against a contractor. The contractor alleged that the arbitrator had failed properly to construe the law and had erroneously interpreted the contract. HELD: The proceedings were fundamentally fair and the alleged errors in law did not rise to the level of misconduct.

In *Moncharsch v Heily & Blase*, 3 Cal 4th 1, 832 P2d 899, 10 Cal Rptr 2d 183 (1992), the court held that an arbitration award may not be vacated for error in law. The risk that an arbitrator might make an error in law is acceptable to parties who voluntarily agree to bear that risk in return for a quick and inexpensive resolution to their dispute. Arbitration awards may be vacated only on those grounds specified in the statute, such as fraud, corruption, undue means, misconduct, and failure to grant a due process hearing. Error in law is not a ground for vacating an award.

The courts are split on whether arbitrators are authorized to award punitive damages in the absence of a contractual provision authorizing such an award. Courts in California, New Mexico, and Alabama have approved awards that included punitive damages, while courts in Florida and Illinois have taken a contrary view.

§ 7.13 Confirm or Vacate Arbitration Award

Confirmation of award. An arbitration award has the legal effect of a contract between the parties: they are legally required to comply with the terms of the award. If the losing party refuses to comply, the winning party may apply to the court to confirm the award. Confirmation is a summary proceeding requiring about 30 days. The petition to confirm shows that a dispute was subject to arbitration, that an arbitration was held, and that an award was issued by the arbitrator. A copy of the award is attached to the petition. The court must confirm the award unless it is vacated or corrected.

If the award is confirmed, judgment is entered on the award. The judgment may then be enforced by the sheriff or marshall, as any other judgment.

Correction of the award. If the award is deficient in arithmetic, spelling, or some other matter of form, the court may correct the award, and then confirm it as corrected. The arbitrator also has jurisdiction to make such corrections at the request of a party, but once an award has been signed and delivered, neither the arbitrator nor the court may make any change of substance. If an award is erroneous or incorrect and it cannot be confirmed or corrected, it must be vacated.

Vacation of award. Courts are reluctant to vacate arbitration awards. Parties usually resort to arbitration because they seek an expedient and efficient resolution that is final. When an award is vacated the parties lose the benefit of the time and expense devoted to the proceedings. They must start all over again with another arbitrator. Nevertheless, an award may be so seriously defective (or the procedure that produced the award so unfair or improper) that the award must be vacated. The number of awards vacated rather than confirmed, however, must be very small (probably one or two out of 100).

Corruption. An award, of course, could be vacated for corruption of the arbitrator.

Due process. Arbitration proceedings must be conducted with due process. The arbitrator must take evidence only at a hearing at which both parties are present, or of which both parties have been given proper notice.

If a party refuses to participate in arbitration proceedings after due notice, the arbitrator may issue an ex parte award only if the arbitration agreement so provides. If the arbitration agreement does not allow the arbitrator to issue an ex parte award, and a party refuses to participate in hearings, then the proponent of arbitration must file, in court, a petition to compel arbitration. If the court finds that the parties agreed to arbitrate the dispute, then it must issue an order compelling the recalcitrant party to participate. Thereafter, if the party, upon due notice, fails to appear, the arbitrator may issue an ex parte award based on evidence submitted by the complaining party.

Arbitration agreement induced by fraud. Occasionally a party who has signed an arbitration agreement refuses to participate in arbitration proceedings, alleging that the agreement was induced by fraud and should be rescinded. This strategy could frustrate the objectives of arbitration because the issue of fraud would have to be decided by a court, and not by the arbitrator, and therefore a full dress fraud trial could become a prerequisite to arbitration. Recognizing a potential for *gaming the system* in bad faith, the courts have held that an arbitration agreement is enforceable even if it is contained in a contract that was induced by fraud, so long as the fraud did not induce the very arbitration clause itself rather than the agreement as a whole.

Rescission of the arbitration agreement. A party to an arbitration may ask the arbitrator to rescind the agreement. Does an arbitrator, by granting rescission, destroy the authority to make an award? *No.* The courts hold that an arbitration agreement survives the rescission of the contract in which it is embedded. The theory is that parties intend their disputes to be resolved by arbitration, even disputes that result in a rescission of the underlying contract.

Social policy. An arbitration award may occasionally be vacated because the award, or the procedure leading up to the award, violates some important social policy. For example, it has sometimes been held that arbitrators cannot decide antitrust cases since arbitration could then be used as a means of voiding the antitrust laws. The recent trend of decision, however, is to allow arbitrators to make final decisions in such cases. It has been suggested in some decisions that an award rendered in proceedings tainted by racial or gender discrimination could be vacated.

Error of law. Some arbitration agreements require that the decision be according to law, and in such cases an award will be vacated if it is contrary to law. Absent such a provision, though, the courts assume the parties who resort to arbitration seek a prompt decision rendered in accordance with the arbitrator's notions of justice and equity whether those notions comply with law or not. It is assumed that parties could care less whether an arbitrator follows the rule of *Hadley v. Baxendale* or observes *the rule against perpetuities* as long as the arbitrator makes a fair and honest decision.

Ex parte communication. Notions of due process require that both parties be present at all times when an arbitrator receives evidence, and an award may be vacated if the arbitrator allows one party to present evidence without giving the other party notice and an opportunity to be present at the hearing. Some ex parte communication may be tolerated if it deals with calendaring and scheduling, but even that is to be avoided if possible. An arbitrator who decides to visit a jobsite should do so with the consent of the parties, or in their presence. An arbitrator should not independently interview witnesses or seek legal advice except at a hearing where both parties are present.

Impression of possible bias. Evidence that a neutral arbitrator is biased, or could be biased, is a ground to vacate an arbitration award. The courts recognize that in most communities the parties who have the knowledge, experience, and qualifications to act as arbitrators of disputes arising in particular industries are likely to be professionally acquainted. A structural engineer, for example, who serves as a neutral arbitrator is likely to be acquainted with one or both parties or their personnel, or their expert witnesses. Mere professional acquaintance, therefore, does not constitute bias. A neutral arbitrator must not, however, decide a case if the arbitrator has a personal or business *relationship* with a party. The award would be vacated.

§ 7.14 Alternative Dispute Resolution

The term "alternative dispute resolution" ("ADR") describes a range of techniques that have been devised to resolve disputes. The development of ADR was made possible by the adoption in 1925 of the Federal Arbitration Act. Before then, courts had been jealous of their prerogatives and had refused to enforce agreements that would "oust them of jurisdiction". In the decades after the 1920's, arbitration steadily gained popularity as society became more litigious and as litigants became more dissatisfied with the perceived inefficiency of the judicial branch.

In recent decades, many factors have combined to make it difficult for courts to function efficiently. Many state legislatures do not give the judiciary sufficient means to accomplish its work. Drug cases have swamped the courts. Anti-crime legislation has increased penalties so criminal defendants are less willing to plea bargain, and the provision of public defenders makes it possible for many defendants to insist on a trial. Therefore the courts in many states have little time to devote to civil business.

Beginning in the 1970's it became known that the need for expeditious resolution of disputes constituted a market that could be served by retired judges, who began to organize as ADR providers in competition with the venerable American Arbitration Association, which had occupied the field almost exclusively during the many decades when the provision of arbitration services was seen as a public service rather than as a profitable business. The AAA meanwhile sought to defend its market, which has lead to many improvements in the system. It is estimated by RAND that 5% of all civil disputes are now handled by ADR rather than the court system, and that the percentage will increase significantly over the next decade.

§ 7.15 Types of ADR

Escalating negotiation. Negotiation by line officers is followed by further negotiation by higher executives and finally by negotiation sessions attended by chief operating officers.

Partnering. Architect, engineer, owner, contractor and subcontractors meet at the beginning of the job in a "retreat" atmosphere to learn to appreciate their own motives and expectations and the motives and expectations of others. They agree to be forthcoming and forthright in dealing with each other, to avoid disputes and claims, and to use ADR rather than go to court.

Dispute review board. A flying squad composed of an engineer, a contractor and a subcontractor (or some such combination eschewing lawyers), called in the event of a dispute to visit the jobsite, interview personnel, investigate the problem, recommend solutions and in some cases dictate the resolution. The DRB is appointed when the contract documents are executed.

Mini trial. Lawyers present their cases through exhibits and the testimony of witnesses in the presence of high executives who are then expected to negotiate a solution.

Mediation. Negotiation facilitated by a mediator whose recommendations are non binding.

Arbitration. Hearings that culminate in a legally enforceable award made by an arbitrator.

Med-arb. Mediation followed by arbitration.

§ 7.16 Mediation

Mediation and arbitration are by far the most popular forms of alternate dispute resolution. Experienced mediators claim success in more than 90% of their cases where "success" is defined to include not only those cases that are settled but also those cases that have not (or not yet) gone to litigation or arbitration. Even when "success" is defined as the actual resolution of a dispute mediation succeeds in well over 75% of cases, which is perhaps unsurprising when one considers that parties who agree to mediation are usually well motivated to resolve their differences.

§ 7.17 Parties to Mediation

Construction industry disputes characteristically involve multiple parties and therefore a mediation may call for the presence of architect, owner, prime contractor, and a number of subcontractors. When a dispute is complex and involves a number of parties, two mediators may be employed to expedite proceedings. The process of mediation requires a succession of meetings between the mediator and one party at a time accompanied by private caucuses of the parties with their advisors. In multiple party cases this process requires considerable down time as parties wait for the attention of the mediator. The process can be expedited by the employment of two mediators who cooperate by dividing issues or parties as the occasion may demand.

§ 7.18 The Mediation Process

Mediation usually starts with a general meeting of all parties and the mediator at which the mediator invites a spokesperson for each party to briefly present its position. The mediator takes careful notes and at the end of this process will usually restate the position of each party to make sure that it is clearly understood. The process of presentation gives the mediator an opportunity to observe the demeanor of the parties and their counsel and to begin to figure out points of potential agreement and points of essential disagreement.

At the general session the mediator will explain to the parties that all statements made during the course of mediation are confidential and protected from disclosure. No party may be permitted or compelled to testify in court or in an arbitration proceeding as to statements made or positions taken during the mediation process.

In some states, the policy against disclosure of events at a mediation is so strong that even evidence of a settlement agreed to by both parties at a mediation is not admissible and therefore such a settlement agreement is unenforceable in the absence of an explicit waiver of the privilege by all parties.

Since the ultimate goal of the mediator is to get the parties to settle, the mediator may ask the parties to sign in advance a waiver of the privilege against disclosure in the case of a settlement reached at the mediation.

The mediator will have insisted on the attendance of officers with authority to settle. The mediator will also have motivated the parties to bring with them to the mediation the claims managers of any insurance carriers who may be interested in resolving the case. Claims managers should also have authority to settle.

At this first general session the mediator may, or may not, depending on the circumstances, ask each party for a response or a rebuttal to the presentation of the other party.

After the general session, the mediator will hold private sessions at which the mediator will attempt to determine the bottom line settlement position of each party and also try to elicit points of agreement so that the scope of the dispute might be reduced.

At these private sessions an experienced mediator will determine whether the parties may have overlooked potential insurance coverage that might contribute to settlement.

The mediator will emphasize the expense of continued litigation and the uncertainties that are inherent in having the dispute decided by a judge, jury, or arbitrator.

During private sessions with the parties the mediator will point out to each party the potential weaknesses in its case and the likelihood that if the party persists in litigation the ultimate decision may be unfavorable.

The mediator may make telephone calls to witnesses or the claims personnel of insurance carriers in order to elicit commitments or information that may facilitate settlement. In order to encourage candor, the mediator may undertake to treat information from one party as confidential from the other.

§ 7.19 Partial Settlement

If the mediator fails to settle all aspects of a dispute it may still be possible to persuade the parties to agree to partial settlement, or to adopt a procedure for resolution of the dispute that will hold down the costs of litigation. For example, the parties might be persuaded to present their cases to an arbitrator in the form of declarations, affidavits and written argument based on stipulated facts in order to reduce litigation expense.

Mediators develop individual styles that often serve them well. While one may lecture, cajole, threaten, reprove and argue, another may plead, implore, pray and beseech. One may exhibit bonhomie, jollity and goodwill while another labors earnestly, long and with severity. A frustrated mediator may make a formal proposal for resolution, and in desperation tell both sides that they can take it or leave it but mediation and the mediator can do no more.

Although most mediations are finished in a single day, others go on for several days separated by days of recess interspersed with telephone conferences. Some mediators make persuasive appeals by telephone to absent insurance or surety managers and will rest at nothing to achieve a successful resolution. For such mediators, the success rate is very high and they are in great demand. To secure the services of such highly reputed mediators, parties are willing to wait for months and to pay handsome fees indeed since thereby they can avoid the truly punishing costs of seeking a solution imposed by a judge or arbitrator.

CHAPTER 8

INDEMNITY, INSURANCE, AND SURETYSHIP

Chapter 8

§ 8.01 Indemnity

Indemnity (called "indemnification" by lovers of legalese) is a three-party concept dealing with legal relationships between *indemnitor*, *indemnitee*, and *claimant*. Although they may be oral, indemnity agreements are almost always in writing. It is customary in the construction industry for the party of greater bargaining position to require the party of lesser bargaining position to provide protection, *indemnity*, against claims arising out of performance by the indemnitor.

An indemnity agreement, to be enforceable, must be clear and explicit. To be clear and explicit, such an agreement must usually be in writing.

> A subcontractor who was digging a trench complained to the prime contractor's supervisor that the operation was dangerous, since the trench might collapse. The supervisor said, "don't worry about it -- we will take care of it if anything happens". The trench did collapse, injuring an employee of the prime contractor. The supervisor reassured the subcontractor that the prime contractor would take care of any problems. The injured worker filed suit against the subcontractor who sought indemnity from the prime contractor based on the oral indemnity agreement. HELD: Indemnity contracts, written or oral, must contain clear and unequivocal language. Here, the statements by the supervisor were ambiguous. Therefore the purported indemnity agreement is unenforceable.

Williams v White Mountain Constr Co, 749 P2d 423 (Colo 1988).

Many indemnity clauses call for indemnity against claims for damages to persons or property. Such an indemnity agreement does not apply to claims that are not founded upon bodily injury or property damage.

> Borough contracted with a design firm to prepare initial plans for a subdivision. The contract provided that the design firm would indemnify the Borough against claims "... incurred for or on

> account of injuries or damages to persons or property . . . ." A road building contractor who encountered difficulties meeting the specifications for the project filed suit against the design firm and the Borough, alleging design deficiencies, negligence, and professional malpractice. The Borough sought indemnity from the design firm. HELD: The indemnity clause in the contract did not apply to such a case, since it only provided indemnity against claims for injuries or damages to persons or property.

Fairbanks N Star Borough v Roen Design Assocs, 727 P2d 758 (Alaska 1986).

> In *Varco-Purden, Inc v Hampshire Constr Co*, 50 Cal App 3d 654, 123 Cal Rptr 606 (1975), an indemnity clause provided that subcontractor would indemnify owner against claims arising out of or in connection with injuries or damages to persons or property sustained in connection with the performance of the work. Part of the work was damaged by fire, and it was contended that the subcontractor was responsible for the fire damage under the indemnity agreement. HELD: As a matter of law, the indemnity agreement only indemnifies the owner against claims by third parties. Here, the owner's property was damaged but there was no claim against the owner by a third party. Therefore the indemnity agreement did not apply to the loss.

§ 8.02 Costs of Defense

An indemnity agreement in its most basic form calls for the indemnitor to pay, on behalf of the indemnitee, any judgment obtained against the indemnitee by a claimant. But most indemnity agreements also require the indemnitor to participate in defending the indemnitee against claims.

Suppose that an indemnity agreement simply provides that K will indemnify O against loss arising out of K's performance of construction work for O. Under this wording, the obligation to indemnify does not arise until O has actually suffered a loss. O would not suffer a loss covered by the indemnity agreement until it had actually paid a judgment entered in favor of a claimant. Immediately upon payment of the loss, K would have the obligation to reimburse O for the amount of the loss.

Now suppose that an indemnity agreement provides that K will indemnify O against claims, demands, liability and loss arising out of K's performance of construction work for O. This language implies that O will be defended by K against such claims, and if a claim should result in a loss, will also pay the loss.

Now suppose that an indemnity agreement provides that K will indemnify and hold harmless and defend O against all claims, demands, liability and loss. Overspray damages a neighbor's building. The neighbor files suit against O. O employs a lawyer to defend O against the suit. Judgment is entered in favor of N against O. O now demands that K reimburse O for the costs of defense, and also pay the judgment. Here, K would be liable for payment of the judgment but not for the costs of defense. K promised to *defend* O, and not pay its costs of defense. If O wanted to take advantage of K's promise to provide a defense, then O would have been required to *tender the defense* of the action to K.

Now suppose O tenders the defense to K, who assumes the defense but provides a lawyer who is not to O's liking. Absent positive evidence of incompetence, K has the right to select the lawyer. If O had wanted to reserve the right to approve the lawyer selected by K, it should have reserved that right in the indemnity agreement.

Now suppose that N, the victim of overspray, sues both K and O for damages. K employs L, its regular attorney, to defend both K and O. An investigation conducted by L reveals that K's superintendent was ordered by O to proceed with painting on a windy day, and did so under protest. This testimony creates a conflict of interest between O and K because the evidence tends to shift responsibility from K to O.

In such a case, the canons of professional ethics prevent L from representing both parties. K is therefore required, in order to provide the promised defense, to employ an independent lawyer to represent the interests of O.

K might argue, with some logic, that since K is obliged to pay any judgments entered in favor of N anyway, the conflict of interest makes no difference. O could respond to this, however, that O has no way of knowing that K will be financially able to pay the judgment that may be entered.

§ 8.03 Indemnity Against One's Own Negligence

An indemnity agreement is not construed so as to protect the indemnitee against its own negligence unless the requirement is expressed in plain language.

Suppose an indemnity agreement provides that K will indemnify O against claims arising out of K's performance of construction work for O. O orders K to perform painting work on a windy day despite K's protests. A neighbor, damaged by overspray, files an action against O for damages. Here, K would not be required to defend O against the claim or to pay any judgment entered against O, because O's liability arose out of its own active negligence.

An indemnity agreement, however, could require K to provide indemnity against losses arising out of O's *passive* negligence. An example of passive negligence is the liability imposed upon owners under the *peculiar risk doctrine*, discussed in § 2.11. The peculiar risk doctrine imposes liability on construction project owners in the absence of negligence.

Some courts have held that an agreement to indemnify a party against the results of its own active negligence is against social policy because the result might be to encourage negligent conduct. The better view, however, is that injury to third parties is at most an unintended and undesired consequence of negligent behavior and therefore social policy does not condemn such an indemnity agreement any more than it condemns insurance.

> In *Arkansas Kraft Corp v Boyed Sanders Constr Co*, 298 Ark 36, 764 SW2d 452 (1989), an indemnity clause provided
>
> > To the extent that, in performance of this order, seller shall do any work or cause any work to be done on any premises of the buyer, then seller shall indemnify and hold buyer harmless against any and all liabilities or claims for injuries or damages to any person or property arising out of such work.
>
> An injured worker brought suit against the owner who sought indemnity from the subcontractor. HELD: The language failed to unequivocally express an intention to indemnify for the indemnitee's

own negligence. The language did not clearly show an intention to indemnify the owner for the owner's own negligence.

Many states have adopted "anti indemnity" statutes that invalidate any agreement in a construction contract to indemnify an indemnitee against its own negligence, or against its own sole negligence.

New Mexico Stat Ann § 56-7-1 (1978) (Repl Pamp 1986) provides that any provision in a construction contract by which a party to the agreement agrees to indemnify the indemnitee against claims arising out of the negligence of the indemnitee is against public policy and void. HELD: The statute voids agreements which attempt to provide for indemnity against liabilities arising from the indemnitee's own negligence. Such liability may not be contracted away by an indemnity agreement.

Sierra v Garcia, 106 Nm 573, 746 P2d 1105 (1987).

In *Johnson v McGough Constr Co*, 294 NW2d 286 (Minn 1980), the indemnity clause provided that the subcontractor would indemnify and save harmless the contractor from all claims including "claims for which the contractor may be, or may be claimed to be, liable". HELD: This was an express provision to indemnify the contractor for liability resulting from its own negligence.

In some states, where an indemnitee and an indemnitor are both negligent, responsibility is allocated on a comparative basis. *Hernandez v Badger Constr Equipment Co*, 28 Cal App 4th 1791, 34 Cal Rptr 2d 732 (4th Dist 1994).

§ 8.04 Agreement to Obtain Insurance

Many construction contracts contain a clause under which the contractor agrees to indemnify the owner against claims and also a provision under which the contractor agrees to provide the owner with insurance against claims. Does an agreement to provide insurance violate the anti-indemnity statute of a state that has such a statute? The answer is no.

In *Holmes v Watson-Forsberg Co*, 488 NW2d 473 (Minn 1992), the employee of a roofing subcontractor slid and fell from a roof. The subcontract provided that the subcontractor would indemnify the contractor against such claims. Minn Stat § 337.02 provided that an indemnification agreement in a construction contract is unenforceable except to the extent that the underlying injury or damage is attributable to a negligent act of the indemnitor. HELD: The anti indemnity statute does not affect the validity of agreements to provide insurance for the benefit of others.

§ 8.05 Statute of Limitations

When an indemnity agreement protects the indemnitee against liability, a cause of action arises and the statute of limitations for enforcement of the indemnity agreement begins to run when the indemnitee becomes liable. The indemnitee becomes liable when a judgment is entered against it. For example, if a contractor agreed to indemnify an owner against liability for bodily injury, the owner would become liable when a judgment is entered in against the owner and in favor of the injured person. It is at that point in time when the contractor would become responsible to perform under the indemnity agreement and it is at that point that the statute of limitations would begin to run.

On the other hand, if a contractor agrees to indemnify an owner against "loss" arising out of bodily injury, the obligation to indemnify would occur only when the owner suffered loss. The owner would suffer loss when it actually paid a judgment. Therefore the obligation to indemnify would not arise until the owner had actually paid the judgment, and that is when the statute of limitations would begin to run.

Suppose now that a contractor agrees to indemnify an owner against claims for bodily injury. The obligation to provide indemnity would arise as soon as a claim was made against the owner by an injured person. The statute of limitations on the indemnity agreement would therefore begin to run when the claim was made.

§ 8.06 Types of Insurance

The types of insurance of most importance in the construction industry are *property* insurance and *liability* insurance.

Property insurance provides insurance against damaged property owned by the insured, or property in which the insured has an insurable interest. *Fire insurance* is a form of property insurance since, in the event of a loss by fire, the insurance carrier pays the property owner money which the property owner may use to rebuild. Property insurance is *two party* insurance because it only involves two parties: the insurance carrier and the insured property owner.

Builder's risk insurance provides insurance against damage to or destruction of a building while it is under construction. Such insurance may be procured either by the owner or the builder. Owner, prime contractor, and subcontractors all have an insurable interest in the continued existence of a building under construction. Although each can theoretically purchase a policy that would cover its insurable interest, it is customary for either the owner or the prime contractor to procure the insurance, and for the insurance to provide that the interests of owner, prime contractor, and subcontractors are all insured.

Liability insurance, is a special form of indemnity contract that involves three parties: the insurance company, the insured, and a claimant. The purpose of liability insurance is not to protect the insured against loss of property, but rather to protect the insured against *claims*.

§ 8.07 Suretyship Distinguished

Because many insurance companies not only write insurance, but also write surety bonds, and because of some superficial similarities, suretyship is often confused with insurance. Suretyship and insurance are alike in that a presumably solvent company undertakes to pay claims and losses. Nevertheless, the basic economic functions of the two regimes are completely different. An insurance company is in the business of paying losses that it anticipates will, in fact, occur. Given that a certain number of fires will occur in the United States in 1997, the function of insurance is to pay for the damage caused by those fires by spreading the risk among a large number of property owners. Each property owner pays an insurance premium that is small relative to the size of the potential loss.

Liability insurance is similar. Insurance companies can predict from their underwriting studies that a certain number of claims are likely to be made against, say, 18-year-old drivers and a lesser number of claims are likely to made against 35-year-old drivers. By adjusting premiums, an insurance company can spread the risk of such claims among a large number of drivers. Each driver is willing to pay a premium for coverage because the amount of a premium is small relative to the risk of financial disaster that could be caused by an uninsured claim.

A performance bond surety, on the other hand, does not insure a premium payer against an anticipated loss, but guarantees that the premium payer will perform its obligations. A surety on a performance bond is in a position similar to an endorser of a promissory note: if the promisor (principal) does not pay the note, the endorser (surety) will do so. Suretyship is an ancient legal concept referred to in the old testament.

> In the multitude of counselors there is safety. He that is surety for a stranger shall smart for it. *Proverbs, 11:14-15.*

The bondsmen of early days developed into the compensated surety companies encountered in modern times. The performance bond surety undertakes that a contractor will properly perform its obligations under a construction contract, and that if the contractor (the principal) does not properly perform, the surety, upon demand, will perform.

Surety companies, naturally, are willing to write bonds only after making a thorough investigation of the qualifications and financial strength of a contractor. Under the law, if a surety is ever called upon to perform the principal's obligations, it is entitled to reimbursement from the principal. As a matter of practice, surety companies also require indemnity agreements from the principal officers and owners of construction companies under which these persons personally undertake to protect the surety against any loss arising out of enforcement of the bond. Therefore if a surety company has properly evaluated the professional competence of the principal (the contractor) and the financial strength of the principal and its officers and owners who are the surety's indemnitors, it will never suffer a loss because the contractor (principal) will never default on a contract or, if it does, the surety will be reimbursed for any loss by the indemnitors.

Property insurance may be seen as a two-party relationship: insurer and insured. If the insured suffers a loss, the insurer pays the loss.

Liability insurance and suretyship are three-party relationships. The insurer or the surety undertakes to pay a loss. In the case of insurance, the promise to pay a loss is made by the insurance company to the prospective *defendant*. (If you are involved in an automobile accident and are sued, we, the insurer, will defend you and pay the loss.)

In a performance bond, the surety promises the prospective *plaintiff* that it will pay the loss. (I, the surety, guarantee you, the owner, that the contractor will not default and if the contractor does default, I will pay the loss.)

In the event of an *insured* loss, the claimant sues the insured and the insurance company defends the insured and pays the loss. In the event of a *bonded* loss, the plaintiff sues the surety company, the surety company defends itself and pays the loss, and files a cross-complaint against the principal and its indemnitors to recoup.

§ 8.08 All Risk Insurance

Builder's risk insurance, although sometimes loosely spoken of as *fire insurance*, is a form of *all risk* insurance. All risk insurance insures not only against fire, but against *all risk of physical loss* except for excluded risks. Many all risk policies, for example, exclude loss from flood or earthquake.

To appreciate the function played by builder's risk insurance, let us return to a consideration of the doctrine of impossibility of performance. Remember that performance of a contract is excused by impossibility. Now suppose that K enters into a contract to build a warehouse for O. When the project is 70% complete, it is heavily damaged by earthquake. The cost of cleaning up the debris and rebuilding to the same percentage of completion would equal 50% of the contract price. Does this partial destruction of the project excuse K's performance? It does not, nor (absent a contractual provision to that effect) does it entitle K to extra compensation for the cost of rebuilding.

It is for this reason that K would be well advised to carry builder's risk insurance on the warehouse project, including earthquake insurance. K undoubtedly has an insurable interest in the project, and could use the proceeds of the insurance to clean up the site and rebuild.

> Insured homeowner employed a painter to paint woodwork. A month after completion of the job, the paint began to blister and peel. The painter attempted to remove the paint by using solvents, but not all paint could be removed, and when the painter attempted to repaint, the paint failed to stick in the areas where paint remover had

> been used. The wood paneling became stained and mottled. The homeowner made a claim against its insurer, which notified homeowner that the damage was not covered by the policy. Judgment for homeowner $1,625.92 AFFIRMED. An all risk policy covers all losses of a fortuitous nature, not resulting from misconduct or fraud, absent an express exclusion. The term *all risk* is not to be given a restrictive meaning. A loss is fortuitous that does not wholly result from an inherent defect in the subject matter and that is not the result of the intentional misconduct or fraud of the insured. A fortuitous loss is one that occurs by chance. A fortuitous event may be said to be one not certain to occur. Negligence of the homeowner would not bar recovery under such a policy. There was no evidence of intentional misconduct or fraud. At most, homeowner was negligent. Since the loss was fortuitous, it is covered by the policy.

Avis v Hartford Fire Ins Co, 283 NC 142, 195 SE2d 545 (1973).

§ 8.09 Sue and Labor Clause

The "sue and labor" clause in an all risk insurance policy bespeaks the ancestry of the modern policy in the underwriting of maritime risks. A typical policy provides "it shall be lawful and necessary for the insured to sue, labor, and travel in the defense, safeguard, and recovery of the property insured". The insurer then agrees to reimburse the insured for costs incurred under the sue and labor clause. Although policy forms may differ, most policies do not subtract the deductible from costs incurred under the sue and labor clause.

> In *American Home Assurance Co v JF Shea Co*, 445 F Supp 365 (DC Cir 1978), the Washington Metropolitan Area Transit Authority and its general contractor were named as insured under an all risk policy that included a sue and labor clause: "It shall be lawful and necessary for the insured . . . to sue, for labor and travel, in the defense, safeguard and recovery of the property insured . . . to the charges whereof, the Company will contribute . . . ." The contractor had erected shoring to support an excavation when a lateral movement caused by a remote slippage plane in the earth caused deflection. After advising the insurer, the contractor "sued and labored" to protect and defend the system. HELD: The costs were

covered under the sue and labor provision and the deductible did not apply.

Under some policy forms, the policy limit does not apply to costs incurred under the sue and labor clause. In one case, homeowners recovered multi-million dollar costs of "suing and laboring" to protect their homes against undermining caused by beach erosion: amounts that were far beyond the policy limits of their insurance policies.

§ 8.10 Subrogation

Subrogation is a legal doctrine that allows one person to enforce legal rights that originally belonged to another person. It is an equitable doctrine that prevents a party who is guilty of wrongful conduct from receiving a windfall by being relieved of the consequences of that conduct by another, innocent, party.

Suppose that a welder employed by S, structural steel subcontractor, starts a fire that destroys a warehouse under construction. O may recover the cost of rebuilding from S, the employer of the negligent welder. O, however, doesn't trouble to file suit against S, since O's loss is covered by builder's risk insurance. But the fact that the builder's risk insurer pays the loss does not relieve S of liability, because the insurer *is subrogated to* O's rights against S.

The same would be true if the builder's risk insurance had been purchased by K. Having paid K the cost of rebuilding, the builder's risk insurer would be subrogated to K's rights against S. Thus is a loss originally borne by a *property* insurance carrier often transferred to a *liability* insurance carrier.

§ 8.11 The Approach of the AIA Contract Documents

Contract documents developed by the American Institute of Architects are in popular use throughout the nation, and serve as a model for many construction contracts.

As we have seen, the owner, the prime contractor, and each subcontractor could purchase builder's risk insurance to cover its insurable interest in the project under construction. This would raise the overall construction cost of the project because it would result in a certain duplication of premium. The subcontractors and the prime contractor would presumably pass the cost of builder's risk insurance on to the owner as part of their cost performing the work.

The AIA documents therefore provide that the owner will provide *all risk insurance* which will name the prime contractor and all subcontractors as additionally insured. The prime contractor is entitled to a copy of the policy and to receive a certificate from the insurance carrier that such insurance is in force. In the event of a loss covered by the policy, it is the duty of the owner to process a claim with the insurance carrier on its behalf and, as trustee, on behalf of the prime contractor and the subcontractors.

In order to implement the philosophy that any insured loss should be covered by the premium paid for the builder's risk insurance, the contract documents provide that owner, contractor and subcontractor each waive all claims against the others for losses covered by the insurance, and on behalf of the builder's risk insurance carrier they waive subrogation. The contract documents also call for the builder's risk insurance carrier to issue an endorsement waiving subrogation.

> Owner employed contractor to construct an addition to an existing clubhouse structure. Fire caused extensive damage to the original clubhouse, the addition, and to personal property of club members. The owner's insurance carrier paid for losses of almost $3,000,000 and brought a subrogation action against the contractor who had built the addition, alleging that the fire was caused by the contractor's negligent construction. Summary judgment for the contractor was AFFIRMED. The contract provided that the owner would purchase and maintain property insurance for the entire work including extended coverage to include all risks for damage including theft, vandalism, and malicious mischief. The contract provided that owner and contractor each waive all rights against the other, and against subcontractors, and architect for damages caused by fire or other perils covered by the all risk insurance. Under the contract, the owner waived all rights of action against the contractor for losses covered by the insurance policy. HELD: These provisions imposed an affirmative duty on the property owner to purchase insurance for the benefit of the contractor. This made the contractor an insured under the policy, and an insurer may not subrogate against its own insured. The insurer was prohibited from

recovering for any damage covered by the policy that the owner was contractually required to obtained.

Insurance Co of N Am v EL Nezelek, Inc, 480 So 2d 133 (Fla Dist Ct App 1985).

In *Harvey's Wagon Wheel, Inc v MacSween*, 96 Nev 215, 606 P2d 1095 (1980), owner employed contractor to expand and remodel the State Line Motel and Casino. The owner amended its all risk insurance policy to include the contractor and its subcontractors as their interests may appear. A fire caused more than $1,000,000 of property damage during the course of construction. Insurer paid owner $1,160,000 under the policy and brought a subrogation claim against the contractor and the painting subcontractor. Summary judgment for contractor and subcontractor AFFIRMED. No right of subrogation can arise in favor of an insurer and against its own insured. Co-insureds are immune from a subrogation claim by their insurer absent an explicit provision to the contrary.

A property insurer filed a subrogation action against a plumbing subcontractor, contending that the subcontractor negligently started a fire that destroyed an apartment complex. A construction contract between the owner and its prime contractor included waiver of subrogation clauses under which owner and contractor waived all rights against each other and subcontractors, and sub-subcontractors, for damages caused by fire. HELD: Insurance carrier cannot subrogate in the face of a contract clause under which its insured waived subrogation rights against a subcontractor.

United States Fidelity & Guar Co v Farrar's Plumbing & Heating Co, 158 Ariz 354, 762 P2d 641 (1988).

Prime contract for a shopping mall project included § 11.3.1 of the AIA general conditions which provides that the owner will purchase property insurance to include the interests of owner, contractor, subcontractors, and sub-subcontractors and that owner and contractor waive all rights against each other and subcontractors and sub-subcontractors for damages caused by perils covered by the insurance. After a loss by fire, the insurance carrier attempted to subrogate against the roofing contractor that allegedly caused the

> fire. HELD: The prime contract was incorporated into the subcontract document, including a waiver of subrogation clause. Such clauses perform a useful function because they prevent disruption and disputes among the parties to a construction project and eliminate lengthy lawsuits. ($417,000 subrogation claim was denied.)

Industrial Risk Insurers v Garlock Equip Co, 576 So 2d 652 (Ala 1991).

§ 8.12 Excluded Risks

An *all risk insurance policy* covers all risk of physical loss except for excluded risks. Risks commonly excluded are losses from flood, earthquake, riot, civil commotion, war, and nuclear reaction. Also excluded are losses caused by faulty construction or faulty design. The precise wording of exclusions is different from one policy to another, and those differences are crucial to determining coverage in a particular case.

Also excluded may be loss from landslide, mudslide, soils movement, soil settlement, or earth movement. Some policies exclude losses *caused by* such risks, and other policies exclude losses *caused by or contributed to by* such risks. Specific wording is crucial.

> An all risk policy excluded damage resulting from earth movement but included earthquake as one of the perils that was insured under its coverage. HELD: Landslide loss was covered, because the evidence supported a finding that the proximate cause of the landslide was an earthquake.

Strubble v United Servs Auto Assn, 35 Cal App 3d 498, 110 Cal Rptr 828 (1973).

Many property losses are caused by a combination of factors, some of which may be covered and some of which may be excluded from coverage under the policy. Although the courts are not entirely in agreement on the coverage of such policies, the better rule appears to be that coverage exists if a covered peril was the moving, efficient, triggering, or proximate cause of the loss.

> A homeowner's insurance policy (an all risk policy) excluded loss "caused by, resulting from, contributed to or aggravated by any

earth movement, including but not limited to earthquake, volcanic eruption, landslide, mud flow, earth sinking, rising or shifting . . . ." Plaintiff's home was damaged because of negligence of a contractor in failing to reinforce the foundation slab and failing to properly prepare subgrade soils. Soils subsided, damaging the home. HELD: The loss was covered. Here, the trial court found that the predominant, moving efficient cause, or prime cause, was the negligence of the contractor. Contractor negligence was the efficient cause of the soil settlement and, since contractor negligence was not excluded from coverage, the loss was covered.

Davis v United Servs Auto Assn, 223 Cal App 3d 1322, 273 Cal Rptr 224 (1990), *review denied*, (Dec 12, 1990).

Losses caused by contractor negligence may also be excluded under some forms of all risk policy.

Heavy rains washed away fill, causing foundations to crack and tilt. The all risk policy excluded coverage for faulty construction. HELD: The efficient proximate cause of the loss was faulty construction of the fill and therefore the ensuing losses were not covered perils.

McDonald v State Farm Fire & Cas Co, 119 Wash 2d 724, 837 P2d 1000 (1992).

§ 8.13 Interpretation of Policy

An insurance policy is usually issued on a standardized form on a take it or leave it basis by a sophisticated insurance carrier to an insurance consumer who may lack detailed knowledge of insurance coverage and may lack the skill or patience to read and fully understand the provisions of a policy. Insurance policies issued to owners and contractors often contain many parts, including coverages, the very names of which are confusing, such as builder's risk coverage, all risk coverage, fire insurance, personal property floater, inland marine coverage, commercial general liability coverage, broad form liability coverage, umbrella coverage, personal injury coverage, collision, non-owned-automobile, workers compensation, employer's liability, and so on. Nevertheless, an insurance carrier has the right to exclude or limit its exposure by the language employed in the policy.

As with any other contract, the courts attempt to interpret insurance policies so as to effectuate the intention of the parties. Because, however, an insurance policy has the characteristics of a contract of adhesion, interpretation is in favor of coverage and such as not to disappoint the reasonable expectations of the insured. Insurance policies usually begin with a few simple words granting coverage, and then go on with paragraph after paragraph of formal, legalistic language that limits, conditions, or excludes coverage. Therefore if language of a policy is such as to defeat the purpose of the policy from the standpoint of the insured, such as to withdraw coverage under circumstances where coverage would reasonably have been expected the language, if ambiguous, will be interpreted in favor of coverage.

In one case, for example, a building that was being remodeled suffered water intrusion that damaged business records, furniture and equipment. The policy excluded coverage for loss caused by faulty workmanship. The court found the word "workmanship" to be ambiguous because it can apply either to a flawed *product* (such as a watch of crude workmanship) or a flawed *process* (such as failing to provide temporary waterproofing during construction). Since the term was ambiguous, it was construed in favor of coverage.

Exclusions in property insurance policies deal with causation: in itself a subject of enormous complexity. In an all risk policy, all risk of physical loss is covered except loss *caused by* certain excluded risks.

The reader may have indulged in amusing reveries that trace an automobile accident to an ultimate cause such as having stopped for a second cup of coffee. With sufficient imagination and tenacity it would seem possible to trace an event to dozens, even hundreds or thousands of causes. Many ingenious scenarios have therefore been proposed by persons determined to find coverage for losses. In one example, it was argued that damage to a building caused by soil settlement, an excluded risk, was in turn caused by contractor negligence, a covered risk. The court bought the argument.

In an important case, the California Supreme Court dealt with damage to a home caused by soil settlement which, in its turn, was caused by a broken sewer lateral. Effusion from the lateral consolidated the soil. It was held that the policy did not exclude the loss because the legal cause was the broken sewer lateral rather than soil settlement.

In determining whether an exclusion applies, the courts look to the primary, direct, efficient cause rather than to remote or secondary causes that might contribute to a loss.

The sophisticated consumer of insurance will employ a consultant or advisor who has made a thorough study of insurance markets and the coverages available. Policies with language differences that seem quite inconsequential, even undetectable, to the diligent and literate layperson portend great economic detriment or benefit depending on the circumstances of a loss. Some policies, for example, exclude losses caused by *or contributed to by* excluded risks. This language defeats the efficient causation analysis and greatly increases the scope of exclusions.

§ 8.14 Practical Application

Under contract documents that follow the AIA pattern, it is the obligation of the owner to provide property insurance and all parties waive any claims against each other arising out of losses covered by the policy. Many claims that might be made against a contractor or subcontractor are such as could be covered by insurance. Windload, for example, might cause deflection or partial collapse of a building under construction. Construction traffic could cause cracking and settlement of roadways or floor slabs. Hydrostatic pressure might cause a retaining wall to deflect. These are examples of physical injury to tangible property within the coverage of a property insurance policy unless excluded. If they are covered, or may be covered, by the property insurance policy called for in the contract documents, then the contractor should call upon the owner to process a claim with the insurance carrier to cover the loss. With waiver of subrogation, then, the cost of repairing the loss will be borne by the insurance carrier rather than owner, contractor, or a subcontractor.

To put the matter in crude terms, the contract provisions dealing with property insurance coverage may constitute a defense to backcharges asserted by an owner against contractor or subcontractor.

> Owner filed an action against contractor and builders risk insurer for damages resulting from defects in a uranium mill built by the contractor. Contractor and a subcontractor filed cross claims against the insurer, claiming to be co-insured under the builders risk policy. The insurer cross claimed against contractor and subcontractor, asserting rights of subrogation. The policy defined the term

"insured" as the owner and "each subcontractor and/or subcontractor or materialman as their interest may appear". Summary judgment for subcontractor was REVERSED. The provisions of the policy were ambiguous, which generally means that the policy should be interpreted favorably to the insured. Under one interpretation, the subcontractor would be insured for losses caused by its own negligence and would be immune from subrogation by the insurer. Summary judgment was improper and a full trial would be required to resolve the ambiguity.

United Nuclear Corp v Mission Ins Co, 97 NM 647, 642 P2d 1106 (1982).

A contract between an owner and a home builder required the owner to provide fire insurance covering the interests of the owner, the contractor, and subcontractors. Under the contract the contractor and subcontractors were to be named as jointly insured under the policy. A subcontractor negligently installed an electrical outlet, and a short circuit caused a fire. The owner failed to provide insurance naming contractor and subcontractors. HELD: When the owner failed to provide the required insurance, the owner became the subcontractor's insurer. Therefore, the owner's insurance company had no rights of subrogation against the subcontractor.

Connor v Thompson Constr & Dev Co, 166 NW2d 109 (Iowa 1969).

In *Berger v Teton Shadows, Inc*, 820 P2d 176 (Wyo 1991), an owner obtained a $120,000 judgment against a subcontractor for negligence causing a fire to a condominium project. The judgment was REVERSED on the ground that the construction contract had required the owner to carry fire insurance. The Court of Appeal held that this provision shifted the risk of loss to the owner's insurance carrier. The only conceivable purpose of a construction contract provision placing an obligation on the owner to carry insurance is to benefit the contractor by providing protection and exculpation from risk of liability for the insured loss.

§ 8.15 Liability Insurance

Liability insurance is called third party insurance because the policy operates on the legal relationships between three parties: an *insurer*, an *insured*, and a *claimant*. A liability insurance policy is a special form of indemnity contract. Its purpose is to indemnify and defend the insured against claims for bodily injury and property damage.

Four forms of liability insurance that may be encountered in the construction industry are *automobile*, *commercial general liability (formerly called comprehensive general liability)*, *personal injury*, and *errors and omissions (or malpractice)*.

The *automobile* coverage takes care of liabilities that may arise out of automobile accidents.

The *personal injury* policy covers an array of exotic risks such as damages for libel, slander, false advertising, and damages for wrongful detainer.

Errors and omissions or *malpractice* insurance is issued to architects, engineers and surveyors to insure them against damages for professional negligence.

Commercial general liability insurance, which will occupy most of our attention in this work, insures a business against damages because of bodily injury and damages because of property damage.

A liability insurance policy with its endorsements runs to many pages, and although some modern policies claim to be written in plain English, the structure and language is very much the same as that developed over centuries. A typical policy begins with a page of declarations showing the amount of insurance, its type, the name of the insured, the basis of calculation of the premium and enumerating the endorsements that are issued along with and as a part of the policy. Next comes the insuring clause which is brief and to the point. This clause tells us that the carrier will pay all damages which the insured becomes legally obligated to pay because of bodily injury or property damage. It is the phrase "damages because of property damage" that provides the essence of coverage of most interest to the construction industry professional, and that will therefore engage most of our attention here. A long section of the policy deals with the exclusions from coverage and another long section provides definitions of some terms that have a very special meaning as used in the policy. There follow endorsements that may enhance or limit coverage.

The profession of underwriting devotes itself to identifying and describing risks of loss, estimating their probability of occurrence among particular classes of insurance customers, and then assigning a premium to be charged for insuring each risk that will spread the cost of the risk among all of the persons insured while providing a profit to the insurance carrier. Competition in the insurance market is such that carriers often, perhaps usually, report underwriting losses that are only made up by the returns on invested capital.

Although technically it may be said that a liability insurance carrier's obligation to make a payment under a policy only arises when a final judgment has been entered against the insured on a claim that is covered by the policy, liability carriers reserve to themselves the right to defend the insured against claims and so, upon notification of a claim, insurers have the right and duty to investigate it and, up to the limits of the policy, they customarily attempt to resolve the claim by payment of a settlement amount. Thus may be avoided the expense of protracted litigation and the hazards of a trial.

Courts recognize that purchasers of insurance, therefore, seek not only indemnity, but also the peace of mind that comes from knowing that their legal position will be defended at the expense of the insurance carrier.

§ 8.16 Bodily Injury Coverage

Bodily injury coverage comes into play when a jobsite accident causes injury to a construction worker or to a bystander. Some courts have interpreted the term "bodily injury" so broadly as to include allegations of emotional distress, particularly if it is alleged that the emotional distress was accompanied by physical symptoms such as changes in blood pressure or gain or loss of weight.

> In *Minnick's, Inc v Reliance Ins Co*, 47 Md App 329, 422 A2d 1028 (1980), homeowners filed an action against a contractor alleging that the contractor had installed defective heating systems and that the defects caused a reduction in the market value of their homes and also had caused emotional distress leading to loss of consortium. Prime contractor filed a cross-complaint against subcontractor, who tendered the defense of the action to its insurance

carrier. The insurance carrier refused to defend. In subcontractor's action against the insurer it was HELD that the policy language defining "accident" encompassed a loss of consortium, since the loss of consortium was a consequence of bodily injury. The insurance carrier was therefore required to defend the subcontractor against the loss of consortium claim.

In *United Pac Ins Co v McGuire Co*, 222 Cal App 3d 467, 271 Cal Rptr 710 (1990), *rehg denied*, (Aug 23, 1990), the court held that emotional distress that does not manifest itself in physical injuries does not fall within the definition of "bodily injury" as it is used in liability insurance policies.

§ 8.17 The Work Exclusion

The most important exclusion affecting contractor and subcontractor insurance coverage is the *work* exclusion. This exclusion is intended to prevent the insurance company from becoming a guarantor of the contractor's performance. The idea behind the work exclusion is that the insurance carrier is not responsible for a defect in a contractor's work if the only property damage caused by the defect is property damage to the contractor's own work. Taking the example of a floor slab on grade, let us assume that the slab, installed by a concrete subcontractor, has cracked because it was installed with high slump concrete on a hot windy day. The only thing damaged is the slab. The owner's claim against the concrete subcontractor for the repair of the cracked slab is not covered by insurance because the damage is to *work performed by the insured.*

Assume on the other hand that a properly installed slab cracks because of improper compaction of underlying soil by the excavation and grading subcontractor. Here, the owner's claim against the excavation and grading subcontractor for the cost of repair the slab would be covered by insurance, since the damage was to work performed by another subcontractor.

The sweep of the exclusion when applied to work performed by or for a prime contractor depends upon whether the prime contractor purchased broad form coverage.

As many policies are structured, the work exclusion applies to damage to work performed *by or on behalf of* the insured. Since all work at a construction project is normally performed either by the prime contractor or on behalf of the prime contractor (which is to say either by the prime contractor's own forces or by a subcontractor) therefore, alluding to the former example, the owner's claim against the prime contractor for the cost of repairing the cracked slab would not be covered by prime contractor's liability insurance regardless of whether the fault lay with the concrete subcontractor or the excavation and grading subcontractor, since in either the damage was to work performed *on behalf of* the prime contractor.

The broad form endorsement, however, omits the four words "or on behalf of" from the work exclusion, which therefore applies only to exclude coverage against claims for damage to work performed by the prime contractor with its own forces. Thus, using the example of the cracked slab, if we assume the prime contractor performed the concrete work with its own forces, and that the prime contractor caused the cracking by using high slump concrete on a hot windy day, then the owner's claim for the cost of repairing the slab would not be covered because damage was to work performed *by* the insured.

If the cause of the damage to the slab was improper compaction by the excavation and grading subcontractor, the owner's claim for repair would still not be covered because, again, damage was to work performed *by the insured.*

Suppose on the other hand that the cracking of the slab caused damage to the quarry tile floor covering installed by tile subcontractor. Here, the owner's claim against the prime contractor for the cost of repairing the tile will be covered because the damage was to work performed by a subcontractor and not to work performed by the prime contractor.

The work exclusion is also known as the *business risk exclusion,* which emphasizes the thought that defective construction is a business risk assumed by a contractor or subcontractor and not a risk to be assumed by a liability insurance carrier.

> In *Century Joint Venture v United States Fidelity & Guar Co*, 63 Md App 545, 493 A2d 370, *cert denied*, 304 Md 297, 498 A2d 1183 (1985), condominium owners filed an action against the condominium developer alleging construction defects. The developer tendered the action to its liability insurance carrier for defense. The carrier denied coverage. Judgment for insurer AFFIRMED. The policy contained a business risk exclusion the

purpose of which was to remove the insurer's obligation to pay for the insured's own defective work or product.

In *Dakota Block Co v Western Cas & Sur Co*, 81 SD 213, 132 NW2d 826 (1965), the insured manufactured concrete blocks with a polyester resin baked onto the surface so the wall of a building could be constructed with a completely finished interior or exterior surface. The manufacturer sold 15,000 square feet of the product to a subcontractor who used it in a project. The wall discolored and cracked and the cost of repair was $9,263. HELD: The damage was not confined to the product of the insured, the concrete blocks, but the fading, discoloring, and cracking diminished the value of the entire building. Therefore the exclusion of damage resulting from injury to the products of the insured did not apply.

In *Hauenstein v Saint Paul-Mercury Indem Co*, 242 Minn 354, 65 NW2d 122 (1954), plaster installed in a hospital shrank, cracked, and required removal and replacement. The liability insurer of the plaster distributor denied coverage, citing an exclusion of "injury to or destruction of any goods or products manufactured, sold, handled, or distributed by the insured". HELD: The application of defective plaster was an "accident" within the meaning of the insurance policy since the damage was completely unexpected and intended from the standpoint of the insured, and the presence of the defective plaster diminished the value of the entire hospital building and therefore the damage was not confined to the product of the insured.

In *Continental Ins Co v Asarco, Inc*, 153 Ariz 497, 738 P2d 368 (1987), contractor negligently caused a partially assembled conveyor belt to collapse, and it caused damage to the conveyor belt system and also to a preexisting structure. HELD: The exclusion of damage to property "the restoration, repair, or replacement of which has been made or is necessary by reason of faulty workmanship" did not apply because damage was to a preexisting structure. Repair was necessary because of the collapse of another structure, not by faulty workmanship to the property that was damaged.

In *Owings v Gifford*, 237 Kan 89, 697 P2d 865 (1985), home buyers filed an action against a homebuilder alleging defective construction. HELD: The policy excluded coverage of "property damage to work performed by or on behalf of the named insured arising out of the work". This exclusion applied to the home which was constructed by the insured. The builder who controls the quality of the work takes the risk of liability for faulty construction as a normal part of business that is not covered by insurance.

§ 8.18 The Faulty Design Exclusion

Contractors and subcontractors often assume some or all of the responsibility for the design of the structures and facilities they install. A design-build contractor, for example, may employ architects and engineers on its own staff and not only build, but also design, a warehouse or a powerplant. A mechanical subcontractor may design, as well as install, a heating and air-conditioning system for a project. Insurance carriers like to isolate the so-called *errors and omissions* risk and charge a separate premium for it. Such losses would then be covered in what we loosely call an architects or engineers malpractice insurance policy.

The errors and omissions risk is therefore often excluded, by special endorsement, from a policy issued to a contractor. The text of the modern exclusionary endorsements withdraws coverage for faulty drawings, plans, specifications, design, inspection, or observation of construction. The contractor or subcontractor who performs *design-build* work should therefore attempt to remove the faulty design exclusion, sometimes at the cost of a substantial additional premium.

§ 8.19 Liability Assumed by Contract

In insurance lingo, the term "liability assumed by contract" refers to an indemnity agreement by which, for example, a subcontractor may assume the liability of a prime contractor for claims made against the prime contractor because of work performed by the subcontractor. One common form of liability insurance policy excludes coverage for liability assumed by contract except for liability assumed under a "sidetrack agreement". ("Sidetrack agreement" is a railroading term the meaning of which is unclear to this author.)

The broad form policies sought and customarily obtained by contractors and subcontractors in the 80's and 90's, however, extends coverage for liability assumed by contract if the contract is a part of the regular business carried out by the insured.

In a crude sense, then, we may conceive that a subcontractor's agreement to indemnify a prime contractor against claims, or a prime contractor's agreement to indemnify an owner against claims, is an *insured* indemnity agreement. This means that the insurance company has an obligation to its insured to pay a judgment entered against the insured on an indemnity agreement.

Now let us return to the hypo where the grading contractor inadequately compacted fill causing damage to a slab. Owner backcharges the prime contractor for the cost of repair and files an action to recover those costs. The prime contractor tenders the defense of the claim to the excavation subcontractor, and the subcontractor is required by its contract to defend and indemnify the prime contractor against the claim. Judgment is entered in favor of the prime contractor and against the subcontractor on the indemnity agreement. Here the insurance carrier that issued the liability assumed by contract coverage would be obliged to pay the judgment.

An esoteric question of insurance coverage is whether the subcontractor's insurance carrier was also obliged to contribute to the cost of defending the prime contractor against the owner's claim. An argument has been made that because of a change in the language of the insuring clause of certain policies issued during the 1980's, the subcontractor's carrier is obliged to contribute to the costs of defending the prime contractor against the owner's claim.

§ 8.20 Occurrence within the Policy Period

Liability insurance is customarily written on a year to year basis, and covers only occurrences that happen during the policy period. A question often arises as to what is the nature of an occurrence that triggers coverage. Suppose, for example, the contractor compacts fill in 1988. A building is constructed on the fill in 1989 and some hairline cracks become visible in the foundations in 1990. Further settlement causes drywall cracking in 1991 and window breakage in 1992. Is the loss covered by the excavation contractor's policy in effect in 1988, 1990, 1991, 1992, or all of them? The specific answer will depend on the language of the policy and the state of the law in the state of the occurrence. There is respectable legal authority for coverage at the time of the negligent act (1988), at the time of first damage (1990), at the time of first manifestation of damage that would be discovered by a reasonable insured (1991) and that each manifestation of damage in a separate occurrence triggering additional coverage (1991 and 1992). The latter is known as the "continuous trigger" rule. Application of the continuous trigger rule can, and does, result in a stacking of coverage in which a series of policies may cover a series of closely related claims. A competing theory, called the "loss in progress" rule, holds that once the loss has begun to occur, additional property damage arising from the same transaction is foreseeable and therefore not insurable, so the entire loss is covered by the policy in effect at the time of first manifestation.

> In *Montrose Chem Corp v Admiral Ins Co*, 3 Cal App 4th 1511, 5 Cal Rptr 2d 358 (1992), Montrose manufactured DDT. Admiral issued four comprehensive general liability policies to Montrose covering the period from October 1982 through March 1986. In a number of lawsuits against Montrose, damages were sought for personal injuries and property damage alleged to have occurred continuously throughout the period when the policies were in effect. HELD: Injury or damage that is continuous or progressive throughout different successive policy periods triggers coverage under all of the policies in effect for all of those periods.
>
> In *Lund v American Motorists Ins Co*, 797 F2d 544 (7th Cir 1986), claimant alleged that a designer builder negligently designed and built an apartment building roof that later collapsed. HELD: Under Wisconsin law, the insurer had an obligation to defend the builder against the claim because the negligent design and construction occurred during the policy period even though the roof did not collapse until after the policy had expired.

§ 8.21 Accident

Liability insurance policies do not provide coverage for property damage that is expected or intended by the insured, but rather for *accidents*. For example, a contractor would not be covered for losses sustained because of sabotage to a job committed by one of its officers motivated by animus against the owner.

Although we often think of an "accident" as a sudden, violent, and unexpected event (such as a train wreck) it is clear that events such as soil settlement, which occur over a long period of time, are also accidental and within the coverage of an insurance policy so long as they are not intended or expected by the insured.

In *Harleysville Mut Cas Co v Harris & Brooks, Inc*, 248 Md 148, 235 A2d 556 (1967), a contractor clearing land made a pile of trees and underbrush, added fuel oil and rubber tires, and burned the mess. The resulting soot and smoke damaged nearby residents, who filed action against the contractor. The contractor's insurer refused to cover the claims. HELD: The contractor's failure to take precautions to prevent a clearly foreseeable damage rendered the damage not an "accident" and therefore the damage was not covered by the policy.

In *Palouse Seed Co v Aetna Ins Co*, 40 Wash App 119, 697 P2d 593 (1985), a dispute arose between an owner and a contractor on a project for the construction of four prefabricated steel buildings, and the contractor walked off the job. The owner obtained a judgment against the contractor for $240,809.19 and sought to recover the amount of the judgment from the contractor's liability insurance company. HELD: Damages flowing from the contractor's walking off the job were neither an "occurrence" nor an "accident" within the meaning of the policy. The contractor's action in walking off the job was intentional, not accidental.

In *Collin v American Empire Ins Co*, 21 Cal App 4th 787, 26 Cal Rptr 2d 391 (1994), Gordon, a tenant in a house owned by Collin, employed a contractor to remodel a house. Gordon removed Collin's furniture and stored it in a warehouse. Collin, when he discovered it, objected both to the remodeling work and to the removal of the property. Collin obtained a judgment against Southwest Design and then sought to recover the amount of the judgment for Southwest's insurance carrier. HELD: The remodeling work was deliberately performed, and therefore not accidental. Likewise, the *conversion* (removal of property) was deliberate and not accidental. Only damages caused by "accidents" are within the coverage of the policy.

In *Bundy Tubing Co v Royal Indem Co*, 298 F2d 151 (6th Cir 1962), claims were made against a manufacturer of thin walled tubing that was used as a material for radiant heating because the material deteriorated in use. HELD: The term "accident" in the liability policy does not exclude claims for negligence or breach of warranty. The claims for cost of reconstruction after failure of the tubing were claims for injury caused by "accident" and were covered by the policy.

§ 8.22 Coverage for Breach of Contract

It is often contended that liability policies do not put a liability insurance carrier in the position of a surety that issues a performance bond, and that a liability insurance policy is no guarantee that a contractor will perform its contract. From this it is argued that there is no coverage for a breach of contract. The better view, however, is that policies cover "damages because of property damage" and it is not relevant whether property damage is caused a breach of contract, negligence, or fortuity.

In *Vernon Williams & Son Constr, Inc v Continental Ins Co*, 591 SW2d 760 (Tenn 1979), a warehouse owner obtained judgment against a contractor based on faulty design and workmanship. HELD: The policy was intended to cover tort, not contract damages. The policy excludes coverage for damage to the contractor's work product and does not cover the cost of correcting the contractor's defective work.

In *Owings v Gifford*, 237 Kan 89, 697 P2d 865 (1985), it was held that a liability policy excluded coverage for property damage that arose out of contractor's faulty construction work, including negligent work. The policy excluded damage to work performed by or on behalf of the named insured. The policy was not a performance bond or a guarantee of contract performance.

§ 8.23 The Duty to Defend

Liability insurance policies provide that the company

> shall pay all damages that the insured becomes legally obligated to pay because of property damage arising out of an occurrence covered by this policy, and the company shall have the right and duty to defend any suit seeking damages on account of such property damage even if the allegations of the suit are groundless or fraudulent.

Courts have recognized that a primary objective of a person who buys an insurance policy is the peace of mind that comes from knowing it will not be ruined by costs of litigation and attorneys fees expended to defend against a claim, even if unmeritorious. It is a striking characteristic of modern construction litigation, in fact, that the costs of defense often exceed the amount of the loss.

Some courts have said that an insurance carrier must determine whether it has a duty to defend from the allegations of the complaint filed by the claimant and facts that are known to the insurance carrier at the time when the insured tenders the defense. If the allegations of the complaint and those facts available to the carrier show that there is a *potential for coverage* then the carrier must provide the defense. Policy language provides that the company shall have the right and duty to defend the insured even if allegations are false or fraudulent. The fact that a claim is false must not deprive the insured of the peace of mind that derives from knowing it will be defended against that claim by the insurance carrier.

An insurance carrier must determine whether it has a duty to defend a claim at the time when the claim is presented to it by the insured. Often, this is just a few days after the insured has been served with a complaint, and the complaint may need to be answered within a few days or even within a few hours.

Many courts have held that the duty to defend arises from the *possibility*, rather from *probability*, that the claim is for damages that are covered by the policy. See, for example, *TJ Picozzi Constr Co v Exchange Mut Ins Co*, 138 AD2d 907, 526 NYS2d 652 (1988).

> In *Trizec Properties v Biltmore Constr Co*, 767 F2d 810 (11th Cir 1985), a contractor tendered the defense of a breach of contract and negligence action arising out of construction of a shopping mall to its insurance carrier. HELD: Under Florida law, the duty to defend depends fully upon the allegations of the complaint filed against the insured. If the complaint alleges facts that are both within and without the scope of coverage, then the insurer must defend the entire suit.
>
> Whether an insurer owes a duty to provide a defense to an insured is determined primarily from the allegations of the complaint. If a complaint alleges an accident or occurrence that

comes within the coverage of the policy, the insurer must defend regardless of the ultimate liability of the insured.

United States Fidelity & Guar Co v Armstrong, 479 So 2d 1164 (Ala 1985). (Contractor and engineering company for design and construction of a city sewage system were sued by adjacent owners, who alleged negligent conduct.)

Fire repair contractor Hurley was sued by Fireman's Fund for fraud and breach of contract. Fireman's Fund alleged that Hurley performed substandard work, used improper materials, charged inflated prices, and billed for services never performed and that a claims manager received kickbacks from Hurley for directing work to Hurley. Hurley tendered the defense of the action to his liability insurance carrier, State Farm. HELD: The Fireman's Fund complaint alleged no facts showing a potential for coverage. 1) The policy covers "accidents". Conspiracy to defraud is not an accident. 2) The policy covers only bodily injury and property damage. The Fireman's Fund complaint sought only economic and punitive damages. By no stretch of the imagination can an action for conspiracy to engage in fraudulent billing practices be deemed to be a claim for accidental bodily injury or property damage.

Hurley Constr Co v State Farm Fire & Cas Co, 10 Cal App 4th 533, 12 Cal Rptr 2d 629 (1992).

An insurance carrier has a duty to defend when a policy is ambiguous and the insured would reasonably expect coverage based on the nature and kind of risk covered by the policy. Alternatively, a duty to defend arises when the underlying suit *potentially* seeks damages within the coverage of the policy. Even if an underlying complaint alleges only intentional misconduct, if it could conceivably be amended to allege merely negligent conduct, such a suit might present the possibility that the plaintiff could obtain damages covered by the policy.

La Jolla Beach & Tennis Club, Inc v Industrial Indemnity Co, 9 Cal 4th 27, 36 Cal Rptr 2d 100, 884 P2d 1048 (1994).

Homeowner filed an action against subcontractor alleging damage from flooding. HELD: The insurer is duty bound to defend irrespective of whether plaintiff can or will ultimately prevail. The allegations of the complaint failed to specify whether the alleged negligence happened before or after operations were completed. Even though completed operations were excluded, there was doubt as to whether the stated facts occurred within the policy period and therefore the insurer was obligated to defend.

Peter Flori v Allstate Ins Co, 120 RI 511, 388 A2d 25 (1978).

General contractor sued concrete supplier alleging that production errors caused concrete to have an insufficient amount of a chemical compound it needed to give strength. The owner required the general contractor to install additional shoring to brace the existing structure at a cost of $169,317.64. The supplier tendered the defense of the action to its insurance carrier, which refused to defend, contending there was no property damage. HELD: The policy covered damages for loss resulting from injury to or destruction of tangible property. Here, the defective concrete caused destruction of the structural integrity of the building, which constituted tangible property damage.

United States Fidelity & Guar Co v Nevada Cement Co, 93 Nev 179, 561 P2d 1335 (1977).

§ 8.24 Withdrawing from the Defense

An insured may tender a claim to an insurance carrier for defense as soon as the claim is made, and at such time it may not be clear whether the claim is for property damage covered by the policy or not. For example, in a soil settlement case it may not be clear whether property damage "occurred" while the policy was in effect. It may not be clear at the time when a claim is first made whether the owner is seeking damages for property damage to work performed by the insured, or property damage to work performed by some other contractor or subcontractor. In such cases, it is customary for an insurance carrier to undertake to investigate the claim, and to defend the insured under a *reservation of rights*. In a reservation of rights letter (which may be many pages in length), the insurer informs the insured of the policy language (usually, the text of exclusions) that it thinks might apply to the claim, but employs a lawyer to defend the insured until it can be determined whether the claim is covered by the policy or not. The carrier often reserves the right to withdraw the defense, and to seek reimbursement of its expenses, if and when it is determined that the claim for damages is not covered by the policy.

Once an insurance carrier has assumed the defense of an insured, it is difficult for it to withdraw even though it may have delivered a reservation of rights letter and even though evidence may come to hand that the claim is not covered by the policy. It is dangerous for the carrier to simply abandon the insured because it loses control of the case and gives the insured an opportunity to assign its rights against the carrier to the claimant under circumstances where it may be difficult for the carrier to keep itself informed of the progress of negotiations and the nature of the claim. To be sure, the insurer may seek relief in court by filing a declaratory relief action, yet the courts are hostile to such an action because it puts the insured in the difficult position of defending itself in the principal case and in the declaratory relief action at the same time. Some courts will accept nothing less than "uncontestable evidence" that the claim is not covered by the policy.

> In *Trovillion v United States Fidelity & Guar Co*, 130 Ill App 3d 694, 474 NE2d 953 (1985), a homeowner filed a defective workmanship suit against a contractor whose insurer defended with a reservation of rights. After investigation, the insurer withdrew from the defense. The homeowner defended itself and prevailed, then brought a declaratory relief against the insurer. The contractor contended that the homeowner's complaint included an allegation of property damage to products other than those furnished by the insured, and that such damage fell within the policy's coverage. HELD: The insurer had no right to withdraw from the defense and wait for the insured to initiate a declaratory relief action. The insurer itself was obliged to seek a declaration of rights. Since the complaint possibly contained a covered claim, and the insurer neither filed a declaratory relief action nor defended under a reservation of rights, it violated its duty to defend and was estopped from raising the coverage issue as defense to the insured's action.
>
> A contractor's insurance carrier assumed the defense of an action against a contractor for faulty construction of a carwash. On the day of trial, counsel employed by the insurance carrier informed the court that a conflict of interest might exist because the insurance carrier wished to reserve the right to assert that the claim was not covered because of the business risk exclusion. HELD: The insurer

> was estopped from raising the conflict of interest issue. An insurer has a duty promptly to notify the insured of possible conflicts of interest. Here, the notice of the conflict was not timely because from the time the complaint was filed the insurer was aware that the business risk exclusion might apply to the claim.

Cozzens v Bazzani Bldg Co, 456 F Supp 192 (ED Mich 1978).

§ 8.25 Independent Counsel

An insurance carrier provides a defense to an insured by employing a qualified law firm to conduct the defense on behalf of the insured. Conflicts of interest, however, may arise between the insurance carrier and the insured. A conflict that often arises is when a contractor files a collection action against an owner who then asserts backcharges (claiming, for example, water intrusion) by way of cross-complaint. The insured may tender the defense of the backcharges to its carrier, and during the conduct of the litigation a conflict of interest may arise because the insured may wish to expedite the litigation and the carrier may prefer delay.

The duty to defend does not include an obligation on the part of the insurance carrier to pursue an affirmative claim for money on behalf of the insured. *Silva & Hill Constr Co v Employers Mut Liab Ins Co*, 19 Cal App 3d 914, 97 Cal Rptr 498 (1971).

A particularly obnoxious and difficult type of conflict may arise dealing with coverage of the policy. Let us assume, for example, that an owner files a complaint against a contractor that contains two causes of action. The first cause of action alleges that the contractor negligently installed a defective parapet cap, without caulking or counterflashing, as a result of which water intrusion damaged the building. The second cause of action alleges that the contractor fraudulently and intentionally and maliciously installed the defective parapet cap. If the jury brings a verdict on count one, the claim is covered by insurance but if the jury brings a verdict on count two, the claim would not be covered and the carrier would not be required to pay the judgment. The carrier would therefore prefer to have the jury find the contractor guilty of fraudulent and malicious conduct.

Now consider the position of the lawyer employed by the insurance carrier to provide the defense. The lawyer may have a longstanding relationship with the insurance carrier: a profitable one that the lawyer takes pains to cultivate. The lawyer is in a position to influence the outcome of the case by defending one count more strongly than the other. The lawyer has professional ethical obligations of good faith and fair dealing to both the insured contractor (the lawyer's client) and the insurance carrier which is paying the bills. Faced with such a situation, a lawyer must either withdraw from the representation or must require the appointment of independent counsel to participate in the defense. When such conflict of interest situations arise, the courts require that independent counsel, selected by the insured, be paid by the insurance carrier for its participation in the defense.

> In *United States Fidelity & Guar Co v Louis A Roser Co*, 585 F2d 932 (8th Cir 1978), plaintiff filed an action against the insured alleging several theories some of which were within and which were without the coverage of a policy issued by the USF&G. USF&G accepted the defense and invited the insured contractor to employ its attorney at its own expense for the defense of the allegations that were not within the coverage of the policy. Contractor employed its own counsel, which billed USF&G, which refused to pay for the representation. HELD: There was a conflict of interest between the carrier and the insured and counsel would be inclined, even acting in good faith, to bend its efforts, however unconsciously, toward establishing that recovery against the insured, grounded on a theory that was not covered by the policy. An attorney cannot represent conflicting interests. However, the conflict did not relieve USF&G of the obligation to provide independent counsel. The insurer must either provide independent counsel to represent the insured or pay the costs incurred by the insured in hiring counsel of its own choice.

§ 8.26 Notice of Loss

Property insurance policies provide that it is the duty of the insured to give prompt notice of a loss. The courts hold, however, that prompt notice is excused unless the insurance carrier can show some positive prejudice caused by failure to give prompt notice.

Most policies provide that any suit against the insurer must be brought within one year after the inception of the loss. Courts have held, however, that the insured has one year after the positive denial of a claim to file an action to recover insurance proceeds.

CHAPTER 9

AFFIRMATIVE ACTION AND PREVAILING WAGES

Chapter 9

§ 9.01 The Programs

We deal in this chapter with two regulatory programs that have little impact on contractors who do private work, but can have a profound effect on public works contractors: affirmative action and prevailing wages. The objectives of these programs are admirable: even noble. The way they work out in administrative and political practice, however, can sometimes seem a parody of bureaucratic arrogance and inefficiency.

The purposes behind prevailing wage laws are to avoid the spectacle of government benefiting from the oppression of workers who receive substandard wages and to secure the benefits of a strong, skilled, and healthy labor force. The objective of affirmative action is to overcome the doleful effect of racial and sexual discrimination and to bring to public contracting the diverse skills of minorities and women that might otherwise be lost. In some states disabled veterans are also targeted for affirmative action.

While the governmental objectives of affirmative action and prevailing wages are laudable, the political objectives have been criticized. The main political support for prevailing wages comes from labor unions and union contractors seeking to avoid competition from non-union (often minority) workers and contractors. Strong political support for affirmative action comes from those who seek racial and sexual preferences and want to avoid, if possible, competition from white males. As with all government programs that seek to closely regulate the marketplace, affirmative action and prevailing wage are subject to bureaucratic abuse.

§ 9.02 Affirmative Action

Affirmative action programs have been adopted by the federal government and by states, cities, counties, and countless commissions, districts, and local agencies. The programs that have been adopted can be divided into two distinct types: quota programs and outreach programs.

Quota programs require that a public works contract bidder provide evidence that specified quotas of the work will be awarded to businesses owned by minorities or women. Outreach programs require a bidder to demonstrate good faith efforts to obtain participation by minority and women owned businesses to attempt to meet participation goals (rather than quotas) established by the public agency.

In 1995, the United States Supreme Court ruled that racial quotas may not be required of public contractors unless an agency has evidence of past discrimination and unless the program is narrowly tailored to repair the effects of past discrimination. Such programs will be subject to strict scrutiny by the courts under the Equal Protection Clause of United States Constitution. Only specific evidence of racial injustice and narrow tailoring of a plan to overcome its effects will justify discrimination against white males in public contracting.

Since the Supreme Court decision, a number of local agencies have abandoned quota programs until they can perform the necessary disparity studies to justify a more narrowly tailored approach to affirmative action. Many affirmative action programs have been tested in court by bidders who contend a contract should have been awarded to them, but was not because of an affirmative action program that does not meet the requirements established by the Supreme Court. In such cases, courts may order an agency to award the contract to the low bidder rather than a bidder who meets the affirmative action requirements of the agency.

A low bidder may also sue the agency for damages. In some states damages may include profits that the bidder would have made if the contract had been awarded to the low bidder, but in other states the damages that the contractor can recover are limited to the cost of preparing the bid.

§ 9.03 Outreach Programs

Many agencies have established outreach programs under which the agency establishes goals for participation by minority and women owned businesses in public contracting. The agency may then require that bidders supply evidence that they have made strenuous good faith efforts to encourage participation by minority and women owned subcontractors and suppliers. Many programs establish criteria for judging whether a bidder has made good faith efforts to attract minority and women owned businesses, among them:

- Helping MBE's and WBE's obtain insurance and bonding capacity

- Advertising for bids in minority and women owned publications

- Cooperating with minority and women oriented associations in soliciting bids

- Soliciting bids from MBE's and WBE's by direct mail

- Following up direct mail solicitations by telephone calls to encourage to MBE's and WBE's to submit bids

- Breaking a project up into small increments of work hat can be performed more readily by MBE's and WBE's

- Supplying MBE's and WBE's with bidding documents, drawings, specifications, and other information to assist them in submitting bids

- Awarding work to MBE's and WBE's who are not the low bidders for their trades

In minority outreach programs the focus is not on meeting a quota, but on demonstrating sufficient efforts to obtain participation by MBE'S and WBE's. Since efforts must be demonstrated by paperwork, bid protests are resolved by agency staff minutely examining MBE/WBE outreach paperwork submitted by each bidder. Reported cases show that agencies have determined the qualifications of bidders based on factors as the number of telephone calls made in attempts to persuade MBE's and WBE's to submit bids, the amount of time taken up on the telephone in these persuasive efforts, and the persistence of the bidder in trying to make sure that faxes inviting participation are delivered.

Disappointed low bidders whose bids are rejected because of insufficient outreach efforts have often bureaucratic nitpicking and point out that evaluation of outreach efforts offers the agency an opportunity to award work to a favored bidder and therefore the MBE and WBE outreach programs can be a screen for favoritism and corruption. Much scrutiny is also devoted to the screening and qualifications of contractors who claim to be minority or women owned and controlled. It is not easy to penetrate the paperwork defenses of a contractor who is determined to make it appear that a business is minority or women owned and controlled when, in actuality, it is owned and controlled by a white man or white men.

§ 9.04 Minorities vs. Women: Do the Same Concepts Apply?

Much ink has been spilled on the question of whether the Supreme Court will treat women and minorities the same. Slavery is a big part of the constitutional justification for minority preferences, so obviously the same reasoning does not necessarily also apply to women and other minorities as applies to blacks. In many states the MBE/WBE question has become politicized. The legal and political environment is fluid and contractors are well advised to keep up-to-date with the latest developments in the agencies with which they wish to do business.

An interesting development in Southern California is the emergence of "MBE-WBE compliance providers" who, for a fee, write the letters, place the ads, send the faxes, make the phone calls, keep the records, and create the paperwork to show compliance with good faith efforts requirements. This development, which is seen by some as a cynical exploitation of a serious social problem, exemplifies to others the marvelous adaptability of the construction industry segment of a market driven economy.

§ 9.05 Prevailing Wages

Contractors on most public projects are required to pay prevailing wages. The labor department of states establish the prevailing wage for journeymen, apprentices, and helpers in the various trades. The prevailing wages are published as part of the contract documents on public projects and the prime contractor and subcontractors are required to pay them. If a subcontractor fails to pay prevailing wages, the agency penalizes the prime contractor and the prime contractor penalizes the subcontractor. In addition to being required to pay backpay to affected workers, the contractor also forfeits to the agency a daily penalty for each worker as to whom there was a failure to pay prevailing wages. (Penalties vary from state to state: $50 to $100 per day per worker is common.)

Contractors are required to keep records showing payment of prevailing wages, known as "certified payrolls", and to make copies of the certified payrolls available to the prime contractor, the agency, and any member of the public. This requirement enables union agents to police the payment of prevailing wages by non-union contractors.

The presence in many states of qualified workers who are willing to work for less than prevailing wages makes it difficult to enforce the laws on all projects. When a local agency does bring charges against a contractor, the contractor is considered guilty until proven innocent. Many prime contractors, in an attempt to protect themselves against defaulting subcontractors, require every worker on the jobsite to sign an affidavit everyday to authenticate compliance with prevailing wage requirements. The reported cases include amusing incidents where workers have been required by their employers to conceal themselves in tool boxes and trash bins to avoid detection by the inspecting authorities. A common ruse is for a contractor to issue checks that comply with prevailing wage requirements, and to require workers to endorse and return the checks to the employer, who then pays less than prevailing wages in cash.

The prime contractor is authorized to withhold from a subcontractor who violates prevailing wage requirements back wages and penalties incurred, and a subcontractor who wishes to challenge the amount withheld must comply with the requirements of a short statute of limitations: typically 90 days.

NATIONAL CONSTRUCTION LAW MANUAL
Table of Cases

Appendix

Selected AIA Forms

INSTRUCTION SHEET

FOR AIA DOCUMENT A101, STANDARD FORM OF AGREEMENT BETWEEN OWNER AND CONTRACTOR where the Basis of Payment is a STIPULATED SUM—1987 EDITION

A. GENERAL INFORMATION

1. Purpose

AIA Document A101 is intended for use on construction projects where the basis of payment is a stipulated sum (fixed price). It is suitable for any arrangement between the Owner and Contractor where the cost has been set in advance, either by bidding or by negotiation.

2. Related Documents

This document has been prepared for use in conjunction with the 1987 edition of AIA Document A201, General Conditi[illegible] of the Contract for Construction, which is adopted into A101 by a specific reference. This integrated set of documents is suitable [illegible]ost projects; however, for projects of limited scope, use of AIA Document A107 may be considered.

The A101 document may be used as one part of the Contract Documents which record the Contract for Construc[illegible] Owner and the Contractor. The other Contract Documents are:

General Conditions (i.e., A201)
Supplementary Conditions
Drawings
Specifications
Modifications

Although the AIA does not produce standard documents for Supplementa[illegible]ns, Draw[illegible]r Specifications, a variety of model and guide documents are available, including AIA's MASTERSPEC.

3. Arbitration

This document incorporates ARBITRATION by adoption of AIA [illegible]ument [illegible]1, which provides [illegible]bitration according to the Construction Industry Arbitration Rules of the Americ[illegible] [illegible]itra[illegible] Associ[illegible]n. Arbitration [illegible]DING AND MANDATORY in most states and under the federal Arbitration Act. In a m[illegible] o[illegible] [illegible]ration provi[illegible]g to future disputes are not enforceable, but arbitration is enforceable if ag[illegible] to afte[illegible] dispu[illegible]ses. A few [illegible] requi[illegible] the contracting parties be especially notified that the written contract cont[illegible] arbit[illegible]n provision by: [illegible]ing on the [illegible]f the document, specific placement of the arbitration provisio[illegible] th[illegible]cum[illegible]or specific di[illegible]ons [illegible]ong the [illegible]es prior to signing the document.

Arbitration provisions have b[illegible] in[illegible] AIA contract form[illegible]e 1888 [illegible]er [illegible]courage alternative dispute resolution procedures and to p[illegible] users [illegible]A do[illegible]nts with lega[illegible]forc[illegible] arb[illegible] provisions when the parties choose to adopt arbitration int[illegible]ntract. In[illegible]uals may, howe[illegible] ch[illegible] delete the [illegible]itration provisions based upon their business decisions with [illegible] ad[illegible] of couns[illegible]o obtain a co[illegible] the [illegible]truc[illegible] Industry Arbitration Rules, write the American Arbitration [illegible]ion, 140 [illegible] 51st Street, New [illegible]rk, N[illegible]20.

4. Use of N[illegible]

If [illegible]mbi[illegible] of [illegible] documents and [illegible]A docu[illegible] is to be used, particular care must be taken to achieve consistency of lan[illegible] and i[illegible]tain owners re[illegible] of o[illegible] contractor agreements and other contract forms which they prepare. [illegible]s s[illegible]e carefully compa[illegible]ndard AIA forms for which they are being substituted before execution of an [illegible] If there are any significant omissions, a[illegible]ions or variances from the terms of the related standard AIA forms, both legal and in[illegible]ce counsel should be consulte[illegible]

5. [illegible]er Forms of Agreement

Letter forms of agreement are generally discouraged by the AIA, as is the performance of a part or the whole of the Work on the basis of oral agreements or understandings. The standard AIA agreement forms have been developed through more than seventy-five years of experience and have been tested repeatedly in the courts. In addition, the standard forms have been carefully coordinated with other AIA documents.

6. Use of Current Documents

Prior to using any AIA document, the user should consult the AIA, an AIA component chapter or a current AIA Documents Price List to determine the current edition of each document.

7. Limited License for Reproduction

AIA Document A101 is a copyrighted work and may not be reproduced or excerpted from in substantial part without the express written permission of the AIA. The A101 document is intended to be used as a consumable—that is, the original document purchased by the user is intended to be consumed in the course of being used. There is no implied permission to reproduce this document, nor does membership in The American Institute of Architects confer any further rights to reproduce them.

A limited license is hereby granted to retail purchasers to reproduce a maximum of ten copies of a completed or executed A101, but only for use in connection with a particular Project. A101 may not be reproduced for Project Manuals. Rather, if a user wishes to include it as an example in a Project Manual, the normal practice is to purchase a quantity of the pre-printed forms and bind one in each of the Project Manuals. Partial modifications, if any, may be accomplished without completing the form by using separate Supplementary Conditions.

Upon reaching agreement concerning the Contract Sum and other conditions, the form may be removed from the manual and such information, except for the signatures, may be added to the blank spaces of the form. The user may then reproduce up to ten copies to facilitate the execution (signing) of multiple original copies of the form, or for other administrative purposes in connection with a particular Project. Please note that at least three original copies of A101 should be signed by the parties as required by the last provision of A101.

B. CHANGES FROM THE PREVIOUS EDITION

1. Format Changes

Two new articles have been added: Article 8, Termination or Suspension; and Article 9, Enumeration of Contract Documents.

2. Changes in Content

The 1987 edition of A101 revises the 1977 edition to reflect changes made in the most recent (1987) edition of A201. It also incorporates alterations proposed by architects, contractors, owners and professional consultants. The following are some of the significant changes made to the contents from the 1977 edition of A101:

Article 1: A specific statement has been added that the Contract represents the entire agreement between the parties, superseding previous negotiations and writings.

Article 2: Space has been provided to describe any exceptions to the description of Contractor's scope of Work.

Article 3: In the title of this article, "Time of Commencement" has been changed to "Date of Commencement."

Article 4: Space has been provided for insertion of the amounts relating to alternates and unit prices.

Article 5: The Progress Payments article has been substantially rewritten and expanded. Detailed directions have been added on how and when payments shall be calculated and applied for.

Article 6: Further details have been added to clarify the conditions under which final payment shall be made by the Owner.

Article 7: The reference to definitions contained in the Conditions of the Contract has been deleted because the A201 document is now specifically adopted by reference under Article 9.

Article 8: This is a new article containing references to the General Conditions.

Article 9: This article is new. The A101 Document and the A201 Document are explicitly enumerated as parts of the Contract Documents. Spaces are provided for information specifically identifying the other Contract Documents, including the Supplementary Conditions, Specifications, Drawings and Addenda, if any.

Signature Page: It is noted above the signature line that this agreement is executed in at least three original copies. See the instructions pertaining to Limited License for Reproduction.

C. COMPLETING THE A101 FORM

1. Prospective bidders should be informed of any additional provisions which may be included in A101, such as liquidated damages or provisions for stored materials, by an appropriate notation in the Bidding Documents and the Supplementary Conditions.

2. Modifications

Users are encouraged to consult an attorney before completing an AIA document. Particularly with respect to contractor's licensing laws, duties imposed by building codes, interest charges, arbitration and indemnification, this document may require modification with the assistance of legal counsel to fully comply with state or local laws regulating these matters.

Generally, necessary modifications may be accomplished by writing or typing the appropriate terms in the blank spaces provided on the form or by Supplementary Conditions, special conditions or amendments included in the Project Manual and referenced in this document. The form may also be modified by striking out language directly on the original pre-printed form. Care must be taken in making these kinds of deletions, however. Under NO circumstances should pre-printed language be struck out in such a way as to render it illegible (as, for example, with blocking tape, correction fluid or X's that completely obscure the text). This may raise suspicions of fraudulent concealment or suggest that the completed and signed document has been tampered with. Handwritten changes should be initialed by both parties to the contract.

It is definitely not recommended practice to retype the standard document. Besides being outside the limited license for reproduction granted under these Instructions, retyping can introduce typographical errors and cloud the legal interpretation given to a standard clause when blended with modifications.

Retyping eliminates one of the principal advantages of the standard form documents. By merely reviewing the modifications to be made to a standard form document, parties familiar with that document can quickly understand the essence of the proposed relationship. Commercial exchanges are greatly simplified and expedited, good-faith dealing is encouraged, and otherwise latent clauses are exposed for scrutiny. In this way, contracting parties can more fairly measure their risks.

3. Cover Page

Date: The date represents the date the Agreement becomes effective. It may be the date that an oral agreement was reached, the date the Agreement was originally submitted to the owner, the date authorizing action was taken or the date of actual execution. It will be the date from which the Contract Time is measured unless a different date is inserted under Paragraph 3.1.

Identification of Parties: Parties to this Agreement should be identified using the full address and legal name under which the Agreement is to be executed, including a designation of the legal status of both parties (sole proprietorship, partnership, joint venture, unincorporated association, limited partnership or corporation [general, closed or professional], etc.). Where appropriate, a copy of the resolution authorizing the individual to act on behalf of the firm or entity should be attached.

Project Description: The proposed Project should be described in sufficient detail to identify (1) the official name or title of the facility, (2) the location of the site, if known, (3) the proposed building type and usage, and (4) the size, capacity or scope of the Project, if known.

Architect: As in the other Contract Documents, the Architect's full legal or corporate titles should be used.

4. Article 1—The Contract Documents

The Contract Documents must be enumerated in detail in Article 9. The Contractor's bid itself may be incorporated into the Contract; similarly, other bidding documents, bonds, etc., may be incorporated, especially in public work.

5. Article 2—The Work of This Contract

Portions of the Work which are the responsibility of persons other than the Contractor and which have not been other[illegible] indicated should be listed here.

6. Article 3—Date of Commencement and Substantial Completion

The following items should be included as appropriate:

Paragraph 3.1
The date of commencement of the Work should be inserted if it is different from the date [illegible] Ag[illegible]ent. It [illegible]ld not be earlier than the date of execution (signing) of the Contract. After the first sentence, enter eit[illegible] the [illegible]ific [illegible]nencement of the Work, or if a notice to proceed is to be used, enter the sentence, "The date of co[illegible]nceme[illegible]all be [illegible]ated by the notice to proceed." When time of performance is to be strictly enforced, the statem[illegible]rting tim[illegible]uld be carefully weighed.

Paragraph 3.2
The time within which Substantial Completion of the Work is to [illegible]ved may [illegible]pressed as a number of days (preferably calendar days) or as a specified date. Any requirements for ea[illegible] Substantial Comp[illegible]on of portions of the Work should be entered here if not specified elsewhere in the Contract Docum[illegible]

Also insert any provisions for liquidated damages relatin[illegible]ilur[illegible]ompl[illegible]on time. Liqui[illegible]amages are not a penalty to be inflicted on the Contractor, but must bear an actu[illegible] and re[illegible]bly [illegible] relationship t[illegible] r's loss if construction is not completed on time. If liquidated damages are t[illegible]ssesse[illegible]ause delayed constr[illegible]n will re[illegible] actual loss to the Owner, the amount of damages due for each day [illegible]hou[illegible] entere[illegible] the Suppleme[illegible] Conditions or [illegible]reement. Factors such as confidentiality or the need to infor[illegible]rac[illegible]ho[illegible] amount of li[illegible]ted[illegible]ages will [illegible]p determine the location chosen.

The provision for liquidate[illegible]mag[illegible]be carefully r[illegible]ed or draft[illegible]wner's attorney, may be as follows:

> The Contractor an[illegible]ontracto[illegible]ety, if any, shall b[illegible]liab[illegible]hall pay [illegible] Owner the sums hereinafter stipulated as liquidated da[illegible]ch calen[illegible]y of delay unt[illegible] Wor[illegible]bsta[illegible]y complete: Dollars
> ($

For furth[illegible]nformation on liq[illegible]ed damages, pe[illegible]rovisions, see AIA Document A511, Guide for Supplementary Conditio[illegible].11.

7. Ar[illegible]4 –Co[illegible]um

[illegible]h 4.1
[illegible]ontract Sum payable to the Co[illegible]

[illegible]aragraph 4.2
[illegible]ntify any alternates described in the Contract Documents and accepted by the Owner. If decisions on alternates are to be made subsequent to execution of A101, attach a schedule showing the amount of each alternate and the date until which that amount is valid.

Paragraph 4.3
Enter any unit prices, cash allowances or cash contingency allowances.

If unit prices are not covered in greater detail elsewhere in the Contract Documents, the following provision for unit prices is suggested:

> The unit prices listed below shall determine the value of extra Work or changes in the Work, as applicable. They shall be considered complete and shall include all material and equipment, labor, installation costs, overhead and profit. Unit prices shall be used uniformly for additions or deductions.

Specific allowances for overhead and profit on Change Orders may be included under this paragraph to forestall disputes over future Change Order costs.

8. Article 5—Progress Payments

Paragraph 5.2
Insert the time period covered by each Application for Payment if it differs from the one given.

Paragraph 5.3
Insert the time schedule for presenting Applications for Payment. Insert the day of the month progress payments are due, indicating whether such day is to be in the same or the following month after receipt by the Architect of the relevant Application for Payment.

The last day upon which Work may be included in an Application should normally be no less than 14 days prior to the payment date, in consideration of the 7 days required for the Architect's evaluation of an Application and issuance of a Certificate for Payment and the time subsequently accorded the Owner to make payment in Article 9 of A201. The Contractor may prefer a few additional days to prepare the Application.

Due dates for payment should be acceptable to both the Owner and Contractor. They should allow sufficient time for the Contractor to prepare an Application for Payment, for the Architect to certify payment, and for the Owner to make payment. They should also be in accordance with time limits established by this Article and Article 9 of A201.

Subparagraph 5.6.1
Indicate the percent retainage, if any, to be withheld when computing the amount of each progress payment.

The Owner frequently pays the Contractor 90 percent of the earned sum when payments fall due, retaining 10 percent to ensure faithful performance. These percentages may vary with circumstances and localities. The AIA endorses the practice of reducing retainage as rapidly as possible, consistent with the continued protection of all affected parties. See AIA Document A511, Gui[illegible]r Supplementary Conditions, for a complete discussion.

Subparagraph 5.6.2
Insert any additional retainage to be withheld from that portion of the Contract Sum allocable to materials and equipm[illegible] the site.

Payment for materials stored off the site should be provided for in a specific agreement and enumera[illegible] Par[illegible]h 7.[illegible]ovisions regarding transportation to the site and insurance protecting Owner's interests should be inclu[illegible]

Subparagraph 5.7.1
Enter the percentage of the Contract Sum to be paid to the Contractor upon Substa[illegible]omp[illegible]n.

Paragraph 5.8
Describe any arrangements to reduce or limit retainages indicated in Subparagr[illegible] 5[illegible]nd 5.6.2, [illegible]ot explained elsewhere in the Contract Documents.

A provision for reducing retainage should provide that the reduction [illegible] be made only if [illegible]chitect judges that the Work is progressing satisfactorily. If the Contractor has furnished a bond, de[illegible]stration [illegible]he surety's conse[illegible] reduction in or partial release of retainage must be provided before such reducti[illegible] effe[illegible] Use o[illegible]A Document G[illegible]s recommended.

9. **Article 6—Final Payment**

   Insert the date by which Owner shall make final pa[illegible]t, if it [illegible]rs from the one [illegible].

   When final payment is requested, the A[illegible] shou[illegible]at all claims h[illegible]ee[illegible]led or sh[illegible]d define those which remain unsettled. The Architect shou[illegible]tain [illegible] Contra[illegible]ertification [illegible]ire[illegible]cle 9 of A201 and must determine that, to the best of the Architect's kn[illegible]ledg[illegible]d according to fin[illegible]pection, [illegible]equi[illegible]nts of the Contract have been fulfilled.

10. **Article 7—Miscellane[illegible] P[illegible]ons**

    Paragraph 7.2
    Enter any ag[illegible]d-upon interest r[illegible]ue on overdue [illegible]

    Parag[illegible]ph 7[illegible]
    Inser[illegible]r provisions [illegible]e.

    [illegible]umeration of Contract Do[illegible]
    [illegible]eration of all Contract Docum[illegible]t be made in this Article.

D. [illegible]ECU[illegible]ON OF THE AGREEMENT

The Agreement should be executed in not less than triplicate by the Owner and the Contractor. Each person executing the Agreement should indicate the capacity in which they are acting (i.e., president, secretary, partner, etc.) and the authority under which they are executing the Agreement. Where appropriate, a copy of the resolution authorizing the individual to act on behalf of the firm or entity should be attached.

THE AMERICAN INSTITUTE OF ARCHITECTS

AIA Document A101

Standard Form of Agreement Between Owner and Contractor

where the basis of payment is a

STIPULATED SUM

1987 EDITION

THIS DOCUMENT HAS IMPORTANT LEGAL CONSEQUENCES; CONSULTATION WITH AN ATTORNEY IS ENCOURAGED WITH RESPECT TO ITS COMPLETION OR MODIFICATION.

The 1987 Edition of AIA Document A201, General Conditions of the Contract for Construction, is adopted in this document by reference. Do not use with other general conditions unless this document is modified.

This document has been approved and endorsed by The Associated General Contractors of America.

AGREEMENT

made as of the day of in the year of Nineteen Hundred and

BETWEEN the Owner:
(Name and address)

and the Contractor:
(Name and address)

The Project is:
(Name and location)

The Architect is:
(Name and address)

The Owner and Contractor agree as set forth below.

ARTICLE 1
THE CONTRACT DOCUMENTS

The Contract Documents consist of this Agreement, Conditions of the Contract (General, Supplementary and other Conditions), Drawings, Specifications, Addenda issued prior to execution of this Agreement, other documents listed in this Agreement and Modifications issued after execution of this Agreement; these form the Contract, and are as fully a part of the Contract as if attached to this Agreement or repeated herein. The Contract represents the entire and integrated agreement between the parties hereto and supersedes prior negotiations, representations or agreements, either written or oral. An enumeration of the Contract Documents, other than Modifications, appears in Article 9.

ARTICLE 2
THE WORK OF THIS CONTRACT

The Contractor shall execute the entire Work described in the Contract Documents, except to the extent specifically indicated in the Contract Documents to be the responsibility of others, or as follows:

ARTICLE 3
DATE OF COMMENCEMENT AND SUBSTANTIAL COMPLETION

3.1 The date of commencement is the date from which the Contract Time of Paragraph 3.2 is measured, and shall be the date of this Agreement, as first written above, unless a different date is stated below or provision is made for the date to be fixed in a notice to proceed issued by the Owner.

(Insert the date of commencement, if it differs from the date of this Agreement or, if applicable, state that the date will be fixed in a notice to proceed.)

Unless the date of commencement is established by a notice to proceed issued by the Owner, the Contractor shall notify the Owner in writing not less than five days before commencing the Work to permit the timely filing of mortgages, mechanic's liens and other security interests.

3.2 The Contractor shall achieve Substantial Completion of the entire Work not later than

(Insert the calendar date or number of calendar days after the date of commencement. Also insert any requirements for earlier Substantial Completion of certain portions of the Work, if not stated elsewhere in the Contract Documents.)

, subject to adjustments of this Contract Time as provided in the Contract Documents.

(Insert provisions, if any, for liquidated damages relating to failure to complete on time.)

ARTICLE 4
CONTRACT SUM

4.1 The Owner shall pay the Contractor in current funds for the Contractor's performance of the Contract the Contract Sum of Dollars ($), subject to additions and deductions as provided in the Contract Documents.

4.2 The Contract Sum is based upon the following alternates, if any, which are described in the Contract Documents and are hereby accepted by the Owner:

(State the numbers or other identification of accepted alternates. If decisions on other alternates are to be made by the Owner subsequent to the execution of this Agreement, attach a schedule of such other alternates showing the amount for each and the date until which that amount is valid.)

4.3 Unit prices, if any, are as follows:

ARTICLE 5
PROGRESS PAYMENTS

5.1 Based upon Applications for Payment submitted to the Architect by the Contractor and Certificates for Payment issued by the Architect, the Owner shall make progress payments on account of the Contract Sum to the Contractor as provided below and elsewhere in the Contract Documents.

5.2 The period covered by each Application for Payment shall be one calendar month ending on the last day of the month, or as follows:

5.3 Provided an Application for Payment is received by the Architect not later than the day of a month, the Owner shall make payment to the Contractor not later than the day of the month. If an Application for Payment is received by the Architect after the application date fixed above, payment shall be made by the Owner not later than days after the Architect receives the Application for Payment.

5.4 Each Application for Payment shall be based upon the Schedule of Values submitted by the Contractor in accordance with the Contract Documents. The Schedule of Values shall allocate the entire Contract Sum among the various portions of the Work and be prepared in such form and supported by such data to substantiate its accuracy as the Architect may require. This Schedule, unless objected to by the Architect, shall be used as a basis for reviewing the Contractor's Applications for Payment.

5.5 Applications for Payment shall indicate the percentage of completion of each portion of the Work as of the end of the period covered by the Application for Payment.

5.6 Subject to the provisions of the Contract Documents, the amount of each progress payment shall be computed as follows:

5.6.1 Take that portion of the Contract Sum properly allocable to completed Work as determined by multiplying the percentage completion of each portion of the Work by the share of the total Contract Sum allocated to that portion of the Work in the Schedule of Values, less retainage of percent (%). Pending final determination of cost to the Owner of changes in the Work, amounts not in dispute may be included as provided in Subparagraph 7.3.7 of the General Conditions even though the Contract Sum has not yet been adjusted by Change Order;

5.6.2 Add that portion of the Contract Sum properly allocable to materials and equipment delivered and suitably stored at the site for subsequent incorporation in the completed construction (or, if approved in advance by the Owner, suitably stored off the site at a location agreed upon in writing), less retainage of percent (%);

5.6.3 Subtract the aggregate of previous payments made by the Owner; and

5.6.4 Subtract amounts, if any, for which the Architect has withheld or nullified a Certificate for Payment as provided in Paragraph 9.5 of the General Conditions.

5.7 The progress payment amount determined in accordance with Paragraph 5.6 shall be further modified under the following circumstances:

5.7.1 Add, upon Substantial Completion of the Work, a sum sufficient to increase the total payments to percent (%) of the Contract Sum, less such amounts as the Architect shall determine for incomplete Work and unsettled claims; and

5.7.2 Add, if final completion of the Work is thereafter materially delayed through no fault of the Contractor, any additional amounts payable in accordance with Subparagraph 9.10.3 of the General Conditions.

5.8 Reduction or limitation of retainage, if any, shall be as follows:

(If it is intended, prior to Substantial Completion of the entire Work, to reduce or limit the retainage resulting from the percentages inserted in Subparagraphs 5.6.1 and 5.6.2 above, and this is not explained elsewhere in the Contract Documents, insert here provisions for such reduction or limitation.)

ARTICLE 6
FINAL PAYMENT

Final payment, constituting the entire unpaid balance of the Contract Sum, shall be made by the Owner to the Contractor when (1) the Contract has been fully performed by the Contractor except for the Contractor's responsibility to correct nonconforming Work as provided in Subparagraph 12.2.2 of the General Conditions and to satisfy other requirements, if any, which necessarily survive final payment; and (2) a final Certificate for Payment has been issued by the Architect; such final payment shall be made by the Owner not more than 30 days after the issuance of the Architect's final Certificate for Payment, or as follows:

ARTICLE 7
MISCELLANEOUS PROVISIONS

7.1 Where reference is made in this Agreement to a provision of the General Conditions or another Contract Document, the reference refers to that provision as amended or supplemented by other provisions of the Contract Documents.

7.2 Payments due and unpaid under the Contract shall bear interest from the date payment is due at the rate stated below, or in the absence thereof, at the legal rate prevailing from time to time at the place where the Project is located.

(Insert rate of interest agreed upon, if any.)

(Usury laws and requirements under the Federal Truth in Lending Act, similar state and local consumer credit laws and other regulations at the Owner's and Contractor's principal places of business, the location of the Project and elsewhere may affect the validity of this provision. Legal advice should be obtained with respect to deletions or modifications, and also regarding requirements such as written disclosures or waivers.)

7.3 Other provisions:

ARTICLE 8
TERMINATION OR SUSPENSION

8.1 The Contract may be terminated by the Owner or the Contractor as provided in Article 14 of the General Conditions.

8.2 The Work may be suspended by the Owner as provided in Article 14 of the General Conditions.

ARTICLE 9

ENUMERATION OF CONTRACT DOCUMENTS

9.1 The Contract Documents, except for Modifications issued after execution of this Agreement, are enumerated as follows:

9.1.1 The Agreement is this executed Standard Form of Agreement Between Owner and Contractor, AIA Document A101, 1987 Edition.

9.1.2 The General Conditions are the General Conditions of the Contract for Construction, AIA Document A201, 1987 Edition.

9.1.3 The Supplementary and other Conditions of the Contract are those contained in the Project Manual dated , and are as follows:

Document	Title	Pages

9.1.4 The Specifications are those contained in the Project Manual dated as in Subparagraph 9.1.3, and are as follows:
(Either list the Specifications here or refer to an exhibit attached to this Agreement.)

Section	Title	Pages

9.1.5 The Drawings are as follows, and are dated unless a different date is shown below:
(Either list the Drawings here or refer to an exhibit attached to this Agreement.)

Number	Title	Date

9.1.6 The Addenda, if any, are as follows:

Number	Date	Pages

Portions of Addenda relating to bidding requirements are not part of the Contract Documents unless the bidding requirements are also enumerated in this Article 9.

9.1.7 Other documents, if any, forming part of the Contract Documents are as follows:

(List here any additional documents which are intended to form part of the Contract Documents. The General Conditions provide that bidding requirements such as advertisement or invitation to bid, Instructions to Bidders, sample forms and the Contractor's bid are not part of the Contract Documents unless enumerated in this Agreement. They should be listed here only if intended to be part of the Contract Documents.)

This Agreement is entered into as of the day and year first written above and is executed in at least three original copies of which one is to be delivered to the Contractor, one to the Architect for use in the administration of the Contract, and the remainder to the Owner.

OWNER	CONTRACTOR
(Signature)	*(Signature)*
(Printed name and title)	*(Printed name and title)*

INSTRUCTION SHEET

FOR AIA DOCUMENT A107, ABBREVIATED FORM OF AGREEMENT BETWEEN OWNER AND CONTRACTOR for Construction Projects of LIMITED SCOPE where the Basis of Payment is a STIPULATED SUM—1987 EDITION

A. GENERAL INFORMATION

1. Purpose

AIA Document A107, an abbreviated form, is intended for use on construction projects of limited scope where the basis of payment is a stipulated sum (fixed fee) and where the combined complexity and length of AIA Documents A101, Owner-Contract[illegible]greement, and A201, General Conditions of the Contract for Construction, are not required. This document may be used on [illegible]ects where the Contractor's compensation has been negotiated, but it is not necessarily suitable where compensation [illegible]ermi[illegible]y bidding. The bidding process involves unknowns and uncertainties which complicate the procurement of cons[illegible] small projects.

2. Related Documents

This document contains abbreviated General Conditions partially derived from the 1987 e[illegible] of [illegible] and [illegible]ld not be used with a separate general conditions document. The A107 document is used as one pa[illegible] th[illegible]tra[illegible]s that record the Contract for Construction between the Owner and Contractor. The other Cont[illegible]ocume[illegible]e:

Supplementary Conditions
Drawings
Specifications
Modifications

Although the AIA does not produce standard documents [illegible] Sup[illegible]entary [illegible]nditions, Drawi[illegible] Specifications, a variety of model and guide documents are available, including AIA [illegible]STE[illegible]C.

3. Arbitration

The A107 document incorporates AR[illegible]N ac[illegible]e Construction [illegible]st[illegible]bitration Rules of the American Arbitration Association. Arbitration is BIN[illegible] AN[illegible]ANDA[illegible] in most sta[illegible]d u[illegible]e fed[illegible] Arbitration Act. In a minority of states, arbitration provisions [illegible]d [illegible] are not enforce[illegible]but arbitr[illegible]is [illegible]ceable if agreed to after the dispute arises. A few states requir[illegible]the co[illegible]ing [illegible]s be especially [illegible]fied [illegible] the [illegible] contract contains an arbitration provision by: a warning o[illegible]f the do[illegible]nt, specific plac[illegible]nt o[illegible]itration provision within the document or specific discussions among the p[illegible]ies [illegible] to sign[illegible]the document.

Arbitration [illegible]ns have b[illegible]cluded in most [illegible]cont[illegible]s si[illegible]88 in order to encourage alternative dispute resolution proc[illegible]es a[illegible]provide[illegible]rs of AIA docum[illegible]eg[illegible]nforceable arbitration provisions when the parties choose to ado[illegible]arbi[illegible]ir contract. Indi[illegible]ay, [illegible]ver, c[illegible]e to delete the arbitration provisions based upon their busines[illegible]isions with t[illegible]dvice of couns[illegible]To obtain a c[illegible]f the Construction Industry Arbitration Rules, write to the American Arbi[illegible]n As[illegible], 140 West 51st [illegible] N[illegible]020.

[illegible]AIA Forms

[illegible]ombination of AIA documents and non-AIA documents is to be used, particular care must be taken to achieve consistency of la[illegible]guage and intent. Certain owners require the use of owner-contractor agreements and other contract forms which they prepare. Such forms should be carefully compared with the standard AIA forms for which they are being substituted before execution of an agreement. If there are any significant omissions, additions or variances from the terms of the related standard AIA forms, both legal and insurance counsel should be consulted.

5. Disclosure Statements

Prior to executing this Agreement, the Owner and the prospective Contractor may reasonably require written evidence of the other party's financial ability to fulfill the respective obligations under the Contract. The Owner may, for instance, provide the Contractor with a letter from the Owner's lender indicating that funds are available to pay for the Work of the Contractor. The Contractor may provide information through a financial statement or on AIA Document A305, Contractor's Qualification Statement.

6. Letter Forms of Agreement

Letter forms of agreement are generally discouraged by the AIA, as is the performance of a part or the whole of the Work on the basis of oral agreements or understandings. The standard AIA agreement forms have been developed through more than seventy-five years of experience and have been tested repeatedly in the courts. In addition, the standard forms have been carefully coordinated with other AIA documents.

7. Use of Current Documents

Prior to using any AIA document, the user should consult the AIA, an AIA component chapter or a current AIA Documents Price List to determine the current edition of each document.

8. Limited License for Reproduction

AIA Document A107 is a copyrighted work and may not be reproduced or excerpted from in substantial part without the express written permission of the AIA. The A107 document is intended to be used as a consumable—that is, the original document purchased by the user is intended to be consumed in the course of being used. There is no implied permission to reproduce this document, nor does membership in The American Institute of Architects confer any further rights to reproduce them.

A limited license is hereby granted to retail purchasers to reproduce a maximum of ten copies of a completed or executed A107, but only for use in connection with a particular Project. A107 may not be reproduced for Project Manuals. Rather, if a user wishes to include it as an example in a Project Manual, the normal practice is to purchase a quantity of the pre-printed forms and bind one in each of the Project Manuals. Partial modifications, if any, may be accomplished without completing the form by using separate S[illegible] plementary Conditions.

Upon reaching agreement concerning the Contract Sum and other conditions, the form may be removed from the man[illegible] uch information, except for the signatures, may be added to the blank spaces of the form. The user may then reproduce up to [illegible] to facilitate the execution (signing) of multiple original copies of the form, or for other administrative purposes [illegible] ecti[illegible] with a particular Project.

B. CHANGES FROM THE PREVIOUS EDITION

1. Format Changes

The article entitled Architect, formerly Article 8, has been retitled and repositioned a[illegible] Adminis[illegible] on of the Contract. The dispute resolution procedures have been consolidated under this new Ar[illegible]

2. Changes in Content

The 1987 edition of A107 revises the 1978 edition to reflect a[illegible] lle[illegible] made in the [illegible] ions of AIA Document A101, an Owner-Contractor Agreement, and AIA Doc[illegible] nt A20[illegible] ner[illegible] ons of the Co[illegible] onstruction. It incorporates alterations proposed by architects, contractors, [illegible] ers and [illegible] essional consultan[illegible] ne of the [illegible] ficant differences in content between this edition and the 1978 edi[illegible] A[illegible] re as [illegible] ws.

Article 1: Space has been provided to d[illegible] xcep[illegible] e descriptio[illegible] of [illegible] actor's scope of Work.

Article 6: Spaces have been provide[illegible] for [illegible] tifying the other C[illegible] ct Docu[illegible] i[illegible] ng the Supplementary Conditions, Specifications, Drawing[illegible] Adde[illegible] an[illegible]

Article 9: The terms of th[illegible] or's war[illegible] have been wri[illegible] to n[illegible] sely p[illegible] alle[illegible] AIA Document A201, and the Shop Drawings requirements hav[illegible] bee[illegible] anded.

Article 10: This [illegible] w article e[illegible] Administration [illegible] C[illegible] nd [illegible] es the former article entitled Architect. Many of the provisions s[illegible] Archit[illegible] with little change. [illegible] visi[illegible] n arbitration have been moved to this article from the article en[illegible] d M[illegible] ovisions.

Article 13 [illegible] ew in[illegible] for effecting [illegible] Wo[illegible] e Construction Change Directive, is now provided for.

[illegible] pr[illegible] on has been added c[illegible] ng [illegible] performance of Work involving asbestos or polychlorinated biphenyl (P[illegible]

Arti[illegible] 9: A provision has been added defining [illegible] dates when the statutes of limitations will commence to run on the [illegible] ontr[illegible] s Work.

C. COMPLETING THE A107 FORM

1. Prospective bidders should be informed of any additional provisions which may be included in A107, such as liquidated damages or payment for stored materials, by an appropriate notice in the Bidding Documents and the Supplementary Conditions.

2. Modifications

Users are encouraged to consult with an attorney before completing an AIA document. Particularly with respect to contractor's licensing laws, duties imposed by building codes, interest charges, arbitration and indemnification, this document may require modification with the assistance of legal counsel to fully comply with state or local laws regulating these matters.

Generally, necessary modifications may be accomplished by writing or typing the appropriate terms in the blank spaces provided on the form or by Supplementary Conditions, special conditions or amendments included in the Project Manual and referenced in this document. The form may also be modified by striking out language directly on the original pre-printed form. Care must be taken in making these kinds of deletions, however. Under NO circumstances should pre-printed language be struck out in such a way as to render it illegible (as, for example, with blocking tape, correction fluid or X's that completely obscure the text). This may raise suspicions of fraudulent concealment, or suggest that the completed and signed document has been tampered with. Handwritten changes should be initialed by both parties to the contract.

It is definitely not recommended practice to retype the standard document. Besides being outside the limited license for reproduction granted under these Instructions, retyping can introduce typographical errors and cloud the legal interpretation given to a standard clause when blended with modifications.

Retyping eliminates one of the principal advantages of the standard form documents. By merely reviewing the modifications to be made to a standard form document, parties familiar with that document can quickly understand the essence of the proposed relationship. Commercial exchanges are greatly simplified and expedited, good-faith dealing is encouraged, and otherwise latent clauses are exposed for scrutiny. In this way, contracting parties can more fairly measure their risks.

3. Cover Page

Date: The date represents the date the Agreement becomes effective. It may be the date that an oral agreement was reached, the date the Agreement was originally submitted to the Owner, the date authorizing action was taken or the date of actual ex[illegible]on. It will be the date from which the Contract Time is measured unless a different date is provided for under Paragraph 2.1.

Identification of Parties: Parties to this Agreement should be identified using the full address and legal name und[illegible] ment is to be executed, including a designation of the legal status of both parties (sole proprietorship, partnersh[illegible] unincorporated association, limited partnership or corporation [general, closed or professional], etc.). [illegible] a co[illegible] the resolution authorizing the individual to act on behalf of the firm or entity should be attached[illegible]

Project Description: The proposed Project should be described in sufficient detail to identify (1) [illegible] official [illegible] of the facility, (2) the location of the site, if known, (3) the proposed building type and usage, and [illegible] size [illegible] capacity [illegible] scope of the Project, if known.

Architect: As in the other Contract Documents, the Architect's full legal or co[illegible] titles s[illegible] be used.

4. Article 1—The Work of This Contract

Portions of the Work which are the responsibility of persons ot[illegible] than the Contract[illegible] which have not been otherwise indicated should be listed here.

5. Article 2—Date of Commencement and Substantial C[illegible]

The following items should be included as app[illegible]te:

Paragraph 2.1

The date of commencement of the [illegible] be inse[illegible] if it differs [illegible] the d[illegible] the A[illegible]ment. It should not be earlier than the date of execution (sign[illegible] th[illegible] either the sp[illegible] date of co[illegible] of the Work, or if a notice to proceed is to be used, ente[illegible]ntence, [illegible] date [illegible] commencemen[illegible] pulated [illegible] notice to proceed." When time of performance is to be s[illegible]rced, the [illegible]ment of starti[illegible]me s[illegible] be ca[illegible]lly weighed.

Paragraph [illegible]

The time [illegible] which Subst[illegible] Completion o[illegible] ac[illegible]ved may be expressed as a number of days (preferably calendar [illegible]ecified date. Any re[illegible]men[illegible]arlier [illegible]antial Completion of portions of the Work should be entered h[illegible] not [illegible] where in the [illegible] Docu[illegible]

Als[illegible]rt a[illegible]ons for liquidate[illegible]ing [illegible]ilure to complete on time. Liquidated damages are not a penalty to be [illegible] the Contractor, but must b[illegible] actu[illegible]d reasonably estimable relationship to the Owner's loss if construction is not [illegible]n time. If liquidated damages ar[illegible] [illegible]ssessed because delayed construction will result in actual loss to the Owner, the [illegible]ount [illegible] damages due for each day lost [illegible] be entered in the Supplementary Conditions or the Agreement. Factors such as [illegible]fidentiality or the need to inform Subcontractors about the amount of liquidated damages will help determine the choice of [illegible]cation.

The provision for liquidated damages, which should be carefully reviewed or drafted by the Owner's attorney, may be as follows:

> The Contractor and the Contractor's surety, if any, shall be liable for and shall pay the Owner the sums hereinafter stipulated as liquidated damages for each calendar day of delay until the Work is substantially complete: Dollars ($).

For further information on liquidated damages, penalties and bonus provisions, see AIA Document A511, Guide for Supplementary Conditions, Paragraph 9.11.

6. Article 3—Contract Sum

Paragraph 3.1

Enter the Contract Sum payable to the Contractor.

Paragraph 3.2

Identify any alternates described in the Contract Documents and accepted by the Owner. If decisions on alternates are to be made subsequent to execution of A107, attach a schedule showing the amount of each alternate and the date until which that amount is valid.

Paragraph 3.3

Enter any unit prices, cash allowances or cash contingency allowances.

If unit prices are not covered in greater detail elsewhere in the Contract Documents, the following provision for unit prices is suggested:

> The unit prices listed below shall determine the value of extra Work or changes in the Work, as applicable. They shall be considered complete and shall include all material and equipment, labor, installation costs, overhead and profit. Unit prices shall be used uniformly for additions or deductions.

Specific allowances for overhead and profit on Change Orders may be included under this paragraph to forestall disputes over future Change Order costs.

7. Article 4—Progress Payments

Paragraph 4.1

Insert the time covered by each Application for Payment, if it differs from the one stated, and provision for retainage, if any.

Paragraph 4.2

Enter any agreed-upon interest rate due on overdue payments.

8. Article 6—Enumeration of Contract Documents

A detailed enumeration of all Contract Documents must be made in this article.

9. Article 21—Other Conditions or Provisions

If minor additions or changes are desired, they may be inserted in this article once the Contractor has been selected. If changes are to be shown to prospective bidders or are extensive in scope, they should be handled by drafting a separate Supplementary Conditions document, similar in format to that described in AIA Document A511, Guide for Supplementary Conditions.

D. EXECUTION OF THE AGREEMENT

Each person executing the Agreement should indicate the capacity in which they are acting (i.e., president, secretary, partner, etc.) and the authority under which they are executing the Agreement. Where appropriate, a copy of the resolution authorizing the individual to act on behalf of the firm or entity should be attached.

AIA Document A107

Abbreviated Form of Agreement Between Owner and Contractor

For CONSTRUCTION PROJECTS OF LIMITED SCOPE where the Basis of Payment is a STIPULATED SUM

1987 EDITION

THIS DOCUMENT HAS IMPORTANT LEGAL CONSEQUENCES; CONSULTATION WITH AN ATTORNEY IS ENCOURAGED WITH RESPECT TO ITS COMPLETION OR MODIFICATION.

This document includes abbreviated General Conditions and should not be used with other general conditions. It has been approved and endorsed by The Associated General Contractors of America.

AGREEMENT

made as of the day of in the year of Nineteen Hundred and

BETWEEN the Owner:
(Name and address)

and the Contractor:
(Name and address)

The Project is:
(Name and location)

The Architect is:
(Name and address)

The Owner and Contractor agree as set forth below.

ARTICLE 1
THE WORK OF THIS CONTRACT

1.1 The Contractor shall execute the entire Work described in the Contract Documents, except to the extent specifically indicated in the Contract Documents to be the responsibility of others, or as follows:

ARTICLE 2
DATE OF COMMENCEMENT AND SUBSTANTIAL COMPLETION

2.1 The date of commencement is the date from which the Contract Time of Paragraph 2.2 is measured, and shall be the date of this Agreement, as first written above, unless a different date is stated below or provision is made for the date to be fixed in a notice to proceed issued by the Owner.

(Insert the date of commencement, if it differs from the date of this Agreement or, if applicable, state that the date will be fixed in a notice to proceed.)

2.2 The Contractor shall achieve Substantial Completion of the entire Work not later than

(Insert the calendar date or number of calendar days after the date of commencement. Also insert any requirements for earlier Substantial Completion of certain portions of the Work, if not stated elsewhere in the Contract Documents.)

, subject to adjustments of this Contract Time as provided in the Contract Documents.

(Insert provisions, if any, for liquidated damages relating to failure to complete on time.)

ARTICLE 3
CONTRACT SUM

3.1 The Owner shall pay the Contractor in current funds for the Contractor's performance of the Contract the Contract Sum of Dollars ($), subject to additions and deductions as provided in the Contract Documents.

3.2 The Contract Sum is based upon the following alternates, if any, which are described in the Contract Documents and are hereby accepted by the Owner:

(State the numbers or other identification of accepted alternates. If decisions on other alternates are to be made by the Owner subsequent to the execution of this Agreement, attach a schedule of such other alternates showing the amount for each and the date until which that amount is valid.)

3.3 Unit prices, if any, are as follows:

ARTICLE 4
PROGRESS PAYMENTS

4.1 Based upon Applications for Payment submitted to the Architect by the Contractor and Certificates for Payment issued by the Architect, the Owner shall make progress payments on account of the Contract Sum to the Contractor as provided below and elsewhere in the Contract Documents. The period covered by each Application for Payment shall be one calendar month ending on the last day of the month, or as follows:

4.2 Payments due and unpaid under the Contract shall bear interest from the date payment is due at the rate stated below, or in the absence thereof, at the legal rate prevailing from time to time at the place where the Project is located.

(Insert rate of interest agreed upon, if any.)

(Usury laws and requirements under the Federal Truth in Lending Act, similar state and local consumer credit laws and other regulations at the Owner's and Contractor's principal places of business, the location of the Project and elsewhere may affect the validity of this provision. Legal advice should be obtained with respect to deletions or modifications, and also regarding requirements such as written disclosures or waivers.)

ARTICLE 5

FINAL PAYMENT

5.1 Final payment, constituting the entire unpaid balance of the Contract Sum, shall be made by the Owner to the Contractor when the Work has been completed, the Contract fully performed, and a final Certificate for Payment has been issued by the Architect.

ARTICLE 6

ENUMERATION OF CONTRACT DOCUMENTS

6.1 The Contract Documents are listed in Article 7 and, except for Modifications issued after execution of this Agreement, are enumerated as follows:

6.1.1 The Agreement is this executed Abbreviated Form of Agreement Between Owner and Contractor, AIA Document A107, 1987 Edition.

6.1.2 The Supplementary and other Conditions of the Contract are those contained in the Project Manual dated , and are as follows:

Document	Title	Pages

6.1.3. The Specifications are those contained in the Project Manual dated as in Subparagraph 6.1.2, and are as follows:
(Either list the Specifications here or refer to an exhibit attached to this Agreement.)

Section	Title	Pages

6.1.4 The Drawings are as follows, and are dated unless a different date is shown below:
(Either list the Drawings here or refer to an exhibit attached to this Agreement.)

Number	Title	Date

6.1.5 The Addenda, if any, are as follows:

Number	Date	Pages

Portions of Addenda relating to bidding requirements are not part of the Contract Documents unless the bidding requirements are also enumerated in this Article 6.

6.1.6 Other documents, if any, forming part of the Contract Documents are as follows:
(List any additional documents which are intended to form part of the Contract Documents.)

GENERAL CONDITIONS

ARTICLE 7
CONTRACT DOCUMENTS

7.1 The Contract Documents consist of this Agreement with Conditions of the Contract (General, Supplementary and other Conditions), Drawings, Specifications, addenda issued prior to the execution of this Agreement, other documents listed in this Agreement and Modifications issued after execution of this Agreement. The intent of the Contract Documents is to include all items necessary for the proper execution and completion of the Work by the Contractor. The Contract Documents are complementary, and what is required by one shall be as binding as if required by all; performance by the Contractor shall be required only to the extent consistent with the Contract Documents and reasonably inferable from them as being necessary to produce the intended results.

7.2 The Contract Documents shall not be construed to create a contractual relationship of any kind (1) between the Architect and Contractor, (2) between the Owner and a Subcontractor or Sub-subcontractor or (3) between any persons or entities other than the Owner and Contractor.

7.3 Execution of the Contract by the Contractor is a representation that the Contractor has visited the site and become familiar with the local conditions under which the Work is to be performed.

7.4 The term "Work" means the construction and services required by the Contract Documents, whether completed or partially completed, and includes all other labor, materials, equipment and services provided or to be provided by the Contractor to fulfill the Contractor's obligations. The Work may constitute the whole or a part of the Project.

ARTICLE 8
OWNER

8.1 The Owner shall furnish surveys and a legal description of the site.

8.2 Except for permits and fees which are the responsibility of the Contractor under the Contract Documents, the Owner shall secure and pay for necessary approvals, easements, assessments and charges required for the construction, use or occupancy of permanent structures or permanent changes in existing facilities.

8.3 If the Contractor fails to correct Work which is not in accordance with the requirements of the Contract Documents or persistently fails to carry out the Work in accordance with the Contract Documents, the Owner, by a written order, may order the Contractor to stop the Work, or any portion thereof, until the cause for such order has been eliminated; however, the right of the Owner to stop the Work shall not give rise to a duty on the part of the Owner to exercise this right for the benefit of the Contractor or any other person or entity.

ARTICLE 9
CONTRACTOR

9.1 The Contractor shall supervise and direct the Work, using the Contractor's best skill and attention. The Contractor shall be solely responsible for and have control over construction means, methods, techniques, sequences and procedures and for coordinating all portions of the Work under the Contract, unless Contract Documents give other specific instructions concerning these matters.

9.2 Unless otherwise provided in the Contract Documents, the Contractor shall provide and pay for labor, materials, equipment, tools, construction equipment and machinery, water, heat, utilities, transportation, and other facilities and services necessary for the proper execution and completion of the Work, whether temporary or permanent and whether or not incorporated or to be incorporated in the Work.

9.3 The Contractor shall enforce strict discipline and good order among the Contractor's employees and other persons carrying out the Contract. The Contractor shall not permit employment of unfit persons or persons not skilled in tasks assigned to them.

9.4 The Contractor warrants to the Owner and Architect that materials and equipment furnished under the Contract will be of good quality and new unless otherwise required or permitted by the Contract Documents, that the Work will be free from defects not inherent in the quality required or permitted, and that the Work will conform with the requirements of the Contract Documents. Work not conforming to these requirements, including substitutions not properly approved and authorized, may be considered defective. The Contractor's warranty excludes remedy for damage or defect caused by abuse, modifications not executed by the Contractor, improper or insufficient maintenance, improper operation, or normal wear and tear under normal usage. If required by the Architect, the Contractor shall furnish satisfactory evidence as to the kind and quality of materials and equipment.

9.5 Unless otherwise provided in the Contract Documents, the Contractor shall pay sales, consumer, use, and other similar taxes which are legally enacted when bids are received or negotiations concluded, whether or not yet effective or merely scheduled to go into effect, and shall secure and pay for the building permit and other permits and governmental fees, licenses and inspections necessary for proper execution and completion of the Work.

9.6 The Contractor shall comply with and give notices required by laws, ordinances, rules, regulations, and lawful orders of public authorities bearing on performance of the Work. The Contractor shall promptly notify the Architect and Owner if the Drawings and Specifications are observed by the Contractor to be at variance therewith.

9.7 The Contractor shall be responsible to the Owner for the acts and omissions of the Contractor's employees, Subcontractors and their agents and employees, and other persons performing portions of the Work under a contract with the Contractor.

9.8 The Contractor shall review, approve and submit to the Architect Shop Drawings, Product Data, Samples and similar submittals required by the Contract Documents with reasonable promptness. The Work shall be in accordance with approved submittals. When professional certification of performance criteria of materials, systems or equipment is required by the Contract Documents, the Architect shall be entitled to rely upon the accuracy and completeness of such certifications.

9.9 The Contractor shall keep the premises and surrounding area free from accumulation of waste materials or rubbish caused by operations under the Contract. At completion of the Work the Contractor shall remove from and about the Project waste materials, rubbish, the Contractor's tools, construction equipment, machinery and surplus materials.

9.10 The Contractor shall provide the Owner and Architect access to the Work in preparation and progress wherever located.

9.11 The Contractor shall pay all royalties and license fees; shall defend suits or claims for infringement of patent rights and shall hold the Owner harmless from loss on account thereof, but shall not be responsible for such defense or loss when a particular design, process or product of a particular manufacturer or manufacturers is required by the Contract Documents unless the Contractor has reason to believe that there is an infringement of patent.

9.12 To the fullest extent permitted by law, the Contractor shall indemnify and hold harmless the Owner, Architect, Architect's consultants, and agents and employees of any of them from and against claims, damages, losses and expenses, including but not limited to attorneys' fees, arising out of or resulting from performance of the Work, provided that such claim, damage, loss or expense is attributable to bodily injury, sickness, disease or death, or to injury to or destruction of tangible property (other than the Work itself) including loss of use resulting therefrom, but only to the extent caused in whole or in part by negligent acts or omissions of the Contractor, a Subcontractor, anyone directly or indirectly employed by them or anyone for whose acts they may be liable, regardless of whether or not such claim, damage, loss or expense is caused in part by a party indemnified hereunder. Such obligation shall not be construed to negate, abridge, or reduce other rights or obligations of idemnity which would otherwise exist as to a party or person described in this Paragraph 9.12.

9.12.1 In claims against any person or entity indemnified under this Paragraph 9.12 by an employee of the Contractor, a Subcontractor, anyone directly or indirectly employed by them or anyone for whose acts they may be liable, the indemnification obligation under this Paragraph 9.12 shall not be limited by a limitation on amount or type of damages, compensation or benefits payable by or for the Contractor or a Subcontractor under workers' or workmen's compensation acts, disability benefit acts or other employee benefit acts.

9.12.2 The obligations of the Contractor under this Paragraph 9.12 shall not extend to the liability of the Architect, the Architect's consultants, and agents and employees of any of them arising out of (1) the preparation or approval of maps, drawings, opinions, reports, surveys, Change Orders, Construction Change Directives, designs or specifications, or (2) the giving of or the failure to give directions or instructions by the Architect, the Architect's consultants, and agents and employees of any of them provided such giving or failure to give is the primary cause of the injury or damage.

ARTICLE 10

ADMINISTRATION OF THE CONTRACT

10.1 The Architect will provide administration of the Contract and will be the Owner's representative (1) during construction, (2) until final payment is due and (3) with the Owner's concurrence, from time to time during the correction period described in Paragraph 18.1

10.2 The Architect will visit the site at intervals appropriate to the stage of construction to become generally familiar with the progress and quality of the completed Work and to determine in general if the Work is being performed in a manner indicating that the Work, when completed, will be in accordance with the Contract Documents. However, the Architect will not be required to make exhaustive or continuous on-site inspections to check quality or quantity of the Work. On the basis of on-site observations as an architect, the Architect will keep the Owner informed of progress of the Work and will endeavor to guard the Owner against defects and deficiencies in the Work.

10.3 The Architect will not have control over or charge of and will not be responsible for construction means, methods, techniques, sequences or procedures, or for safety precautions and programs in connection with the Work, since these are solely the Contractor's responsibility as provided in Paragraphs 9.1 and 16.1. The Architect will not be responsible for the Contractor's failure to carry out the Work in accordance with the Contract Documents.

10.4 Based on the Architect's observations and evaluations of the Contractor's Applications for Payment, the Architect will review and certify the amounts due the Contractor and will issue Certificates for Payment in such amounts.

10.5 The Architect will interpret and decide matters concerning performance and requirements of the Contract Documents on written request of either the Owner or Contractor. The Architect will make initial decisions on all claims, disputes or other matters in question between the Owner and Contractor, but will not be liable for results of any interpretations or decisions rendered in good faith. The Architect's decisions in matters relating to aesthetic effect will be final if consistent with the intent expressed in the Contract Documents. All other decisions of the Architect, except those which have been waived by making or acceptance of final payment, shall be subject to arbitration upon the written demand of either party.

10.6 The Architect will have authority to reject Work which does not conform to the Contract Documents.

10.7 The Architect will review and approve or take other appropriate action upon the Contractor's submittals such as Shop Drawings, Product Data and Samples, but only for the limited purpose of checking for conformance with information given and the design concept expressed in the Contract Documents.

10.8 All claims or disputes between the Contractor and the Owner arising out or relating to the Contract, or the breach thereof, shall be decided by arbitration in accordance with the Construction Industry Arbitration Rules of the American Arbitration Association currently in effect unless the parties mutually agree otherwise and subject to an initial presentation of the claim or dispute to the Architect as required under Paragraph 10.5. Notice of the demand for arbitration shall be filed in writing with the other party to this Agreement and with the American Arbitration Association and shall be made within a reasonable time after the dispute has arisen. The award rendered by the arbitrator or arbitrators shall be final, and judgment may be entered upon it in accordance with applicable law in any court having jurisdiction thereof. Except by written consent of the person or entity sought to be joined, no arbitration arising out of or relating to the Contract Documents shall include, by consolidation, joinder or in any other manner, any person or entity not a party to the Agreement under which such arbitration arises, unless it is shown at the time the demand for arbitration is filed that (1) such person or entity is substantially involved in a common question of fact or law, (2) the presence of such person or entity is required if complete relief is to be accorded in the arbitration, (3) the interest or responsibility of such person or entity in the matter is not insubstantial, and (4) such person or entity is not the Architect or any of the Architect's employees or consultants. The agreement herein among the parties to the Agreement and any other written agreement to arbitrate referred to herein shall be specifically enforceable under applicable law in any court having jurisdiction thereof.

ARTICLE 11

SUBCONTRACTS

11.1 A Subcontractor is a person or entity who has a direct contract with the Contractor to perform a portion of the Work at the site.

11.2 Unless otherwise stated in the Contract Documents or the bidding requirements, the Contractor, as soon as practicable after award of the Contract, shall furnish in writing to the Owner through the Architect the names of the Subcontractors for each of the principal portions of the Work. The Contractor shall not contract with any Subcontractor to whom the Owner or Architect has made reasonable and timely objection. The Contractor shall not be required to contract with anyone to whom the Contractor has made reasonable objection. Contracts between the Contractor and Subcontractors shall (1) require each Subcontractor, to the extent of the Work to be performed by the Subcontractor, to be bound to the Contractor by the terms of the Contract Documents, and to assume toward the Contractor all the obligations and responsibilities which the Contractor, by the Contract Documents, assumes toward the Owner and Architect, and (2) allow to the Subcontractor the benefit of all rights, remedies and redress afforded to the Contractor by these Contract Documents.

ARTICLE 12

CONSTRUCTION BY OWNER OR BY SEPARATE CONTRACTORS

12.1 The Owner reserves the right to perform construction or operations related to the Project with the Owner's own forces, and to award separate contracts in connection with other portions of the Project or other construction or operations on the site under conditions of the contract identical or substantially similar to these, including those portions related to insurance and waiver of subrogation. If the Contractor claims that delay or additional cost is involved because of such action by the Owner, the Contractor shall make such claim as provided elsewhere in the Contract Documents.

12.2 The Contractor shall afford the Owner and separate contractors reasonable opportunity for the introduction and storage of their materials and equipment and performance of their activities, and shall connect and coordinate the Contractor's construction and operations with theirs as required by the Contract Documents.

12.3 Costs caused by delays, improperly timed activities or defective construction shall be borne by the party responsible therefor.

ARTICLE 13

CHANGES IN THE WORK

13.1 The Owner, without invalidating the Contract, may order changes in the Work consisting of additions, deletions or modifications, the Contract Sum and Contract Time being adjusted accordingly. Such changes in the Work shall be authorized by written Change Order signed by the Owner, Contractor and Architect, or by written Construction Change Directive signed by the Owner and Architect.

13.2 The Contract Sum and Contract Time shall be changed only by Change Order.

13.3 The cost or credit to the Owner from a change in the Work shall be determined by mutual agreement.

ARTICLE 14

TIME

14.1 Time limits stated in the Contract Documents are of the essence of the Contract. By executing the Agreement the Contractor confirms that the Contract Time is a reasonable period for performing the Work.

14.2 The date of Substantial Completion is the date certified by the Architect in accordance with Paragraph 15.3.

14.3 If the Contractor is delayed at any time in progress of the Work by changes ordered in the Work, by labor disputes, fire, unusual delay in deliveries, abnormal adverse weather conditions not reasonably anticipatable, unavoidable casualties or any causes beyond the Contractor's control, or by other causes which the Architect determines may justify delay, then the Contract Time shall be extended by Change Order for such reasonable time as the Architect may determine.

ARTICLE 15

PAYMENTS AND COMPLETION

15.1 Payments shall be made as provided in Articles 4 and 5 of this Agreement.

15.2 Payments may be withheld on account of (1) defective Work not remedied, (2) claims filed by third parties, (3) failure of the Contractor to make payments properly to Subcontractors or for labor, materials or equipment, (4) reasonable evidence that the Work cannot be completed for the unpaid balance of the Contract Sum, (5) damage to the Owner or another contractor, (6) reasonable evidence that the Work will not be completed within the Contract Time and that the unpaid balance would not be adequate to cover actual or liquidated damages for the anticipated delay, or (7) persistent failure to carry out the Work in accordance with the Contract Documents.

15.3 When the Architect agrees that the Work is substantially complete, the Architect will issue a Certificate of Substantial Completion.

15.4 Final payment shall not become due until the Contractor has delivered to the Owner a complete release of all liens arising out of this Contract or receipts in full covering all labor, materials and equipment for which a lien could be filed, or a bond satisfactory to the Owner to indemnify the Owner against such lien. If such lien remains unsatisfied after payments are made, the Contractor shall refund to the Owner all money that the Owner may be compelled to pay in discharging such lien, including all costs and reasonable attorneys' fees.

15.5 The making of final payment shall constitute a waiver of claims by the Owner except those arising from:

.1 liens, claims, security interests or encumbrances arising out of the Contract and unsettled;

.2 failure of the Work to comply with the requirements of the Contract Documents; or

.3 terms of special warranties required by the Contract Documents.

Acceptance of final payment by the Contractor, a Subcontractor or material supplier shall constitute a waiver of claims by that payee except those previously made in writing and identified by that payee as unsettled at the time of final Application for Payment.

ARTICLE 16
PROTECTION OF PERSONS AND PROPERTY

16.1 The Contractor shall be responsible for initiating, maintaining, and supervising all safety precautions and programs in connection with the performance of the Contract. The Contractor shall take reasonable precautions for safety of, and shall provide reasonable protection to prevent damage, injury or loss to:

.1 employees on the Work and other persons who may be affected thereby;

.2 the Work and materials and equipment to be incorporated therein; and

.3 other property at the site or adjacent thereto.

The Contractor shall give notices and comply with applicable laws, ordinances, rules, regulations and lawful orders of public authorities bearing on safety of persons and property and their protection from damage, injury or loss. The Contractor shall promptly remedy damage and loss to property at the site caused in whole or in part by the Contractor, a Subcontractor, a Sub-subcontractor, or anyone directly or indirectly employed by any of them, or by anyone for whose acts they may be liable and for which the Contractor is responsible under Subparagraphs 16.1.2 and 16.1.3, except for damage or loss attributable to acts or omissions of the Owner or Architect or by anyone for whose acts either of them may be liable, and not attributable to the fault or negligence of the Contractor. The foregoing obligations of the Contractor are in addition to the Contractor's obligations under Paragraph 9.12.

16.2 The Contractor shall not be required to perform without consent any Work relating to asbestos or polychlorinated biphenyl (PCB).

ARTICLE 17
INSURANCE

17.1 The Contractor shall purchase from and maintain in a company or companies lawfully authorized to do business in the jurisdiction in which the Project is located insurance for protection from claims under workers' or workmen's compensation acts and other employee benefit acts which are applicable, claims for damages because of bodily injury, including death, and from claims for damages, other than to the Work itself, to property which may arise out of or result from the Contractor's operations under the Contract, whether such operations be by the Contractor or by a Subcontractor or anyone directly or indirectly employed by any of them. This insurance shall be written for not less than limits of liability specified in the Contract Documents or required by law, whichever coverage is greater, and shall include contractual liability insurance applicable to the Contractor's obligations under Paragraph 9.12. Certificates of such insurance shall be filed with the Owner prior to the commencement of the Work.

17.2 The Owner shall be responsible for purchasing and maintaining the Owner's usual liability insurance. Optionally, the Owner may purchase and maintain other insurance for self-protection against claims which may arise from operations under the Contract. The Contractor shall not be responsible for purchasing and maintaining this optional Owner's liability insurance unless specifically required by the Contract Documents.

17.3 Unless otherwise provided, the Owner shall purchase and maintain, in a company or companies lawfully authorized to do business in the jurisdiction in which the Project is located, property insurance upon the entire Work at the site to the full insurable value thereof. This insurance shall be on an all-risk policy form and shall include interests of the Owner, the Contractor, Subcontractors and Sub-subcontractors in the Work and shall insure against the perils of fire and extended coverage and physical loss or damage including, without duplication of coverage, theft, vandalism and malicious mischief.

17.4 A loss insured under Owner's property insurance shall be adjusted with the Owner and made payable to the Owner as fiduciary for the insureds, as their interests may appear, subject to the requirements of any applicable mortgagee clause.

17.5 The Owner shall file a copy of each policy with the Contractor before an exposure to loss may occur. Each policy shall contain a provision that the policy will not be cancelled or allowed to expire until at least 30 days' prior written notice has been given to the Contractor.

17.6 The Owner and Contractor waive all rights against each other and the Architect, Architect's consultants, separate contractors described in Article 12, if any, and any of their subcontractors, sub-subcontractors, agents and employees, for damages caused by fire or other perils to the extent covered by property insurance obtained pursuant to this Article 17 or any other property insurance applicable to the Work, except such rights as they may have to the proceeds of such insurance held by the Owner as fiduciary. The Contractor shall require similar waivers in favor of the Owner and the Contractor by Subcontractors and Sub-subcontractors. The Owner shall require similar waivers in favor of the Owner and Contractor by the Architect, Architect's consultants, separate contractors described in Article 12, if any, and the subcontractors, sub-subcontractors, agents and employees of any of them.

ARTICLE 18
CORRECTION OF WORK

18.1 The Contractor shall promptly correct Work rejected by the Architect or failing to conform to the requirements of the Contract Documents, whether observed before or after Substantial Completion and whether or not fabricated, installed or completed, and shall correct any Work found to be not in accordance with the requirements of the Contract Documents within a period of one year from the date of Substantial Completion of the Contract or by terms of an applicable special warranty required by the Contract Documents. The provisions of this Article 18 apply to Work done by Subcontractors as well as to Work done by direct employees of the Contractor.

18.2 Nothing contained in this Article 18 shall be construed to establish a period of limitation with respect to other obligations which the Contractor might have under the Contract Documents. Establishment of the time period of one year as described in Paragraph 18.1 relates only to the specific obligation of the Contractor to correct the Work, and has no relationship to the time within which the obligation to comply with the Contract Documents may be sought to be enforced, nor to the time within which proceedings may be commenced to establish the Contractor's liability with respect to the Contractor's obligations other than specifically to correct the Work.

ARTICLE 19

MISCELLANEOUS PROVISIONS

19.1 The Contract shall be governed by the law of the place where the Project is located.

19.2 As between the Owner and the Contractor, any applicable statute of limitations shall commence to run and any alleged cause of action shall be deemed to have accrued:

- **.1** not later than the date of Substantial Completion for acts or failures to act occurring prior to the relevant date of Substantial Completion;
- **.2** not later than the date of issuance of the final Certificate for Payment for acts or failures to act occurring subsequent to the relevant date of Substantial Completion and prior to issuance of the final Certificate for Payment; and
- **.3** not later than the date of the relevant act or failure to act by the Contractor for acts or failures to act occurring after the date of the final Certificate for Payment.

ARTICLE 20

TERMINATION OF THE CONTRACT

20.1 If the Architect fails to recommend payment for a period of 30 days through no fault of the Contractor, or if the Owner fails to make payment thereon for a period of 30 days, the Contractor may, upon seven additional days' written notice to the Owner and the Architect, terminate the Contract and recover from the Owner payment for Work executed and for proven loss with respect to materials, equipment, tools, and construction equipment and machinery, including reasonable overhead, profit and damages applicable to the Project.

20.2 If the Contractor defaults or persistently fails or neglects to carry out the Work in accordance with the Contract Documents or fails to perform a provision of the Contract, the Owner, after seven days' written notice to the Contractor and without prejudice to any other remedy the Owner may have, may make good such deficiencies and may deduct the cost thereof, including compensation for the Architect's services and expenses made necessary thereby, from the payment then or thereafter due the Contractor. Alternatively, at the Owner's option, and upon certification by the Architect that sufficient cause exists to justify such action, the Owner may terminate the Contract and take possession of the site and of all materials, equipment, tools, and construction equipment and machinery thereon owned by the Contractor and may finish the Work by whatever method the Owner may deem expedient. If the unpaid balance of the Contract Sum exceeds costs of finishing the Work, including compensation for the Architect's services and expenses made necessary thereby, such excess shall be paid to the Contractor, but if such costs exceed such unpaid balance, the Contractor shall pay the difference to the Owner.

ARTICLE 21
OTHER CONDITIONS OR PROVISIONS

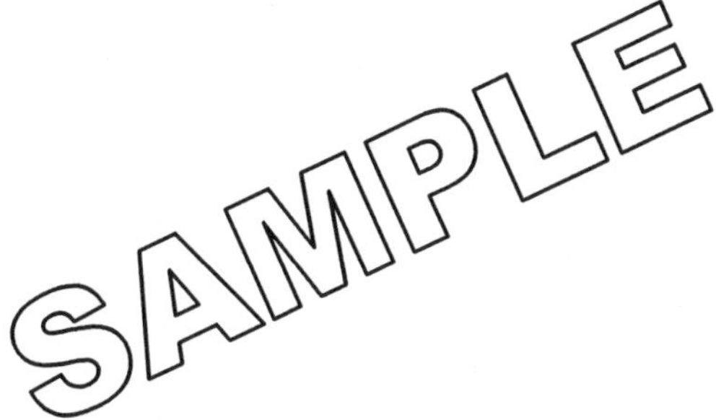

This Agreement entered into as of the day and year first written above.

OWNER	CONTRACTOR
(Signature)	*(Signature)*
(Printed name and title)	*(Printed name and title)*

CAUTION: You should sign an original AIA document which has this caution printed in red. An original assures that changes will not be obscured as may occur when documents are reproduced.

INSTRUCTION SHEET

FOR AIA DOCUMENT A111, STANDARD FORM OF AGREEMENT BETWEEN OWNER AND CONTRACTOR where the basis of payment is the COST OF THE WORK PLUS A FEE with or without a Guaranteed Maximum Price—1987 EDITION

A. GENERAL INFORMATION

1. Purpose

AIA Document A111 is intended for use on construction projects where the basis of payment is the cost of the Work plus a fixed or percentage fee. While the cost-plus-fee arrangement lacks the financial certainty of a lump-sum agreement, it may be desirable when fixed prices on portions of the Work cannot be obtained, when construction must be started before Drawings and Specifica[illegible]s are completed, or under other circumstances.

2. Related Documents

This document has been prepared for use in conjunction with the 1987 edition of AIA Document A201, General C[illegible] Contract for Construction, which is adopted into A111 by a specific reference. This integrated set of d[illegible]uit[illegible] for m[illegible] projects; however, for projects of limited scope, use of AIA Document A117 may be considered.

The A111 document may be used as one part of the Contract Documents which record the C[illegible]tract [illegible] Constru[illegible]n between the Owner and the Contractor. The other Contract Documents are:

- General Conditions (i.e., A201)
- Supplementary Conditions
- Drawings
- Specifications
- Modifications

Although the AIA does not produce standard documents for Sup[illegible]entary Conditions, Drawings [illegible]pecifications, a variety of model and guide documents are available, including AIA'[illegible] ST[illegible]C.

3. Arbitration

This document incorporates ARBITRATION by ad[illegible]n of A[illegible]ocument A201, [illegible] provides f[illegible]tration according to the Construction Industry Arbitration Rules [illegible] Am[illegible] Arbi[illegible]on Associatio[illegible]itrati[illegible] is BIND[illegible] AND MANDATORY in most states and under the federal A[illegible]on[illegible]. In [illegible] of states, a[illegible]itra[illegible]ons relating to future disputes are not enforceable, but arbitration is e[illegible]for[illegible] i[illegible]ed to after the dispute[illegible]. A f[illegible]es r[illegible] that the contracting parties be especially notified that the w[illegible] co[illegible] arbitration [illegible]on b[illegible] a w[illegible] the face of the document, specific placement of the arbitra[illegible]vision w[illegible] the document or speci[illegible] is amo[illegible] parties prior to signing the document.

Arbitration provisions [illegible] included [illegible]ost AIA cont[illegible]rms [illegible] 188[illegible] order to encourage alternative dispute resolution procedure[illegible] to provi[illegible]rs of AIA documents with [illegible] en[illegible]bitration provisions when the parties choose to adopt arbit[illegible] into their co[illegible]t. Individuals [illegible]ose [illegible] delete the arbitration provisions based upon their business d[illegible] the advice of counsel. To [illegible] cop[illegible] the Construction Industry Arbitration Rules, write to the Am[illegible]n A[illegible]ciation, 140 W[illegible] Stree[illegible] York, [illegible] 10020.

4. Use o[illegible]n-AI[illegible]

[illegible]ion of AIA documents and non-AIA d[illegible]ments is to be used, particular care must be taken to achieve consistency of [illegible]gua[illegible] intent. Certain owners require [illegible] owner-contractor agreements and other contract forms which they prepare. [illegible] forms should be carefully compared to the standard AIA forms for which they are being substituted before execution of an a[illegible]ment. If there are any significant omissions, additions or variances from the terms of the related standard AIA forms, both legal and insurance counsel should be consulted.

5. Letter Forms of Agreement

Letter forms of agreement are generally discouraged by the AIA, as is the performance of a part or the whole of the Work on the basis of oral agreements or understandings. The standard AIA agreement forms have been developed through more than seventy-five years of experience and have been tested repeatedly in the courts. In addition, the standard forms have been carefully coordinated with other AIA documents.

6. Use of Current Documents

Prior to using any AIA document, the user should consult the AIA, an AIA component chapter or a current AIA Documents Price List to determine the current edition of each document.

7. Limited License for Reproduction

AIA Document A111 is a copyrighted work and may not be reproduced or excerpted from in substantial part without the express written permission of the AIA. The A111 document is intended to be used as a consumable—that is, the original document purchased by the user is intended to be consumed in the course of being used. There is no implied permission to reproduce this document, nor does membership in The American Institute of Architects confer any further rights to reproduce them.

A limited license is hereby granted to retail purchasers to reproduce a maximum of ten copies of a completed or executed A111, but only for use in connection with a particular Project. A111 may not be reproduced for Project Manuals. Rather, if a user wishes to include it as an example in a Project Manual, the normal practice is to purchase a quantity of the pre-printed forms and bind one in each of the Project Manuals. Partial modifications, if any, may be accomplished without completing the form by using separate Supplementary Conditions.

Upon reaching agreement concerning the Contract Sum and other conditions, the form may be removed from the manual and such information, except for the signatures, may be added to the blank spaces of the form. The user may then reproduce up to ten copies to facilitate the execution (signing) of multiple original copies of the form, or for other administrative purposes in connection with a particular Project. Please note that at least three original copies of A111 should be signed by the parties as required by the last provision of A111.

B. CHANGES FROM THE PREVIOUS EDITION

1. Format Changes

The titles of Articles 3, 4, 5, 12 and 13 have been changed; a new Article 16, Enumeration of Contract Documents, h[illegible], and former Articles 5 and 6 have been combined into a new Article 5, Contract Sum.

2. Changes in Content

The 1987 edition of A111 revises the 1978 edition to reflect changes made in the most recent (1987) edit[illegible]f AIA [illegible]01, General Conditions of the Contract for Construction, and to incorporate alterations propose[illegible] arch[illegible], own[illegible] contractors and professional consultants.

Article 2: Space has been provided to describe any exceptions to the description [illegible] Contrac[illegible] scope [illegible] Work.

Article 3: Language has been added requiring the Owner to excercise best effo[illegible] the Co[illegible]or to perform the Work.

Article 4: The title of this article now refers to the date rather than the ti[illegible]mmenc[illegible]t. The Contractor is now required to notify the Owner before commencing the Work to permit the timel[illegible] mortgages [illegible]other security interests.

Article 5: This article, entitled Contract Sum, combines the for[illegible]er ar[illegible]on Cos[illegible]he Work and Gu[illegible]d Maximum Cost and the former article on Contractor's Fee. The provisions on Gu[illegible]um [illegible] have been ex[illegible] to include further details on Change Orders.

Article 6: This article has been substantially revised t[illegible] for c[illegible]s in the Work with[illegible]thout a [illegible]nteed Maximum Price.

Article 7: Costs to be reimbursed now includ[illegible]custo[illegible] medical health[illegible]fits, [illegible]sts of w[illegible]d spoilage, costs of testing and payment of royalties or fees [illegible]ten[illegible]s, and costs of [illegible] and repair to defective Work not caused by the Contractor.

Article 8: Two new exceptions [illegible] will not be rei[illegible]sed. One is [illegible]yment of the Contractor's personnel at the principal offic[illegible] specifi[illegible] provid[illegible] for under Arti[illegible] other [illegible]ws payment for costs of correction when the cause is not th[illegible]or or th[illegible]tractor's supe[illegible] p[illegible]el.

Article 9: Rebates [illegible] discount[illegible]uing to [illegible] Owner are cre[illegible] to th[illegible] a deduction from the Cost of the Work.

Article 10: Th[illegible] may desig[illegible] specific Subco[illegible] [illegible]m [illegible]ontractor must obtain bids. If a Guaranteed Maximum Price is [illegible]vever, [illegible] Contractor may o[illegible] der if the Owner rejects a Subcontractor selected by the Contr[illegible]

Article [illegible]his artic[illegible]ines two form[illegible] to the Contractor. Separate payment procedures are provided for [illegible]cts [illegible] an[illegible]cts without a Gu[illegible]ce.

[illegible] article on final payment has been subs[illegible]ally rewritten to parallel the provisions of AIA Document A201. Further [illegible] has [illegible]dded on the procedures for ca[illegible]nal payment, including a requirement that the Owner's accountant review th[illegible]tractor's final accounting.

Artic[illegible]14: The reference to the definition of terms contained in the A201 document has been deleted; A201 is now specifically [illegible]dopted by reference into A111. A new sentence has been added noting that references to a specific provision of the General Conditions or another Contract Document include any amendment or supplement to that provision. The provision on interest for overdue payments has been moved to this article from the former article on payments to the Contractor.

Article 15: Provisions have been added concerning termination of contracts with a Guaranteed Maximum Price and suspension of the Project.

Article 16: This new article contains cross-references to the General Conditions.

C. COMPLETING THE A111 FORM

1. Modifications

Users are encouraged to consult an attorney before completing an AIA document. Particularly with respect to contractor's licensing laws, duties imposed by building codes, interest charges, arbitration and indemnification, this document may require modification with the assistance of legal counsel to fully comply with state or local laws regulating these matters.

Generally, necessary modifications may be accomplished by writing or typing the appropriate terms in the blank spaces provided on the form or by Supplementary Conditions, special conditions or amendments included in the Project Manual and referenced in this document. The form may also be modified by striking out language directly on the original pre-printed form. Care must be taken in making these kinds of deletions, however. Under NO circumstances should pre-printed language be struck out in such a way as to render it illegible (as, for example, with blocking tape, correction fluid or X's that completely obscure the text). This may raise suspicions of fraudulent concealment, or suggest that the completed and signed document has been tampered with. Handwritten changes should be initialed by both parties to the contract.

It is definitely not recommended practice to retype the standard document. Besides being outside the limited license for reproduction granted under these Instructions, retyping can introduce typographical errors and cloud the legal interpretation given to a standard clause when blended with modifications.

Retyping eliminates one of the principal advantages of the standard form documents. By merely reviewing the modifications to be made to a standard form document, parties familiar with that document can quickly understand the essence of the proposed relationship. Commercial exchanges are greatly simplified and expedited, good-faith dealing is encouraged, and otherwise latent clauses are exposed for scrutiny. In this way, contracting parties can more fairly measure their risks.

2. Cover Page

Date: The date represents the date the Agreement becomes effective. It may be the date an oral agreement was reached, the [illegible] he Agreement was originally submitted to the Owner, the date authorizing action was taken or the date of actual ex[illegible] the date from which the Contract Time is measured unless a different date is inserted under Paragragh 4.1.

Identification of Parties: Parties to this Agreement should be identified using the full legal name under [illegible] Agre[illegible]t is [illegible] executed, including a designation of the legal status of both parties (sole proprietorship, partnership [illegible] ve[illegible] un[illegible]porated association, limited partnership or corporation [general, closed or professional], etc.). Where appro[illegible]e, a co[illegible] the [illegible]solution authorizing the individual to act on behalf of the firm or entity should be attached.

Project Description: The proposed Project should be described in sufficient detail to i[illegible]fy [illegible] of[illegible]r title of the facility, (2) the location of the site, if known, (3) the proposed building type and usag[illegible](4) the s[illegible]pacity or scope of the Project, if known.

Architect: As in the other Contract Documents, the Architect's full leg[illegible] corpora[illegible]s should be used.

3. Article 2—The Work of This Contract

Portions of the Work which are the responsibility of pers[illegible] oth[illegible]an the [illegible]tractor and whi[illegible] not been otherwise indicated should be listed here.

4. Article 4—Date of Commencement and Subs[illegible]al Co[illegible]on

Paragraph 4.1
The date of commencement of the W[illegible] be [illegible] different fro[illegible] date [illegible]e Agreem[illegible]. It should not be earlier than the date of execution (signing) [illegible]e Co[illegible]act. A[illegible] first sentenc[illegible] ter [illegible]e specific date of commencement of the Work, or if a notice to procee[illegible] to [illegible] the sentence, "Th[illegible] of com[illegible]em[illegible]all be stipulated by the notice to proceed." When time of [illegible]ance [illegible] be [illegible] enforced, t[illegible] tem[illegible]f st[illegible]e should be carefully considered.

Paragraph 4.2
The time within which Sub[illegible]al Comp[illegible]on of the Work [illegible] be [illegible] be expressed as a number of days (preferably calendar day[illegible] specified[illegible] Any requireme[illegible]r earl[illegible]star[illegible]pletion of portions of the Work should be entered here if no[illegible]ecifi[illegible]where [illegible]e Contract Doc[illegible]

Als[illegible]sert [illegible] for liquidated d[illegible] relati[illegible]ailure [illegible]omplete on time. Liquidated damages are not a penalty to be infl[illegible] on the Contr[illegible]r, but must be [illegible]n act[illegible]nd [illegible]ably estimable relationship to the Owner's loss if construction is not comp[illegible] on [illegible]quidated damag[illegible]sse[illegible]cause delayed construction will result in actual loss to the Owner, the [illegible]damages due for each day lost should [illegible]ntered in the Supplementary Conditions or the Agreement. Factors such as [illegible] or the need to inform Subc[illegible] about the amount of liquidated damages will help determine the location [illegible]sen.

[illegible] provision for liquidated damages, which should be carefully reviewed or drafted by the Owner's attorney, may be as follows:

> The Contractor and the Contractor's surety, if any, shall be liable for and shall pay the Owner the sums hereinafter stipulated as liquidated damages for each calendar day of delay until the Work is substantially completed: ($).

For further information on liquidated damages, penalties and bonus provisions, see AIA Document A511, Guide for Supplementary Conditions, Paragraph 9.11.

5. Article 5—Contract Sum

Paragraph 5.1
Enter the method used for determining the Contractor's Fee (lump sum, percentage of Cost of the Work or other method) and explain how the Contractor's Fee is to be adjusted for changes in the Work.

Subparagraph 5.2.1
If applicable, insert a Guaranteed Maximum Price for the Cost of the Work and the Contractor's Fee. Insert specific provisions if the Contractor is to participate in any savings when the final Contract Sum is below the Guaranteed Maximum Price.

Subparagraph 5.2.2
If a Guaranteed Maximum Price is given in Subparagraph 5.2.1, identify any alternates described in the Contract Documents and accepted by the Owner. If decisions on alternates are to be made subsequent to execution of A111, attach a schedule showing the amount of each alternate and the date until which that amount is valid.

Subparagraph 5.2.3
If a Guaranteed Maximum Price is given in Subparagraph 5.2.1, state any amounts agreed for unit prices.

6. Article 7—Costs To Be Reimbursed
Article 8—Costs Not To Be Reimbursed

Modifications to these articles should be included in Paragraph 14.3. Such modifications should be carefully coordinated to ensure consistency between these two articles.

7. Article 12—Progress Payments

Paragraph 12.2
Insert the time period covered by each Application for Payment if it differs from the one given.

Paragraph 12.3
Insert the time schedule for presenting Applications for Payment. Insert the day of the month progress payments are due, indi[illegible] whether such day is to be in the same or the following month after receipt by the Architect of the relevant Application for Paym[illegible]

The last day upon which Work may be included in an Application should normally be no less than 14 days prior t[illegible] date, in consideration of the 7 days required for the Architect's evaluation of an Application and issuance of a Certificate [illegible] and the time subsequently accorded the Owner to make payment in Article 9 of A201. The Contractor m[illegible] few [illegible]tional days to prepare the Application.

Due dates for payment should be acceptable to both the Owner and Contractor. They should all[illegible] su[illegible]nt time [illegible]he Contractor to prepare an Application for Payment, for the Architect to certify payment, and for the O[illegible]o m[illegible]ayme[illegible] They should also be in accordance with time limits established by this Article and Article 9 of A201[illegible]

Clause 12.5.3.3
In contracts with a Guaranteed Maximum Price, indicate the percent retainage[illegible] be with[illegible]om the Contractor's Fee when computing the amount of each progress payment.

Subparagraph 12.5.4
In contracts with a Guaranteed Maximum Price, insert additional reta[illegible], if any, from pro[illegible]s payments to the Contractor above that indicated in Clause 12.5.3.3 or elsewhere in A111. Descri[illegible] arra[illegible]ents f[illegible]iting or reducin[illegible] additional retainage as the Work progresses.

Clause 12.6.2.2
In contracts without a Guaranteed Maximum Price, [illegible]te the [illegible]nt retainage to be w[illegible]d from [illegible]ctor's Fee when computing the amount of each progress paymen[illegible]

Subparagraph 12.6.3
In contracts without a Guaranteed M[illegible]m [illegible] insert [illegible]onal retain[illegible] any[illegible] prog[illegible]s payments to the Contractor above that indicated in Subpara[illegible] 1[illegible] in A111. Des[illegible] arrangem[illegible]g or reducing such additional retainage as the Work prog[illegible]

Subparagraph 12.7.1
Insert the percent retainage, if a[illegible] be sub[illegible]cted from the sh[illegible] the [illegible] Sub[illegible]ract Sum in the Subcontractor's schedule of values when d[illegible]g the ma[illegible]n amount of pa[illegible]t per [illegible]ntra[illegible] be included in each of the Contractor's Applications for Pay[illegible]t.

Subp[illegible]rap[illegible]
Insert [illegible]ercent retain[illegible] if any, to be s[illegible]acted from th[illegible]tion of the Subcontract Sum allocable to materials and equipment [illegible]ed a[illegible]ite [illegible]ulating the maxi[illegible] per[illegible]contractor to be included in each of the Contractor's Applications [illegible]

[illegible]ara[illegible] 12.7.5
In[illegible]he percentage of the Subcontract Sum to be paid to the Subcontractor upon Substantial Completion. Describe any arrangeme[illegible] reduce or limit any retainages indicated in Subparagraphs 12.7.1 and 12.7.2, if not explained elsewhere.

[illegible] Article 14—Miscellaneous Provisions

Paragraph 14.2
Insert any agreed-upon rate of interest chargeable on overdue payments to the Contractor.

Paragraph 14.3
Insert any other provisions which may apply and which are not mentioned elsewhere in the Contract Documents.

9. Article 16—Enumeration of Contract Documents

A detailed enumeration of all Contract Documents must be made in this article.

D. EXECUTION OF THE AGREEMENT

The Agreement should be executed in not less than triplicate by the Owner and the Contractor. Each person executing the Agreement should indicate the capacity in which they are acting (i.e., president, secretary, partner, etc.) and the authority under which they are executing the Agreement. Where appropriate, a copy of the resolution authorizing the individual to act on behalf of the firm or entity should be attached.

THE AMERICAN INSTITUTE OF ARCHITECTS

AIA Document A111

Standard Form of Agreement Between Owner and Contractor

where the basis of payment is the
COST OF THE WORK PLUS A FEE
with or without a Guaranteed Maximum Price

1987 EDITION

THIS DOCUMENT HAS IMPORTANT LEGAL CONSEQUENCES; CONSULTATION WITH AN ATTORNEY IS ENCOURAGED WITH RESPECT TO ITS COMPLETION OR MODIFICATION.

The 1987 Edition of AIA Document A201, General Conditions of the Contract for Construction, is adopted in this document by reference. Do not use with other general conditions unless this document is modified.

This document has been approved and endorsed by The Associated General Contractors of America.

AGREEMENT

made as of the day of in the year of Nineteen Hundred and

BETWEEN the Owner:
(Name and address)

and the Contractor:
(Name and address)

the Project is:
(Name and address)

the Architect is:
(Name and address)

The Owner and Contractor agree as set forth below.

ARTICLE 1
THE CONTRACT DOCUMENTS

1.1 The Contract Documents consist of this Agreement, Conditions of the Contract (General, Supplementary and other Conditions), Drawings, Specifications, addenda issued prior to execution of this Agreement, other documents listed in this Agreement and Modifications issued after execution of this Agreement; these form the Contract, and are as fully a part of the Contract as if attached to this Agreement or repeated herein. The Contract represents the entire and integrated agreement between the parties hereto and supersedes prior negotiations, representations or agreements, either written or oral. An enumeration of the Contract Documents, other than Modifications, appears in Article 16. If anything in the other Contract Documents is inconsistent with this Agreement, this Agreement shall govern.

ARTICLE 2
THE WORK OF THIS CONTRACT

2.1 The Contractor shall execute the entire Work described in the Contract Documents, except to the extent specifically indicated in the Contract Documents to be the responsibility of others, or as follows:

ARTICLE 3
RELATIONSHIP OF THE PARTIES

3.1 The Contractor accepts the relationship of trust and confidence established by this Agreement and covenants with the Owner to cooperate with the Architect and utilize the Contractor's best skill, efforts and judgment in furthering the interests of the Owner; to furnish efficient business administration and supervision; to make best efforts to furnish at all times an adequate supply of workers and materials; and to perform the Work in the best way and most expeditious and economical manner consistent with the interests of the Owner. The Owner agrees to exercise best efforts to enable the Contractor to perform the Work in the best way and most expeditious manner by furnishing and approving in a timely way information required by the Contractor and making payments to the Contractor in accordance with requirements of the Contract Documents.

ARTICLE 4
DATE OF COMMENCEMENT AND SUBSTANTIAL COMPLETION

4.1 The date of commencement is the date from which the Contract Time of Subparagraph 4.2 is measured; it shall be the date of this Agreement, as first written above, unless a different date is stated below or provision is made for the date to be fixed in a notice to proceed issued by the Owner.

(Insert the date of commencement, if it differs from the date of this Agreement or, if applicable, state that the date will be fixed in a notice to proceed.)

Unless the date of commencement is established by a notice to proceed issued by the Owner, the Contractor shall notify the Owner in writing not less than five days before commencing the Work to permit the timely filing of mortgages, mechanic's liens and other security interests.

4.2 The Contractor shall achieve Substantial Completion of the entire Work not later than

(Insert the calendar date or number of calendar days after the date of commencement. Also insert any requirements for earlier Substantial Completion of certain portions of the Work, if not stated elsewhere in the Contract Documents.)

, subject to adjustments of this Contract Time as provided in the Contract Documents.

(Insert provisions, if any, for liquidated damages relating to failure to complete on time.)

ARTICLE 5
CONTRACT SUM

5.1 The Owner shall pay the Contractor in current funds for the Contractor's performance of the Contract the Contract Sum consisting of the Cost of the Work as defined in Article 7 and the Contractor's Fee determined as follows:

(State a lump sum, percentage of Cost of the Work or other provision for determining the Contractor's Fee and explain how the Contractor's Fee is to be adjusted for changes in the Work.)

5.2 GUARANTEED MAXIMUM PRICE (IF APPLICABLE)

5.2.1 The sum of the Cost of the Work and the Contractor's Fee is guaranteed by the Contractor not to exceed Dollars ($), subject to additions and deductions by Change Order as provided in the Contract Documents. Such maximum sum is referred to in the Contract Documents as the Guaranteed Maximum Price. Costs which would cause the Guaranteed Maximum Price to be exceeded shall be paid by the Contractor without reimbursement by the Owner.

(Insert specific provisions if the Contractor is to participate in any savings.)

5.2.2 The Guaranteed Maximum Price is based upon the following alternates, if any, which are described in the Contract Documents and are hereby accepted by the Owner:

(State the numbers or other identification of accepted alternates, but only if a Guaranteed Maximum Price is inserted in Subparagraph 5.2.1. If decisions on other alternates are to be made by the Owner subsequent to the execution of this Agreement, attach a schedule of such other alternates showing the amount for each and the date until which that amount is valid.)

5.2.3 The amounts agreed to for unit prices, if any, are as follows:

(State unit prices only if a Guaranteed Maximum Price is inserted in Subparagraph 5.2.1.)

ARTICLE 6
CHANGES IN THE WORK

6.1 CONTRACTS WITH A GUARANTEED MAXIMUM PRICE

6.1.1 Adjustments to the Guaranteed Maximum Price on account of changes in the Work may be determined by any of the methods listed in Subparagraph 7.3.3 of the General Conditions.

6.1.2 In calculating adjustments to subcontracts (except those awarded with the Owner's prior consent on the basis of cost plus a fee), the terms "cost" and "fee" as used in Clause 7.3.3.3 of the General Conditions and the terms "costs" and "a reasonable allowance for overhead and profit" as used in Subparagraph 7.3.6 of the General Conditions shall have the meanings assigned to them in the General Conditions and shall not be modified by Articles 5, 7 and 8 of this Agreement. Adjustments to subcontracts awarded with the Owner's prior consent on the basis of cost plus a fee shall be calculated in accordance with the terms of those subcontracts.

6.1.3 In calculating adjustments to this Contract, the terms "cost" and "costs" as used in the above-referenced provisions of the General Conditions shall mean the Cost of the Work as defined in Article 7 of this Agreement and the terms "fee" and "a reasonable allowance for overhead and profit" shall mean the Contractor's Fee as defined in Paragraph 5.1 of this Agreement.

6.2 CONTRACTS WITHOUT A GUARANTEED MAXIMUM PRICE

6.2.1 Increased costs for the items set forth in Article 7 which result from changes in the Work shall become part of the Cost of the Work, and the Contractor's Fee shall be adjusted as provided in Paragraph 5.1.

6.3 ALL CONTRACTS

6.3.1 If no specific provision is made in Paragraph 5.1 for adjustment of the Contractor's Fee in the case of changes in the Work, or if the extent of such changes is such, in the aggregate, that application of the adjustment provisions of Paragraph 5.1 will cause substantial inequity to the Owner or Contractor, the Contractor's Fee shall be equitably adjusted on the basis of the Fee established for the original Work.

ARTICLE 7
COSTS TO BE REIMBURSED

7.1 The term Cost of the Work shall mean costs necessarily incurred by the Contractor in the proper performance of the Work. Such costs shall be at rates not higher than the standard paid at the place of the Project except with prior consent of the Owner. The Cost of the Work shall include only the items set forth in this Article 7.

7.1.1 LABOR COSTS

7.1.1.1 Wages of construction workers directly employed by the Contractor to perform the construction of the Work at the site or, with the Owner's agreement, at off-site workshops.

7.1.1.2 Wages or salaries of the Contractor's supervisory and administrative personnel when stationed at the site with the Owner's agreement.
(If it is intended that the wages or salaries of certain personnel stationed at the Contractor's principal or other offices shall be included in the Cost of the Work, identify in Article 14 the personnel to be included and whether for all or only part of their time.)

7.1.1.3 Wages and salaries of the Contractor's supervisory or administrative personnel engaged, at factories, workshops or on the road, in expediting the production or transportation of materials or equipment required for the Work, but only for that portion of their time required for the Work.

7.1.1.4 Costs paid or incurred by the Contractor for taxes, insurance, contributions, assessments and benefits required by law or collective bargaining agreements and, for personnel not covered by such agreements, customary benefits such as sick leave, medical and health benefits, holidays, vacations and pensions, provided such costs are based on wages and salaries included in the Cost of the Work under Clauses 7.1.1.1 through 7.1.1.3.

7.1.2 SUBCONTRACT COSTS

Payments made by the Contractor to Subcontractors in accordance with the requirements of the subcontracts.

7.1.3 COSTS OF MATERIALS AND EQUIPMENT INCORPORATED IN THE COMPLETED CONSTRUCTION

7.1.3.1 Costs, including transportation, of materials and equipment incorporated or to be incorporated in the completed construction.

7.1.3.2 Costs of materials described in the preceding Clause 7.1.3.1 in excess of those actually installed but required to provide reasonable allowance for waste and for spoilage. Unused excess materials, if any, shall be handed over to the Owner at the completion of the Work or, at the Owner's option, shall be sold by the Contractor; amounts realized, if any, from such sales shall be credited to the Owner as a deduction from the Cost of the Work.

7.1.4 COSTS OF OTHER MATERIALS AND EQUIPMENT, TEMPORARY FACILITIES AND RELATED ITEMS

7.1.4.1 Costs, including transportation, installation, maintenance, dismantling and removal of materials, supplies, temporary facilities, machinery, equipment, and hand tools not customarily owned by the construction workers, which are provided by the Contractor at the site and fully consumed in the performance of the Work; and cost less salvage value on such items if not fully consumed, whether sold to others or retained by the Contractor. Cost for items previously used by the Contractor shall mean fair market value.

7.1.4.2 Rental charges for temporary facilities, machinery, equipment, and hand tools not customarily owned by the construction workers, which are provided by the Contractor at the site, whether rented from the Contractor or others, and costs of transportation, installation, minor repairs and replacements, dismantling and removal thereof. Rates and quantities of equipment rented shall be subject to the Owner's prior approval.

7.1.4.3 Costs of removal of debris from the site.

7.1.4.4 Costs of telegrams and long-distance telephone calls, postage and parcel delivery charges, telephone service at the site and reasonable petty cash expenses of the site office.

7.1.4.5 That portion of the reasonable travel and subsistence expenses of the Contractor's personnel incurred while traveling in discharge of duties connected with the Work.

7.1.5 MISCELLANEOUS COSTS

7.1.5.1 That portion directly attributable to this Contract of premiums for insurance and bonds.

7.1.5.2 Sales, use or similar taxes imposed by a governmental authority which are related to the Work and for which the Contractor is liable.

7.1.5.3 Fees and assessments for the building permit and for other permits, licenses and inspections for which the Contractor is required by the Contract Documents to pay.

7.1.5.4 Fees of testing laboratories for tests required by the Contract Documents, except those related to defective or nonconforming Work for which reimbursement is excluded by Subparagraph 13.5.3 of the General Conditions or other provisions of the Contract Documents and which do not fall within the scope of Subparagraphs 7.2.2 through 7.2.4 below.

7.1.5.5 Royalties and license fees paid for the use of a particular design, process or product required by the Contract Documents; the cost of defending suits or claims for infringement of patent rights arising from such requirement by the Contract Documents; payments made in accordance with legal judgments against the Contractor resulting from such suits or claims and payments of settlements made with the Owner's consent; provided, however, that such costs of legal defenses, judgment and settlements shall not be included in the calculation of the Contractor's Fee or of a Guaranteed Maximum Price, if any, and provided that such royalties, fees and costs are not excluded by the last sentence of Subparagraph 3.17.1 of the General Conditions or other provisions of the Contract Documents.

7.1.5.6 Deposits lost for causes other than the Contractor's fault or negligence.

7.1.6 OTHER COSTS

7.1.6.1 Other costs incurred in the performance of the Work if and to the extent approved in advance in writing by the Owner.

7.2 EMERGENCIES: REPAIRS TO DAMAGED, DEFECTIVE OR NONCONFORMING WORK

The Cost of the Work shall also include costs described in Paragraph 7.1 which are incurred by the Contractor:

7.2.1 In taking action to prevent threatened damage, injury or loss in case of an emergency affecting the safety of persons and property, as provided in Paragraph 10.3 of the General Conditions.

7.2.2 In repairing or correcting Work damaged or improperly executed by construction workers in the employ of the Contractor, provided such damage or improper execution did not result from the fault or negligence of the Contractor or the Contractor's foremen, engineers or superintendents, or other supervisory, administrative or managerial personnel of the Contractor.

7.2.3 In repairing damaged Work other than that described in Subparagraph 7.2.2, provided such damage did not result from the fault or negligence of the Contractor or the Contractor's personnel, and only to the extent that the cost of such repairs is not recoverable by the Contractor from others and the Contractor is not compensated therefor by insurance or otherwise.

7.2.4 In correcting defective or nonconforming Work performed or supplied by a Subcontractor or material supplier and not corrected by them, provided such defective or nonconforming Work did not result from the fault or neglect of the Contractor or the Contractor's personnel adequately to supervise and direct the Work of the Subcontractor or material supplier, and only to the extent that the cost of correcting the defective or nonconforming Work is not recoverable by the Contractor from the Subcontractor or material supplier.

ARTICLE 8
COSTS NOT TO BE REIMBURSED

8.1 The Cost of the Work shall not include:

8.1.1 Salaries and other compensation of the Contractor's personnel stationed at the Contractor's principal office or offices other than the site office, except as specifically provided in Clauses 7.1.1.2 and 7.1.1.3 or as may be provided in Article 14.

8.1.2 Expenses of the Contractor's principal office and offices other than the site office.

8.1.3 Overhead and general expenses, except as may be expressly included in Article 7.

8.1.4 The Contractor's capital expenses, including interest on the Contractor's capital employed for the Work.

8.1.5 Rental costs of machinery and equipment, except as specifically provided in Clause 7.1.4.2.

8.1.6 Except as provided in Subparagraphs 7.2.2 through 7.2.4 and Paragraph 13.5 of this Agreement, costs due to the fault or negligence of the Contractor, Subcontractors, anyone directly or indirectly employed by any of them, or for whose acts any of them may be liable, including but not limited to costs for the correction of damaged, defective or nonconforming Work, disposal and replacement of materials and equipment incorrectly ordered or supplied, and making good damage to property not forming part of the Work.

8.1.7 Any cost not specifically and expressly described in Article 7.

8.1.8 Costs which would cause the Guaranteed Maximum Price, if any, to be exceeded.

ARTICLE 9
DISCOUNTS, REBATES AND REFUNDS

9.1 Cash discounts obtained on payments made by the Contractor shall accrue to the Owner if (1) before making the payment, the Contractor included them in an Application for Payment and received payment therefor from the Owner, or (2) the Owner has deposited funds with the Contractor with which to make payments; otherwise, cash discounts shall accrue to the Contractor. Trade discounts, rebates, refunds and amounts received from sales of surplus materials and equipment shall accrue to the Owner, and the Contractor shall make provisions so that they can be secured.

9.2 Amounts which accrue to the Owner in accordance with the provisions of Paragraph 9.1 shall be credited to the Owner as a deduction from the Cost of the Work.

ARTICLE 10
SUBCONTRACTS AND OTHER AGREEMENTS

10.1 Those portions of the Work that the Contractor does not customarily perform with the Contractor's own personnel shall be performed under subcontracts or by other appropriate agreements with the Contractor. The Contractor shall obtain bids from Subcontractors and from suppliers of materials or equipment fabricated especially for the Work and shall deliver such bids to the Architect. The Owner will then determine, with the advice of the Contractor and subject to the reasonable objection of the Architect, which bids will be accepted. The Owner may designate specific persons or entities from whom the Contractor shall obtain bids; however, if a Guaranteed Maximum Price has been established, the Owner may not prohibit the Contractor from obtaining bids from others. The Contractor shall not be required to contract with anyone to whom the Contractor has reasonable objection.

10.2 If a Guaranteed Maximum Price has been established and a specific bidder among those whose bids are delivered by the Contractor to the Architect (1) is recommended to the Owner by the Contractor; (2) is qualified to perform that portion of the Work; and (3) has submitted a bid which conforms to the requirements of the Contract Documents without reservations or exceptions, but the Owner requires that another bid be accepted; then the Contractor may require that a Change Order be issued to adjust the Guaranteed Maximum Price by the difference between the bid of the person or entity recommended to the Owner by the Contractor and the amount of the subcontract or other agreement actually signed with the person or entity designated by the Owner.

10.3 Subcontracts or other agreements shall conform to the payment provisions of Paragraphs 12.7 and 12.8, and shall not be awarded on the basis of cost plus a fee without the prior consent of the Owner.

ARTICLE 11
ACCOUNTING RECORDS

11.1 The Contractor shall keep full and detailed accounts and exercise such controls as may be necessary for proper financial management under this Contract; the accounting and control systems shall be satisfactory to the Owner. The Owner and the Owner's accountants shall be afforded access to the Contractor's records, books, correspondence, instructions, drawings, receipts, subcontracts, purchase orders, vouchers, memoranda and other data relating to this Contract, and the Contractor shall preserve these for a period of three years after final payment, or for such longer period as may be required by law.

ARTICLE 12
PROGRESS PAYMENTS

12.1 Based upon Applications for Payment submitted to the Architect by the Contractor and Certificates for Payment issued by the Architect, the Owner shall make progress payments on account of the Contract Sum to the Contractor as provided below and elsewhere in the Contract Documents.

12.2 The period covered by each Application for Payment shall be one calendar month ending on the last day of the month, or as follows:

12.3 Provided an Application for Payment is received by the Architect not later than the day of the month, the Owner shall make payment to the Contractor not later than the day of the month. If an Application for Payment is received by the Architect after the application date fixed above, payment shall be made by the Owner not later than days after the Architect receives the Application for Payment.

12.4 With each Application for Payment the Contractor shall submit payrolls, petty cash accounts, receipted invoices or invoices with check vouchers attached, and any other evidence required by the Owner or Architect to demonstrate that cash disbursements already made by the Contractor on account of the Cost of the Work equal or exceed (1) progress payments already received by the Contractor; less (2) that portion of those payments attributable to the Contractor's Fee; plus (3) payrolls for the period covered by the present Application for Payment; plus (4) retainage provided in Subparagraph 12.5.4, if any, applicable to prior progress payments.

12.5 CONTRACTS WITH A GUARANTEED MAXIMUM PRICE

12.5.1 Each Application for Payment shall be based upon the most recent schedule of values submitted by the Contractor in accordance with the Contract Documents. The schedule of values shall allocate the entire Guaranteed Maximum Price among the various portions of the Work, except that the Contractor's Fee shall be shown as a single separate item. The schedule of values shall be prepared in such form and supported by such data to substantiate its accuracy as the Architect may require. This schedule, unless objected to by the Architect, shall be used as a basis for reviewing the Contractor's Applications for Payment.

12.5.2 Applications for Payment shall show the percentage completion of each portion of the Work as of the end of the period covered by the Application for Payment. The percentage completion shall be the lesser of (1) the percentage of that portion of the Work which has actually been completed or (2) the percentage obtained by dividing (a) the expense which has actually been incurred by the Contractor on account of that portion of the Work for which the Contractor has made or intends to make actual payment prior to the next Application for Payment by (b) the share of the Guaranteed Maximum Price allocated to that portion of the Work in the schedule of values.

12.5.3 Subject to other provisions of the Contract Documents, the amount of each progress payment shall be computed as follows:

12.5.3.1 Take that portion of the Guaranteed Maximum Price properly allocable to completed Work as determined by multiplying the percentage completion of each portion of the Work by the share of the Guaranteed Maximum Price allocated to that portion of the Work in the schedule of values. Pending final determination of cost to the Owner of changes in the Work, amounts not in dispute may be included as provided in Subparagraph 7.3.7 of the General Conditions, even though the Guaranteed Maximum Price has not yet been adjusted by Change Order.

12.5.3.2 Add that portion of the Guaranteed Maximum Price properly allocable to materials and equipment delivered and suitably stored at the site for subsequent incorporation in the Work or, if approved in advance by the Owner, suitably stored off the site at a location agreed upon in writing.

12.5.3.3 Add the Contractor's Fee, less retainage of percent (%). The Contractor's Fee shall be computed upon the Cost of the Work described in the two preceding Clauses at the rate stated in Paragraph 5.1 or, if the Contractor's Fee is stated as a fixed sum in that Paragraph, shall be an amount which bears the same ratio to that fixed-sum Fee as the Cost of the Work in the two preceding Clauses bears to a reasonable estimate of the probable Cost of the Work upon its completion.

12.5.3.4 Subtract the aggregate of previous payments made by the Owner.

12.5.3.5 Subtract the shortfall, if any, indicated by the Contractor in the documentation required by Paragraph 12.4 to substantiate prior Applications for Payment, or resulting from errors subsequently discovered by the Owner's accountants in such documentation.

12.5.3.6 Subtract amounts, if any, for which the Architect has withheld or nullified a Certificate for Payment as provided in Paragraph 9.5 of the General Conditions.

12.5.4 Additional retainage, if any, shall be as follows:

(If it is intended to retain additional amounts from progress payments to the Contractor beyond (1) the retainage from the Contractor's Fee provided in Clause 12.5.3.3, (2) the retainage from Subcontractors provided in Paragraph 12.7 below, and (3) the retainage, if any, provided by other provisions of the Contract, insert provision for such additional retainage here. Such provision, if made, should also describe any arrangement for limiting or reducing the amount retained after the Work reaches a certain state of completion.)

12.6 CONTRACTS WITHOUT A GUARANTEED MAXIMUM PRICE

12.6.1 Applications for Payment shall show the Cost of the Work actually incurred by the Contractor through the end of the period covered by the Application for Payment and for which the Contractor has made or intends to make actual payment prior to the next Application for Payment.

12.6.2 Subject to other provisions of the Contract Documents, the amount of each progress payment shall be computed as follows:

12.6.2.1 Take the Cost of the Work as described in Subparagraph 12.6.1.

12.6.2.2 Add the Contractor's Fee, less retainage of percent (%). The Contractor's Fee shall be computed upon the Cost of the Work described in the preceding Clause 12.6.2.1 at the rate stated in Paragraph 5.1 or, if the Contractor's Fee is stated as a fixed sum in that Paragraph, an amount which bears the same ratio to that fixed-sum Fee as the Cost of the Work in the preceding Clause bears to a reasonable estimate of the probable Cost of the Work upon its completion.

12.6.2.3 Subtract the aggregate of previous payments made by the Owner.

12.6.2.4 Subtract the shortfall, if any, indicated by the Contractor in the documentation required by Paragraph 12.4 or to substantiate prior Applications for Payment or resulting from errors subsequently discovered by the Owner's accountants in such documentation.

12.6.2.5 Subtract amounts, if any, for which the Architect has withheld or withdrawn a Certificate for Payment as provided in the Contract Documents.

12.6.3 Additional retainage, if any, shall be as follows:

12.7 Except with the Owner's prior approval, payments to Subcontractors included in the Contractor's Applications for Payment shall not exceed an amount for each Subcontractor calculated as follows:

12.7.1 Take that portion of the Subcontract Sum properly allocable to completed Work as determined by multiplying the percentage completion of each portion of the Subcontractor's Work by the share of the total Subcontract Sum allocated to that portion in the Subcontractor's schedule of values, less retainage of percent (%). Pending final determination of amounts to be paid to the Subcontractor for changes in the Work, amounts not in dispute may be included as provided in Subparagraph 7.3.7 of the General Conditions even though the Subcontract Sum has not yet been adjusted by Change Order.

12.7.2 Add that portion of the Subcontract Sum properly allocable to materials and equipment delivered and suitably stored at the site for subsequent incorporation in the Work or, if approved in advance by the Owner, suitably stored off the site at a location agreed upon in writing, less retainage of percent (%).

12.7.3 Subtract the aggregate of previous payments made by the Contractor to the Subcontractor.

12.7.4 Subtract amounts, if any, for which the Architect has withheld or nullified a Certificate for Payment by the Owner to the Contractor for reasons which are the fault of the Subcontractor.

12.7.5 Add, upon Substantial Completion of the entire Work of the Contractor, a sum sufficient to increase the total payments to the Subcontractor to percent (%) of the Subcontract Sum, less amounts, if any, for incomplete Work and unsettled claims; and, if final completion of the entire Work is thereafter materially delayed through no fault of the Subcontractor, add any additional amounts payable on account of Work of the Subcontractor in accordance with Subparagraph 9.10.3 of the General Conditions.

(If it is intended, prior to Substantial Completion of the entire Work of the Contractor, to reduce or limit the retainage from Subcontractors resulting from the percentages inserted in Subparagraphs 12.7.1 and 12.7.2 above, and this is not explained elsewhere in the Contract Documents, insert here provisions for such reduction or limitation.)

The Subcontract Sum is the total amount stipulated in the subcontract to be paid by the Contractor to the Subcontractor for the Subcontractor's performance of the subcontract.

12.8 Except with the Owner's prior approval, the Contractor shall not make advance payments to suppliers for materials or equipment which have not been delivered and stored at the site.

12.9 In taking action on the Contractor's Applications for Payment, the Architect shall be entitled to rely on the accuracy and completeness of the information furnished by the Contractor and shall not be deemed to represent that the Architect has made a detailed examination, audit or arithmetic verification of the documentation submitted in accordance with Paragraph 12.4 or other supporting data; that the Architect has made exhaustive or continuous on-site inspections or that the Architect has made examinations to ascertain how or for what purposes the Contractor has used amounts previously paid on account of the Contract. Such examinations, audits and verifications, if required by the Owner, will be performed by the Owner's accountants acting in the sole interest of the Owner.

ARTICLE 13
FINAL PAYMENT

13.1 Final payment shall be made by the Owner to the Contractor when (1) the Contract has been fully performed by the Contractor except for the Contractor's responsibility to correct defective or nonconforming Work, as provided in Subparagraph 12.2.2 of the General Conditions, and to satisfy other requirements, if any, which necessarily survive final payment; (2) a final Application for Payment and a final accounting for the Cost of the Work have been submitted by the Contractor and reviewed by the Owner's accountants; and (3) a final Certificate for Payment has then been issued by the Architect; such final payment shall be made by the Owner not more than 30 days after the issuance of the Architect's final Certificate for Payment, or as follows:

13.2 The amount of the final payment shall be calculated as follows:

13.2.1 Take the sum of the Cost of the Work substantiated by the Contractor's final accounting and the Contractor's Fee; but not more than the Guaranteed Maximum Price, if any.

13.2.2 Subtract amounts, if any, for which the Architect withholds, in whole or in part, a final Certificate for Payment as provided in Subparagraph 9.5.1 of the General Conditions or other provisions of the Contract Documents.

13.2.3 Subtract the aggregate of previous payments made by the Owner.

If the aggregate of previous payments made by the Owner exceeds the amount due the Contractor, the Contractor shall reimburse the difference to the Owner.

13.3 The Owner's accountants will review and report in writing on the Contractor's final accounting within 30 days after delivery of the final accounting to the Architect by the Contractor. Based upon such Cost of the Work as the Owner's accountants report to be substantiated by the Contractor's final accounting, and provided the other conditions of Paragraph 13.1 have been met, the Architect will, within seven days after receipt of the written report of the Owner's accountants, either issue to the Owner a final Certificate for Payment with a copy to the Contractor, or notify the Contractor and Owner in writing of the Architect's reasons for withholding a certificate as provided in Subparagraph 9.5.1 of the General Conditions. The time periods stated in this Paragraph 13.3 supersede those stated in Subparagraph 9.4.1 of the General Conditions.

13.4 If the Owner's accountants report the Cost of the Work as substantiated by the Contractor's final accounting to be less than claimed by the Contractor, the Contractor shall be entitled to demand arbitration of the disputed amount without a further decision of the Architect. Such demand for arbitration shall be made by the Contractor within 30 days after the Contractor's receipt of a copy of the Architect's final Certificate for Payment; failure to demand arbitration within this 30-day period shall result in the substantiated amount reported by the Owner's accountants becoming binding on the Contractor. Pending a final resolution by arbitration, the Owner shall pay the Contractor the amount certified in the Architect's final Certificate for Payment.

13.5 If, subsequent to final payment and at the Owner's request, the Contractor incurs costs described in Article 7 and not excluded by Article 8 to correct defective or nonconforming Work, the Owner shall reimburse the Contractor such costs and the Contractor's Fee applicable thereto on the same basis as if such costs had been incurred prior to final payment, but not in excess of the Guaranteed Maximum Price, if any. If the Contractor has participated in savings as provided in Paragraph 5.2, the amount of such savings shall be recalculated and appropriate credit given to the Owner in determining the net amount to be paid by the Owner to the Contractor.

ARTICLE 14
MISCELLANEOUS PROVISIONS

14.1 Where reference is made in this Agreement to a provision of the General Conditions or another Contract Document, the reference refers to that provision as amended or supplemented by other provisions of the Contract Documents.

14.2 Payments due and unpaid under the Contract shall bear interest from the date payment is due at the rate stated below, or in the absence thereof, at the legal rate prevailing from time to time at the place where the Project is located.

(Insert rate of interest agreed upon, if any.)

(Usury laws and requirements under the Federal Truth in Lending Act, similar state and local consumer credit laws and other regulations at the Owner's and Contractor's principal places of business, the location of the Project and elsewhere may affect the validity of this provision. Legal advice should be obtained with respect to deletions or modifications, and also regarding requirements such as written disclosures or waivers.)

14.3 Other provisions:

ARTICLE 15
TERMINATION OR SUSPENSION

15.1 The Contract may be terminated by the Contractor as provided in Article 14 of the General Conditions; however, the amount to be paid to the Contractor under Subparagraph 14.1.2 of the General Conditions shall not exceed the amount the Contractor would be entitled to receive under Paragraph 15.3 below, except that the Contractor's Fee shall be calculated as if the Work had been fully completed by the Contractor, including a reasonable estimate of the Cost of the Work for Work not actually completed.

15.2 If a Guaranteed Maximum Price is established in Article 5, the Contract may be terminated by the Owner for cause as provided in Article 14 of the General Conditions; however, the amount, if any, to be paid to the Contractor under Subparagraph 14.2.4 of the General Conditions shall not cause the Guaranteed Maximum Price to be exceeded, nor shall it exceed the amount the Contractor would be entitled to receive under Paragraph 15.3 below.

15.3 If no Guaranteed Maximum Price is established in Article 5, the Contract may be terminated by the Owner for cause as provided in Article 14 of the General Conditions; however, the Owner shall then pay the Contractor an amount calculated as follows:

15.3.1 Take the Cost of the Work incurred by the Contractor to the date of termination.

15.3.2 Add the Contractor's Fee computed upon the Cost of the Work to the date of termination at the rate stated in Paragraph 5.1 or, if the Contractor's Fee is stated as a fixed sum in that Paragraph, an amount which bears the same ratio to that fixed-sum Fee as the Cost of the Work at the time of termination bears to a reasonable estimate of the probable Cost of the Work upon its completion.

15.3.3 Subtract the aggregate of previous payments made by the Owner.

The Owner shall also pay the Contractor fair compensation, either by purchase or rental at the election of the Owner, for any equipment owned by the Contractor which the Owner elects to retain and which is not otherwise included in the Cost of the Work under Subparagraph 15.3.1. To the extent that the Owner elects to take legal assignment of subcontracts and purchase orders (including rental agreements), the Contractor shall, as a condition of receiving the payments referred to in this Article 15, execute and deliver all such papers and take all such steps, including the legal assignment of such subcontracts and other contractual rights of the Contractor, as the Owner may require for the purpose of fully vesting in the Owner the rights and benefits of the Contractor under such subcontracts or purchase orders.

15.4 The Work may be suspended by the Owner as provided in Article 14 of the General Conditions; in such case, the Guaranteed Maximum Price, if any, shall be increased as provided in Subparagraph 14.3.2 of the General Conditions except that the term "cost of performance of the Contract" in that Subparagraph shall be understood to mean the Cost of the Work and the term "profit" shall be understood to mean the Contractor's Fee as described in Paragraphs 5.1 and 6.3 of this Agreement.

ARTICLE 16
ENUMERATION OF CONTRACT DOCUMENTS

16.1 The Contract Documents, except for Modifications issued after execution of this Agreement, are enumerated as follows:

16.1.1 The Agreement is this executed Standard Form of Agreement Between Owner and Contractor, AIA Document A111, 1987 Edition.

16.1.2 The General Conditions are the General Conditions of the Contract for Construction, AIA Document A201, 1987 Edition.

16.1.3 The Supplementary and other Conditions of the Contract are those contained in the Project Manual dated , and are as follows:

Document	Title	Pages

16.1.4 The Specifications are those contained in the Project Manual dated as in Paragraph 16.1.3, and are as follows:
(Either list the Specifications here or refer to an exhibit attached to this Agreement.)

Section	Title	Pages

16.1.5 The Drawings are as follows, and are dated unless a different date is shown below:
(Either list the Drawings here or refer to an exhibit attached to this Agreement.)

Number	Title	Date

16.1.6 The addenda, if any, are as follows:

Number	Date	Pages

Portions of Addenda relating to bidding requirements are not part of the Contract Documents unless the bidding requirements are also enumerated in this Article 16.

16.1.7 Other Documents, if any, forming part of the Contract Documents are as follows:
(List here any additional documents which are intended to form part of the Contract Documents. The General Conditions provide that bidding requirements such as advertisement or invitation to bid, Instructions to Bidders, sample forms and the Contractor's bid are not part of the Contract Documents unless enumerated in this Agreement. They should be listed here only if intended to be part of the Contract Documents.)

This Agreement is entered into as of the day and year first written above and is executed in at least three original copies of which one is to be delivered to the Contractor, one to the Architect for use in the administration of the Contract, and the remainder to the Owner.

OWNER	CONTRACTOR
(Signature)	*(Signature)*
(Printed name and title)	*(Printed name and title)*

AIA **CAUTION: You should sign an original AIA document which has this caution printed in red. An original assures that changes will not be obscured as may occur when documents are reproduced.**

INSTRUCTIONS

FOR AIA DOCUMENT A191, STANDARD FORM OF AGREEMENTS BETWEEN OWNER AND DESIGN/BUILDER—1996 EDITION

A. GENERAL INFORMATION

1. Purpose

AIA Document A191, Standard Form of Agreements Between Owner and Design/Builder, is intended to establish a contractual relationship between an Owner and a Design/Builder. Design/build is a process in which the Owner contracts directly with one entity that is to provide both design and construction services. The Design/Builder's organization may take a variety of legal forms, such as a sole proprietorship, a partnership, a joint venture, or a corporation. An architect or architectural firm may directly contract to perform design/build services or, alternatively, may form a separate corporate entity or joint venture for design/build, although these options are not explicitly stated in the document. The AIA does not currently publish documents governing this type of joint venture.

It is expected that in most situations an architect will wish to establish a separate design/build firm. This firm can then subcontract the design work through the parent architectural firm. This may be accomplished through AIA Document B901, Standard Form of Agreements Between Design/Builder and Architect. To provide guidance for public owners who intend to use the design/build process, the AIA and the Associated General Contractors (AGC) have jointly published the *AIA/AGC Recommended Guidelines for Procurement of Design/Build Projects in the Public Sector.*

AIA Document A191 contains two separate, sequential agreements. The Part 1 Agreement covers services for preliminary design and budgeting. The Part 2 Agreement covers services for final design and construction. It is intended that the parties first enter into the Part 1 Agreement to determine the feasibility and the scope of the Project, and thereafter enter into the Part 2 Agreement. Before signing the Part 1 Agreement the parties should reach substantial agreement on the terms of the Part 2 Agreement, except for the scope of the Project and compensation. Note that the parties may conclude their relationship after the Part 1 Agreement is performed rather than continuing on to the Part 2 Agreement.

Prior to entering into either agreement in this document, architects who wish to act as design/builders should consult their legal counsel, management advisors, and insurance counsel. States may restrict or prohibit design/build practices under statutes that regulate architectural registration, contractor licensing and incorporation of professionals.

2. Related Documents

AIA Document A191 is published in conjunction with the following related documents:

A491, Standard Form of Agreements Between Design/Builder and Contractor
B901, Standard Form of Agreements Between Design/Builder and Architect

These documents are intended to govern the relationships between the Design/Builder and other architects and contractors.

3. Dispute Resolution—Mediation and Arbitration

Both the Part 1 and the Part 2 Agreements incorporate mediation and arbitration by adoption of the Construction Industry Mediation Rules and the Construction Industry Arbitration Rules of the American Arbitration Association. Arbitration is *binding and mandatory* in most states and under the Federal Arbitration Act. In a minority of states, arbitration provisions relating to future disputes are not enforceable, but arbitration is enforceable if agreed to after the dispute arises. In addition, provisions for mediation as a potential precursor to arbitration have been added in both Part 1 and Part 2. A few states require that the contracting parties be especially notified when the written contract contains an arbitration provision by: a warning on the face of the document; specific placement of the arbitration provision within the document; or specific discussions among the parties prior to signing the document.

Arbitration provisions have been included in most AIA contract forms since 1888 in order to encourage alternative dispute resolution procedures and to provide users of AIA documents with legally enforceable arbitration provisions when parties choose to adopt arbitration into their contract. Individuals may, however, choose to delete the arbitration provisions based upon their business decisions with the advice of counsel. To obtain copies of the mediation or arbitration rules, write to the American Arbitration Association, 140 West 51st Street, New York, NY 10020-1203.

4. Use of Non-AIA Forms

If a combination of AIA documents and non-AIA documents is to be used, particular care must be taken to achieve consistency of language and intent. Certain clients require the use of agreements and other contract forms that they prepare. Such forms should be carefully compared to the standard AIA forms for which they are being substituted before execution of an agreement. If there are any significant omissions, additions or variances from the terms of the related standard AIA forms, both legal and insurance counsel should be consulted.

5. Letter Forms of Agreement

Letter forms of agreement are generally discouraged by the AIA, as is the performance of a part or the whole of professional services based on oral agreements or understandings. The standard AIA agreement forms have been developed through more than 80 years of experience and have been tested repeatedly in the courts. In addition, the standard forms have been carefully coordinated with other AIA documents.

6. Use of Current Documents

Prior to using any AIA document, the user should consult the AIA, an AIA component chapter or a current AIA Documents Price List to determine the current edition of each document.

7. Limited License for Reproduction

AIA Document A191 is a copyrighted work and may not be reproduced or excerpted from in substantial part without the express written permission of the AIA. The A191 document is intended to be used as a consumable—that is, the original document purchased by the user is intended to be consumed in the course of being used. There is no implied permission to reproduce this document, nor does membership in The American Institute of Architects confer any further rights to reproduce A191.

A limited license is hereby granted to retail purchasers to reproduce a maximum of ten (10) copies of a completed Part 1 Agreement, with or without signatures, and a maximum of ten (10) copies of a completed Part 2 Agreement, with or without signatures, but only for use in connection with a particular project. Further reproductions are prohibited without the express written permission of the AIA.

A cautionary notice is printed in red on the original version of this document. This notice distinguishes an original AIA document from copies and counterfeits. To ensure accuracy and uniformity of language, purchasers should use only an original AIA document or one that has been reproduced from an original under a special limited license from the AIA. Documents generated by the software AIA Contract Documents: Electronic Format for Windows™ do not contain a red cautionary notice. Documents reproduced in this program may be accompanied by AIA Document D401, Certification of Document's Authenticity. In addition, all documents in this program contain footers that display the license number under which the document was reproduced and the date of expiration of the license.

B. COMPLETING THE A191 FORM

1. Modifications

Users are encouraged to consult their legal and insurance advisors before completing an AIA agreement. Particularly with respect to professional licensing laws, duties imposed by building codes, interest charges, arbitration and indemnification, this document may require modification with the assistance of legal counsel to comply with state or local laws regulating these matters.

Generally, necessary modifications may be accomplished by writing or typing the appropriate terms in the blank spaces provided on the form, or by supplementary conditions or amendments referenced in this document. The form may also be modified by striking out language directly on the original form. Care must be taken in making these kinds of deletions, however. Under NO circumstances should any language be struck out in such a way as to render it illegible (as, for example, with blocking tape, correction fluid, or X's that completely obscure the text). This may raise suspicions of concealment, or suggest that the completed and signed document has been tampered with. Handwritten changes should be initialed by both parties to the contract.

It is not recommended practice to retype the standard document. Besides being outside the limited license for reproduction granted under these Instructions, retyping can introduce typographical errors and cloud the legal interpretation given to a standard clause when blended with modifications, thereby eliminating one of the principal advantages of standard form documents. By merely reviewing the modifications to be made to a standard form document, parties familiar with that document can quickly understand the essence of the proposed relationship. Commercial exchanges are greatly simplified and expedited, good-faith dealing is encouraged, and otherwise latent clauses are exposed for scrutiny. In this way, contracting parties can more confidently and fairly measure their risks.

2. Cover Pages—Part 1 Agreement and Part 2 Agreement

Date: The date represents the date the Agreement becomes effective. It may be the date that an original oral agreement was reached, the date the Agreement was originally submitted to the Owner, the date authorizing action was taken or the date of actual execution. Professional services should not be performed prior to the effective date of the Agreement.

Parties: Parties to the Agreement should be identified using the full address and legal name under which the Agreement is to be executed, including a designation of the legal status of both parties (sole proprietorship, partnership, joint venture, unincorporated association, limited partnership or corporation [general, close or professional], etc.). Where appropriate, a copy of the resolution authorizing the individual to act on behalf of the firm or entity should be attached.

Project: The proposed Project should be described in sufficient detail to identify: (1) the official name or title of the facility; (2) the location of the site; (3) the proposed building usage; and (4) the size, capacity or scope of the Project.

Architectural Services: Although the Architect may not be a party to the Agreement between Owner and Design/Builder, it is customary to identify the Architect in agreements of this kind.

Engineering Services: Parties other than the Architect who will provide normal engineering services should be identified using the full address and legal name under which the Agreement is to be executed, including the discipline with which they are affiliated; their registration number, if any; and their legal relationship to the Design/Builder.

3. Part 1 Agreement

Article 9: Basis of Compensation

Subparagraph 9.1.1
Describe the basis of computing compensation for Basic Services under this subparagraph. Several different methods may be used for various services on a particular project. When more than one method of compensation is used, each method should reference the appropriate services listed in Article 1 and Article 10. This may be done by designating them "Method A," "Method B," etc.

Subparagraph 9.1.2 through Paragraph 9.7
Insert numerical amounts to complete the provisions on payment, Reimbursable Expenses, and rate [illegible] accordance with their accompanying parenthetical notes. These numbers usually are negotiated [illegible] Design/Builder with the Owner. Omission of these numbers may prevent those provisions from becoming effective, except for the rate of interest, which defaults to the prevailing rate.

Article 10: Other Conditions and Services

Paragraph 10.1
Insert date for commencement of Basic Services and number of days [illegible] Basic Services are to be completed.

Paragraph 10.2
Insert Basic Services not described in Article 1.

4. Part 2 Agreement

Article 13: Basis of Compensation

Subparagraph 13.1.1
Insert basis of compensation, [illegible] as [illegible]ulated [illegible] percentage fee [illegible] of the Work; unit prices; and cash allowances or contingencies [illegible]

Subparagraph 13.2 through Subparagraph 13.3.1
Insert numerical a[illegible] comple[illegible] provisions [illegible] Reimbursable Expenses and rate of interest in accordance with their accompanying parenthetical notes. These numbers u[illegible] negotiated by the Design/Builder with the Owner. O[illegible] of these numbers may prevent those [illegible]ons [illegible] becoming effective, except for the rate of interest, which [illegible] the prevailing legal rate.

Article 14: Other Provisions

Paragraph 14.1
[illegible] date of commencement and the number of days allowed for achievement of Substantial Completion.

Paragraph 14.2
Insert Basic Services not described in Article 3.

Paragraph 14.3
Insert Additional Services not described in Article 3.

Paragraph 14.4
State the date of each month on which the Design/Builder shall submit Applications for Payment.

Paragraph 14.5
List elements of the Design/Builder's Proposal, including the title and date of each.

C. CHANGES FROM THE PREVIOUS EDITION

1. Format Changes—Part 1 Agreement and Part 2 Agreement

On the cover pages of both agreements, space has been provided to identify parties other than the Architect who will provide engineering services. In the Part 1 Agreement, Article 1: General Provisions has been deleted and replaced by the new Article 1: Design/Builder. Former Paragraph 1.3, Ownership and Use of Documents, has been moved to

Article 3. Former Articles 2 and 3 have been renumbered, so that the new Article 1 is titled Design/Builder and the new Article 2 is titled Owner.

2. Changes in Content—Part 1 Agreement and Part 2 Agreement

Substantial conceptual changes have been made to both the Part 1 and the Part 2 Agreements, most of which are briefly described below. However, it is strongly recommended that, *prior* to executing the document, users read the Agreements thoroughly to become familiar with these changes.

Articles 1 and 3: Design/Builder

Both Agreements require the Design/Builder to enter into written agreements with the Design/Builder's consultants, including architects and engineers, and the Owner may request copies of those agreements. The Design/Builder is required to provide written notice to the Owner if the Design/Builder believes or is advised that any instructions received from the Owner are in violation of any applicable law.

Article 1: General Provisions

In the Part 2 Agreement, the definition of Contract Documents has been expanded, and Work now is defined as the construction and services to be provided by the Design/Builder to fulfill the Design/Builder's obligations. The Design/Builder must notify the Owner if the Design/Builder believes or is advised by a design professional th[illegible]y instructions received by the Owner are in violation of any applicable law.

Article 2: Owner

The Part 1 Agreement requires the Owner to submit a written program to the Design/Builder a[illegible] [illegible]clo[illegible] info[illegible]mation known to the Owner about the presence of pollutants at the site. Both Agreements a[illegible] [illegible] [illegible]er [illegible]btain independent review of the Design/Builder's documents at the Owner's expense.

Article 3: Ownership and Use of Documents

In the Part 1 Agreement, this new article is derived from former Paragraph 1.3.[illegible] [illegible]diti[illegible]lly d[illegible] the ownership and use of electronic data.

Article 4: Time

The Part 1 Agreement allows the Owner to request, from the [illegible]uilder, a [illegible]dule for performance of services.

Articles 6 and 10: Dispute Resolution—Mediation [illegible]nd [illegible]itratio[illegible]

Formerly titled Arbitration, this article has been revise[illegible] [illegible]bot[illegible] [illegible]eem[illegible]s to allow th[illegible]es to attempt to resolve their disputes through mediation before proce[illegible]ing to [illegible]rati[illegible]

Article 7: Miscellaneous Provisions

The Part 1 Agreement shall be gove[illegible] [illegible] la[illegible] [illegible]ce of the Pro[illegible] [illegible]n th[illegible]art 1 Agr[illegible]ment, Article 7 states that the Design/Builder shall not b[illegible] [illegible]pon[illegible]e for [illegible]ign or the [illegible] of [illegible]ediation of hazardous materials. In case of termination of the Ar[illegible]ec[illegible] [illegible]Builder must n[illegible]entify, i[illegible]tin[illegible] [illegible]other design professional to whom the Owner has n[illegible]tion.

Article 8: Terminati[illegible]

The Owner n[illegible] termin[illegible] [illegible]he Part 1 Agree[illegible]t wit[illegible] [illegible]cau[illegible] [illegible]providing seven (7) days' notice.

Article 8: [illegible] the Work

In th[illegible]rt 2 [illegible]eme[illegible] changes in th[illegible] [illegible] now [illegible]e carried out either through Change Order or Construction Chang[illegible] [illegible]ecti[illegible]

[illegible]rrection of Work

[illegible]e Pa[illegible] [illegible]greement, the term "defect[illegible]" replaces "nonconforming work."

Ar[illegible] 10: Other Conditions and Services

In the Part 1 Agreement, the Owner must enumerate the Owner's preliminary program, budget, and other documents.

Article 11: Miscellaneous Provisions

In the Part 2 Agreement, this article has been revised to further clarify the Design/Builder's obligation to coordinate the Design/Builder's construction and operations with those of the Owner's other contractors. It now requires that a party filing a claim give the other party written notice within a reasonable time, not to exceed 21 days after first observance. The Owner now may assign the Part 2 Agreement to the institution providing construction financing.

Article 14: Other Provisions

The documents comprised by the Design/Builder's Proposal should be listed in the Part 2 Agreement and described with the title and the date.

D. EXECUTION OF THE AGREEMENTS

Each person executing the Agreement should indicate the capacity in which they are acting (i.e., president, secretary, partner, etc.) and the authority under which they are executing the Agreement. Where appropriate, a copy of the resolution authorizing the individual to act on behalf of the firm or entity should be attached.

AIA Document A191

Standard Form of Agreements Between Owner and Design/Builder

THIS DOCUMENT HAS IMPORTANT LEGAL CONSEQUENCES; CONSULTATION WITH AN ATTORNEY IS ENCOURAGED WITH RESPECT TO ITS USE, COMPLETION OR MODIFICATION.

1996 EDITION

TABLE OF ARTICLES

PART 1 AGREEMENT

PART 2 AGREEMENT

AIA Document A191

Standard Form of Agreement Between Owner and Design/Builder

THIS DOCUMENT HAS IMPORTANT LEGAL CONSEQUENCES; CONSULTATION WITH AN ATTORNEY IS ENCOURAGED WITH RESPECT TO ITS USE, COMPLETION OR MODIFICATION.

This document comprises two separate Agreements: Part 1 Agreement and Part 2 Agreement. Before executing the Part 1 Agreement, the parties should reach substantial agreement on the Part 2 Agreement. To the extent referenced in these Agreements, subordinate parallel agreements to A191 consist of AIA Document A491, Standard Form of Agreements Between Design/Builder and Contractor, and AIA Document B901, Standard Form of Agreements Between Design/Builder and Architect.

PART 1 AGREEMENT

1996 EDITION

AGREEMENT

made as of the day of in the year of
(In words, indicate day, month and year.)

BETWEEN the Owner:
(Name and address)

and the Design/Builder:
(Name and address)

For the following Project:
(Include Project name, location and a summary description.)

The architectural services described in Article 1 will be provided by the following person or entity who is lawfully licensed to practice architecture:

(Name and address)	*(Registration Number)*	*(Relationship to Design/Builder)*

Normal structural, mechanical and electrical engineering services will be provided contractually through the Architect except as indicated below:

(Name, address and discipline)	*(Registration Number)*	*(Relationship to Design/Builder)*

The Owner and the Design/Builder agree as set forth below.

TERMS AND CONDITIONS—PART 1 AGREEMENT

ARTICLE 1
DESIGN/BUILDER

1.1 SERVICES

1.1.1 Preliminary design, budget, and schedule comprise the services required to accomplish the preparation and submission of the Design/Builder's Proposal as well as the preparation and submission of any modifications to the Proposal prior to execution of the Part 2 Agreement.

1.2 RESPONSIBILITIES

1.2.1 Design services required by this Part 1 Agreement shall be performed by qualified architects and other design professionals. The contractual obligations of such professional persons or entities are undertaken and performed in the interest of the Design/Builder.

1.2.2 The agreements between the Design/Builder and the persons or entities identified in this Part 1 Agreement, and any subsequent modifications, shall be in writing. These agreements, including financial arrangements with respect to this Project, shall be promptly and fully disclosed to the Owner upon request.

1.2.3 Construction budgets shall be prepared by qualified professionals, cost estimators or contractors retained by and acting in the interest of the Design/Builder.

1.2.4 The Design/Builder shall be responsible to the Owner for acts and omissions of the Design/Builder's employees, subcontractors and their agents and employees, and other persons, including the Architect and other design professionals, performing any portion of the Design/Builder's obligations under this Part 1 Agreement.

1.2.5 If the Design/Builder believes or is advised by the Architect or by another design professional retained to provide services on the Project that implementation of any instruction received from the Owner would cause a violation of any applicable law, the Design/Builder shall notify the Owner in writing. Neither the Design/Builder nor the Architect shall be obligated to perform any act which either believes will violate any applicable law.

1.2.6 Nothing contained in this Part 1 Agreement shall create a contractual relationship between the Owner and any person or entity other than the Design/Builder.

1.3 BASIC SERVICES

1.3.1 The Design/Builder shall provide a preliminary evaluation of the Owner's program and project budget requirements, each in terms of the other.

1.3.2 The Design/Builder shall visit the site, become familiar with the local conditions, and correlate observable conditions with the requirements of the Owner's program, schedule, and budget.

1.3.3 The Design/Builder shall review laws applicable to design and construction of the Project; correlate such laws with the Owner's program requirements; and advise the Owner if any program requirement may cause a violation of such laws. Necessary changes to the Owner's program shall be accomplished by appropriate written modification or disclosed as described in Paragraph 1.3.5.

1.3.4 The Design/Builder shall review with the Owner alternative approaches to design and construction of the Project.

1.3.5 The Design/Builder shall submit to the Owner a Proposal, including the completed Preliminary Design Documents, a statement of the proposed contract sum, and a proposed schedule for completion of the Project. Preliminary Design Documents shall consist of preliminary design drawings, outline specifications or other documents sufficient to establish the size, quality and character of the entire Project, its architectural, structural, mechanical and electrical systems, and the materials and such other elements of the Project as may be appropriate. Deviations from the Owner's program shall be disclosed in the Proposal. If the Proposal is accepted by the Owner, the parties shall then execute the Part 2 Agreement. A modification to the Proposal before execution of the Part 2 Agreement shall be recorded in writing as an addendum and shall be identified in the Contract Documents of the Part 2 Agreement.

1.4 ADDITIONAL SERVICES

1.4.1 The Additional Services described under this Paragraph 1.4 shall be provided by the Design/Builder and paid for by the Owner if authorized or confirmed in writing by the Owner.

1.4.2 Making revisions in the Preliminary Design Documents, budget or other documents when such revisions are:

- **.1** inconsistent with approvals or instructions previously given by the Owner, including revisions made necessary by adjustments in the Owner's program or Project budget;
- **.2** required by the enactment or revision of codes, laws or regulations subsequent to the preparation of such documents; or
- **.3** due to changes required as a result of the Owner's failure to render decisions in a timely manner.

1.4.3 Providing more extensive programmatic criteria than that furnished by the Owner as described in Paragraph 2.1. When authorized, the Design/Builder shall provide professional services to assist the Owner in the preparation of the program. Programming services may consist of:

- **.1** consulting with the Owner and other persons or entities not designated in this Part 1 Agreement to define the program requirements of the Project and to review the understanding of such requirements with the Owner;

.2 documentation of the applicable requirements necessary for the various Project functions or operations;

.3 providing a review and analysis of the functional and organizational relationships, requirements, and objectives for the Project;

.4 setting forth a written program of requirements for the Owner's approval which summarizes the Owner's objectives, schedule, constraints, and criteria.

1.4.4 Providing financial feasibility or other special studies.

1.4.5 Providing planning surveys, site evaluations, or comparative studies of prospective sites.

1.4.6 Providing special surveys, environmental studies, and submissions required for approvals of governmental authorities or others having jurisdiction over the Project.

1.4.7 Providing services relative to future facilities, systems, and equipment.

1.4.8 Providing services at the Owner's specific request to perform detailed investigations of existing conditions or facilities or to make measured drawings thereof.

1.4.9 Providing services at the Owner's specific request to verify the accuracy of drawings or other information furnished by the Owner.

1.4.10 Coordinating services in connection with the work of separate persons or entities retained by the Owner, subsequent to the execution of this Part 1 Agreement.

1.4.11 Providing analyses of owning and operating costs.

1.4.12 Providing interior design and other similar services required for or in connection with the selection, procurement or installation of furniture, furnishings, and related equipment.

1.4.13 Providing services for planning tenant or rental spaces.

1.4.14 Making investigations, inventories of materials or equipment, or valuations and detailed appraisals of existing facilities.

ARTICLE 2
OWNER

2.1 RESPONSIBILITIES

2.1.1 The Owner shall provide full information in a timely manner regarding requirements for the Project, including a written program which shall set forth the Owner's objectives, schedule, constraints and criteria.

2.1.2 The Owner shall establish and update an overall budget for the Project, including reasonable contingencies. This budget shall not constitute the contract sum.

2.1.3 The Owner shall designate a representative authorized to act on the Owner's behalf with respect to the Project. The Owner or such authorized representative shall render decisions in a timely manner pertaining to documents submitted by the Design/Builder in order to avoid unreasonable delay in the orderly and sequential progress of the Design/Builder's services. The Owner may obtain independent review of the documents by a separate architect, engineer, contractor, or cost estimator under contract to or employed by the Owner. Such independent review shall be undertaken at the Owner's expense in a timely manner and shall not delay the orderly progress of the Design/Builder's services.

2.1.4 The Owner shall furnish surveys describing physical characteristics, legal limitations and utility locations for the site of the Project, and a written legal description of the site. The surveys and legal information shall include, as applicable, grades and lines of streets, alleys, pavements, and adjoining property and structures; adjacent drainage; rights-of-way, restrictions, easements, encroachments, zoning, deed restrictions, boundaries and contours of the site; locations, dimensions and necessary data pertaining to existing buildings, other improvements and trees; and information concerning available utility services and lines, both public and private, above and below grade, including inverts and depths. All the information on the survey shall be referenced to a Project benchmark.

2.1.5 The Owner shall furnish the services of geotechnical engineers when such services are stipulated in this Part 1 Agreement, or deemed reasonably necessary by the Design/Builder. Such services may include but are not limited to test borings, test pits, determinations of soil bearing values, percolation tests, evaluations of hazardous materials, ground corrosion and resistivity tests, and necessary operations for anticipating subsoil conditions. The services of geotechnical engineer(s) or other consultants shall include preparation and submission of all appropriate reports and professional recommendations.

2.1.6 The Owner shall disclose, to the extent known to the Owner, the results and reports of prior tests, inspections or investigations conducted for the Project involving: structural or mechanical systems; chemical, air and water pollution; hazardous materials; or other environmental and subsurface conditions. The Owner shall disclose all information known to the Owner regarding the presence of pollutants at the Project's site.

2.1.7 The Owner shall furnish all legal, accounting and insurance counseling services as may be necessary at any time for the Project, including such auditing services as the Owner may require to verify the Design/Builder's Applications for Payment.

2.1.8 The Owner shall promptly obtain easements, zoning variances, and legal authorizations regarding site utilization where essential to the execution of the Owner's program.

2.1.9 Those services, information, surveys, and reports required by Paragraphs 2.1.4 through 2.1.8 which are within the Owner's control shall be furnished at the Owner's expense, and the Design/Builder shall be entitled to rely upon the accuracy and completeness thereof, except to the extent the Owner advises the Design/Builder to the contrary in writing.

2.1.10 If the Owner requires the Design/Builder to maintain any special insurance coverage, policy, amendment, or rider, the Owner shall pay the additional cost thereof, except as otherwise stipulated in this Part 1 Agreement.

2.1.11 The Owner shall communicate with persons or entities employed or retained by the Design/Builder through the Design/Builder, unless otherwise directed by the Design/Builder.

ARTICLE 3

OWNERSHIP AND USE OF DOCUMENTS AND ELECTRONIC DATA

3.1 Drawings, specifications, and other documents and electronic data furnished by the Design/Builder are instruments of service. The Design/Builder's Architect and other providers of professional services shall retain all common law, statutory and other reserved rights, including copyright in those instruments of service furnished by them. Drawings, specifications, and other documents and electronic data are furnished for use solely with respect to this Part 1 Agreement. The Owner shall be permitted to retain copies, including reproducible copies, of the drawings, specifications, and other documents and electronic data furnished by the Design/Builder for information and reference in connection with the Project except as provided in Paragraphs 3.2 and 3.3.

3.2 If the Part 2 Agreement is not executed, the Owner shall not use the drawings, specifications, and other documents and electronic data furnished by the Design/Builder without the written permission of the Design/Builder. Drawings, specifications, and other documents and electronic data shall not be used by the Owner or others on other projects, for additions to this Project or for completion of this Project by others, except by agreement in writing and with appropriate compensation to the Design/Builder, unless the Design/Builder is adjudged to be in default under this Part 1 Agreement or under any other subsequently executed agreement, or by agreement in writing.

3.3 If the Design/Builder defaults in the Design/Builder's obligations to the Owner, the Architect shall grant a license to the Owner to use the drawings, specifications, and other documents and electronic data furnished by the Architect to the Design/Builder for the completion of the Project, conditioned upon the Owner's execution of an agreement to cure the Design/Builder's default in payment to the Architect for services previously performed and to indemnify the Architect with regard to claims arising from such reuse without the Architect's professional involvement.

3.4 Submission or distribution of the Design/Builder's documents to meet official regulatory requirements or for similar purposes in connection with the Project is not to be construed as publication in derogation of the rights reserved in Paragraph 3.1.

ARTICLE 4

TIME

4.1 Upon the request of the Owner, the Design/Builder shall prepare a schedule for the performance of the Basic and Additional Services which shall not exceed the time limits contained in Paragraph 10.1 and shall include allowances for periods of time required for the Owner's review and for approval of submissions by authorities having jurisdiction over the Project.

4.2 If the Design/Builder is delayed in the performance of services under this Part 1 Agreement through no fault of the Design/Builder, any applicable schedule shall be equitably adjusted.

ARTICLE 5

PAYMENTS

5.1 The initial payment provided in Article 9 shall be made upon execution of this Part 1 Agreement and credited to the Owner's account as provided in Subparagraph 9.1.2.

5.2 Subsequent payments for Basic Services, Additional Services, and Reimbursable Expenses provided for in this Part 1 Agreement shall be made monthly on the basis set forth in Article 9.

5.3 Within ten (10) days of the Owner's receipt of a properly submitted and correct Application for Payment, the Owner shall make payment to the Design/Builder.

5.4 Payments due the Design/Builder under this Part 1 Agreement which are not paid when due shall bear interest from the date due at the rate specified in Paragraph 9.5, or in the absence of a specified rate, at the legal rate prevailing where the Project is located.

ARTICLE 6

DISPUTE RESOLUTION—MEDIATION AND ARBITRATION

6.1 Claims, disputes or other matters in question between the parties to this Part 1 Agreement arising out of or relating to this Part 1 Agreement or breach thereof shall be subject to and decided by mediation or arbitration. Such mediation or arbitration shall be conducted in accordance with the Construction Industry Mediation or Arbitration Rules of the American Arbitration Association currently in effect.

6.2 In addition to and prior to arbitration, the parties shall endeavor to settle disputes by mediation. Demand for mediation shall be filed in writing with the other party to this Part 1 Agreement and with the American Arbitration Association. A demand for mediation shall be made within a reasonable time after the claim, dispute or other matter in question has arisen. In no event shall the demand for mediation be made after the date when institution of legal or equitable proceedings based on such claim, dispute or other matter in question would be barred by the applicable statute of repose or limitations.

6.3 Demand for arbitration shall be filed in writing with the other party to this Part 1 Agreement and with the American Arbitration Association. A demand for arbitration shall be made within a reasonable time after the claim, dispute or other matter in question has arisen. In no event shall the demand for arbitration be made after the date when institution of legal or equitable proceedings based on such claim, dispute or other matter in question would be barred by the applicable statutes of repose or limitations.

6.4 An arbitration pursuant to this Paragraph may be joined with an arbitration involving common issues of law or fact between the Design/Builder and any person or entity with whom the Design/Builder has a contractual obligation to arbitrate disputes. No other arbitration arising out of or relating to this Part 1 Agreement shall include, by consolidation, joinder or in any other manner, an additional person or entity not a party to this Part 1 Agreement or not a party to an agreement with the Design/Builder, except by written consent containing a specific reference to this Part 1 Agreement signed by the Owner, the Design/Builder and all other persons or entities sought to be joined. Consent to arbitration involving an additional person or entity shall not constitute consent to arbitration of any claim, dispute or other matter in question not described in the written consent or with a person or entity not named or described therein. The foregoing agreement to arbitrate and other agreements to arbitrate with an additional person or entity duly consented to by the parties to this Part 1 Agreement shall be specifically enforceable in accordance with applicable law in any court having jurisdiction thereof.

6.5 The award rendered by the arbitrator or arbitrators shall be final, and judgment may be entered upon it in accordance with applicable law in any court having jurisdiction thereof.

ARTICLE 7

MISCELLANEOUS PROVISIONS

7.1 Unless otherwise provided, this Part 1 Agreement shall be governed by the law of the place where the Project is located.

7.2 The Owner and the Design/Builder, respectively, bind themselves, their partners, successors, assigns and legal representatives to the other party to this Part 1 Agreement and to the partners, successors and assigns of such other party with respect to all covenants of this Part 1 Agreement. Neither the Owner nor the Design/Builder shall assign this Part 1 Agreement without the written consent of the other.

7.3 Unless otherwise provided, neither the design for nor the cost of remediation of hazardous materials shall be the responsibility of the Design/Builder.

7.4 This Part 1 Agreement represents the entire and integrated agreement between the Owner and the Design/Builder and supersedes all prior negotiations, representations or agreements, either written or oral. This Part 1 Agreement may be amended only by written instrument signed by both the Owner and the Design/Builder.

7.5 Prior to the termination of the services of the Architect or any other design professional designated in this Part 1 Agreement, the Design/Builder shall identify to the Owner in writing another architect or design professional with respect to whom the Owner has no reasonable objection, who will provide the services originally to have been provided by the Architect or other design professional whose services are being terminated.

ARTICLE 8

TERMINATION OF THE AGREEMENT

8.1 This Part 1 Agreement may be terminated by either party upon seven (7) days' written notice should the other party fail to perform substantially in accordance with its terms through no fault of the party initiating the termination.

8.2 This Part 1 Agreement may be terminated by the Owner without cause upon at least seven (7) days' written notice to the Design/Builder.

8.3 In the event of termination not the fault of the Design/Builder, the Design/Builder shall be compensated for services performed to the termination date, together with Reimbursable Expenses then due and Termination Expenses. Termination Expenses are expenses directly attributable to termination, including a reasonable amount for overhead and profit, for which the Design/Builder is not otherwise compensated under this Part 1 Agreement.

ARTICLE 9

BASIS OF COMPENSATION

The Owner shall compensate the Design/Builder in accordance with Article 5, Payments, and the other provisions of this Part 1 Agreement as described below.

9.1 COMPENSATION FOR BASIC SERVICES

9.1.1 FOR BASIC SERVICES, compensation shall be as follows:

9.1.2 AN INITIAL PAYMENT of Dollars ($) shall be made upon execution of this Part 1 Agreement and credited to the Owner's account as follows:

9.1.3 SUBSEQUENT PAYMENTS shall be as follows:

9.2 COMPENSATION FOR ADDITIONAL SERVICES

9.2.1 FOR ADDITIONAL SERVICES, compensation shall be as follows:

9.3 REIMBURSABLE EXPENSES

9.3.1 Reimbursable Expenses are in addition to Compensation for Basic and Additional Services, and include actual expenditures made by the Design/Builder and the Design/Builder's employees and contractors in the interest of the Project, as follows:

9.3.2 FOR REIMBURSABLE EXPENSES, compensation shall be a multiple of ( ) times the amounts expended.

9.4 DIRECT PERSONNEL EXPENSE is defined as the direct salaries of personnel engaged on the Project, and the portion of the cost of their mandatory and customary contributions and benefits related thereto, such as employment taxes and other statutory employee benefits, insurance, sick leave, holidays, vacations, pensions, and similar contributions and benefits.

9.5 INTEREST PAYMENTS

9.5.1 The rate of interest for past due payments shall be as follows:

(Usury laws and requirements under the Federal Truth in Lending Act, similar state and local consumer credit laws and other regulations at the Owner's and Design/Builder's principal places of business, at the location of the Project and elsewhere may affect the validity of this provision. Specific legal advice should be obtained with respect to deletion, modification or other requirements, such as written disclosures or waivers.)

9.6 IF THE SCOPE of the Project is changed materially, the amount of compensation shall be equitably adjusted.

9.7 The compensation set forth in this Part 1 Agreement shall be equitably adjusted if through no fault of the Design/Builder the services have not been completed within ( ) months of the date of this Part 1 Agreement.

ARTICLE 10
OTHER CONDITIONS AND SERVICES

10.1 The Basic Services to be performed shall be commenced on and, subject to authorized adjustments and to delays not caused by the Design/Builder, shall be completed in ( ) calendar days. The Design/Builder's Basic Services consist of those described in Paragraph 1.3 as part of Basic Services, and include normal professional engineering and preliminary design services, unless otherwise indicated.

10.2 Services beyond those described in Paragraph 1.4 are as follows:
(Insert descriptions of other services, identify Additional Services included within Basic Compensation and modifications to the payment and compensation terms included in this Agreement.)

10.3 The Owner's preliminary program, budget, and other documents, if any, are enumerated as follows:

Title Date

This Agreement entered into as of the day and year first written above.

OWNER	DESIGN/BUILDER
(Signature)	*(Signature)*
(Printed name and title)	*(Printed name and title)*

CAUTION: You should sign an original AIA document which has this caution printed in red. An original assures that changes will not be obscured as may occur when documents are reproduced.

AIA Document A491

Standard Form of Agreements Between Design/Builder and Contractor

THIS DOCUMENT HAS IMPORTANT LEGAL CONSEQUENCES; CONSULTATION WITH AN ATTORNEY IS ENCOURAGED WITH RESPECT TO ITS USE, COMPLETION OR MODIFICATION.

AIA Document A201, General Conditions of the Contract for Construction, is adopted in this document by reference. Do not use with other general conditions unless this document is modified. This document comprises two separate agreements: Part 1 Agreement and Part 2 Agreement. This document is intended for use with AIA Document A191, Standard Form of Agreements Between Owner and Design/Builder.

PART 2 AGREEMENT

1996 EDITION

AGREEMENT

made as of the day of in the year of
(In words, indicate day, month and year.)

BETWEEN the Design/Builder:
(Name and address)

and the Contractor:
(Name and address)

For the following Project:
(Include Project name, location and a summary description.)

The Owner is:
(Name and address)

The Architect is:
(Name and address)

The Design/Builder and the Contractor agree as set forth below.

TERMS AND CONDITIONS—PART 2 AGREEMENT

ARTICLE 1
THE CONTRACT DOCUMENTS

1.1 BASIC DEFINITIONS

1.1.1 The Contract Documents consist of the Part 1 Agreement to the extent not modified by this Part 2 Agreement; the Drawings, Specifications and other documents identified in Article 15; the Contractor's Fixed Price proposal or Guaranteed Maximum Price proposal as accepted by the Design/Builder, a copy of which is attached to this Part 2 Agreement as Exhibit 1; this Part 2 Agreement; Conditions of the Contract (General, Supplementary and Other Conditions) issued prior to the execution of this Part 2 Agreement; and Modifications and construction documents issued after execution of this Part 2 Agreement. A Modification is: (1) a written amendment to this Part 2 Agreement signed by both parties, (2) a Change Order, or (3) a Construction Change Directive issued by the Design/Builder.

1.1.2 The term "Work" means the construction and services required by the Contract Documents, whether completed or partially completed, and includes all other labor, materials, equipment and services provided or to be provided by the Contractor to fulfill the Contractor's obligations. The Work may constitute the whole or a part of the Project.

ARTICLE 2
THE WORK OF THIS CONTRACT

2.1 The Contractor shall continue to provide those services set forth in Subparagraphs 2.1.4 through 2.1.8 of the Part 1 Agreement until completion of the construction documents by the Architect and any consultants employed by the Design/Builder. The Contractor shall continue to update and refine the Contractor's detailed cost estimate at intervals agreed upon by the Design/Builder, the Contractor and the Architect.

2.2 The Contractor shall execute the entire Work described in the Contract Documents, except to the extent specifically indicated in the Contract Documents to be the responsibility of others, or as follows:

ARTICLE 3

DATE OF COMMENCEMENT AND SUBSTANTIAL COMPLETION

3.1 The date of commencement is the date from which the Contract Time is measured; it shall be the date designated for commencement of the Work in a written notice to proceed to be issued by the Design/Builder.
(Insert the date of commencement, if it differs from the date of this Agreement or, if applicable, state that the date will be fixed in a notice to proceed.)

3.2 The Contractor shall achieve Substantial Completion of the entire Work not later than
(Insert the calendar date or number of calendar days after the date of commencement. Also insert any requirements for earlier Substantial Completion of certain portions of the Work, if not stated elsewhere in the Contract Documents.)

, subject to adjustments of this Contract Time as provided in the Contract Documents.
(Insert provisions, if any, for liquidated damages relating to failure to complete on time.)

ARTICLE 4

CONTRACT SUM

4.1 FIXED PRICE

4.1.1 If a Fixed Price proposal is the basis of this Part 2 Agreement, the Design/Builder shall pay the Contractor in current funds for the Contractor's performance of this Part 2 Agreement, the Contract Sum in the amount of Dollars ($), subject to additions and deductions as provided in the Contract Documents.

4.1.2 If a Fixed Price proposal is the basis of this Part 2 Agreement, Paragraph 4.2, Articles 5 through 12, and Paragraphs 14.3 through 14.6 are not applicable.

4.2 GUARANTEED MAXIMUM PRICE

4.2.1 If a Guaranteed Maximum Price is the basis of this Part 2 Agreement, the Design/Builder shall pay the Contractor in current funds for the Contractor's performance of this Part 2 Agreement, the Contract Sum consisting of the Cost of the Work as defined in Article 6 and the Contractor's Fee determined as follows:
(State a lump sum, percentage of Cost of the Work or other provision for determining the Contractor's Fee, and explain how the Contractor's Fee is to be adjusted for changes in the Work.)

4.2.2 The sum of the Cost of the Work and the Contractor's Fee is guaranteed by the Contractor not to exceed Dollars ($), subject to additions and deductions by Change Order as provided in the Contract Documents. Such maximum sum is referred to in the Contract Documents as the Guaranteed Maximum Price. Costs which would cause the Guaranteed Maximum Price to be exceeded shall be paid by the Contractor without reimbursement by the Design/Builder.
(Insert specific provisions if the Contractor is to participate in any savings.)

4.2.3 The Guaranteed Maximum Price is subject to the terms and conditions contained in the Contractor's proposal as accepted by the Design/Builder, a copy of which is attached hereto as Exhibit 1.

ARTICLE 5
CHANGES IN THE WORK

5.1 Adjustments to the Guaranteed Maximum Price on account of changes in the Work may be determined by any of the methods listed in Article 7 of the General Conditions.

5.2 In calculating adjustments to the Subcontract Sums of subcontracts (except those awarded with the Design/Builder's prior consent on the basis of cost plus a fee), the definitions of terms found in Article 7 of the General Conditions shall govern over the meanings assigned in Articles 4, 6 and 7 of this Part 2 Agreement to those same terms. Adjustments to subcontracts awarded with the Design/Builder's prior consent on the basis of cost plus a fee shall be calculated in accordance with the terms of those subcontracts.

5.3 In calculating adjustments to the Contract Sum as defined in Paragraph 4.2 of this Part 2 Agreement, the term "Cost of the Work" as found in Article 6 shall govern over the terms "cost" and "costs" as used in Article 7 of the General Conditions, and adjustments to the Contractor's Fee as defined in Subparagraph 4.2.1 of this Part 2 Agreement shall include a reasonable allowance for overhead and profit.

5.4 If no specific provision is made in Subparagraph 4.2.1 for adjustment of the Contractor's Fee in the case of changes in the Work, or if the extent of such changes is such, in the aggregate, that application of the adjustment provisions of Subparagraph 4.2.1 will cause substantial inequity to the Design/Builder or the Contractor, the Contractor's Fee shall be equitably adjusted on the basis of the Fee established for the original Work.

ARTICLE 6
COSTS TO BE REIMBURSED

6.1 The term Cost of the Work shall mean costs necessarily incurred by the Contractor in the proper performance of the Work. Such costs shall be at rates not higher than the standard paid at the place of the Project except with prior consent of the Design/Builder. The Cost of the Work shall include only the items set forth in this Article 6.

6.1.1 LABOR COSTS

.1 Wages of construction workers directly employed by the Contractor to perform the construction of the Work at the site or, with the Design/Builder's agreement, at off-site workshops.

.2 Wages or salaries of the Contractor's supervisory and administrative personnel when stationed at the site with the Design/Builder's agreement.

(If it is intended that the wages or salaries of certain personnel stationed at the Contractor's principal or other offices shall be included in the Cost of the Work, identify in Article 13 the personnel to be included and whether for all or only part of their time.)

.3 Wages and salaries of the Contractor's supervisory or administrative personnel engaged, at factories, workshops or on the road, in expediting the production or transportation of materials or equipment required for the Work, but only for that portion of their time required for the Work.

.4 Costs paid or incurred by the Contractor for taxes, insurance, contributions, assessments and benefits required by law or collective bargaining agreements and, for personnel not covered by such agreements, customary benefits such as sick leave, medical and health benefits, holidays, vacations and pensions, provided such costs are based on wages and salaries included in the Cost of the Work under Clauses 6.1.1.1 through 6.1.1.3.

6.1.2 SUBCONTRACT COSTS

Payments made by the Contractor to Subcontractors in accordance with the requirements of the subcontracts.

6.1.3 COSTS OF MATERIALS AND EQUIPMENT INCORPORATED IN THE COMPLETED CONSTRUCTION

.1 Costs, including transportation, of materials and equipment incorporated or to be incorporated in the completed construction.

.2 Costs of materials described in the preceding Clause 6.1.3.1 in excess of those actually installed but required to provide reasonable allowance for waste and for spoilage. Unused excess materials, if any, shall be handed over to the Design/Builder at the completion of the Work or, at the Design/Builder's option, shall be sold by the Contractor; amounts realized, if any, from such sales shall be credited to the Design/Builder as a deduction from the Cost of the Work.

6.1.4 COSTS OF OTHER MATERIALS AND EQUIPMENT, TEMPORARY FACILITIES AND RELATED ITEMS

.1 Costs, including transportation, installation, maintenance, dismantling and removal of materials, supplies, temporary facilities, machinery, equipment, and hand tools not customarily owned by the construction workers, which are provided by the Contractor at the site and fully consumed in the performance of the Work; and cost less salvage value on such items if not fully consumed, whether sold to others or retained by the Contractor. Cost for items previously used by the Contractor shall mean fair market value.

.2 Rental charges for temporary facilities, machinery, equipment, and hand tools not customarily owned by the construction workers, which are provided by the Contractor at the site, whether rented from the Contractor or others, and costs of transportation, installation, minor repairs and replacements, dismantling and removal thereof. Rates and quantities of equipment rented shall be subject to the Design/Builder's prior approval.

.3 Costs of removal of debris from the site.

.4 Costs of telegrams and long-distance telephone calls, postage and parcel delivery charges, telephone service at the site and reasonable petty cash expenses of the site office.

.5 That portion of the reasonable travel and subsistence expenses of the Contractor's personnel incurred while traveling in discharge of duties connected with the Work.

6.1.5 MISCELLANEOUS COSTS

.1 That portion directly attributable to this Part 2 Agreement of premiums for insurance and bonds.

.2 Sales, use or similar taxes imposed by a governmental authority which are related to the Work and for which the Contractor is liable.

.3 Fees and assessments for the building permit and for other permits, licenses and inspections for which the Contractor is required by the Contract Documents to pay.

.4 Fees of testing laboratories for tests required by the Contract Documents, except those related to defective or nonconforming Work for which reimbursement is excluded by Article 13 of the General Conditions or other provisions of the Contract Documents and which do not fall within the scope of Subparagraphs 6.2.2 through 6.2.4 below.

.5 Royalties and license fees paid for the use of a particular design, process or product required by the Contract Documents; the cost of defending suits or claims for infringement of patent rights arising from such requirement by the Contract Documents; payments made in accordance with legal judgments against the Contractor resulting from such suits or claims and payments of settlements made with the Design/Builder's consent; provided, however, that such costs of legal defenses, judgment and settlements shall not be included in the calculation of the Contractor's Fee or of the Guaranteed Maximum Price, if any, and provided that such royalties, fees and costs are not excluded by Article 3 of the General Conditions or other provisions of the Contract Documents.

.6 Deposits lost for causes other than the Contractor's fault or negligence.

6.1.6 OTHER COSTS

.1 Other costs incurred in the performance of the Work if and to the extent approved in advance in writing by the Design/Builder.

.2 Costs incurred in the performance of the services required in Paragraph 2.1 of this Part 2 Agreement.

6.2 EMERGENCIES: REPAIRS TO DAMAGED, DEFECTIVE OR NONCONFORMING WORK

The Cost of the Work shall also include costs which are incurred by the Contractor:

6.2.1 In taking action to prevent threatened damage, injury or loss in case of an emergency affecting the safety of persons and property, as provided in Article 10 of the General Conditions.

6.2.2 In repairing or correcting Work damaged or improperly executed by construction workers in the employ of the Contractor, provided such damage or improper execution did not result from the fault or negligence of the Contractor or the Contractor's foremen, engineers or superintendents, or other supervisory, administrative or managerial personnel of the Contractor.

6.2.3 In repairing damaged Work other than that described in Subparagraph 6.2.2, provided such damage did not result from the fault or negligence of the Contractor or the Contractor's personnel, and only to the extent that the cost of such repairs is not recoverable by the Contractor from others and the Contractor is not compensated therefor by insurance or otherwise.

6.2.4 In correcting defective or nonconforming Work performed or supplied by a Subcontractor or material supplier and not corrected by them, provided such defective or nonconforming Work did not result from the fault or neglect of the Contractor or the Contractor's personnel adequately to supervise and direct the Work of the Subcontractor or material supplier, and only to the extent that the cost of correcting the defective or nonconforming Work is not recoverable by the Contractor from the Subcontractor or material supplier.

ARTICLE 7

COSTS NOT TO BE REIMBURSED

7.1 The Cost of the Work shall not include:

7.1.1 Salaries and other compensation of the Contractor's personnel stationed at the Contractor's principal office or offices other than the site office, except as specifically provided in Clauses 6.1.1.2 and 6.1.1.3 or as may be provided in Article 13.

7.1.2 Expenses of the Contractor's principal office and offices other than the site office.

7.1.3 Overhead and general expenses, except as may be expressly included in Article 6.

7.1.4 The Contractor's capital expenses, including interest on the Contractor's capital employed for the Work.

7.1.5 Rental costs of machinery and equipment, except as specifically provided in Clause 6.1.4.2.

7.1.6 Except as provided in Subparagraphs 6.2.2 through 6.2.4 and Paragraph 12.5 of this Agreement, costs due to the fault or negligence of the Contractor, Subcontractors, anyone directly or indirectly employed by any of them, or for whose acts any of them may be liable, including but not limited to costs for the correction of damaged, defective or nonconforming Work, disposal and replacement of materials and equipment incorrectly ordered or supplied, and making good damage to property not forming part of the Work.

7.1.7 Any cost not specifically and expressly described in Article 6.

7.1.8 Costs which would cause the Guaranteed Maximum Price, if any, to be exceeded.

11.4.4 Additional retainage, if any, shall be as follows:
(If it is intended to retain additional amounts from progress payments to the Contractor beyond (1) the retainage from the Contractor's Fee provided in Clause 11.4.3.3, (2) the retainage from Subcontractors provided in Subparagraph 11.5 below, and (3) the retainage, if any, provided by other provisions of this Part 2 Agreement, insert provision for such additional retainage here. Such provision, if made, should also describe any arrangement for limiting or reducing the amount retained after the Work reaches a certain state of completion.)

11.5 Except with the Design/Builder's prior approval, payments to Subcontractors included in the Contractor's Applications for Payment shall not exceed an amount for each Subcontractor calculated as follows:

11.5.1 Take that portion of the Subcontract Sum properly allocable to completed Work as determined by multiplying the percentage completion of each portion of the Subcontractor's Work by the share of the total Subcontract Sum allocated to that portion in the Subcontractor's schedule of values, less retainage of percent (%). Pending final determination of amounts to be paid to the Subcontractor for changes in the Work, amounts not in dispute may be included as provided in Article 7 of the General Conditions even though the Subcontract Sum has not yet been adjusted by Change Order.

11.5.2 Add that portion of the Subcontract Sum properly allocable to materials and equipment delivered and suitably stored at the site for subsequent incorporation in the Work or, if approved in advance by the Design/Builder, suitably stored off the site at a location agreed upon in writing, less retainage of percent (%).

11.5.3 Subtract the aggregate of previous payments made by the Contractor to the Subcontractor.

11.5.4 Subtract amounts, if any, for which the Architect has withheld or nullified a Certificate for Payment by the Design/Builder to the Contractor for reasons which are the fault of the Subcontractor.

11.5.5 Add, upon Substantial Completion of the entire Work of the Contractor, a sum sufficient to increase the total payments to the Subcontractor to percent (%) of the Subcontract Sum, less amounts, if any, for incomplete Work and unsettled claims; and, if final completion of the entire Work is thereafter materially delayed through no fault of the Subcontractor, add any additional amounts payable on account of Work of the Subcontractor in accordance with Article 9 of the General Conditions.
(If it is intended, prior to Substantial Completion of the entire Work of the Contractor, to reduce or limit the retainage from Subcontractors resulting from the percentages inserted in Subparagraphs 11.5.1 and 11.5.2 above, and this is not explained elsewhere in the Contract Documents, insert here provisions for such reduction or limitation.)

The Subcontract Sum is the total amount stipulated in the subcontract to be paid by the Contractor to the Subcontractor for the Subcontractor's performance of the subcontract.

11.6 Except with the Design/Builder's prior approval, the Contractor shall not make advance payments to suppliers for materials or equipment which have not been delivered and stored at the site.

11.7 In taking action on the Contractor's Applications for Payment, the Architect shall be entitled to rely on the accuracy and completeness of the information furnished by the Contractor and shall not be deemed to represent that the Architect has made a detailed examination, audit or arithmetic verification of the documentation submitted in accordance with Paragraph 11.4 or other supporting data; that the Architect has made exhaustive or continuous on-site inspections or that the Architect has made examinations to ascertain how or for what purposes the Contractor has used amounts previously paid on account of this Part 2 Agreement. Such examinations, audits and verifications, if required by the Design/Builder, will be performed by the Design/Builder's accountants acting in the sole interest of the Design/Builder.

ARTICLE 12
FINAL PAYMENT

12.1 Final payment shall be made by the Design/Builder to the Contractor when (1) this Part 2 Agreement has been fully performed by the Contractor except for the Contractor's responsibility to correct defective or nonconforming Work, as provided in Article 12 of the General Conditions, and to satisfy other requirements, if any, which necessarily survive final payment; (2) a final Application for Payment and a final accounting for the Cost of the Work have been submitted by the Contractor and reviewed by the Design/Builder's accountants; and (3) a final Certificate for Payment has then been issued by the Architect. Such final payment shall be made by the Design/Builder not more than 30 days after the issuance of the Architect's final Certificate for Payment, or as follows:

12.2 The amount of the final payment shall be calculated as follows:

12.2.1 Take the sum of the Cost of the Work substantiated by the Contractor's final accounting and the Contractor's Fee; but not more than the Guaranteed Maximum Price, if any.

12.2.2 Subtract amounts, if any, which the Architect withholds, in whole or in part, from the final Certificate for Payment as provided in Article 9 of the General Conditions or other provisions of the Contract Documents.

12.2.3 Subtract the aggregate of previous payments made by the Design/Builder. If the aggregate of previous payments made by the Design/Builder exceeds the amount due the Contractor, the Contractor shall reimburse the difference to the Design/Builder.

12.3 The Design/Builder's accountants will review and report in writing on the Contractor's final accounting within 30 days after delivery of the final accounting to the Architect by the Contractor. Based upon such Cost of the Work as the Design/Builder's accountants report to be substantiated by the Contractor's final accounting, and provided the other conditions of Paragraph 12.1 have been met, the Architect will, within seven (7) days after receipt of the written report of the Design/Builder's accountants, either issue to the Design/Builder a final Certificate for Payment with a copy to the Contractor, or notify the Contractor and Design/Builder in writing of the Architect's reasons for withholding a certificate as provided in Article 9 of the General Conditions. The time periods stated in this Paragraph 12.3 supersede those stated in Article 9 of the General Conditions.

12.4 If the Design/Builder's accountants report the Cost of the Work as substantiated by the Contractor's final accounting to be less than claimed by the Contractor, the Contractor shall be entitled to demand arbitration of the disputed amount without a further decision of the Architect. Such demand for arbitration shall be made by the Contractor within 30 days after the Contractor's receipt of a copy of the Architect's final Certificate for Payment; failure to demand arbitration within this 30-day period shall result in the substantiated amount reported by the Design/Builder's accountants becoming binding on the Contractor. Pending a final resolution by arbitration, the Design/Builder shall pay the Contractor the amount certified in the Architect's final Certificate for Payment.

12.5 If, subsequent to final payment and at the Design/Builder's request, the Contractor incurs costs described in Article 6 and not excluded by Article 7 to correct defective or nonconforming Work, the Design/Builder shall reimburse the Contractor such costs and the Contractor's Fee applicable thereto on the same basis as if such costs had been incurred prior to final payment, but not in excess of the Guaranteed Maximum Price, if any. If the Contractor has participated in savings as provided in Paragraph 4.2, the amount of such savings shall be recalculated and appropriate credit given to the Design/Builder in determining the net amount to be paid by the Design/Builder to the Contractor.

ARTICLE 13
MISCELLANEOUS PROVISIONS

13.1 Where reference is made in this Part 2 Agreement to a provision of the General Conditions or another Contract Document, the reference refers to that provision as amended or supplemented by other provisions of the Contract Documents.

13.2 Payments due and unpaid under this Part 2 Agreement shall bear interest from the date payment is due at the rate stated below, or in the absence thereof, at the legal rate prevailing from time to time at the place where the Project is located.
(Insert rate of interest agreed upon, if any.)

(Usury laws and requirements under the Federal Truth in Lending Act, similar state and local consumer credit laws and other regulations at the Design/Builder's and Contractor's principal places of business, the location of the Project and elsewhere may affect the validity of this provision. Legal advice should be obtained with respect to deletions or modifications, and also regarding requirements such as written disclosures or waivers.)

13.3 Other provisions:

ARTICLE 14

TERMINATION OR SUSPENSION

14.1 If the agreement between the Owner and the Design/Builder is terminated, the Design/Builder may terminate this Part 2 Agreement without cause.

14.2 This Part 2 Agreement may be terminated by the Contractor as provided in Article 14 of the General Conditions.

14.3 Upon termination pursuant to Paragraph 14.1 or 14.2, the amount to be paid the Contractor under the provisions for "Termination by the Contractor" in the General Conditions shall be calculated in accordance with Paragraph 14.5 below, except that the Contractor's fee shall be calculated as if the Work had been fully completed by the Contractor, including a reasonable estimate of the Cost of the Work not actually completed.

14.4 This Part 2 Agreement may be terminated by the Design/Builder for cause as provided in Article 14 of the General Conditions; however, the amount, if any, to be paid to the Contractor under the General Conditions shall not cause the Guaranteed Maximum Price to be exceeded, nor shall it exceed the amount the Contractor would be entitled to receive under Paragraph 14.5 below.

14.5 CALCULATION OF PAYMENT UPON TERMINATION

14.5.1 Take the Cost of the Work incurred by the Contractor to the date of termination.

14.5.2 Add the Contractor's Fee computed upon the Cost of the Work to the date of termination at the rate stated in Subparagraph 4.2.1 or, if the Contractor's Fee is stated as a fixed sum in that Subparagraph, an amount which bears the same ratio to that fixed-sum Fee as the Cost of the Work at the time of termination bears to a reasonable estimate of the probable Cost of the Work upon its completion.

14.5.3 Subtract the aggregate of previous payments made by the Design/Builder. The Design/Builder shall also pay the Contractor fair compensation, either by purchase or rental at the election of the Design/Builder, for any equipment owned by the Contractor which the Design/Builder elects to retain and which is not otherwise included in the Cost of the Work under Subparagraph 14.5.1. To the extent that the Design/Builder elects to take legal assignment of subcontracts and purchase orders (including rental agreements), the Contractor shall, as a condition of receiving the payments referred to in this Article 14, execute and deliver all such papers and take all such steps, including the legal assignment of such subcontracts and other contractual rights of the Contractor, as the Design/Builder may require for the purpose of fully vesting in the Design/Builder the rights and benefits of the Contractor under such subcontracts or purchase orders.

14.6 The Work may be suspended by the Design/Builder as provided in Article 14 of the General Conditions; in such case, an adjustment shall be made for increases in the Cost of the Work including an equitable adjustment in the Contractor's Fee caused by suspension, delay or interruption.

ARTICLE 15

ENUMERATION OF CONTRACT DOCUMENTS

15.1 The Contract Documents, except for Modifications issued after execution of this Part 2 Agreement, are enumerated as follows:

15.1.1 The General Conditions are the General Conditions of the Contract for Construction, AIA Document A201, current as of the date of this Agreement. The term "Owner" as used in AIA Document A201 shall mean the Design/Builder. The services of the Contractor and the Design/Builder in the Part 1 Agreement between the Design/Builder and the Contractor supplement those of the Contractor and the Owner, respectively, in A201. Article 6 of the Part 1 Agreement shall not apply to claims or disputes arising during the performance of this Part 2 Agreement.

15.1.2 The Supplementary and other Conditions of the Contract are those contained in the Project Manual dated , and are as follows:

Document	Title	Pages

15.1.3 The specifications are those contained in the Project Manual dated as in Paragraph 15.1.2, and are as follows:
(Either list the Specifications here or refer to an exhibit attached to this Agreement.)

Section	Title	Pages

15.1.4 The drawings are as follows, and are dated , unless a different date is shown below:
(Either list the Drawings here or refer to an exhibit attached to this Agreement.)

Number	Title	Date

15.1.5 The Addenda, if any, are as follows:

Number	Date	Pages

Portions of Addenda relating to bidding requirements are not part of the Contract Documents unless the bidding requirements are also enumerated in this Article 15.

15.1.6 Other documents, if any, forming part of the Contract Documents are as follows:
(List here any additional documents which are intended to form part of the Contract Documents. The General Conditions provide that bidding requirements such as advertisement or invitation to bid, Instructions to Bidders, sample forms and the Contractor's bid are not part of the Contract Documents unless enumerated in this Agreement. They should be listed here only if intended to be part of the Contract Documents.)

This Agreement is entered into as of the day and year first written above and is executed in at least three (3) original copies of which one is to be delivered to the Contractor, one to the Architect for use in the administration of the Contract, and the remainder to the Design/Builder.

DESIGN/BUILDER	CONTRACTOR
______________________	______________________
(Signature)	*(Signature)*
______________________	______________________
(Printed name and title)	*(Printed name and title)*

CAUTION: You should sign an original AIA document which has this caution printed in red. An original assures that changes will not be obscured as may occur when documents are reproduced.

INSTRUCTION SHEET

FOR AIA DOCUMENT A201, GENERAL CONDITIONS OF THE CONTRACT FOR CONSTRUCTION—1987 Edition

A. GENERAL INFORMATION

1. Purpose

AIA Document A201, a general conditions forms, is intended to be used as one of the Contract Documents forming the Construction Contract. In addition, it is frequently adopted by reference into a variety of other agreements, including the Owner-Architect agreements and the Contractor-Subcontractor agreements, in order to establish a common basis for the [illegible]mary and secondary relationships on the typical construction project.

2. Related Documents

The current edition of A201 is incorporated by specific reference into two AIA Owner-Contractor [illegible]ts ([illegible] and [illegible]) and several AIA Owner-Architect agreements (B141, B151, B161 and B181). It may also be adopte[illegible] refe[illegible]e when the prime Agreement between the Owner and Contractor is adopted into a Subcontract, such as [illegible] Docu[illegible] A4[illegible] when the prime Agreement between the Owner and Architect is adopted into Architect-Consulta[illegible] agree[illegible]ts such [illegible]IA Documents C141, C142 and C161. Such incorporation by reference is a valid legal drafting meth[illegible] do[illegible] [illegible]corporated are generally interpreted as part of the respective contract.

The Contract Documents, including A201, record the Contract for Cons[illegible] between [illegible] Owner and Contractor. The other Contract Documents include:

Owner-Contractor Agreement Form (i.e., A101 or A111)
Supplementary and Other Conditions
Drawings
Specifications
Modifications

Also included in the Contract Documents are [illegible]da iss[illegible] prior to execution of the Contra[illegible] other documents listed in the Agreement. The A201 document is consi[illegible] the k[illegible]ne document [illegible]nating the [illegible] parties involved in the construction process. As mentioned a[illegible] dia[illegible] b[illegible], it is a vital d[illegible]ent [illegible] to allo[illegible] the proper legal responsibilities of the parties.

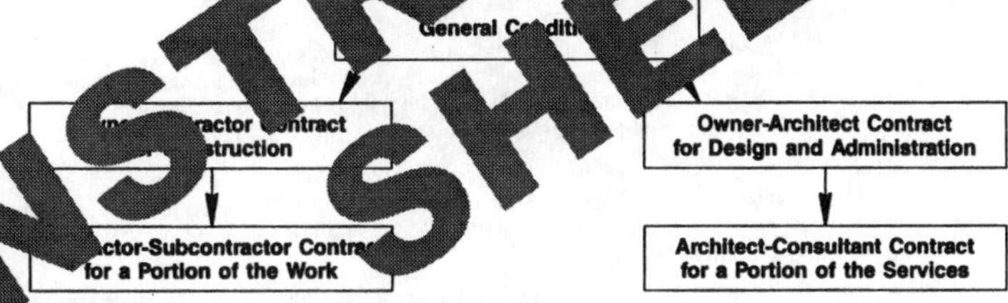

The AIA publishes other General Conditions that parallel A201 for the construction management family of documents (AIA Document A201/CM) and the interiors family of documents (AIA Document A271). For certain federal projects, the AIA publishes Federal Supplementary Conditions (AIA Document A201/SC) for use with A201.

3. Arbitration

The A201 document incorporates ARBITRATION according to the Construction Industry Arbitration Rules of the American Arbitration Association. Arbitration is BINDING AND MANDATORY in most states and under the federal Arbitration Act. In a minority of states, arbitration provisions related to future disputes are not enforceable, but arbitration is enforceable if agreed to after the dispute arises. A few states require that the contracting parties be especially notified that the written contract contains an arbitration provision by: a warning on the face of the document; specific placement of the arbitration provision within the document; or specific discussions among the parties prior to signing the document.

Arbitration provisions have been included in most AIA contract forms since 1888 in order to encourage alternative dispute resolution procedures and to provide users of AIA documents with legally enforceable arbitration provisions when the parties choose to adopt arbitration into their contract. Individuals may, however, choose to delete the arbitration provisions based upon their business decisions with the advice of counsel. To obtain a copy of the Construction Industry Arbitration Rules, write to the American Arbitration Association, 140 West 51st St., New York, NY 10020.

4. Use of Non-AIA Forms

If a combination of AIA documents and non-AIA documents is to be used, particular care must be taken to achieve consistency of language and intent. Certain owners require the use of owner-contractor agreements with general conditions and other contract forms which they prepare. Such forms should be carefully compared with the standard AIA forms for which they are being substituted before execution of an agreement. If there are any significant omissions, additions or variances from the terms of the related standard AIA forms, both legal and insurance counsel should be consulted.

5. Use of Current Documents

Prior to using any AIA document, the user should consult the AIA, an AIA component chapter or a current AIA Documents Price List to determine the current edition of each document.

6. Reproduction

AIA Document A201 is a copyrighted work and may not be reproduced or excerpted from in substantial part withou[illegible] express written permission of the AIA. The A201 document is intended to be used as a consumable—that is, the [illegible] ment purchased by the user is intended to be consumed in the course of being used. There is no implied permission [illegible] this document, nor does membership in The American Institute of Architects confer any further rig[illegible]ro[illegible] the[illegible]

A201 may not be reproduced for Project Manuals. Rather, if a user wishes to include it in a Project M[illegible]al, th[illegible]ma[illegible]tice is to purchase a quantity of the pre-printed forms and bind one in each of the Project Manuals. Mo[illegible]cations [illegible] be [illegible]com-plished through the use of separate Supplementary Conditions, such as those derived f[illegible] AIA [illegible]ment [illegible]11.

Unlike the instruction sheets accompanying some AIA documents, this A201 Instructio[illegible]et [illegible]ot [illegible]cense granting permission to reproduce the A201 document. AIA will not permit the reproduc[illegible]this doc[illegible]t or the use of substantial portions of language from it, except upon written request and receipt of [illegible]mission [illegible] the AIA.

B. CHANGES FROM THE PREVIOUS EDITION

1. Format Changes

The provisions dealing with the rights and re[illegible]nsi[illegible]s of th[illegible]chitect have be[illegible]ved from Ar[illegible] to Article 4, retitled Administration of the Contract, in orde[illegible]on[illegible]Ow[illegible]nd the Cont[illegible] as [illegible]parties to[illegible]e Construction Contract. Miscellaneous Provisions, form[illegible] Arti[illegible]7, is [illegible]cle 13.

2. Changes in Content

The 1987 edition of A20[illegible]evi[illegible]e 1976 e[illegible]n to reflect c[illegible]s in[illegible]truc[illegible]ndustry practices and the law. Comments and assistance in [illegible]vision w[illegible]ceived from nume[illegible]us ind[illegible]ls [illegible]zations, including those representing owners, architects, en[illegible]ers, specifiers, [illegible]al contractors, [illegible]co[illegible] su[illegible]s, attorneys and arbitrators.

Substan[illegible]al c[illegible]een made to the [illegible]doc[illegible]. Th[illegible]cipal changes are as follows.

Articl[illegible] Contractor

[illegible]nt[illegible]e w[illegible]y provision now [illegible]ude[illegible] damage or defect caused by abuse, modifications not executed [illegible]tor, improper or insufficient mainte[illegible]ce, and normal wear and tear under normal usage.

A[illegible]e 4: [illegible]inistration of the Contract

Re[illegible] of Shop Drawings—The provision governing architect's review of shop drawings has been expanded, and now requires [illegible]hat the architect be given sufficient time in his or her professional judgment to conduct an adequate review. The general [illegible]mitation on the purpose of the Architect's review to checking for conformance with the information given and the design concept expressed in the Contract Documents has been retained. In addition, language has been added specifically excluding purposes of checking details that are the responsibility of the Contractor.

Claims and Disputes—Provisions governing the handling of Claims and disputes have been expanded and brought together in a single paragraph to spell out procedures more clearly and sequentially; diagrams of the Change Order and Claims processes may be found on the last page of this Instruction Sheet. In the interest of expediting arbitration proceedings, a notice of demand for arbitration is now required to include all causes of action then known to the party filing the demand. Limitations on consolidation or joinder in arbitration of the Architect or the Architect's employees or consultants have been retained.

Delays Due to Adverse Weather Conditions—Claims for delay due to adverse weather conditions must now be substantiated by data showing that such conditions were out of the ordinary and had an adverse effect on the scheduled construction.

Article 5: Subcontractors

Contingent Assignment of Subcontracts—A new provision assigns Subcontracts to the Owner in the event that the Contract is terminated, and also provides for adjustment of the Subcontractor's compensation if termination has resulted in suspension of the Work for more than 30 days. Both Owner and Subcontractors are thus given a measure of protection from the effects of termination.

Article 7: Changes in the Work

This article has undergone substantial revision, and provides for a new type of document. The Change Order is now required to be signed by the Owner, Contractor and Architect. In the event the Contractor's agreement cannot be obtained, a new document, a Construction Change Directive which is signed by the Owner and Architect, shall be issued. Both of these situations were previously covered by Change Orders. Now they are separated so that they can, if necessary, be handled independently. A diagram of the process may be found on the last page of this Instruction Sheet.

Article 9: Payments and Completion

Substantial Completion—The Substantial Completion provisions now explicitly allow for partial occupancy or use. A Certificate of Substantial Completion covering a portion of Work is provided for, and consent of the insurer of the property is required.

Article 10: Protection of Persons and Property

Asbestos, PCB and Other Hazardous Wastes—The problem of hazardous wastes is addressed, for the first time, in a paragraph prescribing procedures to be followed in the event such substances are encountered on the site. Under its provisions the Work may only proceed in the affected area by written consent of the Owner and Contractor, or in accordance with a determination of the Architect upon which arbitration has not been demanded.

Article 11: Insurance and Bonds

This article has been expanded to cover bonds as well, and it is now provided that bonding requirements [illegible] known to the Contractor in the bidding requirements or at the time the Contract is signed. The Contractor, in [illegible] is required to furnish copies of the bonds on request to any person appearing to be a beneficiary of them.

Owner's property insurance is now required to be written in the full amount of the Contract Sum [illegible] for changes in the Contract Sum effected by Change Order. The coverages to be included on [illegible] all-risk policy [illegible] are given in much greater detail because "all-risk" merely means coverage of all risks not specifically excluded. In addition, the Owner is now required to insure materials stored off-site or in transit.

Article 12: Uncovering and Correction of Work

Correction of Work—The correction period has been extended with respect to Work performed after Substantial Completion, so that such Work is also covered by a one-year correction period.

Article 13: Miscellaneous Provisions

Statutory Limitation Period—A separate paragraph has been included under Miscellaneous Provisions giving the dates of commencement of the statutory limitation period with respect to acts or failures to act occurring at different points in the Project. This paragraph covers a range of [illegible] sets [illegible] commencement date: one for occurrences before Substantial Completion, another for those taking place between Substantial Completion and issuance of the final Certificate for Payment, and a third for those taking [illegible] the final Certificate has been issued.

Article 14: Termination or Suspension of the Contract

Procedures are set out [illegible] suspension of the Contract by the Owner for reasons other than the fault of the Contractor. A provision allowing for termination [illegible] circumstances has been included in [illegible] Document A511, Guide for Supplementary Conditions.

Further details [illegible] these changes may be found in the *[illegible] of Professional Practice* when revised. A side-by-side comparison of the 1976 and 1987 editions of A201 [illegible] for a limited time after publication of the 1987 edition.

C. [illegible] A201 FORM

Modifications

[illegible]ers are encouraged to consult an attorney before using an AIA document. Particularly with respect to licensing laws, duties imposed by building codes, interest charges, arbitration and indemnification, this document may require modification with the assistance of legal counsel to fully comply with state or local laws regulating these matters.

Generally, necessary modifications to the General Conditions may be accomplished by Supplementary Conditions included in the Project Manual and referenced in the Owner-Contractor Agreement. See AIA Document A511, Guide for Supplementary Conditions, for model provisions and suggested format for the Supplementary Conditions.

Because A201 is designed for general usage, it does not provide all the information and legal requirements needed for a specific Project and location. Necessary additional requirements must be provided in the other Contract Documents, such as the Supplementary Conditions. Consult AIA Document A521, Uniform Location of Subject Matter, to determine the proper location for such additional stipulations.

It is definitely not recommended practice to retype the standard document. Besides being a violation of copyright, retyping can introduce typographical errors and cloud the legal interpretation given to a standard clause when blended with modifications. Retyping eliminates one of the principal advantages of standard form documents. By merely reviewing the modifications to be made to a standard form document, parties familiar with that document can quickly understand the essence of the proposed relationship. Commercial exchanges are greatly simplified and expedited, good-faith dealing is encouraged, and otherwise latent clauses are exposed for scrutiny. In this way, contracting parties can more confidently and fairly measure their risks.

D. CHANGE ORDERS AND CLAIMS

The diagrams below are graphic examples of the Change Order and Claims processes under the 1987 edition of AIA Document A201. These diagrams are presented for instructional purposes only, and are not intended to augment or supersede any contract language contained in the document. Users are urged to read the document in its entirety and to consult the relevant contract language regarding the particulars of the processes diagrammed below.

A Change Order may be initiated by the Owner, Contractor or Architect. Typically, upon initiation of the Change Order process, the Architect prepares a copy of AIA Document G709, Proposal Request, and submits it to the Contractor for pricing. This is then conveyed back through the Architect to the Owner, beginning the process diagrammed below.

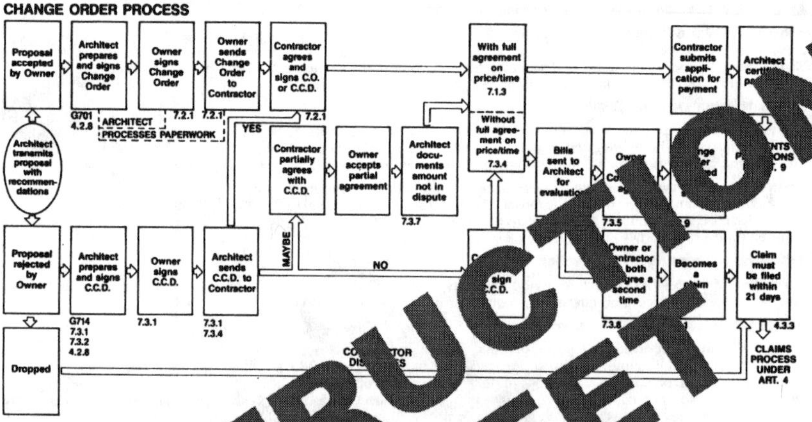

The Claims process may be [illegible]ough a v[illegible] of circumstanc[illegible] inc[illegible]ure to ag[illegible] upon the terms of a Change Order as shown in the diagram ab[illegible] O[illegible]he Claim[illegible]es, the Owne[illegible] Co[illegible]or, t[illegible]er with the Architect, seek resolution of the dispute by follo[illegible]cific ste[illegible]blished in the Co[illegible]ract D[illegible]ents[illegible]cularly in A201. These steps are generalized in the diagram be[illegible]

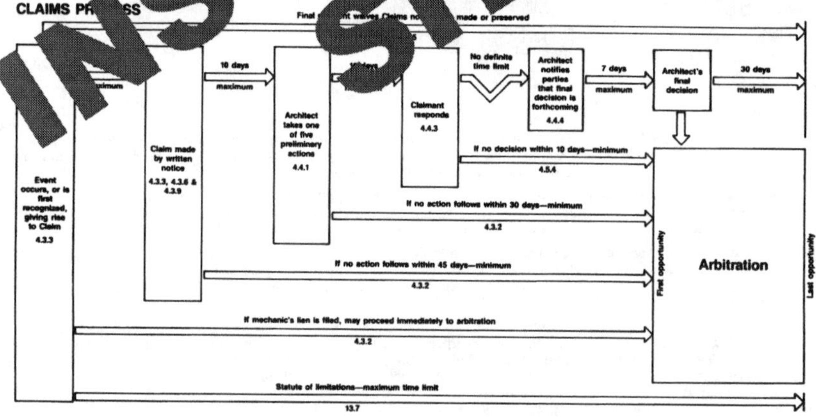

THE AMERICAN INSTITUTE OF ARCHITECTS

AIA Document A201

General Conditions of the Contract for Construction

THIS DOCUMENT HAS IMPORTANT LEGAL CONSEQUENCES; CONSULTATION WITH AN ATTORNEY IS ENCOURAGED WITH RESPECT TO ITS MODIFICATION

1987 EDITION
TABLE OF ARTICLES

This document has been approved and endorsed by the Associated General Contractors of America.

CAUTION: You should use an original AIA document which has this caution printed in red. An original assures that changes will not be obscured as may occur when documents are reproduced.

INDEX

 AIA DOCUMENT A201 • GENERAL CONDITIONS OF THE CONTRACT FOR CONSTRUCTION • FOURTEENTH EDITION

GENERAL CONDITIONS OF THE CONTRACT FOR CONSTRUCTION

ARTICLE 1

GENERAL PROVISIONS

1.1 BASIC DEFINITIONS

1.1.1 THE CONTRACT DOCUMENTS

The Contract Documents consist of the Agreement between Owner and Contractor (hereinafter the Agreement), Conditions of the Contract (General, Supplementary and other Conditions), Drawings, Specifications, addenda issued prior to execution of the Contract, other documents listed in the Agreement and Modifications issued after execution of the Contract. A Modification is (1) a written amendment to the Contract signed by both parties, (2) a Change Order, (3) a Construction Change Directive or (4) a written order for a minor change in the Work issued by the Architect. Unless specifically enumerated in the Agreement, the Contract Documents do not include other documents such as bidding requirements (advertisement or invitation to bid, Instructions to Bidders, sample forms, the Contractor's bid or portions of addenda relating to bidding requirements).

1.1.2 THE CONTRACT

The Contract Documents form the Contract for Construction. The Contract represents the entire and integrated agreement between the parties hereto and supersedes prior negotiations, representations or agreements, either written or oral. The Contract may be amended or modified only by a Modification. The Contract Documents shall not be construed to create a contractual relationship of any kind (1) between the Architect and Contractor, (2) between the Owner and a Subcontractor or Sub-subcontractor or (3) between any persons or entities other than the Owner and Contractor. The Architect shall, however, be entitled to performance and enforcement of obligations under the Contract intended to facilitate performance of the Architect's duties.

1.1.3 THE WORK

The term "Work" means the construction and services required by the Contract Documents, whether completed or partially completed, and includes all other labor, materials, equipment and services provided or to be provided by the Contractor to fulfill the Contractor's obligations. The Work may constitute the whole or a part of the Project.

1.1.4 THE PROJECT

The Project is the total construction of which the Work performed under the Contract Documents may be the whole or a part and which may include construction by the Owner or by separate contractors.

1.1.5 THE DRAWINGS

The Drawings are the graphic and pictorial portions of the Contract Documents, wherever located and whenever issued, showing the design, location and dimensions of the Work, generally including plans, elevations, sections, details, schedules and diagrams.

1.1.6 THE SPECIFICATIONS

The Specifications are that portion of the Contract Documents consisting of the written requirements for materials, equipment, construction systems, standards and workmanship for the Work, and performance of related services.

1.1.7 THE PROJECT MANUAL

The Project Manual is the volume usually assembled for the Work which may include the bidding requirements, sample forms, Conditions of the Contract and Specifications.

1.2 EXECUTION, CORRELATION AND INTENT

1.2.1 The Contract Documents shall be signed by the Owner and Contractor as provided in the Agreement. If either the Owner or Contractor or both do not sign all the Contract Documents, the Architect shall identify such unsigned Documents upon request.

1.2.2 Execution of the Contract by the Contractor is a representation that the Contractor has visited the site, become familiar with local conditions under which the Work is to be performed and correlated personal observations with requirements of the Contract Documents.

1.2.3 The intent of the Contract Documents is to include all items necessary for the proper execution and completion of the Work by the Contractor. The Contract Documents are complementary, and what is required by one shall be as binding as if required by all; performance by the Contractor shall be required only to the extent consistent with the Contract Documents and reasonably inferable from them as being necessary to produce the intended results.

1.2.4 Organization of the Specifications into divisions, sections and articles, and arrangement of Drawings shall not control the Contractor in dividing the Work among Subcontractors or in establishing the extent of Work to be performed by any trade.

1.2.5 Unless otherwise stated in the Contract Documents, words which have well-known technical or construction industry meanings are used in the Contract Documents in accordance with such recognized meanings.

1.3 OWNERSHIP AND USE OF ARCHITECT'S DRAWINGS, SPECIFICATIONS AND OTHER DOCUMENTS

1.3.1 The Drawings, Specifications and other documents prepared by the Architect are instruments of the Architect's service through which the Work to be executed by the Contractor is described. The Contractor may retain one contract record set. Neither the Contractor nor any Subcontractor, Sub-subcontractor or material or equipment supplier shall own or claim a copyright in the Drawings, Specifications and other documents prepared by the Architect, and unless otherwise indicated the Architect shall be deemed the author of them and will retain all common law, statutory and other reserved rights, in addition to the copyright. All copies of them, except the Contractor's record set, shall be returned or suitably accounted for to the Architect, on request, upon completion of the Work. The Drawings, Specifications and other documents prepared by the Architect, and copies thereof furnished to the Contractor, are for use solely with respect to this Project. They are not to be used by the Contractor or any Subcontractor, Sub-subcontractor or material or equipment supplier on other projects or for additions to this Project outside the scope of the

Work without the specific written consent of the Owner and Architect. The Contractor, Subcontractors, Sub-subcontractors and material or equipment suppliers are granted a limited license to use and reproduce applicable portions of the Drawings, Specifications and other documents prepared by the Architect appropriate to and for use in the execution of their Work under the Contract Documents. All copies made under this license shall bear the statutory copyright notice, if any, shown on the Drawings, Specifications and other documents prepared by the Architect. Submittal or distribution to meet official regulatory requirements or for other purposes in connection with this Project is not to be construed as publication in derogation of the Architect's copyright or other reserved rights.

1.4 CAPITALIZATION

1.4.1 Terms capitalized in these General Conditions include those which are (1) specifically defined, (2) the titles of numbered articles and identified references to Paragraphs, Subparagraphs and Clauses in the document or (3) the titles of other documents published by the American Institute of Architects.

1.5 INTERPRETATION

1.5.1 In the interest of brevity the Contract Documents frequently omit modifying words such as "all" and "any" and articles such as "the" and "an," but the fact that a modifier or an article is absent from one statement and appears in another is not intended to affect the interpretation of either statement.

ARTICLE 2

OWNER

2.1 DEFINITION

2.1.1 The Owner is the person or entity identified as such in the Agreement and is referred to throughout the Contract Documents as if singular in number. The term "Owner" means the Owner or the Owner's authorized representative.

2.1.2 The Owner upon reasonable written request shall furnish to the Contractor in writing information which is necessary and relevant for the Contractor to evaluate, give notice of or enforce mechanic's lien rights. Such information shall include a correct statement of the record legal title to the property on which the Project is located, usually referred to as the site, and the Owner's interest therein at the time of execution of the Agreement and, within five days after any change, information of such change in title, recorded or unrecorded.

2.2 INFORMATION AND SERVICES REQUIRED OF THE OWNER

2.2.1 The Owner shall, at the request of the Contractor, prior to execution of the Agreement and promptly from time to time thereafter, furnish to the Contractor reasonable evidence that financial arrangements have been made to fulfill the Owner's obligations under the Contract. *[Note: Unless such reasonable evidence were furnished on request prior to the execution of the Agreement, the prospective contractor would not be required to execute the Agreement or to commence the Work.]*

2.2.2 The Owner shall furnish surveys describing physical characteristics, legal limitations and utility locations for the site of the Project, and a legal description of the site.

2.2.3 Except for permits and fees which are the responsibility of the Contractor under the Contract Documents, the Owner shall secure and pay for necessary approvals, easements, assessments and charges required for construction, use or occupancy of permanent structures or for permanent changes in existing facilities.

2.2.4 Information or services under the Owner's control shall be furnished by the Owner with reasonable promptness to avoid delay in orderly progress of the Work.

2.2.5 Unless otherwise provided in the Contract Documents, the Contractor will be furnished, free of charge, such copies of Drawings and Project Manuals as are reasonably necessary for execution of the Work.

2.2.6 The foregoing are in addition to other duties and responsibilities of the Owner enumerated herein and especially those in respect to Article 6 (Construction by Owner or by Separate Contractors), Article 9 (Payments and Completion) and Article 11 (Insurance and Bonds).

2.3 OWNER'S RIGHT TO STOP THE WORK

2.3.1 If the Contractor fails to correct Work which is not in accordance with the requirements of the Contract Documents as required by Paragraph 12.2 or persistently fails to carry out Work in accordance with the Contract Documents, the Owner, by written order signed personally or by an agent specifically so empowered by the Owner in writing, may order the Contractor to stop the Work, or any portion thereof, until the cause for such order has been eliminated; however, the right of the Owner to stop the Work shall not give rise to a duty on the part of the Owner to exercise this right for the benefit of the Contractor or any other person or entity, except to the extent required by Subparagraph 6.1.3.

2.4 OWNER'S RIGHT TO CARRY OUT THE WORK

2.4.1 If the Contractor defaults or neglects to carry out the Work in accordance with the Contract Documents and fails within a seven-day period after receipt of written notice from the Owner to commence and continue correction of such default or neglect with diligence and promptness, the Owner may after such seven-day period give the Contractor a second written notice to correct such deficiencies within a second seven-day period. If the Contractor within such second seven-day period after receipt of such second notice fails to commence and continue to correct any deficiencies, the Owner may, without prejudice to other remedies the Owner may have, correct such deficiencies. In such case an appropriate Change Order shall be issued deducting from payments then or thereafter due the Contractor the cost of correcting such deficiencies, including compensation for the Architect's additional services and expenses made necessary by such default, neglect or failure. Such action by the Owner and amounts charged to the Contractor are both subject to prior approval of the Architect. If payments then or thereafter due the Contractor are not sufficient to cover such amounts, the Contractor shall pay the difference to the Owner.

ARTICLE 3

CONTRACTOR

3.1 DEFINITION

3.1.1 The Contractor is the person or entity identified as such in the Agreement and is referred to throughout the Contract Documents as if singular in number. The term "Contractor" means the Contractor or the Contractor's authorized representative.

3.2 REVIEW OF CONTRACT DOCUMENTS AND FIELD CONDITIONS BY CONTRACTOR

3.2.1 The Contractor shall carefully study and compare the Contract Documents with each other and with information furnished by the Owner pursuant to Subparagraph 2.2.2 and shall at once report to the Architect errors, inconsistencies or omissions discovered. The Contractor shall not be liable to the Owner or Architect for damage resulting from errors, inconsistencies or omissions in the Contract Documents unless the Contractor recognized such error, inconsistency or omission and knowingly failed to report it to the Architect. If the Contractor performs any construction activity knowing it involves a recognized error, inconsistency or omission in the Contract Documents without such notice to the Architect, the Contractor shall assume appropriate responsibility for such performance and shall bear an appropriate amount of the attributable costs for correction.

3.2.2 The Contractor shall take field measurements and verify field conditions and shall carefully compare such field measurements and conditions and other information known to the Contractor with the Contract Documents before commencing activities. Errors, inconsistencies or omissions discovered shall be reported to the Architect at once.

3.2.3 The Contractor shall perform the Work in accordance with the Contract Documents and submittals approved pursuant to Paragraph 3.12.

3.3 SUPERVISION AND CONSTRUCTION PROCEDURES

3.3.1 The Contractor shall supervise and direct the Work, using the Contractor's best skill and attention. The Contractor shall be solely responsible for and have control over construction means, methods, techniques, sequences and procedures and for coordinating all portions of the Work under the Contract, unless Contract Documents give other specific instructions concerning these matters.

3.3.2 The Contractor shall be responsible to the Owner for acts and omissions of the Contractor's employees, Subcontractors and their agents and employees, and other persons performing portions of the Work under a contract with the Contractor.

3.3.3 The Contractor shall not be relieved of obligations to perform the Work in accordance with the Contract Documents either by activities or duties of the Architect in the Architect's administration of the Contract, or by tests, inspections or approvals required or performed by persons other than the Contractor.

3.3.4 The Contractor shall be responsible for inspection of portions of Work already performed under this Contract to determine that such portions are in proper condition to receive subsequent Work.

3.4 LABOR AND MATERIALS

3.4.1 Unless otherwise provided in the Contract Documents, the Contractor shall provide and pay for labor, materials, equipment, tools, construction equipment and machinery, water, heat, utilities, transportation, and other facilities and services necessary for proper execution and completion of the Work, whether temporary or permanent and whether or not incorporated or to be incorporated in the Work.

3.4.2 The Contractor shall enforce strict discipline and good order among the Contractor's employees and other persons carrying out the Contract. The Contractor shall not permit employment of unfit persons or persons not skilled in tasks assigned to them.

3.5 WARRANTY

3.5.1 The Contractor warrants to the Owner and Architect that materials and equipment furnished under the Contract will be of good quality and new unless otherwise required or permitted by the Contract Documents, that the Work will be free from defects not inherent in the quality required or permitted, and that the Work will conform with the requirements of the Contract Documents. Work not conforming to these requirements, including substitutions not properly approved and authorized, may be considered defective. The Contractor's warranty excludes remedy for damage or defect caused by abuse, modifications not executed by the Contractor, improper or insufficient maintenance, improper operation, or normal wear and tear under normal usage. If required by the Architect, the Contractor shall furnish satisfactory evidence as to the kind and quality of materials and equipment.

3.6 TAXES

3.6.1 The Contractor shall pay sales, consumer, use and similar taxes for the Work or portions thereof provided by the Contractor which are legally enacted when bids are received or negotiations concluded, whether or not yet effective or merely scheduled to go into effect.

3.7 PERMITS, FEES AND NOTICES

3.7.1 Unless otherwise provided in the Contract Documents, the Contractor shall secure and pay for the building permit and other permits and governmental fees, licenses and inspections necessary for proper execution and completion of the Work which are customarily secured after execution of the Contract and which are legally required when bids are received or negotiations concluded.

3.7.2 The Contractor shall comply with and give notices required by laws, ordinances, rules, regulations and lawful orders of public authorities bearing on performance of the Work.

3.7.3 It is not the Contractor's responsibility to ascertain that the Contract Documents are in accordance with applicable laws, statutes, ordinances, building codes, and rules and regulations. However, if the Contractor observes that portions of the Contract Documents are at variance therewith, the Contractor shall promptly notify the Architect and Owner in writing, and necessary changes shall be accomplished by appropriate Modification.

3.7.4 If the Contractor performs Work knowing it to be contrary to laws, statutes, ordinances, building codes, and rules and regulations without such notice to the Architect and Owner, the Contractor shall assume full responsibility for such Work and shall bear the attributable costs.

3.8 ALLOWANCES

3.8.1 The Contractor shall include in the Contract Sum all allowances stated in the Contract Documents. Items covered by allowances shall be supplied for such amounts and by such persons or entities as the Owner may direct, but the Contractor shall not be required to employ persons or entities against which the Contractor makes reasonable objection.

3.8.2 Unless otherwise provided in the Contract Documents:

- **.1** materials and equipment under an allowance shall be selected promptly by the Owner to avoid delay in the Work;
- **.2** allowances shall cover the cost to the Contractor of materials and equipment delivered at the site and all required taxes, less applicable trade discounts;

.3 Contractor's costs for unloading and handling at the site, labor, installation costs, overhead, profit and other expenses contemplated for stated allowance amounts shall be included in the Contract Sum and not in the allowances;

.4 whenever costs are more than or less than allowances, the Contract Sum shall be adjusted accordingly by Change Order. The amount of the Change Order shall reflect (1) the difference between actual costs and the allowances under Clause 3.8.2.2 and (2) changes in Contractor's costs under Clause 3.8.2.3.

3.9 SUPERINTENDENT

3.9.1 The Contractor shall employ a competent superintendent and necessary assistants who shall be in attendance at the Project site during performance of the Work. The superintendent shall represent the Contractor, and communications given to the superintendent shall be as binding as if given to the Contractor. Important communications shall be confirmed in writing. Other communications shall be similarly confirmed on written request in each case.

3.10 CONTRACTOR'S CONSTRUCTION SCHEDULES

3.10.1 The Contractor, promptly after being awarded the Contract, shall prepare and submit for the Owner's and Architect's information a Contractor's construction schedule for the Work. The schedule shall not exceed time limits current under the Contract Documents, shall be revised at appropriate intervals as required by the conditions of the Work and Project, shall be related to the entire Project to the extent required by the Contract Documents, and shall provide for expeditious and practicable execution of the Work.

3.10.2 The Contractor shall prepare and keep current, for the Architect's approval, a schedule of submittals which is coordinated with the Contractor's construction schedule and allows the Architect reasonable time to review submittals.

3.10.3 The Contractor shall conform to the most recent schedules.

3.11 DOCUMENTS AND SAMPLES AT THE SITE

3.11.1 The Contractor shall maintain at the site for the Owner one record copy of the Drawings, Specifications, addenda, Change Orders and other Modifications, in good order and marked currently to record changes and selections made during construction, and in addition approved Shop Drawings, Product Data, Samples and similar required submittals. These shall be available to the Architect and shall be delivered to the Architect for submittal to the Owner upon completion of the Work.

3.12 SHOP DRAWINGS, PRODUCT DATA AND SAMPLES

3.12.1 Shop Drawings are drawings, diagrams, schedules and other data specially prepared for the Work by the Contractor or a Subcontractor, Sub-subcontractor, manufacturer, supplier or distributor to illustrate some portion of the Work.

3.12.2 Product Data are illustrations, standard schedules, performance charts, instructions, brochures, diagrams and other information furnished by the Contractor to illustrate materials or equipment for some portion of the Work.

3.12.3 Samples are physical examples which illustrate materials, equipment or workmanship and establish standards by which the Work will be judged.

3.12.4 Shop Drawings, Product Data, Samples and similar submittals are not Contract Documents. The purpose of their submittal is to demonstrate for those portions of the Work for which submittals are required the way the Contractor proposes to conform to the information given and the design concept expressed in the Contract Documents. Review by the Architect is subject to the limitations of Subparagraph 4.2.7.

3.12.5 The Contractor shall review, approve and submit to the Architect Shop Drawings, Product Data, Samples and similar submittals required by the Contract Documents with reasonable promptness and in such sequence as to cause no delay in the Work or in the activities of the Owner or of separate contractors. Submittals made by the Contractor which are not required by the Contract Documents may be returned without action.

3.12.6 The Contractor shall perform no portion of the Work requiring submittal and review of Shop Drawings, Product Data, Samples or similar submittals until the respective submittal has been approved by the Architect. Such Work shall be in accordance with approved submittals.

3.12.7 By approving and submitting Shop Drawings, Product Data, Samples and similar submittals, the Contractor represents that the Contractor has determined and verified materials, field measurements and field construction criteria related thereto, or will do so, and has checked and coordinated the information contained within such submittals with the requirements of the Work and of the Contract Documents.

3.12.8 The Contractor shall not be relieved of responsibility for deviations from requirements of the Contract Documents by the Architect's approval of Shop Drawings, Product Data, Samples or similar submittals unless the Contractor has specifically informed the Architect in writing of such deviation at the time of submittal and the Architect has given written approval to the specific deviation. The Contractor shall not be relieved of responsibility for errors or omissions in Shop Drawings, Product Data, Samples or similar submittals by the Architect's approval thereof.

3.12.9 The Contractor shall direct specific attention, in writing or on resubmitted Shop Drawings, Product Data, Samples or similar submittals, to revisions other than those requested by the Architect on previous submittals.

3.12.10 Informational submittals upon which the Architect is not expected to take responsive action may be so identified in the Contract Documents.

3.12.11 When professional certification of performance criteria of materials, systems or equipment is required by the Contract Documents, the Architect shall be entitled to rely upon the accuracy and completeness of such calculations and certifications.

3.13 USE OF SITE

3.13.1 The Contractor shall confine operations at the site to areas permitted by law, ordinances, permits and the Contract Documents and shall not unreasonably encumber the site with materials or equipment.

3.14 CUTTING AND PATCHING

3.14.1 The Contractor shall be responsible for cutting, fitting or patching required to complete the Work or to make its parts fit together properly.

3.14.2 The Contractor shall not damage or endanger a portion of the Work or fully or partially completed construction of the Owner or separate contractors by cutting, patching or otherwise altering such construction, or by excavation. The Contractor shall not cut or otherwise alter such construction by the

Owner or a separate contractor except with written consent of the Owner and of such separate contractor; such consent shall not be unreasonably withheld. The Contractor shall not unreasonably withhold from the Owner or a separate contractor the Contractor's consent to cutting or otherwise altering the Work.

3.15 CLEANING UP

3.15.1 The Contractor shall keep the premises and surrounding area free from accumulation of waste materials or rubbish caused by operations under the Contract. At completion of the Work the Contractor shall remove from and about the Project waste materials, rubbish, the Contractor's tools, construction equipment, machinery and surplus materials.

3.15.2 If the Contractor fails to clean up as provided in the Contract Documents, the Owner may do so and the cost thereof shall be charged to the Contractor.

3.16 ACCESS TO WORK

3.16.1 The Contractor shall provide the Owner and Architect access to the Work in preparation and progress wherever located.

3.17 ROYALTIES AND PATENTS

3.17.1 The Contractor shall pay all royalties and license fees. The Contractor shall defend suits or claims for infringement of patent rights and shall hold the Owner and Architect harmless from loss on account thereof, but shall not be responsible for such defense or loss when a particular design, process or product of a particular manufacturer or manufacturers is required by the Contract Documents. However, if the Contractor has reason to believe that the required design, process or product is an infringement of a patent, the Contractor shall be responsible for such loss unless such information is promptly furnished to the Architect.

3.18 INDEMNIFICATION

3.18.1 To the fullest extent permitted by law, the Contractor shall indemnify and hold harmless the Owner, Architect, Architect's consultants, and agents and employees of any of them from and against claims, damages, losses and expenses, including but not limited to attorneys' fees, arising out of or resulting from performance of the Work, provided that such claim, damage, loss or expense is attributable to bodily injury, sickness, disease or death, or to injury to or destruction of tangible property (other than the Work itself) including loss of use resulting therefrom, but only to the extent caused in whole or in part by negligent acts or omissions of the Contractor, a Subcontractor, anyone directly or indirectly employed by them or anyone for whose acts they may be liable, regardless of whether or not such claim, damage, loss or expense is caused in part by a party indemnified hereunder. Such obligation shall not be construed to negate, abridge, or reduce other rights or obligations of indemnity which would otherwise exist as to a party or person described in this Paragraph 3.18.

3.18.2 In claims against any person or entity indemnified under this Paragraph 3.18 by an employee of the Contractor, a Subcontractor, anyone directly or indirectly employed by them or anyone for whose acts they may be liable, the indemnification obligation under this Paragraph 3.18 shall not be limited by a limitation on amount or type of damages, compensation or benefits payable by or for the Contractor or a Subcontractor under workers' or workmen's compensation acts, disability benefit acts or other employee benefit acts.

3.18.3 The obligations of the Contractor under this Paragraph 3.18 shall not extend to the liability of the Architect, the Architect's consultants, and agents and employees of any of them arising out of (1) the preparation or approval of maps, drawings, opinions, reports, surveys, Change Orders, designs or specifications, or (2) the giving of or the failure to give directions or instructions by the Architect, the Architect's consultants, and agents and employees of any of them provided such giving or failure to give is the primary cause of the injury or damage.

ARTICLE 4

ADMINISTRATION OF THE CONTRACT

4.1 ARCHITECT

4.1.1 The Architect is the person lawfully licensed to practice architecture or an entity lawfully practicing architecture identified as such in the Agreement and is referred to throughout the Contract Documents as if singular in number. The term "Architect" means the Architect or the Architect's authorized representative.

4.1.2 Duties, responsibilities and limitations of authority of the Architect as set forth in the Contract Documents shall not be restricted, modified or extended without written consent of the Owner, Contractor and Architect. Consent shall not be unreasonably withheld.

4.1.3 In case of termination of employment of the Architect, the Owner shall appoint an architect against whom the Contractor makes no reasonable objection and whose status under the Contract Documents shall be that of the former architect.

4.1.4 Disputes arising under Subparagraphs 4.1.2 and 4.1.3 shall be subject to arbitration.

4.2 ARCHITECT'S ADMINISTRATION OF THE CONTRACT

4.2.1 The Architect will provide administration of the Contract as described in the Contract Documents, and will be the Owner's representative (1) during construction, (2) until final payment is due and (3) with the Owner's concurrence, from time to time during the correction period described in Paragraph 12.2. The Architect will advise and consult with the Owner. The Architect will have authority to act on behalf of the Owner only to the extent provided in the Contract Documents, unless otherwise modified by written instrument in accordance with other provisions of the Contract.

4.2.2 The Architect will visit the site at intervals appropriate to the stage of construction to become generally familiar with the progress and quality of the completed Work and to determine in general if the Work is being performed in a manner indicating that the Work, when completed, will be in accordance with the Contract Documents. However, the Architect will not be required to make exhaustive or continuous on-site inspections to check quality or quantity of the Work. On the basis of on-site observations as an architect, the Architect will keep the Owner informed of progress of the Work, and will endeavor to guard the Owner against defects and deficiencies in the Work.

4.2.3 The Architect will not have control over or charge of and will not be responsible for construction means, methods, techniques, sequences or procedures, or for safety precautions and programs in connection with the Work, since these are solely the Contractor's responsibility as provided in Paragraph 3.3. The Architect will not be responsible for the Contractor's failure to carry out the Work in accordance with the Contract Documents. The Architect will not have control over or charge of and will not be responsible for acts or omissions of the Contractor, Subcontractors, or their agents or employees, or of any other persons performing portions of the Work.

4.2.4 Communications Facilitating Contract Administration. Except as otherwise provided in the Contract Documents or when direct communications have been specially authorized, the Owner and Contractor shall endeavor to communicate through the Architect. Communications by and with the Architect's consultants shall be through the Architect. Communications by and with Subcontractors and material suppliers shall be through the Contractor. Communications by and with separate contractors shall be through the Owner.

4.2.5 Based on the Architect's observations and evaluations of the Contractor's Applications for Payment, the Architect will review and certify the amounts due the Contractor and will issue Certificates for Payment in such amounts.

4.2.6 The Architect will have authority to reject Work which does not conform to the Contract Documents. Whenever the Architect considers it necessary or advisable for implementation of the intent of the Contract Documents, the Architect will have authority to require additional inspection or testing of the Work in accordance with Subparagraphs 13.5.2 and 13.5.3, whether or not such Work is fabricated, installed or completed. However, neither this authority of the Architect nor a decision made in good faith either to exercise or not to exercise such authority shall give rise to a duty or responsibility of the Architect to the Contractor, Subcontractors, material and equipment suppliers, their agents or employees, or other persons performing portions of the Work.

4.2.7 The Architect will review and approve or take other appropriate action upon the Contractor's submittals such as Shop Drawings, Product Data and Samples, but only for the limited purpose of checking for conformance with information given and the design concept expressed in the Contract Documents. The Architect's action will be taken with such reasonable promptness as to cause no delay in the Work or in the activities of the Owner, Contractor or separate contractors, while allowing sufficient time in the Architect's professional judgment to permit adequate review. Review of such submittals is not conducted for the purpose of determining the accuracy and completeness of other details such as dimensions and quantities, or for substantiating instructions for installation or performance of equipment or systems, all of which remain the responsibility of the Contractor as required by the Contract Documents. The Architect's review of the Contractor's submittals shall not relieve the Contractor of the obligations under Paragraphs 3.3, 3.5 and 3.12. The Architect's review shall not constitute approval of safety precautions or, unless otherwise specifically stated by the Architect, of any construction means, methods, techniques, sequences or procedures. The Architect's approval of a specific item shall not indicate approval of an assembly of which the item is a component.

4.2.8 The Architect will prepare Change Orders and Construction Change Directives, and may authorize minor changes in the Work as provided in Paragraph 7.4.

4.2.9 The Architect will conduct inspections to determine the date or dates of Substantial Completion and the date of final completion, will receive and forward to the Owner for the Owner's review and records written warranties and related documents required by the Contract and assembled by the Contractor, and will issue a final Certificate for Payment upon compliance with the requirements of the Contract Documents.

4.2.10 If the Owner and Architect agree, the Architect will provide one or more project representatives to assist in carrying out the Architect's responsibilities at the site. The duties, responsibilities and limitations of authority of such project representatives shall be as set forth in an exhibit to be incorporated in the Contract Documents.

4.2.11 The Architect will interpret and decide matters concerning performance under and requirements of the Contract Documents on written request of either the Owner or Contractor. The Architect's response to such requests will be made with reasonable promptness and within any time limits agreed upon. If no agreement is made concerning the time within which interpretations required of the Architect shall be furnished in compliance with this Paragraph 4.2, then delay shall not be recognized on account of failure by the Architect to furnish such interpretations until 15 days after written request is made for them.

4.2.12 Interpretations and decisions of the Architect will be consistent with the intent of and reasonably inferable from the Contract Documents and will be in writing or in the form of drawings. When making such interpretations and decisions, the Architect will endeavor to secure faithful performance by both Owner and Contractor, will not show partiality to either and will not be liable for results of interpretations or decisions so rendered in good faith.

4.2.13 The Architect's decisions on matters relating to aesthetic effect will be final if consistent with the intent expressed in the Contract Documents.

4.3 CLAIMS AND DISPUTES

4.3.1 Definition. A Claim is a demand or assertion by one of the parties seeking, as a matter of right, adjustment or interpretation of Contract terms, payment of money, extension of time or other relief with respect to the terms of the Contract. The term "Claim" also includes other disputes and matters in question between the Owner and Contractor arising out of or relating to the Contract. Claims must be made by written notice. The responsibility to substantiate Claims shall rest with the party making the Claim.

4.3.2 Decision of Architect. Claims, including those alleging an error or omission by the Architect, shall be referred initially to the Architect for action as provided in Paragraph 4.4. A decision by the Architect, as provided in Subparagraph 4.4.4, shall be required as a condition precedent to arbitration or litigation of a Claim between the Contractor and Owner as to all such matters arising prior to the date final payment is due, regardless of (1) whether such matters relate to execution and progress of the Work or (2) the extent to which the Work has been completed. The decision by the Architect in response to a Claim shall not be a condition precedent to arbitration or litigation in the event (1) the position of Architect is vacant, (2) the Architect has not received evidence or has failed to render a decision within agreed time limits, (3) the Architect has failed to take action required under Subparagraph 4.4.4 within 30 days after the Claim is made, (4) 45 days have passed after the Claim has been referred to the Architect or (5) the Claim relates to a mechanic's lien.

4.3.3 Time Limits on Claims. Claims by either party must be made within 21 days after occurrence of the event giving rise to such Claim or within 21 days after the claimant first recognizes the condition giving rise to the Claim, whichever is later. Claims must be made by written notice. An additional Claim made after the initial Claim has been implemented by Change Order will not be considered unless submitted in a timely manner.

4.3.4 Continuing Contract Performance. Pending final resolution of a Claim including arbitration, unless otherwise agreed in writing the Contractor shall proceed diligently with performance of the Contract and the Owner shall continue to make payments in accordance with the Contract Documents.

4.3.5 Waiver of Claims: Final Payment. The making of final payment shall constitute a waiver of Claims by the Owner except those arising from:

.1 liens, Claims, security interests or encumbrances arising out of the Contract and unsettled;

.2 failure of the Work to comply with the requirements of the Contract Documents; or

.3 terms of special warranties required by the Contract Documents.

4.3.6 Claims for Concealed or Unknown Conditions. If conditions are encountered at the site which are (1) subsurface or otherwise concealed physical conditions which differ materially from those indicated in the Contract Documents or (2) unknown physical conditions of an unusual nature, which differ materially from those ordinarily found to exist and generally recognized as inherent in construction activities of the character provided for in the Contract Documents, then notice by the observing party shall be given to the other party promptly before conditions are disturbed and in no event later than 21 days after first observance of the conditions. The Architect will promptly investigate such conditions and, if they differ materially and cause an increase or decrease in the Contractor's cost of, or time required for, performance of any part of the Work, will recommend an equitable adjustment in the Contract Sum or Contract Time, or both. If the Architect determines that the conditions at the site are not materially different from those indicated in the Contract Documents and that no change in the terms of the Contract is justified, the Architect shall so notify the Owner and Contractor in writing, stating the reasons. Claims by either party in opposition to such determination must be made within 21 days after the Architect has given notice of the decision. If the Owner and Contractor cannot agree on an adjustment in the Contract Sum or Contract Time, the adjustment shall be referred to the Architect for initial determination, subject to further proceedings pursuant to Paragraph 4.4.

4.3.7 Claims for Additional Cost. If the Contractor wishes to make Claim for an increase in the Contract Sum, written notice as provided herein shall be given before proceeding to execute the Work. Prior notice is not required for Claims relating to an emergency endangering life or property arising under Paragraph 10.3. If the Contractor believes additional cost is involved for reasons including but not limited to (1) a written interpretation from the Architect, (2) an order by the Owner to stop the Work where the Contractor was not at fault, (3) a written order for a minor change in the Work issued by the Architect, (4) failure of payment by the Owner, (5) termination of the Contract by the Owner, (6) Owner's suspension or (7) other reasonable grounds, Claim shall be filed in accordance with the procedure established herein.

4.3.8 Claims for Additional Time

4.3.8.1 If the Contractor wishes to make Claim for an increase in the Contract Time, written notice as provided herein shall be given. The Contractor's Claim shall include an estimate of cost and of probable effect of delay on progress of the Work. In the case of a continuing delay only one Claim is necessary.

4.3.8.2 If adverse weather conditions are the basis for a Claim for additional time, such Claim shall be documented by data substantiating that weather conditions were abnormal for the period of time and could not have been reasonably anticipated, and that weather conditions had an adverse effect on the scheduled construction.

4.3.9 Injury or Damage to Person or Property. If either party to the Contract suffers injury or damage to person or property because of an act or omission of the other party, of any of the other party's employees or agents, or of others for whose acts such party is legally liable, written notice of such injury or damage, whether or not insured, shall be given to the other party within a reasonable time not exceeding 21 days after first observance. The notice shall provide sufficient detail to enable the other party to investigate the matter. If a Claim for additional cost or time related to this Claim is to be asserted, it shall be filed as provided in Subparagraphs 4.3.7 or 4.3.8.

4.4 RESOLUTION OF CLAIMS AND DISPUTES

4.4.1 The Architect will review Claims and take one or more of the following preliminary actions within ten days of receipt of a Claim: (1) request additional supporting data from the claimant, (2) submit a schedule to the parties indicating when the Architect expects to take action, (3) reject the Claim in whole or in part, stating reasons for rejection, (4) recommend approval of the Claim by the other party or (5) suggest a compromise. The Architect may also, but is not obligated to, notify the surety, if any, of the nature and amount of the Claim.

4.4.2 If a Claim has been resolved, the Architect will prepare or obtain appropriate documentation.

4.4.3 If a Claim has not been resolved, the party making the Claim shall, within ten days after the Architect's preliminary response, take one or more of the following actions: (1) submit additional supporting data requested by the Architect, (2) modify the initial Claim or (3) notify the Architect that the initial Claim stands.

4.4.4 If a Claim has not been resolved after consideration of the foregoing and of further evidence presented by the parties or requested by the Architect, the Architect will notify the parties in writing that the Architect's decision will be made within seven days, which decision shall be final and binding on the parties but subject to arbitration. Upon expiration of such time period, the Architect will render to the parties the Architect's written decision relative to the Claim, including any change in the Contract Sum or Contract Time or both. If there is a surety and there appears to be a possibility of a Contractor's default, the Architect may, but is not obligated to, notify the surety and request the surety's assistance in resolving the controversy.

4.5 ARBITRATION

4.5.1 Controversies and Claims Subject to Arbitration. Any controversy or Claim arising out of or related to the Contract, or the breach thereof, shall be settled by arbitration in accordance with the Construction Industry Arbitration Rules of the American Arbitration Association, and judgment upon the award rendered by the arbitrator or arbitrators may be entered in any court having jurisdiction thereof, except controversies or Claims relating to aesthetic effect and except those waived as provided for in Subparagraph 4.3.5. Such controversies or Claims upon which the Architect has given notice and rendered a decision as provided in Subparagraph 4.4.4 shall be subject to arbitration upon written demand of either party. Arbitration may be commenced when 45 days have passed after a Claim has been referred to the Architect as provided in Paragraph 4.3 and no decision has been rendered.

4.5.2 Rules and Notices for Arbitration. Claims between the Owner and Contractor not resolved under Paragraph 4.4 shall, if subject to arbitration under Subparagraph 4.5.1, be decided by arbitration in accordance with the Construction Industry Arbitration Rules of the American Arbitration Association currently in effect, unless the parties mutually agree otherwise. Notice of demand for arbitration shall be filed in writing with the other party to the Agreement between the Owner and Contractor and with the American Arbitration Association, and a copy shall be filed with the Architect.

4.5.3 Contract Performance During Arbitration. During arbitration proceedings, the Owner and Contractor shall comply with Subparagraph 4.3.4.

4.5.4 When Arbitration May Be Demanded. Demand for arbitration of any Claim may not be made until the earlier of (1) the date on which the Architect has rendered a final written decision on the Claim, (2) the tenth day after the parties have presented evidence to the Architect or have been given reasonable opportunity to do so, if the Architect has not rendered a final written decision by that date, or (3) any of the five events described in Subparagraph 4.3.2.

4.5.4.1 When a written decision of the Architect states that (1) the decision is final but subject to arbitration and (2) a demand for arbitration of a Claim covered by such decision must be made within 30 days after the date on which the party making the demand receives the final written decision, then failure to demand arbitration within said 30 days' period shall result in the Architect's decision becoming final and binding upon the Owner and Contractor. If the Architect renders a decision after arbitration proceedings have been initiated, such decision may be entered as evidence, but shall not supersede arbitration proceedings unless the decision is acceptable to all parties concerned.

4.5.4.2 A demand for arbitration shall be made within the time limits specified in Subparagraphs 4.5.1 and 4.5.4 and Clause 4.5.4.1 as applicable, and in other cases within a reasonable time after the Claim has arisen, and in no event shall it be made after the date when institution of legal or equitable proceedings based on such Claim would be barred by the applicable statute of limitations as determined pursuant to Paragraph 13.7.

4.5.5 Limitation on Consolidation or Joinder. No arbitration arising out of or relating to the Contract Documents shall include, by consolidation or joinder or in any other manner, the Architect, the Architect's employees or consultants, except by written consent containing specific reference to the Agreement and signed by the Architect, Owner, Contractor and any other person or entity sought to be joined. No arbitration shall include, by consolidation or joinder or in any other manner, parties other than the Owner, Contractor, a separate contractor as described in Article 6 and other persons substantially involved in a common question of fact or law whose presence is required if complete relief is to be accorded in arbitration. No person or entity other than the Owner, Contractor or a separate contractor as described in Article 6 shall be included as an original third party or additional third party to an arbitration whose interest or responsibility is insubstantial. Consent to arbitration involving an additional person or entity shall not constitute consent to arbitration of a dispute not described therein or with a person or entity not named or described therein. The foregoing agreement to arbitrate and other agreements to arbitrate with an additional person or entity duly consented to by parties to the Agreement shall be specifically enforceable under applicable law in any court having jurisdiction thereof.

4.5.6 Claims and Timely Assertion of Claims. A party who files a notice of demand for arbitration must assert in the demand all Claims then known to that party on which arbitration is permitted to be demanded. When a party fails to include a Claim through oversight, inadvertence or excusable neglect, or when a Claim has matured or been acquired subsequently, the arbitrator or arbitrators may permit amendment.

4.5.7 Judgment on Final Award. The award rendered by the arbitrator or arbitrators shall be final, and judgment may be entered upon it in accordance with applicable law in any court having jurisdiction thereof.

ARTICLE 5

SUBCONTRACTORS

5.1 DEFINITIONS

5.1.1 A Subcontractor is a person or entity who has a direct contract with the Contractor to perform a portion of the Work at the site. The term "Subcontractor" is referred to throughout the Contract Documents as if singular in number and means a Subcontractor or an authorized representative of the Subcontractor. The term "Subcontractor" does not include a separate contractor or subcontractors of a separate contractor.

5.1.2 A Sub-subcontractor is a person or entity who has a direct or indirect contract with a Subcontractor to perform a portion of the Work at the site. The term "Sub-subcontractor" is referred to throughout the Contract Documents as if singular in number and means a Sub-subcontractor or an authorized representative of the Sub-subcontractor.

5.2 AWARD OF SUBCONTRACTS AND OTHER CONTRACTS FOR PORTIONS OF THE WORK

5.2.1 Unless otherwise stated in the Contract Documents or the bidding requirements, the Contractor, as soon as practicable after award of the Contract, shall furnish in writing to the Owner through the Architect the names of persons or entities (including those who are to furnish materials or equipment fabricated to a special design) proposed for each principal portion of the Work. The Architect will promptly reply to the Contractor in writing stating whether or not the Owner or the Architect, after due investigation, has reasonable objection to any such proposed person or entity. Failure of the Owner or Architect to reply promptly shall constitute notice of no reasonable objection.

5.2.2 The Contractor shall not contract with a proposed person or entity to whom the Owner or Architect has made reasonable and timely objection. The Contractor shall not be required to contract with anyone to whom the Contractor has made reasonable objection.

5.2.3 If the Owner or Architect has reasonable objection to a person or entity proposed by the Contractor, the Contractor shall propose another to whom the Owner or Architect has no reasonable objection. The Contract Sum shall be increased or decreased by the difference in cost occasioned by such change and an appropriate Change Order shall be issued. However, no increase in the Contract Sum shall be allowed for such change unless the Contractor has acted promptly and responsively in submitting names as required.

5.2.4 The Contractor shall not change a Subcontractor, person or entity previously selected if the Owner or Architect makes reasonable objection to such change.

5.3 SUBCONTRACTUAL RELATIONS

5.3.1 By appropriate agreement, written where legally required for validity, the Contractor shall require each Subcontractor, to the extent of the Work to be performed by the Subcontractor, to be bound to the Contractor by terms of the Contract Documents, and to assume toward the Contractor all the obligations and responsibilities which the Contractor, by these Documents, assumes toward the Owner and Architect. Each subcontract agreement shall preserve and protect the rights of the Owner and Architect under the Contract Documents with respect to the Work to be performed by the Subcontractor so that subcontracting thereof will not prejudice such rights, and shall allow to the Subcontractor, unless specifically provided otherwise in the subcontract agreement, the benefit of all rights, remedies and redress against the Contractor that the Contractor, by the Contract Documents, has against the Owner. Where appropriate, the Contractor shall require each Subcontractor to enter into similar agreements with Sub-subcontractors. The Contractor shall make available to each proposed Subcontractor, prior to the execution of the subcontract agreement, copies of the Contract Documents to which the Subcontractor will be bound, and, upon written request of the Subcontractor, identify to the Subcontractor terms and conditions of the proposed subcontract agreement which may be at variance with the Contract Documents. Subcontractors shall similarly make copies of applicable portions of such documents available to their respective proposed Sub-subcontractors.

5.4 CONTINGENT ASSIGNMENT OF SUBCONTRACTS

5.4.1 Each subcontract agreement for a portion of the Work is assigned by the Contractor to the Owner provided that:

.1 assignment is effective only after termination of the Contract by the Owner for cause pursuant to Paragraph 14.2 and only for those subcontract agreements which the Owner accepts by notifying the Subcontractor in writing; and

.2 assignment is subject to the prior rights of the surety, if any, obligated under bond relating to the Contract.

5.4.2 If the Work has been suspended for more than 30 days, the Subcontractor's compensation shall be equitably adjusted.

ARTICLE 6

CONSTRUCTION BY OWNER OR BY SEPARATE CONTRACTORS

6.1 OWNER'S RIGHT TO PERFORM CONSTRUCTION AND TO AWARD SEPARATE CONTRACTS

6.1.1 The Owner reserves the right to perform construction or operations related to the Project with the Owner's own forces, and to award separate contracts in connection with other portions of the Project or other construction or operations on the site under Conditions of the Contract identical or substantially similar to these including those portions related to insurance and waiver of subrogation. If the Contractor claims that delay or additional cost is involved because of such action by the Owner, the Contractor shall make such Claim as provided elsewhere in the Contract Documents.

6.1.2 When separate contracts are awarded for different portions of the Project or other construction or operations on the site, the term "Contractor" in the Contract Documents in each case shall mean the Contractor who executes each separate Owner-Contractor Agreement.

6.1.3 The Owner shall provide for coordination of the activities of the Owner's own forces and of each separate contractor with the Work of the Contractor, who shall cooperate with them. The Contractor shall participate with other separate contractors and the Owner in reviewing their construction schedules when directed to do so. The Contractor shall make any revisions to the construction schedule and Contract Sum deemed necessary after a joint review and mutual agreement. The construction schedules shall then constitute the schedules to be used by the Contractor, separate contractors and the Owner until subsequently revised.

6.1.4 Unless otherwise provided in the Contract Documents, when the Owner performs construction or operations related to the Project with the Owner's own forces, the Owner shall be deemed to be subject to the same obligations and to have the same rights which apply to the Contractor under the Conditions of the Contract, including, without excluding others, those stated in Article 3, this Article 6 and Articles 10, 11 and 12.

6.2 MUTUAL RESPONSIBILITY

6.2.1 The Contractor shall afford the Owner and separate contractors reasonable opportunity for introduction and storage of their materials and equipment and performance of their activities and shall connect and coordinate the Contractor's construction and operations with theirs as required by the Contract Documents.

6.2.2 If part of the Contractor's Work depends for proper execution or results upon construction or operations by the Owner or a separate contractor, the Contractor shall, prior to proceeding with that portion of the Work, promptly report to the Architect apparent discrepancies or defects in such other construction that would render it unsuitable for such proper execution and results. Failure of the Contractor so to report shall constitute an acknowledgment that the Owner's or separate contractors' completed or partially completed construction is fit and proper to receive the Contractor's Work, except as to defects not then reasonably discoverable.

6.2.3 Costs caused by delays or by improperly timed activities or defective construction shall be borne by the party responsible therefor.

6.2.4 The Contractor shall promptly remedy damage wrongfully caused by the Contractor to completed or partially completed construction or to property of the Owner or separate contractors as provided in Subparagraph 10.2.5.

6.2.5 Claims and other disputes and matters in question between the Contractor and a separate contractor shall be subject to the provisions of Paragraph 4.3 provided the separate contractor has reciprocal obligations.

6.2.6 The Owner and each separate contractor shall have the same responsibilities for cutting and patching as are described for the Contractor in Paragraph 3.14.

6.3 OWNER'S RIGHT TO CLEAN UP

6.3.1 If a dispute arises among the Contractor, separate contractors and the Owner as to the responsibility under their respective contracts for maintaining the premises and surrounding area free from waste materials and rubbish as described in Paragraph 3.15, the Owner may clean up and allocate the cost among those responsible as the Architect determines to be just.

ARTICLE 7

CHANGES IN THE WORK

7.1 CHANGES

7.1.1 Changes in the Work may be accomplished after execution of the Contract, and without invalidating the Contract, by Change Order, Construction Change Directive or order for a minor change in the Work, subject to the limitations stated in this Article 7 and elsewhere in the Contract Documents.

7.1.2 A Change Order shall be based upon agreement among the Owner, Contractor and Architect; a Construction Change Directive requires agreement by the Owner and Architect and may or may not be agreed to by the Contractor; an order for a minor change in the Work may be issued by the Architect alone.

7.1.3 Changes in the Work shall be performed under applicable provisions of the Contract Documents, and the Contractor shall proceed promptly, unless otherwise provided in the Change Order, Construction Change Directive or order for a minor change in the Work.

7.1.4 If unit prices are stated in the Contract Documents or subsequently agreed upon, and if quantities originally contemplated are so changed in a proposed Change Order or Construction Change Directive that application of such unit prices to quantities of Work proposed will cause substantial inequity to the Owner or Contractor, the applicable unit prices shall be equitably adjusted.

7.2 CHANGE ORDERS

7.2.1 A Change Order is a written instrument prepared by the Architect and signed by the Owner, Contractor and Architect, stating their agreement upon all of the following:

.1 a change in the Work;

.2 the amount of the adjustment in the Contract Sum, if any; and

.3 the extent of the adjustment in the Contract Time, if any.

7.2.2 Methods used in determining adjustments to the Contract Sum may include those listed in Subparagraph 7.3.3.

7.3 CONSTRUCTION CHANGE DIRECTIVES

7.3.1 A Construction Change Directive is a written order prepared by the Architect and signed by the Owner and Architect, directing a change in the Work and stating a proposed basis for adjustment, if any, in the Contract Sum or Contract Time, or both. The Owner may by Construction Change Directive, without invalidating the Contract, order changes in the Work within the general scope of the Contract consisting of additions, deletions or other revisions, the Contract Sum and Contract Time being adjusted accordingly.

7.3.2 A Construction Change Directive shall be used in the absence of total agreement on the terms of a Change Order.

7.3.3 If the Construction Change Directive provides for an adjustment to the Contract Sum, the adjustment shall be based on one of the following methods:

.1 mutual acceptance of a lump sum properly itemized and supported by sufficient substantiating data to permit evaluation;

.2 unit prices stated in the Contract Documents or subsequently agreed upon;

.3 cost to be determined in a manner agreed upon by the parties and a mutually acceptable fixed or percentage fee; or

.4 as provided in Subparagraph 7.3.6.

7.3.4 Upon receipt of a Construction Change Directive, the Contractor shall promptly proceed with the change in the Work involved and advise the Architect of the Contractor's agreement or disagreement with the method, if any, provided in the Construction Change Directive for determining the proposed adjustment in the Contract Sum or Contract Time.

7.3.5 A Construction Change Directive signed by the Contractor indicates the agreement of the Contractor therewith, including adjustment in Contract Sum and Contract Time or the method for determining them. Such agreement shall be effective immediately and shall be recorded as a Change Order.

7.3.6 If the Contractor does not respond promptly or disagrees with the method for adjustment in the Contract Sum, the method and the adjustment shall be determined by the Architect on the basis of reasonable expenditures and savings of those performing the Work attributable to the change, including, in case of an increase in the Contract Sum, a reasonable allowance for overhead and profit. In such case, and also under Clause 7.3.3.3, the Contractor shall keep and present, in such form as the Architect may prescribe, an itemized accounting together with appropriate supporting data. Unless otherwise provided in the Contract Documents, costs for the purposes of this Subparagraph 7.3.6 shall be limited to the following:

.1 costs of labor, including social security, old age and unemployment insurance, fringe benefits required by agreement or custom, and workers' or workmen's compensation insurance;

.2 costs of materials, supplies and equipment, including cost of transportation, whether incorporated or consumed;

.3 rental costs of machinery and equipment, exclusive of hand tools, whether rented from the Contractor or others;

.4 costs of premiums for all bonds and insurance, permit fees, and sales, use or similar taxes related to the Work; and

.5 additional costs of supervision and field office personnel directly attributable to the change.

7.3.7 Pending final determination of cost to the Owner, amounts not in dispute may be included in Applications for Payment. The amount of credit to be allowed by the Contractor to the Owner for a deletion or change which results in a net decrease in the Contract Sum shall be actual net cost as confirmed by the Architect. When both additions and credits covering related Work or substitutions are involved in a change, the allowance for overhead and profit shall be figured on the basis of net increase, if any, with respect to that change.

7.3.8 If the Owner and Contractor do not agree with the adjustment in Contract Time or the method for determining it, the adjustment or the method shall be referred to the Architect for determination.

7.3.9 When the Owner and Contractor agree with the determination made by the Architect concerning the adjustments in the Contract Sum and Contract Time, or otherwise reach agreement upon the adjustments, such agreement shall be effective immediately and shall be recorded by preparation and execution of an appropriate Change Order.

7.4 MINOR CHANGES IN THE WORK

7.4.1 The Architect will have authority to order minor changes in the Work not involving adjustment in the Contract Sum or extension of the Contract Time and not inconsistent with the intent of the Contract Documents. Such changes shall be effected by written order and shall be binding on the Owner and Contractor. The Contractor shall carry out such written orders promptly.

ARTICLE 8

TIME

8.1 DEFINITIONS

8.1.1 Unless otherwise provided, Contract Time is the period of time, including authorized adjustments, allotted in the Contract Documents for Substantial Completion of the Work.

8.1.2 The date of commencement of the Work is the date established in the Agreement. The date shall not be postponed by the failure to act of the Contractor or of persons or entities for whom the Contractor is responsible.

8.1.3 The date of Substantial Completion is the date certified by the Architect in accordance with Paragraph 9.8.

8.1.4 The term "day" as used in the Contract Documents shall mean calendar day unless otherwise specifically defined.

8.2 PROGRESS AND COMPLETION

8.2.1 Time limits stated in the Contract Documents are of the essence of the Contract. By executing the Agreement the Contractor confirms that the Contract Time is a reasonable period for performing the Work.

8.2.2 The Contractor shall not knowingly, except by agreement or instruction of the Owner in writing, prematurely commence operations on the site or elsewhere prior to the effective date of insurance required by Article 11 to be furnished by the Contractor. The date of commencement of the Work shall not be changed by the effective date of such insurance. Unless the date of commencement is established by a notice to proceed given by the Owner, the Contractor shall notify the Owner in writing not less than five days or other agreed period before commencing the Work to permit the timely filing of mortgages, mechanic's liens and other security interests.

8.2.3 The Contractor shall proceed expeditiously with adequate forces and shall achieve Substantial Completion within the Contract Time.

8.3 DELAYS AND EXTENSIONS OF TIME

8.3.1 If the Contractor is delayed at any time in progress of the Work by an act or neglect of the Owner or Architect, or of an employee of either, or of a separate contractor employed by the Owner, or by changes ordered in the Work, or by labor disputes, fire, unusual delay in deliveries, unavoidable casualties or other causes beyond the Contractor's control, or by delay authorized by the Owner pending arbitration, or by other causes which the Architect determines may justify delay, then the Contract Time shall be extended by Change Order for such reasonable time as the Architect may determine.

8.3.2 Claims relating to time shall be made in accordance with applicable provisions of Paragraph 4.3.

8.3.3 This Paragraph 8.3 does not preclude recovery of damages for delay by either party under other provisions of the Contract Documents.

ARTICLE 9

PAYMENTS AND COMPLETION

9.1 CONTRACT SUM

9.1.1 The Contract Sum is stated in the Agreement and, including authorized adjustments, is the total amount payable by the Owner to the Contractor for performance of the Work under the Contract Documents.

9.2 SCHEDULE OF VALUES

9.2.1 Before the first Application for Payment, the Contractor shall submit to the Architect a schedule of values allocated to various portions of the Work, prepared in such form and supported by such data to substantiate its accuracy as the Architect may require. This schedule, unless objected to by the Architect, shall be used as a basis for reviewing the Contractor's Applications for Payment.

9.3 APPLICATIONS FOR PAYMENT

9.3.1 At least ten days before the date established for each progress payment, the Contractor shall submit to the Architect an itemized Application for Payment for operations completed in accordance with the schedule of values. Such application shall be notarized, if required, and supported by such data substantiating the Contractor's right to payment as the Owner or Architect may require, such as copies of requisitions from Subcontractors and material suppliers, and reflecting retainage if provided for elsewhere in the Contract Documents.

9.3.1.1 Such applications may include requests for payment on account of changes in the Work which have been properly authorized by Construction Change Directives but not yet included in Change Orders.

9.3.1.2 Such applications may not include requests for payment of amounts the Contractor does not intend to pay to a Subcontractor or material supplier because of a dispute or other reason.

9.3.2 Unless otherwise provided in the Contract Documents, payments shall be made on account of materials and equipment delivered and suitably stored at the site for subsequent incorporation in the Work. If approved in advance by the Owner, payment may similarly be made for materials and equipment suitably stored off the site at a location agreed upon in writing. Payment for materials and equipment stored on or off the site shall be conditioned upon compliance by the Contractor with procedures satisfactory to the Owner to establish the Owner's title to such materials and equipment or otherwise protect the Owner's interest, and shall include applicable insurance, storage and transportation to the site for such materials and equipment stored off the site.

9.3.3 The Contractor warrants that title to all Work covered by an Application for Payment will pass to the Owner no later than the time of payment. The Contractor further warrants that upon submittal of an Application for Payment all Work for which Certificates for Payment have been previously issued and payments received from the Owner shall, to the best of the Contractor's knowledge, information and belief, be free and clear of liens, claims, security interests or encumbrances in favor of the Contractor, Subcontractors, material suppliers, or other persons or entities making a claim by reason of having provided labor, materials and equipment relating to the Work.

9.4 CERTIFICATES FOR PAYMENT

9.4.1 The Architect will, within seven days after receipt of the Contractor's Application for Payment, either issue to the

Owner a Certificate for Payment, with a copy to the Contractor, for such amount as the Architect determines is properly due, or notify the Contractor and Owner in writing of the Architect's reasons for withholding certification in whole or in part as provided in Subparagraph 9.5.1.

9.4.2 The issuance of a Certificate for Payment will constitute a representation by the Architect to the Owner, based on the Architect's observations at the site and the data comprising the Application for Payment, that the Work has progressed to the point indicated and that, to the best of the Architect's knowledge, information and belief, quality of the Work is in accordance with the Contract Documents. The foregoing representations are subject to an evaluation of the Work for conformance with the Contract Documents upon Substantial Completion, to results of subsequent tests and inspections, to minor deviations from the Contract Documents correctable prior to completion and to specific qualifications expressed by the Architect. The issuance of a Certificate for Payment will further constitute a representation that the Contractor is entitled to payment in the amount certified. However, the issuance of a Certificate for Payment will not be a representation that the Architect has (1) made exhaustive or continuous on-site inspections to check the quality or quantity of the Work, (2) reviewed construction means, methods, techniques, sequences or procedures, (3) reviewed copies of requisitions received from Subcontractors and material suppliers and other data requested by the Owner to substantiate the Contractor's right to payment or (4) made examination to ascertain how or for what purpose the Contractor has used money previously paid on account of the Contract Sum.

9.5 DECISIONS TO WITHHOLD CERTIFICATION

9.5.1 The Architect may decide not to certify payment and may withhold a Certificate for Payment in whole or in part, to the extent reasonably necessary to protect the Owner, if in the Architect's opinion the representations to the Owner required by Subparagraph 9.4.2 cannot be made. If the Architect is unable to certify payment in the amount of the Application, the Architect will notify the Contractor and Owner as provided in Subparagraph 9.4.1. If the Contractor and Architect cannot agree on a revised amount, the Architect will promptly issue a Certificate for Payment for the amount for which the Architect is able to make such representations to the Owner. The Architect may also decide not to certify payment or, because of subsequently discovered evidence or subsequent observations, may nullify the whole or a part of a Certificate for Payment previously issued, to such extent as may be necessary in the Architect's opinion to protect the Owner from loss because of:

- **.1** defective Work not remedied;
- **.2** third party claims filed or reasonable evidence indicating probable filing of such claims;
- **.3** failure of the Contractor to make payments properly to Subcontractors or for labor, materials or equipment;
- **.4** reasonable evidence that the Work cannot be completed for the unpaid balance of the Contract Sum;
- **.5** damage to the Owner or another contractor;
- **.6** reasonable evidence that the Work will not be completed within the Contract Time, and that the unpaid balance would not be adequate to cover actual or liquidated damages for the anticipated delay; or
- **.7** persistent failure to carry out the Work in accordance with the Contract Documents.

9.5.2 When the above reasons for withholding certification are removed, certification will be made for amounts previously withheld.

9.6 PROGRESS PAYMENTS

9.6.1 After the Architect has issued a Certificate for Payment, the Owner shall make payment in the manner and within the time provided in the Contract Documents, and shall so notify the Architect.

9.6.2 The Contractor shall promptly pay each Subcontractor, upon receipt of payment from the Owner, out of the amount paid to the Contractor on account of such Subcontractor's portion of the Work, the amount to which said Subcontractor is entitled, reflecting percentages actually retained from payments to the Contractor on account of such Subcontractor's portion of the Work. The Contractor shall, by appropriate agreement with each Subcontractor, require each Subcontractor to make payments to Sub-subcontractors in similar manner.

9.6.3 The Architect will, on request, furnish to a Subcontractor, if practicable, information regarding percentages of completion or amounts applied for by the Contractor and action taken thereon by the Architect and Owner on account of portions of the Work done by such Subcontractor.

9.6.4 Neither the Owner nor Architect shall have an obligation to pay or to see to the payment of money to a Subcontractor except as may otherwise be required by law.

9.6.5 Payment to material suppliers shall be treated in a manner similar to that provided in Subparagraphs 9.6.2, 9.6.3 and 9.6.4.

9.6.6 A Certificate for Payment, a progress payment, or partial or entire use or occupancy of the Project by the Owner shall not constitute acceptance of Work not in accordance with the Contract Documents.

9.7 FAILURE OF PAYMENT

9.7.1 If the Architect does not issue a Certificate for Payment, through no fault of the Contractor, within seven days after receipt of the Contractor's Application for Payment, or if the Owner does not pay the Contractor within seven days after the date established in the Contract Documents the amount certified by the Architect or awarded by arbitration, then the Contractor may, upon seven additional days' written notice to the Owner and Architect, stop the Work until payment of the amount owing has been received. The Contract Time shall be extended appropriately and the Contract Sum shall be increased by the amount of the Contractor's reasonable costs of shut-down, delay and start-up, which shall be accomplished as provided in Article 7.

9.8 SUBSTANTIAL COMPLETION

9.8.1 Substantial Completion is the stage in the progress of the Work when the Work or designated portion thereof is sufficiently complete in accordance with the Contract Documents so the Owner can occupy or utilize the Work for its intended use.

9.8.2 When the Contractor considers that the Work, or a portion thereof which the Owner agrees to accept separately, is substantially complete, the Contractor shall prepare and submit to the Architect a comprehensive list of items to be completed or corrected. The Contractor shall proceed promptly to complete and correct items on the list. Failure to include an item on such list does not alter the responsibility of the Contractor to complete all Work in accordance with the Contract Documents. Upon receipt of the Contractor's list, the Architect will make an inspection to determine whether the Work or designated portion thereof is substantially complete. If the Architect's inspection discloses any item, whether or not included on the Contractor's list, which is not in accordance with the requirements of the Contract Documents, the Contractor shall, before issuance of the Certificate of Substantial Completion, complete or correct such item upon notification by the Architect. The Contractor shall then submit a request for another inspection by the Architect to determine Substantial Completion. When the Work or designated portion thereof is substantially complete, the Architect will prepare a Certificate of Substantial Completion which shall establish the date of Substantial Completion, shall establish responsibilities of the Owner and Contractor for security, maintenance, heat, utilities, damage to the Work and insurance, and shall fix the time within which the Contractor shall finish all items on the list accompanying the Certificate. Warranties required by the Contract Documents shall commence on the date of Substantial Completion of the Work or designated portion thereof unless otherwise provided in the Certificate of Substantial Completion. The Certificate of Substantial Completion shall be submitted to the Owner and Contractor for their written acceptance of responsibilities assigned to them in such Certificate.

9.8.3 Upon Substantial Completion of the Work or designated portion thereof and upon application by the Contractor and certification by the Architect, the Owner shall make payment, reflecting adjustment in retainage, if any, for such Work or portion thereof as provided in the Contract Documents.

9.9 PARTIAL OCCUPANCY OR USE

9.9.1 The Owner may occupy or use any completed or partially completed portion of the Work at any stage when such portion is designated by separate agreement with the Contractor, provided such occupancy or use is consented to by the insurer as required under Subparagraph 11.3.11 and authorized by public authorities having jurisdiction over the Work. Such partial occupancy or use may commence whether or not the portion is substantially complete, provided the Owner and Contractor have accepted in writing the responsibilities assigned to each of them for payments, retainage if any, security, maintenance, heat, utilities, damage to the Work and insurance, and have agreed in writing concerning the period for correction of the Work and commencement of warranties required by the Contract Documents. When the Contractor considers a portion substantially complete, the Contractor shall prepare and submit a list to the Architect as provided under Subparagraph 9.8.2. Consent of the Contractor to partial occupancy or use shall not be unreasonably withheld. The stage of the progress of the Work shall be determined by written agreement between the Owner and Contractor or, if no agreement is reached, by decision of the Architect.

9.9.2 Immediately prior to such partial occupancy or use, the Owner, Contractor and Architect shall jointly inspect the area to be occupied or portion of the Work to be used in order to determine and record the condition of the Work.

9.9.3 Unless otherwise agreed upon, partial occupancy or use of a portion or portions of the Work shall not constitute acceptance of Work not complying with the requirements of the Contract Documents.

9.10 FINAL COMPLETION AND FINAL PAYMENT

9.10.1 Upon receipt of written notice that the Work is ready for final inspection and acceptance and upon receipt of a final Application for Payment, the Architect will promptly make such inspection and, when the Architect finds the Work acceptable under the Contract Documents and the Contract fully performed, the Architect will promptly issue a final Certificate for Payment stating that to the best of the Architect's knowledge, information and belief, and on the basis of the Architect's observations and inspections, the Work has been completed in accordance with terms and conditions of the Contract Documents and that the entire balance found to be due the Contractor and noted in said final Certificate is due and payable. The Architect's final Certificate for Payment will constitute a further representation that conditions listed in Subparagraph 9.10.2 as precedent to the Contractor's being entitled to final payment have been fulfilled.

9.10.2 Neither final payment nor any remaining retained percentage shall become due until the Contractor submits to the Architect (1) an affidavit that payrolls, bills for materials and equipment, and other indebtedness connected with the Work for which the Owner or the Owner's property might be responsible or encumbered (less amounts withheld by Owner) have been paid or otherwise satisfied, (2) a certificate evidencing that insurance required by the Contract Documents to remain in force after final payment is currently in effect and will not be cancelled or allowed to expire until at least 30 days' prior written notice has been given to the Owner, (3) a written statement that the Contractor knows of no substantial reason that the insurance will not be renewable to cover the period required by the Contract Documents, (4) consent of surety, if any, to final payment and (5), if required by the Owner, other data establishing payment or satisfaction of obligations, such as receipts, releases and waivers of liens, claims, security interests or encumbrances arising out of the Contract, to the extent and in such form as may be designated by the Owner. If a Subcontractor refuses to furnish a release or waiver required by the Owner, the Contractor may furnish a bond satisfactory to the Owner to indemnify the Owner against such lien. If such lien remains unsatisfied after payments are made, the Contractor shall refund to the Owner all money that the Owner may be compelled to pay in discharging such lien, including all costs and reasonable attorneys' fees.

9.10.3 If, after Substantial Completion of the Work, final completion thereof is materially delayed through no fault of the Contractor or by issuance of Change Orders affecting final completion, and the Architect so confirms, the Owner shall, upon application by the Contractor and certification by the Architect, and without terminating the Contract, make payment of the balance due for that portion of the Work fully completed and accepted. If the remaining balance for Work not fully completed or corrected is less than retainage stipulated in the Contract Documents, and if bonds have been furnished, the written consent of surety to payment of the balance due for that portion of the Work fully completed and accepted shall be submitted by the Contractor to the Architect prior to certification of such payment. Such payment shall be made under terms and conditions governing final payment, except that it shall not constitute a waiver of claims. The making of final payment shall constitute a waiver of claims by the Owner as provided in Subparagraph 4.3.5.

9.10.4 Acceptance of final payment by the Contractor, a Subcontractor or material supplier shall constitute a waiver of claims by that payee except those previously made in writing and identified by that payee as unsettled at the time of final Application for Payment. Such waivers shall be in addition to the waiver described in Subparagraph 4.3.5.

ARTICLE 10

PROTECTION OF PERSONS AND PROPERTY

10.1 SAFETY PRECAUTIONS AND PROGRAMS

10.1.1 The Contractor shall be responsible for initiating, maintaining and supervising all safety precautions and programs in connection with the performance of the Contract.

10.1.2 In the event the Contractor encounters on the site material reasonably believed to be asbestos or polychlorinated biphenyl (PCB) which has not been rendered harmless, the Contractor shall immediately stop Work in the area affected and report the condition to the Owner and Architect in writing. The Work in the affected area shall not thereafter be resumed except by written agreement of the Owner and Contractor if in fact the material is asbestos or polychlorinated biphenyl (PCB) and has not been rendered harmless. The Work in the affected area shall be resumed in the absence of asbestos or polychlorinated biphenyl (PCB), or when it has been rendered harmless, by written agreement of the Owner and Contractor, or in accordance with final determination by the Architect on which arbitration has not been demanded, or by arbitration under Article 4.

10.1.3 The Contractor shall not be required pursuant to Article 7 to perform without consent any Work relating to asbestos or polychlorinated biphenyl (PCB).

10.1.4 To the fullest extent permitted by law, the Owner shall indemnify and hold harmless the Contractor, Architect, Architect's consultants and agents and employees of any of them from and against claims, damages, losses and expenses, including but not limited to attorneys' fees, arising out of or resulting from performance of the Work in the affected area if in fact the material is asbestos or polychlorinated biphenyl (PCB) and has not been rendered harmless, provided that such claim, damage, loss or expense is attributable to bodily injury, sickness, disease or death, or to injury to or destruction of tangible property (other than the Work itself) including loss of use resulting therefrom, but only to the extent caused in whole or in part by negligent acts or omissions of the Owner, anyone directly or indirectly employed by the Owner or anyone for whose acts the Owner may be liable, regardless of whether or not such claim, damage, loss or expense is caused in part by a party indemnified hereunder. Such obligation shall not be construed to negate, abridge, or reduce other rights or obligations of indemnity which would otherwise exist as to a party or person described in this Subparagraph 10.1.4.

10.2 SAFETY OF PERSONS AND PROPERTY

10.2.1 The Contractor shall take reasonable precautions for safety of, and shall provide reasonable protection to prevent damage, injury or loss to:

.1 employees on the Work and other persons who may be affected thereby;

.2 the Work and materials and equipment to be incorporated therein, whether in storage on or off the site, under care, custody or control of the Contractor or the Contractor's Subcontractors or Sub-subcontractors; and

.3 other property at the site or adjacent thereto, such as trees, shrubs, lawns, walks, pavements, roadways, structures and utilities not designated for removal, relocation or replacement in the course of construction.

10.2.2 The Contractor shall give notices and comply with applicable laws, ordinances, rules, regulations and lawful orders of public authorities bearing on safety of persons or property or their protection from damage, injury or loss.

10.2.3 The Contractor shall erect and maintain, as required by existing conditions and performance of the Contract, reasonable safeguards for safety and protection, including posting danger signs and other warnings against hazards, promulgating safety regulations and notifying owners and users of adjacent sites and utilities.

10.2.4 When use or storage of explosives or other hazardous materials or equipment or unusual methods are necessary for execution of the Work, the Contractor shall exercise utmost care and carry on such activities under supervision of properly qualified personnel.

10.2.5 The Contractor shall promptly remedy damage and loss (other than damage or loss insured under property insurance required by the Contract Documents) to property referred to in Clauses 10.2.1.2 and 10.2.1.3 caused in whole or in part by the Contractor, a Subcontractor, a Sub-subcontractor, or anyone directly or indirectly employed by any of them, or by anyone for whose acts they may be liable and for which the Contractor is responsible under Clauses 10.2.1.2 and 10.2.1.3, except damage or loss attributable to acts or omissions of the Owner or Architect or anyone directly or indirectly employed by either of them, or by anyone for whose acts either of them may be liable, and not attributable to the fault or negligence of the Contractor. The foregoing obligations of the Contractor are in addition to the Contractor's obligations under Paragraph 3.18.

10.2.6 The Contractor shall designate a responsible member of the Contractor's organization at the site whose duty shall be the prevention of accidents. This person shall be the Contractor's superintendent unless otherwise designated by the Contractor in writing to the Owner and Architect.

10.2.7 The Contractor shall not load or permit any part of the construction or site to be loaded so as to endanger its safety.

10.3 EMERGENCIES

10.3.1 In an emergency affecting safety of persons or property, the Contractor shall act, at the Contractor's discretion, to prevent threatened damage, injury or loss. Additional compensation or extension of time claimed by the Contractor on account of an emergency shall be determined as provided in Paragraph 4.3 and Article 7.

ARTICLE 11

INSURANCE AND BONDS

11.1 CONTRACTOR'S LIABILITY INSURANCE

11.1.1 The Contractor shall purchase from and maintain in a company or companies lawfully authorized to do business in the jurisdiction in which the Project is located such insurance as will protect the Contractor from claims set forth below which may arise out of or result from the Contractor's operations under the Contract and for which the Contractor may be legally liable, whether such operations be by the Contractor or by a Subcontractor or by anyone directly or indirectly employed by any of them, or by anyone for whose acts any of them may be liable:

.1 claims under workers' or workmen's compensation, disability benefit and other similar employee benefit acts which are applicable to the Work to be performed;

.2 claims for damages because of bodily injury, occupational sickness or disease, or death of the Contractor's employees;

.3 claims for damages because of bodily injury, sickness or disease, or death of any person other than the Contractor's employees;

.4 claims for damages insured by usual personal injury liability coverage which are sustained (1) by a person as a result of an offense directly or indirectly related to employment of such person by the Contractor, or (2) by another person;

.5 claims for damages, other than to the Work itself, because of injury to or destruction of tangible property, including loss of use resulting therefrom;

.6 claims for damages because of bodily injury, death of a person or property damage arising out of ownership, maintenance or use of a motor vehicle; and

.7 claims involving contractual liability insurance applicable to the Contractor's obligations under Paragraph 3.18.

11.1.2 The insurance required by Subparagraph 11.1.1 shall be written for not less than limits of liability specified in the Contract Documents or required by law, whichever coverage is greater. Coverages, whether written on an occurrence or claims-made basis, shall be maintained without interruption from date of commencement of the Work until date of final payment and termination of any coverage required to be maintained after final payment.

11.1.3 Certificates of Insurance acceptable to the Owner shall be filed with the Owner prior to commencement of the Work. These Certificates and the insurance policies required by this Paragraph 11.1 shall contain a provision that coverages afforded under the policies will not be cancelled or allowed to expire until at least 30 days' prior written notice has been given to the Owner. If any of the foregoing insurance coverages are required to remain in force after final payment and are reasonably available, an additional certificate evidencing continuation of such coverage shall be submitted with the final Application for Payment as required by Subparagraph 9.10.2. Information concerning reduction of coverage shall be furnished by the Contractor with reasonable promptness in accordance with the Contractor's information and belief.

11.2 OWNER'S LIABILITY INSURANCE

11.2.1 The Owner shall be responsible for purchasing and maintaining the Owner's usual liability insurance. Optionally, the Owner may purchase and maintain other insurance for self-protection against claims which may arise from operations under the Contract. The Contractor shall not be responsible for purchasing and maintaining this optional Owner's liability insurance unless specifically required by the Contract Documents.

11.3 PROPERTY INSURANCE

11.3.1 Unless otherwise provided, the Owner shall purchase and maintain, in a company or companies lawfully authorized to do business in the jurisdiction in which the Project is located, property insurance in the amount of the initial Contract Sum as well as subsequent modifications thereto for the entire Work at the site on a replacement cost basis without voluntary deductibles. Such property insurance shall be maintained, unless otherwise provided in the Contract Documents or otherwise agreed in writing by all persons and entities who are beneficiaries of such insurance, until final payment has been made as provided in Paragraph 9.10 or until no person or entity other than the Owner has an insurable interest in the property required by this Paragraph 11.3 to be covered, whichever is earlier. This insurance shall include interests of the Owner, the Contractor, Subcontractors and Sub-subcontractors in the Work.

11.3.1.1 Property insurance shall be on an all-risk policy form and shall insure against the perils of fire and extended coverage and physical loss or damage including, without duplication of coverage, theft, vandalism, malicious mischief, collapse, falsework, temporary buildings and debris removal including demolition occasioned by enforcement of any applicable legal requirements, and shall cover reasonable compensation for Architect's services and expenses required as a result of such insured loss. Coverage for other perils shall not be required unless otherwise provided in the Contract Documents.

11.3.1.2 If the Owner does not intend to purchase such property insurance required by the Contract and with all of the coverages in the amount described above, the Owner shall so inform the Contractor in writing prior to commencement of the Work. The Contractor may then effect insurance which will protect the interests of the Contractor, Subcontractors and Sub-subcontractors in the Work, and by appropriate Change Order the cost thereof shall be charged to the Owner. If the Contractor is damaged by the failure or neglect of the Owner to purchase or maintain insurance as described above, without so notifying the Contractor, then the Owner shall bear all reasonable costs properly attributable thereto.

11.3.1.3 If the property insurance requires minimum deductibles and such deductibles are identified in the Contract Documents, the Contractor shall pay costs not covered because of such deductibles. If the Owner or insurer increases the required minimum deductibles above the amounts so identified or if the Owner elects to purchase this insurance with voluntary deductible amounts, the Owner shall be responsible for payment of the additional costs not covered because of such increased or voluntary deductibles. If deductibles are not identified in the Contract Documents, the Owner shall pay costs not covered because of deductibles.

11.3.1.4 Unless otherwise provided in the Contract Documents, this property insurance shall cover portions of the Work stored off the site after written approval of the Owner at the value established in the approval, and also portions of the Work in transit.

11.3.2 Boiler and Machinery Insurance. The Owner shall purchase and maintain boiler and machinery insurance required by the Contract Documents or by law, which shall specifically cover such insured objects during installation and until final acceptance by the Owner; this insurance shall include interests of the Owner, Contractor, Subcontractors and Sub-subcontractors in the Work, and the Owner and Contractor shall be named insureds.

11.3.3 Loss of Use Insurance. The Owner, at the Owner's option, may purchase and maintain such insurance as will insure the Owner against loss of use of the Owner's property due to fire or other hazards, however caused. The Owner waives all rights of action against the Contractor for loss of use of the Owner's property, including consequential losses due to fire or other hazards however caused.

11.3.4 If the Contractor requests in writing that insurance for risks other than those described herein or for other special hazards be included in the property insurance policy, the Owner shall, if possible, include such insurance, and the cost thereof shall be charged to the Contractor by appropriate Change Order.

11.3.5 If during the Project construction period the Owner insures properties, real or personal or both, adjoining or adjacent to the site by property insurance under policies separate from those insuring the Project, or if after final payment property insurance is to be provided on the completed Project through a policy or policies other than those insuring the Project during the construction period, the Owner shall waive all rights in accordance with the terms of Subparagraph 11.3.7 for damages caused by fire or other perils covered by this separate property insurance. All separate policies shall provide this waiver of subrogation by endorsement or otherwise.

11.3.6 Before an exposure to loss may occur, the Owner shall file with the Contractor a copy of each policy that includes insurance coverages required by this Paragraph 11.3. Each policy shall contain all generally applicable conditions, definitions, exclusions and endorsements related to this Project. Each policy shall contain a provision that the policy will not be cancelled or allowed to expire until at least 30 days' prior written notice has been given to the Contractor.

11.3.7 Waivers of Subrogation. The Owner and Contractor waive all rights against (1) each other and any of their subcontractors, sub-subcontractors, agents and employees, each of the other, and (2) the Architect, Architect's consultants, separate contractors described in Article 6, if any, and any of their subcontractors, sub-subcontractors, agents and employees, for damages caused by fire or other perils to the extent covered by property insurance obtained pursuant to this Paragraph 11.3 or other property insurance applicable to the Work, except such rights as they have to proceeds of such insurance held by the Owner as fiduciary. The Owner or Contractor, as appropriate, shall require of the Architect, Architect's consultants, separate contractors described in Article 6, if any, and the subcontractors, sub-subcontractors, agents and employees of any of them, by appropriate agreements, written where legally required for validity, similar waivers each in favor of other parties enumerated herein. The policies shall provide such waivers of subrogation by endorsement or otherwise. A waiver of subrogation shall be effective as to a person or entity even though that person or entity would otherwise have a duty of indemnification, contractual or otherwise, did not pay the insurance premium directly or indirectly, and whether or not the person or entity had an insurable interest in the property damaged.

11.3.8 A loss insured under Owner's property insurance shall be adjusted by the Owner as fiduciary and made payable to the Owner as fiduciary for the insureds, as their interests may appear, subject to requirements of any applicable mortgagee clause and of Subparagraph 11.3.10. The Contractor shall pay Subcontractors their just shares of insurance proceeds received by the Contractor, and by appropriate agreements, written where legally required for validity, shall require Subcontractors to make payments to their Sub-subcontractors in similar manner.

11.3.9 If required in writing by a party in interest, the Owner as fiduciary shall, upon occurrence of an insured loss, give bond for proper performance of the Owner's duties. The cost of required bonds shall be charged against proceeds received as fiduciary. The Owner shall deposit in a separate account proceeds so received, which the Owner shall distribute in accordance with such agreement as the parties in interest may reach, or in accordance with an arbitration award in which case the procedure shall be as provided in Paragraph 4.5. If after such loss no other special agreement is made, replacement of damaged property shall be covered by appropriate Change Order.

11.3.10 The Owner as fiduciary shall have power to adjust and settle a loss with insurers unless one of the parties in interest shall object in writing within five days after occurrence of loss to the Owner's exercise of this power; if such objection be made, arbitrators shall be chosen as provided in Paragraph 4.5. The Owner as fiduciary shall, in that case, make settlement with insurers in accordance with directions of such arbitrators. If distribution of insurance proceeds by arbitration is required, the arbitrators will direct such distribution.

11.3.11 Partial occupancy or use in accordance with Paragraph 9.9 shall not commence until the insurance company or companies providing property insurance have consented to such partial occupancy or use by endorsement or otherwise. The Owner and the Contractor shall take reasonable steps to obtain consent of the insurance company or companies and shall, without mutual written consent, take no action with respect to partial occupancy or use that would cause cancellation, lapse or reduction of insurance.

11.4 PERFORMANCE BOND AND PAYMENT BOND

11.4.1 The Owner shall have the right to require the Contractor to furnish bonds covering faithful performance of the Contract and payment of obligations arising thereunder as stipulated in bidding requirements or specifically required in the Contract Documents on the date of execution of the Contract.

11.4.2 Upon the request of any person or entity appearing to be a potential beneficiary of bonds covering payment of obligations arising under the Contract, the Contractor shall promptly furnish a copy of the bonds or shall permit a copy to be made.

ARTICLE 12

UNCOVERING AND CORRECTION OF WORK

12.1 UNCOVERING OF WORK

12.1.1 If a portion of the Work is covered contrary to the Architect's request or to requirements specifically expressed in the Contract Documents, it must, if required in writing by the Architect, be uncovered for the Architect's observation and be replaced at the Contractor's expense without change in the Contract Time.

12.1.2 If a portion of the Work has been covered which the Architect has not specifically requested to observe prior to its being covered, the Architect may request to see such Work and it shall be uncovered by the Contractor. If such Work is in accordance with the Contract Documents, costs of uncovering and replacement shall, by appropriate Change Order, be charged to the Owner. If such Work is not in accordance with the Contract Documents, the Contractor shall pay such costs unless the condition was caused by the Owner or a separate contractor in which event the Owner shall be responsible for payment of such costs.

12.2 CORRECTION OF WORK

12.2.1 The Contractor shall promptly correct Work rejected by the Architect or failing to conform to the requirements of the Contract Documents, whether observed before or after Substantial Completion and whether or not fabricated, installed or completed. The Contractor shall bear costs of correcting such rejected Work, including additional testing and inspections and compensation for the Architect's services and expenses made necessary thereby.

12.2.2 If, within one year after the date of Substantial Completion of the Work or designated portion thereof, or after the date for commencement of warranties established under Subparagraph 9.9.1, or by terms of an applicable special warranty required by the Contract Documents, any of the Work is found to be not in accordance with the requirements of the Contract Documents, the Contractor shall correct it promptly after receipt of written notice from the Owner to do so unless the Owner has previously given the Contractor a written acceptance of such condition. This period of one year shall be extended with respect to portions of Work first performed after Substantial Completion by the period of time between Substantial Completion and the actual performance of the Work. This obligation under this Subparagraph 12.2.2 shall survive acceptance of the Work under the Contract and termination of the Contract. The Owner shall give such notice promptly after discovery of the condition.

12.2.3 The Contractor shall remove from the site portions of the Work which are not in accordance with the requirements of the Contract Documents and are neither corrected by the Contractor nor accepted by the Owner.

12.2.4 If the Contractor fails to correct nonconforming Work within a reasonable time, the Owner may correct it in accordance with Paragraph 2.4. If the Contractor does not proceed with correction of such nonconforming Work within a reasonable time fixed by written notice from the Architect, the Owner may remove it and store the salvable materials or equipment at the Contractor's expense. If the Contractor does not pay costs of such removal and storage within ten days after written notice, the Owner may upon ten additional days' written notice sell such materials and equipment at auction or at private sale and shall account for the proceeds thereof, after deducting costs and damages that should have been borne by the Contractor, including compensation for the Architect's services and expenses made necessary thereby. If such proceeds of sale do not cover costs which the Contractor should have borne, the Contract Sum shall be reduced by the deficiency. If payments then or thereafter due the Contractor are not sufficient to cover such amount, the Contractor shall pay the difference to the Owner.

12.2.5 The Contractor shall bear the cost of correcting destroyed or damaged construction, whether completed or partially completed, of the Owner or separate contractors caused by the Contractor's correction or removal of Work which is not in accordance with the requirements of the Contract Documents.

12.2.6 Nothing contained in this Paragraph 12.2 shall be construed to establish a period of limitation with respect to other obligations which the Contractor might have under the Contract Documents. Establishment of the time period of one year as described in Subparagraph 12.2.2 relates only to the specific obligation of the Contractor to correct the Work, and has no relationship to the time within which the obligation to comply with the Contract Documents may be sought to be enforced, nor to the time within which proceedings may be commenced to establish the Contractor's liability with respect to the Contractor's obligations other than specifically to correct the Work.

12.3 ACCEPTANCE OF NONCONFORMING WORK

12.3.1 If the Owner prefers to accept Work which is not in accordance with the requirements of the Contract Documents, the Owner may do so instead of requiring its removal and correction, in which case the Contract Sum will be reduced as appropriate and equitable. Such adjustment shall be effected whether or not final payment has been made.

ARTICLE 13

MISCELLANEOUS PROVISIONS

13.1 GOVERNING LAW

13.1.1 The Contract shall be governed by the law of the place where the Project is located.

13.2 SUCCESSORS AND ASSIGNS

13.2.1 The Owner and Contractor respectively bind themselves, their partners, successors, assigns and legal representatives to the other party hereto and to partners, successors, assigns and legal representatives of such other party in respect to covenants, agreements and obligations contained in the Contract Documents. Neither party to the Contract shall assign the Contract as a whole without written consent of the other. If either party attempts to make such an assignment without such consent, that party shall nevertheless remain legally responsible for all obligations under the Contract.

13.3 WRITTEN NOTICE

13.3.1 Written notice shall be deemed to have been duly served if delivered in person to the individual or a member of the firm or entity or to an officer of the corporation for which it was intended, or if delivered at or sent by registered or certified mail to the last business address known to the party giving notice.

13.4 RIGHTS AND REMEDIES

13.4.1 Duties and obligations imposed by the Contract Documents and rights and remedies available thereunder shall be in addition to and not a limitation of duties, obligations, rights and remedies otherwise imposed or available by law.

13.4.2 No action or failure to act by the Owner, Architect or Contractor shall constitute a waiver of a right or duty afforded them under the Contract, nor shall such action or failure to act constitute approval of or acquiescence in a breach thereunder, except as may be specifically agreed in writing.

13.5 TESTS AND INSPECTIONS

13.5.1 Tests, inspections and approvals of portions of the Work required by the Contract Documents or by laws, ordinances, rules, regulations or orders of public authorities having jurisdiction shall be made at an appropriate time. Unless otherwise provided, the Contractor shall make arrangements for such tests, inspections and approvals with an independent testing laboratory or entity acceptable to the Owner, or with the appropriate public authority, and shall bear all related costs of tests, inspections and approvals. The Contractor shall give the Architect timely notice of when and where tests and inspections are to be made so the Architect may observe such procedures. The Owner shall bear costs of tests, inspections or approvals which do not become requirements until after bids are received or negotiations concluded.

13.5.2 If the Architect, Owner or public authorities having jurisdiction determine that portions of the Work require additional testing, inspection or approval not included under Subparagraph 13.5.1, the Architect will, upon written authorization from the Owner, instruct the Contractor to make arrangements for such additional testing, inspection or approval by an entity acceptable to the Owner, and the Contractor shall give timely notice to the Architect of when and where tests and inspections are to be made so the Architect may observe such procedures.

The Owner shall bear such costs except as provided in Subparagraph 13.5.3.

13.5.3 If such procedures for testing, inspection or approval under Subparagraphs 13.5.1 and 13.5.2 reveal failure of the portions of the Work to comply with requirements established by the Contract Documents, the Contractor shall bear all costs made necessary by such failure including those of repeated procedures and compensation for the Architect's services and expenses.

13.5.4 Required certificates of testing, inspection or approval shall, unless otherwise required by the Contract Documents, be secured by the Contractor and promptly delivered to the Architect.

13.5.5 If the Architect is to observe tests, inspections or approvals required by the Contract Documents, the Architect will do so promptly and, where practicable, at the normal place of testing.

13.5.6 Tests or inspections conducted pursuant to the Contract Documents shall be made promptly to avoid unreasonable delay in the Work.

13.6 INTEREST

13.6.1 Payments due and unpaid under the Contract Documents shall bear interest from the date payment is due at such rate as the parties may agree upon in writing or, in the absence thereof, at the legal rate prevailing from time to time at the place where the Project is located.

13.7 COMMENCEMENT OF STATUTORY LIMITATION PERIOD

13.7.1 As between the Owner and Contractor:

.1 Before Substantial Completion. As to acts or failures to act occurring prior to the relevant date of Substantial Completion, any applicable statute of limitations shall commence to run and any alleged cause of action shall be deemed to have accrued in any and all events not later than such date of Substantial Completion;

.2 Between Substantial Completion and Final Certificate for Payment. As to acts or failures to act occurring subsequent to the relevant date of Substantial Completion and prior to issuance of the final Certificate for Payment, any applicable statute of limitations shall commence to run and any alleged cause of action shall be deemed to have accrued in any and all events not later than the date of issuance of the final Certificate for Payment; and

.3 After Final Certificate for Payment. As to acts or failures to act occurring after the relevant date of issuance of the final Certificate for Payment, any applicable statute of limitations shall commence to run and any alleged cause of action shall be deemed to have accrued in any and all events not later than the date of any act or failure to act by the Contractor pursuant to any warranty provided under Paragraph 3.5, the date of any correction of the Work or failure to correct the Work by the Contractor under Paragraph 12.2, or the date of actual commission of any other act or failure to perform any duty or obligation by the Contractor or Owner, whichever occurs last.

ARTICLE 14

TERMINATION OR SUSPENSION OF THE CONTRACT

14.1 TERMINATION BY THE CONTRACTOR

14.1.1 The Contractor may terminate the Contract if the Work is stopped for a period of 30 days through no act or fault of the Contractor or a Subcontractor, Sub-subcontractor or their agents or employees or any other persons performing portions of the Work under contract with the Contractor, for any of the following reasons:

.1 issuance of an order of a court or other public authority having jurisdiction;

.2 an act of government, such as a declaration of national emergency, making material unavailable;

.3 because the Architect has not issued a Certificate for Payment and has not notified the Contractor of the reason for withholding certification as provided in Subparagraph 9.4.1, or because the Owner has not made payment on a Certificate for Payment within the time stated in the Contract Documents;

.4 if repeated suspensions, delays or interruptions by the Owner as described in Paragraph 14.3 constitute in the aggregate more than 100 percent of the total number of days scheduled for completion, or 120 days in any 365-day period, whichever is less; or

.5 the Owner has failed to furnish to the Contractor promptly, upon the Contractor's request, reasonable evidence as required by Subparagraph 2.2.1.

14.1.2 If one of the above reasons exists, the Contractor may, upon seven additional days' written notice to the Owner and Architect, terminate the Contract and recover from the Owner payment for Work executed and for proven loss with respect to materials, equipment, tools, and construction equipment and machinery, including reasonable overhead, profit and damages.

14.1.3 If the Work is stopped for a period of 60 days through no act or fault of the Contractor or a Subcontractor or their agents or employees or any other persons performing portions of the Work under contract with the Contractor because the Owner has persistently failed to fulfill the Owner's obligations under the Contract Documents with respect to matters important to the progress of the Work, the Contractor may, upon seven additional days' written notice to the Owner and the Architect, terminate the Contract and recover from the Owner as provided in Subparagraph 14.1.2.

14.2 TERMINATION BY THE OWNER FOR CAUSE

14.2.1 The Owner may terminate the Contract if the Contractor:

.1 persistently or repeatedly refuses or fails to supply enough properly skilled workers or proper materials;

.2 fails to make payment to Subcontractors for materials or labor in accordance with the respective agreements between the Contractor and the Subcontractors;

.3 persistently disregards laws, ordinances, or rules, regulations or orders of a public authority having jurisdiction; or

.4 otherwise is guilty of substantial breach of a provision of the Contract Documents.

14.2.2 When any of the above reasons exist, the Owner, upon certification by the Architect that sufficient cause exists to justify such action, may without prejudice to any other rights or remedies of the Owner and after giving the Contractor and the Contractor's surety, if any, seven days' written notice, terminate employment of the Contractor and may, subject to any prior rights of the surety:

.1 take possession of the site and of all materials, equipment, tools, and construction equipment and machinery thereon owned by the Contractor;

.2 accept assignment of subcontracts pursuant to Paragraph 5.4; and

.3 finish the Work by whatever reasonable method the Owner may deem expedient.

14.2.3 When the Owner terminates the Contract for one of the reasons stated in Subparagraph 14.2.1, the Contractor shall not be entitled to receive further payment until the Work is finished.

14.2.4 If the unpaid balance of the Contract Sum exceeds costs of finishing the Work, including compensation for the Architect's services and expenses made necessary thereby, such excess shall be paid to the Contractor. If such costs exceed the unpaid balance, the Contractor shall pay the difference to the Owner. The amount to be paid to the Contractor or Owner, as the case may be, shall be certified by the Architect, upon application, and this obligation for payment shall survive termination of the Contract.

14.3 SUSPENSION BY THE OWNER FOR CONVENIENCE

14.3.1 The Owner may, without cause, order the Contractor in writing to suspend, delay or interrupt the Work in whole or in part for such period of time as the Owner may determine.

14.3.2 An adjustment shall be made for increases in the cost of performance of the Contract, including profit on the increased cost of performance, caused by suspension, delay or interruption. No adjustment shall be made to the extent:

.1 that performance is, was or would have been so suspended, delayed or interrupted by another cause for which the Contractor is responsible; or

.2 that an equitable adjustment is made or denied under another provision of this Contract.

14.3.3 Adjustments made in the cost of performance may have a mutually agreed fixed or percentage fee.

Printed on Recycled Paper

INSTRUCTION SHEET

FOR AIA DOCUMENT A401, STANDARD FORM OF AGREEMENT BETWEEN CONTRACTOR AND SUBCONTRACTOR—1987 EDITION

A. GENERAL INFORMATION

1. Purpose

AIA Document A401 is intended for use in establishing the contractual relationship between the Contractor and Subcontractor. It is intended that this document, when completed, will adopt by reference a pre-existing Prime Contract between the Contractor and Owner. The completed A401 document will thus form an Agreement whereby the duties and responsibilities of the Contractor under the Prime Contract pass to the Subcontractor with respect to a portion of the Work designated in the completed A401 document.

2. Related Documents

This document has been prepared for use with a Prime Contract which may be based upon the latest editions of [illegible] the following AIA documents:

A101	Owner-Contractor Agreement, Stipulated Sum
A107	Abbreviated Owner-Contractor Agreement, Stipulated Sum
A111	Owner-Contractor Agreement, Cost Plus a Fee
A117	Abbreviated Owner-Contractor Agreement, Cost Plus a Fee
A101/CM	Owner-Contractor Agreement, Stipulated Sum, Construction [illegible] ement [illegible] n
A171	Owner-Contractor Agreement for Furniture, Furnishings [illegible] ment
A177	Abbreviated Owner-Contractor Agreement for Furniture, [illegible] and Equ[illegible]ent
A201	General Conditions
A201/CM	General Conditions, Construction Managemen[illegible] tion
A271	General Conditions, Interiors Edition

3. Arbitration

This document incorporates ARBITRATION by [illegible] ption o[illegible] Construction In[illegible] Arbitration [illegible] of the American Arbitration Association. Arbitration is BINDING [illegible] ND[illegible] RY i[illegible] st states and [illegible] the f[illegible] al Arbitr[illegible] Act. In a minority of states, arbitration provisions relating [illegible] ure [illegible] utes [illegible] nforceable, [illegible] ar[illegible] enforceable if agreed to after the dispute arises. A few states require [illegible] parties be especially [illegible] ed tha[illegible] writ[illegible] ntract contains an arbitration provision by: a warning on [illegible] o[illegible] specific plac[illegible] of t[illegible] arbi[illegible] vision within the document or specific discussions among [illegible] ies prior [illegible] gning the document.

Arbitration provis[illegible] h[illegible] een incl[illegible] in most AIA c[illegible] t fo[illegible] inc[illegible] in order to encourage alternative dispute resolution pro[illegible] and to pr[illegible] users of AIA doc[illegible] ents w[illegible] ally [illegible] ble arbitration provisions when the parties choose to adopt [illegible] tration into thei[illegible] tract. Individu[illegible] ch[illegible] e to delete the arbitration provisions based upon their busine[illegible] ith the advice of [illegible] el. [illegible] n a [illegible] of the Construction Industry Arbitration Rules, write to the [illegible] ric[illegible] Association, 14[illegible] 51st St[illegible] New York, NY 10020.

[illegible] Non-[illegible] Forms

If a [illegible] ination of AIA documents and [illegible] documents is to be used, particular care must be taken to achieve consistency of language and intent. Certain owners require the use of owner-contractor agreements and other contract forms which they prepare. [illegible] ch forms should be carefully compared to the standard AIA forms for which they are being substituted before execution of an agreement. If there are any significant omissions, additions or variances from the terms of the related standard AIA forms, both legal and insurance counsel should be consulted.

5. Letter Forms of Agreement

Letter forms of agreement are generally discouraged by the AIA, as is the performance of a part or the whole of the Work on the basis of oral agreements or understandings. The standard AIA agreement forms have been developed through more than seventy-five years of experience and have been tested repeatedly in the courts. In addition, the standard forms have been carefully coordinated with other AIA documents.

6. Use of Current Documents

Prior to using any AIA document, the user should consult the AIA, an AIA component chapter or a current AIA Documents Price List to determine the current edition of each document.

7. Limited License for Reproduction

AIA Document A401 is a copyrighted work and may not be reproduced or excerpted from in substantial part without the express written permission of the AIA. The A401 document is intended to be used as a consumable—that is, the original document purchased by the user is intended to be consumed in the course of being used. There is no implied permission to reproduce this document, nor does membership in The American Institute of Architects confer any further rights to reproduce them.

A limited license is hereby granted to retail purchasers to reproduce a maximum of ten copies of a completed or executed A401, but only for use in connection with a particular Project.

B. CHANGES FROM THE PREVIOUS EDITION

1. Format Changes

Substantial changes have been made in the format of this document. The Terms and Conditions of the Agreement have been moved to the front of the document and fill-in blanks placed at the back to parallel the format of other similar AIA documents.

2. Changes in Content

The 1987 edition of A401 revises the 1977 edition to reflect changes made in the 1987 edition of AIA Document A201, G[illegible]ditions of the Contract for Construction. It incorporates alterations proposed by subcontractors, architects a[illegible]ter[illegible] parties. Some of the more significant changes are described below according to the order of articles now f[illegible] in [illegible]87 [illegible]n.

Article 1: The title of this article has been changed from "Contract Documents" to "Subcontract Docu[illegible]ts." Th[illegible]finiti[illegible] of Subcontract Documents has been expanded to include applicable modifications to the Prime C[illegible]ct.

Article 2: This article replaces similar and duplicative articles concerning the rights and r[illegible]sib[illegible] of t[illegible]ctor and Subcontractor. A new paragraph has been added to allow the Contractor to require the [illegible]ntractor [illegible]ter into agreements with nominated Sub-subcontractors.

Article 3: A new paragraph has been added requiring the Contractor to no[illegible] Subco[illegible]or of working conditions involving hazardous materials.

Article 4: A new subparagraph has been added requiring the Subcont[illegible]or to sub[illegible] a schedule of val[illegible] Provisions have been added concerning the discovery of asbestos and PCB on the [illegible] The [illegible]ontrac[illegible] warranty no[illegible]des damage caused by abuse, modifications not executed by the Subcontractor, impr[illegible] or [illegible] aintenance, [illegible] wear and tear.

Article 5: Modifications made to the Prime Contract [illegible]ow req[illegible] to be promptly co[illegible]nicated [illegible] Subcontractor.

Article 6: Portions of the arbitration provisio[illegible]ee[illegible]itten [illegible]equire the Co[illegible]or to[illegible]tify the S[illegible]ntractor whenever the Contractor receives a demand for a[illegible]on [illegible], fro[illegible]ner) of a di[illegible]ute [illegible] the Subcontractor's Work.

Article 7: The Subcontractor may [illegible] te[illegible] contract for the s[illegible]easons f[illegible]ich [illegible]ontractor may terminate the Prime Contract. A new subpa[illegible] has [illegible]adde[illegible]wing for ass[illegible]nt [illegible] Su[illegible] to the Owner in the event the Owner terminates the Pri[illegible]ct and e[illegible]o accept the ass[illegible]me[illegible]

Article 9: A new paragraph has b[illegible]dded requiring the Subcon[illegible] to [illegible]ntractor prior to commencement of construction to allo[illegible]ely filing [illegible]ortgages and oth[illegible]curit[illegible]sts.

Article 11: Mo[illegible]sions re[illegible]ing to progress pa[illegible]ave[illegible] consolidated into this rewritten article.

Article [illegible] The [illegible]ditions [illegible]der which fina[illegible] is du[illegible] payable to the Subcontractor are set out in greater detail.

[illegible] 13 [illegible] ins[illegible]rovisions have b[illegible]o c[illegible] both occurrence and claims-made types of policy forms. The [illegible] now required to obtain waiv[illegible] sub[illegible]tion from Sub-subcontractors. The Contractor is required to furnish a c[illegible] covering the payment of oblig[illegible]sing under the Subcontract.

Art[illegible]6: A more detailed enumeration of the Subcontract Documents is now provided for.

C. COMPLETING THE A401 FORM

1. Modifications

Users are encouraged to consult with an attorney before completing an AIA document. Particularly with respect to contractor's licensing laws, duties imposed by building codes, interest charges, arbitration and indemnification, this document may require modification with the assistance of legal counsel to fully comply with state or local laws regulating these matters.

Generally, necessary modifications may be accomplished by writing or typing the appropriate terms in the blank spaces provided on the form or by special conditions adopted by reference. The form may also be modified by striking out language directly on the original pre-printed form. Care must be taken in making these kinds of deletions, however. Under NO circumstances should pre-printed language be struck out in such a way as to render it illegible (as, for example, with blocking tape, correction fluid or X's that completely obscure the text). This may raise suspicions of fraudulent concealment, or suggest that the completed and signed document has been tampered with. Handwritten changes should be initialed by both parties to the contract.

It is definitely not recommended practice to retype the standard document. Besides being outside the limited license for reproduction granted under these Instructions, retyping can introduce typographical errors and cloud the legal interpretation given to a standard clause when blended with modifications.

Retyping eliminates one of the principal advantages of the standard form documents. By merely reviewing the modifications to be made to a standard form document, parties familiar with that document can quickly understand the essence of the proposed relationship. Commercial exchanges are greatly simplified and expedited, good-faith dealing is encouraged, and otherwise latent clauses are exposed for scrutiny. In this way, contracting parties can more fairly measure their risks.

2. Cover Page

Date: The date represents the date the Agreement becomes effective. It may be the date that an oral agreement was reached, the date the Agreement was originally submitted to the Contractor, the date authorizing action was taken or the date of actual execution. It will be the date from which the Contract Time is measured unless a different date is inserted under Paragraph 9.1.

Identification of Parties: Parties to this Agreement should be identified using the full legal name under which the Agreement is to be executed, including a designation of the legal status of both parties (sole proprietorship, partnership, joint venture, unincorp[illegible]ated association, limited partnership or corporation [general, closed or professional], etc.). Where appropriate, a copy of the re[illegible]ion authorizing the individual to act on behalf of the firm or entity should be attached.

Prime Agreement: The date of the Agreement between the Owner and Contractor should be entered.

Owner: The name and address of the Owner should be the same as used on the Prime Contract.

Project Description: The proposed Project should be described in sufficient detail to identify (1) the of[illegible] nam[illegible]itle [illegible] facility, (2) the location of the site, if known, (3) the proposed building type and usage, and (4) the size, ca[illegible]y or sc[illegible] of th[illegible]roject, if known.

Architect: As in the other Contract Documents, the Architect's full legal or corporate [illegible] sh[illegible] be [illegible]

3. Article 8—The Work of This Subcontract

Insert a precise description of the Work of this Subcontract.

4. Article 9—Date of Commencement and Substantial Co[illegible]pleti[illegible]

The following items should be included as appropriate:

Paragraph 9.1
The date of commencement of the Work should b[illegible]rted if [illegible] different from th[illegible] of the Agre[illegible]. It should not be earlier than the date of execution of the Agree[illegible]er [illegible] the [illegible]ic date of co[illegible]cem[illegible] of the W[illegible] or if a notice to proceed is to be used, enter the sentence, "[illegible] date [illegible] comm[illegible] shall be s[illegible]ulat[illegible] notice to proceed."

Paragraph 9.3
The time within which S[illegible]ial Co[illegible]tion [illegible] Work is to [illegible]hie[illegible]ay [illegible]essed as a number of days (preferably calendar days) or as a [illegible] date. Any [illegible]irements for ear[illegible] Sub[illegible] completion of portions of the Work should be entered here if not specified [illegible] the Co[illegible]ct Documents.

Also insert [illegible]isions for [illegible]ted damages re[illegible] to f[illegible] con[illegible]on time. Liquidated damages are not a penalty to be inflicted o[illegible] Sub[illegible]ractor, [illegible] must bear an actu[illegible]estimable relationship to the Contractor's loss if construction is n[illegible]om[illegible] If liquidated dam[illegible] to [illegible]essed [illegible]se delayed construction will result in actual loss to the Contrac[illegible] the amount o[illegible]mages due fo[illegible]ch day lost s[illegible] be entered in the Agreement.

[illegible]ion [illegible] liquidated damages, [illegible] sho[illegible] be carefully reviewed or drafted by the Contractor's attorney, may be as [illegible]

> The Subcontractor and the Subcontra[illegible] surety, if any, shall be liable for and shall pay the Contractor the sums hereinafter stipulated as liquidated damages for each calendar day of delay until the Work is substantially complete:
> ($).

For further information on liquidated damages, penalties and bonus provisions, see AIA Document A511, Guide to Supplementary Conditions, Paragraph 9.11.

5. Article 10—Subcontract Sum

Paragraph 10.1
Enter the Subcontract Sum payable to the Subcontractor.

Paragraph 10.2
Identify any alternates described in the Subcontract Documents and accepted by the Owner and the Contractor. If decisions on alternates are to be made subsequent to execution of A401, attach a schedule showing the amount of each alternate and the date until which that amount is valid.

Paragraph 10.3
Enter any unit prices, cash allowances or cash contingency allowances.

If unit prices are not covered in greater detail elsewhere in the Subcontract Documents, the following provision for unit prices is suggested:

> The unit prices listed below shall determine the value of extra Work or changes in the Work, as applicable. They shall be considered complete and shall include all material and equipment, labor, installation costs, overhead and profit. Unit prices shall be used uniformly for additions or deductions.

6. Article 11—Progress Payments

Paragraph 11.2
Insert the time period covered by each application for payment if it differs from the one given.

Paragraph 11.3
Insert the time schedule for presenting applications for payment.

The last day upon which Work may be included in an application should normally be no less than 14 days prior to the payment date, in consideration of the 7 days required for the Architect's evaluation of the Contractor's Application and issuance of a Certificate for Payment and the time subsequently accorded the Owner to make Payment in Article 9 of A201. The Contractor may prefer that applications be submitted a few additional days prior to the preparation of the Contractor's Application.

Due dates for payment should be acceptable to both the Contractor and Subcontractor. They should allow suffici[illegible] time [illegible]e Contractor to prepare an Application for Payment, for the Architect to certify payment, and for the Owner to mak[illegible] should also be in accordance with the time limits established by this Article and Article 9 of A201.

7. Article 12—Final Payment

Insert provisions for earlier final payment to the Subcontractor, if applicable. When fin[illegible] payme[illegible] reque[illegible] the Architect should ascertain that all claims have been settled or should define those which remain uns[illegible] Th[illegible]hite[illegible] should obtain the Contractor's certification required by Article 9 of A201 and must determine that, to [illegible]st o[illegible]r h[illegible]ge and belief and according to final inspection, the requirements of the Subcontract have been ful[illegible] he Con[illegible]r may also require satisfactory evidence from the Subcontractor that all known indebtedness related to th[illegible]actor's [illegible] has been paid.

8. Article 13—Insurance and Bonds

Paragraph 13.1
Insert types of coverage and limits of liability to be mai[illegible]ned [illegible]e Sub[illegible]ractor.

Paragraph 13.7
If the Subcontractor is to furnish performance [illegible]ymen[illegible]ds, ins[illegible]specific req[illegible]ments.

9. Article 14—Temporary Facilities a[illegible]g C[illegible]

Paragraph 14.1
List temporary facilities, eq[illegible]nt [illegible] furnished by [illegible]ontractor [illegible] S[illegible]ntractor. These are to be furnished free of charge unless o[illegible]se indic[illegible]n this [illegible]aragraph.

Paragraph 14.2
Insert any ap[illegible]le arrang[illegible]ts concerning working co[illegible]ns a[illegible] the Project.

10. Article 1[illegible]ous Provisions

P[illegible]aph 15.2
En[illegible]y ag[illegible] interest rate d[illegible]pa[illegible]ts.

[illegible]Enumeration of Subcontract [illegible]nts
[illegible]detailed enumeration of all Subcontract Documents must be made in this article.

D[illegible]XECUTION OF THE AGREEMENT

Each person executing the Agreement should indicate the capacity in which they are acting (i.e., president, secretary, partner, etc.) and the authority under which they are executing the Agreement. Where appropriate, a copy of the resolution authorizing the individual to act on behalf of the firm or entity should be attached.

THE AMERICAN INSTITUTE OF ARCHITECTS

AIA Document A401

SUBCONTRACT

Standard Form of Agreement Between Contractor and Subcontractor

1978 EDITION

Use with the latest edition of the appropriate AIA Documents as follows:

A101, Owner-Contractor Agreement — Stipulated Sum
A107, Abbreviated Owner-Contractor Agreement with General Conditions
A111, Owner-Contractor Agreement — Cost plus Fee
A201, General Conditions of the Contract for Construction.

THIS DOCUMENT HAS IMPORTANT LEGAL CONSEQUENCES; CONSULTATION WITH AN ATTORNEY IS ENCOURAGED WITH RESPECT TO ITS COMPLETION OR MODIFICATION

This document has been approved and endorsed by the American Subcontractors Association and the Associated Specialty Contractors, Inc.

AGREEMENT

made as of the day of in the year Nineteen Hundred and

BETWEEN the Contractor:

and the Subcontractor:

The Project:

The Owner:

The Architect:

The Contractor and Subcontractor agree as set forth below.

ARTICLE 1
THE CONTRACT DOCUMENTS

1.1 The Contract Documents for this Subcontract consist of this Agreement and any Exhibits attached hereto, the Agreement between the Owner and Contractor dated as of , the Conditions of the Contract between the Owner and Contractor (General, Supplementary and other Conditions), the Drawings, the Specifications, all Addenda issued prior to and all Modifications issued after execution of the Agreement between the Owner and Contractor and agreed upon by the parties to this Subcontract. These form the Subcontract, and are as fully a part of the Subcontract as if attached to this Agreement or repeated herein.

1.2 Copies of the above documents which are applicable to the Work under this Subcontract shall be furnished to the Subcontractor upon his request. An enumeration of the applicable Contract Documents appears in Article 15.

ARTICLE 2
THE WORK

2.1 The Subcontractor shall perform all the Work required by the Contract Documents for

(Here insert a precise description of the Work covered by this Subcontract and refer to numbers of Drawings and pages of Specifications including Addenda, Modifications and accepted Alternates.)

ARTICLE 3
TIME OF COMMENCEMENT AND SUBSTANTIAL COMPLETION

3.1 The Work to be performed under this Subcontract shall be commenced
and, subject to authorized adjustments, shall be substantially completed not later than

(Here insert the specific provisions that are applicable to this Subcontract including any information pertaining to notice to proceed or other method of modification for commencement of Work, starting and completion dates, or duration, and any provisions for liquidated damages relating to failure to complete on time.)

3.2 Time is of the essence of this Subcontract.

3.3 No extension of time will be valid without the Contractor's written consent after claim made by the Subcontractor in accordance with Paragraph 11.10.

ARTICLE 4
THE CONTRACT SUM

4.1 The Contractor shall pay the Subcontractor in current funds for the performance of the Work, subject to additions and deductions authorized pursuant to Paragraph 11.9, the Contract Sum of dollars ($).

The Contract Sum is determined as follows:

(State here the base bid or other lump sum amount, accepted alternates, and unit prices, as applicable.)

ARTICLE 5
PROGRESS PAYMENTS

5.1 The Contractor shall pay the Subcontractor monthly progress payments in accordance with Paragraph 12.4 of this Subcontract.

5.2 Applications for monthly progress payments shall be in writing and in accordance with Paragraph 11.8, shall state the estimated percentage of the Work in this Subcontract that has been satisfactorily completed and shall be submitted to the Contractor on or before the day of each month.

(Here insert details on (1) payment procedures and date of monthly applications, or other procedure if on other than a monthly basis, (2) the basis on which payment will be made on account of materials and equipment suitably stored at the site or other location agreed upon in writing, and (3) any provisions consistent with the Contract Documents for limiting or reducing the amount retained after the Work reaches a certain stage of completion.)

5.3 When the Subcontractor's Work or a designated portion thereof is substantially complete and in accordance with the Contract Documents, the Contractor shall, upon application by the Subcontractor, make prompt application for payment of such Work. Within thirty days following issuance by the Architect of the Certificate for Payment covering such substantially completed Work, the Contractor shall, to the full extent provided in the Contract Documents, make payment to the Subcontractor of the entire unpaid balance of the Contract Sum or of that portion of the Contract Sum attributable to the substantially completed Work, less any portion of the funds for the Subcontractor's Work withheld in accordance with the Certificate to cover costs of items to be completed or corrected by the Subcontractor.

(Delete the above Paragraph if the Contract Documents do not provide for, and the Subcontractor agrees to forego, release of retainage for the Subcontractor's Work prior to completion of the entire Project.)

5.4 Progress payments or final payment due and unpaid under this Subcontract shall bear interest from the date payment is due at the rate entered below, or, in the absence thereof, at the legal rate prevailing at the place of the Project.

(Here insert any rate of interest agreed upon.)

(Usury laws and requirements under the Federal Truth in Lending Act, similar state and local consumer credit laws and other regulations at the Owner's, Contractor's and Subcontractor's principal places of business, the location of the Project and elsewhere may affect the validity of this provision. Specific legal advice should be obtained with respect to deletion, modification, or other requirements such as written disclosures or waivers.)

ARTICLE 6
FINAL PAYMENT

6.1 Final payment, constituting the entire unpaid balance of the Contract Sum, shall be due when the Work described in this Subcontract is fully completed and performed in accordance with the Contract Documents and is satisfactory to the Architect, and shall be payable as follows, in accordance with Article 5 and with Paragraph 12.4 of this Subcontract:

(Here insert the relevant conditions under which, or time in which, final payment will become payable.)

6.2 Before issuance of the final payment, the Subcontractor, if required, shall submit evidence satisfactory to the Contractor that all payrolls, bills for materials and equipment, and all known indebtedness connected with the Subcontractor's Work have been satisfied.

ARTICLE 7
PERFORMANCE BOND AND LABOR AND MATERIAL PAYMENT BOND

(Here insert any requirement for the furnishing of bonds by the Subcontractor.)

ARTICLE 8
TEMPORARY FACILITIES AND SERVICES

8.1 Unless otherwise provided in this Subcontract, the Contractor shall furnish and make available at no cost to the Subcontractor the following temporary facilities and services:

ARTICLE 9
INSURANCE

9.1 Prior to starting work, the Subcontractor shall obtain the required insurance from a responsible insurer, and shall furnish satisfactory evidence to the Contractor that the Subcontractor has complied with the requirements of this Article 9. Similarly, the Contractor shall furnish to the Subcontractor satisfactory evidence of insurance required of the Contractor by the Contract Documents.

9.2. The Contractor and Subcontractor waive all rights against each other and against the Owner, the Architect, separate contractors and all other subcontractors for damages caused by fire or other perils to the extent covered by property insurance provided under the General Conditions, except such rights as they may have to the proceeds of such insurance.

(Here insert any insurance requirements and Subcontractor's responsibility for obtaining, maintaining and paying for necessary insurance with limits equaling or exceeding those specified in the Contract Documents and inserted below, or required by law. If applicable, this shall include fire insurance and extended coverage, public liability, property damage, employer's liability, and workers' or workmen's compensation insurance for the Subcontractor and his employees. The insertion should cover provisions for notice of cancellation, allocation of insurance proceeds, and other aspects of insurance.)

ARTICLE 10
WORKING CONDITIONS

(Here insert any applicable arrangements concerning working conditions and labor matters for the Project.)

GENERAL CONDITIONS

ARTICLE 11
SUBCONTRACTOR

11.1 RIGHTS AND RESPONSIBILITIES

11.1.1 The Subcontractor shall be bound to the Contractor by the terms of this Agreement and, to the extent that provisions of the Contract Documents between the Owner and Contractor apply to the Work of the Subcontractor as defined in this Agreement, the Subcontractor shall assume toward the Contractor all the obligations and responsibilities which the Contractor, by those Documents, assumes toward the Owner and the Architect, and shall have the benefit of all rights, remedies and redress against the Contractor which the Contractor, by those Documents, has against the Owner, insofar as applicable to this Subcontract, provided that where any provision of the Contract Documents between the Owner and Contractor is inconsistent with any provision of this Agreement, this Agreement shall govern.

11.1.2 The Subcontractor shall not assign this subcontract without the written consent of the Contractor, nor subcontract the whole of this Subcontract without the written consent of the Contractor, nor further subcontract portions of this Subcontract without written notification to the Contractor when such notification is requested by the Contractor. The Subcontractor shall not assign any amounts due or to become due under this Subcontract without written notice to the Contractor.

11.2 EXECUTION AND PROGRESS OF THE WORK

11.2.1 The Subcontractor agrees that the Contractor's equipment will be available to the Subcontractor only at the Contractor's discretion and on mutually satisfactory terms.

11.2.2 The Subcontractor shall cooperate with the Contractor in scheduling and performing his Work to avoid conflict or interference with the work of others.

11.2.3 The Subcontractor shall promptly submit shop drawings and samples required in order to perform his Work efficiently, expeditiously and in a manner that will not cause delay in the progress of the Work of the Contractor or other subcontractors.

11.2.4 The Subcontractor shall furnish periodic progress reports on the Work as mutually agreed, including information on the status of materials and equipment under this Subcontract which may be in the course of preparation or manufacture.

11.2.5 The Subcontractor agrees that all Work shall be done subject to the final approval of the Architect. The Architect's decisions in matters relating to artistic effect shall be final if consistent with the intent of the Contract Documents.

11.2.6 The Subcontractor shall pay for all materials, equipment and labor used in, or in connection with, the performance of this Subcontract through the period covered by previous payments received from the Contractor, and shall furnish satisfactory evidence, when requested by the Contractor, to verify compliance with the above requirements.

11.3 LAWS, PERMITS, FEES AND NOTICES

11.3.1 The Subcontractor shall give all notices and comply with all laws, ordinances, rules, regulations and orders of any public authority bearing on the performance of the Work under this Subcontract. The Subcontractor shall secure and pay for all permits and governmental fees, licenses and inspections necessary for the proper execution and completion of the Subcontractor's Work, the furnishing of which is required of the Contractor by the Contract Documents.

11.3.2 The Subcontractor shall comply with Federal, State and local tax laws, social security acts, unemployment compensation acts and workers' or workmen's compensation acts insofar as applicable to the performance of this Subcontract.

11.4 WORK OF OTHERS

11.4.1 In carrying out his Work, the Subcontractor shall take necessary precautions to protect properly the finished work of other trades from damage caused by his operations.

11.4.2 The Subcontractor shall cooperate with the Contractor and other subcontractors whose work might interfere with the Subcontractor's Work, and shall participate in the preparation of coordinated drawings in areas of congestion as required by the Contract Documents, specifically noting and advising the Contractor of any such interference.

11.5 SAFETY PRECAUTIONS AND PROCEDURES

11.5.1 The Subcontractor shall take all reasonable safety precautions with respect to his Work, shall comply with all safety measures initiated by the Contractor and with all applicable laws, ordinances, rules, regulations and orders of any public authority for the safety of persons or property in accordance with the requirements of the Contract Documents. The Subcontractor shall report within three days to the Contractor any injury to any of the Subcontractor's employees at the site.

11.6 CLEANING UP

11.6.1 The Subcontractor shall at all times keep the premises free from accumulation of waste materials or rubbish arising out of the operations of this Subcontract. Unless otherwise provided, the Subcontractor shall not be held responsible for unclean conditions caused by other contractors or subcontractors.

11.7 WARRANTY

11.7.1 The Subcontractor warrants to the Owner, the Architect and the Contractor that all materials and equipment furnished shall be new unless otherwise specified, and that all Work under this Subcontract shall be of good quality, free from faults and defects and in conformance with the Contract Documents. All Work not conforming to these requirements, including substitutions not properly approved and authorized, may be considered defective. The warranty provided in this Paragraph 11.7 shall be in addition to and not in limitation of any other warranty or remedy required by law or by the Contract Documents.

11.8 APPLICATIONS FOR PAYMENT

11.8.1 The Subcontractor shall submit to the Contractor applications for payment at such times as stipulated in Article 5 to enable the Contractor to apply for payment.

11.8.2 If payments are made on the valuation of Work done, the Subcontractor shall, before the first application, submit to the Contractor a schedule of values of the various parts of the Work aggregating the total sum of this Subcontract, made out in such detail as the Subcontractor and Contractor may agree upon or as required by the Owner, and supported by such evidence as to its correctness as the Contractor may direct. This schedule, when approved by the Contractor, shall be used only as a basis for Applications for Payment, unless it be found to be in error. In applying for payment, the Subcontractor shall submit a statement based upon this schedule.

11:8.3 If payments are made on account of materials or equipment not incorporated in the Work but delivered and suitably stored at the site or at some other location agreed upon in writing, such payments shall be in accordance with the Terms and Conditions of the Contract Documents.

11.9 CHANGES IN THE WORK

11.9.1 The Subcontractor may be ordered in writing by the Contractor, without invalidating this Subcontract, to make changes in the Work within the general scope of this Subcontract consisting of additions, deletions or other revisions, the Contract Sum and the Contract Time being adjusted accordingly. The Subcontractor, prior to the commencement of such changed or revised Work, shall submit promptly to the Contractor written copies of any claim for adjustment to the Contract Sum and Contract Time for such revised Work in a manner consistent with the Contract Documents.

11.10 CLAIMS OF THE SUBCONTRACTOR

11.10.1 The Subcontractor shall make all claims promptly to the Contractor for additional cost, extensions of time, and damages for delays or other causes in accordance with the Contract Documents. Any such claim which will affect or become part of a claim which the Contractor is required to make under the Contract Documents within a specified time period or in a specified manner shall be made in sufficient time to permit the Contractor to satisfy the requirements of the Contract Documents. Such claims shall be received by the Contractor not less than two working days preceding the time by which the Contractor's claim must be made. Failure of the Subcontractor to make such a timely claim shall bind the Subcontractor to the same consequences as those to which the Contractor is bound.

11.11 INDEMNIFICATION

11.11.1 To the fullest extent permitted by law, the Subcontractor shall indemnify and hold harmless the Owner, the Architect and the Contractor and all of their agents and employees from and against all claims, damages, losses and expenses, including but not limited to attorney's fees, arising out of or resulting from the performance of the Subcontractor's Work under this Subcontract, provided that any such claim, damage, loss, or expense is attributable to bodily injury, sickness, disease, or death, or to injury to or destruction of tangible property (other than the Work itself) including the loss of use resulting therefrom, to the extent caused in whole or in part by any negligent act or omission of the Subcontractor or anyone directly or indirectly employed by him or anyone for whose acts he may be liable, regardless of whether it is caused in part by a party indemnified hereunder. Such obligation shall not be construed to negate, or abridge, or otherwise reduce any other right or obligation of indemnity which would otherwise exist as to any party or person described in this Paragraph 11.11.

11.11.2 In any and all claims against the Owner, the Architect, or the Contractor or any of their agents or employees by any employee of the Subcontractor, anyone directly or indirectly employed by him or anyone for whose acts he may be liable, the indemnification obligation under this Paragraph 11.11 shall not be limited in any way by any limitation on the amount or type of damages, compensation or benefits payable by or for the Subcontractor under workers' or workmen's compensation acts, disability benefit acts or other employee benefit acts.

11.11.3 The obligations of the Subcontractor under this Paragraph 11.11 shall not extend to the liability of the Architect, his agents or employees arising out of (1) the preparation or approval of maps, drawings, opinions, reports, surveys, Change Orders, designs or specifications, or (2) the giving of or the failure to give directions or instructions by the Architect, his agents or employees provided such giving or failure to give is the primary cause of the injury or damage.

11.12 SUBCONTRACTOR'S REMEDIES

11.12.1 If the Contractor does not pay the Subcontractor through no fault of the Subcontractor, within seven days from the time payment should be made as provided in Paragraph 12.4, the Subcontractor may, without prejudice to any other remedy he may have, upon seven additional days' written notice to the Contractor, stop his Work until payment of the amount owing has been received. The Contract Sum shall, by appropriate adjustment, be increased by the amount of the Subcontractor's reasonable costs of shutdown, delay and start-up.

ARTICLE 12
CONTRACTOR

12.1 RIGHTS AND RESPONSIBILITIES

12.1.1 The Contractor shall be bound to the Subcontractor by the terms of this Agreement, and to the extent that provisions of the Contract Documents between the Owner and the Contractor apply to the Work of the Subcontractor as defined in this Agreement, the Contractor shall assume toward the Subcontractor all the obligations and responsibilities that the Owner, by those Documents, assumes toward the Contractor, and shall have the benefit of all rights, remedies and redress against the Subcontractor which the Owner, by those Documents, has against the Contractor. Where any provision of the

Contract Documents between the Owner and the Contractor is inconsistent with any provisions of this Agreement, this Agreement shall govern.

12.2 SERVICES PROVIDED BY THE CONTRACTOR

12.2.1 The Contractor shall cooperate with the Subcontractor in scheduling and performing his Work to avoid conflicts or interference in the Subcontractor's Work, and shall expedite written responses to submittals made by the Subcontractor in accordance with Paragraphs 11.2, 11.9 and 11.10. As soon as practicable after execution of this Agreement, the Contractor shall provide the Subcontractor a copy of the estimated progress schedule of the Contractor's entire Work which the Contractor has prepared and submitted for the Owner's and the Architect's information, together with such additional scheduling details as will enable the Subcontractor to plan and perform his Work properly. The Subcontractor shall be notified promptly of any subsequent changes in the progress schedule and the additional scheduling details.

12.2.2 The Contractor shall provide suitable areas for storage of the Subcontractor's materials and equipment during the course of the Work. Any additional costs to the Subcontractor resulting from the relocation of such facilities at the direction of the Contractor shall be reimbursed by the Contractor.

12.3 COMMUNICATIONS

12.3.1 The Contractor shall promptly notify the Subcontractor of all modifications to the Contract between the Owner and the Contractor which affect this Subcontract and which were issued or entered into subsequent to the execution of this Subcontract.

12.3.2 The Contractor shall not give instructions or orders directly to employees or workmen of the Subcontractor except to persons designated as authorized representatives of the Subcontractor.

12.4 PAYMENTS TO THE SUBCONTRACTOR

12.4.1 Unless otherwise provided in the Contract Documents, the Contractor shall pay the Subcontractor each progress payment and the final payment under this Subcontract within three working days after he receives payment from the Owner, except as provided in Subparagraph 12.4.3. The amount of each progress payment to the Subcontractor shall be the amount to which the Subcontractor is entitled, reflecting the percentage of completion allowed to the Contractor for the Work of this Subcontractor applied to the Contract Sum of this Subcontract, and the percentage actually retained, if any, from payments to the Contractor on account of such Subcontractor's Work, plus, to the extent permitted by the Contract Documents, the amount allowed for materials and equipment suitably stored by the Subcontractor, less the aggregate of previous payments to the Subcontractor.

12.4.2 The Contractor shall permit the Subcontractor to request directly from the Architect information regarding the percentages of completion or the amount certified on account of Work done by the Subcontractor.

12.4.3 If the Architect does not issue a Certificate for Payment or the Contractor does not receive payment for any cause which is not the fault of the Subcontractor, the Contractor shall pay the Subcontractor, on demand, a progress payment computed as provided in Subparagraph 12.4.1 or the final payment as provided in Article 6.

12.5 CLAIMS BY THE CONTRACTOR

12.5.1 The Contractor shall make no demand for liquidated damages for delay in any sum in excess of such amount as may be specifically named in this Subcontract, and liquidated damages shall be assessed against this Subcontractor only for his negligent acts and his failure to act in accordance with the terms of this Agreement, and in no case for delays or causes arising outside the scope of this Subcontract, or for which other subcontractors are responsible.

12.5.2 Except as may be indicated in this Agreement, the Contractor agrees that no claim for payment for services rendered or materials and equipment furnished by the Contractor to the Subcontractor shall be valid without prior notice to the Subcontractor and unless written notice thereof is given by the Contractor to the Subcontractor not later than the tenth day of the calendar month following that in which the claim originated.

12.6 CONTRACTOR'S REMEDIES

12.6.1 If the Subcontractor defaults or neglects to carry out the Work in accordance with this Agreement and fails within three working days after receipt of written notice from the Contractor to commence and continue correction of such default or neglect with diligence and promptness, the Contractor may, after three days following receipt by the Subcontractor of an additional written notice, and without prejudice to any other remedy he may have, make good such deficiencies and may deduct the cost thereof from the payments then or thereafter due the Subcontractor, provided, however, that if such action is based upon faulty workmanship or materials and equipment, the Architect shall first have determined that the workmanship or materials and equipment are not in accordance with the Contract Documents.

ARTICLE 13
ARBITRATION

13.1 All claims, disputes and other matters in question arising out of, or relating to, this Subcontract, or the breach thereof, shall be decided by arbitration, which shall be conducted in the same manner and under the same procedure as provided in the Contract Documents with respect to disputes between the Owner and the Contractor, except that a decision by the Architect shall not be a condition precedent to arbitration. If the Contract Documents do not provide for arbitration or fail to specify the manner and procedure for arbitration, it shall be conducted in accordance with the Construction Industry Arbitration Rules of the American Arbitration Association then obtaining unless the parties mutually agree otherwise.

13.2 Except by written consent of the person or entity sought to be joined, no arbitration arising out of or relating to the Contract Documents shall include, by consolidation, joinder or in any other manner, any person or entity not a party to the Agreement under which such arbitration arises, unless it is shown at the time the demand for arbitration is filed that (1) such person or entity is substantially involved in a common question of fact or law,

(2) the presence of such person or entity is required if complete relief is to be accorded in the arbitration, (3) the interest or responsibility of such person or entity in the matter is not insubstantial, and (4) such person or entity is not the Architect, his employee or his consultant. This agreement to arbitrate and any other written agreement to arbitrate with an additional person or persons referred to herein shall be specifically enforceable under the prevailing arbitration law.

13.3 The Contractor shall permit the Subcontractor to be present and to submit evidence in any arbitration proceeding involving his rights.

13.4 The Contractor shall permit the Subcontractor to exercise whatever rights the Contractor may have under the Contract Documents in the choice of arbitrators in any dispute, if the sole cause of the dispute is the Work, materials, equipment, rights or responsibilities of the Subcontractor; or if the dispute involves the Subcontractor and any other subcontractor or subcontractors jointly, the Contractor shall permit them to exercise such rights jointly.

13.5 The award rendered by the arbitrators shall be final, and judgment may be entered upon it in accordance with applicable law in any court having jurisdiction thereof.

13.6 This Article shall not be deemed a limitation of any rights or remedies which the Subcontractor may have under any Federal or State mechanics' lien laws or under any applicable labor and material payment bonds unless such rights or remedies are expressly waived by him.

ARTICLE 14
TERMINATION

14.1 TERMINATION BY THE SUBCONTRACTOR

14.1.1 If the Work is stopped for a period of thirty days through no fault of the Subcontractor because the Contractor has not made payments thereon as provided in this Agreement, then the Subcontractor may without prejudice to any other remedy he may have, upon seven additional days' written notice to the Contractor, terminate this Subcontract and recover from the Contractor payment for all Work executed and for any proven loss resulting from the stoppage of the Work, including reasonable overhead, profit and damages.

14.2 TERMINATION BY THE CONTRACTOR

14.2.1 If the Subcontractor persistently or repeatedly fails or neglects to carry out the Work in accordance with the Contract Documents or otherwise to perform in accordance with this Agreement and fails within seven days after receipt of written notice to commence and continue correction of such default or neglect with diligence and promptness, the Contractor may, after seven days following receipt by the Subcontractor of an additional written notice and without prejudice to any other remedy he may have, terminate the Subcontract and finish the Work by whatever method he may deem expedient. If the unpaid balance of the Contract Sum exceeds the expense of finishing the Work, such excess shall be paid to the Subcontractor, but if such expense exceeds such unpaid balance, the Subcontractor shall pay the difference to the Contractor.

ARTICLE 15
MISCELLANEOUS PROVISIONS

15.1 Terms used in this Agreement which are defined in the Conditions of the Contract shall have the meanings designated in those Conditions.

15.2 The Contract Documents, which constitute the entire Agreement between the Owner and the Contractor, are listed in Article 1, and the documents which are applicable to this Subcontract, except for Addenda and Modifications issued after execution of this Subcontract, are enumerated as follows:

(List below the Agreement, the Conditions of the Contract [General, Supplementary, and other Conditions], the Drawings, the Specifications, and any Addenda and accepted Alternates, showing page or sheet numbers in all cases and dates where applicable. Continue on succeeding pages as required.)

This Agreement entered into as of the day and year first written above.

CONTRACTOR	SUBCONTRACTOR
______________________	______________________
______________________	______________________
______________________	______________________

INSTRUCTION SHEET

FOR AIA DOCUMENT B141, STANDARD FORM OF AGREEMENT BETWEEN OWNER AND ARCHITECT—1987 EDITION

A. GENERAL INFORMATION

1. Purpose

AIA Document B141 is a standard form of agreement between Owner and Architect intended for use on construction projects where services are based on the customary five phases: Schematic Design, Design Development, Construction Documents, Bidding or Negotiation, and Construction.

2. Related Documents

B141 is intended to be used in conjunction with AIA Document A201, General Conditions of the Contract for Cons[illegible] it incorporates by reference. It can be used with Architect-Consultant agreements such as AIA Documen[illegible] C142, [illegible]61, C[illegible] or C727.

Other AIA Owner-Architect Agreements available for use in connection with customary services or in[illegible]ial circ[illegible]ances include:

B141/CM	Owner-Architect Agreement, Construction Management Edition
B151	Abbreviated Owner-Architect Agreement for Projects of Limited Sco[illegible]
B161	Owner-Architect Agreement for Designated Services
B161/CM	Owner-Architect Agreement for Designated Services, Constru[illegible] [illegible]gement [illegible]n
B162	Scope of Designated Services (to be used in conjunction with B161 [illegible]161/CM)
B171	Interior Design Services Agreement
B177	Abbreviated Interior Design Services Agreement
B181	Owner-Architect Agreement for Housing Services
B727	Owner-Architect Agreement for Special S[illegible]s
B801	Owner-Construction Manager Agreement
B901	Design/Builder-Architect Agreeme[illegible]

3. Arbitration

This document incorporates ARBITR[illegible] [illegible]ption of the Constru[illegible] Indust[illegible] [illegible]bitrati[illegible] Rules of the American Arbitration Association. Arbitration is BI[illegible] A[illegible] in most sta[illegible] und[illegible] the [illegible]bitration Act. In a minority of states, arbitration provisions re[illegible] to future [illegible]tes are not enforceabl[illegible] [illegible]ration [illegible]forceable if agreed to after the dispute arises. A few states req[illegible] the contra[illegible] parties be esp[illegible] no[illegible] that the written contract contains an arbitration provision by: a warni[illegible] on the fa[illegible] the document, specific plac[illegible] of [illegible]on provision within the document or specific discussions [illegible] the parties [illegible] to signing the d[illegible]ent.

Arbitration [illegible] been included in [illegible] AIA [illegible] fo[illegible] since 1888 in order to encourage alternative dispute resolution [illegible]cedu[illegible] to [illegible]vide users of A[illegible] documents [illegible] legally enforceable arbitration provisions when the parties choose to adop[illegible] arbitration into their contract. In[illegible] [illegible], choose to delete the arbitration provisions based upon their [illegible] decisi[illegible] the advice of co[illegible] a copy of the Construction Industry Arbitration Rules, write the American [illegible] Association, 140 West 51st Street, New [illegible]k, NY 10020.

4. [illegible] of Non-AIA Forms

If a combination of AIA documents and non-AIA documents is to be used, particular care must be taken to achieve consistency of language and intent. Certain owners require the use of owner-architect agreements and other contract forms which they prepare. Such forms should be carefully compared to the standard AIA forms for which they are being substituted before execution of an agreement. If there are any significant omissions, additions or variances from the terms of the related standard AIA forms, both legal and insurance counsel should be consulted. Of particular concern is the need for consistency between the Owner-Architect Agreement and the anticipated General Conditions of the Contract for Construction in the delineation of the Architect's Construction Phase services and responsibilities.

5. Letter Forms of Agreement

Letter forms of agreement are generally discouraged by the AIA, as is the performance of a part or the whole of professional services based on oral agreements or understandings. The standard AIA agreement forms have been developed through more than seventy-five years of experience and have been tested repeatedly in the courts. In addition, the standard forms have been carefully coordinated with other AIA documents.

6. Use of Current Documents

Prior to using any AIA document, the user should consult the AIA, an AIA component chapter or a current AIA Documents Price List to determine the current edition of each document.

7. Limited License for Reproduction

AIA Document B141 is a copyrighted work and may not be reproduced or excerpted from in substantial part without the express written permission of the AIA. The B141 document is intended to be used as a consumable—that is, the original document purchased by the user is intended to be consumed in the course of being used. There is no implied permission to reproduce this document, nor does membership in The American Institute of Architects confer any further rights to reproduce them.

A limited license is hereby granted to retail purchasers to reproduce a maximum of ten copies of a completed or executed B141, but only for use in connection with a particular Project. Further reproductions are prohibited without the express written permission of the AIA.

B. CHANGES FROM THE PREVIOUS EDITION

1. Format Changes

Former Article 1, Architect's Services and Responsibilities, has been subdivided into three new articles. All provisi[illegible] payments to the Architect, including Direct Personnel Expense, Reimbursable Expenses and Architect's Acc[illegible] been consolidated and moved to the end of the document.

2. Changes in Content

The 1987 edition of B141 has been revised to reflect changes made in the 1987 edition o[illegible]IA[illegible]me[illegible]eral Conditions of the Contract for Construction. The following changes in content have been made[illegible]reco[illegible]nda[illegible]wners, AIA members, committees and the AIA board of directors.

Article 2: Scope of Architect's Basic Services

Subparagraphs 2.2.4, 2.3.2 and 2.4.3
The term "Statement of Probable Construction Cost" has been cha[illegible]d to "preliminary [illegible]mate of Co[illegible]truction Cost" to simplify the terminology of the document.

Subparagraph 2.6.5
New language has been added to indicate that the[illegible]itect's[illegible]e vi[illegible]or the pur[illegible]se[illegible]de[illegible]ing that the Work, when completed, will be in accordance with the Contrac[illegible]umen[illegible]note has been add[illegible]alert users[illegible]e form that more extensive site representation is available under[illegible]na[illegible]ices.

Subparagraph 2.6.6
It is noted that the Contractor[illegible]responsible for co[illegible]tion m[illegible]met[illegible]and schedules.

Subparagraph 2.6.8
During construction, [illegible]tions be[illegible] the Owner [illegible]ont[illegible]are to[illegible]directed through the Architect.

Subparagrap[illegible]
The Archite[illegible]Certificates for P[illegible]nt are further q[illegible]d[illegible]icati[illegible]review of construction means or methods or review of Subcont[illegible]tions.

Sub[illegible]graph 2.6.11
It is sp[illegible]cally[illegible]t the Architect'[illegible]jec[illegible]rk is not intended to be exercised for the benefit of the Contractor, [illegible]ors, suppliers, or their agents[illegible]plo[illegible]

[illegible] 2.6.12
[illegible]Architect's review of submittals is further [illegible]ed to limit such review to the information and design concepts expressed in the C[illegible]act Documents. When professional certificates of performance are required from the Contractor, the Architect shall be entitled to rely upon them.

Subparagraph 2.6.13
Preparation of Change Orders and Construction Change Directives by the Architect is a Basic Service, but preparation of supporting documentation and data is now an Additional Service.

Article 3: Additional Services
Three new categories of Additional Services have been consolidated under this new article. The Contingent Additional Services are commenced upon notification of the Owner by the Architect of the need for such services. The other two categories, Project Representation Beyond Basic Services and Optional Additional Services, require the Owner's written approval before or after their commencement to authorize payment for those Additional Services.

Article 4: Owner's Responsibilities
A new Paragraph 4.3 has been added requiring the Owner to furnish evidence that financial arrangements have been made to pay the Architect. The Owner is now required to furnish tests for hazardous materials at the Owner's expense. If the Owner requires the Architect to provide certificates or certifications, the Owner must allow the Architect 14 days for review.

Article 6: Use of Architect's Drawings, Specifications and Other Documents
It is noted that documents prepared by the Architect in addition to the Drawings and Specifications are also the property of the Architect, who retains all common law, statutory and other reserved rights.

Article 8: Termination, Suspension or Abandonment
New provisions allow the Architect to terminate the Agreement if the Owner abandons the Project for more than 90 days or fails to make payments to the Architect.

Article 9: Miscellaneous Provisions
Provisions have been added noting that the Architect has no responsibility for the discovery, removal or disposal of toxic or hazardous substances encountered on the site. Another provision allows the Architect to use representations of the Project in promotional and professional materials.

Article 10: Payments to the Architect
Computer-aided drafting has been added to the list of Reimbursable Expenses.

Article 11: Basis of Compensation
A new provision has been added to indicate when payments are due and payable.

C. MINOR CORRECTIONS IN THIS AND EARLIER PRINTINGS

From time to time, the AIA makes minor corrections and clarifications in its documents as they are repri[illegible] The [illegible] will be indicated on the back of the document at the bottom.

This Instruction Sheet accompanies the 6/92 reprinting of AIA Document B141, 1987 Edition. The us[illegible]hould c[illegible] the [illegible]printing date of the B141 document under consideration to ensure that all of the changes listed b[illegible] ap[illegible]

The following changes were made in the 7/88 reprinting of B141:

Subparagraph 2.6.1
At the end of this subparagraph, the phrase ", unless extended under the t[illegible]bparagra[illegible]3.3" was deleted.

Subparagraph 11.3.2
The term "Basic Services" was substituted for "Additional Service[illegible]

The following changes have been made in this 6/92 repri[illegible]ting [illegible]41:

Subparagraph 2.6.10
In the first sentence, the qualifying phrase ", to the [illegible]st of t[illegible]chit[illegible]wledge, infor[illegible]belief," has been relocated. The sentence now reads "The Architect's certific[illegible] for pa[illegible]t shall constitute a[illegible]sentatio[illegible]he Owner, based on the Architect's observations at the site as provi[illegible] S[illegible]graph[illegible].5 and on the [illegible]omprising the[illegible]ractor's Application for Payment, that, to the best of the Archi[illegible]wle[illegible]on and belie[illegible] W[illegible]as progre[illegible]d to the point indicated and the quality of the Work is in [illegible]danc[illegible]ith the[illegible]act Docum[illegible]"

Paragraph 4.5
In the last sentence, the [illegible] Projec[illegible] been[illegible]apitalized.

D. COMPLETING [illegible] B141 F[illegible]

1. Mod[illegible]atio[illegible]

Users [illegible]ncou[illegible]onsult an attor[illegible] [illegible]n AIA document. Particularly with respect to professional licensing [illegible] by building codes, [illegible], arbitration and indemnification, this document may require modification [illegible]ance of legal counsel to fully comply [illegible]h state or local laws regulating these matters.

[illegible]erally, necessary modifications may be a[illegible]plished by writing or typing the appropriate terms in the blank spaces provided [illegible] form, or by supplementary conditions, special conditions or amendments referenced in this document. The form may also be modified by striking out language directly on the pre-printed form. Care must be taken in making these kinds of deletions, however. Under NO circumstances should pre-printed language be struck out in such a way as to render it illegible (as, for example, with blocking tape, correction fluid or X's that completely obscure the text). This may raise suspicions of fraudulent concealment, or suggest that the completed and signed document has been tampered with. Handwritten changes should be initialed by both parties to the contract.

It is definitely not recommended practice to retype the standard document. Besides being outside the limited license for reproduction granted under these Instructions, retyping can introduce typographical errors and cloud the legal interpretation given to a standard clause when blended with modifications.

Retyping eliminates one of the principal advantages of the standard form documents. By merely reviewing the modifications to be made to a standard form document, parties familiar with that document can quickly understand the essence of the proposed relationship. Commercial exchanges are greatly simplified and expedited, good-faith dealing is encouraged, and otherwise latent clauses are exposed for scrutiny. In this way, contracting parties can more fairly measure their risks.

2. Cover Page

Date: The date represents the date the Agreement becomes effective. It may be the date that an oral agreement was reached, the date the Agreement was originally submitted to the Owner, the date authorizing action was taken or the date of actual execution. Professional services should not be performed prior to the effective date of the Agreement.

Identification of Parties: Parties to this Agreement should be identified using the full legal name under which the Agreement is to be executed, including a designation of the legal status of both parties (sole proprietorship, partnership, joint venture, unincorporated association, limited partnership or corporation [general, closed or professional], etc.). Where appropriate, a copy of the resolution authorizing the individual to act on behalf of the firm or entity should be attached.

Project Description: The proposed Project should be described in sufficient detail to identify (1) the official name or title of the facility, (2) the location of the site, if known, (3) the proposed building type and usage, and (4) the size, capacity or scope of the Project, if known.

3. Article 11—Basis of Compensation

Paragraph 11.1
Insert the dollar amount of the initial payment.

Subparagraph 11.2.1
Sample language is provided below for describing four methods of computing compensation.

Compensation—Multiple of Direct Personnel Expense: "Compensation for services rendered by Principals, employe[illegible] sional consultants shall be based on a Multiple of Direct Personnel Expense in the same manner as [illegible] S[illegible]agraph 11.3.2."

Compensation—Professional Fee Plus Expenses: "Compensation shall be a Fixed Fee of Doll[illegible]) plus compensation for services rendered by Principals, employees and professional consultan[illegible] the [illegible] man[illegible]s described in Subparagraph 11.3.2."

Compensation—Stipulated Sum: "Compensation shall be a stipulated sum of Dollars ($)."

Compensation—Percentage of Construction Cost: "Compensation shall be base[illegible] on [illegible] the follo[illegible]ing Percentages of Construction Cost, as defined in Article 5:

For portions of the Project to be awarded under:

A single stipulated-sum construction contract:	pe[illegible] %)
Separate stipulated-sum construction contracts:	[illegible] (%)
A single cost-plus construction contract:	perc[illegible] %)
Separate cost-plus construction contra[illegible]	percent[illegible] %)"

Subparagraph 11.2.2
For compensation based on pr[illegible]sio[illegible] [illegible]enses, stipulated [illegible]r perce[illegible] of [illegible]ruction Cost, insert the percentages of total payment payab[illegible] [illegible]ch se[illegible] ph[illegible] [illegible]ervices. The[illegible] [illegible]cent[illegible] may [illegible] each Project and do not necessarily have a direct relations[illegible] time a[illegible] [illegible]rts of the Arch[illegible]ct.

Because phases may overlap [illegible]e, these [illegible]rcentages have [illegible] exp[illegible] [illegible]ly for each phase, rather than cumulatively. This facilitate[illegible] when se[illegible] are being provi[illegible] in mo[illegible] on[illegible] at a time.

Subparagr[illegible] 11[illegible]
Inse[illegible] b[illegible] [illegible]sation for Proje[illegible] [illegible]senta[illegible] Beyond [illegible]sic Services.

Subp[illegible]raph 1[illegible]
[illegible] a[illegible] and Principals and [illegible] classified in accordance with the AIA publication *Compensation Guidelines [illegible]al/Engineering Services,* insert:

(a) [illegible]ncipals' time at the fixed rate of Dollars ($) per hour.
For the purposes of this Agreement, the Principals are: (list Principals)

(b) Supervisory time at the fixed rate of Dollars ($) per hour.
For the purposes of this Agreement, supervisory personnel include: (Describe supervisory personnel by job title, such as Project Architect.)

(c) Technical Level I time at the fixed rate of Dollars ($) per hour.
For the purposes of this Agreement, Technical Level I personnel include: (Describe by job title, such as Senior Designer, Specifier, etc.)

(d) Technical Level II time at the fixed rate of Dollars ($) per hour.
For the purposes of this Agreement, Technical Level II personnel include: (Describe by job title, such as Junior Designer, Senior Draftsman, etc.)

(e) Technical Level III and clerical time at the fixed rate of Dollars ($) per hour.
For the purposes of this Agreement, Technical Level III and clerical personnel include: (Describe by job title, such as Junior Draftsman, Secretary, etc.)

If a multiple of Direct Personnel Expense is used, insert: "Principals' and employees' time at a multiple of ( ) times their Direct Personnel Expense as defined by the AIA publication *Compensation Guidelines for Architectural/Engineering Services.*"

If a multiple of direct salaries is used, the term "Direct Salaries" should be substituted for Direct Personnel Expense above.

Subparagraph 11.3.3
Insert the multiple to be used to determine the cost to the Architect of Additional Services of consultants as defined in Article 3 or Article 12.

Subparagraph 11.4.1
Insert the multiple to be used to determine the amount due the Architect, Architect's employees or consultants for Reimbursable Expenses as described in Paragraph 10.2 or Article 12.

Subparagraph 11.5.1
Insert the number of months beyond which the Architect shall be compensated for Basic Services on the same basis as for Additional Services.

Paragraph 11.5.2
Insert the percentage rate and basis (monthly, annual) of interest charges.

Article 12—Other Conditions or Services

Insert provisions, if any, on additional phases of services, Additional Services, special compensation arrangemen[illegible] other [illegible] sultants, the choice of project delivery method or any other conditions.

E. EXECUTION OF THE AGREEMENT

Each person executing the Agreement should indicate the capacity in which they are acting (i[illegible], p[illegible]nt, [illegible]ner, etc.) and the authority under which they are executing the Agreement. Where appropriate, a copy [illegible]eso[illegible] au[illegible]he individual to act on behalf of the firm or entity should be attached.

THE AMERICAN INSTITUTE OF ARCHITECTS

AIA Document B141

Standard Form of Agreement Between Owner and Architect

1987 EDITION

THIS DOCUMENT HAS IMPORTANT LEGAL CONSEQUENCES; CONSULTATION WITH AN ATTORNEY IS ENCOURAGED WITH RESPECT TO ITS COMPLETION OR MODIFICATION.

AGREEMENT

made as of the day of in the year of Nineteen Hundred and

BETWEEN the Owner:
(Name and address)

and the Architect:
(Name and address)

For the following Project:
(Include detailed description of Project, location, address and scope.)

The Owner and Architect agree as set forth below.

TERMS AND CONDITIONS OF AGREEMENT BETWEEN OWNER AND ARCHITECT

ARTICLE 1
ARCHITECT'S RESPONSIBILITIES

1.1 ARCHITECT'S SERVICES

1.1.1 The Architect's services consist of those services performed by the Architect, Architect's employees and Architect's consultants as enumerated in Articles 2 and 3 of this Agreement and any other services included in Article 12.

1.1.2 The Architect's services shall be performed as expeditiously as is consistent with professional skill and care and the orderly progress of the Work. Upon request of the Owner, the Architect shall submit for the Owner's approval a schedule for the performance of the Architect's services which may be adjusted as the Project proceeds, and shall include allowances for periods of time required for the Owner's review and for approval of submissions by authorities having jurisdiction over the Project. Time limits established by this schedule approved by the Owner shall not, except for reasonable cause, be exceeded by the Architect or Owner.

1.1.3 The services covered by this Agreement are subject to the time limitations contained in Subparagraph 11.5.1.

ARTICLE 2
SCOPE OF ARCHITECT'S BASIC SERVICES

2.1 DEFINITION

2.1.1 The Architect's Basic Services consist of those described in Paragraphs 2.2 through 2.6 and any other services identified in Article 12 as part of Basic Services, and include normal structural, mechanical and electrical engineering services.

2.2 SCHEMATIC DESIGN PHASE

2.2.1 The Architect shall review the program furnished by the Owner to ascertain the requirements of the Project and shall arrive at a mutual understanding of such requirements with the Owner.

2.2.2 The Architect shall provide a preliminary evaluation of the Owner's program, schedule and construction budget requirements, each in terms of the other, subject to the limitations set forth in Subparagraph 5.2.1.

2.2.3 The Architect shall review with the Owner alternative approaches to design and construction of the Project.

2.2.4 Based on the mutually agreed-upon program, schedule and construction budget requirements, the Architect shall prepare, for approval by the Owner, Schematic Design Documents consisting of drawings and other documents illustrating the scale and relationship of Project components.

2.2.5 The Architect shall submit to the Owner a preliminary estimate of Construction Cost based on current area, volume or other unit costs.

2.3 DESIGN DEVELOPMENT PHASE

2.3.1 Based on the approved Schematic Design Documents and any adjustments authorized by the Owner in the program, schedule or construction budget, the Architect shall prepare, for approval by the Owner, Design Development Documents consisting of drawings and other documents to fix and describe the size and character of the Project as to architectural, structural, mechanical and electrical systems, materials and such other elements as may be appropriate.

2.3.2 The Architect shall advise the Owner of any adjustments to the preliminary estimate of Construction Cost.

2.4 CONSTRUCTION DOCUMENTS PHASE

2.4.1 Based on the approved Design Development Documents and any further adjustments in the scope or quality of the Project or in the construction budget authorized by the Owner, the Architect shall prepare, for approval by the Owner, Construction Documents consisting of Drawings and Specifications setting forth in detail the requirements for the construction of the Project.

2.4.2 The Architect shall assist the Owner in the preparation of the necessary bidding information, bidding forms, the Conditions of the Contract, and the form of Agreement between the Owner and Contractor.

2.4.3 The Architect shall advise the Owner of any adjustments to previous preliminary estimates of Construction Cost indicated by changes in requirements or general market conditions.

2.4.4 The Architect shall assist the Owner in connection with the Owner's responsibility for filing documents required for the approval of governmental authorities having jurisdiction over the Project.

2.5 BIDDING OR NEGOTIATION PHASE

2.5.1 The Architect, following the Owner's approval of the Construction Documents and of the latest preliminary estimate of Construction Cost, shall assist the Owner in obtaining bids or negotiated proposals and assist in awarding and preparing contracts for construction.

2.6 CONSTRUCTION PHASE—ADMINISTRATION OF THE CONSTRUCTION CONTRACT

2.6.1 The Architect's responsibility to provide Basic Services for the Construction Phase under this Agreement commences with the award of the Contract for Construction and terminates at the earlier of the issuance to the Owner of the final Certificate for Payment or 60 days after the date of Substantial Completion of the Work, unless extended under the terms of Subparagraph 10.3.3.

2.6.2 The Architect shall provide administration of the Contract for Construction as set forth below and in the edition of AIA Document A201, General Conditions of the Contract for Construction, current as of the date of this Agreement, unless otherwise provided in this Agreement.

2.6.3 Duties, responsibilities and limitations of authority of the Architect shall not be restricted, modified or extended without written agreement of the Owner and Architect with consent of the Contractor, which consent shall not be unreasonably withheld.

2.6.4 The Architect shall be a representative of and shall advise and consult with the Owner (1) during construction until final payment to the Contractor is due, and (2) as an Additional Service at the Owner's direction from time to time during the correction period described in the Contract for Construction. The Architect shall have authority to act on behalf of the Owner only to the extent provided in this Agreement unless otherwise modified by written instrument.

2.6.5 The Architect shall visit the site at intervals appropriate to the stage of construction or as otherwise agreed by the Owner and Architect in writing to become generally familiar with the progress and quality of the Work completed and to determine in general if the Work is being performed in a manner indicating that the Work when completed will be in accordance with the Contract Documents. However, the Architect shall not be required to make exhaustive or continuous on-site inspections to check the quality or quantity of the Work. On the basis of on-site observations as an architect, the Architect shall keep the Owner informed of the progress and quality of the Work, and shall endeavor to guard the Owner against defects and deficiencies in the Work. *(More extensive site representation may be agreed to as an Additional Service, as described in Paragraph 3.2.)*

2.6.6 The Architect shall not have control over or charge of and shall not be responsible for construction means, methods, techniques, sequences or procedures, or for safety precautions and programs in connection with the Work, since these are solely the Contractor's responsibility under the Contract for Construction. The Architect shall not be responsible for the Contractor's schedules or failure to carry out the Work in accordance with the Contract Documents. The Architect shall not have control over or charge of acts or omissions of the Contractor, Subcontractors, or their agents or employees, or of any other persons performing portions of the Work.

2.6.7 The Architect shall at all times have access to the Work wherever it is in preparation or progress.

2.6.8 Except as may otherwise be provided in the Contract Documents or when direct communications have been specially authorized, the Owner and Contractor shall communicate through the Architect. Communications by and with the Architect's consultants shall be through the Architect.

2.6.9 Based on the Architect's observations and evaluations of the Contractor's Applications for Payment, the Architect shall review and certify the amounts due the Contractor.

2.6.10 The Architect's certification for payment shall constitute a representation to the Owner, based on the Architect's observations at the site as provided in Subparagraph 2.6.5 and on the data comprising the Contractor's Application for Payment, that the Work has progressed to the point indicated and that, to the best of the Architect's knowledge, information and belief, quality of the Work is in accordance with the Contract Documents. The foregoing representations are subject to an evaluation of the Work for conformance with the Contract Documents upon Substantial Completion, to results of subsequent tests and inspections, to minor deviations from the Contract Documents correctable prior to completion and to specific qualifications expressed by the Architect. The issuance of a Certificate for Payment shall further constitute a representation that the Contractor is entitled to payment in the amount certified. However, the issuance of a Certificate for Payment shall not be a representation that the Architect has (1) made exhaustive or continuous on-site inspections to check the quality or quantity of the Work, (2) reviewed construction means, methods, techniques, sequences or procedures, (3) reviewed copies of requisitions received from Subcontractors and material suppliers and other data requested by the Owner to substantiate the Contractor's right to payment or (4) ascertained how or for what purpose the Contractor has used money previously paid on account of the Contract Sum.

2.6.11 The Architect shall have authority to reject Work which does not conform to the Contract Documents. Whenever the Architect considers it necessary or advisable for implementation of the intent of the Contract Documents, the Architect will have authority to require additional inspection or testing of the Work in accordance with the provisions of the Contract Documents, whether or not such Work is fabricated, installed or completed. However, neither this authority of the Architect nor a decision made in good faith either to exercise or not to exercise such authority shall give rise to a duty or responsibility of the Architect to the Contractor, Subcontractors, material and equipment suppliers, their agents or employees or other persons performing portions of the Work.

2.6.12 The Architect shall review and approve or take other appropriate action upon Contractor's submittals such as Shop Drawings, Product Data and Samples, but only for the limited purpose of checking for conformance with information given and the design concept expressed in the Contract Documents. The Architect's action shall be taken with such reasonable promptness as to cause no delay in the Work or in the construction of the Owner or of separate contractors, while allowing sufficient time in the Architect's professional judgment to permit adequate review. Review of such submittals is not conducted for the purpose of determining the accuracy and completeness of other details such as dimensions and quantities or for substantiating instructions for installation or performance of equipment or systems designed by the Contractor, all of which remain the responsibility of the Contractor to the extent required by the Contract Documents. The Architect's review shall not constitute approval of safety precautions or, unless otherwise specifically stated by the Architect, of construction means, methods, techniques, sequences or procedures. The Architect's approval of a specific item shall not indicate approval of an assembly of which the item is a component. When professional certification of performance characteristics of materials, systems or equipment is required by the Contract Documents, the Architect shall be entitled to rely upon such certification to establish that the materials, systems or equipment will meet the performance criteria required by the Contract Documents.

2.6.13 The Architect shall prepare Change Orders and Construction Change Directives, with supporting documentation and data if deemed necessary by the Architect as provided in Subparagraphs 3.1.1 and 3.3.3, for the Owner's approval and execution in accordance with the Contract Documents, and may authorize minor changes in the Work not involving an adjustment in the Contract Sum or an extension of the Contract Time which are not inconsistent with the intent of the Contract Documents.

2.6.14 The Architect shall conduct inspections to determine the date or dates of Substantial Completion and the date of final completion, shall receive and forward to the Owner for the Owner's review and records written warranties and related documents required by the Contract Documents and assembled by the Contractor, and shall issue a final Certificate for Payment upon compliance with the requirements of the Contract Documents.

2.6.15 The Architect shall interpret and decide matters concerning performance of the Owner and Contractor under the requirements of the Contract Documents on written request of either the Owner or Contractor. The Architect's response to such requests shall be made with reasonable promptness and within any time limits agreed upon.

2.6.16 Interpretations and decisions of the Architect shall be consistent with the intent of and reasonably inferable from the Contract Documents and shall be in writing or in the form of drawings. When making such interpretations and initial decisions, the Architect shall endeavor to secure faithful performance by both Owner and Contractor, shall not show partiality to either, and shall not be liable for results of interpretations or decisions so rendered in good faith.

2.6.17 The Architect's decisions on matters relating to aesthetic effect shall be final if consistent with the intent expressed in the Contract Documents.

2.6.18 The Architect shall render written decisions within a reasonable time on all claims, disputes or other matters in question between the Owner and Contractor relating to the execution or progress of the Work as provided in the Contract Documents.

2.6.19 The Architect's decisions on claims, disputes or other matters, including those in question between the Owner and Contractor, except for those relating to aesthetic effect as provided in Subparagraph 2.6.17, shall be subject to arbitration as provided in this Agreement and in the Contract Documents.

ARTICLE 3
ADDITIONAL SERVICES

3.1 GENERAL

3.1.1 The services described in this Article 3 are not included in Basic Services unless so identified in Article 12, and they shall be paid for by the Owner as provided in this Agreement, in addition to the compensation for Basic Services. The services described under Paragraphs 3.2 and 3.4 shall only be provided if authorized or confirmed in writing by the Owner. If services described under Contingent Additional Services in Paragraph 3.3 are required due to circumstances beyond the Architect's control, the Architect shall notify the Owner prior to commencing such services. If the Owner deems that such services described under Paragraph 3.3 are not required, the Owner shall give prompt written notice to the Architect. If the Owner indicates in writing that all or part of such Contingent Additional Services are not required, the Architect shall have no obligation to provide those services.

3.2 PROJECT REPRESENTATION BEYOND BASIC SERVICES

3.2.1 If more extensive representation at the site than is described in Subparagraph 2.6.5 is required, the Architect shall provide one or more Project Representatives to assist in carrying out such additional on-site responsibilities.

3.2.2 Project Representatives shall be selected, employed and directed by the Architect, and the Architect shall be compensated therefor as agreed by the Owner and Architect. The duties, responsibilities and limitations of authority of Project Representatives shall be as described in the edition of AIA Document B352 current as of the date of this Agreement, unless otherwise agreed.

3.2.3 Through the observations by such Project Representatives, the Architect shall endeavor to provide further protection for the Owner against defects and deficiencies in the Work, but the furnishing of such project representation shall not modify the rights, responsibilities or obligations of the Architect as described elsewhere in this Agreement.

3.3 CONTINGENT ADDITIONAL SERVICES

3.3.1 Making revisions in Drawings, Specifications or other documents when such revisions are:

- **.1** inconsistent with approvals or instructions previously given by the Owner, including revisions made necessary by adjustments in the Owner's program or Project budget;
- **.2** required by the enactment or revision of codes, laws or regulations subsequent to the preparation of such documents; or
- **.3** due to changes required as a result of the Owner's failure to render decisions in a timely manner.

3.3.2 Providing services required because of significant changes in the Project including, but not limited to, size, quality, complexity, the Owner's schedule, or the method of bidding or negotiating and contracting for construction, except for services required under Subparagraph 5.2.5.

3.3.3 Preparing Drawings, Specifications and other documentation and supporting data, evaluating Contractor's proposals, and providing other services in connection with Change Orders and Construction Change Directives.

3.3.4 Providing services in connection with evaluating substitutions proposed by the Contractor and making subsequent revisions to Drawings, Specifications and other documentation resulting therefrom.

3.3.5 Providing consultation concerning replacement of Work damaged by fire or other cause during construction, and furnishing services required in connection with the replacement of such Work.

3.3.6 Providing services made necessary by the default of the Contractor, by major defects or deficiencies in the Work of the Contractor, or by failure of performance of either the Owner or Contractor under the Contract for Construction.

3.3.7 Providing services in evaluating an extensive number of claims submitted by the Contractor or others in connection with the Work.

3.3.8 Providing services in connection with a public hearing, arbitration proceeding or legal proceeding except where the Architect is party thereto.

3.3.9 Preparing documents for alternate, separate or sequential bids or providing services in connection with bidding, negotiation or construction prior to the completion of the Construction Documents Phase.

3.4 OPTIONAL ADDITIONAL SERVICES

3.4.1 Providing analyses of the Owner's needs and programming the requirements of the Project.

3.4.2 Providing financial feasibility or other special studies.

3.4.3 Providing planning surveys, site evaluations or comparative studies of prospective sites.

3.4.4 Providing special surveys, environmental studies and submissions required for approvals of governmental authorities or others having jurisdiction over the Project.

3.4.5 Providing services relative to future facilities, systems and equipment.

3.4.6 Providing services to investigate existing conditions or facilities or to make measured drawings thereof.

3.4.7 Providing services to verify the accuracy of drawings or other information furnished by the Owner.

3.4.8 Providing coordination of construction performed by separate contractors or by the Owner's own forces and coordination of services required in connection with construction performed and equipment supplied by the Owner.

3.4.9 Providing services in connection with the work of a construction manager or separate consultants retained by the Owner.

3.4.10 Providing detailed estimates of Construction Cost.

3.4.11 Providing detailed quantity surveys or inventories of material, equipment and labor.

3.4.12 Providing analyses of owning and operating costs.

3.4.13 Providing interior design and other similar services required for or in connection with the selection, procurement or installation of furniture, furnishings and related equipment.

3.4.14 Providing services for planning tenant or rental spaces.

3.4.15 Making investigations, inventories of materials or equipment, or valuations and detailed appraisals of existing facilities.

3.4.16 Preparing a set of reproducible record drawings showing significant changes in the Work made during construction based on marked-up prints, drawings and other data furnished by the Contractor to the Architect.

3.4.17 Providing assistance in the utilization of equipment or systems such as testing, adjusting and balancing, preparation of operation and maintenance manuals, training personnel for operation and maintenance, and consultation during operation.

3.4.18 Providing services after issuance to the Owner of the final Certificate for Payment, or in the absence of a final Certificate for Payment, more than 60 days after the date of Substantial Completion of the Work.

3.4.19 Providing services of consultants for other than architectural, structural, mechanical and electrical engineering portions of the Project provided as a part of Basic Services.

3.4.20 Providing any other services not otherwise included in this Agreement or not customarily furnished in accordance with generally accepted architectural practice.

ARTICLE 4

OWNER'S RESPONSIBILITIES

4.1 The Owner shall provide full information regarding requirements for the Project, including a program which shall set forth the Owner's objectives, schedule, constraints and criteria, including space requirements and relationships, flexibility, expandability, special equipment, systems and site requirements.

4.2 The Owner shall establish and update an overall budget for the Project, including the Construction Cost, the Owner's other costs and reasonable contingencies related to all of these costs.

4.3 If requested by the Architect, the Owner shall furnish evidence that financial arrangements have been made to fulfill the Owner's obligations under this Agreement.

4.4 The Owner shall designate a representative authorized to act on the Owner's behalf with respect to the Project. The Owner or such authorized representative shall render decisions in a timely manner pertaining to documents submitted by the Architect in order to avoid unreasonable delay in the orderly and sequential progress of the Architect's services.

4.5 The Owner shall furnish surveys describing physical characteristics, legal limitations and utility locations for the site of the Project, and a written legal description of the site. The surveys and legal information shall include, as applicable, grades and lines of streets, alleys, pavements and adjoining property and structures; adjacent drainage; rights-of-way, restrictions, easements, encroachments, zoning, deed restrictions, boundaries and contours of the site; locations, dimensions and necessary data pertaining to existing buildings, other improvements and trees; and information concerning available utility services and lines, both public and private, above and below grade, including inverts and depths. All the information on the survey shall be referenced to a project benchmark.

4.6 The Owner shall furnish the services of geotechnical engineers when such services are requested by the Architect. Such services may include but are not limited to test borings, test pits, determinations of soil bearing values, percolation tests, evaluations of hazardous materials, ground corrosion and resistivity tests, including necessary operations for anticipating subsoil conditions, with reports and appropriate professional recommendations.

4.6.1 The Owner shall furnish the services of other consultants when such services are reasonably required by the scope of the Project and are requested by the Architect.

4.7 The Owner shall furnish structural, mechanical, chemical, air and water pollution tests, tests for hazardous materials, and other laboratory and environmental tests, inspections and reports required by law or the Contract Documents.

4.8 The Owner shall furnish all legal, accounting and insurance counseling services as may be necessary at any time for the Project, including auditing services the Owner may require to verify the Contractor's Applications for Payment or to ascertain how or for what purposes the Contractor has used the money paid by or on behalf of the Owner.

4.9 The services, information, surveys and reports required by Paragraphs 4.5 through 4.8 shall be furnished at the Owner's expense, and the Architect shall be entitled to rely upon the accuracy and completeness thereof.

4.10 Prompt written notice shall be given by the Owner to the Architect if the Owner becomes aware of any fault or defect in the Project or nonconformance with the Contract Documents.

4.11 The proposed language of certificates or certifications requested of the Architect or Architect's consultants shall be submitted to the Architect for review and approval at least 14 days prior to execution. The Owner shall not request certifications that would require knowledge or services beyond the scope of this Agreement.

ARTICLE 5
CONSTRUCTION COST

5.1 DEFINITION

5.1.1 The Construction Cost shall be the total cost or estimated cost to the Owner of all elements of the Project designed or specified by the Architect.

5.1.2 The Construction Cost shall include the cost at current market rates of labor and materials furnished by the Owner and equipment designed, specified, selected or specially provided for by the Architect, plus a reasonable allowance for the Contractor's overhead and profit. In addition, a reasonable allowance for contingencies shall be included for market conditions at the time of bidding and for changes in the Work during construction.

5.1.3 Construction Cost does not include the compensation of the Architect and Architect's consultants, the costs of the land, rights-of-way, financing or other costs which are the responsibility of the Owner as provided in Article 4.

5.2 RESPONSIBILITY FOR CONSTRUCTION COST

5.2.1 Evaluations of the Owner's Project budget, preliminary estimates of Construction Cost and detailed estimates of Construction Cost, if any, prepared by the Architect, represent the Architect's best judgment as a design professional familiar with the construction industry. It is recognized, however, that neither the Architect nor the Owner has control over the cost of labor, materials or equipment, over the Contractor's methods of determining bid prices, or over competitive bidding, market or negotiating conditions. Accordingly, the Architect cannot and does not warrant or represent that bids or negotiated prices will not vary from the Owner's Project budget or from any estimate of Construction Cost or evaluation prepared or agreed to by the Architect.

5.2.2 No fixed limit of Construction Cost shall be established as a condition of this Agreement by the furnishing, proposal or establishment of a Project budget, unless such fixed limit has been agreed upon in writing and signed by the parties hereto. If such a fixed limit has been established, the Architect shall be permitted to include contingencies for design, bidding and price escalation, to determine what materials, equipment, component systems and types of construction are to be included in the Contract Documents, to make reasonable adjustments in the scope of the Project and to include in the Contract Documents alternate bids to adjust the Construction Cost to the fixed limit. Fixed limits, if any, shall be increased in the amount of an increase in the Contract Sum occurring after execution of the Contract for Construction.

5.2.3 If the Bidding or Negotiation Phase has not commenced within 90 days after the Architect submits the Construction Documents to the Owner, any Project budget or fixed limit of Construction Cost shall be adjusted to reflect changes in the general level of prices in the construction industry between the date of submission of the Construction Documents to the Owner and the date on which proposals are sought.

5.2.4 If a fixed limit of Construction Cost (adjusted as provided in Subparagraph 5.2.3) is exceeded by the lowest bona fide bid or negotiated proposal, the Owner shall:

.1 give written approval of an increase in such fixed limit;

.2 authorize rebidding or renegotiating of the Project within a reasonable time;

.3 if the Project is abandoned, terminate in accordance with Paragraph 8.3; or

.4 cooperate in revising the Project scope and quality as required to reduce the Construction Cost.

5.2.5 If the Owner chooses to proceed under Clause 5.2.4.4, the Architect, without additional charge, shall modify the Contract Documents as necessary to comply with the fixed limit, if established as a condition of this Agreement. The modification of Contract Documents shall be the limit of the Architect's responsibility arising out of the establishment of a fixed limit. The Architect shall be entitled to compensation in accordance with this Agreement for all services performed whether or not the Construction Phase is commenced.

ARTICLE 6
USE OF ARCHITECT'S DRAWINGS, SPECIFICATIONS AND OTHER DOCUMENTS

6.1 The Drawings, Specifications and other documents prepared by the Architect for this Project are instruments of the Architect's service for use solely with respect to this Project and, unless otherwise provided, the Architect shall be deemed the author of these documents and shall retain all common law, statutory and other reserved rights, including the copyright. The Owner shall be permitted to retain copies, including reproducible copies, of the Architect's Drawings, Specifications and other documents for information and reference in connection with the Owner's use and occupancy of the Project. The Architect's Drawings, Specifications or other documents shall not be used by the Owner or others on other projects, for additions to this Project or for completion of this Project by others, unless the Architect is adjudged to be in default under this Agreement, except by agreement in writing and with appropriate compensation to the Architect.

6.2 Submission or distribution of documents to meet official regulatory requirements or for similar purposes in connection with the Project is not to be construed as publication in derogation of the Architect's reserved rights.

ARTICLE 7
ARBITRATION

7.1 Claims, disputes or other matters in question between the parties to this Agreement arising out of or relating to this Agreement or breach thereof shall be subject to and decided by arbitration in accordance with the Construction Industry Arbitration Rules of the American Arbitration Association currently in effect unless the parties mutually agree otherwise.

7.2 Demand for arbitration shall be filed in writing with the other party to this Agreement and with the American Arbitration Association. A demand for arbitration shall be made within a reasonable time after the claim, dispute or other matter in question has arisen. In no event shall the demand for arbitration be made after the date when institution of legal or equitable proceedings based on such claim, dispute or other matter in question would be barred by the applicable statutes of limitations.

7.3 No arbitration arising out of or relating to this Agreement shall include, by consolidation, joinder or in any other manner, an additional person or entity not a party to this Agreement, except by written consent containing a specific reference to this Agreement signed by the Owner, Architect, and any other person or entity sought to be joined. Consent to arbitration involving an additional person or entity shall not constitute consent to arbitration of any claim, dispute or other matter in question not described in the written consent or with a person or entity not named or described therein. The foregoing agreement to arbitrate and other agreements to arbitrate with an additional person or entity duly consented to by the parties to this Agreement shall be specifically enforceable in accordance with applicable law in any court having jurisdiction thereof.

7.4 The award rendered by the arbitrator or arbitrators shall be final, and judgment may be entered upon it in accordance with applicable law in any court having jurisdiction thereof.

ARTICLE 8

TERMINATION, SUSPENSION OR ABANDONMENT

8.1 This Agreement may be terminated by either party upon not less than seven days' written notice should the other party fail substantially to perform in accordance with the terms of this Agreement through no fault of the party initiating the termination.

8.2 If the Project is suspended by the Owner for more than 30 consecutive days, the Architect shall be compensated for services performed prior to notice of such suspension. When the Project is resumed, the Architect's compensation shall be equitably adjusted to provide for expenses incurred in the interruption and resumption of the Architect's services.

8.3 This Agreement may be terminated by the Owner upon not less than seven days' written notice to the Architect in the event that the Project is permanently abandoned. If the Project is abandoned by the Owner for more than 90 consecutive days, the Architect may terminate this Agreement by giving written notice.

8.4 Failure of the Owner to make payments to the Architect in accordance with this Agreement shall be considered substantial nonperformance and cause for termination.

8.5 If the Owner fails to make payment when due the Architect for services and expenses, the Architect may, upon seven days' written notice to the Owner, suspend performance of services under this Agreement. Unless payment in full is received by the Architect within seven days of the date of the notice, the suspension shall take effect without further notice. In the event of a suspension of services, the Architect shall have no liability to the Owner for delay or damage caused the Owner because of such suspension of services.

8.6 In the event of termination not the fault of the Architect, the Architect shall be compensated for services performed prior to termination, together with Reimbursable Expenses then due and all Termination Expenses as defined in Paragraph 8.7.

8.7 Termination Expenses are in addition to compensation for Basic and Additional Services, and include expenses which are directly attributable to termination. Termination Expenses shall be computed as a percentage of the total compensation for Basic Services and Additional Services earned to the time of termination, as follows:

.1 Twenty percent of the total compensation for Basic and Additional Services earned to date if termination occurs before or during the predesign, site analysis, or Schematic Design Phases; or

.2 Ten percent of the total compensation for Basic and Additional Services earned to date if termination occurs during the Design Development Phase; or

.3 Five percent of the total compensation for Basic and Additional Services earned to date if termination occurs during any subsequent phase.

ARTICLE 9

MISCELLANEOUS PROVISIONS

9.1 Unless otherwise provided, this Agreement shall be governed by the law of the principal place of business of the Architect.

9.2 Terms in this Agreement shall have the same meaning as those in AIA Document A201, General Conditions of the Contract for Construction, current as of the date of this Agreement.

9.3 Causes of action between the parties to this Agreement pertaining to acts or failures to act shall be deemed to have accrued and the applicable statutes of limitations shall commence to run not later than either the date of Substantial Completion for acts or failures to act occurring prior to Substantial Completion, or the date of issuance of the final Certificate for Payment for acts or failures to act occurring after Substantial Completion.

9.4 The Owner and Architect waive all rights against each other and against the contractors, consultants, agents and employees of the other for damages, but only to the extent covered by property insurance during construction, except such rights as they may have to the proceeds of such insurance as set forth in the edition of AIA Document A201, General Conditions of the Contract for Construction, current as of the date of this Agreement. The Owner and Architect each shall require similar waivers from their contractors, consultants and agents.

9.5 The Owner and Architect, respectively, bind themselves, their partners, successors, assigns and legal representatives to the other party to this Agreement and to the partners, successors, assigns and legal representatives of such other party with respect to all covenants of this Agreement. Neither Owner nor Architect shall assign this Agreement without the written consent of the other.

9.6 This Agreement represents the entire and integrated agreement between the Owner and Architect and supersedes all prior negotiations, representations or agreements, either written or oral. This Agreement may be amended only by written instrument signed by both Owner and Architect.

9.7 Nothing contained in this Agreement shall create a contractual relationship with or a cause of action in favor of a third party against either the Owner or Architect.

9.8 Unless otherwise provided in this Agreement, the Architect and Architect's consultants shall have no responsibility for the discovery, presence, handling, removal or disposal of or exposure of persons to hazardous materials in any form at the Project site, including but not limited to asbestos, asbestos products, polychlorinated biphenyl (PCB) or other toxic substances.

9.9 The Architect shall have the right to include representations of the design of the Project, including photographs of the exterior and interior, among the Architect's promotional and professional materials. The Architect's materials shall not include the Owner's confidential or proprietary information if the Owner has previously advised the Architect in writing of the specific information considered by the Owner to be confidential or proprietary. The Owner shall provide professional credit for the Architect on the construction sign and in the promotional materials for the Project.

ARTICLE 10
PAYMENTS TO THE ARCHITECT

10.1 DIRECT PERSONNEL EXPENSE

10.1.1 Direct Personnel Expense is defined as the direct salaries of the Architect's personnel engaged on the Project and the portion of the cost of their mandatory and customary contributions and benefits related thereto, such as employment taxes and other statutory employee benefits, insurance, sick leave, holidays, vacations, pensions and similar contributions and benefits.

10.2 REIMBURSABLE EXPENSES

10.2.1 Reimbursable Expenses are in addition to compensation for Basic and Additional Services and include expenses incurred by the Architect and Architect's employees and consultants in the interest of the Project, as identified in the following Clauses.

10.2.1.1 Expense of transportation in connection with the Project; expenses in connection with authorized out-of-town travel; long-distance communications; and fees paid for securing approval of authorities having jurisdiction over the Project.

10.2.1.2 Expense of reproductions, postage and handling of Drawings, Specifications and other documents.

10.2.1.3 If authorized in advance by the Owner, expense of overtime work requiring higher than regular rates.

10.2.1.4 Expense of renderings, models and mock-ups requested by the Owner.

10.2.1.5 Expense of additional insurance coverage or limits, including professional liability insurance, requested by the Owner in excess of that normally carried by the Architect and Architect's consultants.

10.2.1.6 Expense of computer-aided design and drafting equipment time when used in connection with the Project.

10.3 PAYMENTS ON ACCOUNT OF BASIC SERVICES

10.3.1 An initial payment as set forth in Paragraph 11.1 is the minimum payment under this Agreement.

10.3.2 Subsequent payments for Basic Services shall be made monthly and, where applicable, shall be in proportion to services performed within each phase of service, on the basis set forth in Subparagraph 11.2.2.

10.3.3 If and to the extent that the time initially established in Subparagraph 11.5.1 of this Agreement is exceeded or extended through no fault of the Architect, compensation for any services rendered during the additional period of time shall be computed in the manner set forth in Subparagraph 11.3.2.

10.3.4 When compensation is based on a percentage of Construction Cost and any portions of the Project are deleted or otherwise not constructed, compensation for those portions of the Project shall be payable to the extent services are performed on those portions, in accordance with the schedule set forth in Subparagraph 11.2.2, based on (1) the lowest bona fide bid or negotiated proposal, or (2) if no such bid or proposal is received, the most recent preliminary estimate of Construction Cost or detailed estimate of Construction Cost for such portions of the Project.

10.4 PAYMENTS ON ACCOUNT OF ADDITIONAL SERVICES

10.4.1 Payments on account of the Architect's Additional Services and for Reimbursable Expenses shall be made monthly upon presentation of the Architect's statement of services rendered or expenses incurred.

10.5 PAYMENTS WITHHELD

10.5.1 No deductions shall be made from the Architect's compensation on account of penalty, liquidated damages or other sums withheld from payments to contractors, or on account of the cost of changes in the Work other than those for which the Architect has been found to be liable.

10.6 ARCHITECT'S ACCOUNTING RECORDS

10.6.1 Records of Reimbursable Expenses and expenses pertaining to Additional Services and services performed on the basis of a multiple of Direct Personnel Expense shall be available to the Owner or the Owner's authorized representative at mutually convenient times.

ARTICLE 11
BASIS OF COMPENSATION

The Owner shall compensate the Architect as follows:

11.1 AN INITIAL PAYMENT of Dollars ($)
shall be made upon execution of this Agreement and credited to the Owner's account at final payment.

11.2 BASIC COMPENSATION

11.2.1 FOR BASIC SERVICES, as described in Article 2, and any other services included in Article 12 as part of Basic Services, Basic Compensation shall be computed as follows:

(Insert basis of compensation, including stipulated sums, multiples or percentages, and identify phases to which particular methods of compensation apply, if necessary.)

11.2.2 Where compensation is based on a stipulated sum or percentage of Construction Cost, progress payments for Basic Services in each phase shall total the following percentages of the total Basic Compensation payable:

(Insert additional phases as appropriate.)

Schematic Design Phase:	percent (%)
Design Development Phase:	percent (%)
Construction Documents Phase:	percent (%)
Bidding or Negotiation Phase:	percent (%)
Construction Phase:	percent (%)
Total Basic Compensation:	one hundred percent (100%)

11.3 COMPENSATION FOR ADDITIONAL SERVICES

11.3.1 FOR PROJECT REPRESENTATION BEYOND BASIC SERVICES, as described in Paragraph 3.2, compensation shall be computed as follows:

11.3.2 FOR ADDITIONAL SERVICES OF THE ARCHITECT, as described in Articles 3 and 12, other than (1) Additional Project Representation, as described in Paragraph 3.2, and (2) services included in Article 12 as part of Additional Services, but excluding services of consultants, compensation shall be computed as follows:

(Insert basis of compensation, including rates and/or multiples of Direct Personnel Expense for Principals and employees, and identify Principals and classify employees, if required. Identify specific services to which particular methods of compensation apply, if necessary.)

11.3.3 FOR ADDITIONAL SERVICES OF CONSULTANTS, including additional structural, mechanical and electrical engineering services and those provided under Subparagraph 3.4.19 or identified in Article 12 as part of Additional Services, a multiple of ( ) times the amounts billed to the Architect for such services.

(Identify specific types of consultants in Article 12, if required.)

11.4 REIMBURSABLE EXPENSES

11.4.1 FOR REIMBURSABLE EXPENSES, as described in Paragraph 10.2, and any other items included in Article 12 as Reimbursable Expenses, a multiple of ( ) times the expenses incurred by the Architect, the Architect's employees and consultants in the interest of the Project.

11.5 ADDITIONAL PROVISIONS

11.5.1 IF THE BASIC SERVICES covered by this Agreement have not been completed within ( ) months of the date hereof, through no fault of the Architect, extension of the Architect's services beyond that time shall be compensated as provided in Subparagraphs 10.3.3 and 11.3.2.

11.5.2 Payments are due and payable ( ) days from the date of the Architect's invoice. Amounts unpaid ( ) days after the invoice date shall bear interest at the rate entered below, or in the absence thereof at the legal rate prevailing from time to time at the principal place of business of the Architect.

(Insert rate of interest agreed upon.)

(Usury laws and requirements under the Federal Truth in Lending Act, similar state and local consumer credit laws and other regulations at the Owner's and Architect's principal places of business, the location of the Project and elsewhere may affect the validity of this provision. Specific legal advice should be obtained with respect to deletions or modifications, and also regarding requirements such as written disclosures or waivers.)

11.5.3 The rates and multiples set forth for Additional Services shall be annually adjusted in accordance with normal salary review practices of the Architect.

ARTICLE 12
OTHER CONDITIONS OR SERVICES

(Insert descriptions of other services, identify Additional Services included within Basic Compensation and modifications to the payment and compensation terms included in this Agreement.)

This Agreement entered into as of the day and year first written above.

OWNER

ARCHITECT

(Signature)

(Signature)

(Printed name and title)

(Printed name and title)

INSTRUCTION SHEET *AIA DOCUMENT B141/CMa*

FOR AIA DOCUMENT B141/CM, STANDARD FORM OF AGREEMENT BETWEEN OWNER AND ARCHITECT, CONSTRUCTION MANAGEMENT EDITION—JUNE 1980 EDITION

A. GENERAL INFORMATION

1. Purpose

This Document is intended as the basis for the agreement between the Owner and the Architect for architectural services when a Construction Manager is used on the Project. It provides a choice of several methods of compensation, and the parties may select the appropriate one.

2. Related Documents

This Document is intended to be used in conjunction with the following AIA Documents:

a) A101/CM, Owner-Contractor Agreement, Construction Management Edition
b) A201/CM, General Conditions of the Contract for Construction, Construction Management Edition
c) B801, Owner-Construction Manager Agreement

3. Use of Non-AIA Forms

If a series of non-AIA documents or a mixture of AIA Documents plus non-AIA documents are to be used, particular care must be taken to achieve consistency of language and intent. Certain owners require the use of owner-contractor agreements and other contract forms prepared by them. Such forms should be carefully compared to the standard AIA forms for which they are being substituted before executing an agreement. If there are any significant omissions, additions or variances from the terms of the related standard AIA forms, both legal and insurance counsel should be consulted. Of particular concern is the need for consistency between the Owner-Architect Agreement and the anticipated General Conditions of the Contract for Construction in the delineation of the Architect's Construction Phase services and responsibilities.

4. Letter Forms of Agreement

Letter forms of agreement are generally discouraged by the AIA, as is the performance of a part or the whole of professional services based on oral agreements or understandings. The standard AIA Agreement forms have been developed through more than sixty years of experience and have been tested repeatedly in the courts. In addition, the standard forms have been carefully coordinated with other AIA Documents, including the various Architect-Consultant Agreement forms, the Owner-Contractor Agreements and the General Conditions of the Contract for Construction. The necessity for specific and complete correlation between these documents and any Owner-Architect Agreement used is of paramount importance.

5. Use of Current Documents

Prior to using any AIA Document, the user should consult the AIA or an AIA component to determine the current edition of each Document.

6. Reproduction

AIA Document B141/CM is a copyrighted document, and may not be reproduced or excerpted from in substantial part without the express written permission of the AIA. Purchasers of B141/CM are hereby entitled to reproduce a maximum of ten copies of the completed or executed document for use only in connection with the particular Project. AIA will not permit the reproduction of this Document in blank, or the use of substantial portions of, or language from, this Document, except upon written request and after receipt of written permission from AIA.

B. CHANGES FROM THE PREVIOUS EDITION

1. Format Changes

The compensation provisions have been moved to a position near the end of the Document rather than preceding the Terms and Conditions. Also, the language dealing with alternative methods of computing compensation has been deleted from the Agreement form and is now provided as part of this Instruction Sheet for incorporation by the user.

2. Changes in Content

Numerous changes in content have been made in response to experience with the previous edition, the recognition of concerns of Owners, and the recommendations of AIA members, committees, legal and insurance counsel. The following are some of the significant changes made to the content of the 1975 Edition of B141/CM:

a) **Architect's Services:** Under the Schematic Design, Design Development and Construction Documents Phases, the requirement for the Architect to submit a Statement of Probable Construction Cost has been eliminated. The Architect now has the responsibility to provide the Construction Manager with drawings and other documents for the purpose of preparing an estimate of Construction Cost.

b) **Construction Administration:** Subparagraphs 1.5.7 and 1.5.8 have been modified utilizing the term "Project Certificate for Payment" and require the Construction Manager's recommendation prior to the Architect's action on Applications for Payment.

Subparagraph 1.5.12, dealing with the Architect's authority to require testing and reject nonconforming Work, requires action be taken only after consultation with the Construction Manager.

Subparagraph 1.5.14, pertaining to Change Orders, requires the Architect to review and sign or take other appropriate action on Change Orders *prepared by the Construction Manager.*

Subparagraph 1.7.6 has been added making the providing of services in connection with alternative designs for cost estimating or bidding purposes additional services.

c) **The Owner's Responsibilities:** Paragraph 2.4 has been added stating that the Owner shall retain a Construction Manager and outlining the Construction Manager's duties and responsibilities.

d) **Construction Cost:** Subparagraph 3.1.2 outlines what the construction cost will include and specifically mentions the Construction Manager's compensation and costs.

Subparagraph 3.2.4 outlines the procedure to be followed in the event the project budget or fixed limit of construction cost is exceeded by the sum of the lowest bona fide bids or negotiated proposals. Note that it is the Construction Manager's responsibility to prepare a detailed cost estimate (provided for in B801); and the Architect is required to modify the drawings and specifications as necessary to comply with the fixed limit without additional cost to the Owner, *only* if the Architect has concurred in the Construction Manager's estimate of Construction Cost.

e) **Reimbursable Expense:** This edition provides for reimbursement for reproductions, postage and handling of all drawings, specifications and other documents except those for the use of the Architect and the Architect's consultants.

Expense of any additional insurance coverage or limits requested by the Owner in excess of that normally carried by the Architect or the Architect's consultants will be reimbursable.

f) **Payments to the Architect:** The percentage of the total fee to be paid for each phase of the Work is removed from this Article and is included in Article 14.

Compensation for administration of the Construction Contract beyond the period initially established shall be as set forth in Paragraph 14.[illegible]

g) **Ownership and Use of Documents:** Revised to conform with the [illegible] edition of AIA Document B141.

C. COMPLETING THE B141/CM FORM

1. **Modifications**

As with all AIA Documents users are encouraged to consult an attorney with respect to completing the form. Generally, any necessary modifications can be accomplished by describing in Article 15 changes to the printed text. Legal counsel should also be sought concerning the effect of state and local law on the terms of the Agreement, particularly with respect to registration laws, duties imposed by building codes, interest charges and arbitration.

Cover Page

Date: The date represents the date as of which the Agreement becomes effective. It may be the date that an oral agreement was reached, the date the Agreement was originally submitted to the Owner, the date authorizing action was taken, or the date of actual execution. Professional services should not be performed prior to the effective date of the Agreement.

Identification of Parties: Parties to this Agreement should be identified using the full legal name under which the Agreement is to be executed, including a designation of the legal status of both parties (sole proprietorship, partnership, joint venture, unincorporated association, limited partnership or corporation [general, close or professional], etc.).

Project Description: The proposed Project should be described in sufficient detail to identify (1) the official name or title of the facility, (2) the location of the site, if known, (3) the proposed building type or usage, and (4) the size, capacity or scope of the Project, if known.

3. Article 14—Basis of Compensation

Paragraph 14.1

Insert the amount of the retainer, if any, and indicate whether it will be credited to the first, last, or proportionately to all of the payments on the Owner's account.

Paragraph 14.2, Subparagraph 14.2.1

Compensation—Multiple of Direct Personnel Expense

"Compensation for services rendered by Principals and employees shall be based on a Multiple of Direct Personnel Expense in the same manner as described in Subparagraph 14.4.1, and for the services of professional consultants as described in Subparagraph 14.4.2."

The Architect may wish to include a method of computing Direct Personnel Expense, such as by using a percentage of employee salaries.

Compensation—Professional Fee Plus Expenses

"Compensation shall be based on a Professional Fee of ______________ dollars ($) plus compensation for services rendered by Principals and employees in the same manner as described in Subparagraph 14.4.1, and for the services of professional consultants as described in Subparagraph 14.4.2."

Compensation—Stipulated Sum

"Compensation shall be a Stipulated Sum of ______________ dollars ($)."

Compensation—Percentage of Construction Cost

"Compensation shall be based on one of the following Percentages of Construction Cost, as defined in Article 3:

For portions of the Project to be awarded under:

A single, stipulated sum construction contract:

______________ percent (%)

Separate, stipulated sum construction contracts:

______________ percent (%)

A single, cost-plus construction contract:

______________ percent (%)

Separate, cost-plus construction contracts:

______________ percent (%)."

Paragraph 14.2, Sugparagraph 14.2.2

If applicable, insert the percentages of compensation payable for each separate phase of services. Percentages contained in previous Owner-Architect agreements should be expressed as follows:

Schematic Design Phase:	fifteen percent (15%)
Design Development Phase:	twenty percent (20%)
Construction Documents Phase:	forty percent (40%)
Bidding or Negotiation Phase:	five percent (5%)
Construction Phase:	twenty percent (20%)
Total:	one hundred percent (100%)

Because phases may overlap in time, these percentages have been expressed separately for each phase, rather than cumulatively. This facilitates billing when services are being provided during more than one phase at a time.

Paragraph 14.3

[illegible] AIA Document B352, Duties, Responsibilities and Limitations of Authority of the Architect's Project Representative, [illegible] the agreed compensation arrangement for such services. If this is to be determined at a later date, such as at the time of commencement of the Construction Phase, so indicate.

If a cost of living escalation is to be included, the amount or percentage increase should be stated if it can be determined in advance.

Paragraph 14.4, Subparagraph 14.4.1

If billing rates are used and employees are classified in accordance with the AIA publication *Compensation Guidelines for Architectural and Engineering Services*, insert:

"1. Principals' time at the fixed rate of ______________ dollars ($) per hour. For the purposes of this Article, the Principals are:

2. Supervisory time at the fixed rate of ______________ dollars ($) per hour. For the purposes of this Article, Supervisory personnel include those in the following positions:

3. Technical Level I time at the fixed rate of ______________ dollars ($) per hour. For the purposes of this Article, Technical Level I personnel include those in the following positions:

4. Technical Level II time at the fixed rate of ______________ dollars ($) per hour. For the purposes of this Article, Technical Level II personnel include those in the following positions:

5. Technical Level III time at the fixed rate of ______________ dollars ($) per hour. For the purposes of this Article, Technical Level III personnel include those in the following positions:

These billing rates shall be adjusted annually (semi-annually), in accordance with the Architect's adjustments in compensation for Principals and employees." (Add agreed upon limitations.)

NOTE: The rates above will normally be the total compensation. For a more detailed explanation, refer to *Compensation Guidelines*.

If a Multiple of Direct Personnel Expense is used, insert:

"Principals' and employees' time at a multiple of ________ ( ) times their Direct Personnel Expense as defined in Article 4."

If a multiple of direct salaries is used, the term "direct salaries" should be substituted for Direct Personnel Expense above, and this should be noted in Article 15.

Paragraph 14.4, Subparagraph 14.4.2

Insert the multiplier applied to consultant billings used to cover the costs of administration, responsibility for consultants' work, coordination and profit.

Paragraph 14.5

Insert the multiplier, if any, applied to reimbursable expenses used to cover the costs of administration.

Paragraph 14.6

Establish a due date for payment and insert the percentage rate and basis (monthly, annual) and the time (such as a number of days) after the due date for payment on which interest charges will begin to run. This should be carefully checked against state usury laws which may set a limit on the rate of interest which may legally be charged. In addition, federal truth in lending and similar state and local consumer protection laws may require setting forth the annual percentage rate and other disclosures or waivers for certain types of transactions or with certain types of clients. Advice of legal counsel should be sought on such matters.

Paragraph 14.7, Subparagraph 14.7.2

Insert the amount of time after which the compensation shall be subject to renegotiation or adjustment. If the firm requires periodic adjustments in hourly rates and multiples, this should be stated, along with any limitations on the amount of upward adjustment which may be made.

4. **Article 15—Other Conditions or Services**

Here insert the following types of provisions:

Additional phases, such as Predesign, Site Analysis or Postconstruction, and the services provided in each
Identification of Additional Services, if any, provided under the Basic Compensation
Other Additional Services, and any special compensation arrangements for them
Description of consultants, if any, provided under the Basic Compensation
Procedure for award of Construction Contracts (i.e., bidding or negotiation)
Fixed Limit of Construction Cost
Fixed Time of Performance
Modifications to any services or conditions
Other additional conditions

Note that any changes in the duties of the Architect during the Construction Phase must be considered with extreme care and correlated with the terms of A201/CM, General Conditions of the Contract for Construction, Construction Management Edition.

D. **EXECUTION OF THE AGREEMENT**

Each person executing the Agreement should indicate the capacity in which they are acting (i.e., president, secretary, partner, etc.) and the authority under which they are executing the Agreement. Where appropriate, a copy of the resolution authorizing the individual to act on behalf of the firm or entity should be attached.

THE AMERICAN INSTITUTE OF ARCHITECTS

AIA Document B141/CM

CONSTRUCTION MANAGEMENT EDITION

Standard Form of Agreement Between Owner and Architect

1980 EDITION

THIS DOCUMENT HAS IMPORTANT LEGAL CONSEQUENCES; CONSULTATION WITH AN ATTORNEY IS ENCOURAGED.

This document is intended to be used in conjunction with AIA Documents B801, 1980; A101/CM, 1980; and A201/CM, 1980.

AGREEMENT

made as of the day of in the year of Nineteen Hundred and

BETWEEN the Owner:

and the Architect:

For the following Project:
(Include detailed description of Project location and scope.)

the Construction Manager:

The Owner and the Architect agree as set forth below.

TERMS AND CONDITIONS OF AGREEMENT BETWEEN OWNER AND ARCHITECT

ARTICLE 1

ARCHITECT'S SERVICES AND RESPONSIBILITIES

BASIC SERVICES

Unless modified by Article 15, the Architect's Basic Services shall be provided in conjunction with, and in reliance upon, the services of a Construction Manager as described in the Standard Form of Agreement Between Owner and Construction Manager, AIA Document B801, 1980 Edition. They shall consist of the five Phases described in Paragraphs 1.1 through 1.5, inclusive, and include normal structural, mechanical and electrical engineering services, and any other services included in Article 15 as part of Basic Services.

1.1 SCHEMATIC DESIGN PHASE

1.1.1 The Architect shall review the program furnished by the Owner to ascertain the requirements of the Project and shall review and confirm the understanding of these requirements and other design parameters with the Owner.

1.1.2 The Architect shall provide a preliminary evaluation of the program and the Project budget requirements, each in terms of the other, subject to the limitations set forth in Subparagraph 3.2.1.

1.1.3 The Architect shall review with the Owner and the Construction Manager site use and improvements; selection of materials, building systems and equipment; construction methods and methods of Project delivery.

1.1.4 Based on the mutually agreed upon program and the Project budget requirements, the Architect shall prepare, for approval by the Owner, Schematic Design Documents consisting of drawings, outline specifications and other documents illustrating the scale and relationship of Project components.

1.1.5 At intervals appropriate to the progress of the Schematic Design Phase, the Architect shall provide schematic design studies for the Construction Manager's review, which will be made so as to cause no delay to the Architect.

1.1.6 Upon completion of the Schematic Design Phase the Architect shall provide the drawings, outline specifications and other documents approved by the Owner for the Construction Manager's use in preparing an estimate of Construction Cost.

1.2 DESIGN DEVELOPMENT PHASE

1.2.1 Based on the approved Schematic Design Documents and any adjustments authorized by the Owner in the program or the Project budget, the Architect shall prepare, for approval by the Owner, the Design Development Documents consisting of drawings, outline specifications and other documents to fix and describe the size and character of the entire Project as to architectural, structural, mechanical and electrical systems, materials, and such other elements as may be appropriate.

1.2.2 At intervals appropriate to the progress of the Design Development Phase, the Architect shall provide design development documents for the Construction Manager's review, which will be made so as to cause no delay to the Architect.

1.2.3 Upon completion of the Design Development Phase, the Architect shall provide the Construction Manager with drawings, outline specifications and other documents approved by the Owner for use in preparing a further estimate of Construction Cost, and shall assist the Construction Manager in preparing such estimate of Construction Cost.

1.3 CONSTRUCTION DOCUMENTS PHASE

1.3.1 Based on the approved Design Development Documents, and any further adjustments in the scope or quality of the Project or in the Project budget authorized by the Owner, the Architect shall prepare, for approval by the Owner, Construction Documents consisting of Drawings and Specifications setting forth in detail the requirements for the construction of the Project.

1.3.2 The Architect shall keep the Construction Manager informed of any changes in requirements or in construction materials, systems or equipment as the Drawings and Specifications are developed so that the Construction Manager can adjust the estimate of Construction Cost appropriately.

1.3.3 The Architect shall assist the Owner and the Construction Manager in the preparation of the necessary bidding information, bidding forms, the Conditions of the Contracts, and the forms of Agreement between the Owner and the Contractors.

1.3.4 The Architect shall assist the Owner and the Construction Manager in connection with the Owner's responsibility for filing documents required for the approvals of governmental authorities having jurisdiction over the Project.

1.4 BIDDING OR NEGOTIATION PHASE

1.4.1 The Architect, following the Owner's approval of the Construction Documents and the latest estimate of Construction Cost, shall assist the Construction Manager in obtaining Bids or negotiated proposals by rendering interpretations and clarifications of the Drawings and Specifications in appropriate written form. The Architect shall assist the Construction Manager in conducting pre-award conferences with successful Bidders.

1.5 CONSTRUCTION PHASE-ADMINISTRATION OF THE CONSTRUCTION CONTRACT

1.5.1 The Construction Phase will commence with the award of the initial Contract for Construction and, together with the Architect's obligation to provide Basic Services under this Agreement, will end when final payment to all Contractors is due, or in the absence of a final Project Certificate for Payment or of such due date, sixty days after the Date of Substantial Completion of the Project whichever occurs first.

1.5.2 Unless otherwise provided in this Agreement and incorporated in the Contract Documents, the Architect, in cooperation with the Construction Manager, shall provide administration of the Contracts for Construction as set forth below and in the 1980 Edition of AIA Document A201/CM, General Conditions of the Contract for Construction, Construction Management Edition.

1.5.3 The Architect and the Construction Manager shall advise and consult with the Owner during the Construction Phase. All instructions to the Contractors shall be forwarded through the Construction Manager. The Architect and the Construction Manager shall have authority to act on behalf of the Owner only to the extent provided in the Contract Documents unless otherwise modified by written instrument in accordance with Subparagraph 1.5.18.

1.5.4 The Architect shall visit the site at intervals appropriate to the stage of construction, or as otherwise agreed by the Architect in writing, to become generally familiar with the progress and quality of Work and to determine in general if Work is proceeding in accordance with the Contract Documents. However, the Architect shall not be required to make exhaustive or continuous on-site inspections to check the quality or quantity of Work. On the basis of such on-site observations as an architect, the Architect shall keep the Owner informed of the progress and quality of Work, and shall endeavor to guard the Owner against defects and deficiencies in Work of the Contractors.

1.5.5 The Architect shall not be responsible for, nor have control or charge of, construction means, methods, techniques, sequences or procedures, or for safety precautions and programs in connection with the Project, and shall not be responsible for Contractors' failure to carry out Work in accordance with the Contract Documents. The Architect shall not be responsible for, nor have control over, the acts or omissions of the Contractors, Subcontractors, any of their agents or employees, or any other persons performing any Work, nor shall the Architect be responsible for the Construction Manager's obligations as an agent of the Owner.

1.5.6 The Architect shall at all times have access to Work wherever it is in preparation or progress.

1.5.7 Based on the Architect's observations at the site, the recommendations of the Construction Manager and an evaluation of the Project Application for Payment, the Architect shall determine the amounts owing to the Contractors and shall issue a Project Certificate for Payment in such amounts, as provided in the Contract Documents.

1.5.8 The issuance of a Project Certificate for Payment shall constitute a representation by the Architect to the Owner that, based on the Architect's observations at the site as provided in Subparagraph 1.5.4 and on the data comprising the Project Application for Payment, Work has progressed to the point indicated; that, to the best of the Architect's knowledge, information and belief, the quality of Work is in accordance with the Contract Documents (subject to an evaluation of Work for conformance with the Contract Documents upon Substantial Completion, to the results of any subsequent tests required by or performed under the Contract Documents, to minor deviations from the Contract Documents correctable prior to completion, and to any specific qualifications stated in the Project Certificate for Payment); and that the Contractors are entitled to payment in the amount certified. However, the issuance of a Project Certificate for Payment shall not be a representation that the Architect has made any examination to ascertain how or for what purpose the Contractors have used the monies paid on account of the Contract Sums.

1.5.9 The Architect shall be the interpreter of the requirements of the Contract Documents and the judge of the performance thereunder by both the Owner and the Contractors. The Architect shall render interpretations necessary for the proper execution or progress of Work, with reasonable promptness and in accordance with agreed upon time limits. The Architect shall render written decisions, within a reasonable time, on all claims, disputes and other matters in question between the Owner and the Contractors relating to the execution or progress of Work or the interpretation of the Contract Documents.

1.5.10 All interpretations and decisions of the Architect shall be consistent with the intent of, and reasonably inferable from, the Contract Documents, and shall be in writing or in graphic form. In the capacity of interpreter and judge, the Architect shall endeavor to secure faithful performance by both the Owner and the Contractors, shall not show partiality, and shall not be liable for the result of any interpretation or decision rendered in good faith in such capacity.

1.5.11 The Architect's decision in matters relating to artistic effect shall be final if consistent with the intent of the Contract Documents. The Architect's decisions on any other claims, disputes or other matters, including those in question between the Owner and the Contractor(s), shall be subject to arbitration as provided in this Agreement and in the Contract Documents.

1.5.12 The Architect shall have authority to reject Work which does not conform to the Contract Documents, and whenever, in the Architect's reasonable opinion, it is necessary or advisable for the implementation of the intent of the Contract Documents, the Architect shall have authority to require special inspection or testing of Work in accordance with the provisions of the Contract Documents, whether or not such Work be then fabricated, installed or completed; but the Architect shall take such action only after consultation with the Construction Manager.

1.5.13 The Architect shall receive Contractors' submittals such as Shop Drawings, Product Data and Samples from the Construction Manager and shall review and approve or take other appropriate action upon them, but only for conformance with the design concept of the Project and with the information given in the Contract Documents. Such action shall be taken with reasonable promptness so as to cause no delay. The Architect's approval of a specific item shall not indicate approval of an assembly of which the item is a component.

1.5.14 The Architect shall review and sign or take other appropriate action on Change Orders prepared by the Construction Manager for the Owner's authorization in accordance with the Contract Documents.

1.5.15 The Architect shall have authority to order minor changes in Work not involving an adjustment in a Contract Sum or an extension of a Contract Time and which are not inconsistent with the intent of the Contract Documents. Such changes shall be effected by written order issued through the Construction Manager.

1.5.16 The Architect, assisted by the Construction Manager, shall conduct inspections to determine the Dates of Substantial Completion and final completion and shall issue appropriate Project Certificates for Payment.

1.5.17 The Architect shall assist the Construction Manager in receiving and forwarding to the Owner for the Owner's review written warranties and related documents assembled by the Contractors.

1.5.18 The extent of the duties, responsibilities and limitations of authority of the Architect as a representative of the Owner during construction shall not be modified or extended without the written consent of the Owner, the Contractors, the Architect and the Construction Manager, which consent shall not be unreasonably withheld.

1.6 PROJECT REPRESENTATION BEYOND BASIC SERVICES

1.6.1 If the Owner and the Architect agree that more extensive representation at the site than is described in Paragraph 1.5 shall be provided, the Architect shall provide one or more Project Representatives to assist the Architect in carrying out such responsibilities at the site.

1.6.2 Such Project Representatives shall be selected, employed and directed by the Architect, and the Architect shall be compensated therefor as mutually agreed between the Owner and the Architect, as set forth in an exhibit appended to this Agreement, which shall describe the duties, responsibilities and limitations of authority of such Project Representatives.

1.6.3 Through the observations of such Project Representatives, the Architect shall endeavor to provide further protection for the Owner against defects and deficiencies in Work, but the furnishing of such Project representation shall not modify the rights, responsibilities or obligations of the Architect as described in Paragraph 1.5.

1.7 ADDITIONAL SERVICES

The following services are not included in Basic Services unless so identified in Article 15. They shall be provided if authorized or confirmed in writing by the Owner, and they shall be paid for by the Owner as provided in this Agreement, in addition to the compensation for Basic Services.

1.7.1 Providing analyses of the Owner's needs, and programming the requirements of the Project.

1.7.2 Providing financial feasibility or other special studies.

1.7.3 Providing planning surveys, site evaluations, environmental studies or comparative studies of prospective sites, and preparing special surveys, studies and submissions required for approvals of governmental authorities or others having jurisdiction over the Project.

1.7.4 Providing services relative to future facilities, systems and equipment which are not intended to be constructed during the Construction Phase.

1.7.5 Providing services to investigate existing conditions or facilities, or to make measured drawings thereof, or to verify the accuracy of drawings or other information furnished by the Owner.

1.7.6 Providing services in connection with alternative designs for cost estimating or bidding purposes.

1.7.7 Providing coordination of work performed by separate contractors or by the Owner's own forces.

1.7.8 Providing services in connection with the work of separate consultants, other than the Construction Manager, retained by the Owner.

1.7.9 Providing interior design and other similar services required for or in connection with the selection, procurement or installation of furniture, furnishings and related equipment.

1.7.10 Providing services for planning tenant or rental spaces.

1.7.11 Making revisions in Drawings, Specifications or other documents when such revisions are inconsistent with written approvals or instructions previously given, are required by the enactment or revision of codes, laws or regulations subsequent to the preparation of such documents, or are due to other causes not solely within the control of the Architect.

1.7.12 Preparing Drawings, Specifications and supporting data and providing other services in connection with Change Orders. If Basic Compensation is to be adjusted according to adjustments in Construction Cost, to the extent that any Change Order not required by causes solely within the control of the Architect results in an adjustment in the Basic Compensation not commensurate with the services required of the Architect, compensation shall be equitably adjusted.

1.7.13 Making investigations, surveys, valuations, inventories, detailed appraisals of existing facilities, and services required in connection with construction performed by the Owner.

1.7.14 Providing consultation concerning replacement of any Work damaged by fire or other cause during construction, and furnishing services as may be required in connection with the replacement of such Work.

1.7.15 Providing services made necessary by the failure of performance, the termination or default of the Construction Manager; by default of a Contractor; by major defects or deficiencies in the Work of any Contractor; or by failure of performance of either the Owner or any Contractor under the Contracts for Construction.

1.7.16 Preparing a set of reproducible record drawings showing significant changes in Work made during construction based on marked-up prints, drawings and other data furnished to the Architect.

1.7.17 Providing extensive assistance in the utilization of any equipment or system such as initial start-up or testing, adjusting and balancing, preparation of operation and maintenance manuals, training personnel for operation and maintenance, and consultation during operation.

1.7.18 Providing services after issuance to the Owner of the final Project Certificate for Payment, or in the absence of a final Project Certificate for Payment, more than sixty days after the Date of Substantial Completion of the Project.

1.7.19 Preparing to serve or serving as a witness in connection with any public hearing, arbitration proceeding or legal proceeding.

1.7.20 Providing services of consultants for other than the normal architectural, structural, mechanical and electrical engineering services for the Project.

1.7.21 Providing any other services not otherwise included in this Agreement or not customarily furnished in accordance with generally accepted architectural practice.

1.8 TIME

1.8.1 The Architect shall perform Basic and Additional Services as expeditiously as is consistent with professional skill and care and the orderly progress of the Project. Upon request of the Owner, the Architect shall submit for the Owner's approval a schedule for the performance of the Architect's services which shall be adjusted as required as the Project proceeds, and which shall include allowances for periods of time required for the Owner's review and approval of submissions and for approvals of authorities having jurisdiction over the Project. The Architect shall consult with the Construction Manager to coordinate the Architect's time schedule with the Project Schedule. This schedule, when approved by the Owner, shall not, except for reasonable cause, be exceeded by the Architect.

ARTICLE 2
THE OWNER'S RESPONSIBILITIES

2.1 The Owner shall provide full information regarding requirements for the Project, including a program which shall set forth the Owner's design objectives, constraints and criteria, including space requirements and relationships, flexibility and expandability, special equipment and systems and site requirements.

2.2 The Owner shall provide a budget for the Project based on consultation with the Architect and the Construction Manager, which shall include contingencies for bidding, changes during construction and other costs which are the responsibility of the Owner. The Owner shall, at the request of the Architect, provide a statement of funds available for the Project and their source.

2.3 The Owner shall designate a representative authorized to act in the Owner's behalf with respect to the Project. The Owner, or such authorized representative, shall examine the documents submitted by the Architect and shall render decisions pertaining thereto promptly to avoid unreasonable delay in the progress of the Architect's services.

2.4 The Owner shall retain a construction manager to manage the Project. The Construction Manager's services, duties and responsibilities will be as described in the Agreement Between Owner and Construction Manager, AIA Document B801, 1980 Edition. The Terms and Conditions of the Owner-Construction Manager Agreement will be furnished to the Architect and will not be modified without written consent of the Architect, which consent shall not be unreasonably withheld. Actions taken by the Construction Manager as agent of the Owner shall be the acts of the Owner, and the Architect shall not be responsible for them.

2.5 The Owner shall furnish a legal description and a certified land survey of the site, giving, as applicable, grades and lines of streets, alleys, pavements and adjoining property; rights-of-way, restrictions, easements, encroachments, zoning, deed restrictions, boundaries and contours of the site; locations, dimensions and complete data pertaining to existing buildings, other improvements and trees; and full information concerning available service and utility lines both public and private, above and below grade, including inverts and depths.

2.6 The Owner shall furnish the services of soil engineers or other consultants when such services are deemed necessary by the Architect. Such services shall include test borings, test pits, soil bearing values, percolation tests, air and water pollution tests, ground corrosion and resistivity tests including necessary operations for determining subsoil, air and water conditions, with reports and appropriate professional recommendations.

2.7 The Owner shall furnish structural, mechanical, chemical and other laboratory tests, inspections and reports as required by law or the Contract Documents.

2.8 The Owner shall furnish such legal, accounting and insurance counseling services as may be necessary for the Project, including such auditing services as the Owner may require to verify the Project Applications for Payment or to ascertain how or for what purposes the Contractors have used the monies paid by or on behalf of the Owner.

2.9 The services, information, surveys and reports required by Paragraphs 2.5 through 2.8, inclusive, shall be furnished at the Owner's expense, and the Architect shall be entitled to rely upon their accuracy and completeness.

2.10 If the Owner observes or otherwise becomes aware of any fault or defect in the Project, or nonconformance with the Contract Documents, prompt written notice thereof shall be given by the Owner to the Architect and the Construction Manager.

2.11 The Owner shall furnish the required information and services and shall render approvals and decisions as expeditiously as necessary for the orderly progress of the Architect's services and Work of the Contractors.

ARTICLE 3
CONSTRUCTION COST

3.1 DEFINITION

3.1.1 The Construction Cost shall be the total cost or estimated cost to the Owner of all elements of the Project designed or specified by the Architect.

3.1.2 The Construction Cost shall also include at current market rates, including a reasonable allowance for overhead and profit, the cost of labor and materials furnished by the Owner and any equipment which has been designed, specified, selected or specially provided for by the Architect. It shall also include the Construction Manager's compensation for services, Reimbursable Costs and the cost of work provided by the Construction Manager.

3.1.3 Construction Cost does not include the compensation of the Architect and the Architect's consultants, the cost of the land, rights-of-way, or other costs which are the responsibility of the Owner as provided in Article 2.

3.2 RESPONSIBILITY FOR CONSTRUCTION COST

3.2.1 The Architect, as a design professional familiar with the construction industry, shall assist the Construction Manager in evaluating the Owner's Project budget and shall review the estimates of Construction Cost prepared by the Construction Manager. It is recognized, however, that neither the Architect, the Construction Manager nor the Owner has control over the cost of labor, materials or equipment, over the Contractors' methods of determining Bid prices, or over competitive bidding, market or negotiating conditions. Accordingly, the Architect cannot and does not warrant or represent that

Bids or negotiated prices will not vary from the Project budget proposed, established or approved by the Owner, if any, or from the estimate of Construction Cost or other cost estimate or evaluation prepared by the Construction Manager.

3.2.2 No fixed limit of Construction Cost shall be established as a condition of this Agreement by the furnishing, proposal or establishment of a Project budget under Subparagraph 1.1.2 or Paragraph 2.2, or otherwise, unless such fixed limit has been agreed upon in writing and signed by the parties to this Agreement. If such a fixed limit has been established, the Construction Manager will include contingencies for design, bidding and price escalation, and will consult with the Architect to determine what materials, equipment, component systems and types of construction are to be included in the Contract Documents, to make reasonable adjustments in the scope of the Project, and to include in the Contract Documents alternate Bids to adjust the Construction Cost to the fixed limit. Any such fixed limit shall be increased in the amount of any increase in the Contract Sums occurring after the execution of the Contracts for Construction.

3.2.3 If Bids are not received within the time scheduled at the time the fixed limit of Construction Cost was established, due to causes beyond the Architect's control, any fixed limit of Construction Cost established as a condition of this Agreement shall be adjusted to reflect any change in the general level of prices in the construction industry between the originally scheduled date and the date on which Bids are received.

3.2.4 If a fixed limit of Construction Cost (adjusted as provided in Subparagraph 3.2.3) is exceeded by the sum of the lowest figures from bona fide Bids or negotiated proposals, plus the Construction Manager's estimate of other elements of Construction Cost for the Project, the Owner shall (1) give written approval of an increase in such fixed limit, (2) authorize rebidding or renegotiation of the Project or portions of the Project within a reasonable time, (3) if the Project is abandoned, terminate in accordance with Paragraph 10. 2, or (4) cooperate in revising the Project scope and quality as required to reduce the Construction Cost. In the case of item (4), the Architect shall modify the Drawings and Specifications as necessary to comply with the fixed limit, without additional cost to the Owner if the Architect has concurred in the Construction Manager's estimate of Construction Cost, but subject to compensation as an Additional Service under Subparagraph 1.7.11 if the Architect has not so concurred. The providing of such service shall be the limit of the Architect's responsibility arising from the establishment of such fixed limit, and having done so, the Architect shall be entitled to compensation for all services performed in accordance with this Agreement, whether or not the Construction Phase is commenced.

ARTICLE 4
DIRECT PERSONNEL EXPENSE

4.1 Direct Personnel Expense is defined as the direct salaries of all the Architect's personnel engaged on the Project, and the portion of the cost of their mandatory and customary contributions and benefits related thereto, such as employment taxes and other statutory employee benefits, insurance, sick leave, holidays, vacations, pensions and similar contributions and benefits.

ARTICLE 5
REIMBURSABLE EXPENSES

5.1 Reimbursable Expenses are in addition to the compensation for Basic and Additional Services and include actual expenditures made by the Architect and the Architect's employees and consultants in the interest of the Project for the expenses listed in the following Subparagraphs:

5.1.1 Expense of transportation in connection with the Project; living expenses in connection with out-of-town travel; long distance communications; and fees paid for securing approval of authorities having jurisdiction over the Project.

5.1.2 Expense of reproductions, postage and handling of Drawings, Specifications and other documents, excluding reproductions for the office use of the Architect and the Architect's consultants.

5.1.3 Expense of data processing and photographic production techniques when used in connection with Additional Services.

5.1.4 If authorized in advance by the Owner, expense of overtime work requiring higher than regular rates.

5.1.5 Expense of renderings, models and mock-ups requested by the Owner.

5.1.6 Expense of any additional insurance coverage or limits, including professional liability insurance, requested by the Owner in excess of that normally carried by the Architect and the Architect's consultants.

ARTICLE 6
PAYMENTS TO THE ARCHITECT

6.1 PAYMENTS ON ACCOUNT OF BASIC SERVICES

6.1.1 An initial payment as set forth in Paragraph 14.1 is the minimum payment under this Agreement.

6.1.2 Subsequent payments for Basic Services shall be made monthly and shall be in proportion to services performed within each Phase of services, on the basis set forth in Article 14.

6.1.3 If and to the extent that the period initially established for the Construction Phase of the Project is exceeded or extended through no fault of the Architect, compensation for Basic Services required for such extended period of Administration of the Construction Contracts shall be computed as set forth in Paragraph 14.4 for Additional Services.

6.1.4 When compensation is based on a percentage of Construction Cost, and any portions of the Project are deleted or otherwise not constructed, compensation for such portions of the Project shall be payable to the extent services are performed on such portions, in accordance with the schedule set forth in Subparagraph 14.2.2, based on (1) the lowest figures from bona fide Bids or negotiated proposals, or (2) if no such Bids or proposals are received, the most recent estimate of Construction Cost for such portions of the Project.

6.2 PAYMENTS ON ACCOUNT OF ADDITIONAL SERVICES

6.2.1 Payments on account of the Architect's Additional Services, as defined in Paragraph 1.7, and for Reimbursable Expenses, as defined in Article 5, shall be made monthly upon presentation of the Architect's statement of services rendered or expenses incurred.

6.3 PAYMENTS WITHHELD

6.3.1 No deductions shall be made from the Architect's compensation on account of penalty, liquidated damages or other sums withheld from payments to Contractors, or on account of changes in Construction Cost other than those for which the Architect is held legally liable.

6.4 PROJECT SUSPENSION OR ABANDONMENT

6.4.1 If the Project is suspended or abandoned in whole or in part for more than three months, the Architect shall be compensated for all services performed prior to receipt of written notice from the Owner of such suspension or abandonment, together with Reimbursable Expenses then due and all Termination Expenses as defined in Paragraph 10.4. If the Project is resumed after being suspended for more than three months, the Architect's compensation shall be equitably adjusted.

ARTICLE 7
ARCHITECT'S ACCOUNTING RECORDS

7.1 Records of Reimbursable Expenses and expenses pertaining to Additional Services and services performed on the basis of a Multiple of Direct Personnel Expense shall be kept on the basis of generally accepted accounting principles and shall be available to the Owner or the Owner's authorized representative at mutually convenient times.

ARTICLE 8
OWNERSHIP AND USE OF DOCUMENTS

8.1 Drawings and Specifications as instruments of service are and shall remain the property of the Architect whether the Project for which they are made is executed or not. The Owner shall be permitted to retain copies, including reproducible copies, of Drawings and Specifications for information and reference in connection with the Owner's use and occupancy of the Project. The Drawings and Specifications shall not be used by the Owner on other projects, for additions to this Project, or for completion of this Project by others provided the Architect is not in default under this Agreement, except by agreement in writing and with appropriate compensation to the Architect.

8.2 Submission or distribution to meet official regulatory requirements or for other purposes in connection with the Project is not to be construed as publication in derogation of the Architect's rights.

ARTICLE 9
ARBITRATION

9.1 All claims, disputes and other matters in question between the parties to this Agreement arising out of or relating to this Agreement or the breach thereof, shall be decided by arbitration in accordance with the Construction Industry Arbitration Rules of the American Arbitration Association then obtaining unless the parties mutually agree otherwise. No arbitration arising out of or relating to this Agreement shall include, by consolidation, joinder or in any other manner, any additional person not a party to this Agreement except by written consent containing a specific reference to this Agreement and signed by the Architect, the Owner and any other person sought to be joined. Any consent to arbitration involving an additional person or persons shall not constitute consent to arbitration of any dispute not described therein or with any person not named or described therein. This agreement to arbitrate and any agreement to arbitrate with an additional person or persons duly consented to by the parties to this Agreement shall be specifically enforceable under the prevailing arbitration law.

9.2 Notice of the demand for arbitration shall be filed in writing with the other party to this Agreement and with the American Arbitration Association. The demand shall be made within a reasonable time after the claim, dispute or other matter in question has arisen. In no event shall the demand for arbitration be made after the date when institution of legal or equitable proceedings based on such claim, dispute or other matter in question would be barred by the applicable statute of limitations.

9.3 The award rendered by the arbitrators shall be final, and judgment may be entered upon it in accordance with applicable law in any court having jurisdiction thereof.

ARTICLE 10
TERMINATION OF AGREEMENT

10.1 This Agreement may be terminated by either party upon seven days' written notice should the other party fail substantially to perform in accordance with its terms through no fault of the party initiating the termination.

10.2 This Agreement may be terminated by the Owner upon at least seven days' written notice to the Architect in the event that the Project is permanently abandoned.

10.3 In the event of termination not the fault of the Architect, the Architect shall be compensated for all services performed to the termination date, together with Reimbursable Expenses then due and all Termination Expenses as defined in Paragraph 10.4.

10.4 Termination Expenses include expenses directly attributable to termination for which the Architect is not otherwise compensated, plus an amount computed as a percentage of the total Basic and Additional Compensation earned to the time of termination, as follows:

.1 20 percent if termination occurs during the Schematic Design Phase; or

.2 10 percent if termination occurs during the Design Development Phase; or

.3 5 percent if termination occurs during any subsequent Phase.

ARTICLE 11
MISCELLANEOUS PROVISIONS

11.1 Unless otherwise specified, this Agreement shall be governed by the law of the principal place of business of the Architect.

11.2 Terms in this Agreement shall have the same meaning as those in the 1980 Edition of AIA Document A201/CM, General Conditions of the Contract for Construction, Construction Management Edition.

11.3 As between the parties to this Agreement: as to all acts or failures to act by either party to this Agreement, any applicable statute of limitations shall commence to run and any alleged cause of action shall be deemed to have accrued in any and all events not later than the relevant Date of Substantial Completion of the Project, and as to any acts or failures to act occurring after the relevant Date of Substantial Completion of the Project, not later than the date of issuance of the final Project Certificate for Payment.

11.4 The Owner and the Architect waive all rights against each other, and against the contractors, consultants, agents and employees of the other, for damages covered by any property insurance during construction, as set forth in the 1980 Edition of AIA Document A201/CM, General Conditions of the Contract for Construction, Construction Management Edition. The Owner and the Architect shall each require appropriate similar waivers from their contractors, consultants and agents.

ARTICLE 12
SUCCESSORS AND ASSIGNS

12.1 The Owner and the Architect, respectively, bind themselves, their partners, successors, assigns and legal representatives to the other party to this Agreement, and to the partners, successors, assigns and legal representatives of such other party with respect to all covenants of this Agreement. Neither the Owner nor the Architect shall assign, sublet or transfer any interest in this Agreement without the written consent of the other.

ARTICLE 13
EXTENT OF AGREEMENT

13.1 This Agreement represents the entire and integrated agreement between the Owner and the Architect and supersedes all prior negotiations, representations or agreements, either written or oral. This Agreement may be amended only by written instrument signed by both the Owner and the Architect.

13.2 Nothing contained herein shall be deemed to create any contractual relationship between the Architect and the Construction Manager or any of the Contractors, Subcontractors or material suppliers on the Project; nor shall anything contained in this Agreement be deemed to give any third party any claim or right of action against the Owner or the Architect which does not otherwise exist without regard to this Agreement.

ARTICLE 14
BASIS OF COMPENSATION

The Owner shall compensate the Architect for the Scope of Services provided, in accordance with Article 6, Payments to the Architect, and the other Terms and Conditions of this Agreement, as follows:

14.1 AN INITIAL PAYMENT of dollars ($) shall be made upon execution of this Agreement and credited to the Owner's account as follows:

14.2 BASIC COMPENSATION

14.2.1 FOR BASIC SERVICES, as described in Paragraphs 1.1 through 1.5, and any other services included in Article 15 as part of Basic Services, Basic Compensation shall be computed as follows:
(Here insert basis of compensation, including fixed amounts, multiples or percentages, and identify Phases or parts of the Project to which particular methods of compensation apply, if necessary.)

14.2.2 Where compensation is based on a Stipulated Sum or Percentage of Construction Cost, payments for Basic Services shall be made as provided in Subparagraph 6.1.2, so that Basic Compensation for each Phase shall equal the following percentages of the total Basic Compensation payable:

(Include any additional Phases as appropriate.)

Schematic Design Phase:	percent (%)
Design Development Phase:	percent (%)
Construction Documents Phase:	percent (%)
Bidding or Negotiation Phase:	percent (%)
Construction Phase:	percent (%)

14.3 FOR PROJECT REPRESENTATION BEYOND BASIC SERVICES, as described in Paragraph 1.6, compensation shall be computed separately in accordance with Subparagraph 1.6.2.
(Here insert basis of compensation which may be a stipulated sum for a given period of time or a Multiple of Direct Personnel Expense as defined in Article 4. If a Multiple of Direct Personnel Expense is used, the Multiple should be clearly stated.)

14.4 COMPENSATION FOR ADDITIONAL SERVICES

14.4.1 FOR ADDITIONAL SERVICES OF THE ARCHITECT, as described in Paragraph 1.7, and any other services included in Article 15 as part of Additional Services, but excluding Additional Services of consultants, compensation shall be computed as follows:

(Here insert basis of compensation, including rates and/or Multiples of Direct Personnel Expense for Principals and employees, and identify Principals and classify employees, if required. Identify specific services to which particular methods of compensation apply, if necessary.)

14.4.2 FOR ADDITIONAL SERVICES OF CONSULTANTS, including additional structural, mechanical and electrical engineering services and those provided under Subparagraph 1.7.20 or identified in Article 15 as part of Additional Services, a multiple of ( ) times the amounts billed to the Architect for such services.

(Identify specific types of consultants in Article 15, if required.)

14.5 FOR REIMBURSABLE EXPENSES, as described in Article 5, and any other items included in Article 15 as Reimbursable Expenses, a multiple of ( ) times the amounts expended by the Architect, the Architect's employees and consultants in the interest of the Project.

14.6 Payments due the Architect and unpaid under this Agreement shall bear interest from the date payment is due at the rate entered below, or in the absence thereof, at the legal rate prevailing at the principal place of business of the Architect.

(Here insert any rate of interest agreed upon.)

(Usury laws and requirements under the Federal Truth in Lending Act, similar state and local consumer credit laws and other regulations at the Owner's and Architect's principal places of business, the location of the Project and elsewhere may affect the validity of this provision. Specific legal advice should be obtained with respect to deletion, modification or other requirements such as written disclosures or waivers.)

14.7 The Owner and the Architect agree in accordance with the Terms and Conditions of this Agreement that:

14.7.1 IF THE SCOPE of the Project or the Architect's services is changed materially, the amounts of compensation shall be equitably adjusted.

14.7.2 IF THE SERVICES covered by this Agreement have not been completed within ( ) months of the date hereof, through no fault of the Architect, the amounts of compensation, rates and multiples set forth herein shall be equitably adjusted.

ARTICLE 15
OTHER CONDITIONS OR SERVICES

This Agreement entered into as of the day and year first written above.

OWNER	ARCHITECT